CW01163549

JINNAH
India – Partition – Independence

JINNAH

India – Partition – Independence

JASWANT SINGH

OXFORD
UNIVERSITY PRESS

OXFORD
UNIVERSITY PRESS

Great Clarendon Street, Oxford OX2 6DP

Oxford University Press is a department of the University of Oxford.
It furthers the University's objective of excellence in research, scholarship,
and education by publishing worldwide in

Oxford New York

Auckland Cape Town Dar es Salaam Hong Kong Karachi
Kuala Lumpur Madrid Melbourne Mexico City Nairobi
New Delhi Shanghai Taipei Toronto

with offices in

Argentina Austria Brazil Chile Czech Republic France Greece
Guatemala Hungary Italy Japan Poland Portugal Singapore
South Korea Switzerland Turkey Ukraine Vietnam

Oxford is a registered trade mark of Oxford University Press
in the UK and in certain other countries

Copyright © Jaswant Singh 2010

The moral rights of the author have been asserted

First published by Rupa & Co., New Delhi 2009

This edition by Oxford University Press 2010

All rights reserved. No part of this publication may be reproduced, translated,
stored in a retrieval system, or transmitted, in any form or by any means,
without the prior permission in writing of Oxford University Press.
Enquiries concerning reproduction should be sent to
Oxford University Press at the address below.

This book is sold subject to the condition that it shall not, by way
of trade or otherwise, be lent, re-sold, hired out or otherwise circulated
without the publisher's prior consent in any form of binding or cover
other than that in which it is published and without a similar condition
including this condition being imposed on the subsequent purchaser.

ISBN 978-0-19-547927-0

Not for sale in India.

Typeset in Adobe Garamond Pro
Printed in Pakistan by
Kagzi Printers, Karachi.
Published by
Ameena Saiyid, Oxford University Press
No. 38, Sector 15, Korangi Industrial Area, PO Box 8214
Karachi-74900, Pakistan.

To those that lost their all in the 'partition'
'....*Dawn was theirs,*
And sunset and the colours of the earth.'
Rupert Brooke, *The Dead*

CONTENTS

List of Illustrations	xi
Acknowledgements	xiii
Introduction: A Complex Opening	1
1. India and Islam	10
2. Jenabhai to Jinnah: The Journey	50
3. The Turbulent Twenties	98
4. Sharpening Focus—Narrowing Options	129
5. A Short Decade—A Long End Game	177
6. Sunset of the Empire—'Post-dated Cheque on a Collapsing Bank'	235
7. A War of Succession—Diverging Paths	284
8. Stymied Negotiations?	336
9. Mountbatten Viceroyalty: The End of the Raj	366
10. Pakistan: Birth–Independence: The Quaid-i-Azam's Last Journey	400
11. In Retrospect	408

Appendices

Appendix to Chapter 1

Appendix I: The Simla Delegation and the Formation of the Muslim League	449

Appendices to Chapter 2

Appendix I:	Minto-Morley Reforms (1909)	452
Appendix II:	The Official British Opinion on the Montagu-Chelmsford Reforms	453
Appendix III:	Lucknow Pact	454

Appendix to Chapter 5

Appendix I:	The Elections of 1937	456

Appendices to Chapter 6

Appendix I:	The Cripps Mission Plan, 1942	458
Appendix II:	The C.R. Formula, 1943	458
Appendix III:	Gandhi's Offer as Revealed in his Letter to Jinnah, 24 September 1944	459
Appendix IV:	The Desai Formula	460
Appendix V:	Wavell on Gandhi-Jinnah talks 30 September 1944	460

Appendices to Chapter 8

Appendix I:	The Wavell Plan, 1945	462
Appendix II:	The Muslim Legislators' Convention, 1946	463
Appendix III:	Muslim League's Memorandum to the Cabinet Mission	464
Appendix IV:	Congress Proposals to the Cabinet Mission	464
Appendix V:	The Cabinet Mission Plan, 1946	465
Appendix VI:	The 3 June 1947 Statement	466
Appendix VII:	Wavell–Gandhi–Nehru – 27 September 1946 Post-Calcutta killings	467
Appendix VIII:	Wavell–The Viceroy's Journal Ed. by Penderel Moon	469
Appendix IX:	Note by Field Marshal Sir C. Auchinleck	471
Appendix X:	The Long-Term Plan	477

Appendix XI:	The Congress submitted panel of 15 names for the proposed Executive Council	478
Appendix XII:	Results of the 1946 Elections	479

Appendix to Chapter 10

Appendix I:	Quaid-i-Azam's Message to Hindustan 7 August 1947	480

Appendices to Chapter 11

Appendix I:	Mr Jinnah's Presidential Address to the Constituent Assembly of Pakistan	481
Appendix II:	Speech Delivered by Maulana Azad at Jama Masjid of Delhi on 23-10-1947	484
Appendix III:	Dialogue between the Author, Lloyd and Susanne Rudolph, Professors of Political Science Emeritus, University of Chicago	486

Endnotes	493
Index	539

LIST OF ILLUSTRATIONS

1. An elegant Jinnah
2. Jinnah relaxing
3. Barrister Jinnah
4. Jinnah. H.J. Rustomjee and Homi Rustomjee
5. Meeting of the Indian National Congress and All-India Muslim League
6. Jinnah with his Doberman and West Highland Terrier
7. Jinnah with daughter Dina
8. Jinnah with sister Fatima and daughter Dina
9. Muslim League leaders
10. Round Table Conference, London, 1931
11. Jinnah with Subhas Bose
12. All-India Muslim League, 26th Session
13. At 10 Aurangzeb Lane, 1944-45
14. Reception at Indira House
15. Jinnah arriving in Karachi
16. Quaid-i-Azam Jinnah at opening of the State Bank of Pakistan
17. At Quetta Railway Station, 1945
18. With Louis Fischer
19. With Muslim League Women's Guard
20. With sister Fatima
21. Jinnah in his study
22. Jinnah in Jodhpur breeches
23. As Barrister-at-Law (top and bottom)
24. On holiday (top and bottom)
25. Quaid-i-Azam Governor-General Mohammad Ali Jinnah

ACKNOWLEDGEMENTS

My quest for writing a political biography of Mohammad Ali Jinnah goes back a long way, but really as a thought, the seed of the idea lying dormant for many years, certainly until 1999, when fortuitous circumstances made its planting possible. This was during Prime Minister Atal Behari Vajpayee's historical bus journey to Lahore in 1999. I accompanied the prime minister to Minar-e-Pakistan, (it is a 60-metre high tower to mark the place where the All-India Muslim League adopted a resolution for the creation of Pakistan on 23 March 1940) returning from where I was struck by the thought there existed no biography of Jinnah written by a political figure from India. It was then that I decided to fill the gap; however, yet again, between that thought and subsequent action, the gap lengthened.

It was only in 2004 when a processing of this work actually began. It was the period when I was out of office and had a fair amount of time to reflect, to research and to write.

It is then that my first consultations also started; a large number of those whom I spoke with wondered why I was venturing on this path at all and as most well-wishers do, cautioned me against doing so. However, I persisted, for, it was a journey of my own, of my rediscovery and a clearer understanding of why India had been partitioned in 1947.

After much deliberation, I did venture forth, and now, finally, the 'book' is here. It has taken me five years to write, rewrite, check, cross-check, seemingly an endless process. My list of those to whom I am deeply grateful is very long, but the very first acknowledgement has to be to Dr Z.H. Zaidi, editor-in-chief of the Quaid-i-Azam Papers Project, National Archives of Pakistan. When contacted he was immediately of great help, and remained so, consistently, corresponding on his charmingly antiquated manual typewriter. In this age, I wondered, of proliferating computers and vastly more efficient printers? Dr Zaidi had instantly offered all assistance and unstintingly, unceasingly he gave it. Thank you very much, Doctor Sahib.

The research for this book involved consulting an intimidating wealth of books, all chronicling that period, all works of great learning, experience, passion, and remarkable merit. The Endnotes section lists them, my acknowledgements being but the markers of my obligations.

Raghvendra Singh was a marvel of assistance in my endeavours; relentlessly searching out new books, new sources and references with intrepid ability. He helped greatly with early drafting too, that difficult crafting of raw paper into book. Thank you, Raghvendra.

This work had threatened, as most such books do to keep growing, for this subject is immensely demanding. Besides, books do tend to acquire a life and a will of their own. However, the 'boundaries' of this work had to be defined, for in any event, boundaries, territory, limits—all these confining words—form the central basis of this work, of those divisions that were thrust on the Indian subcontinent, in 1947. The world now calls us 'South Asia'.

The writing of this book has been a grave responsibility, as sensitivities are acute and just below the surface of the skin. After all, the Partition of India has been the defining event of the twentieth century, for all of us. The wounds that it inflicted have not healed; not yet.

That is also why the number of those upon whom I relied, and sought advise from, would run into several pages, if I detailed all that they gave—so many friends, colleagues and advisors. They are all examples of selfless assistance; all of them, without exception, in and out of India, cheerfully suffering the infliction of having to 'force read' an often disorganised and incomprehensible manuscript. I was corrected on facts, inevitably, also on opinions, often gently, sometimes not so; occasionally with robust persuasiveness and I was also oft times disagreed with, but that after all is inherent in the subject.

This work is saturated with emotions; it has to be, for how do you separate what Gandhi termed 'vivisection' from pain and feelings and emotions. Historiographers will doubtless frown upon such an approach, I know, but then I do not write as a cold, linear narrator of events alone. Of such accounts we are now weary.

It was a pleasure and a great privilege to have so many attend to the manuscript so assiduously. It is the theme that drew them: an account of Mohammad Ali Jinnah's public life and his political journey from being an 'ambassador of Hindu-Muslim unity' to the Quaid-i-Azam of Pakistan.

ACKNOWLEDGEMENTS

Thank you all, very sincerely: M.J. Akbar, Maj.-Gen. (Retd.) Bhatia, William Dalrymple, David Goodall, Wajahat Habibullah, Polly O'Hanlon, Mani Shankar Iyer, Vivek Katju, Sunil Khilnani, Pratap Bhanu Mehta, A.G. Noorani, T.C.A. Raghavan, Anthony Ramsay, Susanne Rudolph, Lloyd Rudolph, K.C. Singh, Manvendra Singh, Strobe Talbott, B.G. Verghese and the research team of Anjan Bhowmick, Abhishek Dixit and Natarajan Swaminathan.

A special vote of thanks to the research team, particularly Ashwini Channan; he helped me mould the raw clay of an idea into this book. Without his stewardship I doubt whether this book would have reached the publishers.

Sanjana Roy Choudhury, with outstanding professionalism and great dedication, painstakingly worked on my fault-ridden manuscript(s), repeatedly, patiently, and then yet again, until finally it now emerges as a finished work.

All mistakes, faults, omissions, lapses are, of course, all mine and I alone am responsible for what I have written.

This book is about the Partition of India in 1947; it is from that the title emerges:

JINNAH
India – Partition – Independence

I also gratefully acknowledge the contributions made by Mr Hameed Haroon, proprietor of *Dawn* newspaper and his senior journalist, a veteran in the calling—Mr Ardeshir Cowasjee; both of whom so graciously gave me permission to use Jinnah's photographs from their respective personal collections. It is from these albums that I have selected some, those which to my eyes, represent Jinnah's epic journey.

To Sir Dorab Tata Trust, whose support has been generous and spontaneous, and to whom I owe a great deal: Thank you.

Jaswant Singh

INTRODUCTION
A Complex Opening

The Opening Pages of Indo-Islamic History

Within a few years of Hazrat Muhammad's (PBUH) death in AD 632 Arab invasions started; 'the armies of Islam' fanning out from the 'Hejaz, spreading rapidly through Persia, Iraq, Maghreb, the Levant' and the Byzantine lands. By the eighth century AD, catholic Spain had submitted to the sword of Islam, which now knocked on the peripheries of today's France. The Arabs by now held the largest, and the most 'powerful empire in the world, from the Bay of Biscay to the shores of the Indus, and from the Aral Sea to the Upper Nile'. By AD 662, the spreading influence of the Khalifa began touching the land frontiers of Hindustan, too, but neither the Umayyads nor the Abbasids[1] succeeded in moving farther in land. Contrary to the generally held views, it took the Arabs several attempts, and close to four hundred years to gain a foothold in India and that too at great cost. It was not until the eleventh century that the kingdoms of Kabul, Zabul and Sindh finally succumbed to the Arabs.

The first of the sea invasions of India was earlier, in AD 636, when three Arab naval expeditions, to Thana, to Gujarat and to coastal Sindh, were repulsed. Overland the raid on Debal in AD 662, the first in Sindh, ended in a rout for the Arabs, as did efforts of successive Khalifas. Khalifa Walid, chiding the governor of Iraq, when permission to invade Sindh was again sought said, 'This affair will be a source of great anxiety, so we must put it off, for every time the army goes on such an expedition, vast number of Musalmans get killed. Think no more of such designs'.[2]

But Hejjaj, the governor of Iraq did finally succeed in organising an expeditionary force under his son-in-law and cousin Mohammad bin Qasim to avenge the ignominious defeat suffered at the hands of Raja Dahir of Sindh. To Mohammad bin Qasim, his parting words were: 'I swear by God that I am determined to spend the wealth of whole Iraq that is in my possession on this expedition and that the flame of my fire will not go down until I take the revenge'.[3]

Debal was conquered in AD 712, when Raja Dahir, engaging Mohammad bin Qasim, was killed in an open battle. His queen performed 'jauhar', while their son lived on to resist the Arabs. Soon thereafter, Mohammad bin Qasim was recalled to Iraq by the new Khalifa—Sulaiman and Raja Dahir's son retrieved most of his kingdom.

In the ninth and tenth centuries, the powers of the Abbasid Khalifas declined greatly resulting in a loss of their ability to support envoys in distant lands. Most accounts of Arab travellers in India of the tenth century speak of only two independent Arab principalities then that of Multan and Mansurah. Al-Istakhri,[4] writing in AD 951 about Multan records: 'there is an idol [here] held in great veneration by the Hindus and every year people from the most distant parts undertake pilgrimages to it…when the Indians make war upon them and endeavour to seize the idol, the inhabitants bring it out, pretending that they will break it and burn it. Upon this the Indians retire, otherwise they would destroy Multan'. Wolsdey Haig rightly describes the Arab conquest of Sindh as 'a mere episode in the history of India which affected only a fringe of that vast country…The tide of Islam, having overflowed, Sindh and the lower Punjab ebbed leaving some jetsam on the sand'.

As Dr Ram Gopal Mishra, author of *Indian Resistance to Early Muslim Invaders up to 1206 AD* observes: 'the kingdoms of Kabul and Zabul too, had valiantly defied the Arabs for over two centuries. For another 175 years, the ruling dynasties of these kingdoms, the Shahis, held out. Kabul then comprised the Kabul river valley and extended up to the Hindukush. It included the present areas of Lamghan, Jalalabad, Peshawar and Charsadda in the south, bordering Kashmir in the North and Persia in the west.'

The kingdom of Zabul lay to the south of Kabul and north of Baluchistan (Gedrosia)[5] comprising the upper valley of the Helmand river with Seistan forming a part of this kingdom.

After conquering Persia in AD 643, the Arabs attacked the valley of Kabul in AD 650. Abdullah ibn Amir, the governor of Basra, wanted to subdue Seistan. Though this expedition failed, Seistan was finally conquered by the Arabs in AD 653 to be lost again soon after. Various other attempts to re-conquer Seistan were resisted stoutly, their resistance making the kings of Kabul and Zabul part of the then prevailing Arab folklore, they were the heroes of many Arab stories about 'holy wars on the frontiers of Hind'.

Kalhana,[6] author of the epic poem *Rajatarangini* has numerous verses in praise of these 'Hindu Shahi'. Gradually, however, they were pushed towards Punjab where finally in AD 1026, their long struggle against an ascendant Islam ended. Writing some 130 years after the demise of these kingdoms, Kalhana, plaintively observed that 'the very name of the Shahis seems to have vanished from the region, for people were wont to ask whether, "with its kings, ministers, and its courts, it ever was or was not?"'

This phase transformed over time and gradually over the centuries evolved into frequently repeated forays, primarily for loot of the inestimable wealth of the land. Some came in those centuries in a frenzy of Islamic zeal destroying whatever non-Islamic symbol, structure or image fell their way; they were the early iconoclasts of Islam destroying what for them were 'symbols of Satan'. Conquest, dynastic rule and 'invaders becoming Indians' came last. The three broad categorisations cannot in any fashion be delineated with geometric precision for it was not as if one followed the other in an orderly manner, movement of the first evolving into the next. Accompanying these invasions, came a new experience for India, conversion of the unbelievers to Islam, until a time arrived when, finally, Islam itself got transformed by India, intermeshing with it and ultimately being absorbed by it as an integer. All this, upon which we have now spent but a few sentences, in reality, took almost a millennium and a half to evolve.

India's involvement with these diverse strands of Islam covered the entire range of human experience, encapsulating within the geographical spread of the subcontinent a journey that travelled from arriving as a conquering faith, adopting the country as home and then finally dividing this very homeland with the faithful abandoning it. Islam had come to India principally with the invading Islamic forces; fuelled by the lure of a 'throne' and of rulership over these rich, fertile, bountiful lands of Hind. In consequence, Islam became the faith of a conquering invader, acquiring the identity of a foreign, Islamic outsider.

How did Islam with ease first become Indian, then struggled to become a geographical supernumerary to it, to this great spread of what was their own 'home'. From being the faith of kings, emperors and the rulers of India, for a period of time, it then became the faith of the 'separator', of those that divided the land, expelling itself (notionally) from India and moving voluntarily to the eastern and western peripheries of it; relegating such of the faith that remained within India to a life of perpetual self-questioning and doubt about their true identity. For those that 'remained' were then questioned, humiliatingly: 'Where do you actually belong?' These bewildered, abandoned faithful rightly therefore, now lament—'Are we also not of the *ummah* (an Arabic word which means 'community' or 'nation')?' Besides, what then of the Muslim League's boast of being the 'sole and the exclusive representative of all the faithful'? The League had claimed that it was the true upholder of Islam's ideological authenticity; also of representing a substantive Muslim consensus, therefore, it demanded, rather presupposed, just a single Muslim medium—and asserting its identity as a different conceptual 'nation', claimed a separate land for itself which is why this agonising question continues to grate against our sensibilities: 'Separate' from what? And, what of those that do not so separate 'geographically'? How do you divide a geographic (also geopolitical) unity? Simply by drawing lines on maps? Through a 'surgical operation', Mountbatten had said, and tragically Nehru and Patel and the Congress party had assented, Jinnah, in any event having demanded adopting to just such a recourse.

The Muslim League in that sense triumphed under Jinnah's leadership, for he achieved what he had set out to. The League was his political instrument and his acumen enabled him to exploit the accumulated weaknesses of the Congress party's mistakes, principally from the 1930s onwards; upon which he heaped the British Empire's critical enfeeblement, post-Second World War, carving out for himself a Pakistan; even if 'moth-eaten' and from birth.

Many commentators have reflected upon this, as have C.H. Philips and Mary Doreen Wainwright in a book *The Partition of India: Policies & Perspectives 1935-1947*. They have expressed a view that this path of the League's triumph is well enough known even though it might now have gone somewhat hazy. It is this path that we travel over again.

For this, in essence, was also Mohammad Ali Jinnah's political journey. How could, or rather why did, a person of such central importance to the front rank of India's political leadership for almost the first forty-seven years of the twentieth century relegate himself to a fringe of it? It is then also a journey of this transcendental idea of 'Hindu-Muslim unity'; what quest, which urge thereafter made Jinnah travel the road to its very antipodal extreme: from being the symbol, 'ambassador', as Gopal Krishna Gokhale first said and, subsequently, Sarojini Naidu eloquently expressed—'of Hindu-Muslim unity', to becoming the principal proponent and voice of separation between the two; the architect of Pakistan; and in Ayesha Jalal's unique phrase...'its Sole Spokesman'? Or was he at all any of this? Was it collective human folly that created Pakistan? Lloyd and Susanne Rudolph[7] in a thought provoking lecture have posed this question with elegant lucidity: 'Jinnah continued to be perceived as 'liberal, eclectic and secular to the core'; committed to India's unity, he was thought of by Viceroy Lord Linlithgow as 'more Congress than the Congress'.[8] 'So what happened? How could so cataclysmic an event as Partition occur when it hadn't even been imagined as late as the 1940s?' And no intelligible definition of it existed uptil as late as 1946. How and why did this 'ambassador of Hindu-Muslim unity', the liberal constitutionalist, an Indian nationalist—Mohammad Ali Jinnah, become, in Viceroy Lord Wavell's phrase, a 'Frankenstein monster',[9] working to dismember that very world which had so generously created him?

There are some other, to my mind, equally important aspects of this great tragedy of India's Partition deserving of our reflection. Did not this Partition of India, vivisecting the land and its people question the very identity of India itself? If, as Jinnah asserted, 'Muslims of India were a separate nation' then axiomatically what was/is India? Jinnah asserted in his later years that 'India is not one nation'. If it is not 'one nation', then what are we, even as a residue? Are we but a conglomerate of communities? Or a collection of 'many nations', as Jinnah had rather casually put it while describing India as a residue of communities. But certainly all this India is not and not because I say so, but because history affirms so, and we assert that as a nation we give equal rights, (adding with justifiable pride) to all citizens, also a common citizenship. Then how, rather why did we then, also why do we now, confer selectively identified separative, religious, caste and community identities, thus effectively and functionally fragmenting that very unity of India about which we so proudly declaim everywhere? For this support of affirmative action is for the needy, a helping hand of 'reservations', to assist in overcoming historical, social inequalities but we err gravely in perpetuating such politically misconceived social engineering. After all, this was precisely Jinnah's central, and consistent, demand as the 'sole spokesman of Muslims'; for he, too, wanted the insurance of a specified ratio of representation for the Muslims in elective bodies and government jobs. To this Gandhi had demurred, as had others at least to start with, but bewilderingly later, scrambled to competitively climb that very, ever lengthening ladder of slippery and divisive reservations. But this thought outstrips the chronology of our narrative of Jinnah's 'journey'.

Let us reverse the gaze. It is ironical that amongst the great constitutionalists of those times, and there were several, Jinnah and Nehru became the principal promoters of 'special status for Muslims'; Jinnah, directly, Nehru, indirectly. As all Indian citizens constitutionally were and are equal, then Jinnah by directly demanding a 'special' status for Muslims and Nehru through contesting Jinnah's right as their 'sole spokesman', became advocates of establishing different categories amongst Indian citizens. The irony of it is galling when sadly, (though, of course in retrospect) we observe that both of them, these two great Indians of their times were either actually, or in effect, competing to become the 'spokesman of Muslims' in India. This approach arose, principally, because they were, both in effect, so deeply imbued by European thought, percepts and societal subscriptions that they, tragically, became far removed from the core of Indian cultural consciousness. Then who, we wonder, remained to speak for a united India? Sadly, only Mahatma Gandhi.

The cruel truth is that this partitioning of India has actually resulted in achieving the very reverse of the originally intended purpose; partition, instead of settling contention between communities has left us a legacy of markedly enhanced Hindu, Muslim, Sikh or other such denominational identities, hence differences. Affirmative action, reservations for Muslims, other castes and communities, unfortunately, does not dissolve those identities; it heavily underscores them, waters their roots, perpetuating differences through the nutrient of self-interest being poured constantly in separateness. Reservation results finally in compartmentalising society, hence, ultimately in fragmenting national identity. That is what 'special reservation' for Muslims in India did.

But then, this is only a field sketch of the ground that was then traversed. What of the historical period of which we talk? The easy answer is that this 'period' lies broadly between 1857 and 1947. The trauma of the first, (1857), was marked by a violent usurpation of the symbols of sovereignty of India by rough, freebooting traders from a foreign land. The essence and authority of Mughal India (North India, broadly) had admittedly begun to decline in the eighteenth century, but 1857 was a violent seizure. And that is the backdrop against which we travel those defining four decades of the twentieth century; from the Simla delegation of 1906 to the Independence of India Act 1946. It is these four decades (1906-47) that transformed the very identity of the entire Indian subcontinent and in a very significant manner influenced events and issues globally, too. The journey was from 'special reservations', which had a built-in bias in the arithmetic of democratic representation to finally, a vivisection of the land itself. This effectively defines the conceptual, the territorial and the historical limits of this tragic journey. I venture on this perilous path, to search, for I must know for myself; what happened? 'What brought about this great cataclysm of 1947? For an event of such transforming consequences, clearly all cannot hold uniform views, they are sharply divergent.

'A view widely held in India, for example, is that partition was a tragedy—a vivisection'—and discussions in India, therefore, tend to be focused upon identifying reasons and apportioning blame for this 'failure to maintain the unity of the subcontinent', as well as mitigating the terrible consequences of division. With admirable detachment the blame is often laid at the feet of the Congress leaders: had they done this, or refrained from doing that, partition could have been avoided. In Pakistan, on the other hand, where naturally it cannot be accepted that partition should have been avoided, there is a tendency to plumb the growth of 'Muslim nationalism' into the depths of history, and connect that with a kind of a 'seeming inevitability of the establishment of a Muslim state/nation'.

That, in essence, is also the genesis of both this search and the book proper: the conceptual canvas on which we work; the construct, however, of the book is even simpler, it has to be if we are to trace our journey through all those many challenges, the great climbs and the abysmal pitfalls of those epochal decades.

There is need to share a difficulty here. Is the present account, doubtless one amongst many of that trauma of a partitioning of India; is this account merely a recapitulation of those happenings; a linear narrative of events simply recounted? A method that a friend from Scotland recently wrote to me about, explaining that the 'father of history', Herodotus, adopted: 'history as a systematically tested compilation of materials'. Or is it to be what that great Arab historian Ibn Khaldun reflected history to be, rather ought to be, in his epic treatise *The Muqaddimah*?[10]

> The (writing of history) requires numerous sources and much varied knowledge. It also requires a good speculative mind and thoroughness, which lead the historian to the truth and keep him from slips and errors. If he trusts historical information in its plain transmitted form and has no clear knowledge of the principles resulting from custom, the fundamental facts of politics, the nature of civilisation, or the conditions governing human social organisation, and if, furthermore, he does not evaluate remote or ancient material through comparison with near or contemporary material, he often cannot avoid stumbling and slipping and deviating from the path of truth. Historians, Quran commentators and leading transmitters have committed frequent errors in the stories and events they reported. They accepted them in the plain transmitted form, without regard for its value. They did not check them with the principles underlying such historical situations, nor did they compare them with similar material. Also, they did not probe with the yardstick of philosophy, with the help of knowledge of the nature of things, or with the help of speculation and historical insight. Therefore, they strayed from the truth and found themselves lost in the desert of baseless assumptions and errors.[11]

I can scarcely add or remove even one word from this brilliant, yet so succinct, a laying down of the parameters within which I must remain, and the criteria that I must endeavour to fulfil as I attempt an interpretive account of Jinnah's evolution as the 'Quaid-i-Azam of Pakistan'.

I accept that all accounts are subjective; they cannot be otherwise, after all, any account or interpretation of that searing period which forced a vivisection upon an ancient cultural unity—India—can hardly be shoe-horned into any *a-priori* determinations, theories or even claims of objectivity, neither in narrative, nor certainly in analysis or interpretation. Why was this ancient entity broken: Why? That is the question that haunts us, as each viewer narrates what is seen and made out of that tragic kaleidoscope by him or her.

Could the answer to this great and tormenting question, be found through any occidental philosophical determinations? I believe not. Then, is it to be found in a straight recapitulation of events? Again, clearly, no. For unless we ourselves almost live in that period, and breathe those very contentions, join in the great debates of those years as participants, as closely as we can, not merely be ex post-facto narrators of events, or commentators upon past happenings, unless we do this very minimum we will fail to capture the passions of those times. And without living those passions any commentary on that great oscillation of history through the jaundiced prisms of our respective viewpoints will be but a very sad parody of an epic tragedy.

1

INDIA AND ISLAM

India—Islam—Nationhood

Our enquiry into the road traversed by Mohammad Ali Jinnah, from being an ambassador of Hindu-Muslim unity to the Quaid-i-Azam of Pakistan begins here. If an assertion of that highly questionable thesis that 'Muslims are a separate nation' led to the creation of Pakistan, then why did an integral part of that very 'Muslim nation', reject the notion in its entirety and separate, yet again, in violence, indescribable human suffering and death? Why did Bangladesh opt out? This, we need to reflect upon, in some detail, but before that Islam's journey in India; how, also why, did that which grew in India opt for the 'smallness' of a separation from it?

It makes a fascinating tapestry; this experience of Islam in India from invasion to accommodation, resulting in a kind of integrated assimilation, where, after fretting against that very oneness to then reject India, seek a separate Islamic nation, and finally, through a 'surgical' operation hurriedly settle for a 'moth-eaten Pakistan'? How is it that the Indian subcontinent of an undivided India, home to more Muslims than, for example, the entire Middle East, did not become the global standard-bearer of this noble faith choosing instead to be cut up? Was that because Islam was always a foreign intrusion here, living as if not entirely at home, therefore, it must depart someday, for that is what partition is. Or, is it that during the course of almost a millennia and a half, 'Islam, Islamic traditions, and Muslims' became entirely indigenous; of and from this very soil; an undeniable part of this 'multi-layered, cultural sediment of the Indian subcontinent'? And if that be correct then why and how did Mohammad Ali Jinnah assert, and more significantly why did we, Jawaharlal Nehru, Vallabhbhai Patel, that entire generation of Congress leaders accept this fallacious notion that 'Muslims (and why in India alone?) are a separate nation', and permit our nation to be vivisected? That also is our enquiry.[1]

It is, of course self-evident that Islam is not, just as Christianity or Zoroastrianism are not indigenous to India, for born elsewhere Islam came to India wielding the evangelising sword of the invader, in consequence it arrived as an outsider and, at least initially, remained just that (an alien faith). But India is a cultural ocean, rivers of many faiths empty here; in that same vein Islam, too, is a part of those cultural layers, absorbed by what exists, mixing then with the rest to become an inseparable part of the marvel that is India. The problem lay, still does, in attempting to separate, to keep distinctly apart this one particular strata from India's foundational layer. That foundation is Vedic, though some historians like to dispute this; whereafter comes the Indic, the indigenous. It is much later that the more recent layers of the Indo-Islamic or the Indo-Anglian come into reckoning. The late Girilal Jain has reasoned convincingly that 'Islam is a totality'. He has written to say: 'The modern mind just cannot comprehend Islam precisely because it is a totality. Islamic society is rooted in the religion of Islam: it is not the other way about. The point needs to be heavily underscored that Islamic society is theocentric not theocratic'.

The advent of Islam (Muslims) into India was in three broad waves, spread over almost eight centuries. The first were the Arabs, in the seventh and eighth centuries AD, they came into Sindh, fought a few skirmishes and left. Just about forty kilometres south of Karachi lies the now largely abandoned settlement of Banbhore, often asserted as the first port of call of Mohammad bin Qasim, (though this is questioned). It is believed that the very first mosque in India was also built here in Banbhore. This now lies in ruins. (On the other hand, Malabar Coast claims the distinction of the first mosque, too, but the genealogy of mosques in India is not central to our enquiry.) The forays of the Afghans and the Persians were the next wave between the tenth and eleventh centuries AD, followed then by the Turkic-Mongol invasions between the twelfth and sixteenth centuries. From that very first invasion by Mohammad bin Qasim, hardly any Arab stayed back in Hind, just as very few from amongst the later Persian invaders like Nadir Shah did. Of the Afghans and the Mughals (the Turkic-Mongols) a similar conclusion cannot be drawn. A number of Afghans continued to live in India and made it their home, as did the Mughals who over time got assimilated and became 'Hindustani' in every sense. Again, our principal concern is not a recounting of these waves of invasions by Islamic forces, only a brief analysis of some of the historiographical oddities of the period detains us here.

The advent of Persianised Turks into India is routinely characterised by historians as 'Muslim conquest'. This, to my mind, is an oddity, for to term this entire period from the thirteenth to the eighteenth century as the 'Muslim era' is wrong, also, simplistic. Principally, because there is a significant conceptual and terminological error here, which over the centuries has got embedded. The query being: are we to term an invasion, any invasion for that matter by the faith or the religious beliefs of the invader: Islamic/pagan/ancestor-worshipper/shamanist or whatever; or establish identity by ethnicity and the place of origin of the invader? When we relate these invasions of India with other comparable historical encounters elsewhere, then this oddity stands out as even more sharply contrasted. Why do we not, for example, speak of a 'Christian conquest' of America? Or why is it that the Columbus, post-AD 1492 period is not called America's 'Christian era'? Though Spain defined its conquests of Central and South America in unambiguously Christian terms, their (Spanish) destruction of an entire way of life, of fully flowering civilisations in that continent is termed simply as Spanish conquests. Why? All that great pillage of pristine lands is never called 'Christian depredation'; why again? And here I cannot resist mentioning the obvious: How is it that British conquest (granted, in stages) of India is just 'British' and not 'Christian'? It is this kind of standard historiographic practice or shorthand that has given birth to our fixations with such misleading phraseology, which is why this nagging question remains: Why make an exception in the case of Islam alone? And from where therefore, has this notion of an Islamic conquest of India found such a secure hold amongst the historians of India?[2] This notion persists, even in the twenty-first century. It has many damaging consequences, one of them eventually became Jinnah's assertion of being the champion of a separate 'nation' within India, hence wanting a different geographical space. This could be carved only from what existed in India, and that is what the invaders (the British) finally did in 1947. But we move, too fast, again.

Because most Indo-Persian chroniclers of medieval India identified Islam with the fortunes of their royal patrons, therefore, with sycophantic inaccuracy they reduced accounts of those reigns into such hagiographical nonsense as: 'India's history' begins only from when Muslims began to rule areas around Delhi/Agra/Malwa. This attitude can be traced from the beginnings of the Turkish rule, an ironic oddity being that even as the Delhi Sultanates were consolidating their hold here,[3] the land of the birth of Islam was itself then being subjected to devastating Mongol invasions. That titanic Mongol energy and the ferocity of their invasions uprooted many Persianised Turks from their homelands in Iran and Central Asia, driving several of them towards Hindustan where they sought refuge, found sanctuary, often service in those still new Sultanates of Delhi. By AD 1258 the Abbasid capital of Baghdad had been razed and the office of the Khalifa of Islam taken over by the Turks. This effectively questioned not just the principal symbol of Islamic authority but also its institutions, ecclesiastical and temporal. In consequence, a markedly preservative mentality got embedded in this large refugee community that had sought shelter in Delhi. Many of the traumatised escapees carried with them vivid memories of the inhuman ferocity of the Turkic-Mongol destructions. Which is why having found in this adopted homeland, Hindustan, a sanctuary the shelter itself became a focus of their remaining Islamic world. Thereafter, these elite administrators, men of arms and of letters then began to equate (habitually) the impress of Muslim presence in Hind with both sovereignty and with Islam itself.[4] And Hind,[5] as it has always done, gave sanctuary, but not all of itself. For then that latent nationalism, call it Indian or Bharatiya or Hindu or whatever you will, began to assert itself. That was also, roughly the time that Al Beruni came to this land—to Hind, as part student, part refugee, complaining that:

> ...the Hindus believe that there is no country but theirs, no nation like theirs, no kings like theirs, no religion like theirs, no science like theirs. They are haughty, foolishly vain, self-conceited, and stolid. They are by nature niggardly in communicating that which they know, and they take the greatest possible care to withhold it from men of another caste among their own people, still much more, of course, from any foreigner.

Little wonder that thereafter this separation of the invader from the invaded, Muslim from the Hindu began to permeate our social consciousness and fabric.

There has then to be taken note of Hindustan's approach to such emigrants, invaders or refugees, and how they were ordinarily referred to; for the phraseology of such reference always conveys, as effectively now as it did then, either acceptance, rejection or a kind of tolerant indifference: to illustrate 'Paki', 'nigger', 'Hun', 'chink' or whatever. From the eighth to the fourteenth centuries, reference to these aliens was not so much by their religion, as by their linguistic or national identity, for example, more typically, and more often as Turks (*Turuska*), Khorasani, or Irani or Arab, etc; or then as *maleccha,* an outsider, an alien. (This word was not originally a pejorative term of rejection, it came to be so considered [interpreted] only much later). However, for the Muslims whether invader, refugee or resident, a non-believer, that is a Hindu, was a 'kafir', for he was not of the faith. Despite this and whatever medieval Indo-Persian chroniclers might have recorded, their contemporary Hindus did not regard the religious faith or traditions of the newcomers as sufficiently remarkable to warrant identifying them solely by their faith, or only as Muslims. Rather, they were accommodated as just another alien group that had arrived in India, some to invade others to shelter. On a somewhat autobiographical note, in my own childhood more often than not the word used for the identification of a Muslim visitor, from distant parts to our home was 'a Turk has come to visit'. That is why this question becomes central, if the Hindus did not always categorise the occurrence of such invasions as purely Islamic conquests, or a Muslim as only that, then how and why did all these categories, all identified by faith alone, as 'Muslim', become the defining term of use for historians in the colonial and the post-colonial era? I do not have an answer to this, nor a definitive answer to another question that surfaces: Is not Indian historiography, therefore, (at least in part) responsible for creating a mindset of separateness, and that, too, only from Islam, or fixedly as Hindus and Muslims? Why then did it not, ever, term the European Imperialists (British, French, Portuguese) as Christian invaders? British India remains British—not Christian, in contrast, say, to the term Muslim India. Why?

I find that orientalist scholars, colonial administrators, religious reformers, even 'nationalist' historians, have laboured strenuously to first establish, and then perpetuate, such dichotomies by distinguishing between the foreign and indigenous only in terms of faith and that, too, almost entirely in respect of Muslims and Hindus alone, never for example—Christian, and always projecting the current identity backwards in time.

Lloyd Rudolph, professor emeritus at the University of Chicago, has observed that 'assuming the existence of a contemporary concept or institution such as a 'nation' and reading it back in historical time, say finding an 'Indian, or Hindu, or Muslim nation prior to late nineteenth or twentieth century' would not be appropriate'. He cites Benedict Anderson's phrase[6] 'Imagined communities', reasoning that personalities, like Sir Sayyid Ahmad Khan and Jinnah, in reality also first 'imagined' a Muslim community and then Muslims and nation in India. So, of course, did Indian nationalists, like Nehru or the Hindu nationalists, like Madan Mohan Malaviya. It is Benedict Anderson who 'opened up the idea that nationalism is constructed, contested, and changing. He did a lot to bury the notion that there is an essential or natural, or primordial community, identity or nation', in which sense 'from music to food to dress, what is 'national' or 'ethnic' or Muslim…is always constructed.'[7]

In the case of Islam, for instance, scholars focused on seventh century Arabia to describe Islam's essential qualities, value systems and nature. This is understandable, but only up to a point. When, however, Max Weber,[8] goes to the extent of characterising Islam as the 'national, Arabic, warrior religion,'[9] it is a strange manner of universalising that characteristic, besides being so misleading. Such descriptions of Muslims, over time, established a norm; it stereotyped Muslims by asserting their faith in Islam first, then geographically linking that with the Arab world, whereafter conceptually, as if all Arabs were always endowed with overabundant attributes of 'warriors'. And so successfully has all this been done that such notions persist with remarkable tenacity till today. On the other hand, evidence revealing the large indifference of Hindustan and Hindwis towards Muslims as Muslims, until a separateness began to be asserted by the Muslims themselves, suggests that this political question of whether 'Muslims are a separate nation' was fundamentally misplaced, which is why it became and still remains so divisive. I can, up to a point, understand Jinnah's persistence with this notion, but not at all the Congress party's acceptance of it. Though, I do accept that there existed other and significant grounds for alienation; different faith and worship rituals, some different social norms, certain specific and mutually unacceptable customs or dietary preferences; also the many historical abrasions on the memory templates of the Hindus, be it invasions, killings, loot, and whatever the original intention of the invader all these grate; they still do.

Islamic Traditions of India[10]

To understand how and why Islam became (despite all the loot and rapine and pillage) a part of India's cultural landscape requires a much deeper understanding of the nature of this land and its people, then a grasp of the enormous body of India's Islamic traditions; examinations that we cannot really undertake here as that is not the primary focus of our search. However, we must acknowledge that the Islamic traditions of India do reflect a variety of sects, linguistic communities and social classes, all called by the term and thriving as Muslims. In India, Muslims never were and still are not a homogenous, monolithic community just as they are not so in Pakistan, however much the political community of both the countries might want them to be, principally for the selfless purpose of electoral benefits to themselves. This is tragic, for it is attitudes such as these that fix separateness, generating a traffic of response and counter-response that constantly moves apart, in turn decreasing social intercourse and becoming, again, a factor for encouraging hostility, which yet again helps in perpetuating political exploitation.

There is another aspect meriting underscoring. How did the Quran Sharif, revealed to the Prophet in Arabic, his native language, get mediated to India, to a non-Arabic speaking region and people? And how then did India become home to almost a third of the world's Muslim population? Clearly, Islam was, and had to have been, translated into something Indian; translation here is not simply a limitedly linguistic effort, rather a broader absorption process through cultural and societal assimilation; via language, social intercourse and by the Quran itself being adapted to Indian literary genres and modes of communication. Of course, the use of the Perso-Arabic script gradually facilitated a direct transmission of Islamic terms, and the ideas that they carried; for eventually all this became the Indian Islamic vernacular tradition. Whereafter, concepts originally expressed in Arabic gradually entered the Indian Muslims' thought streams, principally by becoming a part of their idiom, scripts and their vernacular of communication too.

India's Islamic traditions (Indo-Islamic) served then to both shape Islam to the existing cultures of India and also to connect the Muslims from our (Indian) cultures to a wider, global community of faith. As it came to be, these Islamic traditions displayed two distinctive strands—one stretching from Lahore to Delhi then south to Hyderabad, with offshoots radiating from Delhi—east towards Patna, and west to Ahmedabad. The pronounced style here was Persian. Beyond this—in parts of Sindh, Thar Parkar or Nagarparkar, Rajputana, Tamil Nadu, Malabar, Kashmir and Bengal, Islam remained imbued of the local styles and idioms.[11]

In areas where the Persian Islamic traditions were dominant that distinctive culture (Perso-Islamic) began to represent the culture of the rulers, these were/are the ashraf,[12] the global people, whose ancestors had come from other cultures, or so they averred, and some certainly had but most only so claimed. The *ashraf* had a well-defined vision of themselves; indeed they still do. They asserted that as they had come from elsewhere it was to rule; that this wielding of power was their natural right. They cultivated and cherished Perso-Islamic standards conduct and manners, being prepared to accept in their world such of the Hindus—as for example the Kayastha and Kashmiri Brahmins—who helped them with the business of running a government, and who willingly absorbed some external elements of Muslim culture. But they hesitated, by and large, to accept the proselytised, for they had been drawn mostly from the poor. For the *ashraf* these converts had little to do with their world, these were the *musallahs,* the hewers of wood and the fetchers of water, they were the atrap.[13] By the eighteenth century the very basis on which Perso-Islamic culture rested in India began to weaken, and to do so very rapidly. By the beginning of the nineteenth century Muslim 'power' had been reduced to Awadh, to Hyderabad and the North-Western border lands. Perhaps because this period also saw a flowering of Islam, the eighteenth and early nineteenth centuries therefore became, a period of the highest refinement of Persianate culture in India. With this blooming also came the end; does not an Arab saying wisely caution: 'Once the House is built the decline starts'.

Of this decline of the once great Taimurids and the resultant chaos, amongst the most moving accounts is the testimony of C.B. Saunders, officiating commissioner and agent to the lieutenant governor, who when examined by the judge advocate on Friday, 12 February 1858, during that pretence of a trial of the last Mughal emperor, Bahadur Shah Zafar, testified:

Question: Can you give the court any information as to the circumstances under which the kings of Delhi became subjects and pensioners of the British government in India?
Answer: Shah Alam, Emperor of Delhi, after having his eyes put out and having suffered every indignity from the hands of Ghulam Kadir, fell into the hands of the Mahrattas in the year 1788. The Emperor, although vested with nominal authority over the city of Delhi, was kept in confinement, more or less rigorous, until the year 1803, when General Lake having seized Aligarh, marched with the British troops against Delhi. The Mahratta Army drawn out at Patparganj, six miles from Delhi, was attacked by General Lake and utterly routed. The city and fort having been evacuated by the Mahrattas, the Emperor Shah Alam sent a message to General Lake, applying for the protection of the British Authorities, and on 14 September 1803, the date since rendered more memorable by the successful assault in 1857, the British troops entered Delhi: from that time the Kings of Delhi have become pensioned subjects of the British Government, and have exchanged the state of rigorous confinement in which they were held by the Mahrattas, to one of more lenient restraint under the British rule. The Prisoner succeeded to the titular sovereignty of Delhi in 1837. He had no power whatever beyond the precincts of his own Palace: he had the power of conferring titles and dresses of honour upon his own immediate retainers, but was prohibited from exercising that power on any others. He and the heir-apparent alone were exempted from the jurisdiction of the Company's local courts: but were under the orders of the Supreme Government.

Q: Was there any limit to the number of the prisoner's armed retainers?
A: The prisoner requested Lord Auckland to be permitted to entertain as many men in his service as he thought proper. The governor-general, in reply, accorded permission to his entertaining as many men as he could payout of the income allotted to him.

Q: Can you state the amount of pension granted by the government to the prisoner at the time of the outbreak?
A: He was in receipt of a stipend of one lakh of rupees per mensem, of which 99,000 rupees were paid at Delhi, and 1,000 at Lucknow to the members of his family mere. He also was in receipt of revenue to the amount of one

and a half lakhs of rupees per annum from the crown lands, in the neighbourhood of Delhi. He also received a considerable sum from ground-rents of houses and tenements in the city of Delhi.

And thus ended the great Mughalia Sultanate (Mughal dynasty) which is why 1857 was but an obituary, there really remained nothing more to end after General Lake's conquest.

How Patrons Then Became Petitioners

From about AD 1830 onwards this Perso-Islamic culture withered, rather collapsed, and with bewildering speed. The prime cause was, of course, the increasingly confident assertion of a new and emerging power: the conquering culture of Britain; they (the British) were already the administrators of large parts of India; trade, its protection and enhancement had, almost as of right, led to ownership of land and conquest of territory in parts of India. However, this collapse was not a consequence of British assertiveness alone, for while the British dismantled the cultural fabric from without, both the Hindus and the Muslims of the period undermined it from within. Whereafter, the shock of that great uprising of 1857 finally shattered the remaining illusions of Perso-Islamic power; 1857 also smashed the grip of Persianate aesthetics.[14] There was another, an unintended consequence of this decline. For the British it was principally 1857 that made them conscious of Muslims as Muslims; consequently they then began to endow the community with a separate (from the Hindu) political character. This did not happen immediately, and not quite as decisively as the written word might suggest, but certainly within a decade or so from 1857 the British had begun to treat the Muslims as a political collectivity; they treated them as occupying one of the two pans of the political balance of India.

Here is how Thomas Metcalf had summed up a rather typical British attitude to the uprising of 1857: 'The first sparks of disaffection, it was generally agreed, were kindled by the Hindu sepoys...but the Muslims then fanned the flames of discontent and placed themselves at the head of the movement for they saw in these religious grievances the stepping stone to [regaining] political power'. In the view of the British, it was Muslim intrigue and Muslim leadership that converted a sepoy Mutiny into a political conspiracy, aimed at the extinction of the British Raj.[15] Sir George Campbell too, describes the bitterness of British feelings towards Muslims, as he encountered them in the North Western provinces of India.[16] 'It was at Meerut that I first realized the strong feelings against Mohammadans (for they) had no excuse from the caste grievances which was the immediate occasion of the Mutiny. We were disappointed when Mohammadan sepoys in regular regiments went with the rest. We were also aggrieved when the irregular cavalry, generally Mohammadan, who we had thought will stand by us, went too'.

However, appearances were deceptive, and recognised as such by the then governor general, Lord Canning, also by others in high places. The original 'military mutinies', Canning assessed, were 'sparked off by Hindu sepoys, who feared for their caste, their honour and their self-respect. The civil risings in Awadh, Bihar and Central India were mostly Hindu led'. A 'majority of the rebellious Talukdars of Awadh were also Hindu', the Rani of Jhansi, Tatya Tope and Nana Saheb were all Hindus. In the Gorakhpur region the commissioner noted that it were certain tribes of the higher castes of Rajputs who displayed the most marked hostility.[17] In contrast the Muslims themselves were as divided by personal, class and regional affiliations as were the Hindus, experiencing exactly the same pressures. In 1857, amongst the Muslim princes and aristocrats the likes of the Nizam of Hyderabad, and the Nawabs of Rampur, Karnal, Muradabad and Dacca remained loyal to the British, whereas the Nawabs of Farukhabad and Danda turned against them. 'Some Muslim officials went one way and,' [human behaviour]—'some the other'. In Aligarh and Rohilkhand they were mostly with the uprising, but Muslims of Bengal, who had perhaps suffered the most economically from the expropriatory ways of the British East India Company were not sufficiently persuaded to bestir themselves or to raise even their voice in protest. That is why the foundation of the East India Company's seat in India remained undisturbed. In the Punjab, Muslims joined with the Sikhs and formed part of the reinforcements for the British troops on the ridge outside Delhi, However, the Pathans, Rajputs and Bundelas, whose lands and estates had been acquired in the last fifty years participated with robust vigour in this struggle; but the 'Mohammadans and Zamindars of Bihar, and parts of Benaras, whose subjection to the British was relatively recent, did not generally join in this uprising'. Curiously, Muslim communities most given to religious fanaticism like the Faraizis and the Moppillas in South India remained entirely uninvolved.[18]

Canning, in a formal assessment of the causes of 1857, and the part taken in it by Muslims summed up:

> It is true that Mohammadans in many parts of India are ill-disposed towards the British government and have at various times excited disturbances...It is also true that every Mohammadan would gladly see the day when his faith should again be in the ascendant and would infinitely prefer Mohammadan to British rule. But allowing this to be an accurate exposition of their secret aspirations it cannot militate against facts which tend to show that the Mohammadans only took a partial share in the Mutiny and that [too] after its development.[19]

With the recapture of Delhi, in September 1857, dire vengeance visited upon the hapless Muslims of this city. Bahadur Shah Zafar was put through the indignity of a mock trial and exiled to Rangoon; Mughal princes were beheaded, summarily; with Hodson[20] boasting about it, wine glass in hand. Worse, a great catastrophe then befell the Muslim intelligentsia of Delhi, and such of them as wanted to return to the city, their home, after the ruthless quelling of 1857 were required to pay a fine. Prime Minister Palmerston wrote to Canning that 'every civil building connected with (the) Mohammadan tradition, (a not so oblique a reference to Jama Masjid) should be levelled to the ground without regard to antiquarian veneration or artistic predilection'.[21] As condign and retributary punishment followed, though scarcely even a pretence at observing judicial processes was demonstrated, the backbone of the economic strength of the rural communities of North India was broken through wholesale confiscation of property in the affected provinces. Here the approach of the British usurpers was guided only by an overwhelming desire to avenge the upsurge of 1857, that was the principal motivation and they remained blind to communities in execution.

This great trauma of 1857 marked the formal end of a long period of Muslim political primacy, and notwithstanding their survival as a major interest group, 1857 did definitely destroy their self-image as 'rulers'. Despite this shattered image, Muslims remained a major social interest group, ready whenever an opportunity arose to assert their position as one of the two great political communities of India. Eighteen fifty-seven could not destroy the Muslim as a 'weight in the religious, social and political balance of British India'.[22] But they had perforce to adapt, as indeed had all others, and were required to conduct their affairs and behaviour exactly as the English wanted. 'They could compete in the race of life, but not by using the old weapons of arms and statecraft. Their paragons would now not be Akbar or Aurangzeb, it is the British who would dictate',[23] What is surprising is the number of Muslims willing to make such a transition, and somewhat against the conventional historical belief that Muslims suffered unduly after 1857, they did not, on the contrary, politically and economically many certainly benefited.

Eighteen fifty-seven did though, cause an inevitable shift in the land holding traditions and patterns of the Muslim community; those with a 'Mughal past losing to those with a British future'.[24] Even before 1857, a new class of Muslim landlords, comprising largely such as were ready to serve the British as deputy collectors and *sadar amin*,[25] or similar other posts, also those who had gained through land auctions had become ascendant. After 1857 these loyalists, more typically those who had turned British rule to their profit became Sir Sayyid Ahmad Khan's followers, promoting western education for their community and collaborating politically and administratively with the British.[26]

Without doubt old Muslim families suffered grievously, paying a price for 1857; their sense of honour was outraged, their self-pride broken through economic deprivation, their lifestyle altered permanently; Mughal princesses, past 1857, led a broken and violated life. The British then, in an act of continuing humiliation, patronisingly granted to the scions of the nobility pensions, insulting both in the very act of grant and the paltry amounts doled out so gracelessly. British attitude towards Muslims for about a decade after 1857 expressed a dualism: accepting them (the Muslims) as an important interest group, yet combining that acceptance with 'severe rebuffing of any political pugnacity'.[27] After 1857, the British began to fear that they could actually be driven out of India, an apprehension that never hereafter left them, and was never dismissed as an impossibility. This fear always combined with an assessment that such a contingency could occur, and like a flash, but only when, and if, the two great fanaticisms of India combined: of caste and of religion. But it was also here that lay their safety, a scope for exploiting existing divisions in society. The British believed, again not wrongly, that the inherent antagonisms of Indian society, principally those between the Muslims and the Hindus, (though they never really fully understood either of the two faiths, only exploited their characteristics) will always need an impartial umpire, namely themselves. Despite this it is difficult to place all blame on the British, that they alone divided the two communities so as to facilitate their rule; it was more that finding divisions already existing, these were rubbed raw by the British whenever they could do so, exploitatively.

An unexpected, perhaps inevitable but nevertheless, sad consequence of the multiple traumas of 1857 was a decline in the status of Persian in India. In consequence the *ashraf* suffered most, some of the rational sciences, those distinctive contributions of Iran and Central Asia to Indian Islam, began to lose their relevance and were in the process cultivated less and less. Instead traditions that emphasised the study of the Quran and the *hadith*[28] and which mingled with the *Naqshbandi*[29] accent on reform became ascendant in Islamic thinking. Seeds of introspective Sufism, planted long back by Sheikh Ahmad Sarhindi,[30] began to flower. Besides, Indian Islam began moving more towards the orthodox, with a sharper, more fundamentalist hue. The *ashraf* did not, or could not, resist this change for they, (besides, other factors) were far too ease loving to be in the front ranks of the energetic wielders of this proselytising sword of Islam.

The reformist movements of the nineteenth century, of course drew Muslims, but mainly from outside the former ruling circles, and about them Sayyid Ahmad of Bareilly[31] was openly critical. These aimed not so much at restoring the Mughal dynasty or any form of Mughal aristocracy, more to re-creating a kind of a facsimile of the early Muslim community, and to regaining a part at least, of that lost spirit. Even Sayyid Ahmad believed that the Muslims would one day be 'inspired to conquer India again, but this time for God'. And, such messages clearly appealed to the entire strata of Muslim society, as strongly then as they do now.

We need to focus here on two important Muslim personalities of the period, of very different origins, totally antithetical political philosophies and examine their impress upon the Muslims of India. The first is Sir Sayyid Ahmad Khan.

In 1838, (the year his father died), Sayyid Ahmad Khan was nearly twenty-two years old. Though his father had been an employee of the remnants of the Mughal establishment in the Red Fort of Delhi, Sayyid

Ahmad Khan chose to take leave of the Fort and opt for a service with the Company Bahadur. He was astute enough to read the trend of his times to his advantage. Sayyid Ahmad Khan knew nothing then of the legal procedures, or of the law courts established by the British. His uncle, Maulvi Khalilullah Khan, *sadar amin* in Delhi, therefore, took him under his wings, and thus launched Sayyid Ahmad's career as an employee of the British Raj. This also laid the foundations of his lifelong anglo-philia.

In those tumultuous days of 1857 Sayyid Ahmad's career took him to Delhi, then to Agra, to Fatehpur Sikri, and finally to Bijnor. His attempts at rescuing the European population and of taking over the administration of Bijnor are described in ample detail in his biography *Hayat-i-Javed* by Altaf Hussain Hali. When in 1859, a special commission was set up to examine the confiscation of Indians' property, post-1857, two Europeans, commissioner of Rohilkhand and the judge of Muradabad and just one Indian, Sayyid Ahmad Khan found a place on it.

Sayyid Ahmad Khan's is the most prominent of the names associated with the Aligarh Movement. Some other public figures connected with it in those early years were Syed Mehdi Ali Khan (1837-1907), Maulvi Nazir Ahmad (1830-1912) and Maulvi Samiullah Khan (1834-1908). It could not have been that Sayyid Ahmad, who had for long lived in Delhi and had close family connections with the Fort would fail to notice the devastation that had befallen the city, but he belonged to that class of the 'sharif', ('*ashraf*') who are renowned for their attachment to power, the privileges that go with office and for their knack in sticking with the seats of power. If their own status had to be maintained it needed a fast demonstration of loyalty to the British, an adaptation of the British power. For the adherents of the Aligarh Movement the only way to that sinecure was to adopt things 'European' and that too, with some urgency even if it involved a considerable cultural shift. For those of the Aligarh Movement this was an easy way to build bridges between their own and the imperial world of the British.

The Muslims of the ilk of Sayyid Ahmad Khan, like Syed Amir Ali and Nawab Abdul Lateef, the modernists of those times, advocated that their co-religionists keep aloof from the Congress. On the other hand, the Congress, even then appreciated the importance of Muslim support for retaining its supposedly national character. As only two out of a total of seventy-two delegates of the first Congress were Muslims and that too fairly unimportant members of the community, the Reception Committee of the second Congress took particular care to ensure a markedly better Muslim representation. In reaction, Sayyid Ahmad Khan, in an article in the *Aligarh Institute Gazette* of 23 November 1886, condemned the 'Congress movement as seditious'. Even at this second Congress in Calcutta in 1886, they were only 33 Muslim participants in a total of 431 delegates, and again none were prominent Muslims.

Sayyid Ahmad came into an open conflict with the Congress from 1887. For the third Congress, Badruddin Tyabji had been invited to chair the session and several students from Mohammadan Anglo-Oriental College, Aligarh were likely to attend the session. In consequence, the proportion of Muslim participation improved markedly. This alarmed Sayyid Ahmad Khan, who in a public speech delivered on 28 December 1887, sketched the first outlines of his Muslim policy. He categorically warned against the 'disaster that the Muslims would court if they supported the Congress'.

In the meantime, the Congress had then been demanding that Indian members find a due place in the Imperial and Provincial Councils, but through elections. For Sayyid Ahmad this meant representation in the councils only of the majority, (the Hindus) and this too, permanently. It is in this context that he, for the first time, asserted that the Muslims were a separate 'people', a 'separate nation'. For these views, statements and such activities, Sayyid Ahmad Khan was trenchantly criticised by Lala Lajpat Rai. Late in 1888, Lalaji accused Sayyid Ahmad of going back on his earlier statements, also that the Congress had demanded nothing more than what Sayyid Ahmad had himself advocated in his book *The Causes of the Indian Revolt*, and also accused Sayyid Ahmad of opposing the Congress just so as to flatter British officials.

In 1893 Sayyid Ahmad founded the Mohammadan Anglo-Oriental Defence Association, 'to protect the political interest of Muslims'. In 1896, Sayyid Mahmud (Sayyid Ahmad's son) and Theodore Beck (principal of Aligarh College) drew up a scheme on behalf of this association, dealing with the question of Muslim representation in Imperial and Provincial Councils. Their scheme asked for a 'parity in representation' not just in these higher councils but also in municipalities and districts and where the Muslims totalled 25 per cent or more of the population. An important feature of this scheme was a suggestion that

Muslim members of such councils and local bodies should be elected only by Muslims. The Muslim press, not surprisingly, welcomed the scheme. This Sayyid Mahmud-Beck scheme, acted as the seed, eventually becoming the tree of the Muslim political movement for a separate Muslim state, whether in or out of India

The other significant personality of those times, almost contemporaneous with Sayyid Ahmad was Sayyid Jamal ad-Din 'al-Afghani' (1839-97). He is recorded as having visited India around 1855-56 and was very deeply affected by what he saw and experienced. It is perhaps this visit to India that eventually converted him into becoming a bitter critic of the British rule, a transformation no doubt caused by what he later heard about 1857. That is why for Afghani, Sayyid Ahmad Khan was like a partisan of his great enemy, the British, which is why he could not, rather just would not, accept what Sayyid Ahmad Khan stood for or represented.

Afghani's views were astonishingly correct for those times; he advocated nationalism of a linguistic and territorial variety, implying a unity of Hindus and Muslims, with little said about unity amongst Indian Muslims or with Muslims of other lands.[32] He was not a pan-Islamist, at least not then, affectively refuting such notions through his writings. 'There is no happiness except in nationality', he wrote, 'and there is no nationality except in language, and a language cannot be called a language [until it] embraces all affairs that those [engaged] in manufacture and trade need for use in their work'.[33] Which is perhaps why Afghani advocated the need for a common language so as to bring together individuals, tribes and groups into one unified national unit. This was an expression of a specific preference for the linguistic over religious nationalism, the former, in Afghani's views, being more unifying and more durable:

> In the human world the bonds that have been extensive...[are] two. One is...unity of language of which nationality and national unity consist, and the other is religion There is no doubt that the unity of language is more durable for survival and permanence in this world than unity of religion since it does not change in a short time in contrast to the latter.[34]

He advocated the teaching and learning of the national language, which would then encourage development of ties to the nation's past and make learning so much more accessible to so many more people than if the teaching was done in a foreign language. 'Encouragement of a national language is a requisite to national unity and patriotism; thus Indians should translate modern knowledge into their own language, especially Urdu'.[35] These views were astonishingly current, considering that they were expressed in the mid-nineteenth century.

Afghani was also against such religious conservatives as were opposed to western learning. He held that the principles of the *shari'a* (Islamic law) were in no way against the spread of science and learning, rather the opposite, for useful knowledge strengthened religion as it enabled its adherents to come into wealth, position and glory. 'English arts and industries are necessary, but they should be spread through translation into one's own language'.[36] Afghani well understood the context of his times and, therefore, rather than emphasising religious unity, stood for linguistic unity. His anti-imperialist and anti-British purpose was best served by this approach, an approach that in every sense was the opposite of Sir Sayyid Ahmad Khan's.

Muslim Reform Movements

As with any other religion, when faced by decline in its appeal recourse, is often sought in introspection. Post-1857, Islam in India too, went through such a process. Contemporaneously with Sayyid Ahmad of Bareilly there then rose, in Bengal, religious movements closer to the soil, to the daily life and struggles of the Muslim cultivator—the Faraizi[37] movement. The peasant struggles of Dadu Mian and Titu Meer[38] had idioms similar to that of Sayyid Ahmad of Bareilly; for all of these Muslim reformists spoke of the need for a purified Islam. Such reform movements contributed then to a gradual transformation of the Indian Muslim community from an 'aggregate of believers into a political association with a will for joint action'.[39] Essentially, such movements worked for a rejection of the medieval, Persianised, soft Islam in India, and a return to the earlier, purer, harder forms of Islam. Besides, these movements were not of the city halls and the elegant *baithaks* or sitting chambers of the *ashraf*, they went out and preached against customs that so many Muslims had absorbed from, and begun sharing with, Hindus: 'they must not adopt these Hindu ways', preached forcefully the reformists; for India could 'not (be) like home, (it was) like a habitat'.[40] These religious and social activities of Dadu Mian and Titu Meer in

Bengal, or Sayyid Ahmad of Bareilly resulted, in time, in the adoption of a sharp edged, combative, communal language. In addition, these movements also dealt a blow to the upper middle-class Muslim culture, which by then was already in decline. Poetry, painting, the cultivation of the senses, that urbane nostalgia of gentlemen, whether Muslim or Hindu for better days, all collapsed when confronted by the harsh exigencies of religious rectitude, just as they had had to surrender to the demanding (and humiliating) realities of straitened economic circumstances post 1857. The cruel whiplashes of time gave birth to renewed religious fervour, as a kind of repentant atonement, and equally, a demonstration of reformed and ardent faithfulness. Experience of adversity does do this, always, to all faiths, not Islam alone.

At the leading edge of this Islamic reform, was Deoband, founded in 1867 by Ulema imbued with the tradition of Shah Waliullah.[41] They believed that education should no longer be for the purpose of training Muslims for serving the Empire, instead it ought to train them in the art of 'survival' in a world where Muslims had no power. And yet, as would always happen, many *ashraf* continued even in early twentieth century to draw on their memory of a Perso-Islamic base for psychological and civilisational sustenance, reasoning that as their forbears had come to India to rule, power and its wielding was in their blood; it was their birthright, and it is this right that remained as their just and inevitable due. 'It was but a question of time for power to return to them', so at least they reasoned amongst themselves.

This attitude lay, perhaps still does, at the heart of most Muslim politics, certainly in the first half of the twentieth century, also in today's Pakistan, and is currently in a diluted form in India, too. This thought both infused, and inspired, the writings of the Aligarh Movement as demonstrated by the persistence with which the All-India Muslim League continued to assert the political importance of Muslims; also in the power-worship that infused so much of Iqbal's poetry and led not just to the development of a demand for Pakistan it continues still to confuse so much of the current political thought in India. While not at all devaluing the importance of the many other factors that contributed to the birth of Pakistan this was perhaps also the last striking expression of Perso-Islamic values in India, which had been revealed to be, like other values of early twentieth century, imbued with complex contradictions, several paradoxes and a self-defeating inwardness.

Deoband, this great Islamic seminary, some distance out of Delhi, and now renowned internationally as one of the great centres of Islamic learning was in the early years of its founding supported entirely by voluntary contributions. The students were drawn solely from Muslim society, though not just from North India or UP but also from Punjab, Bengal and even from Afghanistan; some came from Iran too. The course of study was strictly traditional. No English was taught, and of course, no sciences. Cut off from government employment and by tradition from the small crafts, except printing and book binding, Deoband graduates flocked to the *madrasas* of Muslim India, maintaining the system of first educating and then dividing these educated Muslims from the rest. Deoband's leading lights were mostly former students of the Delhi Madrasa started by Shah Waliullah and destroyed by the British in 1857, and they were, at least some of them, survivors of the battlefields of that uprising.

The Barelwis, another reformist group often paired in opposition to the Deobandis, began to take shape in 1880s. Representing Barelwi views, Ahmad Riza Khan's[42] assessment that interests of Hindus and Muslims were intrinsically opposed was the guiding thought; for him the Christians were at least 'people of the Book', but the Hindus, were irredeemable, they are *kafirs*. Despite such hard views, the Barelwis had doctrinal differences with the Deobandis, into which ecclesiastical minefield I dare not enter, inspiring as it had a fatwa war between the two (Deoband and Barelwis) in the late nineteenth and early twentieth centuries. This division, true to form, was later exploited by the British to neutralise the Deobandis and to entrap the Barelwis in the loyalist camp: *Quad Erat Demonstrandum*.

Islam—Image and Reality

Writing in November 1888, the then viceroy of India, Lord Dufferin described the Muslims of British India as 'a nation of some 50 million, with their monotheism, their iconoclastic fanaticism, their animal sacrifices, their social equality and their remembrance of the days when, on their own at Delhi, they reigned supreme....'.[43] This last bit, about 'reigning supreme', accurately captures the self-image that the modern, educated, Indian Muslims had of themselves in the late nineteenth and early twentieth centuries. This self-image was a consequence of yearning for a past long gone, a thirst for that bygone era, of regaining, some at least, of those glories. Such irrational nostalgia had consequences, some extremely damaging, as we shall see in the later chapters. It spurred the Muslims to first demand a special political position in British India, and then in the 1940s, they moved, from seeking parity with the Hindu majority to a separate, self-governing statehood, their own land, a Pakistan for themselves because they held that Muslims were a separate nation, and not because Dufferin had so termed them.

Paradoxically, in their quest for a land of their own it was this self-image that first got lost, it most inexplicably went into oblivion with Partition; for now there was a land but no glory, and for that strand of Muslims who now found themselves abandoned in India, they of course, lost entirely their dreams of bygone glories. Highlighting the illusory nature of such a self-image is the observation by many that such views would actually have startled the Muslims of that earlier, pre-British period when they were, in reality, the dominant political entity over large parts of India. Scattered unevenly over a subcontinent the size of West Europe, divided by sectarian beliefs, dietary habits, social norms, dress, occupation and so often by language, the Muslims of India's middle centuries never thought of themselves as a unity, and certainly never acted as one. They just could not, for this went against the very grain of being in India, being an Indian, and also being an Indian Muslim.

Let us go back for a moment to when Islam first came to India. Persian and Arab traders had engaged in commerce on the West Coast of India from pre-Islamic times. With the rise of Islam, these very traders adopted the faith, became Muslim merchants, entering into the trade as an inheritance, and converting to Islam because that had become the faith pervading their lands. The first Muslim fleet is said to have appeared at Thane, near Bombay, in AD 636, during the Caliphate of Umar, just four years after the death of the Prophet. Land approaches to India had always been the preferred routes of access and it was over land that invasions in Sindh in the seventh and eighth centuries had occurred. By the eleventh and twelfth centuries, the Muslims had gained near total domination over both the land and sea routes to India. On land, the places where Muslims had, by this time settled along with trade and trading posts lay in Malabar, Konkan, or the West Coast of India.

Early Muslim settlers in northern India had come raiding as invaders, or with the invaders, in recurring waves of immigration. Sindh, as we have already noted was raided [invaded] by the Arabs in seventh/eighth century; in consequence a tiny Muslim community had come into existence there. Similarly, western Punjab saw the emergence of a local community of Muslims following upon the invasion of Mahmud of Ghazna in the eleventh century. Between this invasion and that of Mohammad Ghauri, that is between the eleventh and the late twelfth century there sprang up several Muslim settlements in northern India. This foothold of the Ghaznavids in Punjab lent itself to becoming the springboard of expansion, facilitating a movement further east. Nearly half a century before the Ghaurian conquest isolated pockets of Muslim migrants had appeared in northern India and even during the epochal period of Rathore dynasties in Kannauj, there were Muslim governors in Varanasi.

But so long as their commercial activity brought revenue to the Hindu rulers, they remained mostly welcome. They were also welcome for volunteering enrolment in the armies of Hindu rulers as mercenaries. But welcome or not, they continued to push their way into the heart of India through military expeditions, by land and by sea, strengthening their position as immigrants. From the first Muslim fleet to the major invasions of Qasim and Ghazni, there were in between many forays on many occasions, especially from AD 1080 to 1114; and then AD 1133 and 1169.[44] It mattered little if some failed in their efforts as long as their total numbers and influence continued to rise. And of course, the characteristic Hindu spirit of tolerance, of a kind of indifference towards the religious pursuits and affairs of others helped. However, by this period they (Hindus) certainly did not appreciate or welcome any marked proselytising activity by the Muslims. As this could not be immediately stopped by them, here too, they became largely indifferent.

Between the establishment by Ghaznavid rule and the battle of Tarain,[45] there is a gap of more than 150 years. However, these two landmark events are interconnected, being separated only in time. For, Muslim rule, in one form or another had continued in the Punjab throughout this period, although with varying degrees of spread, depth, and effectiveness. Which is why, Ghauri's ultimate success lay in establishing a recognisable rule in Punjab and Delhi, so vital for extension of Muslim kingdoms in India. This had another consequence, the presence of one or another form of Muslim rule in India stimulated an increase in the numbers of the faithful. For one, Muslim rulers actively encouraged conversion, then they endowed Muslim scholars and centres of learning, also conferred land grants and pensions but only to Muslim scholars. Very occasionally, in the heat of a campaign, invading forces also made some of those taken captive profess Islam on the pain of death. Occasionally, a Muslim ruler might offer a tributary chieftainship or rights over land as a precondition of conversion. Mostly they created situations wherein conversions became convenient, to remain steadfast to one's faith, as say devotedly a Hindu, instantly invited penalties, amongst which lay the infamous 'jazia'.[46]

Besides, as the area under Muslim rule gradually expanded the number of Muslims also, naturally, went up. In Indian life then conversion meant not much more than a change of fellowship, much less of conduct or inner life—although the latter did, in time, obviously occur. A convert to Islam joined a new social group, which was never really in harmony with the aggregate of other Muslims in India for those most intimate of social relations: marriage, inter-dining, and ritual observances. Beside, leaving old associates did not necessarily mean leaving all old ways behind because even new co-religionists would not immediately accept the recent convert on an equal footing, certainly not for a generation or two during which period they remained *mussalahs,* a step lower or different to being a pure born Muslim.

Muslim *maulvis, qazis, pirs* and *faqirs* too, did not demand of recent converts any immediate and total abandonment of their old faith, habits or social ties. They were tolerant of deviations from the letter of the Muslim law in, for example, rules of inheritance. When members of a dominant land-holding family converted to Islam those in 'jajmani'[47] relationship to them, on account of consanguinity, followed suit. This was more a matter of convenience than a consequence of religious transformation or new-found religious fervour. The achievements of Muslim rulers varied but like the British in India, after their initial military successes they were content being consistently more diplomatic than martial; maintaining their rule through useful political alliances, and more importantly, through a suggestion of force rather than its actual use. Muslim rule in India, like the British Raj, or for that matter most governance in India is more a matter of tolerant acceptance by the *ryot* (the ruled), an indifferent acquiescence, not always a consequence of giving in to forceful domination. Besides, ruling from just one central authority in India is always more notional than real; in this vast and varied land it can hardly be otherwise.

Writing in 1871, the Bengal civil servant Sir William Hunter[48] described the 'musalmans as in all respects...a race ruined under British rule'. By overlooking that this observation applied more to lower or south Bengal, most historians accepted this blanker verdict as final, and then extended it as depicting the fate of Muslims in all of British India. Yet, for other Muslims, in Punjab for example, British rule had brought security; for those in Bombay who were engaged in shipping and commerce it brought wealth; for some in British service in the North-West Provinces it brought land grants as rewards. The only generalisation possible being that gradually the British changed the criteria of success in Indian society, from the military to commercial: their lure became 'accept the British and gain material favours', and so many got hooked, readily and totally.

The British, by early nineteenth century were no doubt themselves rather awed by what they had achieved on the by-lines of their commercial exploitation of India: consequently, they remained carefully respectful of the prevalent Mughal culture of North India. Even though they had virtually occupied Delhi, they worked, at first, pragmatically to accommodate the nominal supremacy of Shah Alam. Nonetheless, this, of course, had all to end, and it did, slowly but relentlessly through obdurate British assertiveness in refusing to recognise the Mughal emperor's rights. By 1857, the British had convinced themselves that the Mughals in Delhi had become an anomaly. Their existence now, was a matter of indifference even to the Muslim population of the East India Company's territories. There was little in that to grieve for, as such is the fate of any enfeebled dynasty or ruler, not just that of the later Mughals; it is uniformly the same, in India or elsewhere, as then so now in the twenty-first century, too.

A continuing search for a new role, a new relevance, some responsibility, a position in life to which they were accustomed, made the Muslim community begin to reach outwards. It was this impulse that finally persuaded Muslims of India to resort to political activism; else they reckoned they would be rendered as even more irrelevant. The Hindus, better educated, more accommodative were already astir. The Indian National Congress (INC) had been in existence since 1885, from during the viceroyalty of Lord Dufferin, who for so long as he remained in that eminent position, routinely invited the Congress members to his annual garden party.

This search resulted in an initiative: that of petitioning for a share in power, and it is this that finally caused the Simla delegation of 1906 to come about. From this petitioning was born the separate electorates of the Indian Councils Act of 1909, which gave to the Muslims a separate constitutional identity, but within the limited ambit of the then prevailing democratic modes, and of course always as subjects of the Empire. This, in part, was also an outcome of the steps taken by Viceroy Curzon (1898-1905). However, we are moving far too fast: about all this and Curzon's partitioning of Bengal, that one single move, administratively sound but politically disastrous, proving conclusively the theory of unintended consequences, we now briefly refer.

THE LANGUAGE DIVIDE

Outside of the particularities and rituals of the two faiths, what also separated them was the medium of education, the language used, and the curriculum adopted; they were entirely different and separate. Schools of teaching tended to be attached (mostly) to temples, mosques and such other congregational centres. The medium of instruction here was different: Sanskrit, Hindi or the regional language for Hindu schools just as Persian, Arabic or Urdu were standard for the Muslim. Though Hindu students could, and were, admitted to Muslim schools, Muslims were hard to come by at Hindu establishments. Also, while Hindus severally took to learning Urdu or Persian, it was seldom that a Muslim was fluent in Sanskrit, though Hindi was even then, as now, a commonly-used medium.

This schooling system, native to the country, continued through the first half of the nineteenth century even as more modern establishments, (in their educational curriculum), had begun to appear. Though Muslims were freely entering government establishments then, in proportion that is to their population, yet, an assumption became common amongst leading Muslims of North India that their community did not have the advantage of English education.

The situation in Bengal was entirely different, as indeed it was, for example in South India. However, we examine only Bengal where Muslims were educationally backward. This was for a variety of reasons, amongst which, prominently was the 'Wahabi influence'.[49] While North India had a Sir Sayyid as an ardent reformer, Bengal, where the need was perhaps greater, had no such benefactor. Syed Ameer Ali, Nawab Abdul Lateef and such other Muslim leaders of Bengal did emphasise that Urdu ought to be for the Muslims what Bengali was to the Hindus of Bengal; yet, it never did acquire the same status. A fact never left unstressed being that there was too much of a Hindu influence in an ordinary Bengali school.

In the 1870s, there arose a conflict between the protagonists of Hindi and Urdu.

Though the Hindus never did really abandon Urdu, the superiority of this camp language, its usability and other attractions provoked Hindi protagonists to protest in Bihar, then a part of Bengal. In consequence, the government of Bengal issued orders for the use of Hindi in the court offices of Bihar whereafter Devanagari[50] was made the exclusive script of use in Bihar for official documents, The doggedness with which this order was followed antagonised Muslims and the controversy travelled then to provinces like NWFP. Here the reverse manifestation occurred: a failure to introduce Devanagari in the provinces, like in Punjab or NWFP became a cause for grievance amongst the Hindus.

For both communities, the question of language and script had more than any ordinary significance. For Hindus, Hindi as a language was purged of Arabic and Persian influence, and for the Muslims, Urdu came to signify power and influence; the Arabic script, in consequence, acquired a completely unwarranted religious significance. This was by the second half of the nineteenth century by when Urdu had indeed replaced Persian as a language of the government. In the literary circles of the north and western province, much of the drive against Persian and Urdu came from people like Pundit Pratap Narain Mishra[51] and Bhartendu Harishchandra,[52] famous names who switched loyalty, also their medium of expression, from Urdu to Hindi. Wishing to break the patronage in government jobs for the Urdu speaking elite, Bhartendu Harishchandra's pro-Hindi paper *Kavi Vachan Sudha*, frequently gave expression to the attitude of such civil service hopefuls: 'The Muslims, it is true, might suffer by the change from Persian to Nagri script but they are only a small portion of the community and the interests of the few must always yield to the many'.[53] It was Benares from where emerged the main inspiration for the pro-Hindi agitation. Here Raja Shiv Prasad[54] from the 1870s, mainly through the efforts of Bhartendu Harishchandra, helped Hindi acquire a body of literature, also its form as a language. Much of this activity involved Hindi translation of Bengali works. The Arya Samajists also found that they could use Hindi and the Devanagari script for facilitating contact with the masses.

The campaign for Hindi and Devanagari script was possibly just one prominent aspect of a growing awareness for the protection and promotion of Hindu interests. Certain others like cow protection movement and holding processions on religious occasions, were more specifically oriented towards the religious interests of the Hindus.

Unfortunately, an assertion of these religious interests at municipal level tended to push the political parties increasingly towards conducting themselves as religious parties. This trend further weakened the already strained cross-communal alliances, with the result that the Urdu-speaking elite broke away at many places, an unfortunate development, for it had held together for long the Hindu and Muslim components.

Within Hindu society, as a reaction to the social influences exerted by the British rule, there then arose movements attempting reforms, for example the Brahmo Samaj[55] of Calcutta (1828), the Prarthana Samaj[56] of Bombay and the Arya Samaj (1875).[57] These attempts at reform, when directed against orthodox Hinduism did not remain unchallenged. The founding of Brahmo Samaj was immediately countered by the foundation of Dharma Sabha.[58] The spread of the Arya Samaj also inspired orthodox reaction, culminating in the formation of Bharat Dharma Maha Mandal.[59] It was the Sanatanis[60] who were primarily responsible for the formation of the Hindu Sabha[61] of the United Province in mid-1910, essentially as a reaction against the extension of a separate electorate in favour of Muslims at the municipal level. The Hindu Sabha spread beyond Punjab and the United Provinces into Bihar, Bengal and Central Provinces and included the Bombay Presidency, too.

In the final analysis it was more the fact rather than any prospects of a partitioning of Bengal that crystallised Muslim opinion against an anti-partition agitation launched by the Hindus. This was largely a consequence of a stir amongst Hindus of rural Bengal, who opposed Partition, consistently, both before and after it had occurred; their appeal being based largely on popular Hindu religious sentiment. In historical terms this division of Bengal and then a joining of the separated East

Bengal with Assam, planted yet another poisonous seed which continues to bedevil the entire region till this day: of unchecked, illegal immigration in Assam, and of this destructive Muslim electorate politics of the region. For the Muslims of Bengal, adjoining areas of Assam and its rich, fertile lands were (are) a continuous temptation, a natural hinterland for their ballooning numbers to expand into; first to encroach upon, as almost by right and then to usurp. Political activism, separate identities, assertive claims of political equality with Hindus, (by Muslims) all had by now arrived, and all this within a half century of 1857. Then again, in less than fifty years from this reawakened Muslim and Hindu political activism, that is, from the beginning to mid-twentieth century, the logic of a sponsored and an unreal Hindu-Muslim political equalism led inevitably to the separation of the two. 'As you sow so shall you reap,' we are told, trite no doubt to repeat this over used axiom, but here it is nevertheless very apt, for having sown the seeds of separation, what started limitedly as separate electorates kept growing and spreading until it finally became a demand for a separate nation.

Let us pause in that fateful year of 1905. Once this new, Eastern Bengal, a Muslim majority province had got established, leading Muslims then began to see clearly its many advantages, and with this vision new self-interests took birth. That is why any Hindu led, anti-partition agitation appeared (to the Muslims) as an interference in what they considered by then as already 'theirs', a rightful due, their own Muslim province. Limited issues like Minto's acceptance of Fuller's resignation[62] in August 1906, over the Government of India's refusal to support reprisals against school agitators in Serajganj[63] came across as a victory for the Hindu agitators just when Muslims in this Muslim majority province were basking in the then unfamiliar sun of official favour. This eventually brought the Muslims of East Bengal politically nearer to their co-religionists in North India, again totally unexpectedly.

However, all this was of little avail, for in the new province of Eastern Bengal things became worse. As Lovett records in the *History of the Indian National Movement*:

> As purely sentimental appeals were ineffectual to excite sufficient popular sympathy, the (Hindu) leaders of the anti-partition movement, searching for a national hero endeavoured to import from Bombay the cult of Shivaji and

appealed to the religion of the multitude by placing their efforts under the patronage of Kali, the goddess of strength and destruction.[64]

The many dice of fate were already rolling, unstoppably, as we are now able to see, but we do so with that helpless clarity of hindsight.

Almost unavoidably, the Congress identified itself with this agitation. In turn, the Muslims, galvanised by these events persuaded their leaders to realise that the call of the times was for assertive action, and that it was a must for sheer self-preservation. It is in consequence of all these agitations that the famous Simla Deputation to Lord Minto was organised in 1906. But about that, too, in some detail later.

POLITICS OF IDENTITY

In this period of shift and of transformation, an important development in Muslim polity was the emergence of a young Muslim element. This was at the beginning of the twentieth century. This young element drawn mostly from lawyers and professionals, quite often members of landowning families but now better endowed with education and awareness, was politically an assertive lot, they emerged challenging the existing, the conservatives. These young came largely from the United Provinces, and included people like Mohammad Ali,[65] his brother Shaukat Ali and Hakim Ajmal Khan.[66] Conservatives of the ilk of Nawab Saheb Dhaka were alarmed at the vehemence of protests voiced by these 'younger' elements, as for example, when Muhsin al-Mulk gave in to the government over Urdu.[67] It is this alarm that probably accounts for Wiqar-ul-Mulk's[68] abortive efforts, between 1901 and 1903, to found a Muslim political association in the United Provinces under conservative leadership. However, all these various pieces of the Muslim patchwork needed to be put together, somehow given an aim and an objective to work for.

The British did just that, via Morley and Minto,[69] who were determined to influence Indian opinion for their own sake, of smoother governance in India. Besides, those disturbing echoes of 1857 were still being heard in the Imperial corridors, 'were the Hindus and Muslims to come together we will be in grave difficulties,' went the fearful counsels of Imperial advisers. These apprehensions were greatly sharpened by a rise of the nationalist movement in mid-1880s, in which Hindu intelligentsia—being the more advanced—was naturally more prominent. The first session of the INC was held at Bombay in 1885. It was attended by only two Muslims. The second one held in Calcutta the following year was attended by 33, and the sixth in 1890 by 156 Muslim delegates out of a total of 702, or 22 per cent. As more and more Muslims were drawn to the movement, the British government became restive. To win the Muslims back to the ranks of the loyal followers then became the recognised, official policy of the British.

In a letter dated 11 May 1906 to Lord Minto, then the viceroy, Lord Morley, the secretary of state for India, referring to a conversation he had had with the Prince of Wales, during his visit to India, wrote: 'He (the Prince) talked of the National Congress rapidly becoming a great power...There it is, (the Congress) whether we like it or not'. But interestingly an angle existed to this princely observation. Syed Mohammad Zauqi, editor of a 'loyal' paper *Al-haq,* had accompanied the Prince of Wales on his India visit as a local press representative. Zauqi describes his encounters with Muslim leaders, specially with Syed Hussain Bilgrami (Imad-ul-Mulk).[70] In a letter to Jinnah, but very much later in 1943, Zauqi recalled those events and encounters which had led to the establishment of the Muslim party and also on the origins of the Simla Depuration. In this a rather detailed, but retrospective account is given of the origins of the Simla Deputation and the formation of the Muslim League. This is placed in the Appendix, for interest though its authenticity cannot be vouchsafed.

Zauqi's story apart, on 4 August 1906, Muhsin al-Mulk, then secretary of the Aligarh College had written to his principal about Archibold, who was visiting Simla:

> You must have read and thought over Mr John Morley's speech on the Indian budget. It is very much talked of among the Mohammadans of India and is commonly believed to be a great success achieved by the National Congress. You are aware that the Mohammadans already feel a little disappointed, and young educated Mohammadans seem to have a sympathy for the Congress and this speech will produce a greater tendency in them to join the Congress. I have got several letters drawing attention particularly to the new proposal of elected representatives in the Legislative Councils. They say that the existing rules confer no rights on Mohammadans; and no Mohammadans get into the Councils by election. If the new rules, now to be drawn up

introduce 'election' on a more extended scale, the Mohammadans will hardly get a seat and no Mohammadans will get into the Councils by election.[71]

Minto saw Muhsin al-Mulk's letter on 8 August 1906 and sent it on to Morley. On 10 August, Archibold, the viceroy's secretary, informed Muhsin al-Mulk that Minto would receive a 'Muslim deputation' and hear their grievances. This finally happened on 1 October 1906, when Minto received a deputation of thirty-five Muslims, from all the provinces of British India barring the NWFP. An address was then presented to the viceroy, claiming: 'For Muslims a 'fair share' in such extended representation as was now being considered for India,[72] but that 'fair share' should be computed not merely by reference to the numerical strength of Muslims in India but also by reference to their 'political importance', and to the contribution which they make to the defence of the empire'.[73] After remarking that 'representative institutions' of the 'European type' were alien to the people of India, this address went on to assert that such representation as the 'Muslims had hitherto been granted in the Legislative Councils had been inadequate and without the approval of those whom the nominees had been selected to represent'. Furthermore, a Muslim was unlikely to be selected by the electoral bodies, as now constituted, unless in 'sympathy with the majority', which it followed would necessarily be a Hindu. In which case, it was put across: 'He would not be a true representative of (the) Muslims'; because they 'are a distinct community with additional interests...not shared by other communities and...have hitherto suffered (as) they have not been adequately represented'. The address proposed that a

> fixed proportion of Muslims, on Municipal and District Boards...be returned by separate electorates, that the proportion of Muslims on provincial councils should be established with due regard to the Muslim community's political importance and proportion to be returned by an electoral college composed of Muslims only, and that a similar arrangement should be adopted for the Imperial (Viceroy's) Legislative Council, appointment by election being preferred over appointment by nomination.[74]

Minto's response was encouraging. He welcomed 'the representative character of the deputation for expressing the views and aspirations of the enlightened Muslim community of India';[75] and announced:

> that in any system of representation whether it affects a Municipality, a District Board or a Legislative Council, in which it is proposed to introduce or increase an electoral organisation, the Mohammadan community should be represented as a community...I am entirely in accord with you; please do not misunderstand me I make no attempt to indicate by what means the representation of communities can be obtained, but I am firmly convinced, as I believe you to be, that any electoral representation in India would be doomed to mischievous failure which aimed at granting a personal enfranchisement regardless of the beliefs and traditions of the communities composing the population of this continent.[76]

It is this one single step, acknowledged and encouraged by Minto, among of course, various other factors, which we examine in subsequent chapters that contributed to a 'separation' mentality. And indisputably this rejection of personal enfranchisement and acceptance of the device of reservation, based on religion, finally moved the Muslim political personality of India towards an eventual separation for which a sentiment had been growing ever since Sir Sayyid Ahmad Khan refused to have anything to do with the Indian National Congress.[77] But a question arises: Did the British do no more than simply acknowledge what already existed? Or did they, in fact, incite, create or encourage a separatist tendency? as a number of historians assert. Also, was this Simla Deputation, in Maulana Mohammad Ali Jauhar's words, 'a command performance'? Or was it more a consequence of the existing situation than any cause of separateness? There are, and will perhaps always remain, two schools of thought about this. But there is another, an even more worrisome, query that confronts us here. Elections, the very first step of democratic representation are to unite through electing public representatives jointly, that is by providing a platform and giving a voice, through vote, to all eligible adults; but what if the process of democratically electing itself becomes divisive, as clearly in this case it did?

By this time, Jinnah had been a Congressman of the Pherozeshah Mehta group, (the moderate group of the Congress, which amongst others included Dadabhai Naoroji, Gopal Krishna Gokhale and their group included Tilak, Bipin Chandra Pal and Lala Lajpat Rai.) and also, secretary to Dadabhai Naoroji who was presiding over the Calcutta Congress. This Simla Deputation did not amuse Jinnah at all. *Gujarati* a newspaper of Bombay, published a letter from Jinnah regarding this deputation and the memorial placed by it before the viceroy. Jinnah's letter had earlier been addressed to *The Times of India* but for some reason, it found no room in the columns. His letter, questioning the very locus-standi of the deputationist says:

> Dear Sir, It has been given out in the papers including your paper that a representative deputation of Mahomadans of India is going to wait upon the Viceroy on the 1 October. May I know whoever elected the gentlemen who are supposed to represent Bombay? It is such a pity that some people are always assuming the role of representatives without the smallest shadow of ground or foundation for it. I know of no meeting of the Mahomadan community that appointed these worthies to represent Bombay. Then another thing is this: May I know what is the object of the deputation? Nobody up to now knows what the deputation proposes to do. Is this the way to speak in the name of millions without even informing them what is going to be done for them, to say nothing of the fact that nothing has been done to ascertain the real views of the Mahomadans of this city in the matter?

Interesting light is also thrown on the origin and nature of H.H. the Aga Khan's performance by an entry in Lady Minto's Diary under the date 3 October 1906. Referring to the death of Nawab Mohsin-ul-Mulk, the great Mohammadan leader, one finds the following mentioned as among his good points: 'He it was who engineered the recent Mohammadan deputation'. Again, an entry dated 1 October 1906, which is set down as 'a very eventful day, and epoch in Indian history', is rather illuminating. That evening Lady Minto received a letter from an official (name not disclosed) which ran: 'I must send Your Excellency a line to say that a very big thing has happened today, a work of statesmanship that will affect India and Indian history for many a long year. It is nothing less man the pulling back of 62 millions of people from joining the ranks of the seditious opposition'.

This device of the communal electorates served its purpose so well, in the manner devised that a decade later we find a successor secretary of state for India, Montagu, and the viceroy, Lord Chelmsford, placing on record their observation:

> Division by creeds and classes means the creation of political camps organised against each other, and teaches men to think as partisans and not as citizens...We regard any system of communal electorates, therefore, as a very serious hindrance to the development of the self-governing principle.

The authors of the Montford scheme of Reforms then add: 'That the principle works so well that once it has been fully established, it so entrenches communalism that one could hardly then abandon the principle even if one wished to do so'.[78] And thus the system of communal franchise got embedded via the Montford Reforms. Lord Olivier, secretary of state for India in the Labour Government under Ramsay MacDonald, admitted it in as many words:

> No-one with any close acquaintance of Indian affairs will be prepared to deny that on the whole there is a predominant bias in British officialdom in India in favour of the Muslim community, partly on the ground of closer sympathy but more largely as a make-weight against Hindu nationalism.[79]

How then is one to pronounce authoritatively on such events of great import, a century after they occurred? Some aspects, though, are clear. Of all the British officials it was only Harcourt Butler, then deputy commissioner at Lucknow who criticised this whole idea of Muslims meeting in Lucknow, then drafting an address for the viceroy, and also for not following his advice. Butler had assertively opposed any demand for separate electorates, also this idea of a fixed proportion of Muslim appointments in the civil services He placed on record his views unambiguously: 'This whole business since Fuller's retirement till now has been organised by Muhsin al-Mulk and Imad al-Mulk of Bilgram in a hurry'?[80] Dunlop Smith's letter (viceroy's private secretary) though, to Muhsin al-Mulk advising on how the Simla address should be framed also suggested that 'Muslims should seek representation by 'nomination' rather than by 'election'.' The members of the Simla Deputation carried an assurance of receiving a sympathetic hearing from the British, also that they had a fair chance of success, for had not Minto in his letter of 8 August 1906, written to Morley that 'it was necessary to give full value to the importance of other interests besides those so largely represented by Congress'.[81] Sir Denzil Ibbetson, then lieutenant-governor of the Punjab, wrote to Dunlop Smith on 10 August 1906:

> I have heard from other quarters also what Mahsin ul-Mulk says about the aspirations of the younger generations of Mohammadans. Their aspirations are perfectly natural. But it would be a calamity if they were to drive...them into the arms of the Congress party; for at present the educated Mohammadan is the most conservative element in Indian society.[82]

Precisely, for the members of Simla Deputation, too, were mostly the conservative elements of Muslim society: but they were a self-appointed lot, and the younger Muslim element had practically no representation in this deputation.

British officials continued to assure Minto that this Simla Deputation was 'truly representative of the Muslims' and warned against the 'great threat to the stability of British rule that would arise should there be any Muslim discontent', (shadows of 1857, again). It remained to Harcourt Butler who alone continued to caution for he knew 'that the seed of Muslim political organisation needed the sun of British favour to grow into an all India'[83] plant, and the viceroy's patronage was just that. Writing to the law member of the Government of India, on 16 September 1906, Butler held that anti-Hindu feeling was about the only common platform'[84] on which the Muslims had gathered at Lucknow to draft the Simla address. Was this deputation the outcome then of a marriage of convenience between British political necessity (keep Muslims placated and away from the Congress), and Muslim interests, principally from UP? Inherent in all this was an underlying assumption, that as the 'British rule in India was here to stay', they must and will therefore, remain as the final arbiters. All this finally resulted in the passage of the Indian Councils Act, 1909. Through this the 'Government of India amplified (that) call for help from conservative Muslims into an alarm siren'.[85]

What follows is an interesting extract from the journal of Mary, Countess of Minto, regarding separate electorates:

> When Mr Gandhi attended the Round-Table Conference in London, the Maharaja of Bikaner [late Maharaja Sir Ganga Singhji] brought him up to me at a party, to be introduced.
> 'Do you remember my name?' I [Mary] asked.

'Remember your name!' exclaimed Mr Gandhi. 'The Minto-Morley Reforms have been our undoing. Had it not been for the separate electorates then established we should have settled our differences by now.'

'You forget, Mr Gandhi,' I replied, 'that the separate electorates were proposed by your leader and predecessor, Mr Gokhale.'

'Ah!' said Mr Gandhi with a smile. 'Gokhale was a good man, but even good men may make mistakes.'

'Yes,' said a Punjab landowner on the Council at the Indian office, who was standing near by, 'and if Lord Minto had not insisted on separate electorates, we Mohammadans should not be in existence.'

To the charge that the principle of separate representation for Muslims would exacerbate, if not actually create, communal differences, the official response was always that 'such differences already existed'. Replying to an address by the Hindu Sabha of Lahore against separate electorates, Dunlop Smith suggested that the viceroy ought to inform the Hindu Sabha that 'any government fit to rule the country for a day must take into account the differences in religions which exist';[86] also that the answer to the claim that the 'political interests of Hindus and Muslims, and other communities were identical was that Muslims and others did not think so'.[87]

Minto's (and his officials') stand for separate Muslim electorates owed much to the Muslim desire itself to have that distinction. Besides, Minto was fearful of Muslim disaffection, (1857 again!). He passed Harcourt Butler's views on to Morley, 'that at heart many Muslims were against the British government in India, that the Muslim landowning classes and the Muslim lawyer and professional classes were drifting apart';[88] that 'out of the tangle of warring ideas are slowly emerging or re-emerging the two persistent parties in Indian politics—the party for the Government and the party against it'.[89] Earlier Minto had informed Morley that, 'though the Mohammadan is silent, he is very strong'. However, after they had won Morley's acceptance of such separate electorates, the Muslims began demanding disproportionately higher number of seats on the Councils, above what Minto had found appropriate, and also to object to the proposal that Muslims should also have votes in general constituencies. Minto was then quick to join with Morley in reminding them of their client status, also that they alone were not important to British interests, as the conservative Muslim believed they were, Hindus were, after all, the best organised elements in India, whatever Sir Lancelot Hare might say.'[90] As Morley pithily then put it, the British had to be 'careful lest in picking up their Muslim parcels they drop their Hindu one'.[91]

Hindsight and clarity of thought, now informs us that this path of electoral separateness for ensuring an appropriate share in the political office of the country could only become more insatiably demanding, and there being no ultimate levelling out it would always result in creating greater inequalities. The concluding opinion came from Morley with his well-known declaration in the House of Lords on 17 December 1908: 'If I were attempting to set up a parliamentary system in India, or if it could be said that this chapter of reforms led directly or necessarily up to the establishment of a parliamentary system in India, I, for one, would have nothing at all to do with it'. It ought thereafter to have been abundantly clear what the Imperial intent was. And yet another step had got engraved on the memory templates of those times; fate was dragging us towards political separateness, and we went unheedingly along, for we did not even read the warning signals that had by then begun to flash.

It was in these circumstances that Muslims, now conferred with the identity of a separate political community, equipped themselves with a political organisation. It was essentially the self-appointed, from almost the whole of India, who had as 'Muslim leaders', gathered together for this Simla deputation. Inevitable and convenient, too, that a formal Muslim political organisation ought to now emerge from the chrysalis of this very Simla process. On 30 December 1906, members of the Mohammadan Educational Conference met at Dacca and converted themselves into the All-India Muslim League (AIML). Though most members of the Simla Deputation found representation on the provisional committee of the League, through being formally so appointed at Dacca, the foundations of the League had not yet set. Nawab Salimullah of Dacca, earlier absent from the Simla Deputation, was now the initiator of this process, having circulated a scheme for a Muslim All-India Confederacy. As an early forerunner of things to come Muslims from the United Provinces were even then not prepared to yield to the Muslims of Bengal. This young lawyer element of UP, well represented at Dacca, were a restive and an impatient lot, and they asserted themselves. Twenty-five members of the fifty-five strong Provisional Committee declined to support the loyalist line favoured by the landlords and government pensioners. To paper over these cracks a neutral resolution was adopted. At this stage, no attempt was made to spell out the nature of the Muslim political interests needing protection or promotion. This was clearly not the time for any such initiative; the League at this stage was, after all, just a loyalist body.

As is only normal, the AIML remained a rather feeble infant for several decades after being baptised. Financially, it was dependent on the subventions of the Muslim nawabs and princes. In the agitation of 1909, against the electoral college scheme, many of the telegrams calling upon the government to hold fast to a scheme of separate electorates were sent more on behalf of local Anjumans than the Muslim League. In 1910, in the first elections held under the Morley-Minto reforms, the Muslim League failed to act as an organisation; it did not even present itself to the new Muslim electorate as a political party and had no recognisable political platform. Such of its elements as were elected to the enlarged Legislative Councils, despite these shortcomings, gained electoral success only on account of their local and personal prestige, and not because they were members of the Muslim League. The most dramatic revelation of the League's political limitations was its incapacity to even protest effectively against a British decision, widely construed as a blow to Muslim interests to revoke, in 1911, the partition of Bengal; indeed the Muslim League as a political organisation was not even counted as a factor in discussions leading to this decision about annulling that fateful 'partition'. Writing to the then lieutenant-governor of United Provinces, in February 1910, Minto had specifically refused to accept the League as the sole representative Muslim body, to which one ought naturally refer for an opinion on any question of importance. It is a very long distance, as we shall see in subsequent chapters, that the League travelled from this observation to actually becoming the 'sole representative Muslim body', and for Mohammad Ali Jinnah to be the 'sole spokesman' of the Muslims.

Going back, the membership of the League was skeletal, and as per the annual report of the AIML, in early 1920 it did not cross the 1200. Chaudhri Khaliquzzaman recalled how the League lived merely on paper during the Khilafat days, and how afterwards a 'new set of Nawabs' wrested control of it. They merely attended the annual sessions and received praise from their equally honourable hosts for having undertaken such a tedious journey at 'great inconvenience to themselves; then, for staying as guests in the discomfort of unfamiliar lodgings, whereafter to have to suffer those unfamiliar (but rather delicious) dishes; though plenty of *pan* (betel) to chew and cigarettes to smoke perhaps mitigated some of their discomfort'. What an enchanting world of the *ashraf* that must have been, this playing at national politics, and so self-importantly. The proceedings of the League, after the session, were duly sent to the press, this though, would always be long after the British officials had already received complete versions of every word spoken at the meeting from their own loyal sources. 'The end of the session was the end of the organisation for that year and no one took notice of what had been said, few even remembered a month later what had been discussed, [only] the records of the Government of India maintained all'.[92]

In the early years, the AIML was really more like an amateur playing not in a command performance, but to an invited audience'.[93] The British and the conservative Muslims, both, had succeeded through separating the electorates on a very narrow, property-based franchise, in isolating the young Muslim element from both the radical Congress politicians and from Muslims outside the charmed circles of the durbar invitees. However, they underestimated the resilience of the young Muslims. This younger lot had votes as graduates; in addition, they canvassed for larger popular support by working with those who had the ear of Muslims outside the British educational system, the Ulema, the Muslim religious scholars, and in this manner to seriously then bid for the leadership of the Muslim League. By conceding separate electorates, the British had conferred upon Muslims a distinctive political role in British India. It is a totally different matter that with time the British awakened to the fact that the writing of the script for that role had got snatched out of their hands, that they had ceased to now call the shots that made the Muslims obey; the theory of unintended consequences had asserted itself, again.

Those Muslims who had organised the Simla Deputation and who with eager British assistance, had secured separate electorates, were in reality now more concerned about preserving their own quality of life, their status and their standing against their own lower orders, than achieving any electoral domination over the Hindus. The Muslims of the Simla Deputation had sought more the certainty of their own co-option, their own hierarchical status continuing in the Empire. The possibility of a political or ideological independence from the British, they did not, for all their emphasis on their 'Muslim-ness', even seriously contemplate perhaps did not even consider then.

It is here that Mohammad Ali Jinnah arrived to etch his own, as also the political future of the Muslims of India on the copperplate of time. In succeeding chapters, we examine Jinnah's evolution as the founder of Pakistan, for the founding of which it seems the ground had already been prepared by this complex sequence of events. These events, in time culminated in the great tragedy of 1947. So many millions were then uprooted and death and vengeance stalked this ancient land of India. A bitter and ironic thought strikes us here, forcefully, when reflecting on this cruel vivisection. Was Jinnah's search actually for regaining, at least, some of the glitter of that lost past, or was it just for adequate political space in this new, democratic order now fast emerging in India; in essence how to not get drowned in an unseeing, uncaring sea of majoritarianism? Is it this last that was the quest? And, is it our failure to grasp the import of this need that led to 1947? We attempt to answer these questions, too, in succeeding chapters.

2

JENABHAI TO JINNAH: THE JOURNEY

Kathiawar—Sindh

In the preceding chapter we journeyed with Islam's growth in India, though, it is just not possible to condense adequately, certainly not in the space of only one chapter the totality of that epic saga, of Islam's advent and growth in India, a journey of many centuries, covering the entire range of human experience. Through the grinding passage of time, the challenge of altering circumstances, and the robust insolence of those conquering traders from a distant island—Britain; the Muslims, rulers in large parts of India, until then patrons of power and dispensers of favours, sank slowly to the humiliating position of petitioners in the durbars of the *firangi*. The trading British had brought with them the very same freebooting spirit and attributes of dare-devilry that the early Muslim invaders had come endowed with. Then the Muslim spirit had been to either conquer or to perish, not too dissimilar an approach from what these new arrivals came imbued with. Britain was a very long way away, and in any event as the journey back was as perilous as the challenge of staying on in India; better then to stay and conquer.

When Mohammad Ali Jinnah entered the Indian political scene, though the Muslim League did not exist then, a reawakened Muslim consciousness was certainly there, as were those very first stirrings of demands for more authority in the hands of Indians. The Imperial British were being urged to yield political space to the natives, in which they could at least play at being the moulders of their own political destiny; but, obviously, all this had to be within strictly controlled limits and with no dilution of the imperial authority, indeed to enhance that authority by creating an illusion of sharing without actually doing so.

It was the turn of the century. Great Britain was at the height of its imperial glory, Queen Victoria reigned majestically supreme, the lords, the ladies and the sahibs who ruled on her behalf in India saw not a speck of cloud obstructing their imperial vision; not one troublesome dot existed then on the horizon of their future. How, in such a scenario, a rather impecunious Khoja, socially very far from the *ashraf* of India, not the inheritor of either family wealth, standing or name, did this young entrant to the cosmopolitan world of Bombay, etch his name so boldly and so indelibly on the social and political firmament of India? That was Mohammad Ali Jinnah, from Kathiawar.

Tucked below the Great Rann of Kutch, skirting the Arabian Sea which lies to the west and stretching landwards into the fertile and well watered lands of 'hundred kingdoms', literally 'Saurashtra', in the Indian state of Gujarat lies Kathiawar—freely translated 'the region of the Kathis'; inhabited by fine Kathiawari horses; beautiful Kathi women, astute traders and so many rich business families—Hindu and Muslim.

Now spare a moment for the accompanying, rather rough map of the region, marked on it in bold are some place names, for example: Porbander; Jamnagar; Rajkot; Gondal; Ganod; Paneli. They all lie within a radius of roughly two hundred miles, and we are in the declining years of the nineteenth century. The cataclysms of Oudh, of the Indo-Gangetic plains, have left this part of India largely untroubled. Islam has, of course, been here right from before that paralysing sack of the great temple of Somnath by Ghazna, in AD 1024. Gujarat has also by then had several Muslim governors; oppressions of Mohammad Shah Begra, for example, remain in the memory of this land and its people, as also the challenge mounted to Begra, as ballads inform us, by Rathore chieftains from the adjoining desert fastnesses of Mallani, (today's Barmer district in Rajasthan). Kathiawar is the land where Krishna breathed his last; it is one of the four great pilgrimage centres for the Hindus. As for the Muslims, Patan then provided the port through which the annual Haj pilgrimages, by the sea route then set sail. In this land is also Porbander from where Mohandas Karamchand Gandhi's family originally came. Mohandas was Karamchandji's fourth offspring, born on 2 October 1869, (some twelve years after the great upheaval of 1857) at Rajkot, where the elder Gandhi then held the important post of the diwan[1] of that state.

Gujarat (District Map)

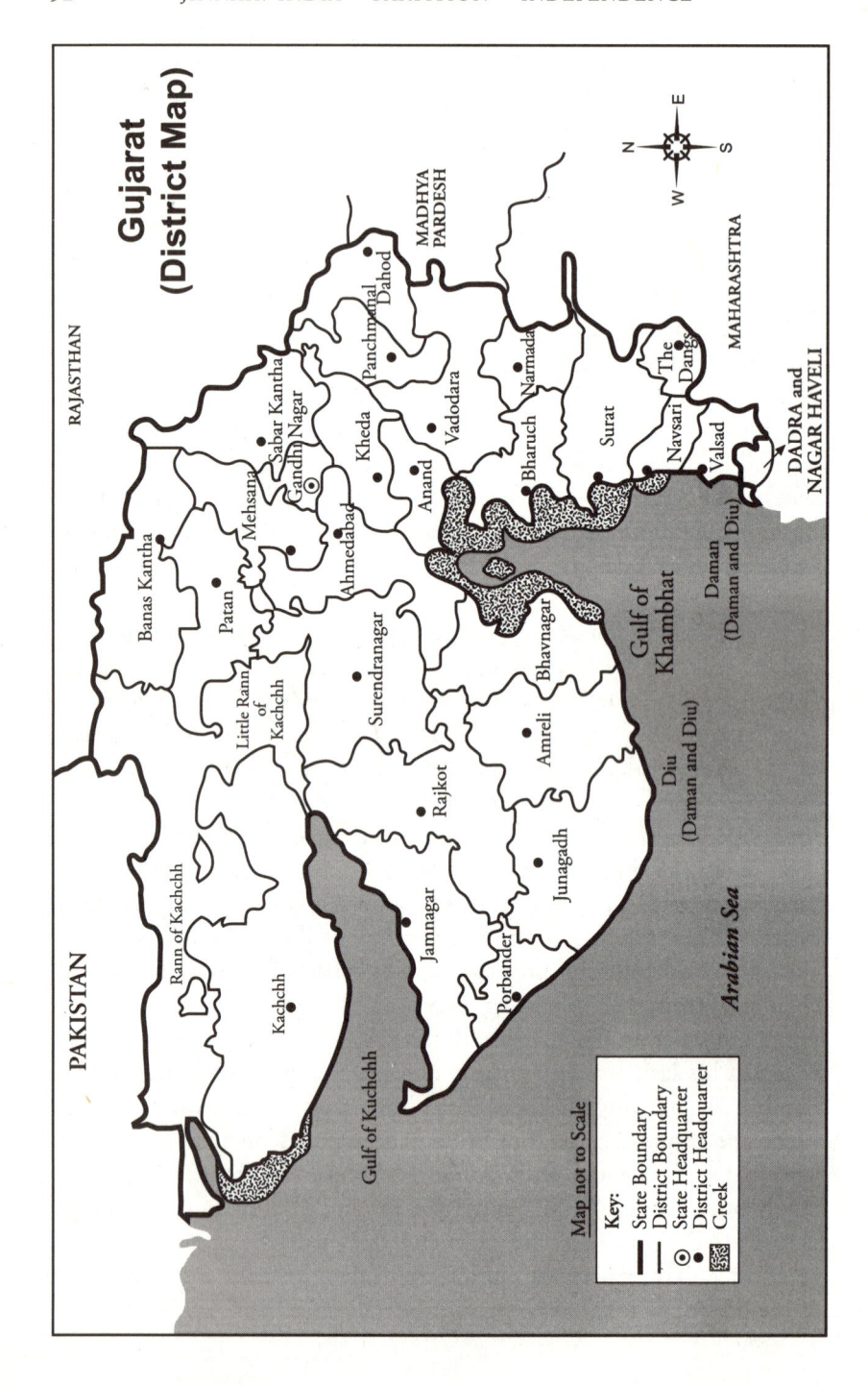

Some fifty-odd miles to the south-west of Rajkot lies the village of Paneli. It was then part of a small Kathiawari principality by the name of Gondal. In Paneli lived a family of Khoja Muslims,[2] who like the Bohras[3] were, and still are, essentially peace-loving traders, accommodative, non-combative with none of the supposed attributes earlier cited.

Poonjabhai, along with his three sons, Valjibhai, Nathubhai, Jenabhai and a daughter Maanbai had always lived in Paneli. Like many others of his ilk, Poonjabhai earned his living working handlooms. The youngest of Poonjabhai's sons, Jenabhai, risked leaving Paneli and moved to nearby Gondal. This was the first step. The next, in comparison, was a giant leap—in time, space and in circumstances, and ultimately in consequences, too. Thereafter, Jenabhai moved to Karachi, sailing for that port city around 1875. In Karachi he ventured into trade, and given his native ability, prospered. Karachi, like Bombay or other ports of India, was where British firms had then established their trading posts. And here fortuitous trading circumstances brought Jenabhai in contact with Frederick Leigh-Croft. This proved to be the turning point in Jenabhai's fortunes and of immense advantage to his entire family and, of course, to himself, in several ways.

In Karachi, on 25 October or December 1876, (for this matter of the exact date of Jinnah's birth remained undecided for sometime) was born a son to Mithibai and Jenabhai. As is customary Jenabhai the father decided upon the name, the mother agreed and the *qazi* performed the necessary rituals. In Kathiawar most of the male members of Poonjabhai's family had names strikingly similar to those of the Hindus. However, Karachi was different; it had a significant Muslim presence, besides as all other children in the neighbourhood had regular Muslim names a strange sounding one would place the newborn at a clear disadvantage. It was considered appropriate, therefore to name the first-born as Mohammad Ali Jenabhai, the last a customary suffix being really the patronym.

For the ceremony of 'Aqiqah',[4] young Mohammad Ali's parents took him to the *dargah* of Hassan Pir, all the way back to Ganod, a few miles off Paneli. Mohammad Ali's head was then shaved ceremoniously, for it was, as it still is, believed that the miraculous and supernatural powers of Hassan Pir would bestow on Mohammad Ali (or on any other with faith in the Pir) a great future: and so Mithibai, the devout and loving mother had prayed and sought blessings.

Mohammad Ali's primary education was not formal. As was then customary, a teacher came to their home in Karachi to teach the Gujarati language, their mother tongue. When he was nine, Mohammad Ali was put in a primary school, from where a year later he shifted to Sindh Madrassah-tul-Islam[5] spending three and a half years there. After Sindh Madrassah young Mohammad Ali was shifted to the Church Mission School of Karachi. However, after some time, upon the advice of Frederick Leigh-Croft, Mohammad Ali was sent to London, primarily to learn the intricacies of shipping, in which trade Jenabhai, the father, was then engaged. Croft had assured an apprenticeship in London to young Mohammad Ali. For the parents this opportunity was too good to decline. Before leaving for London, Mohammad Ali was, as was then the custom, married to Emi Bai. She was eleven to his sixteen; the year was 1892.

He left for London in the first week of November 1892, but before that, and quite suddenly, his father's family fortunes suffered. A court judgment in one of the pending cases, announced in the month of May 1892, went against Jenabhai; in consequence his property was placed at the disposal of the court. Under such circumstances, with the honour and prestige of the family at stake, as the decreed amount was not readily payable, the father thought it best to send his son abroad. After his son's departure Jenabhai declared himself insolvent. In January 1893 processes were set afoot for realising the debt money through an attachment of property. This then compelled Jenabhai to move again, this rime to Bombay, where he took up residence in Durga Mohalla,[6] in July 1893, a locality just outside Fort, Bombay.

Very little is known of young Mohammad Ali's early experiences in England, except that as a Karachi-born Kathiawari youth, to start with, he felt greatly alone in this strange land, was troubled by the cold climate, was uncomfortable in the midst of all those aliens and was not until then fluent enough in English language. He was on a paid assignment, courtesy Leigh-Croft, at Grahams' Head Office in London, working as a business apprentice. As knowledge of law helped in this business, one thing led to another and Mohammad Ali Jenabhai developed an interest in law. Whereafter, flexibility in admission rules, along with other factors, encouraged him to sit for admission tests for the Bar and in June 1893, he was admitted to Lincoln's Inn. An apocryphal story informs us that he chose this particular Inn because on one of the New Hall's main entrances he saw a fresco depicting the image of Prophet Muhammad (PBUH) among the group of lawgivers of the world.

JENABHAI—JINNAH IN ENGLAND

In London, Dadabhai Naoroji now arrived in Jinnah's life, as an inspiration and a benefactor. Gandhi, recollecting his arrival in London, for he too had gone there for study, reminisced: 'I found that the Indian students had free access to Naoroji at all hours of the day. Indeed, he was in the place of father to everyone of them, no matter to which province or religion they belonged. He was there to advise and guide them in their difficulties. I have always been a hero worshipper, and so Dadabhai became like a real 'Dada' to me'.[7] Dadabhai Naoroji was elected to the House of Commons in July 1892, Indian students having then enthusiastically campaigned for him, though, Jinnah could not participate as in July 1892 he was still in Karachi. However, then Jinnah must surely have participated in the celebratory gathering on 23 January 1893.

Thereafter, Jinnah regularly attended the proceedings of the House of Commons as a visitor. Indeed, in his enthusiasm he had once said, 'I want to be in London and enter Parliament where I hope to wield some influence. There I shall meet British statesmen on a footing of equality.' This youthful enthusiasm could have been on account of Dadabhai's work for India in the British Parliament. Fatima Jinnah, his sister, recalling those days, writes: 'My brother said to me, when I learnt that Lord Salisbury in one of his speeches had ridiculed Dadabhoy as a 'black man', warning Finsbury constituency not to elect him, I was furious. If Dadabhoy was black, I was blacker; and if this was the mentality of our political 'masters', then we could never get a fair deal at their hands. From that day I have been an uncompromising enemy of all forms of colour bar. I worked for the Old Man (Dadabhai) with a vengeance. Fortunately, he won by a majority of three votes. However thin the majority, jubilation among Indian students in London was tremendous. As I sat in the galleries, listening to the maiden speech of the Old Man in the Commons, I felt a new thrill within me'. Jinnah developed great respect and admiration for Dadabhai Naoroji, who later was to exert a significant influence on his political identity. Jinnah remained a devout friend of the 'Old Man', though much younger in years. The two together rendered yeoman service to the Indian National Congress in the early years of its existence.[8]

Fortunately for Jinnah that year (1893) was the last when aspirants for a career in law could obtain admission by qualifying in an examination known at that time by the curious nomenclature of 'Little Go'. As in the following year regulations were being changed, requiring of Jinnah two additional years to be called to the Bar, he decided wisely, to give up his apprenticeship with Grahams and attempt to get through the 'Little Go'. For this he was required to appear in three papers: English language, English history and Latin. The third, for most Indians was, as it would still be, a very hard deal. To gain even rudimentary acquaintanceship with the language required at least two years, by which time this facility of concessional entrance examination would be gone. But there did exist a rule whereby Indians could be exempt from the Latin paper if the Masters of the Bench, of the relevant Inn, were satisfied otherwise of the aspiring students' performance. Jinnah applied for this exemption.

The Masters, the Special Council of the Lincoln's Inn accepted his plea and excused him from the Latin portion of the preliminaries. The examination was held on 25 May 1893; Jinnah was through. The first tentative steps of this future legal luminary had been taken. And it is also here that he dropped the by now superfluous, also perhaps a somewhat curious sounding suffix (under those circumstances) to his name, the word 'bhai', and changed the spelling of it, too. He now became what he was to remain for the rest of his life: Mohammad Ali Jinnah.

There was also a transition in the way that Jinnah had not just changed his name but also kept altering the spelling of his name; it travelled from being Mohomedalli Jinnahbhai, to a jettisoning of 'Jennabhai' and adopting to 'Jinnah'; then on to Mahomed Alli Jinnah, and yet again then, dropping of the second 'l' from Ali, and still later adopting an additional 'm' to Mohamed, leading finally to the version Mohammad Ali Jinnah.

This is not a small point. Any social psychologist would no doubt read much into these alterations. But clearly it points us to an evolution of the personality of the future Quaid-i-Azam. These changes being denotive, touchingly, of both a transformation of the personality and of

London 25th April 1893.

To,
    The Masters of the Bench of
      the honourable society of Lincoln's Inn

Sirs
      I most humbly & respectfully beg to inform you that I intend to appear for the preliminary exam.
      Having heard that I shall be examined in the Latin Language I request you in this petition to grant me dispensation for the following reasons.
      I. Being a native of India I have never been taught this language.
      II. I know several of Indian languages which we are required to learn as first classes or second languages.
      III. Thus having spent my time in learning other languages which are required there I have not been able to learn the Latin Language & which if I be compelled to learn will take some years to pass my required exam.
      I hope you will kindly comply with my request considering the reasons to be satisfactory.

      I remain sir
      yours most humble & obedient servant
Mahomedalli Jinnahbhai
    40 Claybury Road
    West Kensington
      W.

35 Russell Rd
Kensington
W
30th March 96.

To The Steward
Lincoln's Inn

Sir, I beg to inform you that I am desirous of dropping the ending of my name namely bhai – meaning Mr as I explained to you. It being customary in India at the time of my admission I happened to give the name after that fashion. I shall feel much obliged if you can and will alter it without it causing you any great inconvenience the name should be M. A. Jinnah or in full Mahomed Alli Jinnah

Hoping you will see that it is altered at any rate before my call.

Yours faithfully
M. A. Jinnah

how a still very young Jinnah was attempting to find exactly that name which would fit the personality he thought that he would be in the years ahead.

Completing his studies in England, Jinnah returned to India in 1896 but it was not to Karachi, there was, in reality no reason for him to do so. It was to Bombay that he came and while he had been away from India his child bride Emi Bai had died, as had his mother. Bombay thus became his home for the next fifty-one years. At first Jinnah moved into the Railway Hotel near the high court and waited for clients. Life then for him was not easy. As Syed Pirzada has said in a film, in part on Jinnah's life that, 'Jinnah used to say that when I started I did not have enough money even to travel by tram or by bus. I walked most of the time. There is always room at the top but there is no lift; you have to struggle.' And struggle he did; he struggled very hard. Jinnah was to later say, 'As you would know, for two or three years before I became a magistrate I had a very bad time and I used to go every other day to the Watson's Hotel beneath the road. It was a famous hotel in those days and I used to take on to a game of billiards for a wager, and that is how I supplemented my otherwise meagre resources.' Watson's Hotel is now in a rundown state. The solitary reminder of its existence now is just a 'W' on its railing.

He was enrolled in the high court of judicature in Bombay on 24 August 1896, and soon thereafter was sworn in as an advocate (OS). In the register of the Bombay High Court records show Mohammad Ali Jinnah's enrolment as a member of the Bombay High Court Bar on 24 August 1896.[9] Gandhi, upon his return from England had enrolled in 1891. Mohammad Ali Jinnah was then just twenty; his great legal and political career stretched ahead of him.

Notwithstanding the early difficulties that he faced, the timing of Jinnah's return to India was fortuitous, for his father was then involved in serious litigations at the district courts at Karachi. Jinnah took it upon himself to conduct the cross-examinations and prepare their defence. He won the case for his father.[10] Jinnah's professional legal career had begun and he was soon amongst the best at the Bombay Bar. Thereafter, he was admitted to the chambers of John Molesworth Macpherson, then the acting advocate-general of Bombay. In the words of Sarojini Naidu, this was 'a courteous concession, the first of its kind ever extended to an Indian, which its recipient always remembered as a beacon of hope in the dark distress of his early struggles'.[11] Sir Chimanlal Setalvad has commented that: 'Macpherson had a large practice. His language and diction were perfect. During this apprenticeship, Jinnah gained a forensic foundation; but, except for occasional briefs, he made little headway up the ladder of his profession',[12] It was only in 1900 that the first opportunity came Jinnah's way when he joined as a presidency magistrate, an appointment considered quite prestigious then for a young lawyer.

Following this appointment, a news item, filled with parochial pride had appeared in the *Sind Gazetteer*, a Karachi daily, on 10 May 1900 lauding the achievement in these words: 'The Khoja Community of Karachi is to be congratulated on the appointment of Mr Mohamed Ali Jinnah to be the Third Presidency Magistrate of Bombay. He is the son of Mr Jenabhai, who is one of the old (sic) and most respected merchants of Karachi. Mr Mohamed Ali Jinnah passed the Bar examination when he was quite young, and was, on his return, enrolled as an Advocate of the Bombay High Court'. Jinnah, at this time, was only twenty-four years old.

Jinnah's great dedication and interest in law was marked by irreproachable integrity. He was for sometime in the Chambers of Sir George Lowndes, who later became the law member of the Viceroy's Executive Council, and later still a member of the Privy Council. 'Lowndes, a very clear and a lucid mind, had an extremely forceful and impressive manner of advocacy. When Jinnah was reading in his Chamber, Lowndes' opinion was sought (about) some speech that Tilak had delivered. There was going to be a conference on this prior to which Lowndes asked of Jinnah 'whether he had read the brief, and what he thought of it'. Jinnah responded that, 'he had not touched the brief, and would not look at it, as he wanted to keep himself free to criticise the Government for prosecuting a great patriot like Tilak.'[13]

Mohammad Ali Jinnah's reputation as a lawyer in Bombay had become formidable by then. After being interrupted during a hearing thrice by the judge who said 'rubbish' on each occasion, Jinnah said, 'Nothing but rubbish has passed from Your Lordship's mouth throughout the day.'[14] Jinnah had commenced legal practice when racial prejudice and discrimination against Indians in the bar was widely in evidence, but very soon, only on the strength of his capability in conducting cases, he won a handsome practice. To achieve this in the company of eminent lawyers of those times was a testimonial to his abilities as an advocate, to his determination and his character.

The Khojas, it is recognised are converts from the Hindu Lohana[15] caste. Jinnah belonged to the Ithna Ashari sect of the Shia,[16] Khoja Muslim community. Khojas, given their beliefs and religious practices do not easily fit any stereotype. Bernard Lewis, in a comment has described them as 'Hindus under a thin Muslim veneer'.[17] Theirs is a unique blend of Hindu and Muslim practice under the over-arching umbrella of Islamic faith. Sarojini Naidu in 1917, must have linked Jinnah's liberal personality trait to his Khoja ancestry when she said, "That Jinnah was Hindu by race and Muslim by religion—it may not be wholly idle to fancy something a little symbolic in the Khoja parentage of a child destined to become 'an ambassador of Hindu-Muslim unity".'[18]

The Khojas, like the Bohras and the Memons, are known for their wealth, their trading and business abilities and are essentially of peace-loving nature. They have their bases principally in Surat, Bharuch, Ahmedabad, Karachi and Bombay, all strung along the western edge or coast of India. It is from these bases that they controlled a considerable part of the Bombay Presidency's internal trade, plus lucrative external trade with East Africa and Mauritius, also trade within Bombay city. In terms of English language education, however, they remain not particularly advanced. This was then not any debilitating backwardness, for in their own language—Gujarati—they remain as well-versed as the most advanced of Hindus, besides as a community they chose not to be burdened by this education in English, having little need for it. Being a predominantly trading community, they managed and continue to do so, admirably, in their own language—Gujarati. Also obtaining a government job or post was (still is) for them, no criteria of success. Their spiritual head is the Aga Khan, though Jinnah never really acknowledged him as such.

Preoccupation with trade and industry naturally affected their political outlook. At a time when competition for government service was a source of communal assertiveness, the Khojas, as a relatively self-contained and prosperous community, were little affected by this virus. This has always remained their attribute, and in contrast to a majority of their co-religionists, the Khojas are not given to combative Muslimness. Moreover, as members of the commercial world of Bombay they had very sound commercial reasons for combining with members of all other communities; they had to, how else would they continue to obtain trading and financial benefits?

Jinnah, though, was an exception to all these generalisations. He had not the trader's instincts of conciliation, accommodation or pursuit of profit, not at all. He was by nature determined and combative. His nationalism was not born of any self-interest; it was a by-product of his free spirited nature, his exposure to England, his thriving legal practice, which he had earned on his own merit. He was largely a self-educated, a self-made man, anxious as a youth that his merit should gain recognition and be duly rewarded. He had not the assets of birth, lineage or social status that most other barristers of his time came equipped with. Having been exposed to English mores he resented greatly the double standards practised by them, one set in their own country and another, a markedly different one for, and in, India. Like so many others who had been through the Inns of Court, Jinnah upon return became committed to 'the eradication of British insolence on the one hand; and of a feeling of inferiority and mortification by the Indians, on the other'. Zealous for reform, his enthusiasm was always marked by his sense of constitutional propriety, for which characteristic his great legal practice was to account. He was typical of those who earned influence through their own efforts, on merit and by remaining committed to principles. Possessing no other tools he employed these very attributes and his principles to combat India's imperial overlords.

Jinnah's early training as a lawyer no doubt affected his attitude to relations between the Muslim community and the government. Having reached where he had despite personal and family difficulties, he believed that others, too, must seek no special treatment, in the field of education or elsewhere. When he appeared before the Public Services Commission on 11 March 1913, he was asked by Lord Islington[19] whether he was not concerned that under a system of simultaneous examinations the backward communities would be at a disadvantage? Jinnah was firm in his views: 'I would have no objection if the result happens to be, of which I am now doubtful, that a particular community has the preponderance, provided I get competent men.' 'It has been represented to me,' queried Islington further, 'that difficulties might arise if you put a Hindu in charge of Mohammedan population. Do you think that a Hindu who got a few more marks than an educated and influential

Mohammedan would make a better and more efficient administrator when he was in charge of a population which was largely Mohammedan?' 'I say,' replied Jinnah, 'that in that case you will be doing the greatest injustice to the Hindu.... I do not see why a Hindu should not be in charge of a district where the majority happens to be Mohammedan.' In Jinnah's early years, it was views such as these that made him a member of the Indian National Congress, and not of the Muslim League.[20]

Hector Bolitho, the first official biographer of Jinnah, appointed by the government of Pakistan, quoting Percival Spear from *Jinnah, The Creator of Pakistan* writes: 'To personal integrity, devotion to principles must be added courage, an absence of petty thought or motives. Whether holding the balance between Swaraj and government forces in the Assemblies of the mid-twenties, or facing contumacious resistance in the all-parties discussions, or pursuing a lonely course against the prestige and authority of Gandhi, the determination of an imperial government immersed in a world war, or standing firm against the pressures of the post-war negotiations Jinnah was not found wanting in courage'.

For many years, including the time of his marriage, Jinnah had lived in an old Goanese bungalow, on Mount Pleasant Road. After Ruttie's death in 1929, he continued to live there until he went to England in 1930. Upon return in 1934, he demolished the old Goanese bungalow and built the present, Jinnah House. During the two years of its being built, he lived in a rented home on Little Gibbs Road, a little higher up Malabar Hill. These years were an 'amalgam of loneliness, mental and moral celibacy', and an 'integrity, so intense that it was a form of self-torture'. His virtues were intense, his faults trivial in contrast.

Jinnah—Political Beginnings

Jinnah's political life began along with his legal practice when he returned from Britain. He then joined the Anjuman-i-Islam,[21] a prominent representative Muslim body, in 1897.[22] Badruddin Tyabji, a judge of the Bombay High Court since 1895, then headed the Anjuman, and he thus naturally became Jinnah's Muslim mentor. This was fortuitous because this greatly helped Jinnah in both his public and legal career, especially when it came to guidance about the role of Muslims in the Congress. Having presided over the Congress in 1887, Tyabji had then immediately come under pressure from Sayyid Ahmad Khan, who asked him to stay away, to distance himself from this body as in Sayyid Ahmad's opinion the 'Congress was not an organisation that helped the Muslim cause'. Tyabji had then asked for a prorogation of the Congress for at least five years in view of the Muslim sentiments, and he did not attend Congress sessions thereafter. Jinnah came close to Tyabji in the initial years of his involvement with Anjuman-i-Islam, at a time when he had already been close to Dadabhai Naoroji, a Congressman and a Parsi. Besides, Congress politics in Bombay, in those years were dominated by the Parsis, and names like Pherozeshah Mehta, Dinshaw Wacha and others were then the identifying personalities of the party in that city. Fortunately for Jinnah, Anjuman-i-Islam representatives in Bombay did not feel threatened by the Congress, for the Parsis dominating the Bombay Congress then were a free spirited and a thinking lot. Besides, the Parsi group in the Bombay Congress banked upon the support of Gokhale and Jinnah to counterbalance leaders, like Tilak, whose nationalism was then considered to be Hindu. The Parsis also then dominated the legal circles of Bombay, for as a community they had the benefit of English language education earlier than the others, also their aptitude enabled them to relate better with the Raj and its officialdom.

Which is why, Jinnah soon joined a Committee formed to oversee the coronation ceremonies of King Edward VII, along with Tyabji. He participated in a Congress Reception Committee meeting on 28 July 1904, over which Pherozeshah Mehta presided, but refused to be drawn into any controversy over the issue of forming a separate political body for the Muslims.[23] In the same year, 1904, Bombay Congress decided to send a delegation to England to influence the British political opinion on the issue of 'self government'. The Bombay Presidency Association recommended two names, that of Gokhale and Jinnah. The Provincial Congress Committee endorsed Jinnah's name but at the central level Tilak objected. The reason was political as Jinnah was then identified with the Pherozeshah Mehta group.[24]

Moving ahead in time we now join the Congress at Surat, and not at Nagpur, as had been originally planned; this witnessed a split in the party. Though not a Tilak stronghold, the Surat Session ended in unruly scenes with the pro-changers staging a walkout, to return to the parent body only after a decade, in 1916. By then the two great stalwarts

Gokhale and Mehta were no more. Jinnah, therefore, tried afresh to befriend and work with Tilak. The British, happy at this split in the Congress moved fast and in 1908, arrested Tilak on charges of sedition. It was on this occasion that Jinnah had stepped in boldly and filed an application for bail on behalf of Tilak, in the Bombay High Court before Justice D.D. Davur, an Indian judge. The judge, on one pretext or another, at first, kept postponing the date of hearing and then finally, rejected the bail application without assigning any reason. Justice Davur also maintained that no observation was needed from the bench until the case came up for trial. Unfortunately, despite all his efforts, Jinnah was not permitted by Tilak to act as his defence counsel as Tilak, being himself a law graduate chose to plead his case personally in the High Court.

While paying Tilak a tribute in August 1920, Jinnah had said: 'Mr Tilak was a shrewd practical politician. After the split at Surat where I came to know him first in 1907, Mr Tilak's party in the Indian National Congress had a very small voice and remained in a minority. Mr Tilak's conviction (by Mr Justice Davur) in a case for sedition removed him from the political arena for nearly six years, this was a savage sentence. I was given a retainer for his defence and was instructed to make an application for bail which was refused by Mr Justice Davur...There arose a serious difference of opinion between him and myself as a Counsel, because I refused to adopt any line, as a Counsel, except what I considered best for his defence'.[25] This trial continued for eight days, and on 13 July 1908 it came up for judgment. Tilak was sentenced to six years rigorous imprisonment, for which 'justice', Justice Davur was rewarded with a Knighthood. Jinnah was bitter in his criticism of the dinner organised for Justice Davur to celebrate and refused to attend.[26]

With the kind of views that he then held, the great distance that he had travelled, in experience, in growth as a civic being, in evolution as an independent minded and a thinking Indian; his success after the initial years of struggle, as a reformist with Islam sitting lightly on him, Jinnah, to start with, could hardly follow any other politics than that which he did. His thought was for freedom from the insolent might of the ruling British; his political arena had to be, indeed could only be, national. His thinking could not, seldom did, in fact, adjust to the provincial milieu. It is here that he faced all his significant political disjuncts: how to ride the national scene without there being any province wholly behind him? Further, he faced the quandary of how to relate to this newly established Muslim League while being a committed member of the Congress? He could scarcely ignore the League and yet to adopt it, as his chosen political vehicle, at this stage of his life (still in his thirties) was to bind himself to a very narrow sectarian focus. Attending the meetings of the Muslim League as a member of the Congress party was clearly a way out.[27] To this decision Jinnah added a caveat, his statement in the autumn of 1913—'loyalty to the Muslim League and the Muslim interest would in no way and at no time imply even the shadow of disloyalty to the national cause to which his (Jinnah's) life was dedicated'. Was this to enable him to straddle this chasm on a bridge of apparent principles? But was it principles? or a baser calculation of having a foot in both camps ? There exist advocates of both views.

The other, and entirely understandable, was the all important matter of a political constituency. Here again Jinnah was clearly disadvantaged, he faced a complex dilemma. For one, he was not an oratorically theatrical or pulpit bashing rabble rouser. His whole persona was of a self contained, reserved man who worked on reason, clarity of thought, and by the incisiveness of his expression. 'As long as politics was consultative, his position was not to be questioned. With increasing politicisation, democratisation and the trend becoming more participatory',[28] it became important that a 'national level politician be connected with the provincial and local political trends', too.[29] And it is here that Jinnah lost his inclusive, all-India platform, he had to overcome far too many handicaps, amongst which was the unmatched impress of Gandhi on India's masses. Let us spend some time trying to understand the dynamics of the interaction between these two titans of India's freedom movement. It is a daunting venture but vital for our enquiry.

Comparing Gandhi and Jinnah is an extremely complex exercise but important for they were, or rather became, the two foci of the freedom movement. Gandhi was doubtless of a very different mould, but he too, like Jinnah, had gained eminence and successfully transited from his Kathiawari origins to become a London barrister before acquiring a political personality. Yet there existed an essential difference here. Gandhi's birth in a prominent family, his father was, after all, a *diwan* (prime minister) of an Indian state helped immeasurably. No such advantage of birth gave Jinnah a leg-up, it was entirely through his endeavours. Gandhi, most remarkably became a master practitioner of the politics of protest. This he did not do by altering his own nature, or language of discourse, but by transforming the very nature of politics in India. He transformed a people, who on account of prolonged foreign rule had acquired a style of subservience. He shook them out of this long, moral servitude. Gandhi took politics out of the genteel salons, the debating halls and societies to the soil of India, for he, Gandhi—was rooted to that soil, he was of it, he lived the idiom, the dialogue and discourse of that soil: its sweat; its smells and its great beauty and fragrances, too.

Some striking differences between these two great Indians are lucidly conveyed by Hector Bolitho in *In Quest of Jinnah*. He writes: 'Jinnah was a source of power'. Gandhi...an 'instrument of it...Jinnah was a cold rationalist in politics—he had a one track mind, with great force behind it'. Then: 'Jinnah was potentially kind, but in behaviour extremely cold and distant'. Gandhi embodied compassion—Jinnah did not wish to touch the poor, but then Gandhi's instincts were rooted in India and life long he soiled his hands in helping the squalid poor.

Not so Jinnah: for having been uprooted repeatedly in his childhood, then moved too frequently, he neither easily belonged nor did he relate with comfort. Besides being the quintessential constitutionalist, he had to follow a different course; for him to adapt to the changing times, to the dusty trails of rural India was not at all easy. That is why he found it so difficult, by around 1920, to maintain his position at the national level given Gandhi's arrival and rapid ascendancy. Besides, there was no province, not one, not then, not later, that he could rely upon totally as his exclusive parish. His lack of ability to adapt to the integrative politics of the masses always remained a problem. Whereafter, his status as a Muslim, it must be accepted, further handicapped his position at the national level, for in nationalist politics the scene had already got crowded; as a Muslim, yes, there was a role for him to play but only in the second rank. For Jinnah, a secondary status was galling, what he had always sought and mostly attained was the centre stage; yet, now how could he, when so many factors constantly kept pushing him to the periphery of it?

Lloyd and Susanne Rudolph, professors of political science, emeritus, University of Chicago, in correspondence with me have shared thoughts, briefly, on the same theme. They hold: 'Jinnah couldn't stand Gandhi but his reasons I believe were markedly different from those driving his 'hatred' of Nehru. Almost from the beginning of Gandhi's entry into national politics in the 1915-20 era, Jinnah thought of him not only as a rival but also as 'a poseur, a fake, and a demagogue'. They shared an English experience that included common mentors, patrons and admirers and studying for and becoming a barrister. And they shared the common patronage in India of Gokhale, a 'moderate' and a liberal.' Jinnah acquired the style of an English gentleman and the views of a liberal. Gandhi did too, for a time, as photos of him as a successful barrister in South Africa and as his efforts to secure the rights of British subjects for the Indian minority in South Africa attest. But by the time Gandhi returned to India from twenty-one years in South Africa he had begun to shed his identity as an English gentleman and to add to his liberal creed a commitment to be a man of and for the people, the ordinary people of India's towns and villages.

Jinnah remained committed to his three-piece suits, his lorgnette, his cigarette holder and the King's English. No Gujarati for him, and no political language that invoked religion. Jinnah excelled in parliamentary politics, the kind of politics that the moderate Gokhale was good at and that the extremist Tilak scorned. Gandhi combined a liberal concern for deliberative, non-violent politics evident in the politics of *satyagraha* with the extremist tactics of direct action. His was an out of doors politics of the public sphere and of public opinion rather than an indoors politics of the halls of parliament and the corridors of power. When Gandhi donned the clothes and style of the common man, then later shed even these for the bare minimum of the poorest villager, Jinnah was progressively repelled and increasingly convinced that Gandhi was demagogue and a fake. For decades Jinnah resented and resisted Gandhi's common man politics until, on 16 August 1946, he called for direct action to defend Islam and in support of Pakistan. Jinnah then became the demagogue he deplored and detested in Gandhi. He had come to fight fire with fire—but doing so didn't bring him closer to Gandhi. At the same time, he had, over the years, developed a wary respect for the man who, for most of his political career, outshone and outgunned him. Toward the end, he practised the highest form of flattery, imitation. He, too, [like Gandhi in reality was of the Congress, the final arbiters] would be the sole spokesman.

Jinnah saw Congress as his adversary and his nemesis. It was Congress versus the Muslim League, two parties contending for power in an independent Indian state that led to partition. Gandhi unlike Nehru did not share the view that Congress should take power in an independent Indian state. For him, Congress was a vehicle for the independence movement and for a constructive work movement. He rarely took interest in Congress party affairs. In his last will and testament written the day before he was assassinated on 30 January 1948, he called on the Congress party to disband itself. Contending for power in an independent Indian state and assuming and using power in that state appalled and repelled him. In his last will and testament he called on Congress party workers to form a Lok Sevak Sangh where they could engage in constructive work in the towns and villages of India. Gandhi was a man of civil society dedicated to achieving individual and national *swaraj*, not to seizing and using state power. That was what Nehru wanted. In this context it made sense for Gandhi to tell Mountbatten that he should call on Jinnah to be the prime minister of the interim government, and for the Muslim League to form the government (covered in detail in chapter 9). Gandhi wanted India's independence, not Congress rule, and in that he didn't attract the kind of animosity and distrust that Jinnah directed at Nehru.

Sarojini Naidu recounts meeting Jinnah just when he was getting a feel of India's politics. This was at the Calcutta session of the Congress, in 1906, (the year in which the Muslim League was launched in Dacca) by which time Jinnah was already a private secretary to Dadabhai Naoroji, who (Dadabhai) at the Calcutta Congress, for the first time, enunciated the ideal of self-government. In 1906, as Naoroji's private secretary, Jinnah was being thought of both as a shining young lawyer and a promising politician. He was fast coming into his own. Hereafter, Jinnah for several years regularly attended the Congress' annual sessions. As I recall (from reading Martin Green's book titled *Gandhi: New Age-Revolutionary*) both Jinnah and Gandhi sought to be in the good graces of Sarojini Naidu. I believe Jinnah and Sarojini Naidu overlapped in England. Jinnah tried his hand in theatre and may have thought of an acting career. Sarojini and he shared an interest in the arts, she as a poet and writer, he in the theatre. Green, as I recall, pictures something like a rivalry for the good graces of this talented lady. In an Indian context she seems to have gravitated to Gandhi.

It was on two issues, both related to Muslims that Jinnah had intervened at the Calcutta Congress. After all, he was a Muslim delegate to the Congress and how could he ignore Muslim concerns. His first intervention was on the validity of 'wakf-i-aulad'[30] and the second on the issue of reservation. He undoubtedly argued for the Muslim cause but simultaneously stressed the possibility of using the Congress platform and that too, on an equal footing alongside the Hindus.[31] His amendments were accepted in that Congress meet.

In October of that year, 1906, he took a more serious and assertive political step. He went on to question the very representative status of the delegation led by Aga Khan to the viceroy.[32] He was of the view that the Congress represented the Muslims no less, in fact, was the only 'true political voice in the country'.[33] He also opposed this whole pursuit of separate electorates through a memorandum forwarded to Lord Minto by the Bombay Presidency Association. (Jinnah's letter in *Gujarati*, 7 October 1906.)[34]

The Aga Khan, whom Jinnah was opposed to all his life, writing in his memoirs on the question of separate electorates has said: 'Who then was our doughtiest opponent in 1906? A distinguished Muslim barrister in Bombay, Jinnah had always been on friendly terms but at this juncture he came out in bitter hostility towards all that I and my friends had done and were trying to do. He was the only well-known Muslim to take up this attitude, but his opposition had nothing mealy-mouthed about it; he said that our principle of separate electorates was dividing the nation against itself, and for nearly a quarter of a century, he remained our most inflexible critic and opponent'.[35]

Then came the change. In a letter to the editor of *The Times of India*, dated 20 February 1909, Jinnah rook a markedly different stand, he (for the first time?) accepted that the Muslims were 'entitled to a real and substantial representation in the new reforms',[36] but the real question was how this ought to be done; 'whether to have separate electorates at all stages, from rural Boards to the Viceregal Council? Or something less and if so, then what level?' On the basis of population Muslims would become entitled to representation of about 25 per cent. 'But if this share could be enhanced to a weightage equivalent to a third then this whole business of communal representation could be dispensed with',[37] Jinnah reasoned, 'otherwise, there was no alternative but to retaining the reservation system'. In addition, at a meeting of the Muslims of Bombay held on 13 August 1909, Jinnah successfully proposed that if the alternatives available for Muslim representation in the Bombay Legislative Council were election by separate electorates, or selection by nomination, preference should be given to the former—election.

With time his views on this sensitive matter changed further, though gradually. Jinnah's demeanour during the twenty-fifth session of the Congress at Allahabad, on 26-29 December 1910, plainly demonstrated this change and his mounting uneasiness. His personal views on the issue of separate electorates had become by then not so totally at variance with those of a majority of his co-religionists. Under pressure, however, from several Congress leaders he moved a resolution that was carried unanimously: 'This Congress strongly deprecates the extension or application of the principle of separate communal electorates to municipalities, district boards or other local bodies'.[38] But in the performance of this task he was uncharacteristically hesitant, also brief: 'I did not intend to speak at all, but in response to the wishes of a great many leaders of the Congress I have agreed to move this resolution before you', he said.* However, he remained opposed to separate electorates that was emphasised by his observations at the Agra Session of the Muslim League in 1913: Special representation or separate electorate, said Jinnah, would get them only 'two water-tight compartments'.[39] Herein lay his dilemma; real, and difficult to resolve, for he was not, per se, opposed to constitutional safeguards to protect the interest of the Muslims as a minority, otherwise, he would never have advocated that the aim of the Muslim League ought to be achieving a self-government as suited to the realities of India. Yet how was he to be true to his beliefs, his nature, and simultaneously to Muslim interests, and his constituency that remained essentially Muslim?

In the autumn of 1910, Jinnah was elected by the Muslims of the Bombay presidency as their representative to the Viceroy's Legislative Council, defeating Maulvi Rafiuddin who was the president of the Bombay Muslim League. In this Council just a month after his election, Jinnah entered into a heated verbal exchange with no less than the viceroy himself—Lord Minto. This contention arose from a resolution on indentured labour for Natal. Jinnah held that this had 'aroused the feelings of all classes in the country to the highest pitch of indignation

---

* For a comprehensive analysis of the Morley-Minto reforms, please see Appendix 1.

and horror at the harsh and cruel treatment that is meted out to Indians in South Africa'.[40] Lord Minto objected that 'cruel' was 'rather a strong word'. Jinnah stood his ground and responded—'I should feel inclined to use much stronger language, My Lord, but I am fully aware of the constitution of this Council which I do not wish to trespass for a single moment, but I do say this that the treatment that is meted out to Indians is the harshest which can possibly be imagined, and, as I said before, the feeling in this country is unanimous'.[41] This was unusual as it was perhaps for the first time that the government was criticised so clearly, and to the face of the viceroy.

Jinnah did not also suffer the pressures that influenced many of his north Indian compatriots, elected through limited communal franchises. In Bombay those Muslims who were wealthy enough to qualify for a vote, were not inclined to keep Islam in the forefront. Which is why all through Jinnah's long association with his constituency in Bombay, which lasted with a few interruptions until the Partition, he continued to be re-elected, though not just on the strength of the Muslim votes alone for many Parsis and Hindus, too, voted for him. In the Viceroy's Council, Jinnah found himself sitting alongside some of India's most eminent men then, fellow Congressmen like Bhupendra Nath Basu, Dinshaw Wacha, Srinivas Sastri, Mazhar-ul-Haq, Tej Bahadur Sapru and Madan Mohan Malaviya. Whereas others like Raja Sahib of Mahmudabad or Sir Ali Imam, with whom, too, Jinnah developed close relations, were of different political persuasions.

In the Council every liberal measure drew his willing support, as did issues of national importance like Gokhale's Elementary Education Bill (1912), or the later Primary Education Bill (1917), and of course, the Special Marriage Bill[42] to which conservative India was then strongly opposed. His endeavours were always directed towards securing new options for educated Indians like the earlier mentioned demand for simultaneously holding Indian Civil Services examination in India and in England (1917), but this was only one of them.

Jinnah did not attend the Congress Session of 1911 and 1912. Though not yet formally a member, he did attend the Muslim League Sessions of 1910 and 1912. These were the times when his attention was engaged in matters of Muslim *Wakfs*, and he exerted such a marked influence on the League that even without becoming its member, he was successful in changing its constitution. This paved the way for his joining the League in 1913.[43]

He was formally invited to attend the Muslim League Council Meeting at Bankipur, on 31 December 1912, whilst he was still a member of the Congress party. This meeting, with the Aga Khan presiding, adopted a resolution laying down the aims of the Muslim League. Clause 4 of this resolution elaborated that one of the aims should be the attainment of a system of self-government suitable to India. Though a leading member from Mazhar-ul-Haq group objected to this phrase self-government suitable to India, Jinnah intervened to stoutly defend the resolution, as framed, and praised the League for having placed the right ideal before the community, and though a member of the Congress he knew that the Congress was wrong in this matter and thought that the League should be congratulated for going a step ahead of the Congress in this. The change in the League's constitution, its loyalist stance, and its demand for self-government were no mean achievements. Jinnah had to struggle hard against the old guard of the Muslim League, like Nawab Viquar-ul-Mulk, Maulvi Mushtaq Hussain and Nawab Abdullah Khan.[44] But Jinnah had his supporters too, in Raja Sahib Mahmudabad and Syed Wazir Hassan. Aga Khan's neutrality also helped him. The government was obviously unhappy at these developments and tried hard to convince the League leaders to resist this change. Sir James Meston, then the lieutenant governor of United Provinces and Sir Harcourt Butler, member of the Viceroy's Executive Council attempted to undo what Jinnah and his group had achieved. But Jinnah by now was destined to grow at the all-India level.[45]

In April 1913, Jinnah along with Gokhale sailed for Britain, a stay that kept him out of India for six months. While he was away there occurred in India the infamous Kanpur mosque incident. There were riots in the city and protests spread far beyond Kanpur. Mohammad Ali Jauhar and Wazir Hassan were deputed by the movement leaders to go to England and press for the Muslim case before the secretary of state and the home government.[46] Mohammad Ali Jauhar, before his departure expressed a desire to enlist Jinnah's support while in England.[47] Jinnah conveyed assent but in favour of a broader idea, that of Indian unity. He also deplored the secretary of state for refusing to grant an interview to the Indian delegation. Jinnah, upon his return, also took part in the deliberations of Anjuman-i-Islam, which held a meeting to welcome the return of the delegation.[48] Jinnah had by now truly come into his own. He was following an independent line and his popularity, both as a Congress leader and as that of the League was an established fact. At this juncture, not only was he taking steps to bring about unity between the League and the Congress, he was also striking a balance between the Moderates and the Extremists. In politics now all factions gave him recognition—the Extremists, the Moderates, the Muslims, the Hindus, the Parsis and others.

WITH BOTH THE CONGRESS AND THE MUSLIM LEAGUE

On the eve of his return from London towards the end of 1913, Jinnah formally then also joined the All-India Muslim League, as some of his friends in that organisation expressly urged him to. This rather unique cross-representation drew a questioning comment from Sarojini Naidu, with Jinnah's sense of honour requiring his sponsors to make a solemn, preliminary covenant that 'loyalty to the Muslim League and the Muslim interest would in no way and at no time imply even the shadow of disloyalty to the larger national cause to which his [Jinnah's] life was dedicated'.[49]

Upon return to India Jinnah went first to the twenty-eighth session of the Congress, at Karachi (13 December 1913) and then hurried to Agra and attended the seventh session of the Muslim League (26-28 December). He was perhaps the first ever to have moved the same resolution, that for Council Reforms, at the Karachi session of the Congress and the League session at Agra. It was at his instance that the Congress had then adopted a rather ambitious resolution demanding a change in the structure and functions of the council of the secretary of state in London. At the session of the League a resolution on communal representation resulted in a heated debate. It had been moved by Maulvi Rafi-ud-Din, who had asked for its adoption without much discussion, reasoning that it had been passed unanimously for six of the past years, this is effectively at every sitting of the League. This resolution ran: '...that in the interests of Mussulman community, it is absolutely necessary that the principle of communal representation be extended to all the self-governing public bodies, and respectfully urges that a provision for the adequate and effective representation of Mussalmans on municipal and district boards is a necessary corollary of the application of the principle to the Imperial and Provincial Legislative Council, and at the same time essential to the successful working of those public bodies'.

Apprehending that such a resolution could hurt the prospects of Hindu-Muslim accord, Mohammad Ali[50] proposed that a consideration of this question—of communal representation in self-governing bodies be postponed for a year, arguing that it would be to the ultimate interest of India for the Hindus and the Muslims 'to merge together'. He emphasised that though in the past, 'Hindus had always opposed separate representation...but this year out of regard for Muslims, the Congress had not opposed it. The Muslims must (therefore) now show that they were prepared to meet the Hindus halfway'.[51] The proposer, Mohammad Ali was strongly supported by Jinnah. He urged the Muslims 'to consider the question dispassionately, not from the point of view of present gain, but of lasting advantage in the future'. He cautioned his co-religionists that 'by demanding special representation they would get only two watertight compartments'. The Aga Khan also supported this stand of Mohammad Ali and of Jinnah but fruitlessly as the proposal was defeated and the originally worded resolution adopted.

After three years in the Viceroy's Council, Jinnah remained dissatisfied with the progress. Members of government listened politely to any number of eloquent speeches but showed no inclination whatsoever towards doing anything else, principally because they felt no need to, besides the Council really had no powers. Also, non-official members were a kind of a permanent minority, their right was limited to speaking during the budget debate, to asking questions, and to introducing Private Members' Bills, subject of course, to government's approval. A frustrated Jinnah decided, therefore, to not contest the coming election and, though he was nominated by the viceroy for the 1913 session to pilot the Muslim *Wakf* Validating Act to its adoption; he did not again sit as an elected member until 1915. His disenchantment went further and he began to work for reforms outside the Council, and not from the platform of the Congress alone, but simultaneously with the Muslim League, too. Though initially as the League evolved Jinnah considered the organisation as too narrow and still undefined. Jinnah was helped significantly in the pursuit of this policy by the emergence now, in

Lucknow, where the League was headquartered of a group of like-minded figures, like Raja Sahib of Mahmudabad, with whom Jinnah had worked in the Viceroy's Council. The group included Wazir Hassan, the secretary of the League, Syed Nabiullah, later the chairman of the Lucknow Municipal Board, and Samiullah Beg, an advocate at the Lucknow Bar. With the exception of Raja Sahib Mahmudabad, all these personages were lawyers, and were successful in their profession. Consequently, they shared Jinnah's political views but unlike him were mainly interested in reform at the provincial level. Their realism made them recognise that provincial demands were what had a chance of succeeding, and these too, only if presented under a national umbrella. It was Wazir Hassan, the League's secretary, who reshaped the League's creed in 1912, and it was he, supported by Raja Sahib Mahmudabad, who in the years that followed steered a difficult course, but unfailingly with skill and thus kept the League in the centre of nationalist politics. In UP the League's Lucknow leadership did not really command respect and their advocacy of cooperation with the Congress appeared to many as weak, a surrender, or even as suicidal for the League.

The 1909 Council Reforms, having extended the franchise and increased the number of elected members, brought in their wake a far larger number of local grievances, more than had ever earlier been the case or even anticipated. For one the educated, the professionals, and the articulate, to improve their own positions had taken to politics in a more systematic manner. Secondly, by making election to the provincial council largely dependent on the votes of members of municipal and district boards, it greatly increased competition for positions in those primary local bodies, (in essence for local government). This inevitably introduced factionalism, followed by communalism, whereafter came further Hindu-Muslim divide; and all this despite the existence of general electorates.

Jinnah's endeavours at reforms within his community soon got him entangled in a complex web of the provincial versus all India interests, and politics. This challenging tangle remained unresolved until Partition and has actually continued even after. The dilemma being that Jinnah's realm was the national, he was an all-India politician; that is where he sought a voice and devolution of power. However, he could not simultaneously contend with the viceroy's recalcitrance, have no sympathetic allies in the provinces, and yet avoid getting drawn into provincial rivalries, conflicts or be involved with that very limited mindset. This was for him, in those early years, a problem and remained until very late in his political life, an unresolved dilemma.

By 1914, Jinnah's reputation as an all-India leader had been fully established. Tilak, having completed his sentence of imprisonment, was back in India from Mandalay, and Gandhi was also then on his way back to India. At this juncture what lay before Jinnah was the stupendous challenge of not only attaining unity between Moderates and Extremists but also between the Hindus and Muslims. For this cause attempts at rapprochement between Gokhale and Tilak were made. Jinnah also engaged with Gokhale to evolve a common constitutional formula around which all political forces of India could unite. Gokhale did evolve just such a formula but it was still only at a draft stage in February 1915 when sadly he died. This draft formula, thereafter, could only be made public in August 1917, by Aga Khan while in London. Termed as the 'Gokhale Scheme', it provided for a governor for each province with a Cabinet of six, three Indian and three European members. The Executive was to be responsible to the Legislature. The services were to be provincialised. The viceroy and his council was to have nominal control. Jinnah had endeavoured to unite all political forces behind this formula, but just then Gokhale's death, at such a juncture, meant a great loss to him.[52] There was also then the challenge of the abolition of the Khilafat. In this Jinnah was perhaps the first leader of an all-India stature to have warned the British of the consequences of reducing the status of the Khalifa. This occurred when Jinnah was president of the Muslim League in December 1916. He repeated this warning in September 1919 to Prime Minister David Lloyd George cautioning him of the possible reactions such a step could have among Muslims in India. In January 1920, he was part of the Khilafat delegation that waited upon Viceroy Lord Chelmsford. The Khilafat Conference, then in March 1920 sent a delegation to meet the prime minister in England but it was rebuffed. This was followed by the Treaty of Sevres (15 May 1920) proposing dismemberment of the Ottoman Empire. Coincidentally, the Hunter Committee Report on the Punjab disturbances of April 1919 was made public twelve days later: Dyer had been let off lightly; the Turkish Empire was being dismembered. Under this double impact, public opinion in India was outraged, in reaction the Muslim League and the Congress called their special sessions at Calcutta in September 1920.[53]

Presiding over this special session of the League, at Calcutta on 7 September 1920, Jinnah deplored the resolution passed by the House of Lords in support of Dyer. Describing the members of that Chamber he termed them as the blue and brainless blood of England. He also warned the British of the consequences which would force them to adopt a path of non-cooperation, though not necessarily emulatory of Gandhi.

When the Congress met in its special session the only prominent leader who supported Gandhi on his non-cooperation resolution was Motilal Nehru, Lala Lajpat Rai, C.R. Das, Bipin Chandra Pal, Annie Besant, Madan Mohan Malaviya and Jinnah all stood against Gandhi's move, but Gandhi still carried the day. This special session of Congress at Calcutta[54] heralded the arrival of the Gandhian era in Congress politics. This resolution on non-cooperation, proposed by Gandhi, was passed by 1886 votes to 884. Clearly an open clash between Gandhi and Jinnah was now only a matter of time; this occurred on 3 October 1920. Annie Besant had resigned as president of the Home Rule League, and Gandhi had taken over as the new president. To bring the goal of the Home Rule League in line with the programme that had just been adopted by the Congress, Gandhi wanted to change its creed and also its name. Jinnah opposed Gandhi but without any success and in protest he too, resigned from the Home Rule League.[55]

The thirty-fifth session of the Congress at Nagpur (26-31 December 1920) confirmed the changed creed of the Congress, it sought to attain *swaraj* within one year. Jinnah was the only dissenting voice; he demonstrated courage in going up to the rostrum and opposing the resolutions relating to the proposed change in creed, and about non-cooperation. His objection to the creed centred on the lack of clarity on the issue of *swaraj* as to what it actually meant. As for non-cooperation being a weapon for attaining swaraj, he found it not only politically unsound, but also illogical. A resolution of the Muslim League session, convened concurrently in Nagpur, under the presidentship of M.A. Ansari affirmed League's support for non-cooperation, and another resolution echoed the Nagpur Congress Resolution regarding the change of creed. For the time being everyone appeared to be following Gandhi. Jinnah, realising that it was not his day, left Nagpur the same day.[56]

The Ahmedabad Session (1921) of the Congress, under the de facto leadership of Gandhi was finally the great watershed. In that session there were no chairs or tables for the delegates. Everyone had to sit on the ground. People wore *khadi* and were lodged in *khaddar* tents, all required to spin *khadi*. Jinnah was also present at Ahmedabad where he was attending the Congress Session for the last time. He was perhaps the only individual to be seen in foreign clothes, complete with collar, tie, and was found not spinning the *charkha*.⁵⁷

In the six-year period of 1912 to 1918, while Jinnah and the Lucknow politicians pursued their policy of cooperation with the Congress, local conflicts continued to provide an effective enough dampener to their efforts. In UP, at the Agra Session of the league in 1913, Jinnah and Mazhar-ul-Haq had attempted to persuade the League not to pass its routine resolution favouring separate electorates in local governments. This, as earlier, was voted down by the municipal politicians of UP. Two years later in Bombay, in 1915, when for the first time both the Congress and the Muslim League were holding their session in the same city, local rivalries almost wrecked the possibility of a joint approach to the question of reform. Jinnah and his colleagues carried the day against Cassim Mitha⁵⁸ and his henchmen by locking themselves up in the Taj Mahal hotel and holding their session in private. In 1915 and 1916, when the UP Municipal Bill was introduced the provincial interests were fully aroused, for this Bill proposed a large-scale devolution of power to the municipalities, thus sharpening communally oriented demands, for it seemed to the aspirants that the power of municipal patronage was now within their grasp. Inevitably, this inflamed the issue of separate versus joint electorates and brought it to a head. The provincial satraps sought a communal alliance at the provincial level advising a surrender of local advantage for provincial profit, a difficult trade off in the best of circumstances. Jinnah, was of course, not involved in any such communal wrangles of UP, though he was very much a part of a national settlement, at Lucknow in 1916.⁵⁹ But these provincial tangles severely restricted his capacity for manoeuvre, so much so that his views on separate electorates finally altered, and that, too, radically. In 1913, he was still a passionate advocate of joint electorates; by 1916 he had begun to argue with the Congress leaders that unless the Muslims' demand for separate electorates was conceded a settlement would not be reached. This is where Jinnah, the Muslim leader first begins to emerge; the compelling rationale for this transformation being the existing political reality of the country, his own largely notional political constituency, and his public standing.

What did this mean for Jinnah? In the first place—great personal disappointment for it was the policy of Hindu-Muslim cooperation that he had got enshrined in the 1916 Lucknow Pact. Admittedly, from Jinnah's point of view, his personal bargaining position at the all-India level had got strengthened, but as a Muslim, and not as an ambassador of Hindu-Muslim unity. Yet, and paradoxically, to maintain this position, to further strengthen chances of reforms at the all-India level, he had to ally himself with the provincial aspirants. Only in that manner could he pursue a policy of reform both at the national and provincial levels.

What was the government's response to all this? To stand firm at the all-India level and to make only some minor concessions at the provincial level. Jinnah received practically no political payoff even after having helped to keep the Congress and the League together right up to the point of Montagu's visit to India.[60] His own distress and frustration at this are clear. His speech to the Imperial Legislative Council on 7 September 1918, transparently brings this out: 'Now my Lord, may I know why the Government of India is to remain so sacred and not to be touched? Is there no department in the Government of India which could not be brought under the control of the legislature?...Why, I ask should there not be simultaneous advance?'[61]

Following upon these reforms, devolution of power took place though, almost entirely in the provinces. Despite Jinnah, and his ilk of professionals, lawyers and doctors having worked so assiduously for reform, clearly it was not they who benefited. They simply could not for reasons of Empire, as any devolution of power to them would have enfeebled the central imperial authority and systems. In reality, devolution got so designed and then implemented on the ground, also in the provinces that it actually augmented the powers of patronage of the Raj; hence the allies of the British, largely the rural landed gentry. This did lead to some urban professionals of the Muslim League to retiring in frustration from public life, like Wazir Hassan, who after 1920, became more intent on his legal career or gravitated towards the path of agitation, but by then this platform of agitation was also about to be usurped. Hereafter, this form of protest became the sole preserve of the Congress, until well in to the fateful 1940s.

Jinnah—The Constitutional Reformist

Even a cursory study of the freedom movement informs us that communal accord between the Hindus and Muslims almost always moved in tandem with constitutional reform; whenever the first, that is communal amity was present, the other, reforms by the Raj followed almost axiomatically, as a Hindu-Muslim combine always greatly troubled the British.

Montford Reforms (Montagu-Chelmsford Reforms) of 1919,* when finally introduced was the first time ever that the Imperial British had shed a thin sliver of executive authority. Amongst other contributory causes for this development was also the unstated pressure exerted by a united Congress-League stand. Had such pressure not been there, it is highly unlikely that any British initiative would have been forthcoming.

Jinnah's contribution towards this united stand was significant. It was he who endeavoured and succeeded in creating an ideational unity between the League and the Congress. In addition, he had them committed to a demand for reforming the Indian Council during the League and the Congress sessions of 1913, where it was Jinnah who had moved the resolution for Council Reforms, in both the Congress and the Muslim League sessions. The intent of these resolutions was a share in the power of governance of India between the secretary of state for India and Indian members of the council, by having at least one-third Indian representatives, elected by a constituency composed of the elected members of the Indian central and provincial legislatures. A bill to this effect was to be moved by the secretary of state for India in the British parliament. To lobby for these Indian aspirations a deputation (upon Jinnah's initiative) then visited Britain and a bill was finally moved by Lord Crewe, then the secretary of state, which got adopted by the House of Commons but rejected by the Lords. There were other consequences of this, though, and not all were beneficial. To add to Jinnah's disappointment, a revengeful Raj now exerted pressure vindictively, for a postponement of the annual session of the Muslim League, scheduled for December 1914, rationalising this fiat on grounds of the outbreak

---

* The official British version of self-government, envisaged as a step towards it in the Montford Reforms was at variance with what Congress understood it to be. At Appendix II is a note that brings out quite clearly the different viewpoints.

of the First World War. Of course, not just Jinnah, but others too, had difficulty in accepting both this facile explanation and the preceding order.

Jinnah, now a member of the Muslim League Council, continued to concentrate his efforts, despite the imperial opposition towards convening the Muslim League session in Bombay. This move, in turn, was vehemently opposed by the Raj supporters amongst the Bombay Leaguers, like Haji Cassim Mitha and Maulana Rafiuddin, who acted largely upon suggestions from Lord Willingdon, then governor of Bombay. Jinnah did finally succeed and in December 1915, sessions of both the League and the Congress were held in the same city, for the first time, largely again on account of Jinnah's initiative.

At these sessions of the two principal political parties an admirable spirit of cooperation prevailed between the Hindu and Muslim leadership. These sessions appointed separate committees, which after consultations evolved a common constitutional formula for the next instalment of reforms. In holding the meetings of these committees it was again Jinnah who worked assiduously. It is from such initiatives that was eventually born the famous statement of Gokhale's about Jinnah being an 'ambassador of Hindu-Muslim Unity'; of which testimonial Jinnah made substantial use later for forging a consensus for the Lucknow Pact of 1916. Credit also accrues to Jinnah for making leaders, like Tilak, agree to the issue of separate electorates, which support helped greatly in keeping other stalwarts, like S.N. Banerjee, otherwise vehemently opposed to the idea of separate electorates, in check.

Jinnah was elected president of the sixteenth Bombay Provincial Conference in October 1916, the second Muslim to be conferred with such a position after M.R. Sayani. In his presidential address to this conference, Jinnah expounded his views on the central and provincial aspects of the constitution, ideas that later got incorporated in December 1916 in Lucknow, and are now commonly referred to as the Lucknow Pact. This was amongst the first of the joint schemes of reforms proposed by the Congress and the League, the foundational commitment of it being that the two parties would work together for *swaraj*, or self-government within the shortest possible time. It was also Jinnah's initiative that a decision at Lucknow was taken by the League and the Congress to appoint a joint committee, to draft a bill to be carried to

London for introduction in the British Parliament, for which purpose a joint deputation was also planned.

This proposal could not materialise, for His Majesty's Government was in no position to entertain any Indian politicians during the War. Instead, therefore it was decided to send Edwin S. Montagu, then the secretary of state for India, to visit and ascertain views directly. He came to India in November 1917 and returned after a stay of almost six months, by April 1918, by when he had prepared his constitutional report. This was published in early July 1918.

Jinnah, during this period also functioned as the joint leader of the two Home Rule Leagues, that of the Congress and the Muslim League, enjoying the confidence of all communities, enabling him to arrange three joint deputations to Montagu; the first headed by Tilak on behalf of the Congress and the Muslim League; the second by Annie Besant on behalf of the two All-India Home Rule Leagues; and the third he led himself on behalf of the two Bombay Presidency Home Rule Leagues. Jinnah, of course, was also a part of the first two deputations. Apart from this, Jinnah met Montagu on a number of occasions to press for reforms for which his contribution, his abilities and his other qualities subsequently received handsome recognition from Montagu in his book, *An Indian Diary*.

When the Montford Report was finally published, there arose serious disagreements amongst the Indian leaders which could be settled only after some hectic parleys by Jinnah. An agreement was finally arrived at resulting in a joint deputation of the Congress and the Muslim League to proceed to England. This was for recommending such improvements in the Montford Report as could then be incorporated in the bill to be moved in Parliament. Unfortunately, the timing was again wrong, for, the British would just not entertain any such delegations during the war years, preferring a limited discussion at the Legislative Council level in India, but this was not acceptable to Jinnah. The government, therefore, as a compromise and a palliative went ahead, again, by forming a committee for the purpose.

In any event, Jinnah did not consider the Montford Report a substantial enough step towards Home Rule. To him provincial autonomy largely depended on the nature and extent of division of the reserved and the transferred subjects under diarchy. He correctly apprehended that half-hearted diarchy could well reduce the position of

Indian ministers to that of mere bystanders. He believed that some of the provinces were competent enough to manage their own affairs and therefore, in such provinces, all the subjects should be transferred to Indians. Not acceptable, specifically, were provisions that empowered provincial governors to disallow introduction of bills or motions in the Legislative Assembly relating to reserved subjects. The 20 August 1917 announcement had talked of responsible government, which word Jinnah interpreted as meaning a transfer of all powers to Indian hands, for to him freedom of the country was inseparable from responsible government.

The government benches in the Legislative Assembly were then understandably perturbed by such assertions, which, for the likes of Jinnah, was no deterrence. These ideas for improving the Montagu-Chelmsford Report were explained in his evidence before the Southborough Committee in January 1919 in Bombay. However, his observations to the Joint Parliamentary Committee in the August of that year (1919 were far more elaborate and blunt. This committee had been appointed by Parliament to review the Government of India Bill (1919) by interviewing Indian political leaders, who could later be called to London for giving evidence.

What strikes greatly is that at this stage, when most of his colleague were not even ready for freedom of India, Jinnah was clearly and forcefully advocating his constitutional ideas for leading India to freedom. The role of the civil services, judiciary and executive were all explained by Jinnah, lucidly and in detail. While giving evidence before the Joint Select Committee on the Government of India Bill Jinnah gave his reasons:

> But are we asking for responsible government today, although we have ten per cent of the population that can get into the electorate? We are not. What do you find in Canada? In Canada people had no municipal franchise even, they had no municipal experience when complete responsible government was established in Canada...Therefore, I say this argument that we have not got on electorate is without justification. There is no warrant for it.

Jinnah favoured a federal constitution in which all the residuary powers would rest with the provinces. He did not favour the office of the secretary of state for India in the shape that it then existed, holding that the viceroy and the governors must be shorn of their autocratic powers. It was only in matters of public security, law and order that they should have discretionary powers, but they must be made responsible to the legislature, which body must enjoy all powers including financial. Nomination of members in the formation of legislative bodies, centre or provincial was to be dispensed with, all seats being filled through elections based on an electorate of ten or twelve per cent of the population. Amongst various other proposals was that governors being appointed must be from amongst men of eminence in the public life of England so that they could bring fresh thought into the Indian society; provincial subjects should all be transferred to Indian hands who should then be responsible to the provincial legislatures not governors. This is almost exactly what Jinnah later suggested as improvements to the Montford Report and the Government of India Bill 1935.*

Subsequently, of course, Gandhi differing with Jinnah on the working of these reforms carved his own path and went to civil disobedience and the agitational methodology of *satyagraha*. Until 1920, though, Jinnah had successfully kept the Indian political forces together, simultaneously exerting pressure on the government. With this new Gandhian methodology, that pressure dissipated and the British Raj remained for three more decades.

GANDHI AND JINNAH: THE TWO INCOMPATIBLE KATHIAWARIS

We have earlier, though very briefly, considered these two great but incompatible Indians, both born of Kathiawari trading communities but not endowed with much other similarities. One was devoutly and expressly Hindu, the other but a casual votary of Islam. One shaped religion to his political ends; the other shunned it on grounds of principle. Gandhi, in a very real sense was deeply under the influence of Tolstoy (it is after Tolstoy that he had named his settlement in South Africa) and Henry David Thoreau; Jinnah recognised the political impress only of Dadabhai and Gokhale. Gandhi led his personal life publicly; Jinnah led even his public life close to his chest. These two, in

---

* It is both instructive and perhaps symptomatic of a certain inability to break out of the existing mould that certain fundamentals of the Montford proposals have travelled, down the years, largely unaltered, decade after decade, all the way through various constitutional reforms in India, including, finally, the Constitution of independent India adopted in 1950.

one fashion or another, not just deeply influenced events of those momentous decades of India's freedom struggle but actually shaped them. Gandhi admitted failure in his quest; Jinnah, it is apocryphally suggested boasted that 'he won Pakistan with the help of just a typewriter and a clerk'. It is a fascinating theme, a study of these two great Indians. This sub-chapter can attempt no more than an outline sketch.

Although the families of both Jinnah and Gandhi had once lived just about forty miles or so apart in Kathiawar, (Gujarat), this adjacency of their places of origin did nothing to bring their politics close together. In their very first meeting, at the Gurjar Sabha in January 1915, convened to felicitate Gandhi upon his return from South Africa, in response to a welcome speech, with Jinnah presiding, Gandhi had somewhat accommodatingly said he was 'glad to find a Muslim not only belonging to his own region's Sabha, but chairing it'.[62] Gandhi had singled out Jinnah as a Muslim, though, neither in appearance nor in conduct was Jinnah anywhere near to being any of the stereotypes of the religious identity ascribed by Gandhi. Jinnah, on the other hand, was far more fulsome in his praise.

Gandhi had reached India by boat in January 1915 when many leaders including Jinnah and Gokhale went to Bombay to give him an ovatious welcome. By this date Jinnah had already emerged as an all-India leader and was committed to attaining his stated goals of unity, not just between the Muslims and the Hindus, Extremists and Moderates, but also among various classes of India. To receive Gandhi, Jinnah had forsaken attending the Madras Congress meet of 1914. Gandhi, upon reaching Bombay had been warmly welcomed by Jinnah who wanted to enlist his services for the cause of Hindu-Muslim unity. It was because of his popularity and standing that Jinnah had been invited to preside over a garden party given by the Gurjar Sabha, an association of the Gurjar (Gujar) community, arranged to welcome Mr and Mrs Gandhi, on his arrival on 13 January 1915.

In his presidential address, Jinnah 'welcomed...Mr and Mrs Gandhi, not only on behalf of Bombay but on behalf of the whole of India.' He impressed upon Gandhi that the greatest problem was 'to bring about unanimity and cooperation between the two communities so that the demands of India (from Imperial Britain) may be made absolutely unanimously.' For this he desired 'that frame of mind, that state, that condition which they had to bring about between the two communities, when most of their problems, he had no doubt, would be easily solved'. Jinnah went to the extent of saying: 'Undoubtedly he [Gandhi] would not only become a worthy ornament but also a real worker whose equals there were very few.' This remark was greatly applauded by a largely Hindu audience, accounts of that meeting report. Gandhi, however, was cautious and somewhat circuitous in his response. He took the plea that he would study all the Indian questions from 'his own point of view', a reasonable enough assertion; also because Gokhale had advised him to study the situation for at least a year before entering into politics. This, too, was all right but then, needlessly he thanked Jinnah for presiding over a Hindu gathering. This was an ungracious and discouraging response to Jinnah's warm welcome and had a dampening effect.

Gandhi, somewhat hesitant at first, could, in that early phase, see no other route but of following Gokhale, Jinnah and some of the other moderate leaders. This was also because Tilak had also by then, come around to the moderate line. Gandhi did cooperate with all of them, but only until about 1920, after which his clearly became the prominent voice and position. Besides, by then (1920) Gandhi had won acceptance from the British government too, even though that was through the good offices of Gokhale, who 'exerted the full weight of his prestige and influence upon the Viceroy, Lord Hardinge to bring the Government of India solidly behind Gandhi'.[63] This was the period when the British government, very concerned about Jinnah, his Hindu-Muslim unity moves were endeavouring hard to keep the All-India Muslim League away from the Indian National Congress.[64]

In a sense Jinnah's position goes back a year, to May 1914, when he had led a Congress delegation to England to lobby with the secretary of state and other members of parliament for opening up the Council of India to at least three non-official Indians, who could be elected by the Imperial and Provincial Legislative Councils. He appeared then as a kind of potential political heir to the great trio of the early years of the twentieth century: Naoroji-Mehta-Gokhale;[65] and, of course, of the leadership of the Congress, too, certainly in India's West. The India Office, however rejected these demands outright. It was in any event an ill-timed initiative for just about then the First World War had broken out. While Jinnah was so engaged, Gandhi, upon the outbreak of war urged his countrymen to 'think Imperially'.[66] He also took the lead in organising a Field Ambulance Training Corps, in London, to help the Allies. One hears echoes of similar efforts by him in South Africa and during the Boer War, but this was in a sharp contrast to Gandhi's approach and policy during the Second World War. In any event, Gandhi's leadership at this time had almost an entirely religiously provincial character, Jinnah, on the other hand was then doubtless imbued by a non-sectarian, nationalistic zeal.

THE LUCKNOW PACT—1916

To examine this rather momentous pact, we have to travel with events as they evolved into a Congress-Muslim League joint formulation, of a scheme of reforms in 1916, which later came to be referred to as the Lucknow Pact of 1916. The All-India Congress Committee, chaired by Pandit Madan Mohan Malaviya in April 1916, had framed the original but still tentative proposal: for discussion in the Congress Provincial Committees. In August the All-India Muslim League conducted a similar exercise with Jinnah steering the discussions. The League finalised its recommendation by November 1916 whereafter a joint meeting of the Congress and the Muslim League was held at Calcutta on 17 November 1916. This was presided by that haloed name and Bengal leader, Surendra Nath Banerjee. Largely due to Jinnah' continuous and untiring efforts a consensus was finally reached and his sterling contributions duly recognised when in a League Council meeting he was appointed the president of the next League Session, in Lucknow, scheduled for December 1916. This choice was greatly applauded in the Congress circles, too. With astute handling of complex negotiations, and with the invaluable support of Tilak in the Congress, a joint scheme of reforms was then evolved by the two parties. This, to give its full name, came to be known as Congress-League Joint Scheme of Reforms, or more simply and practically as the Lucknow Pact. This was made possible by the 'signal service of Jinnah to the cause of Hindu-Muslim unity'[67] as recorded by the *Bombay Chronicle* of 1 January 1916.

This Lucknow Pact was an agreement at the national level on principles, whereby, both the Congress and the Muslim League would share power in the executive and the legislature. This pact was more specific in scope than what had earlier been envisaged in Gokhale's Scheme.[68] The Congress, as per the pact, would have a two-thirds representation in the Central Executive and the Legislature, while the Muslim League would get one-third. Some special safeguards were agreed upon for religious matters, all such issues needing for their passage the support of three-fourth members of the concerned community. Separate electorate for the Muslims was recognised as a principle of cardinal importance. It was adopted after necessary assurances from Jinnah, backed by Tilak. In this unity effort Jinnah was the arch culprit as he himself would say later in a self-deprecatory mode.[69]

These leadership roles in the Congress, respectively, of Jinnah and Gandhi got reversed within just six years of Gandhi's return. By 1920, Gandhi had come fully into his own; that is by the Nagpur Congress, from where onwards Jinnah got increasingly marginalised in the Congress party. It is not that either of them altered their political personalities, rather during these six years the entire Indian political scene got transformed, and these two reacted to the changes as they best judged. Besides, by 1920, Gandhi, too, had gathered around him a recognisable Muslim support plus a great deal of financial support. It was Gandhi who then became the rallying spirit behind India's freedom movement; a status that Jinnah never really attained. From Amritsar, to Calcutta to Nagpur (all respectively Congress sessions), Gandhi grew from strength to strength. By 1920, and the Nagpur Congress session, the Congress party was now unquestioningly behind Gandhi.

As for Jinnah, earlier often called the Muslim Gokhale, had it not been for the war perhaps he could have remained central to the Congress, and simultaneously also been the principal spirit of the Muslim League, endeavouring through his constitutional methods a political rapprochement between the two parties and the Hindus and the Muslims, certainly politically. The First World War changed all that: had fate willed otherwise? Or was Jinnah outwitted, out-manoeuvred? Or, even more tragically, was it that being Muslim he was from the very beginning disadvantaged? In this heartless race of political influence in India, Jinnah always carried a heavy handicap then, also later.

Just months before the war Jinnah's political demands had been rejected in England. Yet, ironically it were these very demands that later got announced by Montagu for a responsible government for India, and in just three years this announcement had got translated into an enabling legislation. Jinnah, in the process was robbed of a major political platform, rather had it pulled away from under his political feet. The other major factor, or contributor to Jinnah's relegation in the Congress was ironically the break up of the Ottoman Empire, following which came the abolition of the Caliphate and an arrival on the Indian political scene of the mesmerising (temporarily) Ali brothers—Mohammad Ali Jauhar and Shaukat Ali Jauhar. This removed, at least temporarily the Muslim plank, too, as an option for Jinnah. Rather morosely he then communicated with the then governor of Bombay, Sir George Lloyd, to let White Hall know that 'all the value and goodwill that one hoped from your reforms is being rapidly submerged on account of the actions of two or three men (Gandhi and the Ali brothers?) and feeling has never been worse than at present since the Mutiny'.[70]

But there were other consequences of the First World War that followed. For one it conveyed to India and to Indians that Asians could defeat the 'white man'. They had drawn some inspiration from Japan defeating the Russian forces in 1905, during the Russo-Japanese War. Besides, the First World War events now in Europe and Arabia, exposed lay Indians to a greatly accelerated timetable of political expectations. Indian soldiers saw Europe, and the 'vilayat'[71] at first hand, also white troops in a very different role. This shortened the fuse of their popular patience, too, as began to be commented. This was a god-sent opportunity to muster mass support and Gandhi having developed his programmes earlier in South Africa seized it instantly. The war had caused frustration, also ambivalence even among the Muslims in India. While Jinnah had remained aloof from any involvement in pan-Islamic activities, Gandhi, a proto-typical Hindu, chose to ride this tiger of the Khilafat agitation. During the years of Gandhi's rise to power, he had avoided competing with the leadership of any public organisation throughout the war. However, at the same time he had courted the Arya Samajists (Swami Shraddhanand), and the Congress, also the Home Rule League leaders. Jinnah understood the phenomenon of Gandhi and his rise to popular fame but could not counter it, for as he explained to Meston,[72] in 1917:

> The extremists have a definite programme, impracticable perhaps, but appealing keenly to the pride of the people. The moderates have no particular creed except to trust the Government. If they go on the platform and ask audiences to trust Government, the people immediately challenge them and ask them to say what the Government is going to do for them.

The moderates are unable to reply. The Government has not confided its intentions to them; and they are shouted down. The extremists on the other hand, are definite, plausible, and unless they break the law, there is nothing to show that the Government disapproves of their propaganda.[73]

Time and again, as in this and in other such circumstances it has been proven that in a contest between an extreme and a moderate viewpoint the former scores, almost always, even if temporarily.

While Jinnah had persisted with constitutional, legislative reforms also communal rapprochement, Gandhi had gone to Champaran, to Ahmedabad and to Kheda,[74] from success to success and he was by then dearly carrying the masses with him, there was no disputing his appeal or his position. Jinnah, on the other hand, had no such mass following, even the Muslim majority provinces were not with him. Yet, and paradoxically it is precisely during these years that Jinnah's nationalism irked the British. By early 1918, Willingdon, then governor of Bombay had come to club him with Pandit Madan Mohan Malaviya, Bal Gangadhar Tilak and Annie Besant 'who were among those extremists who had no feeling of their duty towards [the] Empire in a crisis'.[75] Chelmsford was equally frustrated by Jinnah's outspoken criticism in council. Sir George Lloyd, Willingdon's successor had later warned Montagu against 'Jinnah and Mrs Naidu...both fair of speech and black of heart—real irreconcilables'.[76]

Jinnah resigned from the Viceroy's Council in protest against the passage of Rowlatt Acts, in the April of 1919. By then he had already been elected president of the Bombay Home Rule League following Annie Besant's internment in 1917. Jinnah's letter of resignation to the Viceroy is eloquent: '...by passing this Bill, Your Excellency's Government have...ruthlessly trampled upon the principles for which Great Britain avowedly fought the war. The fundamental principles of justice have been uprooted and the Constitutional rights of the people have been violated...when there is no real danger to the State, by an over fretful and incompetent bureaucracy which is neither responsible to the people nor in touch with real public opinion'.[77]

Jinnah had resigned his Council seat in Simla not to rouse mass feelings but to shift the venue of his politics from the Viceroy's Council to what he believed would be a more responsive venue: White Hall. He tendered his resignation feeling 'that under the prevailing conditions, I can be of no use to my people in the council...In my opinion the Government that passes such laws in times of peace forfeits the claim to be called a civilized Government...I still hope that the Secretary of State for India will advice His Majesty to signify his disallowance of this black act'.[78]

Jinnah went to London in the summer of 1919, leading this time, a Muslim League deputation, to appeal to Montagu and to present a testimony before Lord Selborne's Select Committee on Reforms. His success was modest. He returned to Bombay convinced that 'if India were to send...real representatives to London, a great deal could (still) be done', and he himself was prepared to serve as one of those 'permanent émigré representatives'.[79] His prescription sounded much like that voiced several decades earlier by William Wedderburn and Gokhale.[80] Though his path to dominion status for a united India could have proved the swiftest, most rational and least painful, it evoked no welcoming response then from the political leadership of a Post-First World War Delhi.

Gandhi–Jinnah and the Khilafat Movement

Gandhi's work on the Punjab atrocities enquiry, his commitment to the Khilafat cause and his close association with the Ali brothers, Shaukat and Mohammad Ali, had won for him great popularity. Gandhi would say: 'born of the same mother, belonging to the same soil', Hindus and Muslims must love one another. On the issue of Khilafat his usual response was—'if the Hindus and Muslims are brothers, it is their duty to share each other's sorrows.' Seldom earlier, had such camaraderie been witnessed between Hindus and Muslims.

Edmund Chandler's description of those times in the *Atlantic Monthly* illustrates: 'The politician who could unite these incompatible currents in a combined stream would have won half the battle of independence'. Thus the 'Hindu-Moslem' entente, from the Indian point of view, is the most important political movement of the century. When in the April of 1919, the Hindu, Swami Shraddhanand, ascended the pulpit of the Jama Masjid, at Delhi, and addressed the people the precedent was described in the Mohammedan press in India as the most remarkable event in recent Islamic history. Then in December, Gandhi was elected president of the Khilafat Conference at Delhi. It was about this time that the political catchword, 'Allah-u Akbar and Om (the mystic Hindu formula) are one name', began to be repeated everywhere, and the Mussulmans, to appease Hindu sentiment, forsook the slaying of cows. This was only the beginning of Gandhi's association with the Moslem extremists. At a later stage he became so far the champion of Islam as to make civil obedience to the Government of India contingent upon a rectification of the Treaty of Sevres. This is best illustrated by Gandhi's approach to Palestine and the very identity of Israel.

During the 1937 Arab revolt in Palestine, the Jewish Agency sent Herman Kallenbach, a German-Jewish architect, to India to seek Mahatma Gandhi's aid. Kallenbach, an excellent choice had been a major worker with Gandhi in his South African campaigns and, despite a separation of many years, the two remained the closest of friends.

In July 1937, Kallenbach returned with messages for Moshe Shertock of the Agency's Political Department and Chaim Weizmann, the Zionist leader, stating that Gandhi was willing to help bring about a settlement in Palestine, along with the following written statement of principle which is to be found in the Central Zionist Archives:

'Assuming Zionism is not a material movement but represents the spiritual aspiration of the Jews, the introduction of Jews in Palestine under the protection of British and other arms, is wholly inconsistent with spirituality. Neither the Mandate nor the Balfour Declaration can therefore be used in support of sustaining Jewish immigration into Palestine, in the teeth of Arab opposition.

In my opinion the Jews should disclaim any intention of realizing their aspiration under the protection of arms and should rely wholly on the goodwill of Arabs.

No exception can possibly be taken to the natural desire of the Jews to found a home in Palestine. But they must wait for its fulfilment, till Arab opinion is ripe for it.' The only response of the Jewish Agency was to send Gandhi a parcel, without a covering note, containing a twenty-five page account of Zionism.

A year later, Gandhi further damaged his credentials and capacity to intervene via a newspaper article entitled 'The Jews', written in response to the *Reichskristallnacht* pogrom of 9-10 November 1938. 'Palestine belongs to the Arabs in the same way that England belongs to the English', he declared. 'It is wrong and inhuman to impose the Jews on the Arabs'. Jews could only settle in Palestine, as he had already told the Agency, 'by the goodwill of the Arabs': 'If I were a Jew and were born in Germany and earned my livelihood there, I would claim Germany as my home even as the tallest Gentile German may...I am convinced that if someone with courage and vision can rise amongst them (the Jews) to lead them in non-violent action the winter of their despair can be turned into a summer of hope'. Zionist protests were loud and long.

Simone Panter-Brick focuses on this 'extraordinary moment in Gandhi's life' when he imagined he could make a 'difference' in Palestine. She underscores this key relationship between Gandhi and Kallenbach which offered a 'bridge between Gandhi and the Zionist movement'. The context here was of the 'Palestine Mandate and the progress of Zionist' settlements into the 1930s. She also provides another context of Gandhi's alliance with 'Indian Muslims in the Khilafat Movement after the First World War'.

Panter-Brick then explains how Gandhi's views of the Arab-Zionist struggle in Palestine ought to be viewed through the prism of Indian politics of the 1930s. As Wm. Roger Louis states in his brief but excellent preface to the book: 'It is no whitewash of British imperialism to say that Gandhi's tactics could not have succeeded in Nazi Germany or the Soviet Union or even French Indo-China. So the desire to intervene in Palestine itself was driven by Gandhi's concern to foster Hindu-Muslim unity, by adopting an emotive Muslim issue with which he could forge national unity as he had attempted in the Caliphate protest'.

Gandhi, of course, was morally entitled to throw his whole force into the Islamic movement so long as his belief in the righteousness of the Turk's cause was sincere. To his critics, however, he appeared to be backing a cause which he must know to be wrong, out of political expediency. What conceivable traffic can there be between the apostle of gentleness—the liberator of his own people—and the truculent Turk, that he should join in a campaign to perpetuate a regime of repression like the Osmanali's? However, Gandhi was quite frank about his position. He did not pretend to be interested in Turkey. As for the subject races, he still believed, in spite of Turkey's record of massacre-made majorities, that Christians, Arabs, and Jews might enjoy their birthright and remain autonomous within the Ottoman Empire, under the protection of guarantees. 'By helping the Mohammedans of India,' he said, 'at a critical moment of their history, I want to buy their friendship.' And so long as he believed in their wrongs, it was a perfectly straight deal. The 'Hindu-Moslem Entente was the first essential in Indian nationalism.'

For an even more graphic description of the events of that period I rely on Swami Shraddhanand's own version:

> The 4th of April 1919 was a red letter day in Delhi. It was the first Friday after the indiscriminate shooting and congregational prayers were to be offered in the great Jumma Masjid. A notice had been sent round by responsible Musalmans inviting the public to join the Memorial Meeting called for invoking God's blessings on the Hindu-Muslim Martyrs.
>
> As usual I was making a round of the city when scores of Hindu of gentlemen told me that our Musalman brethren insisted on the Hindus going inside the Masjid and joining the Memorial Meeting and asked my advice as to the course they should adopt. The reason of the enquiry was this: Non-Muslims had no right of entry into the great mosque without the sanction of the Mosque Managing Committee, especially when *Namaz* was going on. I asked them to wait and went to consult Mr Abdul Rahman Vakeel whose office was close by. Mr Abdur Rahman advised me not to go without consulting Hakeem Saheb. As Hakeem Sahib was not at home, I returned to *my* ashram determined not to go out till Namaz and memorial service [were] over....
>
> I was busy writing when by 1 p.m. about fifty Mussulman gentlemen boarded my humble lodgings and lovingly forced me down. A tonga was waiting. In (sic) the way they requisitioned several conveyances one faster than the other till an empty motor car was found. I was then hurried on and reached the southern steps of the Jumma Masjid. I saw some people about to come down but when they saw me ascending the steps, shouts of 'Mahatma Gandhi ki Jaya' and 'Hindu-Musalman ki Jaya' went forth and all of them turned back. The gathering inside could not be less than thirty thousand. I was going to sit behind the last man when other Musalman brethren came running and took me inside the buildings and then outside, where a permanent wooden pulpit stood for the preachers' use. Maulvie Abdul Majeed was addressing the audience. He stopped, waiting for me to go up: I hesitated. A hundred voices urged me to go up. After ascending two steps I again hesitated. The huge audience was up on its legs and with one voice called upon me to go up. When I reached the pulpit, they sat down.
>
> I expected Maulvie Abdul Majeed to go on with his sermon. But he stopped with the remark: 'You have heard what the Quran Majeed says about the blood of the Martyrs. Swami Shraddhanand will now tell you that the Holy Veda, which is believed to be the revelation according to our Hindu brethren, inculcates the same teachings.' It was a sudden call. I had to stand

up. I recited the Vedic verse which inculcated the Fatherhood and the Motherhood of God.

त्वं हि नः पिता वसो त्वं माता शतक्रतो बभूविथ: । अधाते सत्रमीमहे

I called upon the huge audience to bear testimony to the innocence of the martyrs and ended with calling upon them to fall at the feet of Him who was the Father and the Mother of all.

Those, who were present, can well describe the scene. And when I thrice repeated, 'Om shanti, Ameen!' and the whole audience followed me with one reverberating voice, it was an inspiring spectacle. I came down and left with the audience whose faces showed how impressed they were.

This was followed by Hindu Sadhus addressing from Muslim pulpits in Masjids and Musalman divines addressing mixed audiences in Hindu Temples, in all parts of the country. In spite of all that has occurred after that grand scene I am still impressed with its memory and am living in the hope that clouds of doubt will disappear and the bright light of the sun of Faith and Truth will shine forth again with all its splendour.

Inside, this beautiful scene was being acted and outside the great mosque the armoured cars and the Military and the Police were provokingly in evidence. But the people, exhorted by their leaders, kept their temper admirably.

But this 'tide of togetherness' soon ran out; the turbulent twenties arrived, the situation reverted to what it had been and the communal situation deteriorated. Dr B.R. Ambedkar, a contemporary of Gandhi later observed in his book *Pakistan, or, The Partition of India:* 'It is a notorious fact that many prominent Hindus who had offended the religious susceptibilities of the Muslims either by their writings or by their part in the Shudhi movement have been murdered by some fanatic Musalmans. [But the] first to suffer was Swami Shradhanand, who was shot by Abdul Rashid on 23 December 1926. This was followed by the murder of Lala Nanakchand, a prominent Arya Samajist of Delhi. Rajpal, the publisher of *Rangila Rasool,* was stabbed by Ilamdin on 6 April 1929 while he was sitting in his shop. Nathuramal Sharma was murdered by Abdul Qayum in September 1934. It was an act of great daring, for Sharma was stabbed to death in the Court of the Judicial Commissioner of Sindh where he was seated awaiting the hearing of his appeal against his conviction...for the publication of a pamphlet on the history of Islam. Khanna, the Secretary of the Hindu Sabha, was severely assaulted in 1938 after the Session of the Hindu Maha Sabha held in Ahmedabad and very narrowly escaped death'.

The *Times of India* of 30 November 1927 in its column, 'Through Indian Eyes' stated: 'It is reported that for earning merit for the soul of Abdul Rashid, the murderer of Swami Shradhanand, in the next world, the students and professors of the famous theological college at Deoband finished five complete recitations of the Quran and had planned to finish daily a lakh and a quarter recitations of Quranic verses. Their prayer was "God Almighty may give the *marhoom* (i.e., Rashid) a place in the 'a '*ala-e-illeeyeen* (the summit of the seventh heaven)".'

3

THE TURBULENT TWENTIES

Hindu-Muslim Conflicts of the 1920s

In these troubled decades, the more the efforts made towards lasting communal amity and a joint Hindu-Muslim plank, perversely, the greater became an upsurge in communal conflicts. Such periodic bursts had of course, been experienced earlier too, for instance, in the twentieth century between 1904-14, and 1917-18.[1] Those earlier periods had, in one fashion or another, all coincided with steps taken towards devolution of political power in India; for even as Muslim domination declined, Hindus more easily filled the vacated space, generating protests, which in turn invited reaction and thus sparking conflicts. In addition, as political power slowly passed from the British to Indian hands the process of transference itself put immense pressure on Hindu-Muslim relations. Besides, this method (perhaps born of circumstances) of transferring (British) power in slow and small instalments sharpened existing divisions within society, and issues like reservation of seats etc. fostered additional points of communal abrasion. Hindu-Muslim relations in the 1920s were also dogged by several movements that had arisen as protests and the very expression of these protests, in turn, gave birth to additional, reactive movements. All these, relate sadly, to the darker aspects of the Hindu-Muslim interaction. Besides, as earlier mentioned, the Council Reforms of 1919 rather than helping to bring together, in fact had divided the communities. In addition, a temporary collapse of the Non-Cooperation Movement during this period drove another wedge in the aspirations for a national political coalition which, to a considerable extent, had covered traditional divisions. One definite casualty of all this became the slogan of 'Hindu-Muslim Unity', which either came to be reinterpreted pejoratively now or was reviled, in press, in public, and by Hindus and Muslims alike. With the Press Act repealed and alliance between the Congress and Muslim Khilafatists falling apart, the press, too, reverted to its tradition of sensational reportage of communal conflicts.

The Hindu-Muslim unity witnessed during the Khilafat agitation of 1920-21 did not last long. With the Khilafat abolished and the Non-Cooperation Movement called off by Gandhi, the common front against the British soon crumbled. The Montford reforms, brought to the Indian polity through the Act of 1919—diarchy being its main feature, ushered an era of electoral political competition, however limited the electorate and even if at the district and the provincial level only. With these reforms came separate electorates, the two communities—Hindus and Muslims—were now brought, in what can only be termed as democratic competition, and this over and above existing social abrasions. Despite impressive attempts by several political personalities in both the parties that spirit of cooperation of the 1920-21 period, between Hindus and Muslims could not be revived.

Differences over petty matters often became issues of violent discord, like playing music before mosques, holding tazia processions or killing of cows during Id, and such, easily descended into communal violence and killings. There were, for example, serious communal clashes in 1923, in Multan and Amritsar. A communal movement—Tanzeem and Tabligh was thereafter started by the Muslims, to organise the community as virile warriors. In reaction the Hindu Mahasabha, too, sought to strengthen the Hindus and the Sangathan movement was the answer to that search: promoting physical culture. Swami Shraddhananda, started the Shuddhi (purification) movement, attempting to bring back within the Hindu fold such as had converted to Islam earlier, like for example, the Malkana Rajputs. These developments, the 'Sangathan' and 'Shuddhi' were, predictably, denounced by the Muslims, the movements causing rift between the two communities.

The Hindu Mahasabha also sought to strengthen the Hindus by admitting the depressed classes to the rights and privileges of the higher classes. The Muslims suspected that the object of the removal of untouchability was not the absorbing of these communities into Hindu society, but to use them as auxiliaries. This, too, then added to the list of suspicious activities in the minds of the Muslims. A competitive manifestation of zeal, for conversion and re-conversion was then witnessed amongst both Muslims and Hindus. Witnessing these dangerous trends Mohammad Ali Jauhar in his 1923 presidential address of the League observed: 'My belief is that both sides are working with an eye much more on the next decennial census than on heaven...and I frankly confess that it is on such occasions that I sigh for the days when our fore-fathers settled things by cutting heads rather than [through] counting them.'

There then, occurred a major crisis, in the Malabar. In August 1921, from the west coast of southern India, there began to appear reports of a revolt among the Moplahs.[2] Such unrests had a history; they were not new and were therefore, not a surprise. However, this time it became a major rebellion, eventually involving some 50,000 people directly and finally drawing a response from the British Indian military on a scale that was later termed as 'the only internal operations worthy of being dignified with the name of a war since...1857'.[3] The government version described this rebellion as the outcome of the Congress-Khilafat campaign against the government. The ideology of the Khilafat, so explained the British Raj,[4] had imparted a religious fervour.

In the Punjab, where memories were still fresh of the martial law that had followed the Rowlatt Acts, concerns instantly got raised that the excesses of 1919 could well get repeated in the Malabar. The *Bande Mataram,* a Lahore newspaper edited by the venerable public figure of Lala Lajpat Rai, was direct and bitter in its condemnation. Lalaji termed the 'Khilafat Movement being responsible' for kind of reasoning of the Raj as 'an imaginary cause', asserting instead, and with reason, that, 'if these disturbances are due to the Khilafat agitators or Khilafat resolutions they ought to have first of all taken place in Karachi or Sind'.[5] Such newspapers as wished to sustain their stance against the government and in favour of Hindu-Muslim unity, despite being confronted now by daily accounts of new atrocities against the Hindus pouring in from the south, found it immensely difficult to maintain their position. The consequence of the Malabar riots travelled north fast and seriously damaged inter-religious relations here, too.

In the face of these communal cross currents the Congress, as it tends to, got caught in a pincer of competing interests. On the practical side, these conflicts could hardly have come at a worse time, for all principal leaders of the Congress were then in prison, there was uncertainty about the future direction of its programmes, and the party was falling short of funds. On the ideological front the Congress, committed to Hindu-Muslim unity found these conflicts eroding the very foundation of that ideal. There were, of course, some expectations that the Congress might mediate the disputes and it did make a few tentative efforts but without any success, for such timid attempts carried neither conviction nor commitment.

In its emphasis on Hindu interests, Punjab was now well ahead of the United Provinces where the first Hindu Sabha had not been founded until 1911, and where the movement was not put on any established basis until 1915. The year 1922 actually proved to be a turning point in the history of the Hindu Mahasabha, and largely on account of events that dramatised Muslim threat to the Hindu community. News from Malabar about the Moplah revolt had continued to command space in the press, and in the autumn of 1922 that got coupled with additional news of more atrocities against the Hindus, on this occasion from within Punjab.

During Muharram, in September 1922, there occurred a major communal riot in Multan, of which the Hindus bore the brunt. Pandit Madan Mohan Malaviya, then in Punjab to investigate the matter of Akali Sikh troubles of Guru-ka-Bagh,[6] visited and addressed large meetings in Amritsar and Lahore and spoke about these recent riots in Multan. At Lahore, he related details of heart-rending incidents from the riot effected city and criticised Hindus for their failure to stand up in their own defence.

The impact of the Moplah rebellion combined with Muharram riots in Multan was long lasting. In the six years that followed, an evocation of Malabar and Multan got woven as a kind of a rallying cry appealing to the Hindus to stand up for the community's resurgence. At the Hindu Mahasabha's annual session in December 1922, held just after those of other all-India organisations at the common meeting place of Gaya, Pandit Madan Mohan Malaviya set the tone. He proposed the formation of Hindu Sabhas in every village. The resolutions of this session while echoing Malviya's speech evidenced a much more militant stance.[7]

Meanwhile, Muslim efforts during the middle of 1920s to counteract Hindu movements were, for the most part, not so well-coordinated, also not as effective. An attempt was made to foster physical culture troops under the name Ali Ghol,[8] as a counterpart to the Mahabir Dal of the Mahasabha, but the results were spotty. There was just one single effort to construct a full equivalent to sangathan,[9] and that amounted to little more than the work of one man. In 1924, Dr Saifuddin Kitchlew, an associate of Shaukat Ali launched the Tanzeem movement. He gained some support from the Central Khilafat Committee, established an Urdu language daily in Amritsar called *Tanzim*, and began a round of speaking engagements to raise both funds and a following. Though the Muslim response to Sangathan was scattered and did not generate any new institution, it was of little comfort to the Hindus who remained rooted in their conviction that the Muslims, strongly entrenched, needed to be confronted.

Another factor which then contributed (still does) to Hindu-Muslim strife was the periodic coincidence of their main festivals. Particularly problematic was, (and is), for example, the coincidence of *Ram Lila* or *Dussherra* with the observance of *Muharram*[10] and *Bakr Id*.[11] Incidents of cow slaughter and the playing of music before mosques had, as it still does, a continuing potential for disruption of peace. Which is why festivals got associated with almost all communal conflicts of the 1920s, so much so, that British observers then began to refer to the 'Hindu-Muslim' clashes of the period, derisively as the 'cow-music' question.

From about 1923 onward, India then witnessed a series of communal riots that further deteriorated the political atmosphere. The Calcutta riots of 1923, riots in Delhi, Gulbarga and Kohat in 1924 are only some examples of major communal conflagrations in the period of all these, the most serious occurred in Kohat in NWFP, a province with an overwhelmingly large Muslim population, over 92 per cent. The trouble arose over a pamphlet published by the Sanatan Dharm Sabha, Kohat, that contained an anti-Islamic poem. This, in turn, was as a reaction or reply to an equally offensive anti-Hindu poem published in a Muslim newssheet. The Muslim community at Kohat rose against this disturbing poem, and despite Hindus adopting resolutions regretting the error, drastic action was sought against them. The Muslims of Kohat took an oath of extreme revenge.

The district administration failed to assess the seriousness of the situation. Violence broke out on 9 September 1924, and continued for some days leading to looting, arson, and widespread killing of Hindus. The failure of the government to protect them caused deep resentment throughout India. When Gandhi attempted to visit Kohat, he was refused permission by the viceroy. The popular demand of an independent enquiry was also not heeded; instead, the government held an internal inquiry of its own and predictably, it exonerated the local officials.

The manner in which the Congress, the Muslim League and the Hindu Mahasabha reacted to the Kohat tragedy is illustrative of the manner in which communal questions were then looked at. Motilal Nehru had moved a resolution on this subject, in the Congress conclave, scrupulously avoiding casting blame on any party, as he himself admitted later the 'resolution was a non-controversial one and committed Congress to nothing'.[12] The Muslim League felt that the killings in Kohat of Hindus was not unprovoked, on the contrary, gross provocations had been offered to the religious sentiments of Musalmans and the Hindus were the first to resort to violence. Lala Lajpat Rai, speaking for Hindu Mahasabha had asked, 'Whether even admitting that the Hindus were at fault, was their fault such that it deserved the punishment inflicted on them?'

A joint enquiry into the Kohat riots was also held by Gandhi and Shaukat Ali. Since Gandhi had been denied permission to go to Kohat, this enquiry was conducted at Rawalpindi. In their findings, the two, Gandhi and Shaukat Ali, differed. To Shaukat Ali, the firing and burning incidents were accidental; he also disbelieved that the Muslims had organised a general jihad against the Hindus. Gandhi, on the other hand, expressed that Muslim fury on 10 September knew no bounds. Had the Hindus not been evacuated from their places and taken to the Cantonment, not many would have lived.

Hindu-Muslim relations continued to deteriorate in 1925 and 1926 with riots occurring in Delhi, Allahabad, and Calcutta. It is significant that during this period of great communal tension, Gandhi kept himself aloof, probably giving up as hopeless any attempt at harmony. It is instructive that communal riots were confined to only the British territory, whereas Indian states were almost entirely free from them—a riot in 1924 at Gulbarga in Nizam's territory possibly being the only unfortunate exception.

Rashtriya Swayamsevak Sangh (RSS)

The Rashtriya Swayamsevak Sangh was established in Nagpur in 1925 by Dr K.B. Hedgewar, who founded it. He was a staunch Congressman, having joined the party in 1915. Dr Hedgewar had in fact been getting increasingly irked at the factional divisions in the Congress party and the Gandhian method of non-cooperation he considered unsuited to the challenge of freedom struggle. In addition to British domination, what also disturbed Dr Hedgewar was the threat from Muslims, the Nagpur riots of 1923 profoundly impacting upon him.

The distinguishing features of the RSS stood them apart: uniformed volunteers wearing khaki shorts, its military-style marching was all indicative of an attempt to make Hindu society more cohesive and strong. The first task assigned to the RSS by Dr Hedgewar was to protect pilgrims against the rapacity of Muslim *fakirs* and Brahmin priests during the festival of Ramnavmi in 1926.

In those earlier years, Muslims would not allow the Ganesh Chaturthi processions to pass through their locality, or a mosque. Specially, after the Nagpur riots of 1927, Dr Hedgewar found the Hindus tentative, unsure of participating in the festival. He thus took the onus of leading the Ganesh procession, all through this confrontationist route, as more and more Hindus joined him.

Prof. Rosalind O'Hanlon,* Oxford University, has expressed a very persuasive point, that 'the legalistic approach of the British did much to prolong the communal clashes. In essence, their approach was to invite all parties to pursue the rights and wrongs of their cases—a clash over the precedence of a procession, a dispute over music before a mosque— through the courts. In the view of the British, a 'precedent' was everything. Naturally, therefore, the leaders of each faction felt honour bound to take up the cause on each side, and disputes were dragged out and further embittered'.

This very brief sketch of the religious and social determinants of an otherwise rooted Hindu-Muslim question provides us with both a backdrop to the political developments influencing both communities, as also an essential integral; that the internal fuel which consistently stoked the fires of strife, separation and supremacy, even as accord was sought and worked for was this social divide. While politically self-rule, Hindu-Muslim unity and such issues dominated political thinking, socially, divides of faith, belief, and practice continued to strain the fabric, often tearing it apart.

---

* Prof Rosalind O'Hanlon is a chairperson of Indian History & Culture at the Institute of Oriental Studies, Oxford University.

This was, in brief, the social backdrop of the momentous developments that followed in the decade of the twenties.

THE GULF WIDENS

With the outbreak of the First World War, change arrived and at a greatly accelerated pace. It began to be said more often that the British were, after all, not born to rule. The First World War, and Indian troops fighting European forces on European soil conveyed many messages, already examined in an earlier chapter. The collapse of the Ottoman Empire and the abolition of the Khalifa of Islam[13] followed the Treaty of Sevres,[14] which amongst myriad other unintended consequences, did temporarily bring together the Hindus and the Muslims on a political platform. This reaction to the abolition of the Khalifa of Islam, from which was born the Khilafat Movement, demonstrated yet again the theory of unintended consequences.

Because of all these factors coinciding in time, what would otherwise have been seen as a welcome initiative of the ruling British, just two years earlier, was now received with scepticism. This sentiment marked the Indian response when the Council Reforms of 1919 finally got introduced. Nevertheless, by then had arisen other impediments: tragic, traumatic and ultimately divisive, generating disillusionment all around. That was the Jallianwala Bagh massacre of 13 April 1919. This caused such an enormous wave of revulsion throughout the country and provoked such an all-India campaign of protest that every other initiative of the Raj paled into insignificance. It was this Jallianwala Bagh, which in turn, gave Gandhi, earlier an advocate of working with the Allies, his launching pad of public protest and non-cooperation. From here onwards the Congress rapidly swung away from moderation to civil disobedience, a change demonstrated most forcefully by the Home Rule League, which transformed itself from a constitutional league into a political body, but with this we will deal in subsequent chapters.

The Congress and the Muslim League at their sessions, at Lucknow, in 1916, had both agreed to give the Muslims separate electorates in all provincial legislatures and had conceded to them a special weightage in Hindu majority provinces, too. This provided the basis for a working cooperation between these two communities as also their respective political organisations, the Congress and the Muslim League. In this session, K.M. Munshi, in his *Pilgrimage to Freedom,* describes the events in striking prose: 'In a sense Jinnah dominated the Congress and the League (both) at that time. He had played the key role in preparing a draft constitution for India and getting it adopted by the sessions both of the Congress and of the League. The historical Lucknow Pact was an integral part of this constitution. Under it, the Muslims led by the League promised to work with the Hindus to achieve freedom in return for the Congress conceding to the Muslims separate electorates with weightage far in excess of their numerical strength'.[15]

This was the very same Jinnah who later got denounced as the destroyer of Hindu-Muslim unity, and simultaneously venerated as the creator of Pakistan; he also became the instigator of 'direct action' and the destroyer of the cultural unity of India. However, all this lies ahead, here it suffices to record that his entry into the Congress, in 1906, was as a nationalist Muslim and his signal contribution, certainly, until 1916 was the Lucknow Pact, exemplifying Hindu-Muslim unity.

However, change was already in the air, paths were separating, not just by Gandhi's adoption of Khilafat and Jinnah's opposition to that but also the entire Home Rule League[16] issue: 'Gandhi', reports K.M. Munshi, 'changed the object of the Home Rule League from self-government within the British Empire to complete *Swaraj* [and] freedom from all ties with Britain. Further, in the aims of the League, the words "by peaceful and legitimate means" were substituted for "by constitutional means". When Jinnah protested that under the Rules of the Home Rule League its constitution could not be changed except by a three-fourths majority and not without a proper notice being given, [this] 'resolution… had been passed by a simple majority, Gandhi, who presided, overruled the objection. Thereafter, Jinnah with nineteen other members (including Munshi) left the Home Rule League'. Munshi has recorded the effect of this development: 'When Gandhiji forced Jinnah and his followers out of the Home Rule League and later also from the Congress, we all felt, with Jinnah, that *a movement of an unconstitutional nature,* [civil disobedience] sponsored by Gandhiji with the tremendous influence he had acquired over the masses, would inevitably result in widespread violence, thus barring the progressive development of self-governing institutions based on a partnership between educated Hindus and Muslims. *To generate coercive power in the masses would only provoke mass conflict between the two communities, as in fact it did. With his keen sense of realities* Jinnah firmly set his face against any dialogue with Gandhiji on this point'. Munshi continues: 'Another event of importance was Gandhi's support to the agitation led by [the] two brothers, Mohammad Ali and Shaukat Ali, against the abolition of the Khilafat in Turkey after the First World War, for the Khalifa was the spiritual head of the Muslims'.[17] That the Khilafat agitation was essentially religious is clear from Gandhi's own statement in *Young India* of 20 October 1921 wherein he wrote: 'I claim that with us both the Khilafat is the central fact, with Maulana Mohammad Ali because *it is his religion*, with me because, in laying down my life for the Khilafat, I ensure the safety of the cow from the Mussalman knife,[18] *that is my religion*'.

Gandhi, adopted the Khilafat cause, as an aid to communal harmony, for he sincerely believed that by supporting the Khilafat agitation he would achieve Hindu-Muslim unity. According to Munshi, though, Jinnah warned[19] 'Gandhiji not to encourage fanaticism of Muslim religious leaders and their followers. Indeed, he was not the only person who foresaw danger in the Khilafat Movement. Srinivasa Sastri [also] wrote to Sri P.S. Siwaswamy Aiyar '...I fear the Khilafat Movement is going to lead us into disaster'. In addition, many other writers have also expressed the view that Gandhiji's support of the Khilafat agitation was a mistake. Years later, in one of his numerous interviews with Richard Casey, then the governor of Bengal, Gandhi shared that: 'Jinnah had told him that he (Gandhi) had ruined politics in India by dragging up a lot of unwholesome elements in Indian life and giving them political prominence, *that it was a crime to mix up politics and religion the way he had done*'.[20] (Emphasis added)

The Lucknow Pact of 1916 is a striking example of what could be achieved by men of resolve and goodwill and yet in the final round still failed to deliver. Jinnah along with Tilak was among the main actors who had brought about the 1916 Lucknow Pact. Jinnah had himself travelled some distance, from being an uncompromising opponent of separate electorates to a modified accommodation of that concept, but all this was for a larger national objective of Hindu-Muslim unity. Clearly, Jinnah often did change his position, but only exceptionally his methods of political operation; he would not, rather could not, temperamentally support an agitational mode, which Gandhi had adopted as his principal instrument. Jinnah's staying within the confines of constitutional methods, Gandhi's much greater public appeal, resulting in his rapid political ascendancy, and the larger political trends of the Council Reforms of 1919, began to shut many political doors for Jinnah. Moreover, as this gulf widened an eventual parting of ways became inevitable; perhaps that was also inherent in the personalities of the two principal actors; in the very dynamic of the unfolding events, also no doubt, in this quickening pace of global developments; for the twilight of the empire had now begun to descend.

Let us recapitulate briefly the principal events of that period. The first, of course, were the Council Reforms of 1909. Under these, the government was not answerable to the Legislative Council, and irrespective of what the Council determined, was not obliged to heed their decisions. With the 1919 Act this changed; the government's monopoly of power now got diluted; remarkably so, for the Raj, this was actually an act of voluntarily giving up some share, albeit tiny, of imperial authority, and this was also a first ever. The power so shed now transferred to Indian hands, consequently, placing upon the government an obligation to obtain the cooperation of others for a proper administration of the Raj.

Montagu-Chelmsford Reforms (also called Montford Reforms) were implemented under the legislated authority of the Government of India Act 1919. This Act introduced diarchy in the provinces, the executive was bifurcated, whereby certain departments, for the first time, were put in charge of elected ministers who were then responsible to the legislature; the rest stayed as they were, with government officials, principally members of the Governor's Executive Council heading them. As it is these reforms had not really been welcomed wholeheartedly whereafter, two grave errors combined and added to the difficulties in their implementation: the first was the passing of the Rowlatt Act allowing preventive detention; and the second, General Dyer's unthinkably cruel and mindless massacre of innocents in Jallianwalla Bagh. These came together gravely hampering any proper functioning of the Act of 1919. Besides, now Gandhi, too, launched his non-violent, Non-Cooperation Movement against the British.

Yet, these very Council Reforms of 1919 also set in motion trends of such lasting import that they influenced events materially, until well into the 1930s. For one, when it came to the second council elections of 1923, it became clear that politics at the national level would, henceforth, have to more satisfactorily attend to the demands of provinces, and that this, in turn, would markedly influence what in the absence of any better phrase we continue to call an all India platform. However, not so recognised or voiced in the twenties, this until now unstated and unvoiced question of central importance to Indian policy and governance now began to be raised: what should be the form of governance in India, federal, decentralised governance or unitary, centralised rule?

To the existing contentions of separate electorates, therefore, got added the controversies of diarchy now. For the newly elected there was now the lure of office, with which came attendant authority and patronage. Inevitably, thereafter, competition for such positions became acute, in turn, adding to the already existing separation of Hindus and Muslims. Lure of office pulled apart, divisively, and here again Hindu/Muslim, caste, community, the sectional became the dominant interest. What followed then was again predictable: a complete domination of the transferred departments by just one community (as for example in Punjab); and a deliberate flaming of communal passions for political advantage (as in the United Provinces) became oft used political tools, (why cavil, they still are). In consequence, what suffered was Hindu-Muslim unity; what got accented was a communal divide, for there had now come into existence an additional tool of contention. The Montford reforms aimed at devolution of power, but without diluting, in effect, any of the existing authority of the British Raj, or, for that matter in any manner reducing the effectiveness of the governance of India. But as in the political dynamics of the national struggle here, too, provincial interests came in conflict with the all India, and the British, to maintain their authority—both central and provincial, almost always relied more on the provinces; for in any event, the reins of the Centre they held firmly in their hands, the provinces were diverse and distant, but they must still be kept in tow, therefore they must submit.

For achieving all this, apart from the landed rich, the British banked largely on the Muslims, wherever they were in a majority and in those provinces, too, where they were not. In turn for the Muslims it was vital that separate electorates be retained, and it was only the government in Delhi that could do so. Here what greatly troubled them (the Muslim leadership) was the prospect of the Hindus, someday, getting control of the Centre. Driven by self-interest, Muslim provincial groups, almost always aligned with the British government in Delhi; because for them a benign Delhi was a surer guarantee of preserving their (Muslim) interests. Which is why the Council Reforms of 1919, also became a kind of a watershed in Hindu-Muslim relations, because instead of cementing they contributed to further dividing them.

While the Council Reforms of 1919 were not of any great help to Jinnah and his politics at the national level, diarchy did thwart his ambitions. The Congress policy of non-cooperation had also prevented his entry into the National Assembly in 1920.[21] His dilemmas were real and several, he just could not (or would not?) adopt agitationist methods of protest by fully lending his support to Gandhi's non-cooperation. Yet he could not afford to entirely alienate the Congress either.

In the summer of 1921, Jinnah had visited England and lobbied for a constitutional response, as an answer to Gandhi's civil disobedience movement. He suggested that if Punjab's wrongs were righted[22] and the constitution amended to allow for acceptable provincial autonomy, and if some diarchy were introduced in the Central Government then India might be restored to normalcy. Yet again, his appeal went unheeded, for even if there had existed some sympathy for what Jinnah was advocating, there was no mandate that Secretary of State Montagu had to revise the constitution.

A brief analysis of Punjab and Bengal (Muslim majority provinces) and United Provinces, politically crucial for the Muslims would help us understand the situation better as it unfolded in the 1920s.

The Muslims of Bengal like the Hindus were not a monolithic, united group. The Congress Swarajists[23] under the leadership of C.R. Das succeeded in carrying several layers of Muslim opinion along with them in the 1923 provincial elections. All these had largely flowed from the Bengal Pact.[24] However, diarchy was rendered as practically unworkable in Bengal because of the legislative unity of Hindus and Muslims, but this very unity made a section of the Hindus uncomfortable.

Undoubtedly, the Calcutta riots of April 1926[25] contributed significantly to breaking this fragile alliance of the two communities. In consequence, by the time of the 1926 Bengal elections, the two had fallen apart and Congress got hardly any Muslim support. Despite the Bengal Pact of 1923, by 1926 the Swarajists had also floundered in their effort to keep their Muslim supporters together.

In the west of India political activity in Punjab, which had until then been largely an urban phenomenon shifted focus, post-1920s, to rural areas. Consequently, the centre of Muslim politics also shifted—from

Malwa to Majha.[26] In contrast to Bengal, here the rural Muslim leadership was a favoured community. They had also clearly benefited from the Act of 1919.

However, Punjab's record on communalism was perhaps the worst in India. Just before the elections of 1923, when people like C.R. Das, Nehru, Azad and Sarojini Naidu visited the province, (in March 1923) they found the situation virtually beyond control. It has to be understood that there was an inbuilt conflict of interests between a Muslim majority working the 1919 reforms, and a highly literate, professional and politically aware urban Hindu minority, suffering the unintended adverse consequences of the 1919 reforms. A reconstitution of municipal committees did then take place, under the terms of Municipal Amendment Act,[27] but it benefited, again, only the Muslims, and that too, unrealistically. Though, no Hindu seats, as such, were lost but providing for extra Muslim seats changed the entire balance of power in several municipalities, thus in the process, generating even greater Hindu discontent.

On top of all this Gandhi's attacks then on the Arya Samaj[28] added to the existing discontents, for the Samaj was then a very significant influence in the Punjab, indeed much more so than Gandhi or the Congress. After the Kohat riots[29] of September 1924, a large number of Hindus left the Frontier, actually being transported away through arrangements made by the government itself, seeking refuge as far away as in Rawalpindi. No one then asked of the government: 'why, when their principal responsibility is to preserve order, protect the citizens and not escort them away from their own homes, was such a step taken?' These displaced, disenchanted, and discontented urban Hindus slowly began to reorder their political priorities. The first manifestation of this became visible in December 1924, when Gandhi visited Lahore in an effort to improve communal relations. On that occasion, the urban Hindu of Punjab stood disapprovingly aloof, even from the Mahatma's efforts, and this was when Gandhi strode the Indian political firmament as a colossus.

By 1925, the urban Hindus of the Punjab had not only identified the working of the political system as the cause of their communal difficulties, they had also taken a firm stand against any further political concessions, certainly not until their existing difficulties had at least been attended to. Perhaps, on account of this the results of the 1926 elections were disastrous for the Congress. Loss of support among Muslims by the Congress was much more marked than by the Swarajists. Whatever little Muslim support remained was because the Congress had not yet fully repudiated separate electorates. This was finally done at the Gauhati Congress of 1926, where a resolution was moved for the abolition of separate electorates. Though this resolution was overruled because of strong interventions by Motilal Nehru and Gandhi, time was now not far away when Motilal Nehru would be compelled to take a different stand on this issue in order to retain the support even of his closest followers. This was the situation within the Congress towards the second half of the 1920s, a backdrop necessary for us to grasp before examining Jinnah's position.

Jinnah's role in the Central Assembly, as leader of the Independent Party and the Swarajists[30] had got separated from the very beginning, their respective political ideologies leading them in different directions. However, initially there had been a period of cooperation, even of cordiality, for the two parties were then agreed about making a national demand, calling for provincial autonomy and some responsibility in the Central Government. On 18 February 1925, Motilal Nehru moved this demand. Even before he had moved it, the government made clear that it would not consider any concessions. All that was offered was a departmental enquiry to examine justifiable complaints within the terms of the Act and no more. Nevertheless, when it came to expressing their disappointment at such attitudes of the British, the Swamrajists and the Independents fell apart.

In Lord Reading's view, Jinnah was then making a bid for national leadership and his activities over the next three months buttress that impression. He first attempted to achieve this by direct methods. After the Assembly session had ended, he returned to Bombay and held almost daily conferences with Motilal Nehru, M.R. Jayakar, Purushotamdas Thakurdas, and Vithalbhai Patel, all with a view to producing a new, inclusive constitutional party. Gandhi also participated in a number of these discussions, as did C.R. Das. Ultimately, however, Jinnah's efforts floundered on the rock of Congress' internal differences. Nehru and Das were under pressure from Gandhi and, though they did not always bow to his dictates, they were wary of his hold to so openly ally with those who repudiated his (Gandhi's) creed. It was only after the promulgation of the Bengal ordinance in October 1924,[31] when Gandhi agreed to suspend the Non-Cooperation Movement and go to the extent of offering the Swarajists charge of the Congress organisation that Jinnah's ambitions stood any chance of being fulfilled, but by then, as so often happens, new obstacles had surfaced.

Jinnah was simultaneously also attempting to revive the Muslim League. He persuaded his colleagues in the League Council Session at Delhi in March 1924 to agree to a Session at Lahore to bolster his chances of receiving a response from the viceroy on the national demand. Unfortunately, his choice of Lahore was ill-judged because Punjab was the only province where the Muslims were willingly and successfully working diarchy, of course, to their own advantage. For which reason the Punjabi Muslims were obviously the most active supporters of a policy of constitutional advance, certainly not of reining them back. Yet if, somehow such a demand did come from the Muslim League, then that would be a crushing rejoinder to all those who argued that communal differences were an obstacle to constitutional advancement. Moreover, Jinnah, as the man who had secured Muslim support for this purpose, would, in the process add to his own political stature. Therefore, at least, it must have seemed then. This was a complex tussle: diarchy versus provincial autonomy; and it would go on for long, even after Partition, in India and in Pakistan.

Fazli Husain[32] was keen on provincial autonomy, but he was wary of offering Jinnah his support too easily, which is why he made sure that his supporters were present in overwhelming strength at the Lahore meeting of the Muslim League. This paid dividend for when the main resolution defining the Muslim position emerged from the Subjects Committee it was almost entirely a Punjabi affair. Obviously, this was then resented by Muslims from provinces where they were in a minority, but that is where their resentment remained, it did not translate into any change of policy by the league, certainly not then.

Within a week of the Lahore session, Motilal Nehru and Jinnah were invited to sit as non-official members on the Reforms Enquiry Committee, (Muddiman Committee),[33] which was an extended version of the departmental enquiry promised by Hailey[34] in February. Nehru would have liked to accept this invitation but opposition from the Swarajist executive obliged him to decline it. Jinnah, on the other hand, being less subject to external pressures of this kind accepted. And this gave him an ideal opportunity to pursue his ambitions for reform, to explore the views of others, and where necessary, to convert them to his point of view. His questions to witnesses suggest three main preoccupations. He sought firstly, to show that diarchy had failed and that the constitution needed overhauling; secondly, to counter the argument that communal tension was an obstacle to advance; and thirdly, to discover terms on which a new Lucknow Pact (of the 1916 variety) could be structured. He met with considerable opposition from the chairman, Sir Alexander Muddiman, who was also the Home member, and from Sir Mohammad Shafi, the Law member, who had been put on the committee only to represent the communal point of view. Jinnah, though, received cooperation from the Punjabi Muslims who were anxious for reforms and were willing to minimise the significance of communal tension in order to achieve their desired objective. Besides, he had the UP Muslims also supporting him.

The work of the Reforms Enquiry Committee, when completed, suddenly came across a roadblock. Jinnah, along with Sir Tej Bahadur Sapru and Sivaswamy Iyer declined to sign this report, offering instead a Minority Report. In this, they condemned diarchy unequivocally and demanded the introduction of provincial autonomy and responsibility in the Central Government. On 3 December 1924, when the Reforms Enquiry Committee Report was finally signed, Jinnah's ambitions looked like being fulfilled. The government, by its promulgation of the Bengal Ordinance,[35] had provided a real spur to unity. For one, Gandhi, by his suspension of Non-Cooperation Movement had paved the way for a new accretion of strength to the Congress. Then on 21 November, an All-Party Conference met in Bombay and set up a representative committee to devise a United Front against the government.

However, Jinnah was still wary; he did not relish taking part in unity discussions based on other people's terms. Whereas the suspension of non-cooperation did open the option of his rejoining the Congress, yet when he considered attending the Belgaum session in 1924, he found himself in two minds. Jinnah had always wanted the Swarajists to adopt purely constitutional methods but he had no desire to fight their battles for them. His own position, both as leader of the Independents and as president of the Muslim League was secure, and he did not wish to compromise his chances of negotiation with the Congress as an equal by becoming a party in advance to the decisions of the Congress itself. Similar considerations influenced his participation in the All-Party

Conference, too. That is why he agreed to sit on Gandhi's Unity Committee, but on the condition that its decisions were not to be taken by vote, for majority decisions, he reasoned, were clearly born of differences of opinion, and he was prepared to subscribe only to such agreements as were voluntarily and unanimously adopted by all. For Jinnah, the leading political light of the Muslims, but a numerical minority, this was an intelligent man's way out of the trap of decisions by votes, and also of the perils of majoritarianism.

During the Lahore Session of the League in May 1924, a committee had been appointed to formulate a constitution for it, in consultation with other organisations. This was Jinnah's initiative and he had invested some hope in it. This theme was proposed to the Congress also, of consultations, but it was not welcomed by them; also his proposal of holding a joint session at Belgaum—joint between the Congress and the Muslim League, this got turned aside rather brusquely. Jinnah had yet again failed to make any dent in the congealed prejudices of the Congress. Indeed, some of the members of the Council of the Muslim League were so troubled by this rather offhand treatment that they rejected the suggestion of even holding their session at the same place as the Congress.

More significant still was the attempt made by Gandhi and the Ali brothers to solve the communal tangle in the Punjab by political means. Early in December 1924, they visited Lahore and offered the Muslims proportional representation in the legislatures and services in exchange for the abolition of separate electorates. This offer amounted to, at least seemed like an affront, to the League's claim to solely represent the Muslims and a clear indication of Congress's unwillingness to accept the terms already decided upon at Lahore. The suggestion was, of course, not ultimately accepted but it emphasised again to Jinnah, how the political forces were aligning.

Though relations between the League and the Congress had by now become testy, both Jinnah and the Swarajists remained anxious for a settlement. When Motilal Nehru learned that the League had decided to hold its session at Bombay, he urged Jinnah to change the venue to Belgaum, and Jinnah, though he claimed it was too late to do so, did postpone the meeting for several days, so as to allow for attendance at the Congress meet. At the League session, the then president, Syed Raza Ali, warned his audience against a merger with the Congress. However,

Jinnah, whilst acknowledging the differences that had emerged over separate electorates, renewed his plea for an attempt at a settlement, and he was not entirely unsuccessful. The Constitution Committee of the League, appointed at Lahore, was refashioned to accommodate a significantly larger Congress Muslim element, and presumably, as a result of Gandhi's intervention, this new committee was subsequently co-opted bodily on the Unity Committee of the All Party Conference.

At this stage, the main obstacle to a settlement came from the Hindus of the Punjab and the United Provinces. Lala Lajpat Rai, the Punjabi Swarajist leader, was slowly being alienated from the national leadership, and like Malaviya and Chintamani, he found the call of danger to the Hindu a more potent message; besides this was also Lalaji's own creed. Thereafter, Lala Lajpat Rai, between 26 November and 17 December 1924, published thirteen articles in *The Tribune* criticising Muslim insistence on absolute rights, castigating Jinnah as a recruit to the communalist Muslim party and condemning communal electorates. With considerable prescience, he then shared with his readers that communal electorates once accepted would never be abolished, not without a civil war, also that to accept them was to divide the country into a Hindu India and another which would be Muslim India; and that as the Punjabi Muslims were unwilling to grant weightage to minorities it would be better to partition the Punjab, and jf necessary Bengal, too, and to establish a federation of autonomous Hindu and Muslim states.[36] At the same time, in a circular to prominent Hindus of all provinces, he condemned the Congress for its part in the Lucknow Pact and urged them to make the Hindu Mahasabha their political mouthpiece. This call, met with a ready response at Belgaum where the Mahasabha's activities took a distinctly political turn, for the first time. A committee was then appointed to formulate Hindu opinion on the communal question. Amongst others, it had Lala Lajpat Rai, Raja Narendra Nath, Chintamani, Raja Sir Rampal Singh, Jairamdas Daulatram of Sindh and Moti Lal Nehru's Swarajist Allies from the Central Provinces, B.S. Moonje and N.C. Kelkar.

When the All-Party Conference reconvened at Delhi on 23 January 1925 the chances of a new Lucknow Pact dimmed further, if they had in reality, ever seriously resurfaced. There were too many misunderstandings and certainly all the substantial ones needed resolving before any progress could be made. On 28 January 1925, this All-Party Conference was therefore, adjourned for a month. That, in effect, marked the end of this effort, for after this January session, Jinnah ceased to take any further interest in the venture. It was, however, a significant indicator to the future that the Hindu Mahasabha was able to hold the Congress at bay, and even Nehru and Gandhi, though keen for a settlement, were not prepared to make concessions in the face of opposition from the Mahasabha. They chose instead to leave it well alone. In a communiqué issued at Delhi on 2 March 1925 Motilal Nehru and Gandhi informed that there was now no likelihood of a settlement; and just three days later, in Bombay, Gandhi told reporters that he intended to put the Hindu-Muslim problem to one side'.[37]

After the failure of this conference, the political distance between Motilal Nehru and Jinnah widened. For Motilal Nehru confronted by this trenchant criticism of the Hindu Mahasabha, altering his stance became necessary; he now turned more obstructionist in the Assembly. Jinnah, on the other hand, despite his sense of disappointment, refused to lend support to what he considered as the wrecking tactics of the non-cooperationists. In the spring of 1925, the two, for the first time, began to disagree publicly. This United Front against the Central Government had finally collapsed. An aside is necessary here. Motilal Nehru and Mohammad Ali Jinnah's social relations, despite their growing political separation remained cordial to the very last.

Though Jinnah was keen that the Muddiman Report be debated, the government postponed this matter. In the interim, the Viceroy Lord Reading visited England, not to discuss political reforms rather, to devise a formula for staunching nationalist fires. He had viewed the Muddiman Committee as merely an expedient, essentially to hold the situation in check, and contrary to Jinnah's expectations, he had been totally unimpressed by Jinnah's policy of rational protest. In 1924, with a Labour government in office and the Nationalists in control of the Assembly Reading had been strained; in 1925, with Conservatives back in office and Jinnah and Nehru in political confrontation, he was strengthened and consequently decided to stand firm.

On 7 July 1925, in the House of Lords, Lord Birkenhead put paid to any remaining hopes of immediate reform. Though he did not entirely rule out the possibility of an early statutory commission, he did make it plain that no concession could be expected until Indian leaders had first cooperated in the working of the Reforms. This speech eventually became a turning point for India's politics of confrontation. Until then, Motilal Nehru's leadership and Swarajist tactics had remained unchallenged and victory at the all-India level seemed possible. With this ultimatum, however, both options now stood rejected. Many 'provincial battalions (then) withdrew from battle and made overtures to the enemy'.[38] Consequently, Motilal Nehru was obliged to cease front-line operations and to take up the task of quelling mutiny in his own ranks instead. To do that effectively, he had to eventually quit the legislature and revert to Gandhi's path of non-cooperation.

Jinnah was even more disappointed for he had lost more. After all, it was principally his policy that had suffered a reverse and when the Muddiman Report was finally debated, his patience gave way to a mood of unrestrained exasperation: 'I again here ask the Government, I ask Lord Birkenhead, I ask Lord Reading, what is your answer to those men who have cooperated with you? None. Your answer to me as one who has not non-cooperated with you is this: 'Will you bring a section of the politically minded people, who happen to be the largest political party, will you bring them down to their knees? Will you bring Pandit Motilal Nehru to bow before the throne at Vice-regal Lodge and say: Sir, I am humble. I crawl before you, and will you now graciously be pleased to give me a Royal Commission?' Is that what you want? What has Pandit Motilal Nehru been doing in this Assembly? Has he not been cooperating with you? I want to know what more [do] you want, and may I know what evidence, what proof, documentary or oral, do you want me to produce or adduce that the responsible leaders are willing to cooperate with you? Have you no eyes, have you no ears, have you no brains?'[39]

This was the speech of a man who had fought and lost an important battle, for unlike Nehru, Jinnah had no outlet left, no solace in non-cooperation. All he could do was to take up Birkenhead's challenge and work the Reforms, for whatever they were worth. In July 1925, he again made overtures to Jayakar, the Bombay Swarajist, and in November, he also tried to form a party with discontented Congressmen from the Central Provinces. Yet the more he moved towards Congress dissidents, the further he moved away from the most powerful elements in the Muslim League. This paradox could not easily be resolved. To support Motilal Nehru was to support a policy of non-cooperation but to also move towards a possible Hindu-Muslim unity; on the other hand, to support his opponents in the League was to support a policy of cooperation with the Raj but of Hindu-Muslim antagonism. Jinnah, sought both, but their inherent contradictions were not easy to resolve. In near despair, he escaped to Europe in 1926, as a member of the Skeen Committee and did not become active again until after the elections of that year.

On 20 March 1927, a conference of Muslims met in Delhi, to decide on the issue of separate electorates. The charter of demand now became broader: it included the separation of Sindh from Bombay; reforms for the Frontier and Baluchistan; representation by population in the Punjab and Bengal; and 33 per cent reservations for the Muslims in the Central Legislature. This conference had been convened largely on Jinnah's initiative, and he was taking a stand totally different to what his position had earlier been, say during the Lucknow Pact of 1916, particularly on the issue of separate electorates. He must have fully assessed that his present stand would certainly invite opposition from the Muslims of the provinces. Despite that he took it, for his stand was yet another attempt, in a long series of such attempts to solve this complex national tangle; and his initiative was a response to Congress' expanding mass appeal, too.

Viceroy Irwin anticipating events had interpreted this difficulty, 'whatever Jinnah's original intentions (and these were by no means clear at the time), the result of his initiative was to widen rather than diminish the breach between the two communities'.[40] The result of this initiative illustrated two recurring features of the all-India political scenario obtaining then: importance of provincial Muslim opinion and the reluctance of the Hindu Mahasabha to accept any terms that failed to fully address the interest of the Hindus. However, the response of provincial Muslims did not help the situation either in reality; however, neither the Hindu Mahasabha nor the Muslim League can be seriously faulted for working fixedly for safeguarding the well-being, as they saw it, of their respective communities. That, after all, was the very basis of their political existence.

On 29 March 1927, seeing the way things were going, Jinnah issued a statement to the press making it clear that his four proposals, just cited had either to be accepted in full or rejected totally.[41] However, this, too, did not improve the situation. Indeed, when the Hindu Mahasabha met at Patna on 16 April of that year (1927) Jinnah's statement was used as the reason for not discussing the offer at all. The provincial Muslim response was also not encouragingly better; they (the provinces) had begun to resist Jinnah's all-India initiatives fearing a possible diminution in the powers that they (the provinces) held then. Several supporters of the original offer had now begun to change tack. As Muddiman put it, while commenting on a draft-despatch relating to these events: 'It is a case of manoeuvring for a political position and as usual the Muslims will be out manoeuvred but neither side can deliver the goods even if they wish to...'.[42]

THE MUSLIM LEAGUE SPLITS

Back then to the Punjab. Ever since Jinnah's March 1927 initiative, the Punjab Muslim League had been suspicious of his intentions, they apprehended a dilution of their provincial primacy against an all-India agenda. In October 1927, when the Muslim League Council met at Simla they had prevented Jinnah from holding the annual session at Madras fearing he might engineer a verdict in favour of a national agenda. They made plain, therefore, as did the UP contingent that the League must meet in North India. Jinnah, in consequence gave up both—a joint session with the Congress, and a League meet at Lahore. Instead, he began to lobby for Calcutta. However, Calcutta appeared as even less suitable to the Punjab politicians. Because Punjab had voted for cooperation, it was of vital importance to them that the All-India Muslim League meet be held in a province where their policy would receive local support. Because of the preparations made by Firoz Khan Noon the Muslim League Council meeting held at Delhi on 20 November 1927, became a triumph for the Punjabis. Even in the face of opposition from Jinnah and the Ali brothers, a verdict was recorded in favour of Lahore, with Sir Mohammad Shafi as president designate. This, for Jinnah, was as unsatisfactory as was a Calcutta meeting for the Punjabis, and if he was not to lose his standing it was essential that this decision be reversed. Mohammad Yakub, his Assembly colleague, agreed wholeheartedly, and encouraged Dr Kitchlew, then the secretary of the League to call another meeting of the Council, whilst simultaneously urging Dr Ansari[43] to use his influence to secure a majority for Calcutta, where the Aga Khan would then preside.

As a result, on 11 December 1927 the Council met again. Only twenty-three members attended, and though Firoz Khan Noon and his followers were by physical count a majority, on this occasion, absentee votes swung the decision in Jinnah's favour. By eighty-four votes (seventy-four absentees) to fifty-four (forty-one absentees), the previous decision (about Lahore) was reversed, and Calcutta decided upon for the session. Jinnah had won, but it was a pyrrhic victory for Firoz Khan Noon, Sir Mohammad Iqbal, Hasrat Mohani, and a number of Noon's Punjabi followers left the meeting, they were striking out on their own, the League had separated. As a result of this clash at Delhi, in 1927, there came into existence two Muslim Leagues, one meeting later at Lahore and the other at Calcutta. Sir Mohammad Shafi, who had been elected president for both council meetings, presided at the Lahore session, and Maulvi Mohammad Yakub at Calcutta. Predictably, the Lahore resolutions followed those earlier adopted by the Punjab Muslim League. (13 November 1927). More than the resolutions what was of greater significance was a consolidation of the UP and Punjab Muslims through this process. Those who attended Jinnah's League at Calcutta, in December 1927, were the same who had attended his meeting at Delhi in March, except that the Frontiersmen and the urban constitutionalists from the Muslim majority provinces had by then also left him.

At the Muslim League Session at Calcutta, the question of a declaration in favour of Independence was not officially raised,[44] which in itself was a comment on both the fragmented thinking of the die-hard 'Khilafatists' and the ascendancy of the Independents, as represented by Jinnah, Ali Imam and Mohammad Yakub. They clearly dominated this session, with Jinnah as the permanent president, Yakub as the president of the session, and Ali Imam as the mover of the resolution. Their position was pragmatic and not outside the mainstream of constitutionalist politics, consequently they were disinclined to declare either for Independence or even an unconditional boycott.

The Calcutta League organisers had laid great emphasis upon communal unity. However, it became clear during the proceedings that Jinnah's four proposals would not be accepted, not totally, not even in this Bengal meet. Consequently, as for these four proposals, though the League remained anxious to cement their alliance with the Congress, they were now obliged to make more credible their own negotiating position. The League resolution on this question made it plain therefore, that only when the Frontier had received the reforms, and when Sindh had actually been constituted as a separate province, would the proposal of separate electorates be dropped.

At the invitation of Congress, cautiously though, the League leaders agreed then to participate in an All-Party Conference at Delhi. When this Delhi conference finally convened on 12 February 1928, it became apparent that an agreement would not be easy. Pandit Madan Mohan Malaviya, who was increasingly under shadow of being too inclined towards the Congress was further pushed into a corner by Moonje, who refused to agree either to the separation of Sindh or any reservation of seats for majorities (e.g. for Muslims in the Punjab). Jinnah met this intransigence by reiterating the terms of the League's Calcutta session, and there followed the inevitable deadlock. From Jinnah's point of view, this was totally unsatisfactory. His faction of the League had already been isolated and it now appeared that he was in danger of losing his entire political following. So back he went to the Viceroy's House and urged Irwin, once more, to make a change in the arrangements for the Statutory Commission. Either appoint a mixed commission, he said, or failing that, a body of Indian commissioners with twin powers and responsibilities. Not surprisingly, his appeals we disregarded. Irwin could assess that Jinnah's influence was now on the wane and therefore, found no reason why such a falling star needed to be conciliated. This was Jinnah's dilemma. He had failed to get a seat on the commission, and had also failed to find such a platform for boycott as would command at least minimal Muslim approval. How could he then participate in these All Party Conferences any more—without a united party and an acceptable stand? The only sensible course for him was retreat. On 17 March 1928, he, therefore, withdrew the Muslim League delegation from the Conference and by May 1928 he was in England.

Paradoxically, this withdrawal of the League and Jinnah's departure for Europe had a marked dampening effect on the All-Party Conference, too. For most Congressmen, Jinnah was 'the only man to deliver the goods on behalf of the Muslim League'.[45] The conference, therefore decided, 'that a small committee, viewing the communal problem as a whole in relation to the constitution might succeed in finding a way our'.[46] Motilal Nehru was, once again, appointed chairman and there were nine other members.[47] The bulk of the work of this Committee fell on five men—Motilal Nehru, Shuaib Qureshi, Mangal Singh, Aney and Sapru, though Jawaharlal Nehru also attended many of the later sessions and some of the more important meetings.

Between 5 and 22 June 1928, this Committee met for several hours, every day, at Motilal Nehru's house at Allahabad. It made progress on the general outlines of the Constitution but not on the communal question which remained intractable. Finally, on 7 July 1928 it arrived at a compromise formula according to which all members were announced as being opposed to reservation of seats, whether for the majority or minorities.

There was an unusual aspect of the Committee's deliberations, though not officially a member, Jawaharlal Nehru had played a part in several of its more important sessions. After the meetings of 6 and 7 July, by Motilal's own admission, he—Jawaharlal, became one of the 'chief draftsmen of the Report',[48] writing a significant portion of it. While it was Motilal who wrote sections dealing with the communal question, it was Jawaharlal, in reality who had prepared much of the material. The determination of the author (Motilal Nehru) to face the problem and to solve it, his condemnation of communal organisations for not wanting to change the existing structure of society were clearly his own authorship, but this voicing of aspirations that in a free India political parties would be formed on an 'economic basis', has a thought content, a style and a philosophy distinctly that of the son, Jawaharlal, not the father.

This Nehru Report was then published on 21 August 1928. The constitution which the report recommended was the most radical until then, and though its communal provisions have received greater subsequent attention, its political recommendations were no less controversial, contributing to germinating a fresh crop of communal dissensions. The national government envisaged in this report was to be unitary, not federal, with residuary powers, too, vested in the Central Government. This, predictably, became the most unacceptable recommendation, with many opponents vociferously objecting. In the communal sphere, the report recommended the abolition of both separate electorates and a granting of weightage for minorities. It also rejected the Muslim demand for any reservation for majorities and, of course, no sharing of 33 per cent of the seats at the Centre. Only the Muslims from the Northwest had reasons to be satisfied, for both a separation of Sindh from Bombay and an equal status for the Frontier received the committee's recommendation.

The All-Party Conference, the originator of the committee, met thereafter at Lucknow, a week later, on 28 August 1928, to consider this Report. Recognising Jinnah's absence the two Nehrus were urged to postpone the conference. They appeared to concede the point without actually doing so; gracelessly the conference was postponed by just one day. The Nehrus were not keen to be conciliatory to Jinnah, and all 'religious bodies', including the two Sikh organisations were also excluded, attendance being kept to just a hundred. It is not surprising therefore, that the meeting produced the results that it did.

The only murmur of dissent came from Shaukat Ali[49] over the abolition of reservation for majorities. He broke with Motilal Nehru on this, denounced him for making concessions to the Hindu Mahasabha, and he also broke with those Muslims who supported Motilal Nehru. This (Shaukat Ali's repudiation of the Nehru Report) was a great embarrassment for the Congress. However, a more serious challenge came from those provincial forces with which the government had banked hopes.

In Motilal Nehru's reckoning, despite the somewhat graceless manner of not accommodating Jinnah's convenience when the Report was to be finally considered by the full committee, he (Jinnah) still remained the most important factor and personality, still of crucial consequence. If he could be won over, this Nehru Report would acquire the needed prestige. Motilal Nehru therefore, deputed Purshotamdas Thakurdas to persuade Jinnah before Shaukat Ali could do any further damage. When Jinnah returned to India, he did not immediately proclaim his support for Nehru's recommendations, instead, with uncharacteristic caution he chose to first sound Muslim opinion. The Lucknow Muslim League Council Meeting, which he convened for the purpose proved less conclusive than Jinnah would have liked and no decision was forthcoming. This absence of unanimity made it difficult, indeed even impolitic for him to open negotiations with the Congress on the subject.

It is this impasse that had then led Motilal Nehru to lament at the Calcutta Congress in December 1928: 'It is difficult to stand against the foreigner without offering him a united front. [But] It is not easy to offer a united front while the foreigner is in our midst domineering over us.' Jawaharlal, too, had thought deeply on the causes of the 'communal deadlock that frustrated' the (1928) Nehru report and blocked the Round Table conference, he came to a somewhat similar conclusion that this 'political bargaining and haggling' would not take the country far, because 'whatever offer we make, however high our bid might be, there is always a third party which can bid higher and, what is more, give substance to its words. This third and controlling party inevitably plays the dominant role and hands out its gifts to the prize of its choice'.

Events, however, kept rolling and decisively. Before the League next met at Calcutta in the December of 1928, another powerful section of support seceded. This was the Khilafat Section which had already repudiated the Nehru Report; clearly, the indefatigable Ali Brothers had been working overtime. When the League did finally meet in Calcutta, it decided to elect a delegation for the All-Parties Convention, authorising them to settle all outstanding communal issues. Subsequently, after a joint meeting of the Muslim League and Khilafat delegates with the subcommittee of the All Parties Convention, Jinnah and T.A.K. Shervani[50] put forward the following demands; these had now grown from the earlier four to the present seven. [Some commentators, though have recorded these as six].[51]

In all probability, Jinnah was responsible for this demand of a 33 per cent representation at the Centre. This had been one of his four proposals in March 1927, and he had every reason to stick to it unbendingly, principally, because his Muslim followers in the Central Assembly, and particularly those from the minority provinces had been very critical of the Nehru report on precisely this issue. Jinnah's insistence in defence of this demand, that the extra seats should be distributed to give weightage to the minority provinces, is no doubt a reflection of his appreciation of this sentiment.

The reception to these demands by the All-Parties Convention Sub-Committee could easily have been predicted. Of its thirty-seven members eleven were Hindus, Sikhs, and Christians of the Punjab, one was a leading opponent of the separation of Sindh, and six were leading lights of the Hindu Mahasabha. This demand for 33 per cent representation at the Centre was supported by Gandhi and by Sir Tej Bahadur Sapru but opposed by the Hindu Mahasabha and the Sikhs. The demand about residuary powers remaining with the provinces was opposed by both the Mahasabha and the Liberal Federation, though both Sapru and Chintamani were prepared to re-examine the schedules of subjects. Neither Gandhi nor Motilal Nehru intervened during discussion on this important point. The demand for reservation on the basis of population in Bengal and Punjab, if adult suffrage was not adopted, was skirted by means of the formula: 'We do not contemplate any such contingency'.[52] The demand regarding Sindh was rejected on the grounds that it involved altering the agreement reached at Lucknow. In the open session, Jinnah tried again to change the verdict of the committee. He told the audience that the modifications suggested were 'fair and reasonable; that no country had succeeded in establishing its independence without making provision for its minorities; and that a Hindu-Muslim settlement was essential for the political progress of the country'.[53] Though he was supported by Dr Sapru, Jinnah met with a highly reasoned opposition from M.R. Jayakar, who told the convention that Jinnah 'represented only a small minority of Muslims and that it was not worthwhile making concessions because it would make no difference to the Muslim community as a whole'.[54] 'Besides,' he said, 'Jinnah was on their side anyway, and would do his best to bring the Muslim League with him.'[55] Jinnah's reply shows how clearly he realised the isolation of his position: 'It is essential that you must get not only the Muslim League but the musulman of India and here I am not speaking as a Musulman but as an Indian. And it is my desire to see that we get seven crores of Musulmans to march along with us in the struggle for freedom. Would you be content if I were to say, I am with you? (But) do you want or do you not want Muslim India to (also) go along with you?'[56] Very powerful advocacy and a good question, but Jayakar had already answered it. The convention rejected Jinnah's offer and this brought Jinnah, to the *'parting of the way'* which Hector Bolitho quotes:

10 March 1952—*Notes on Talk with Jamshed Nusserwanjee*
A dear old Parsee gentleman. A theosophist who came to see me at the Metropole Hotel. He wore a long white coat and check grey hat. He recommended me to see Kanji Dwarkadas when I go to Bombay. He said he was an old friend of Jinnah and then used a nice phrase; he said, 'His memory is very beautiful.'

He said of Jinnah. 'He was emotional and affectionate, but he was unable to demonstrate it. All was control, control!'

Then, 'I saw him once in tears. It is a fine thing that I can tell you. It was in 1927 [1928], during the Congress session in Calcutta.' He paused then and said, 'I shall write it out for you.'

Again, of Jinnah, 'There was some kind of loneliness about Jinnah. A lonely man.'

Next day, Jamshed Nusserwanjee bought me the following notes:

'The Parting of the Ways'

During the Congress session at Calcutta in 1927 [All Parties National Convention in December 1928], a telegram came from Mr Jinnah, who was in Delhi, saying that he and six other colleagues of the Muslim League would like to meet and discuss certain points with the Congress committee—these were their demands for a settlement with Congress. Mr Jawaharlal Nehru was President of the Congress. Most of the leaders were against the plan, but Mahatma Gandhi prevailed upon them to invite Mr Jinnah and his party to Calcutta. They came and Mr Jinnah placed the demands of his party before a special committee, but they rejected them. There were eighteen against and two for: those two were Mahatma Gandhi and myself. Mr Jinnah returned to his hotel in tears. Mahatma Gandhi went to his room, sadly, at 3 a.m., and span on his spinning wheel until 6 o' clock in the morning. About 8:30 next morning, Mr Jinnah and his party left for Delhi. I went to see him off at the station. He shook hands with me and these were his words, 'Well, Jamshed, this is the parting of the ways'.

Thereafter, Mr Jinnah rejected all proposals, even the All-Party resolutions, consistently. He would not trust the Congress leaders. He attempted to reach reconciliation at the Round Table Conference in London, but there again he was disappointed. But these are matters of records.

However, that was not to be, not yet anyway.

The circumstances responsible for repeatedly forcing Jinnah into the wilderness were extremely complex. They went far beyond the individual attitudes of politicians of that period, reflecting more the very workings of the political system then obtaining. Early in the 1920s, though the forces of provincialism did occasionally impinge on the all-India scene, the real conflict of interest remained between the 'nationalist' and the 'provincial politician'. Only when the Montagu-Chelmsford Reforms got the legitimacy of an Act, did this conflict of interest become explicit and pointed. The fascination of studying this period lies in observing the political reactions of the principal actors as they struggled with the constraints of the system. Jinnah's central difficulty, remained the absence of a 'solid political base', besides, he was a 'consultative' politician in an age of political agitations. Consequently, however sincere his 'nationalism', he could only survive by acting as a broker between Muslim politicians in the provinces and his Congress colleagues at the Centre. He was not himself engaged in any provincial politics, he could not be. Nevertheless, he did attempt to fashion the existing provincial clay into a shape that would suit his all-India purposes. His task was like that of a 'sculptor required to work on materials that constantly change their texture'. As the provinces threw up new demands, necessarily, Jinnah too was then obliged to change his political objectives. In 1927, he put forward four proposals; in 1928 they became six; and in 1929, fourteen.[57]

Ultimately, negotiations between Jinnah and the Congress no longer remained productive. Jinnah was constantly looking over his shoulder at the provinces, and so often that he was no longer actively engaged in the same battle as the Congress. He did not, really could not, accede to the Congress programme merely as an individual; he wanted, and he needed to, take a large body of Muslims with him, that was his political imperative. Yet those very Muslims whose activities forced Jinnah to alter his all-India negotiating position were the provincial political opponents of the swelling ranks of the Congress. Here lay the core of Jinnah's dilemma; he either had to be in the Congress camp or in the Muslim camp; but he simply could not be in both. It was this cruel logic and its continuous whiplash of demands which ultimately turned Jinnah into becoming the Quaid-i-Azam of Pakistan. Just as those Congressmen who favoured Independence and non-cooperation were now beginning to challenge the Nehrus and Saprus, similarly, Muslims of the various legislatures were now declaring their allegiance to the King Emperor, and their respect for constitutional norms, thus putting the question to Jinnah: 'Are you with us, or are you not?'

The Indian body politic was being divided, the government and the Muslims on one side, Hindus on the other, and as the Congress then embarked on the dusty trails of protest and civil disobedience towards Dandi, in the footsteps of the Mahatma, the beneficiaries of the system (Muslims) rallied to the defence of the Raj and the system.

4

SHARPENING FOCUS—NARROWING OPTIONS

In the 1920s Mohandas Karamchand Gandhi had been back in India for just about five years, Jinnah, on the other hand, had been politically active for fifteen. Gandhi having worked actively in South Africa for twenty-one years, upon return to India, very soon gained political primacy by taking politics out of the comfortable debating chambers of the cities and into the heart of India: in that dusty, neglected, always derided rural India.

Issues that dominated the political scene then circled around: Swaraj; freedom; self-rule; but how? In one leap or through slow, gradual devolution of power? The other was Hindu-Muslim unity, for if it was a free and an undivided India that was sought, then beyond any question Hindu-Muslim unity was of central importance. This worthy objective, though, was not so easily achieved, not till an independent self-governing India offered to all Indians, all communities, all faiths, freedom not just from the British regime but also from the real or imaginary fears of majoritarian domination. In the path of this unity stood many centuries of unhappy, accumulated experiences, a residue of the shadows and overhangs of history. Discernibly the British Empire was now in decline, and seeing that the Muslims yearned for the glories of their lost past; they sought freedom from the British Raj but not in its place the possibility of a Hindu dominated India. The Hindus, on the other hand, after many centuries of subjugation saw real freedom dawning, finally, and they saw that they could well soon be, at last, both the arbiters and the masters of their own destiny: *'Door hato, Door hato ai dunia walo, Hindustan hamara hai',* Pradeep had so boldly distilled the principal emotion of those times. But whose Hindustan was it to be? Almost all discussions, negotiations, and talks then circled around these objectives: how to reconcile conflicting interests, mutual fears, rational or imaginary?

How, in other words, to share sovereignty as justly and equitably as possible, principally between the Hindus and the Muslims, and of course the Sikhs and others, too, and also simultaneously, find a just answer to the complexity of the princely states of India, which were almost six hundred in number. Collectively they comprised a major slice of the pre-1947 Indian body-politic—two-fifths of the area and one-third of the population of the country. Questions also got voiced: Where does paramountacy go when the British, also, finally go? All these we need to dwell upon, but focused principally on Jinnah's endeavours in this great turmoil of India.

However, before that what was happening in a post-First World War Great Britain? The end of that war to end all wars, had also ended the period of the ascendancy of British imperial power; the flower of their youth had been robbed of them; the new age of American hegemony had arrived. Besides, the Treaty of Sevres 1922, had redefined the political geography not just of Arabia but the geo-politics of the entire world, paradoxically it resulted in a 'peace that ended all peace'.[1] For what peace remained now? Or what peace could possibly remain in the circumstances? New countries were getting created by breaking up the existing countries, arbitrarily, at times almost whimsically, simply by drawing lines on paper and on sand. In India, we should have read those times (also the lines) more carefully, there was then, sadly, not sufficient awareness of the portents of these developments. The Spanish Civil War and the aftermath of the Great October Revolution sweeping through not just the established order of Russia but blowing away many European crowns and monarchies; this attracted Jawaharlal Nehru more, not the deliberate fracturing of the Arabian Peninsula and Mesopotamia. A great pity, for he ought to have paid more heed to our neighbours. However, it was the European struggles that attracted him more; for after all we were the true anglophiles of those times, we aped them best amongst all the ruled, even as we struggled against their rule. We went always to Europe not to those great cities, the great centres of civilisation, our historical and cultural kin: Baghdad, Istanbul/Ankara, Cairo, Teheran.

In Great Britain, according to Ian Bryant Wells: 'In the late '20s it became apparent to the Tory government [of Stanley Baldwin] that the strength of the Labour Party was growing and it would soon...form a government. The Tories decided [therefore] to convene a statutory commission to investigate political reform for India early to ensure the continuation of their own policies in India...The government's motivation to exclude Indians from the statutory commission originated from within the Government of India. In 1926, the newly arrived viceroy, Lord Irwin, found himself surrounded by advisers from the Punjab branch of the service. These advisers, particularly Sir Malcom Hailey and Geoffrey de Montmorency, were the driving force behind this all white commission'.[2]

Lord Irwin made efforts to secure dominion status for India and was supported by Prime Minister Ramsay MacDonald, also by Stanley Baldwin, then the leader of the Conservative Party in Parliament, and by far the largest component of MacDonald's National Government. A debate in the House of Commons on Irwin's declaration began on Friday, 8 November 1929. The prime minister spoke for dominion status and Baldwin announced Conservative support. However, a third of the Conservative members did not agree. 'They had listened glumly to their leader; their applause for him had been perfunctory...The diehards were...violently opposed...Winston [Churchill] was almost demented with fury... 'Churchill's first attack came in the pages of the *Daily Mail*. 'Britain', he wrote: 'had rescued India from ages of barbarism...Self-government was unthinkable...And it was absurd to contemplate [Dominion Status]...If the Viceregal proposal was adopted the British Raj would be replaced by a Gandhi Raj...'[3]

Under these circumstances, a seven-member Statutory Commission was appointed. This was led by Sir John Simon, a barrister and an MP of the Liberal Party. It had a composition of four Conservative and two Labour MPs and reached Bombay on 3 February 1928. It was charged with examining the workings of the Montagu-Chelmsford Reforms of 1919, as mandated to be done decennially. There are several reasons cited for its earlier than required appointment, amongst which were political pressure in India for self-rule and as already expressed, Stanley Baldwin's assessment of an impending Labour victory; in this lay the origins of the Simon Commission. What, however, continued to be the dominant themes in India were Hindu-Muslim unity, representation for Muslims, and freedom. It is to these themes that we must attend first.

A central tenet of Gandhi's political and social thought was Hindu-Muslim unity. Gandhi had grasped this better than any other Congressman, with perhaps, the exception perhaps of the Swarajists.[4] That is why he had lent support to the Khilafat agitation, though, attended by great controversy and in retrospect, both wrongly and destructively. He focused on the abolition of the Khilafat only as a religious issue and had no hesitation in affirming that.[5] Gandhi judged that by supporting the Khilafat agitation he would cement Hindu-Muslim unity, that this abolition had wounded the Muslim psyche. He was correct in this assessment but had not taken on board a crucial point, that this abolition of the Khilafat was a step taken centrally by the Turks themselves, through a revolution led by Mustafa Kemal Pasha. Of course, Gandhi knew all this but he was overlooking the import of it in the hope that this salve of support to the Muslims on their emotional wound might, perhaps bond them with the Hindus against the British. It did do so, though for a very short period and tragically, in time, it resulted in the opposite consequence.

From Hindu-Muslim unity to dominion status was an obvious and the logical next step. Above all, this would prevent a partitioning of the country and when, rather if, coordinated with the precepts of the Lucknow Pact of 1916 of which Jinnah was himself the leading proponent, fears of majoritarianism would also be significantly assuaged. On this question of dominion status the penetrating analysis of Lloyd Rudolph and Susanne Hoeber Rudolph in their perceptive essay entitled, 'The Road not Taken' cannot be bettered.[6]

'The first public dash between Gandhi and his political heir-to-be, Jawaharlal Nehru, occurred in December 1927, at the Congress' annual session in Madras. The issue that divided them was whether the Indian National Congress should keep dominion status as its political goal or abandon it and adopt a new goal, 'complete independence' [purna swaraj]. Gandhi was for dominion status. Nehru for complete independence. The struggle went on for two years. It was resolved in 1929 at the annual session in Lahore with Nehru's installation as president of the Indian National Congress and the Congress' adoption of complete independence as the national movement's political objective.

While both goals involved sovereign autonomy, they brought with them different expectations and commitments. Dominion status carried with it allegiance to the Crown, participation in imperial institutions and, 'at least partially engaging with British politics and public opinion.' Dominion status also meant that there would be negotiations about the conditions in India under which the transfer of power would occur. For example, the British were likely to insist on provisions for minority rights and representation. Complete independence, on the other hand, carried overtones of anti-imperialism, unitary nationalism and majoritarian democracy. 'It amounted to a severance of ties, a political rupture that would...leave the shape of the successor state in nationalist hands.... Complete independence also meant that the successor state was unlikely to share sovereignty with the minority community'.

Gandhi and Nehru brought different historical understandings to the concept of dominion status. Gandhi having spent the first twenty-one years of his political life in South Africa, as a member of an Indian minority fighting for rights in the face of an incipient apartheid regime had experience of this system. In South Africa, the British Crown and imperial citizenship were a potential source of rights and redress against oppression. Gandhi, whilst in South Africa had sought legal help in London by visiting there'. He had cooperated with the British by raising 'a medical corps to aid the English in the Zulu and Boer Wars and (had) recruited for the British Army in World War I'. But Nehru 'younger than Gandhi...viewed imperialism and capitalism as evil forces in world politics'. He too, liked English ways and had English friends but 'politically the British empire was the enemy'.

This issue of dominion status became urgent in 1927. In December of that year the Congress resolved on a total boycott of the Simon Commission. So, too, did the Muslim League and the Swarajists. As Ian Wells put it: 'The Simon Commission reminded the nationalist movement of its common foe and many Indian politicians, including Jinnah, who had moved away from the Congress returned to its fold... 'Jinnah,' Wells continues: 'was at the centre of the protest and promoted a united front for the boycott of the commission'. For he (Jinnah) like Gandhi, Motilal Nehru and Sapru were agreed that the time had come for Britain to grant India dominion status. In the event, the Commission's report of May 1930 rejected 'all ideas of transfer of power and made no mention of Dominion Status'.

It is from this impasse that was born a Round Table Conference. On 31 October 1929, Viceroy Irwin announced that a conference would be held in London on Indian constitutional reform and held out the prospect of this conference advancing the cause of dominion status for India. Indian nationalists for their part already had their own version of constitutional reform, the 1928 Nehru Report, examined in some detail in Chapter III. One of the principal recommendations of this Report had been Dominion Status for India. In turn this became the context for Jawaharlal Nehru's successful effort at Congress' annual meeting in Madras, in December 1929, to repudiate this report and to reject dominion status as the political objective of the Congress, to then replace it with *purna swaraj* or complete independence. However, we are going faster than the events themselves.

Gandhi, in 1927, continuing to abide by Hindu-Muslim unity, as the highest priority, had remained committed to dominion status, holding that this would help to foster and maintain that unity, but he would not ensure it. Of course, he worked on other measures, too, for this unity. One was to ensure that Dr M.A. Ansari, a distinguished and much respected Muslim elder statesman, be elected as Congress president at the Madras annual session. This, it was hoped, would serve to reassure the Muslim community. And, in an echo of the 1916 Lucknow Pact, Gandhi did expect Ansari to contribute to a pact among the communities, something along the lines that Jinnah had come close to realising in early 1927, via his Delhi Proposals.[7]

As Lloyd and Susanne put it: 'Gandhi's plan was cross-cut by a request from Motilal Nehru, a Gandhi confidant and Congress stalwart, to have his son, Jawaharlal, elected Congress president. Gandhi told Motilal that it was premature for this to happen. At this conjuncture, Gandhi was convinced that Hindu-Muslim unity took precedence over (any) generational change in Congress' leadership. Ansari was elected, and Jawaharlal was accommodated by being moved from being one of several INC general secretaries to becoming "*the* working secretary", a more elevated post'.

However, Jawaharlal had other priorities. He had just returned from an extended European tour toward the end of December 1927, just in time for the Congress' annual session in Madras. It appears that he had been 'transformed by his experience as a delegate to the International Congress Against Colonial Oppression and Imperialism in Brussels'.[8] With this new 'consciousness of imperialism and revolutionary change, Nehru now found Gandhi's 1920s concentration on constructive work in India's villages and on spinning *khadi* on a *charkha* tame and humdrum'. Six years had passed since the momentous Gandhi-led non-cooperation campaign for self-rule. Nehru and others thought it was about to succeed when Gandhi fearing the escalation of violence after

Chauri Chaura, had called it off. As Madhu Limaye says: 'The Jawaharlal who returned to India at the end of 1927 was a changed person. He had drunk deep at the fountain of Marxism, and was full of anti-imperialism, complete independence and socialism.' Class politics, not communal harmony was now uppermost in Jawaharlal Nehru's mind. For, against Gandhi's advice to stay with the moderate course in INC-Raj relations, Nehru took the lead at the 1927 annual session in pressing for and passing radical resolutions. One resolution replaced dominion status with complete independence as the Congress objective, another attacked imperial wars.

Gandhi reacted sharply to Nehru's attack on his carefully crafted strategy'. In a letter dated 4 January 1928, he told Nehru:

> You are going too fast. You should have taken time to think and become acclimatized. Most of the resolutions you framed and got carried could have been delayed for one year. Your plunging into the 'republican army' [by replacing dominion status, which called for allegiance to the British Crown, with 'complete independence' which didn't] was a hasty step.

Then came a less than veiled attack on Nehru's new-found revolutionary fervour:

> But I do not mind these acts of yours [the badly-timed, ill-judged resolutions] so much as I mind your encouraging mischief-makers and hooligans. I do not know whether you still believe in unadulterated non-violence. But even if you have altered your views, you could not think that unlicensed and unbridled violence is going to deliver the country. If careful observation of the country in the light of your European experience convinces you of the error of the current ways and means, by all means enforce your views, but do please form a disciplined party...Until that day, it is your duty as working secretary of the Indian National Congress to devote your whole energy to the central resolution, i.e., Unity....

An angry Nehru replied on 11 January 1928: 'It amazes me to find you [...who are always so careful with your words and language] using language which appears to me wholly unjustified...you have...specially selected some resolutions for...criticism and condemnation...You have referred to discipline...May I remind you that you are member of the Working Committee and it is an extraordinary thing for a member on the morrow of the Congress to criticize...its principal resolutions'. Nehru then cut to the substance: 'You have described the Independence Resolution as 'hastily conceived and thoughtlessly passed'. [Given the attention that Nehru and others over the last five years and at the annual session have given to the subject]...no stretch of language can justify the use of the words 'hastily conceived' [or] 'thoughtlessly passed'....a demand for independence and all that implies has come to mean a very great deal for me and I attach more importance to it than to almost anything else...I doubt if anyone outside a small circle understands your position...The liberals [for example, Sir Tej Bahadur Sapru, and Motilal Nehru] and the Muslims [such as Jinnah] may have their doubts about impendence.' Nehru admitted, 'and say they prefer dominion status' but 'whether they like it or not, it passes my comprehension how a national organisation can have as its ideal and goal dominion status. *The very idea suffocates and strangles me'.* [Emphasis added]

Nehru then turned to the more general questions of Gandhi's ideas and leadership, questions which bear more directly on the modernity—postmodernity divide. 'You know how intensely I have admired you and believed in you as a leader...I have done so in spite of the fact that I hardly agreed with anything that some of your previous publications—*India Home Rule* [*Hind Swaraj*], etc.—contained. I felt and feel that you were and are infinitely greater than your little books. [S]ince you have come out of prison [February 1924] something seems to have gone wrong....You...repeatedly changed your attitude...most of us were left in utter bewilderment...I have asked you many times what you expected to do in the future and your answers have been far from satisfying... you...said that...you expected the khadi movement to spread rapidly [but]...the miracle has not happened...I am beginning to think, if we are to wait for freedom till khadi becomes universal in India we shall have to wait till the Greek Kalends[9]...our khadi work is almost wholly divorced from politics...What then can be done? You say nothing...you only criticize and no helpful lead comes from you...'

Nehru then turns directly to worldview. 'Reading many of your articles in *Young India*—your autobiography, etc.—I have often felt how very different my ideals were from yours...You misjudge greatly, I think, the civilization of the West and attach too great importance to its many failings....I neither think that the so-called *Ramaraj* was very good in the past, nor do I want it back. I think that western or rather industrial civilization is bound to conquer India...Everybody knows these defects [of industrialism] and the utopias and social theories are meant to remove them'.

Nehru then juxtaposed his modern understanding of the cause and cure for India's poverty to Gandhi's post-industrial view. 'You have advocated...claims of...the poor in India...I doubt very much if the fundamental causes of poverty are touched by [your remedy of village employment and constructive work]....You do not say a word against the semi-feudal zamindari [landlord] system...or against the capitalist exploitation of both the workers and the consumers'.

Let us pause to underline some of the positions Nehru takes in his letter of 11 January 1928. Industrial or modern civilisation is bound to conquer India; its defects will be removed by western [read Fabian and/or Marxian] 'utopias and social theories'; charkha spinning and the making and wearing of khadi deadens rather then awakens the spirit and practice of *swaraj;* feudalism and capitalism must be attacked and removed if India is to overcome its poverty; and Gandhi is 'infinitely greater than [his]...little books...' [for example, *Hind Swaraj*] whose reading makes Nehru realise 'how very different my ideals...[are] from yours...'

It wasn't always this way. In the early and mid-1920s, before his European trip, Nehru spoke as if he held Gandhian views. He condemned violence and affirmed the efficacy of non-violence. 'The choice for us,' he (had) said in 1923, 'is between Lenin and Mussolini on the one side and Gandhi on the other.' Free India should not become a cheap replica of Western countries. Bringing the message of khadi to the people was a way of avoiding such a result.

On 17 January 1928, Gandhi responded to Nehru's denial of his Gandhian self. He tells Nehru that he must have been heroically suppressing his true self all these years. He is free to 'revolt against me'. The articles criticising Nehru and the work of the Madras annual session were a misfire all around. 'I had no notion of the terrible extent of [our] differences'. 'While you were in that state [of self-suppression], you overlooked the very things which appear to you now as my serious blemishes'. Similar criticisms on previous occasions weren't noticed because, while 'you [were] under stupefaction, these things did not jar you as they do now'.

Gandhi was clear about what was to be done. '...If [as you say] I am wrong I am evidently doing irreparable harm to the country...it is your duty to rise in revolt against me...' 'The differences between you and me appear to me to be so vast and radical that there seems no meeting ground between us. I can't conceal from you my grief that I should lose a comrade so valiant, so faithful, so able and so honest as you have always been...But this dissolution of comradeship—if dissolution must come—in no way affects our personal intimacy'. Gandhi then turned to how to begin (attempt?) their separation and rivalry. 'I suggest a dignified way to unfurl your banner. Write to me a letter for publication showing your differences. I will print it in *Young India* and write a brief reply...If you do not want to take the trouble of writing another letter, I am prepared to publish the letter [of 11 January 1928] that is before me...I consider that letter a frank and honest document'.

Lloyd and Susanne elaborate: 'Nehru was "shocked and pained" by Gandhi's 17 January 1928 letter. But he quickly decided not to accept Gandhi's invitation to go into opposition, a positioning that would have meant challenging his mentor and patron. Instead, Nehru backed down. His 11 January letter was impulsive and ill-considered. Gandhi was not to publish it. He pledged not to intentionally or directly criticize Gandhi's views or positions. "No one has moved me and inspired me more than you...There can be no question of our personal relations suffering. But even in the wider sphere am I not your child in politics, though perhaps a truant and errant child?" Perhaps this "remarkable correspondence" offers us a way to understand "how the resolution of...differences over dominion status and complete independence led to the partition of India?"'

This January 1928 conflict between Gandhi and Nehru was, in reality, an argument about the Congress' grand strategy. Should the country's goal be dominion status or complete independence? Answers were being prepared for the Simon Commission, appointed to look into constitutional advance, which was about to arrive in India on 22 February 1928. Its composition—as we have seen its seven members included no Indian and it was dominated by conservative Tories—was an insult to Indian nationalists and particularly infuriated the younger generation of which Nehru was a leader.

Gandhi wanted the Congress to have a version of dominion status on offer. It would, unlike Nehru's complete independence demand, help to reassure the minorities, particularly the Muslims, that self-government would include minority rights and representation as well as majority rule. And it would help to assure the great Muslim majority provinces, Punjab and Bengal, and the princely states, both important parts of the independence equation, that the new state would find a way to provide for their autonomy in the shared sovereignty of a federal system.

Gandhi's preference for dominion status was, of course, strongly influenced by his South Africa experiences and learning process. That is why he held it as a more preferred choice than complete independence. In addition weighed in its favour was his awareness that the Indian negotiating position should be within striking distance of British parliamentary and public opinion. The British Parliament would have to legislate on the subjects of Indian constitutional reform and self-government, and access to that legislature and the British judiciary would be of immense help in the early days.

Such a negotiating position, proposing advances that had some chance of being accepted by Parliament, had in fact been prepared over more than a decade, and it was this position that Gandhi chastised Nehru for demolishing. In 1916 the Lucknow Pact between the Congress and the League, in which the two organisations were united in support of self-government and a parliamentary system for India, provided for separate electorates along with reserved seats for Muslims and weightage, granting a larger proportion of seats to the minority community than its share of the population. And this had been the negotiating position for the reforms of 1918.

The Nehru Report of 1928 was drawn up in anticipation of the next step in the self-governing process. It called for dominion status but withdrew the Lucknow Pact's commitment to separate electorates and to weightage. Instead of reserving one-third of the seats in the central legislature as Jinnah, on behalf of the Muslim League, had requested, the Nehru Report limited Muslim representation to 25 per cent, roughly the Muslim community's share of the population. 'The atmosphere at the [All Parties] conference', Wells writes, 'was distinctly hostile to Jinnah...The rejection of [Jinnah's]...six points [the most important of which was that one-third of the elected representatives of both houses of the Central Legislature should be Mussalmans] was to be expected, considering the views of Jawaharlal Nehru and the younger nationalists in Congress, the high [Hindu] Mahasabha representation at the conference, as well as the number of Hindus from the Punjab present for the deliberation...the Liberals under Sapru were prepared to concede many of the Muslim League's demands [but] the Congress was not'.

Despite his treatment at the All Parties Conference that adopted the Nehru Report, 'Jinnah', Wells argues, 'still saw himself as a nationalist and continued to harbour a dream to unite the Hindu and Muslim communities to strive for a common political goal'. Throughout 1928 he persisted in his efforts to bring the two communities together. Like Gandhi but unlike Nehru and the younger generation of nationalists, Jinnah saw the Hindu-Muslim question as a national problem, not a communal dispute. At the end of 1928, Jinnah still saw Hindu-Muslim unity as a byword for swaraj and he retained his faith in constitutional methods as the (only) way it could be achieved.

Although Jawaharlal initially went along with the [Motilal] Nehru Report of 1928 he soon found its acceptance of communal representation and commitment to dominion status unacceptable. He had after all returned from his European tour a changed man. 'His Gandhian ideological commitments were overlaid, perhaps displaced, by an anti-imperialist socialist ideology. His nationalist understanding changed too; he was now committed to an integral nationalism that was consistent with uniform citizenship and majoritarian democracy. Class replaced other social categories, notably religion, as his way of understanding the political process. In rejecting communal representation and dominion status he was rejecting key aspects of a pluralist state and a multi-cultural society in India, for example, minority representation, safeguards, and a federalized state. It is important to remember that Nehru wrote to Gandhi that the very thought of dominion status "suffocated and strangled" him'.[10]

In this context A.G. Noorani writes: 'It was Nehru who insisted on "blindly" following "British practice and procedure" in India's plural society by refusing to recognize the need for safeguards for minorities, especially the Muslims'. Safeguards [for example, reserved seats for Muslims] and weightage [allocating a higher proportion of legislative seats than a minority's share of the population] were not needed; Indian citizens, regardless of their religion or caste, would have constitutionally guaranteed uniform rights and that was good enough. In any case, safeguards played into the hands of Britain's divide and rule strategy. Such questions draw their meaning and urgency from the existence and concerns of India's religious and social minorities, "minorities" who "feel endangered by the monopoly sovereignty claims of the Congress' majoritarianism".'

In the 1920s, at the provincial as well as the all-India level, minorities had acquired political consciousness and identities and had begun to seek a voice, a due representation, and were asserting their rights. India's existence as one country depended on the willing support of its Muslim community for an independent Indian nation, yet paradoxically, that is exactly where lay the source of the Muslim fear, of their future in an Independent India. Would they not then face the tyranny of the permanent majority—the Hindu? A response denying any such possibility drew only groans of disbelief, the past many centuries and the shadows of history obscured both vision and thought.

In the event, the expectations of both Gandhi and Nehru were defeated by British domestic political developments beyond their control. Prime Minister Ramsay MacDonald's tottering national government was too divided and too hostile to grant India the dominion status that Lord Irwin as viceroy had cried for and that the 1928 [Motilal] Nehru Report had also recommended. Besides, this goal of dominion status was rendered an academic point by the December 1929 decision of the Congress to demand full independence.

What the Pandit Motital Nehru Report of 1928 did achieve was a totally unintended objective, it convinced the various Muslim groups that they had to, for safeguarding their own interests come under one single umbrella—that of the All-India Muslim Conference,[11] (as distinctly apart from the Muslim League) and there must be a united view that is put across. This Nehru Report of 1928, running totally counter to the Lucknow Pact of 1916 had as we have already noted, recommended an abolition of elections on the basis of separate electorates, also weightage for the minority provinces, both these impacted directly on Muslim representation in minority provinces, such as United Provinces, Bihar and others in this category, and it reduced their numbers in the Central Assembly. Not unnaturally, therefore, Jinnah and his colleagues in the Central Assembly now greatly perturbed, made a common cause with the Muslim provincial leaders. A Muslim Conference was therefore, convened in Delhi on 31 December 1928 under the Aga Khan's chairmanship. The chief architect of this move was Fazli Hussain, then the leader of the Unionist Party in Punjab.

Those that responded and attended were broadly of two categories: groups like the Punjab Unionists, and the politically aware UP Muslims, or those who had now wearied of this seemingly endless confrontation with the ruling British, particularly after it became clear that Jinnah's negotiations with Congress were getting the community nowhere. In this category came the Muslim majority provinces, the Frontiersmen, the Punjabi and Bengali urban constitutionalists and the minority province Khilafatists, plus Sindh. This Muslim Conference recommended full provincial autonomy; a true federation; Muslim majority in Punjab and Bengal; separate electorates: weightage in the Muslim minority provinces and retention of the existing one-third representation for Muslims in the Central Legislature.

Jinnah did not attend this Muslim Conference at Delhi in December 1928, but in March 1929, after a meeting with Conference representatives who sought to invite him to be their spokesman, he (Jinnah) drew up his famous fourteen poims.[12] These were accepted by the Muslim Conference as their credo and were sent to the Nehru Committee. Motilal Nehru's reactions were dismissive; he felt that such demands did not belong to the realm of practical politics. 'He is simply trying to reinstate himself with his followers', he wrote to Gandhi in August 1929, 'by making [these] preposterous demands...I am quite clear in my own mind that the only way to reach a compromise with the truly nationalist Muslims is to ignore Mr Jinnah and the Ali brothers altogether'.[13] This Muslin Conference representation had not got anywhere.

The Muslim Conference met its next serious challenge when the Simon Commission Report was published in May 1930. However, before this, preparations for Simon had themselves got riddled with disputes. Mindful of such possibilities and born from his own experience of the Muddiman Committee[14] (see Chapter 2), Jinnah had come to attach importance to the composition and status of the personnel of any Indian constitutional enquiry. In one of his speeches in the Legislative Assembly, as far back as in March 1926, Jinnah had asked of the government for the appointment of a Statutory Commission, for which a provision existed in the 1919 Act. He had even then made quite clear that 'the personnel of that Commission should be such as would satisfy the people...if you are going to appoint a Royal Commission', he had reasoned, 'it is no use appointing it unless you have a Commission which will command the confidence and the respect of the people'. A week before the personnel of the Simon Commission were to be announced, Jinnah was invited by Lord Irwin and informed confidentially of the decision of the government about the composition of the proposed Commission. Recording his impression of Jinnah's mood at this interview Irwin wrote: 'I had a long talk with Jinnah today. He listened very attentively and at the end said that he did not quite see what he had to say if the matter had been already decided. He then professed to dwell at some length upon the usual objections to the Commission being purely Parliamentary; that it savoured of the nature of a judicial inquest in which Indians were in the dock; that it was wounding [to] the national pride and hurting to national sentiment. He feared that the resentment that would be created by the Parliamentary Commission would be such as to submerge the proposal about the Select Committee[15] of the Legislature going home, a proposal which in itself he recognized to be of considerable constitutional value. We discussed the things generally on these lines for some time, but he did not give me any indication that he changed his view of the results he anticipated. He professed himself very gloomy as to the reception with which the announcement would meet'.[16]

Irwin had already done enough in India, especially through his appeals to the Indian leaders and his efforts at bringing about communal peace to earn Jinnah's 'sincere respect and affection'.[17] Therefore, despite the gloom that Irwin had detected in Jinnah at the interview, Jinnah acted with restraint. During the week after the interview, Jinnah urged Irwin to do his utmost and secure the inclusion of at least two Indians on the Commission, without disclosing any secret, to the leaders of all parties in India to withhold expression of individual opinion committing the country in any way. He also called upon Indian leaders to discuss jointly the terms of the proposals, after they have appeared in cold print, and determine upon a common policy of action. It was widely speculated in India then that the British Labour party would assert itself on India's side in this matter, wrongly as subsequent events were to prove. The Labour Parliamentary party, in an official statement on the subject issued two days after the announcement, advised 'Indian opinion to await the results of the debates in Parliament before finally deciding its attitude to the Commission'.[18] A leading British daily had also predicted 'a possible change in the Indian Commission'.[19] On 14 November 1927, i.e. a week after the announcement of the Commission, Jinnah sent the following telegram to Fenner-Brockway of the Independent Labour Party in Britain:

> The exclusion of Indians from the Commission is fundamentally wrong. The amendments proposed so far and reported are equally impossible. No self-respecting and accredited representative of India would associate with or serve on the Commission unless invited on absolutely equal terms and with equal rights. I appeal to the Labour party to demonstrate their sympathy with Indian feeling by action and in response to Indian public opinion at least to refuse to allow any member of their party to serve on Commission which excludes Indians and which is calculated to humiliate and wound the self-respect of the people of India.[20]

The Tory government ultimately succeeded in getting the necessary support of the Labour Party in Parliament and on 26 November 1927, the Royal Warrant appointing the Commission was signed. The next day, Jinnah, in a press interview, expressed his by now definite opinion that 'India cannot participate in this policy and share in the work of the Commission, in any form, at any stage, because it is a complete negation of India's status as a partner'.[21] All the Indian newspapers of December were full of reports of Jinnah's efforts to create a public opinion against the proposed Commission and of his disagreement with a number of his prominent co-religionists in the Punjab. His activities culminated in the following remarks in his presidential address at the Muslim League session in Calcutta on 1 January 1928: 'Constitutional war has been declared [by the Muslim League] on Great Britain. Negotiations for a settlement are not to come from our side. Let the Government sue for peace. We are denied equal partnership and we will resist the new doctrine to the best of our power. The Jallianwala Bagh was physical butchery. The Simon Commission is the butchery of our soul. By appointing an exclusively white Commission, Lord Birkenhead has declared our unfitness for self-government. I welcome Pandit Malaviya and I welcome the hand of fellowship extended to us by the Hindu leaders from the platform of Congress and the Hindu Mahasabha. For to me this offer is more valuable than any concession which the British Government can make. Let us then grasp the hand of fellowship. This is indeed a bright day, and for achieving this unity our thanks are due to Lord Birkenhead'.[22] Strong stuff all this. Simon and the eponymous

Commission had at least got all the Indian parties speaking of unity if not actually reach it.

Jinnah sailed for England in May 1928, accompanied by Srinivasa Iyengar, president of the Indian Congress at the time, and Dewan Chamanlal. He stayed there for six months for which period Irwin continued to receive reports from England about Jinnah's endeavours at influencing the British Labour Party and the India Office for the inclusion of Indian representatives on the Simon Commission. To not much avail though, for Jinnah returned to India in October 1928, without either any encouraging results or even much hope. In an interview to *The Times of India* on 26 October 1928, immediately after his return to Bombay, Jinnah warned his countrymen that it was the biggest folly on their part 'to expect any substantial help from anyone party in England and that the 'one hope for India' was 'unity between Hindus and Muslims.' However, despite the earlier discussed 1928 Nehru Report, Jinnah was not without hope of settling this communal question, and applied himself afresh to achieving just that objective.

In the March of 1928, Jinnah had already suggested to Irwin two ways of resolving the difficulty—'one was by turning Simon's Commission into a mixed Commission; and the other was by establishing a twin Indian Commission with parallel authority'.[23] Jinnah had offered to take the brunt of the attack in India if either of his suggestions was accepted. Irwin received a similar suggestion from Sir Chimanlal Setalvad in June 1928. Irwin took up these suggestions with conviction, to the extent that it nearly caused a diplomatic clash with the then secretary of state for India. Lord Birkenhead, who saw in these suggestions an undue Indian pressure for concession which according to him, (Birkenhead) if conceded would only expand. On Irwin's insistence, the suggestions were, however placed before the British Cabinet, whereas Secretary of State Birkenhead leaned heavily on his colleagues and secured a decision against Irwin.

Hereafter, Irwin's political efforts shifted from India to Britain. He looked towards going home sometime in the middle of 1929, so as to get an opportunity and an advantage to talk to the leadership directly, in Britain, on the complexities of the Indian question. Then suddenly the clouds parted: Birkenhead resigned from India Office in October 1928, this removed an obstacle for Irwin. In June 1929, just before he was to leave for home on four months' leave, the Labour party came to power in Britain and Anthony Wedgwood Benn was appointed secretary of state for India. This further facilitated Irwin's task, for his ideas had by now advanced beyond merely the personnel of the Simon Commission. He saw no further use in the Commission or in the recommendations that it might make. Confiding to George Lane-Fox, a member of the Simon Commission, who was related to Irwin's family: 'What really matters here more is what is going to be the political temper of India by the time you have finished and your work has to be put into operation. It is really worth a great deal to try and avoid having to launch any plans in a general atmosphere of hostility and resentment.'

Five months later, towards the end of November 1929, Irwin again wrote, this time to the Archbishop of Canterbury:

> I feel more and more clearly myself that the effective choice of policy is going to lie between doing very little and doing something pretty substantial... There are ample justifications of course for the first, but I cannot resist the conclusion that its broad effect over years must be to drive Indian politics more and more to the left; whereas it seems to me that there is a chance that we might get an adequate amount of agreement on the lines of the second.[24]

At this stage, Irwin had two objectives: to restore confidence in India of British intentions about their political future, this having suffered on account of Sir Malcolm Hailey's speech of 8 February 1924 in the Legislative Assembly.[25] Secondly, Irwin wanted a Round Table Conference of representative Indians and their counterparts in Britain to work out the future Indian constitution in an atmosphere of harmony. A demand for such a conference had earlier got raised, as far back as 1922, through that 'conference of leaders', held in Bombay, in the middle of January 1922, to address the Punjab (Jallianwala Bagh) and the Khilafat wrongs and to discuss the demand of swaraj. Jinnah had then taken a leading part in the conference. A Round Table Conference had also been demanded in a resolution adopted by the Legislative Assembly in February 1924. Which is why now, in a speech that he delivered in the Legislative Assembly early in 1929, Irwin revisited the idea, but only after the Simon Commission had reported its views. 'I tell this Assembly again, and through them India, that the declaration of 1917 stands, and will stand for all time as the solemn pledge of the British people to do all that can be done by one people to assist another to attain full national political stature, and that the pledge so given will never be dishonoured. And, as actions are commonly held more powerful than words, I will add that I should not be standing before you here today...if I believed that the British people had withdrawn their hand from [that] solemn covenant'.[26]

By the middle of 1930, the Simon Commission Report, though deprived of even its remaining authority, first by the boycott and then the viceroy's offer of a Round Table Conference, had still to complete its task by formally presenting it. Sir Fazli Hussain from Punjab apprehended that because the Commission had been appointed by the Parliament in London, it could still prove dangerous for the Muslim Conference interests, if the Report that it presented did not specifically mention the issue of Muslim majorities.

As it transpired, the Report did not do any of this but it did not also grant what had been sought: the separation of Sindh; and the NWFP's demand for equal status had also been neglected. For Baluchistan, too, the report envisaged no change at all. Then on top of all this, Simon maintained a totally unsympathetic attitude towards separate electorates; further, in the Central Legislature, the Commission recommended the abolition of separate representation. The Report did not even consider the Muslim demand for majorities by separate electorates in Punjab and Bengal. Patently, for the Muslim Conference, this Report was a great discouragement and to many it felt akin to an open challenge; and to the moderates a deliberate provocation.

Under such circumstances, it was largely Fazli Hussain, who then damage controlled the Muslim position vis-à-vis the government. First, he placated the Frontier Muslims by approaching the officials; then gradually he brought them around to appreciating the importance for reforms in the Frontier region. Then, he secured the Muslim position in the majority provinces by working for maximum provincial autonomy. On the question of minorities he argued that he was not interested in the question of religion or culture, more about representation in local bodies and services. All along, Fazli Hussain argued that Simon Commission had done great injustice by making its recommendations on the basis of the Lucknow Pact of 1916. He emphasised that recognition of Muslim majorities in Punjab and Bengal was not to be made subject to a surrendering of the principle of weightage in the minority provinces. Fazli Hussain's voice was that of the provinces, for him the question of Muslim representation in Punjab and Bengal was distinctly apart, that stood on its own. His view was that no change should be made at the centre until the provinces had established themselves. However, once a decision had been made, in principle, that certain subjects were to be transferred, he endeavoured to limit them to the very minimum. He also argued against the Simon Commission's recommendations for indirect election to the Assembly, on the grounds that that would transfer power into the hands of either provincial caucuses or place Congress in a dominating position in the Legislative Assembly. Fazli Hussain had remained apprehensive about the nature of power that would eventually be devolved, until suggestions about the First Round Table Conference, until now only floating got crystallised. In this complex background, the First Round Table Conference was finally called in London for November 1930.

THE FIRST ROUND TABLE CONFERENCE—12 NOVEMBER 1930

In May 1929 before going home, Irwin had a long, personal talk with Jinnah who briefed him comprehensively on his ideas about the proposed conference and followed that up with a letter to the British prime minister, Ramsay MacDonald, arguing the need for of reiterating the pledge(s) of dominion status and of convening a Round Table Conference. In his statement of 31 October 1929, to the Central Assembly, Irwin was able to deliver both, thus giving India all that Jinnah and men of his thinking had demanded; which was much more than any other viceroy had been willing to, or had until then been able to give.

Jinnah's response to Irwin's announcement was to take up the challenge of making a success of this offer as a personal responsibility; he felt it was his moral duty to do so. The Congress, in the interim, had issued their 'Leaders' Manifesto', which insisted that the Round Table Conference should meet not to discuss by when dominion status had to be established but to frame a scheme for the Dominion Constitution of India. These different priorities were in reality two different approaches: the first accepted dominion status as a given; a starting point to be advanced from, therefore advocated this as the practical course; the second, stood for framing a Dominion Constitution, as a precondition. This was the cautious, step-by-step, legalistic path—'get the detailed specifics accepted before moving on to consenting to the general'. The question was not which one of these was a better approach but what would have moved India with greater dispatch towards the twin objectives of unity and freedom. With that as the yardstick starting with dominion status, as a given, would have contributed significantly more to greater unity, generated much more goodwill and moved faster towards the final objective of freedom.

Jinnah now had to first reconcile with Gandhi and the Congress therefore, when he met Irwin in Bombay, immediately after the latter's return to India to discuss the three matters of practical importance: composition of the conference; its date; and the question of amnesty for political prisoners—Jinnah had already been in direct and indirect, communication with Gandhi. From then till almost end December 1929, Jinnah, along with Sir Tej Bahadur Sapru, worked indefatigably to bring about just such a meeting between the viceroy and the Congress leaders. This finally took place on 23 December 1929, the participants met Gandhi, Motilal Nehru, Sir Tej Bahadur Sapru, Vithalbhai Patel and Jinnah, besides, of course, the viceroy. Gandhi and Motilal appeared, to the viceroy, to be attending the meeting, under duress, (of the young men in the Congress?) determined to extract prior assurances, and that is precisely what they sought, an assurance that the only purpose of the conference would be to consider the details of a constitution for dominion status. This, as already observed, was a characteristic subtlety. If the conference was to go first to the details of the proposal, *before* the principle of it had been accepted then many contentious issues like federal vs central, reservations, representation in central legislature, etc., could easily stymie the entire initiative. Moreover, for this the responsibility would then shift away from the Congress. However, this was patently not in the sphere of the viceroy's authority to give, even if he had wanted to. The meeting, therefore, failed. Irwin recounting the meeting commented: 'Sapru, Jinnah and Patel (Vithalbhai) were frankly disgusted' with the attitude adopted at the meeting by Gandhi and Motilal, The options had now narrowed further.

In all this, there was already a degree of foreclosure of options, for towards the end of 1929, in Lahore, the Congress had already adopted a resolution for Independence, and in March 1930 it resumed countrywide civil disobedience. Jinnah, now feared, and with justification, that this path of agitation/satyagraha and the inevitable

British response of suppression would destroy his preferred path. He, therefore, urged the viceroy to set a date for convening the Round Table Conference and also to have the list of 'invitees shown to him', in case Jinnah had 'some suggestions to make'.[27]

At this juncture, Sir Tej Bahadur Sapru, in association with M.R Jayakar, made another effort for peace between the Congress and the government. They got the two Nehrus (father and son) to meet Gandhi, as both by then had been imprisoned in consequence of civil disobedience and were lodged in separate jails. This effort also failed, principally because Gandhi felt that that was not an appropriate time for securing any honourable settlement. Upon which Jinnah, counseled the viceroy on 19 August 1930, to take a firm stand with Indian nationalists. Jinnah, now with only London to look forward to, in preparation, by mid August 1930, had already invited Dr Muhammad Iqbal to preside over the Muslim League's session, as he would be away in London. This long awaited Round Table Conference was finally called in London for the autumn of 1930. It would launch a new phase in India's efforts at freedom through constitution making.

Interest (and importance) now got focused on who the representatives from India would be; who would say what and speak for whom. For Fazli Hussain the choice of appropriate representatives who could effectively articulate the Muslim Conference's case was the new priority also the next challenge. In his view, held with justification, because of leaders, like Jinnah, who were principally interested in responsibility at the Centre a clear danger existed that in hands such as Jinnah's the interests of the provincial Muslim case could well go by default. 'Frankly,' Fazli Hussain wrote to Sir Malcolm Hailey, 'I do not like the idea of Jinnah doing all the talking and of there being no one strong minded enough to make a protest in case Jinnah starts expressing...views...[that are] not the accepted Indian Muslim views'. Jinnah and Muhammad Shafi were then amongst the well-known lawyers of India. They were both well acquainted with political debates at the highest level and were no doubt sterling representatives of the Muslims, but a 'provinces' man was still needed. Fazli Hussain's counterbalancing choice, therefore, fell upon Zafrullah Khan, and Shafaat Ahmed from the United Provinces, along with Nawab Saheb of Chhatari'.[28]

Despite all these precautions Fazli Hussain remained uneasy, for there was an inbuilt discord between all India concessions and provincial gains. Representatives of these two views had never come to a head in India, having lobbied their respective causes to the Government of India separately and independently. However, in London both would be present, they would be sitting around the same table and would have to put their respective cases to a new arbiter, the Labour Government. Also, pressure for a settlement was now far more demanding on the all India politicians. Indian liberals like Sir Tej Bahadur Sapru and Srinivasa Sastri feared that a prolongation of Congress led non-cooperation was a serious threat to their political future, they were therefore, naturally anxious to return to India with some positive achievement, which in turn might persuade the Congress to return to the constitutional path. The Indian liberals also aimed at acquiring a measure of responsibility at the Centre, for which purpose they put forward the idea of a federation of British India and the princely states. However, to achieve this, yet again, it was necessary that the communal question be first settled, to this end they then adopted a generous attitude towards the Muslim demands. On the other hand, men like Jinnah and Muhammad Shafi were equally anxious to come across as national leaders. This was very broadly the setting of the Conference, though still not totally, for we have not examined the stand of the princes. Nevertheless, for the moment we will not delve into the complexities of princely India.

Jinnah sailed for London on 4 October 1930. The Round Table Conference convened on 12 November 1930; H.H. Aga Khan was elected leader of the Muslim delegation with his headquarters at the Ritz Hotel in London. The first Plenary Session of this conference began with a formal inauguration in the House of Lords, presided over by His Majesty King George V. The Aga Khan, was subsequently elected as the chairman of the British-Indian section of the conference, that is, of all the Indian representatives except the princes. The conference, moving thereafter to St. James's Palace settled down to its task. The major parties at the conference had arrived with defined, settled ideas and solutions; they had their representative claims to put across, after which efforts at reconciliation of positions were to be attempted here. In the process, the British would obviously be presented with a series of contradictory claims and counterclaims.

Therefore, a united front was the obvious priority and the first step in that direction was by finding a way of bridging the gulf between the Muslim and Hindu sections of the British-Indian delegation. Only when that had been achieved, it was reasoned, could one offer to the 'British representatives a conjoint proposal for the constitutional reforms'.[29] Pre-eminent among those whose effort was devoted towards achieving this was the then Nawab Saheb of Bhopal.[30] He and the Aga Khan conceptualised independent India as a federal state, in which authority and power remained with the Central Government, the constituents having autonomous rights and functions.

Sir Chimanlal Setalvad in his book *Recollections and Reflections,* also a participant has recorded: 'After we reached London well in advance for the Round Table Conference, it was arranged that some representatives of Hindus and of Muslims should meet to consider the question of a communal settlement. Sapru, Sastri, myself, Jayakar, Moonje and Ambedkar were deputed for this meeting and the Aga Khan, Jinnah and one other gentleman represented the Muslims...When we first met, I put the question to the Aga Khan, whether if we arrived at a satisfactory settlement on other points he would agree to joint electorates. He said, "if you satisfy our demands on all other matters we would agree to joint electorates, with reservation of seats for Muslims." I put a further question, "If we come to a settlement on all matters including joint electorates, will the Muslim delegates support the national demand at the Conference?" His answer was characteristic. He said, 'In that event you lead and we follow".'

Sir Chimanlal then states that along with Sapru, Sastri they would have agreed immediately to the demands, but they 'were seriously disappointed in the attitude of Jayakar and Moonje'. He laments that 'a great opportunity was thus lost'. The Aga Khan too in his memoirs refers to these discussions as follows: 'In his memoirs, Sir Chimanlal Setalvad has referred to these offers of mine and his evidence at least stands firmly on record that if the First Round Table Conference did not achieve all that was expected of it, and if, ultimately, not only was 'Dominion Status' not brought about, but India had to be partitioned, some at least of the beginnings of these momentous happenings are to be found in the Hindu delegation's refusal to accept my offer'.

At first several of the Muslim delegates, in particular Jinnah, were, as they had been long before the conference, suspicious of the idea of a federation. Its dangers, to them were neither remote nor unimportant; to associate a growing democracy with a number of princely states in which personal rule was the established norm and to which could also be added a continuing danger, that since a majority of the ruling princes were Hindu, there could occur a serious diminution of the political influence of the Muslim community, in the federation as a whole. The Aga Khan, however, carried a conviction that whatever the temporary difficulties, this federal scheme still remained the most acceptable solution to India's political problems; it was an opportunity, he felt, that might never recur, and that if it required a compromise (or compromises) to make it effective, well then, that would relatively be a small price to pay.

The ruling princes, too, had given a kind of partial assent to some form of a federal government. The guarantees now sought were that the Muslim majorities in the Punjab and Bengal should not, by some legalistic proviso be reduced into minorities; further that Sindh be separated from Bombay; plus reforms in the NWFP, and finally assurance of statutory reservation of a certain proportion of places in the army and in the civil service for Muslims. This kind of a comprehensive platform, it was reasoned, would enable the Muslim delegation to offer a united front to the British. The Aga Khan suggested a united command, under a chosen Indian leader, which he would then get the Muslim community to accept.[31]

In his memoirs, Sir Chimanlal Setalvad has mentioned that if the First Round Table Conference did not achieve all that was expected, and if, ultimately, not only was dominion status not brought about but India had to be partitioned, some at least of the beginnings of those momentous happenings are to be found in the Hindu delegations' refusal to accept the Aga Khan's offer. Sapru and Sastri were not averse to accepting the Muslim proposals, but they were intimidated by the opposition of their colleagues, and of course, of the Hindu Mahasabha.

To quote the Aga Khan's sentiments: 'Had my views been accepted... later history would have taken a profoundly different course, and there would...have long since been in existence a Federal Government of India, in which Muslims and Hindus would have been partners in the day-to-day administration of the country...I must say I was always suspicious that our work might not procure any real or lasting results because the great realities of India in 1930 were being forgotten...It was forgotten that there were, first and foremost and all the time, fundamental differences between the Muslim(s) and Hindu(s)...and that these differences were most apparent between the Muslims of the two Northwestern and Eastern sections of India and the Hindu majority in the rest...It was forgotten that the intelligentsia—although only ten per cent of the total Hindu population—numbered between forty and fifty million, and could not possibly be dismissed 'as a mere microscopic minority'. It was forgotten that they desired the British to quit India, bag and baggage, finally and forever; this was the aim for which they laboured and strove, and indeed [this] was brought to pass in 1947...It was forgotten that the Princes, for all their wealth, ability, personal charm, prestige and sincere loyalty to the British connection, had in fact very little power or influence'.[32]

By the middle of November 1930, even the Indian liberals could not make progress, as negotiations had got deadlocked on the question of electorates and other issues pertaining to residuary powers. When they resumed, Punjab now emerged as one of the main stumbling blocks to any agreement. The Sikhs and Hindus would not agree to a majority by separate electorates, Fazli Hussain attributing most of the trouble on the British side to the attitude of the Labour Party and on the Indian side to Jinnah, Nawab Bhopal, Mohammad Shafi and Fazlul Haq. What he (Fazli Hussain) feared most was that the Muslims would give up separate electorates so as to strengthen the case for devolution at the Centre. He remained staunchly opposed to this, representing to the viceroy that any discussion on the basis of joint electorates in London will not have the support of the Muslim community in India. He deplored the Labour government's insistence that Muslims should not have a majority. At the same time it began insidiously to be hinted that the two Punjabi Muslim representatives at the Round Table Conference, Muhammad Shafi and Zafrullah Khan, came from the Sikh areas of Punjab; therefore Shafi, boycotted by the Hindus and Sikhs will have his views severely curtailed and that Zafrullah Khan, the barrister from Sialkot was not even a proper Mohammedan as he was an *Ahmedia*. This last was a cruel barb; such thinking doubtless did afflict the north Indian Muslims' mind, but it was destructive and was later to have many adverse consequences.

Despite Fazli Hussain's efforts, it was in reality the polarisation of political feeling in India that prevented the conference from coming to any agreement. It also became clear that the princes and the politicians had divergent aims.

Jinnah's speech at the open session had emphasised the need for action. He had then said, 'I must express my pleasure at the presence of Dominion Prime Ministers and representatives. I am glad that they are here to witness the birth of a new Dominion of India which would be ready to march along with them within the British Commonwealth of Nations'.[33] Sir Malcolm Hailey, former governor of Punjab and the United Provinces, reporting to Lord Irwin on the Muslim delegation, wrote: 'The Aga Khan does not give them a lead, but professes himself willing to follow the majority. Jinnah is of course, a good deal mistrusted; he did not at the opening of the Conference say what his party had agreed to, and they are a little sore in consequence. He declined to give the Conference Secretariat a copy of his speech in advance as all the others had done. But then Jinnah, of course, was always the perfect little bounder and as slippery as the eels which his forefathers purveyed in Bombay market'.[34]

Jinnah, responding to Lord Peel, former secretary of state for India in Baldwin's Tory government from 1922 to 1924, and then leading the Conservative Party's delegation, had emphasised that the Simon Commission's Report was 'dead'.[35] Even to the Federal Structure Committee, to which Jinnah was assigned, he made it quite plain that no constitution could work unless provisions giving a sense of security to the Muslims and other minorities were embodied.

This First Round Table Conference sharply highlighted Jinnah's many dilemmas, and of all the many commentators *The Manchester Guardian* most clearly and succinctly focused them: 'Mr Jinnah's position at the Round Table Conference was unique. The Hindus thought he was a Muslim communalist, the Muslims took him to be a pro-Hindu, the Princes deemed him to be too democratic. The British considered him a rabid extremist with the result that he was everywhere but nowhere. None wanted him'.[36]

Jinnah himself reflected on his role at the conference in a later public speech at Lahore on 2 March 1936: 'I displeased the Muslims, I displeased my Hindu friends because of the 'famous' 14 points. I displeased the Princes because I was deadly against their underhand activities and I displeased the British Parliament because I felt right from the beginning and I rebelled against it, and said that it was all [a] fraud. Within a few weeks I did not have a friend left there'.[37]

The Gandhi–Irwin Pact

Irrespective of how the conference actually ended, at its closure there had to be some conclusion, some future course of action delineated. Prime Minister Ramsay MacDonald therefore, announced that His Majesty's Government was prepared to accept 'devolution of power at the Centre if the legislature could be constituted on a federal basis'.[38] This was a bargaining chip for the Indian liberals to display, not really any answer to the communal problem, for unless the Congress was fully involved with the constitution-making process along with the Muslim League, what progress could there be? Nevertheless, to encourage this initiative the Government of India released leading members of the Congress so that they could reconsider their position in light of developments around the First Round Table Conference. This eventually resulted in consultations between Gandhi and Viceroy Irwin, which in turn contributed to what came later to be termed as the Delhi Pact of 5 March 1931. On the basis of this pact the government suspended rule by ordinance and agreed to release political prisoners; in turn, the Congress agreed to suspend all civil disobedience, to accept dominion status as its objective, and to attend the Second Round Table Conference. Though, the Government of India was ready to concede some ground to get the Congress back into the constitution-making process, it patently could not do so at the cost of their (the government's) provincial allies.

When this Delhi Pact (also often called Gandhi–Irwin Pact) was signed, it appeared that the Congress had gained a good deal more than the government had actually intended to concede. Another unintended message that reached rural India was that the Congress had won a great victory, therefore, '*Ram Raj*'[39] was now not far. The Civil Disobedience Movement, having been suspended the situation was now under control of the government, but then a simultaneous suspension of the coercive powers of the government opened many other avenues for the Congress to reassert its influence. Many leading Congressmen thereupon seized the opportunity, particularly when on 10 March 1931, Jawaharlal Nehru through a circular, communicated to the Congress rank and file that this Pact was 'a truce only and no final peace'.[40] 'Just before the Pact,' bemoaned the collector of Allahabad 'things were improving and the rent was [again] beginning to come in and it appeared that the 'no-rent' campaign was shortly to be broken. But then,' he continued, '[this] Pact has had an extremely bad effect. It was being construed as a victory for the tenants. The payment of rent has [again] fallen'. Though the Congress had undertaken to discontinue this campaign, in reality it continued, and effectively, for which tenant farmer would give up a share of his hard-earned labour if he could avoid paying it altogether.

The Muslim Conference particularly, and the Muslims generally, had a vague sense of having in some manner been 'betrayed'. Added to this was a sense of hurt and outrage about some serious communal rioting in the United Provinces that occurred around this time, and which left a traumatic effect on the entire north Indian Muslim mind. All this made the Muslim Conference more strident in its demands, wanting, for the first time that fundamental rights should be made justiciable; that Muslims be subject only to their own personal law in all matters relating to religious observances; and that no government should, at any time, have any powers to alter this law. These were grave developments, of deep import. They demonstrated the anxiety of minority province Muslims, illustrating simultaneously a growing convergence, yet again, of the political and the religious. Hand in hand with these went other demands designed to widen still further the scope of provincial autonomy. A striking example of this was an outlandish proposal, put forward in all seriousness, though not formally, by Firoz Khan Noon that the army be also provincialised. His suggestion was that the control of the army should not, post British devolution of power, pass on to the Centre, devolving instead to the provinces, for should there be communal disorders, what if the army remained at the beck and call of the Hindus, who, he feared, could then be in control of the Centre'. The Muslims of Punjab and the Unionist Party were beginning to see this devolution of power to the Centre more as a threat, not only to its provincial political interests but also to its privileged position in the Imperial military machine.

Just as the government had made some conciliatory gestures to the Congress, in turn, the Congress had also begun making conciliatory moves towards the Muslims. By the terms of the Delhi Pact, Gandhi had committed himself to attending the Second Round Table Conference and obviously assessed that his position would be strengthened if he could reach London as the communicator of the demands of a united India. Which is why after the Pact had been signed, he (Gandhi) began to say that it would be useless to go to London without a prior settlement of the communal question; that he was prepared to give the Muslims all they wanted as a prize for an agreement; though it is doubtful whether Gandhi himself was convinced of the Congress supporting such a proposal when the Non-Cooperation Movement had itself been a statement that a joint demand by the two communities was not feasible. Nevertheless, pursuing this objective Gandhi did meet the Muslim Conference Working Committee, in Delhi, early in April 1931 but the talks soon got deadlocked, as they had done earlier in London, and again principally over the question of separate electorates. The existing differences within the Congress, and between the Congress and the Nationalist Muslims, prevented him from making any concessions at all.

On the communal question, therefore, by May 1931, Gandhi proposed that Lord Irwin himself ought now to arbitrate, endeavouring all this while to maintain the Congress' claim as a representative of the whole of India but without involving it in negotiations for a settlement. This was a real dilemma, for were the Congress to shut doors on negotiations, its position would suffer in London, and if it got involved in negotiations then that would divide their own support base.

There were, no doubt, Muslims within the Muslim Conference, as also in the Congress who were prepared to work for and achieve a settlement. The Conference Khilafatists, too, were not averse to a settlement with the Congress. The urban constitutionalists of Punjab showed a similar inclination. Muhammad Shafi's advocacy in the Round Table Conference had further enraged the Unionists, besides, their (Unionist's) ascendancy in the Punjab in the 1920s had not benefited the settlement seekers in any manner. To some extent, even Iqbal fell into the same category, he was an urban Muslim of Kashmiri descent, he commanded a popular poet's enormous appeal but had little in common with the bulk of the Unionists and, was therefore, prepared to consider a settlement with the Congress if that secured advantage to the Muslims. However, unlike Muhammad Shafi, Iqbal was amenable to Fazli Hussain's influence and thus became an important factor in subsequent negotiations.

Muslims in the Congress, all committed to a united India keenly sought a settlement. For people like Ansari, Khaliquzzaman and Sherwani the going so far had all along been difficult but they had stoutly refused to be browbeaten by the Ali brothers and had continued to work with the Congress. The Lahore Session of the Congress in 1929, where the Nehru Report of 1928, had been allowed to lapse had greatly disillusioned them. It was over this very report that they had broken with so many of their co-religionists and friends. *Purna Swaraj* (complete freedom) was now to be attained through a civil disobedience movement in which Muslims would obviously not figure prominently, and for the duration of the agitation, negotiations for any communal settlement would inevitably get suspended. This frustration led, early in 1930, for Ansari, Khaliquzzaman and Sherwani to resign their respective posts in the Congress, remaining but ordinary *'four anna'* [41] members. Sherwani even made some attempts to come to terms with the Muslim League, endeavouring simultaneously to somehow get the Congress back into a conciliatory mode. For the Congress Muslims this Gandhi–Irwin Pact was therefore, a very welcome development.

Though Muslim members of the Congress took a lead in attempting a settlement in April 1931, they remained firm on the question of electorates, wanting the measure and method of representation in the federal and provincial legislatures to be settled on the basis of joint electorates and adult suffrage. Accordingly, a Round Table Conference of all Muslim organisations was suggested. For the Muslim Conference this initiative was potentially dangerous, Fazli Hussain did not want to be involved in discussing such terms as would imply that the existing demands of the Conference were negotiable. He, therefore, tried closing ranks on these issues and also dissuaded Iqbal and Shafi from holding separate parleys with Nationalist Muslims. Despite Fazli Hussain's advice, Shafi, Iqbal, Shaukat Ali and others did meet the Nationalist Muslims but no recognisable agreement emerged from that. At such a meeting with the Nationalist Muslims on 19 June 1931, a formula agreeable to Fazli Hussain of continued weightage in minority provinces and recognition of Muslim majorities in Punjab and Bengal, but with no adult suffrage and no joint electorates[42] was mooted for negotiation. This non-starter brought the negotiations with the Nationalist Muslims to an end.

It is in this overall context that the agreement between Irwin and Gandhi has to be seen. The pact had created a semblance of a lull, following as it did those turbulent days of the Civil Disobedience Movement, all that generated discord and high emotions. This pact had been endorsed by the Karachi Congress practically unanimously, but in an atmosphere of continuing hostility towards the British regime. The fact that the viceroy had entered into an agreement with the Congress had created in the rank and file of the Congress an illusion of triumph, not any mood of cooperation with the Raj but as was then commonly remarked 'a spirit of defiant triumphalism'.

There were doubts about Gandhi's participation in the Round Table Conference till almost literally the last minute. This delay of course, raised anxiety but also spawned a crop of speculative theories: there were hitches; there were moral difficulties that Gandhi had voiced; the officials were breaking the pact; the Hindu-Muslim problem had to be solved first: there had been a change of heart with Gandhi (which he often did have), or worse, the British had had a change of heart, so on and so forth. Gandhi had, indeed, threatened a breakdown of this truce on grounds of his 'conscience'. On the other hand, that initial euphoria over the Gandhi–Irwin Pact had begun to wane, as was inevitable, and always happens when untenable initial expectations meet with reality. Consequently, these Congress tactics then came in for a great deal of questioning by the public, Gandhi tried to meet this complex situation by sending out a chargesheet against local officials alleging breaches of the Delhi Pact. Willingdon's, (for by then he had replaced Irwin as viceroy), reply to the chargesheet was an immediate and an unequivocal refusal to let anyone interfere with the working of His Majesty's Government. The situation at once became tense: the political atmosphere got surcharged, again. Anxious conversations between Lord Willingdon and Gandhi followed, The time was approaching for the Indian delegates to leave for the Round Table Conference but the last train for the boat to England had already left; Willingdon's conversations had grown tense and after the tension had reached a peak, the situation made intensely dramatic, suddenly Gandhi announced his agreement with Willingdon's offer. A special train, waiting, rushed him to Bombay. Willingdon had sacrificed no vital position nor surrendered any interests of the government. 'What had Gandhi gained?

THE SECOND ROUND TABLE CONFERENCE—BACKDROP

In the meantime, the international context for negotiations turned unexpectedly adverse during this Second Round Table conference. A number of commentators, (amongst them Wells and Lloyd Rudolph have observed): 'The collapse of the world economy with the onset of a world economic depression, particularly as the depression affected the two largest economies, the British and the US, precipitated the abandonment of the gold standard first in Britain [21 September 1931], later in the US [January 1933], where rapidly rising unemployment, and sharp declines in national income resulted.* MacDonald's Labour government resigned on 24 August. He then formed a national coalition government of Conservatives, Liberals, and Labourites. This, too, resigned on 27 October 1931, two-thirds of the way through the second Round Table Conference, necessitating fresh elections'. The general election of October 1931 returned MacDonald's coalition with a majority and this government, dominated by the Conservatives, unsympathetic, to an extent even hostile to Indian aspirations for self-government, continued until the next general election of June 1935.

Barely had the world recovered from the great depression and the demise of the Gold Standard when the Second World War broke out; the world was now caught in yet another global conflict. This outbreak of war in September 1939 launched an endgame that eventually resulted in India's Partition and Independence. It is for all these reasons that the Second Round Table Conference of 1931 became so very ill-timed. It was taking place in the background of loss of jobs in Britain, rising unemployment, collapse of a coalition and the ensuing general elections. Indian constitutional discussions unavoidably then got pushed into the background, in consequence, the conference lurched about aimlessly in uncertain anxiety, to such an extent that Muslim delegates threatened a walk-out being persuaded finally, to stay but only on a watching brief. The return, after the elections, of a government dominated by the Conservatives gave currency to fresh rumours about the real designs of this new government. Despite all these discouraging circumstances, the conference did meet but rather irregularly, relegating its various committees to the task of dealing mostly with procedural irrelevancies. This was not just untidy; it was a shabby way of dealing with India's problems. For days together the open session of the conference could not even be convened, and when at last it did take place that, ironically, happened to be Gandhi's 'day of silence'. This was on 30 November 1931; the conference began in the morning, but all through the long

---

*A similar economic meltdown rook place in September–November 2008.

speech-making that followed few would come to grips with burning constitutional issues, and when finally at midnight, Gandhi broke his silence, sadly his speech offered nothing, only as a commentator put it 'righteous bitterness'. No doubt was left thereafter that the Congress would soon be reverting to civil disobedience.

In any event, hostility with the Muslim Conference had got sharpened from the very start when Gandhi had attempted to take Ali Imam and M.A. Ansari as Congress nominees. The Muslim Conference predictably, treated this move as a deliberate attempt to undermine its Islamic credentials as the comprehensive representative of the Muslims. These fruitless contentions did give Fazli Hussain the needed leverage to secure Ansari's exclusion from the Congress team. This Round Table Conference did not produce any surprises either. With Gandhi refusing to take part in any discussion on the communal question, except as a mediator, the situation was only marginally different from what it had been in 1930. As on the previous occasion, the Liberal lot from India found the Muslim delegation prepared to come to terms but once again Punjab proved to be an insurmountable barrier to any general agreement.

The Aga Khan remembers Gandhi reaching London in November 1931, as the sole representative of the Congress accompanied by Sarojini Naidu. While describing his meeting with Gandhi he recollected:

> It took place in our capacity as delegates to the Second Round Table Conference and occurred at midnight in my own room at the Ritz Hotel. We posed together for the press photographers, and then settled down to our conversation. I opened it by saying to Mahatmaji that were he now to show himself a real father to India's Muslims, they would respond by helping him, to the utmost of their ability, in his struggle for India's independence, Mahatmaji turned to face me. 'I cannot in truth say,' he observed, 'that I have any feelings of paternal love for Muslims. But if you put the matter on grounds of political necessity, I am ready to discuss it in a co-operative spirit. I cannot indulge in any form of sentiment'.

This would be characteristically impish, also perhaps humorous but for the cold douche at the very outset that it became. The chill that this created, writes the Aga Khan 'pervaded the rest of our conversation. I felt that, whereas I had given prompt and ready evidence of a genuine emotional attachment and kinship, there had been no similar response from the Mahatmaji'. The Aga Khan then continues:

Years later—in 1940—I reminded him of this. He said that he completely recollected the episode. 'I am very, very sorry,' he said then, 'that you misunderstood that answer of mine. I didn't mean that I was aware of no emotional attachment, no feeling for the welfare of Muslims. I only meant that I was conscious of full blood brotherhood, yes, but not of the superiority that fatherhood would imply.'

'And I, on my side,' 'had only meant in that word 'father' to show respect for the frailty of his age—nor, of course, frailty in health or mental capacity—and not to him at any superiority.'

This unfortunate initial misunderstanding over words had more than a transient effect. It created an impression, which persisted not just that night but throughout the Round Table Conference, wrote the Aga Khan 'that our attempts to reach a Muslim- Hindu entente were purely political and without the stabilizing emotional ties of long fellow citizenship and admiration for one another's civilisation and culture. Thus there could be no cordiality about any entente we might achieve; we were driven back to cold politics, with none of the inspiring warmth of emotional understanding to suffuse and strengthen our discussions'.

He was right in arriving at such a conclusion, sad but accurate.

On the Second Round Table Conference proper the Aga Khan goes on to say: [These are a part of his memoirs, no doubt subjective as the Aga Khan's own observations are. I recount them here because they transport vividly a feel of those times, certainly in the Conference and of the Conferees.]

This preliminary talk did not take us far. Thereafter we had a further series of conversations—usually at midnight in my rooms at the Ritz—I myself presiding as host, and Mr Jinnah and Sir Mohammad Shafi negotiating on one side, and Mahatma Gandhi on the other. They were informal talks and no record was kept. I said little and left the bulk of the discussion to Mr Jinnah and Sir Mohammad Shafi, and to other delegates who from time to time took part, notably Sir Zafrullah Khan, Mr Shaukat Ali and the late Shaff'at Ali Khan…Always the argument returned to certain basic points of difference: Was India a nation or two nations? Was Islam merely a religious minority, or were Muslims in those areas in which they were in a majority to have and to hold special political rights and responsibilities? The Congress attitude seemed to us doctrinaire and unrealistic. They held stubbornly to their one-nation theory, which we knew to be historically insupportable. We maintained that before the coming of the British Raj the various regions of the Indian subcontinent had never been one country, that the Raj had created an artificial and transient unity, and that when the Raj went, that unity could not be preserved and the diverse peoples, with their profound racial and religious differences, could not remain fellow-sleepers for all time but they would awake and go their separate ways...However close, therefore, we might come to agreement on points of detail, this ultimate disagreement on principle could not be bridged....

He adds: 'The Mahatma sought to impose a first and fundamental condition: that the Muslims should, before they asked for any guarantees for themselves, accept Congress' interpretation of swaraj—self-government—as their goal. To which Mr Jinnah very rightly answered that since the Mahatma was not imposing this condition on the other Hindu members of the various delegations attending the Round Table, why should he impose it on the Muslims? Here was another heavy handicap...Jinnah then further argued: 'Our conditions were the same throughout; very few powers at the Centre, except in respect of defence and external affairs; all other powers to be transferred, and especially to those provinces in which there were Muslim majorities—the Punjab, Bengal, Sind, Baluchistan and the Northwest Frontier. We were adamant because we knew that the majority of the Muslims who lived in Bengal and the Punjab were adamant'. To which the Aga Khan adds: 'Mahatma Gandhi fully recognised the importance of having us in his camp. Who knows?—perhaps he might have seen his way to accept our viewpoint, but Pundit Malaviya and the Hindu Mahasabha exerted great pressure against us, deploying arguments based on abstract political doctrines and principles which, as the partition of 1947 proved, were totally unrelated to the realities of India.

As time went on such hair-splitting became finer and finer, the arguments more and more abstract: a nation could not hand over unspecified powers to its provinces; there was no constitutional way of putting a limit on the devices by which a majority could be turned into a minority—fascinating academic issues, but with little or no connection with the real facts and figures of Indian life'.

If Begum Shah Nawaz, representative to the Second Round Table Conference and the daughter of Muhammad Shafi is to be relied upon, in her recollection of events she records:

There was a time when the Muslims and Liberals had agreed amongst themselves, and a settlement did indeed seem possible. Shafi had ordered sweets and drinks and the Muslim delegates had assembled in the Aga Khan's rooms at the Ritz to celebrate the occasion. But the party failed to start. For Gandhi, who had gone to secure the agreement of the Sikhs and the Hindu Mahasabha, came back without it. He said upon return, "Gentlemen, I am sorry to report that I have failed in my efforts for settlement. The Sikhs and the Mahasabhaites are not prepared to accept the terms proposed by us."

'There was a hush in the room, '…and most of us felt like shedding bitter tears'. Shafi had an alternative proposal. He said to Gandhi, "Let us, the Muslims and the Congress come to a settlement tonight on these very terms." Gandhi replied, "Shafi, I know my limitations and I cannot do it." And so the party broke up. Shafi and his daughter returned home, "and when we reached our flat, father broke down completely and fainted".[43]

Gandhi's refusal to commit himself to terms which the Hindu Mahasabha and Sikhs would not accept was part of the same policy which he had followed in India in the summer of 1931. He was prepared to be a mediator but would not (could not?) take sides. Gandhi knew the power of a communal appeal, and he also knew what it would mean for Congress if he committed himself publicly to stand against Hindu demands. Under the existing electoral system, and until such time as it did not become clear as to what concessions were actually forthcoming, such a public stand would only mean loss of support for the Congress. It was far better, Gandhi must have calculated, to let the government make the decision and carry the attendant unpopularity rather than get the Congress into doing it. And so having been through the ordeal of negotiations with other delegates, Gandhi put the ball firmly back into the government's court. In the Minorities Sub-Committee, he confessed to being sad and humiliated by his failure to produce a settlement, but he attributed it to the fact that the delegation had been selected by the government. What, in effect, he wanted to say was that it was the government which was demanding communal agreement as the price for discussing political concessions, but such an agreement would be possible only if the government *first* announced the concessions. How sad, how ironic and how utterly tragic this circular hair splitting—'Have a 'communal' agreement and then get concessions', said the Raj; 'No, announce the concessions first then we will agree amongst ourselves as communities', was the rejoinder.

Not long after this Second Round Table Conference had ended, the Congress resumed Civil Disobedience that, in any event, was inherent in the very logic of the situation. Despite all outward show of conciliation, a polarisation of political forces at the provincial level, had by 1928, so divided Indian politics into clearly opposing communal camps that it all seemed futile. For a brief period, and that, too only after the Gandhi–Irwin Pact, both the Congress and the government had adopted more flexible positions, but alas, that was a very brief episode.

In India, before the Second Round Table Conference, Congress had doubtless gained more. However, in London, the advantage reverted to the Imperial Government, it succeeded in making the Congress look like just another body, amongst the many that were then relevant, and this strengthened the Raj's hands in Britain, particularly when the next period of repression in India began. As for the Muslims, the Round Table Conference did nothing to safeguard their position. They were now no longer sure that if and when a decision did finally come, it would be in their favour, which is why as the 'Communal Award'[44] approached, they too, turned belligerent.

When Gandhi returned to India, the main issue before the government was the Congress party's cooperation in further constitutional discussions. But so long as the 'no-rent' activities in the United Provinces, and preparation for conflict[45] in the NWFP continued, cooperation was just not possible. Within six months, therefore, the government's authority got completely re-established; no-rent campaign in the United Provinces died down, and the agitation in the Frontier was suppressed. It was time, therefore, to act.

Gandhi was imprisoned on 4 January 1932 and lodged in the Yeravada jail. Within a few days of his imprisonment, the Indian liberals issued a manifesto demanding his release. Other parties, too, followed suit. The press also clamoured for Gandhi's release. However, Willingdon would not agree, not until the Civil Disobedience Movement had first been withdrawn. This clamour for Gandhi's release continued in the press, in the legislature and even on the floors of the House of Commons, till Sir Samuel Hoare made a statement in the Commons that: 'there will be no question of making [any] bargain with the Congress as a condition of its co-operation'.[46]

The Second Round Table Conference had ended towards the end of 1931, and had thrown up several issues requiring resolution. In consequence, three committees were set up to consult Indian public opinion on questions of 'franchise'; 'finance': and the 'position of the [Princely] states' under a federal constitution. The Franchise Committee under Lord Lothian toured the whole country taking evidence whereafter it recommended a marked increase of the electorate, from seven to thirty-six million: property, though, remained the main qualification apart from education. Special electorates were also created for women. The Federal Finance Committee, with Sir Eustace Percy as chairman, submitted its report in May 1932 laying out an elaborate financial arrangement for the federal and provincial governments, which it was hoped, will assure a smooth working of the new constitution. The States Committee traced the origin and development of the political relationship between the states and the British Indian government and laid down broad principles for a future settlement.

Under the chairmanship of the viceroy a Consultative Committee, composed of nineteen representative member of the Round Table Conference was thereafter formed in early 1932, to work out the details of federation. Its working continued to be considerably hampered because of some Muslim members refusing to discuss any proposals until the Communal Award had been announced. This Muslim reluctance was born of an apprehension that central responsibility would be conceded on terms favouring the Congress party and Muslim interests either ignored or certainly neglected. Willingdon, by January 1933, smoothed over their (Muslim) doubts about participating in the Consultative Committee but while agreeing to serve, they refused to discuss any question that related to devolution of power at the Centre unless their demands had also been met. By the end of February 1932, this effectively brought the Committees' work to a halt, whereafter, Willingdon had no alternative but to adjourn proceedings. The other committees were similarly affected, though, their work did, to an extent, facilitate the convening of the Third Round Table Conference.

Communal Award

In the second session of the Second Round Table Conference Gandhi had opposed separate electorates to any other than the Muslims and had taken a very determined stand against reservation of seats for the Harijans. Upon return to India, an agreed solution to this vexed question of communal representation had to be found. Under such circumstances, in August 1932, Prime Minister Ramsay MacDonald announced a Communal Award. This proposed, among other things, a reservation of a number of seats for the Depressed Classes, (as the Harijans/Dalits were then termed) in a special constituency, and a specified number of reserved seats. Five months before the publication of the award, Gandhi had written to the secretary of state intimating his resolve to resist with his life any establishment of separate electorates for the depressed classes. This, he held, would drive a wedge through the Hindu society and actually accentuate further degradation of the 'depressed'. On 18 August 1932, the day following the announcement of the award, Gandhi confirmed to the prime minister his earlier decision and announced that unless, by 20 September, this award, as affecting the 'Harijans',[47] was not amended he would enter upon a fast unto death, 'as an atonement'.[48]

On the appointed day, Gandhi entered upon his fast. This roused the whole of India; days for national fasts were announced; national prayer days were also declared and the entire country witnessed packed meetings, again, after a gap of just eight months. The final outcome of all this was an agreement, reserving 148 seats for Harijans, as against the earlier proposed 'separate constituencies', as had been announced by MacDonald.

Willingdon was, by now, clearly a worried man: he decided that under the circumstances the only practical solution was to strengthen the Central Government by introducing greater degree of responsibility. From November 1931 to March 1932 this became the principal theme of his correspondence with Sir Samuel Hoare, then the secretary of state for India.

Just as Willingdon's efforts to strengthen the Centre illustrates one side of the Imperial dilemma, his determination to win back Muslim support explains the other. The Muslim Conference had also given an ultimatum, until the end of June 1932, demanding a clear announcement of the decision on Reforms, failing which they, too, would launch a direct action programme. It became clear then that no further constitutional progress was possible without a settlement. The fear was that irrespective of what was finally decided upon, the Raj would become weaker. Therefore, the questions confronting the viceroy were stark: was Muslim provincialism to be encouraged? What then, of the Centre? Strengthening the Centre further having been rejected, the only alternative was to strengthen the provinces. This amounted to granting a victory to Punjab and for Muslim provincialism, thus no gain for Jinnah and his politics, and of no benefit to the Congress either. In such a backdrop, the third Round Table Conference got announced.

The secretary of state on 27 June 1932, made an announcement in the House of Commons, that since it would require time for the proposed Indian federation to be constituted, responsibility in the provinces would now be instituted without waiting for the completion of all steps required for the actual inauguration of federation. The secretary of state also proposed setting up a Joint Parliamentary Committee, which would invite representatives of Indian opinion to examine the reform proposals before they were formally introduced in Parliament.

This outraged the Liberals in the UK, who took it as an affront, concluding that the conference method was being abandoned and joint consultations and deliberations ended. The Labour Opposition took the same view. The Indian press, notably the element that had declared for a boycott of the conference and had the strongest moral and spiritual affinity with the Disobedience Movement, was loud in condemning the announcement. Resignations from the Liberal members of Consultative and other committees soon followed. The government could not alienate that section of Indian opinion which had stood by them. On 5 September the government, therefore, announced that select representatives of British India and the states would again be invited to a conference in London, and that this would be around the middle of November 1932. The threatening clouds that had so ominously gathered in the Indian sky equally quickly dispersed.

THE THIRD ROUND TABLE CONFERENCE (1932): THE BACKDROP

The Third Round Table Conference was a business-like body, smaller in composition, free of rhetorical discourses and learned enunciations about political principles which had so hindered the preceding conference's deliberations, the picture though, was still not encouraging. The interests involved were so varied, the differences so much more accented, instead of having been whittled by time that consequently the delegates dispersed with the most important questions left unsettled. However, neither Britain nor India could afford to waste any further time, enough opportunities had already been given to the parties concerned to formulate some agreed proposals, reasoned the British but without results. The conference ended and the participants left without coming to any final decisions. The Indian liberals came back dissatisfied; the princes came back, at least some of them, like so many doubting 'Thomases'. The viceroy could grasp the significance of the atmosphere, but he simply could not allow it to fester. Therefore, the first step he took was to call all the delegates for lengthy interviews, to see how the Indian liberals and others views could be accommodated in the proposed constitution.

Jinnah had attended only the first of the two sessions of this conference. The Third would not even have taken place, but for the strong stand taken by the Hindu liberal leaders of India, especially Sapru and Jayakar. Samuel Hoare, then secretary of state for India, yielded to the pressure of these Indian liberals. However, the selection of the Indian delegates to this session had been made carefully so that only conservative and provincial elements could be present. Jinnah stood no chance for selection at this session or for the Joint Parliamentary Committee. He was not even invited to give evidence before the Parliamentary Committee, while many Indians and Britons were. However, there is no reason to doubt that Jinnah would have agreed to serve on the third session of the conference, and also to be a delegate to the Parliamentary Committee, or be a witness before this Committee if such an offer had been made to him by the government. After all, despite disappointments at the conference he had not withdrawn and had continued to work till the end at both sessions of the conference.

Though Gandhi did not attend the Third Round Table Conference, there was present a sizeable element of advanced Indian nationalists drawn from outside the ranks of Congress. Looking back on what happened during the course of this conference, the Aga Khan regretted Jinnah's absence as much as that of Gandhi. It was, he said, 'extremely unfortunate that we Muslims did not insist on having Mr Jinnah with us; had he been a member of the delegation he might have subscribed to what I consider was the most valuable result of these Round Table Conferences'. That, according to the Aga Khan, was: 'the Joint Memorandum, which—for the first time in the history of Indo-British relations—put before the British Government a united demand on behalf of all communities, covering practically every important political point at issue. It propounded what would have been, in effect, a major step forward—the penultimate step indeed before Dominion Status. By it we sought to ensure continuity in the process of the further transfer of responsibility. It was signed by all the non-official Indian delegates. It was a claim for the transfer to Indian hands of practically every power except certain final sanctions which would be reserved to the British Government. Had a constitution been granted along these lines, later critical situations—declaration of war in 1939, the problems which faced the Cripps Mission in 1942, and the final and total transfer of authority—might all have been much less difficult. Had this constitution been fully established, it would have, in due course, been comparatively a simple operation to lop off those reserve powers which in the draft marked the final stage of constitutional devolution.

Was the Aga Khan being too optimistic in recollection? Or unrealistic? Such speculation is no longer relevant for events were moving almost autonomously, agreement or not. In any event during the course of evidence that the Aga Khan gave before the Joint Committee on the Government of India Bill, he submitted: 'I accept the term "Responsible Government", though as an ideal my preference is for self-government... But the facts of the situation have to be recognized..."Responsible Government" must be our way toward evolving in the future some plan more suited to a Congress of great states, such as India will become, and I believe the way will be found in something akin to the American federal plan'. He further added, 'Despite all (as we thought) its merits, our Joint Memorandum was disowned by Congress, and therefore the British government felt compelled in their turn to reject it'. However, these then were the Aga Khan's views, they could hardly be central to the tormented pulls and pushes of the political streets of British India; or indeed even in the durbars of the princely states.

Having been so excluded from these constitutional discussions, Jinnah spent the major part of the years 1932-34 in England. Was this a self-imposed exile? A retirement from Indian political life, or what? He bought himself a spacious house in the then fashionable Hampstead and enrolled his only child Dina in a private school nearby. About this being a self-imposed exile a great deal of speculation persists. Such an interpretation though, would grossly misread Jinnah's resolve and his committed nationalism. There were some factors though, personal and public, which made him stay in London, more as break, a kind of a sabbatical. He was, of course, by then in a kind of a political 'no man's land' (Wells) but there was his serious disagreement with Willingdon, too, Indeed, he had mentioned to Durga Das, 'I came away to London because I did not wish to meet that wretched Viceroy'.[49]

This was obviously an afterthought for the animosity was old standing. Jawaharlal Nehru's virulent dislike of Jinnah and his constant stream of correspondence with Gandhi, adversial to Muslim interests turned him cynical towards both the Congress and the British Civil Service, for he had come to learn of their disinclination to serve under Indian ministers. Nehru, on the other hand, was scathing in his critical observances; to illustrate: 'Jawaharlal's reaction was sharp when Jinnah had informed the conference on 5 September 1931 that: "The new constitution should provide for reasonable guarantees to Muslims and if they are not provided, the new constitution is sure to break down".'[50] Jawaharlal branded this 'an amazing farrago of nonsense and narrow-minded communalism'.[51] He was even more scathing in his condemnation of 'Jinnah's ridiculous 14 points'.[52] By the end of September, Jinnah's continued demand that his Fourteen Points be accepted in their entirety had brought Jawaharlal's biting sarcasm to the surface: 'I wonder if any purgatory would be more dreadful for me than to carry on in this way. If I had to listen to my dear friend Mohammad Ali Jinnah talking the most unmitigated nonsense about his 14 points for any length of time I would consider the desirability of retiring to the South Sea Islands where there would be some hope of meeting with some people who were intelligent enough or ignorant enough not to talk of the 14 points.'[53]

How, in reality, could there be any effective Jinnah-led League and a Nehru-led Congress? A parting, a partition had to come, eventually.

Besides there was also the personal aspect. Jinnah's personal life, with the radiance of his romantic marriage to young Ruttie (Ratanbai Petit)—had begun to sour under the unyielding glare and heat of the political demands of India's freedom struggle. His marriage needed time and attention, but then so did his commitment to India's Independence. In consequence his personal life suffered. Ruttie and he both went through great pain, they separated and yet he maintained a close relationship with her. She, after a long illness, died in 1929; his own health then began to suffer greatly, he was after all already in his late fifties, was a chain smoker and under great political stress. Besides, he now had the responsibility of a child. He needed a break, a change, a different environment, at least for sometime.

Sorely disappointed by the Round Table Conferences, the impasse in Hindu-Muslim relations and the stolid immobility of the imperial British, made Jinnah reflect and question where his life was now headed. 'Make an attempt at joining British politics through a membership of the House?' he mused, and though attracted temporarily by the idea, he realised, no British party would accept him, he was already too 'big' for them, besides India always beckoned, continuously.

Soon after the publication of a White Paper on Indian Constitutional Reform in March 1933, he publicly expressed his views on it, in London. Here he evaluated the proposals contained in this Paper for political progress in India, criticised the powers and functions of the governor-general and provincial governors and the numerous safeguards contained in it, pointing out the difficulty in setting up the all-India federation under the scheme. He reacted with an oft-quoted note: 'I am convinced that there is no hope for India without real and genuine Hindu-Muslim unity which can only be achieved by Hindus who are in a majority. There must be a real change of heart. It is then alone that India will command respect all over the world and her voice will become really effective. It is futile to expect important changes favourable to India from the Select Committee as long as India is divided.' His deepest disappointment was this continuing failure to achieve Hindu-Muslim unity. In a later speech, in 1938, to the students of Aligarh Anglo-Muslim College he had poured his anguish:

I received the shock of my life at the... meetings of the Round Table Conference, I saw the face of danger, the Hindu sentiment, the Hindu mind, the Hindu attitude led me to the conclusion that there was no hope of unity. I felt very pessimistic about my country. The position was most unfortunate. The Mussalmans were like dwellers in No-Man's Land: they were led by either the flunkeys of the British government or the camp followers of the Congress. Whenever attempts were made to organise the Muslims, toadies and flunkeys on the one hand, and traitors in the Congress camp on the other, frustrated the efforts. I began to feel that neither could I help India, nor change the Hindus' mentality; nor could I make the Mussalmans realise their precarious position. I felt so disappointed and so depressed that I decided to settle down in London. Not that I did not love India, but I felt so utterly helpless.[54]

This is a moving admission, whatever the merits and demerits of its contents.

After an interval of two months during August and September 1933, the Joint Parliamentary Committee sat, in collaboration with the Indian delegates, and heard over 120 witnesses. Among those from Britain and India who tendered their evidence before the Committee and held extreme views were Sir Michael O'Dwyer, Winston Churchill and Dr B.S. Moonje. The reports of much that was said by these witnesses must have increased Jinnah's frustration. He came to India in January 1934, in a gloomy mood. Speaking at a meeting held in his honour, at Bombay, on 20 January 1934, by the Bombay Muslim Students' Union under the chairmanship of M.C. Chagla, Jinnah expressed his inability 'to see any light' and asked his audience as to 'what is it that I can do?' He again lamented the absence of political harmony in India and repeated his plea for unity:

There was not one crystallised object before the country to be presented before the British government. There was not one organisation which could claim to speak for the (sic) united India, and there was not one leader behind whom the whole country was prepared to stand. Unless, therefore the leaders in the country forgot their differences and reviewed the situation afresh, there was the danger of this 'White Paper being foisted on India....

Unless you forget your visions of the distant future and think of the immediate danger and unless you achieve unity, there is no hope, and the British Raj must control the essential departments of this country.

Before returning to England, Jinnah stayed in India for four months—from January to April 1934, during which time he worked towards that very unity which he had urged before the Muslim students of Bombay. On the initiative of the Aga Khan, who was also in India at this time, the split that had occurred in the Muslim League in 1927 was now repaired, whereupon, in February 1934, Jinnah announced his willingness to accept the office of the president of the Muslim League. Then, having finished with the preliminaries of the reorganisation of the League, he again made a bid to settle the communal question. He devised a new communal formula under which he offered to the Hindus acceptance of separate electorates provided in the Communal Award 'for the present on the understanding that, after a period to be agreed upon, joint electorates was to be substituted for separate electorates'. Negotiations between Jinnah and Pandit Madan Mohan Malaviya ensued immediately thereafter. However, these negotiations too, broke down soon. The interests of the provinces had cropped up again, particularly the representation of Muslims in the Punjab and Bengal provincial legislatures. Jinnah issued a long statement in which he gave details of the negotiations with Pandit Malaviya and left for England in April 1934. The Report of the Parliamentary Committee was published in November 1934. It was also the time when elections to the Legislative Assembly were held and Jinnah was elected to the Assembly unopposed from the Muhammadan Urban-Bombay City constituency. He returned to India in December 1934, to resume his political activities at a time when the constitutional discussions in London had come to an end and the centre of gravity of the political scene had shifted back to India. A new scenario was now developing, there was a new force that was emerging in Europe—Nazi Germany. Besides, by now, he was being invited by the Muslim League factions to preside over a unified Muslim League, as S.S. Pirzada has recorded in his edited work *Foundations* (Vol. II, pp. 194-228). 'The very same Fazli Hussain who in 1930 had written that Jinnah was doing mischief at the R.T.C. [22 December 1930, Fazli Hussain's Diary, papers Vol. 6] now invited Jinnah writing to him to say that "Muslim India cannot afford to lose you. Men of clear vision, independent judgement and strength of character are very few".'[55]

Percival Spear in his essay *'Jinnah, The Creator of Pakistan'* had observed 'Bolitho in his writings did comment that Jinnah had apparently greatly damaged his political career in the twenties by standing up as a champion of Hindu-Muslim Unity. His return to India in 1934 was thus saddled with this thought, also rather a forlorn hope. Which is why he resisted Iqbal's persuasive separatism until the Congress had made it clear that there could be no political cooperation with the League only a kind of subordination or absorption. What finally made Jinnah a "communalist" was this Congress totalitarianism; "Congress *hubris* rather than Jinnah's wounded vanity precipitated" the great change of approach'.

5

A SHORT DECADE—A LONG END GAME

THE MUSLIM LEAGUE—1935

The Muslim League that Mohammad Ali Jinnah was invited to preside over was no dynamic political instrument. In this League of 1935-36, all the top rungs of leadership were almost entirely occupied by titled gentry, nawabs, zamindars and the inevitable time servers and favour seekers found in all political organisations, whether of those times, or with appropriate variations of the current generation. This leadership did want to serve the Muslim cause but only so long as it did not affect their own individual positions adversely in any manner, socially or with the imperial authorities. In any event from its very birth in 1906, the Muslim League's activities had almost always been indoor; genteel, polite discussions of the *ashraf* hardly of consequence to anyone but themselves. Even its annual sessions were held either in well-decorated *pandals* or in big halls where only a few visitors were allowed entry and that, too, by invitation. Mass movements were, till then, unknown to the Muslim League. Its Central Office, upon the founding of the League in 1906 had functioned from Aligarh, where it was really an adjunct of the Muhammedan Anglo-Oriental College (MAO), and could hardly be considered a separate political body. Besides, Aligarh had been the centre of most Muslim activities, particularly political, since Sir Sayyid Ahmed's days. It was in 1910, that the League finally shifted its office to Lucknow. Its income from membership and annual subscriptions continued to remain insufficient, not enough to even maintain an office, much less organise any other activity. In Lucknow it functioned on a grant from Raja Sahib Mahmudabad, of rupees three thousand, annually. Unlike the Congress, the League, in the initial years, did not have a sufficiency of moneyed benefactors.

Of course, during the Khilafat movement days even this meagre living had dried up, then the League had barely existed and that, too, only on paper, holding its session wherever Khilafat conferences or the Congress sessions were being held. The end of the session of the League was the end of the organisation for that particular year and except in the official records of the Government of India no one else took any notice of what the 'League' had said or done. The human material was the same, as for example of the Khilafat, but no cause existed to inspire and arouse the League, or the Muslims as they had been during the Khilafat agitation of 1914-22. There was no session of the Muslim League in 1935, and as for the Khilafat Committee it, too, had long ceased to hold its sessions. This rather moribund state of the League was an accurate index of an important fact: that the real centre of gravity of Muslim politics lay in the provinces, there just was not any recognisable cause or sustainable all India activity that it could undertake.

Provincial elections were now due. With that in mind Khaliquzzaman, in February 1936, sent notices for holding a meeting of the League at Delhi. Jinnah was invited to attend, as president. It was during this meeting that the idea of merging the Muslim Unity Board with the Muslim League was discussed with Jinnah. Describing the meeting in his book *Pathway to Pakistan,* Khaliquzzaman quotes Jinnah as saying:

> I would like to see the Muslim League organisation purified and revived, and with that end in view I am going to hold a Muslim League session on 10 May 1936, at Bombay where I would ask the Muslim League to give me a mandate to form a Parliamentary Board for the forthcoming elections.... And I promise to you that in that Board I shall give people of your party a majority. If we have to fight elections on the Muslim ticket, it would not be in the interest of either of us to split our votes. Let us therefore, fight from the common platform of the Muslim League Parliamentary Board.[1]

Muslims, in 1936, were politically divided and there appeared no reasonable chance of putting up a united front for the central or the provincial legislatures through a well-knit party. This lack persuaded Jinnah to start negotiations with Maulana Ahmad Saeed, secretary of the Jamiat-ul-Ulema-i-Hind to fight the forthcoming 1937 elections on a common Muslim platform. Even that minimum could be done only if the Muslim Unity Board was to compromise with the Muslim League, as the Unity Board having won one-third of the Muslim seats in the

Central Assembly, from the 1934 elections considered itself to be the 'real Muslim platform'. For political organisations, even if already redundant, to give up standing born of demonstrated electoral success, is near impossible; and yet a satisfactory answer had to be found for the 1937 provincial elections, they were now just over the horizon. This was vital for it is not fully realised that the Muslim League between 1937-47 was the first purely political movement of the Indian Muslims. Sir Sayyid Ahmad Khan's earlier efforts had concentrated on the educational and cultural improvement of the Muslims, and not simply that he went further' and actually 'discouraged...active political participation' by the Muslims.

Jinnah was entirely political, even if not then voiced in as many words. Clearly he wanted a Muslim territory; not any Islamic state; on which issue there had simmered a difference of opinion for long between Raja Sahib Mahmudabad, the youngest member of the League working committee and himself.

Yet, because in the early thirties Muslims were hopelessly divided and the League was (still) a negligible force, in the 1937 elections it gained a mere 4.8 per cent of the Muslim vote. In Hector Bolitho's book *In Quest of Jinnah* is recorded a conversation between the author and A.B. (Sonny) Habibullah. This was on 2 April 1952, it contains Sonny Habibullah saying:

'I was one of Jinnah's first disciples in the revived Muslim League and I was with him four years, from 1936 to 1940. In 1938 or 1939, a rather Nazi-minded man addressed Jinnah as the leader of my Nation. Jinnah said, 'I may be your leader, but not of a separate nation'.

'Jinnah had a tremendous ego and was always susceptible to flattery....Up to 1943 he would tolerate, even enjoy (an) argument. But after that, when his health began to fail, he became impatient, refused to argue, and preferred 'yes men'. But his smile was always infectious, and his movement, when he threw his head back and laughed, was quite charming.

'His impatience' (was monumental); 'he discarded Mahmudabad for saying, 'My leader must not be the ablest politician, but the man who is closest to God'. He [Jinnah] eliminated Ismail Khan, President of the UP Muslim League, because he would always oppose Jinnah when he thought him wrong.'

The Elections of 1937—The Opening Moves

The British authorities, under the impression that the morale of the Congress had been broken by the prolonged detention of its leaders, seemed to view with little apprehension the outcome of the first general elections in 1937. It is not as if the Congress party was a solid phalanx of uniformly inspired members. Many Congress leaders, particularly of the Left wing, had no doubt spoken of their plans to wreck the Constitution from within. However, the party was torn by internal dissensions at the top and all the principal lieutenants of Mahatma Gandhi had threatened resignation from the Working Committee (as the party's central executive was called) unless Jawaharlal Nehru, in his capacity as the president, abandoned the policy of preaching socialism as the goal for the Congress. Even the principal leadership of the party was troubled. Nehru's European import of socialism worried them greatly. In an outspoken letter to Nehru, who was then the president of the Congress, Dr Rajendra Prasad, Sardar Patel, C. Rajagopalachari, Acharya Kripalani and other members of the working committee warned him at the end of June, 1936 in unambiguous terms:

> We are of opinion that through your speeches and those of the other socialist colleagues and the acts of other socialists, the Congress organisation has been weakened throughout the country without any compensating gain. The effect of your propaganda on the political work immediately before the nation, particularly the programme of election has been very harmful and we feel that in the situation created we cannot shoulder the responsibility of organizing and fighting the coming elections. It is not without much reluctance that we have, therefore, decided to tender our resignation from the Working Committee.

Of course, this did get resolved amicably and in time but it also demonstrated the extent of discomfort with Jawaharlal Nehru's 'Europeanised' thinking.

When, therefore, the election process started Jinnah was hopeful that an even-handed approach would perhaps keep differences between the National Agriculturalist Party (NAP) and the Muslim Unity Board manageable in the UP. He nominated both, Nawab Saheb of Chattari and Chaudhri Khaliquzzaman to the All-India Muslim League Parliamentary Board (AIMLPB) but very shortly after he had done so,

Nawab Chattari, along with Sir Muhammad Yousuf of the NAP, publicly announced their resignations issuing statements justifying their own party and explaining differences with the Muslim League.

Sir Muhammad Yousuf referred to his fear of socialism, and like Nawab Chattari took the plea that that could be combated only through joint efforts of both the Hindus and Muslims, adding that the circumstances in UP were markedly different from the rest of India. What he said about political compatibility with Khaliquzzaman's group was more explicitly stated than by Chattari. He said:

> We made it clear to you through Nawabzada Liaquat Ali Khan that it may still be possible for us to act on the Parliamentary Board but only if we were allowed to stand on the Muslim League as well as the National Agriculturist Party ticket, and further, if the fifty men representing these provinces on the League Council were allowed to set up a Provincial Parliamentary Board where our representation would be adequate. But the rules of the Parliamentary Board recently passed definitely preclude the possibility of any such cooperation among us.[2]

Jinnah, needing an all India Muslim body and platform, then held wide-ranging meetings, in Delhi, on 27 and 28 April 1936, before finally releasing a list of Parliamentary Board members. During the course of these deliberations Liaquat Ali Khan cautioned against over representation to anyone group. Then followed complicated but typical negotiations resulting in a rather complex scheme, details of it being so tedious that it is best for us not to get detained by them here. It suffices to record that after the accord names were finally announced in May 1936, by Jinnah. Predictably, soon thereafter, on 8 and 9 June, Raja Sahib Salempur and Chaudhri Khaliquzzaman raised fresh objections, this time to the terms agreed upon in Lahore.

To resolve these differences, the Raja Sahib of Mahmudabad, the Raja of Salempur and Chaudhri Khaliquzzaman met Jinnah and Liaquat Ali Khan again in Lahore, where another formula was evolved which read:

> It is agreed that all the members of the Council of the All-India Muslim League from the UP, excluding four representatives from Delhi, shall be invited to the proposed conference for the purpose of constituting Provincial Board of UP; as it is agreed that the total number should be one hundred (if possible), the remaining 44 to be nominated would be as follows: 18 by

Nawabzada Liaquat Ali Khan and 26 by Nawab Ismail Khan. This is agreed to by the members present except Mr Khaliquzzaman who says he will abide by this decision.[3]

Little wonder that this 'formula' did not end all contentious, it was near impossible to grasp its meaning, therefore, Nawab Chattari and Sir Muhammad Yousuf, who had both not been present in the second Lahore meeting sent in their resignations. Liaquat Ali Khan now suspected foul play, he feared that the Khaliquzzaman group was having a clandestine affair with the Congress. In any event some of them had, in the past, been and some were even now associated with the Congress.

Subsequent events further eroded this rather complicated and difficult to grasp Lahore formula. Raja Sahib Mahmudabad had privately informed Liaquat Ali Khan that a meeting was scheduled for 9 July 1936 to select twenty-six members of Nawab Ismail's quota. However, instead of selecting twenty-six members (as per the Lahore formula), this meeting decided instead to convene a conference of 'three hundred'! Liaquat Ali Khan protested and back went the ball to Jinnah. Before this could create further complications there followed Liaquat Ali Khan's suggestion that if a larger number of Muslims were to be invited, than had earlier been agreed to in Lahore, then the invitees must be of a 'representative character'. This was rejected. It was now his turn, the loyal Liaquat Ali to rebel. He wired Jinnah of his inability to work on the Board. He also released a statement labelling the UP Parliamentary Board as 'unrepresentative'.

It is possible to find some ground for Liaquat Ali Khan's apprehensions. With Khaliquzzaman would get inducted into the ranks of the Muslim League a group acting, in reality, as surrogates of the Congress. Rafi Ahmed Kidwai, as a matter of typical electoral tactics could well have deviously persuaded Chaudhri Khaliquzzaman, Nawab Muhammad Ismail Khan, and other Muslim Congressmen to contest the elections on the ticket of the Muslim League, (a standard practice in the electoral politics of India). The ultimate beneficiary of such trickery would only have been the Congress, and every one knew that Khaliquzzaman had been a member of the Congress party till the announcement of the elections.

In such a setting, the ideological merits of the contending factions were hardly any basis for political preference. Though the Muslim League had certainly spoken of working for electoral compatibility with the Congress, it was not prepared to obliterate itself in the process. Yet, this is precisely what Jawaharlal Nehru had demanded and Jinnah disputed, and it was precisely this, the existence of the League as a separate body, which Khaliquzzaman was now threatening. The resistance that Liaquat Ali Khan offered to Khaliquzzaman was aimed ultimately at preserving the League.

Jinnah, steering clear of such incomprehensible disputations, in his first statement, following the constitution of this All-India Muslim League Central Parliamentary Board made clear that he wanted to 'make the Board as representative as possible'. His efforts centred on 'accommodating and unifying all existing factions of the Muslim League', and even after the defection of Nawab Chattari and Sir Muhammad Yousuf he desisted taking any rigid stand, and even as these factional controversies raged Jinnah kept himself distant from them, wary of adopting any doctrinaire position. His tone remained far more conciliatory than that of lieutenants like Khaliquzzaman. According to a report of a speech he made in Calcutta:

> Jinnah referring to his critics observed that there was a feeling in one section that the Muslims would be dragged into the fold of the reactionaries. On the other hand there was misgiving among the conservative section that Muslims might be led by Jinnah to the Congress or [the] extreme left. Jinnah replied that the 'Muslims alone should judge for themselves where to go. Why should the critics go on making prophesies?' So long as separate electorates existed, the separate organisation of Musalmans was an inevitable corollary. But that did not mean that such a position was an ideal one or that he was satisfied with it. He had however to deal with realities and would do his best in the circumstances.[4]

The Bombay Session of the Muslim League was held on 10 May 1936, presided over by Sir Wazir Hassan. Most of the landed gentry of UP had found it far too uncomfortable to undertake this long journey, in the heat of summer, along almost the spine of India. Besides, many had already joined the Agriculturist Party in UP, and had also come to know of the settlement reached between Jinnah and the Unity Board. At this Bombay meet Jinnah was given the right, by the League, to nominate a Parliamentary Board of at least thirty-five from all over India. This Board was to prepare its own election manifesto and to take all necessary steps to contest the forthcoming elections.

Jinnah had also visited Bengal to assess the chances of the Muslim League Parliamentary Board's position in that province. The two well-known leaders of Bengal, Fazlul Haq[5] and Khwaja Nazimuddin[6] were, as usual, pulling in different directions. Fazlul Haq was preparing to fight the elections on the Krishak Praja Party[7] ticket while Khwaja Nazimuddin and his group were willing to fight on the Muslim League platform.

In the elections that followed the cultivating tenants of United Provinces, for the first time, decided to record a protest against prevailing conditions. In all the earlier elections (before 1937) they had consistently voted for their zamindar's candidates, but on this occasion they refused to be so influenced. The zamindars remained ignorant of all this till the last day, so much so that Sir Harry Haig, the governor of UP, also remained convinced that the Congress would not be able to secure more than 60 out of a total of 144 Hindu seats. In the end, in UP the Congress secured 134 out of a total of 144 seats, a clean sweep. The Muslim League won 29 of the 36 they had contested on the Muslim League ticket, another signal victory. Yet, not one single Muslim was elected on the Congress ticket, a disastrous signal for the future but only if it were read clearly.

Even as the process of announcing the election results was on, Babu Rajendra Prasad, in a press statement, had said that the 'Congress would not co-operate in the legislature with any other group or party'.[8] This rather hasty statement by Rajendra Prasad queered the pitch from the very beginning.

It is necessary that this is brought into account when reviewing negotiations between the Congress and the Muslim League in the UP for a representation of the latter in the provincial cabinet. The crucial question for Nehru in these negotiations was not so much as to how many representatives of the Muslim League ought to find a place in the cabinet. It was much more a concern that Nehru had whether after inducting such League members, the UP cabinet would be able to maintain its cohesion. Nehru's own part in these negotiations was small. Soon after the elections he had a spell of ill-health which kept him bound to Anand Bhawan. In all developments he was of course consulted by Abul Kalam Azad (who conducted the negotiations on behalf of the Congress) but these decisions did not really rest with Nehru. Indeed G.B. Pant, Rafi Ahmed Kidwai, K.M. Ashraf, P.D. Tandon and other members of the UP legislature exercised equal influence, on the ultimate result of the negotiations. The most important consideration with the provincial Congress leaders, as with Nehru, was that if the 'Muslim League, with its landlord support, joined the cabinet, the Congress programme for agrarian reform, particularly the abolition of zamindari, would be jeopardised. This fear was not groundless, the stubborn opposition of the Muslim League to land reform in the UP during the years 1937, proving so clearly enough.

By May 1937 all the results of the provincial elections had been declared. A coalition was now attempted and parleys began as described in some detail in *Pathway to Pakistan,* by Khaliquzzaman, who on behalf of the Muslim League had taken the initiative. He writes:

> I met Nehru on 12 May, 1937, for the last time at Anand Bhawan. I had only to impress upon him the necessity, in the Legislative Assembly, of cooperation between the Congress and the Muslim League, which in my opinion would once and for all put an end to British interference in Indian affairs and pave the way for the complete independence of the country. Quite contrary to my views, he (Nehru) believed that the Hindu-Muslim question in India was confined to a few Muslim intellectual landlords and capitalists who were cooking up a problem which did not, in fact, exist in the mind of the masses. He ridiculed the idea of Muslims having any separate organisation carried on within the precincts of the Legislature. In support of the dangers involved in keeping party factions alive he cited the civil war in Spain and instances in other countries of Europe. I pointed out to him that the Muslim problem of India was unique, that no parallel could be found anywhere in the world [therefore] drawing parallels from what might apply to Canada or other western countries was [to] completely ignore the history of India and the magnitude of the Muslim problem in the country. I further said that democracy was for the good of the country but the country should not be sacrificed at the altar of a system of Government borrowed from the West, which had never had to face a problem approaching in similarity to that presented by India. We could not agree and I had to leave disappointed.[9]

Totally separated from the above incident, there then took place another development—a meeting of the Ulema, of UP, was held in

Allahabad on 17 May 1937. They (Ulema) decided to leave the Muslim League Parliamentary Board and to go over to the Congress, unconditionally. This happened a mere five days after Khaliquzzaman had met Jawaharlal Nehru, thus strengthening Nehru's line of thinking though, it was Maulana Abul Kalam Azad who had actually managed this shift of the Ulema. In the meantime Pandit Pant also met Khaliquzzaman over the question of sharing cabinet seats in case of a coalition. Khaliquzzaman, in response, asked for 33 per cent of the total strength of the cabinet. He was then asked whether he (Pant) would have any voice in the selection of the Muslim League Ministers. He had replied: 'As much voice as I should have in your (Congress) selection.'

On 5 July 1937, the Congress agreed to accept office and Maulana Abul Kalam Azad came to Lucknow a week later, on 12 July, to meet with Khaliquzzaman. To quote him (Khaliquzzaman) again:

> 'What would be the attitude of the Muslim party in the assembly if on any issue between the British Government and the Congress, the Congress decides to leave the Assembly, and resigns?' Maulana Azad had asked. I replied: 'If we are a coalition Government, surely it will be our moral duty to leave the Assembly with the Congress. Coalition presupposes cooperation on a wider basis.' Then suddenly he asked me: 'Will you have Hafiz Ibrahim as your colleague in the Cabinet?' I said: 'No! My colleague in the Cabinet will be Nawab Ismail Khan because he enjoys the confidence not only of my party but of the Muslims in the Province.' Thereafter he said: 'Will you give it to me in writing that the League will also leave the Assembly if the Congress decides to retire?' I said: 'My word should be enough. If, however, the Congress wants it, it is here.'

Maulana Abul Kalam Azad came back to Lucknow on 15 July 1937 to talk to Khaliquzzaman again, this time accompanied by Pandit Govind Ballabh Pant. Khaliquzzaman takes up the account:

> After some preliminary talk the Maulana handed over to me a two-page typed note which I was supposed to sign as a price for Muslim League Coalition with the Congress. Here is the note:
> 'The Muslim League group in the United Provinces Legislature shall cease to function as a separate group. The existing members of the Muslim League Party in the United Provinces Assembly shall become part of the Congress Party and will fully share with other members of the Party their privileges and obligations as members of the Congress Party. They will similarly be

empowered to participate in the deliberations of the Party. They will likewise be subject to the control and discipline of the Congress Party in equal measure with other members and the decisions of the Congress Party, as regards work in the Legislature and general behaviour of its members, shall be binding on them. All matters shall be decided by a majority vote of the Party, each individual member having one vote.

'The policy laid down by the Congress Working Committee for their members in the Legislature along with instructions issued by the competent Congress bodies pertaining to their work in such Legislatures shall be faithfully carried including these members.

'The Muslim League Parliamentary Board in the United Provinces will be dissolved, and no candidates will thereafter be set up by the said Board at any bye-election. All members of the Party shall actively support any candidate that may be nominated by the Congress to fill up any vacancy occurring hereafter.

'All members of the Congress party shall abide by the rules of the Congress party and offer their full and genuine cooperation with a view to promoting the interests and prestige of the Congress.

'In the event of the Congress Party deciding on resignation from the Ministry or from the Legislature the members of the above-mentioned group will also be bound by that decision.'

'To this typed statement, defining the terms, Maulana Azad had appended a short note: 'It was hoped that if these terms were agreed to and the Muslim League group of members joined the Congress Party as full members that group would cease to exist as a separate group. In the formation of the Provincial Cabinet it was considered proper that they should have representatives.'

'After going through the note I said: 'Maulana, this is a very strange document. You want me to sign the death warrant of the Muslim League Parliamentary Board as well as the Muslim League organisation, which I am representing. I have no other capacity in which to talk to you except as the representative of the Muslim League Parliamentary Board. Besides there are many other matters in this note which are very objectionable. I cannot sign this document.'

'Then a long discussion was started, word by word, sentence by sentence, and it continued till about eight o'clock. When I was leaving Pantji said: 'Well, I shall let you know the final position of the Congress in a day or two.'

'A few days later, I telephoned to Maulana and asked him whether he would agree to the following proviso to the agreement: 'Provided that the Muslim League Party members in the UP Assembly will be free to vote in accordance with their conscience, on communal matters.' The Maulana seemed to have been very much upset over this message on the phone, and told me that a reply to this would have to be considered and to be conveyed to me after some time. In the evening Pantji asked me on the phone, 'What do you mean by communal matters?' I replied: 'Pantji, we have had enough to deal with in our lives over communal questions and you know what they include. But for your information I can say that they include religion, religious ceremonies, language, culture, services etc.' He asked when I would be returning, I replied, 'Next morning, both Nawab Ismail Khan and I shall be reaching Lucknow.'

'From Lucknow station we went straight to Pantji's residence where we found Maulana Abul Kalam Azad taking his tea. We handed the document back to Maulana and told him that on 27 July 1937, when the Assembly session started we should be sitting in the opposition and would face the consequences'.'[10]

Whatever the other merits and demerits of this 'coalition controversy' in UP, unquestionably the events of 1937 had a tremendous, almost a traumatic effect upon Jinnah. The tide of provincial autonomy had come and gone and left him high and dry. The real tragedy was not the failure of his party to secure two seats on its own terms in the UP cabinet; but this collapse, like a house of cards of the assumptions on which he had conducted his policies for twenty years. He had pinned his hopes on separate electorates and on organizing Muslims on a separate political platform, on the formation of as many Muslim-majority provinces as possible by redrawing provincial boundaries, and on weighted representation for Muslims in provinces where they were in a minority. His 'Fourteen Points' had been practically conceded in the new constitution. However, all these safeguards had not yielded the fruit he had hoped from them. In the Muslim-majority provinces where indeed the Muslim League could legitimately have hoped to be voted to office, it had met with an electoral disaster of the first magnitude.[11] In the Sindh legislative assembly the League had won three seats, in Punjab only one, and in the North-West Frontier Province none at all. In Bengal it had won a third of the Muslim (and one-sixth of the total) seats in the legislative assembly, but here, too, it did not occupy a commanding position. Party alignments in Muslim-majority provinces had cut across religion; Sir Sikandar Hayat Khan in the Punjab, Fazlul Haq in Bengal, and Sir Ghulam Husain Hidayatullah in Sindh had not responded to Jinnah's appeal for 'Muslim unity', and seemed to be swayed by personal, and class interests rather than by religious affiliations.

Dr Zaidi observes acutely this

> experience of contesting the elections of 1936-37 and forming ministries under conditions of responsible government revealed the inner dynamics of Indian politics. It brought to surface both majority and minority attitudes in a new and striking way. The most significant of these was the Congress tendency towards a one-party polity in India that assumed the submersion of other Indian parties. Another was the emergent unity of Muslim India.

In the experiences of these years Jinnah learned vital lessons in practical politics, such as a purely theoretical approach would never have taught him. He and the Muslim League went into the 'elections as idealists; they emerged from the aftermath as political realists. The change could hardly have been more significant for India and the shape of her independent future.'[12]

He further records that this 'Muslim solution of the Indian political and communal problem was put forward publicly—probably for the first time—by Maulana Hasrat Mohani in his presidential address to the Muslim League session held at Ahmedabad towards the end of December 1921. With slight variations of emphasis or detail, it formed the substance of the various demands put forward in the twenties and thirties by most of the prominent Muslim organisations and leaders on behalf of their community. Attempts were being made concurrently to provide with an adequate rationale the Muslim demand to dominate the provinces where the Muslims were in a majority. The Indian Muslims, it was urged, were a 'nation' by themselves, totally different from the other 'nations' in India, and as such entitled to exercise their right of self-determination and to establish a homeland for themselves where they could work out their destiny according to their own ideas of Islamic culture and polity. While some, such as Muhammad Iqbal in 1930, favoured 'the creation of a Muslim India [with-] in India', others, such as Rahmat Ali in 1933, advocated the total separation of 'Muslim India' from the rest of India and the creation of a new Muslim state ('Pakistan'). The results of the 1937 elections came as a great shock and surprise to the communally-minded Muslims. They showed that the Muslims were weak, divided and disorganised'.

This one single event has generated a variety of comments from a wide range of informed opinion, yet, one common thread runs through all. However, argued as a purely theoretical, academic point and whatever other justifications are advanced in support of the Congress stand, essentially Nehru's stand and this step of rejecting a coalition with the League, ultimately had disastrous consequences for unity. The Congress could scarcely have wished away the presence of the Muslims in UP, or for that matter anywhere else in India. Acceptance of their presence as citizens had implicit a right of their democratic representation; after all, that is what the whole debate had been from 1909 to 1919 and in all the Round Table Conferences. Nehru's doctrinaire approach begs many questions, rather repeats them: In an elective democracy are numbers all? If India is unique, as it is, then how can the examples of Spain, Italy or Europe or for that matter, their modes, practices and personages be any guides, leave alone becoming the principal markers of democratic practice in India?

As K.M. Munshi in his *Pilgrimage to Freedom* summed up: 'At that time it did not appear to be formidable; but as events were to show ten years later, it was the beginning of the end of united India....'[13] The year 1937, thereafter became the critical watershed, compelling me to repeat an agonising query first voiced at the beginning of this book that, if democracy is representation then how and why instead of uniting did it begin to divide India? And, most painfully and pertinently, why does it continue to do so still?' We remain with 1937 for a little while longer.

THE YEAR 1937—A WATERSHED IN DEMOCRATIC POLITICS? ELECTIONS IN THE UNITED PROVINCES (CONTD.)

Jinnah, consistent in his ambition of filling the role of an all-India politician at the centre: was still largely dependant on demonstrable electoral strength in the provinces, which is why he worked assiduously to sustain this political partnership in UP even though Jinnah had little inclination for the demands of mass politics, he differed hardly at all from most of the Congressmen of that period. Nehru's biographer, S. Gopal characterises Jinnah and his politics in this manner:

> When Jinnah took up again, in 1936, the leadership of the Muslim League, he was still a nationalist who had no wish to support, or rely on, foreign rule. Indeed his aloofness, brittle ability and anti-imperialist attitude made him as disliked by the British as any Congressman. He had been the chief

architect of the Lucknow Pact of 1916, between the Congress and the League and his hope now was for another similar understanding. He, therefore, secured the election as president of the League not of any loyalist contender but of Sir Wazir Hassan, a retired judge of Lucknow whose family had close links with the Congress leadership in the U.P. The election manifesto of the League, drafted by Jinnah himself, was very similar to that of the Congress, and in the League's parliamentary board there were representatives of Muslim organisations such as the Jamiat-ul-Ulema, which stood in support of the Congress.[14]

But that the Congress, in reality had accepted this task of winning the Muslim seats by delegating them to the UP Muslim League Parliamentary Board (UPMLPB), had an implied message; that in the event of the Congress forming the government after the elections, the UPMLPB would provide the Muslim component of the Cabinet. According to Sitaramayya, the official historian of the Congress: 'The Congress and Muslim League had actually worked in unison to select Muslim candidates for the elections'. The Congress contested only nine seats and left the rest to the UPMLPB. The 'intimacy of consultations' went so far as to allow Rafi Ahmad Kidwai, after his defeat in the general elections, to contest a bye-election unopposed. All this led people to believe, and with reason, that there would be a coalition ministry after the elections. As it transpired the Congress won a clear majority—134 seats in a house of 228. However, this was a kind of a lopsided success because the Congress had not won a single Muslim seat whereas the UPMLPB had won 29 of a total of 66 Muslim seats.

These negotiations between the Muslim League and the Congress, for a coalition broke down primarily because the Congress, filled with its sense of majority, set such very hard conditions for inducting the League ministers into the cabinet that the leader of the UPMLPB, Khaliquzzaman had no option but to turn them down. Doubts arise whether the Congress was interested more in absorbing the UP Muslim League than in forming a coalition with it. This, under the prevailing circumstances, was an impossible goal to achieve, irrespective of whether it was desirable. How conceivably could the Muslim League accept its own liquidation as a precondition for a coalition? Paradoxically, the Congress achieved the very reverse of this, all such attitudinising gave the Muslim League a new lease of life and set in motion a process that culminated eventually in the partition of India.

In defence of Nehru, S. Gopal says:

> Any agreement would in effect have accepted that politics were a matter of alliances between upper-class groups, and betrayed all Muslims who thought in non-communal terms, (also abandoning) the economic programme on which Jawaharlal had been laying so much stress. No such agreement could have endured for the League had no long-term economic or social objectives. The only incentive where its leaders were concerned was the hope of office, and once this was fulfilled, the cracks were bound to widen.... In these circumstances, little importance can be attached to the talks with Khaliquzzaman, and no weighty consequences followed their failure.[15]

Neither the analysis nor the conclusion of the author are sustained by events as they unfolded.

A rationale advanced by Nehru reasoned that to start with there had been no formal agreement to form a coalition ministry, therefore, the question of the consequences attendant upon its breaking up did not arise. Technically this was perhaps accurate, but it was clearly an empty, legalistic argument, for implicit in an electoral alliance with the League was the prospect of a coalition were the Congress to take office. The other rationale frequently advanced is of the ideological gulf that separated the League and the Congress. If this was meant to be the difference between a clearly sectarian (the Muslim League) and a supposedly secular party (the Congress), then that argument, too, is difficult to sustain for long because the Congress had allied with the same sectarian party for the purposes of electioneering. Also, if the reference was to the conservatism of the UPMLPB, as contrasted with the supposedly advanced politics of Nehru (hardly so of the Congress as a whole) then several arguments can be put forward to contradict the notion: Khaliquzzaman and Ismail Khan were generally regarded as Congress-minded Muslims and there were many members of the UPMLPB whose political views were as radical as those of any Congressman. Even the social composition of the UP Muslim League was far less reactionary than it became subsequently. At this time most Muslim zamindars, though nominally members of the League, were fighting the elections either as independents or as nominees of the National Agriculturalist Party. Besides, Khaliquzzaman and Nawab Ismail Khan were no more conservative than, for example, the members of the Bengal Congress who had determinedly opposed tenancy and credit reform in that province. Besides, Sardar Patel was not exactly a votary of Nehruvian socialistic thinking. Finally, it has been argued that the ideological distance between two parties was borne out by the fundamental difference in the way in which they conceptualized freedom from British rule. In the context of accepting office in 1937, this difference was more apparent than real, as Jinnah showed in the course of his address at the 25th session of the All-India Muslim League in Lucknow in October 1937:

> 'A great deal of capital is made out of phrases for the consumption of the ignorant and illiterate masses. Various phrases are used such as Purna Swaraj, self-government, complete independence, responsible government, substance of independence and dominion status. There are some who talk of complete independence...Those who talk of complete independence the most, mean the least of what it means (sic). Was the Gandhi-Irwin pact in consonance with complete independence? Were the assurances that were required before offices could be accepted and the Provincial Constitution could be worked consistent with Purna Swaraj, and was the resolution, after the assurances were refused, accepting offices and working the Provincial Constitution enacted by the British Parliament, and forced upon the people of India by Imperialistic power, in keeping with the policy and programme and the declarations of the Congress party? Does wrecking mean working? These paper declarations, slogans and shibboleths are not going to carry us anywhere. What India requires is a completely united front and honesty of purpose, and then by whatever name you may call your government is a matter of no consequence so long as it is a government of the people, by the people, for the people.

Jinnah's central argument of unity between the Congress and the League was unimpeachable. Whatever the Congress' real motives in taking up office (wrecking the government, certainly did not constitute as one of them), it had agreed to work the 1935 constitution, and having done so it was, for so long as it was in office, a constitutionalist organisation in the same position, vis-à-vis the British authorities and the British crown as all the other parties. Therefore, the argument that insuperable political differences ruled our a coalition is also not sustainable.

The year 1937 and Congress policies post the elections of that year had another consequence. By mid-1939, Jinnah had strengthened the control of the All-India Muslim League on all the provincial Leagues, to the extent where he could now prevent them from making agreements without referring to the central party organisation. The provinces learnt that to rival Congress, an all India status, a political stand and party organisation were vital, this, for the Muslim League had become a question of survival as a Muslim body. This helped Jinnah who now began spreading his influence and ensuring that his authority prevailed in the provinces too. This was a development of very significant long-term consequences, again born essentially of 1937.

There was then this other controversy born of Nehru's programme of mass contact, again theoretically valid but in practice disastrous.

Nehru's reiterated argument that the time for pacts with an elitist Muslim organisation like the League had gone, direct mass contact with the Muslims of India was the need of the hour was theoretically a stand that could be advocated by any political party active in India, but it was not timely, it was unrealistic; (being based on a wrong assessment of the Muslim mind and psyche), inconsistent; (for the Congress had often adopted a totally anti-podal position), and counter productive, the last as it spurred the Muslim League to become even more unreasonably assertive. If all this was what the Congress now truly subscribed to then surely it ought not to have worked with the Muslim League at all, from the very beginning of and during the elections. It should also not have felt the need to fight subsequent bye-elections with the 'mullahs and green flags', as in many instances it did. While Nehru wrote to N.A. Sherwani chiding him for his request for maulvis for his election campaign, this disapproval did not extend to making Sherwani actually give up all such assistance of the ulema. The Congress, also, should not have felt the need to use Maulana Azad to win the Jamiat-ul-Ulema-i-Hind to its side, for, after all what did maulvis have to do with an approach that based itself upon 'socio-economic solidarities, unimpeachable secular credentials and radical programmes', as according to Nehru, for example, in Spain, or elsewhere in Europe?

Another argument against an alliance was that to form a coalition government with the League would be to accept that the Congress did not represent the Muslims. However, then it had already demonstrated this very deficiency, by first making that open, initial statement of contesting a mere nine seats in the Muslim constituencies, of the UP, and, shockingly for a 'secular body', none at all in Bengal. The Congress had recruited Muslims, but even in that age of mass politics, always through the aid of allied Muslim organisations. During the Non-

Cooperation Movement and the early twenties that 'aid' had been the Khilafatists, Gandhi had surmised that supporting them was a short cut to Muslim support, that it failed is a separate issue. During Civil Disobedience, in the absence of a strong Muslim ally, Muslim participation dropped sharply. Through the thirties and the forties, the Congress relied not so much on Muslim Congressmen as upon Muslim organisations independent of it, such as the Jamiat-ul-Ulema-i-Hind, the Ahrars,[16] the Muslim Unity Board,[17] the Momin Conference[18] and so on. Similarly, in 1937 the Muslim League, in informal alliance with the Congress, had won 29 seats in the UP. Extending this alliance into a coalition government would have been in keeping with past practice—the only difference being that the context now was both legislative institutions and the political executive, not any more just agitational politics.

Why then did the Congress not come to terms with the League? The immediate reason for a repudiation of the electoral alliance was obviously the heady arithmetics of the elected numbers, the Congress having obtained a legislative majority. This electoral alliance had been undertaken when the Congress was unsure of such an outcome and, therefore, needed an ally to make up the numbers should it not reach them, irrespective of whether it decided to wreck the constitution from the inside after, or work it. Once it had achieved a majority on its own, it then saw no need to make any concessions to electoral allies, numerically smaller, therefore now redundant. This was unalloyed majoritarianism, arguable somewhat perhaps in theory, disastrous in consequences.

Where then does an intelligible and rational explanation of the Congress stand lie? Part of it is to be found in the political ideology of the Congress, that of their self-adopted style called secularism and majoritarian democracy. This platform of assumed secularism by the Congress was part of its basis towards claims to be a national party.

'Secularism' Debate

Debate on the term 'secularism', was [is] in reality a by-product of the European socio-political history getting transferred directly to India as a colonial discourse, which is why its practical applicability in the Indian context became adversarial from the very beginning. Hindu became a word of communal identification, and almost always as that faith, belief or practice which unwaveringly contested the merit-worthy idea of 'secularism'. A direct, western contextual meaning could just not be, or perhaps would not be elaborated by political scientists, sociologists, or other activists of India, for they found that it could not be correctly applied to the Indian societal fabric. For example, to T.N. Madan, it appears incompatible with Indian religious traditions; Partha Chatterjee thinks that secularism as an ideology cannot come to terms with majoritarian communalism; this is a curious euphemism, but routine for left-leaning thinking to adopt, the implied deduction being that minority communalism, would be more acceptable and could still qualify for being termed as 'secular', or nearly so. There are some that suggest that as India is Hindu in nature it can never be truly 'secular'. Herein lies a very great misconception, principally about the essence of this, Hindu, or Sanatan thought.

Post-partition, 'secularism' as a political thought, platform or an ideology has been widely and variously interpreted. Some equate it to a kind of a vague tolerance, thus allowing space for religion in political life. While Gandhi unhesitatingly used the religious idiom, indeed religion itself to assert equality, others like Jawaharlal Nehru held to 'secularism' as a tenet of the state, which ought to remain divorced from religion, though, of course, elements of 'mild Nehruvian celebration of India's Hindu culture were allowed to mingle with that notion', This interpretation was falsely and parochially applied as it held that the Congress, whatever it did, alone was 'secular', and always so, none other.

These others position 'secularism', as being synonymous with the Indian idea of *sarva-dharma-sambhava,* where all religious beliefs are in harmony. This is modified to replace dharma with the word panth, a more accurate way to convey the essence. There are those who assert that what the West has lately arrived to as 'secularism', India has long had, as a living philosophical tradition, going back many millennia; implying thereby that the Muslim community was/is responsible for communal antagonisms.[19]

After the 1937 elections, where it had contested very few Muslim seats and had been routed even in these, the Congress still continued to see itself as a national party because it now switched emphasis on to its assumed 'secularism', this then became a substitute for Muslim support.

This was really spurious reasoning, simply because the party called itself secular, therefore, it was national, and because of this self-adopted nomenclature of national it was automatically representative of all Indians, regardless of what the election results demonstrated does not carry any conviction. This idea of 'secularism', just the idea not the fact, thereafter became more important than any empirical reality. This illusionist tendency had been foreshadowed in Jawaharlal Nehru's own address to the Faizpur Congress,[20] where he had made his famous assertion chat there were only two forces in the country, the Congress representing 'nationalism' and the British representing 'imperialism'. A few months later, with obvious reference to Jinnah's assertion that the party of the Muslims was the third force, Nehru wrote[21] that third parties were unimportant because the Congress was charged with a 'historic destiny'; but that self-assumed 'destiny' was certainly not intended to lead the country down the path of vivisection.

This self-adopted conviction about the Congress being secular, allowed Nehru to interpret the party's disastrous performance in the Muslim constituencies of UP as actually a hopeful augury. 'Though the Muslim nominees of the Congress have been defeated in the UP, I refuse to believe that the Congress has no hold on the Muslim masses', and continuing in the same vein added '…our very failure on this occasion has demonstrated that success is easily in our grasp and (that) the Muslim masses are increasingly (?) turning to the Congress'.[22] According to Nehru the Congress had failed with the Muslims because it had failed to work amongst them. This was perhaps true, also that the League had hardly any organisational structure (a valid observation) but the League did have a base even if that was totally sectarian and was dominated by provincial interests.

Nehru believed that the Muslims in the UP were in a ferment, They were fed up with ineffectual communal leadership. They wished to climb out of the communal rut and to line up with the forces of freedom and progress. The elections had '…gone some way to lay the ghost of communalism'.[23] In so far as a section of the Muslims was alienated from the Congress, it was the urban as opposed to the rural Muslims. 'I am sure that when the next opportunity comes we shall not lose a single Muslim seat in the rural areas though I am not quite certain about the urban seats'.[24] Given this kind of optimistic unreality for an assessment of the 1937 elections it is not at all surprising that Nehru was so sanguine about the Congress taking office in the UP without the Muslim League.

The second feature of the Congress' political ideology allowing it to ignore this demonstrated lack of support with the Muslim electorate was its commitment to a 'Congress kind' of Westminster model of majoritarian democracy, a simple majority in the legislature being enough to form the government, the arithmetic constituting the only legitimacy, but in India a complex social arithmetic also operated, and it did so simultaneously. This notion blinded Nehru and many other Congressmen to the fact that under the system of separate electorates (and the Congress had agreed to play the electoral game according to the rules of the 1935 constitution), a government (any), entirely majoritarian and not reasonably inclusive of minorities, (in this instance, Muslim MLAs) would be seen as an unrepresentative government. There were others, of course, within the Congress, and there were (are still) many of this ilk, for whom this political model was a means to the end of showing the Muslim minority in the UP its 'place'.

When the Congress formed a government with almost all the Muslim MLAs sitting on the Opposition benches, non-Congress Muslims were suddenly faced with this stark reality of near total political powerlessness. It was brought home to them, like a bolt of lightning, that even if the Congress did not win a single Muslim seat, as had happened now, (in the 1937 elections) so long as it won an absolute majority in the House, on the strength of the general (Hindu) seats, it could and would form a government entirely on its own, unless Muslim politicians altogether surrendered their separate political identity, in which case they would hardly be elected in the first place. Yet again this carried a very serious and damaging message for the future of a united India: that in a majoritarian minded, Congress ruled India there was no place for the Muslims, indeed, for any political minority, unless the Congress found itself in a corner, then it would ally with anyone.

Speaking of the decision not to form a coalition Ministry, the *History of the Freedom Movement in India* records: 'There is no doubt that the decision of the Congress leaders was extremely unwise and it was bound to have disastrous consequences. The Muslims now fully realized that as a separate community, they had no political prospects. The Congress ultimatum was the signal for the parting of the ways, which, by evitable stages, led to the foundation of Pakistan'.

In his *Transfer of Power in India*, V.P. Menon wrote: 'The Congress decided to have homogenous ministries on its own and chose Muslim ministers from among those who were members of the Congress party. This was the beginning of a serious rift between the Congress and the League and was a factor which induced neutral Muslim opinion to turn to the support of Jinnah'.[25]

In his autobiography, *India Wins Freedom*, Maulana Abul Kalam Azad, who was the president of the Congress from 1939 to 1946, speaking of the aftermath of the 1937 elections, wrote: 'If the UP League's offer of cooperation had been accepted, the Muslim League party would for all practical purposes have merged in the Congress. Jawaharlal's action gave the Muslim League in the UP a new lease of life...It was from the UP that the League was reorganised. Mr Jinnah took full advantage of the situation and started an offensive which ultimately led to partition'.[26] In his biography of Nehru, Brecher commented:

> The immediate and most far-reaching effect of the Congress victory at the polls was a widening of the breach with the Muslim League. Flushed with success the Congress adopted an imperious attitude to all other political patties, a 'Himalayan blunder', for which it was to pay dearly in the years to come. Nehru himself set the tone with his haughty remark in March 1937. 'There are only two forces in India today, British imperialism and Indian nationalism as represented by the Congress.' Jinnah was quick to retort: 'No, there is a third party, the Mussulmans.' History was to bear him out.[27]

Writing in 1969, Shiva Rao referred to the 1937 elections and said that it was significant that even after the elections, Jinnah was not thinking of a separate state of Pakistan:

> In a public statement, shortly after the elections in 1937 he declared, 'nobody will welcome an honourable settlement between the Hindus and the Muslims more than I and nobody will be more ready to help it': and he followed it with a public appeal to Gandhi to tackle this question. The latter's response was somewhat depressing: 'Wish I could do something, but I am utterly helpless. My faith in unity is bright as ever; only I see no daylight but impenetrable darkness and in such distress I cry out to God for light'.[28]

God, it transpires was sadly not then willing to illuminate the Congress path with wisdom or light, and more than Gandhi, it is unlikely that anyone else in the Congress had a better access to the Creator's ear, he was unquestionably a devout Hindu, certainly more than Nehru whose thinking and path (sadly language and idiom, too) was lit up more by imported western notions than by India's great wealth of faith, thought and wisdom.

This refusal by the Congress to induct the League ministers on any but the harshest terms, had two other crucial consequences. First, UP's Muslim politicians were then forced to rethink both their political strategy and their objectives. As briefly examined earlier, recognising that the Congress would not deal with them at the provincial level the Muslim Leaguers of UP turned to Jinnah and the All-India Muslim League, for that vitally needed pan-Indian Muslim solidarity only which, they reasoned, would extract the needed concessions from the Congress at both the national and the provincial levels. By late 1937, the Congress stand had discredited all the coalition efforts of Khaliquzzaman and Nawab Ismail Khan, and after this there was no real chance for any provincial accommodation. Hereafter, Jinnah began to hold out for all-India settlements of the communal problem and to insist upon a formal recognition by the Congress of the Muslim League as the only all India organisation representing the Muslims. He reasoned that unless this 'sole spokesman', and the League as the only organisation stand was not forcefully asserted, the Congress would not concede even that which was the League's reasonable due. And, this very Jinnah and Khaliquzzaman who had so far maintained an anti-zamindar stance, during the period that they were in informal alliance with the Congress, now changed tack and accepted most of the Muslim notables of the 'UP, both for funds and for the sake of Muslim solidarity,

The Congress was in office for over two years. The general impression of these years, amongst the Muslims was not at all favourable to the Congress regime. Irrespective of whether all the instances quoted by the League were true or false, a general feeling among the Muslims of all classes was that 'Hindu raj' had arrived.

There was another and a very serious consequence: having directly experienced this lack of the effectiveness of separate electorates, or even weighted representation as a means for attaining executive authority or even a check upon it. UP's Muslim politicians now began to look for a formulation that would more effectively get them access to political office. If the limitations of a minority status had to be repudiated and yet effective voice achieved then what was that to be? It is from this search that the concept of parity eventually was born. There must be, the reasoning went, a politically effective parity between the majority and a minority and this was a must, irrespective of numbers; also despite all the theories and the logic of elected majority in a democracy. For only parity could get them the needed voice, therefore, only such a claim would now be appropriate for representatives of a nation, as Jinnah claimed Muslims of India to be.

There was yet another, and a lasting consequence of this decision by the Congress, it was this serious denting of the Congress' self-adopted claims of being 'secular', more than ever before. They were now the ruling party, therefore, they became directly responsible for policy, administration and for maintaining law and order in UP, should anything go wrong, and in a large province like UP they would go wrong, it is the Congress that would directly be in the line of critical fire. With representatives of the Muslim electorate sitting almost totally in the opposition, should hereafter any issue, susceptible to communal controversy arise, the actions of such a Congress government, with no Muslim voice, would inevitably then become doubly suspect. Then the Muslim electorate of UP having decisively rejected the Congress candidates, their claims of still being a national party would rest totally on how effectively they demonstrated this commitment to a platform of convincing communal oneness and harmony. For the Muslim population of the United Provinces, all such Congress assertions of 'secularism' had now to be demonstrated in practice and on the ground. Additionally, if the inevitable accusations by the Muslim politicians in the opposition were to be deflected, the Congress Party and government, had both to conduct their affairs beyond reproach, to show themselves as scrupulously, even-handedly, totally non-partisan. This under the then prevailing circumstances of UP was near impossible.

That is why, this breakdown of coalition negotiations between the UP Congress and the UP Muslim League became a watershed in the history of pre-partition provincial politics of UP. This rupture transformed the organisation and political programmes of the Muslim League, it set the Congress on a course which eroded its image, and ultimately, alienated a bulk of the Muslims of UP. More tellingly, this one single event continued to cast its long shadow over the tone, content, and tenor of India's political debate and rhetoric for the next decade; and it contributed significantly, to an eventual partitioning of the country in 1947.

As for Jinnah, his task now became clearer, post the recently concluded elections of 1937, the overriding necessity now became a real building up of the Muslim League as the 'sole spokesman' of the Muslims. In this task Jinnah was, of course, helped by many factors and events, but also by the policies of both the Congress and the British government. 'In politics', he had once said, 'one has to play one's game as on the chess board'. Jinnah, therefore, recognised that his opening move had to be a revitalisation of the Muslim League. Since that would take time, Jinnah reasoned that the Muslim League ought not to be in any hurry to reach a settlement, considering especially the latest practical experience of a settlement attempted with the Congress. He therefore, concluded that as the ultimate power lay with the British, it was only they who could share or transfer any portion of that power, thus, he had no need now to come to any terms with the Congress. In the meanwhile, the best course open to the League was to strengthen its own organisation and only thereafter enter into negotiations with the Congress. And all this while, he had to continue to voice opposition to British rule, and all this he did in ample measure.

The other question: whether the Congress ought to accept office or not, then came to a head, this demanded an early resolution. The central issue here was the possibility of using the special powers of the governors. Congress leaders, under instruction from their All-India Committee, demanded an undertaking that a governor would not use these special powers vested in him by Section 93 of the Government of India Act of 1935.[29] This was a very difficult call, and as no such undertaking was forthcoming, the Congress refused accepting office.

For Viceroy Linlithgow, this was an early setback. Meanwhile, in provinces where the Congress did not have majorities the formation of the ministries went uninterruptedly ahead. By March 1937, Gandhi was now beginning to get uneasy, wondering if the Congress had got trapped in a blind alley of its own making? He, therefore, advised the Congress to work out a formula for negotiating options with the governors, in other words possible escape clauses. Seeing this impasse of the Congress' own making Syed Wazir Hassan, who had been president of the last session of the Muslim League, issued a statement that as forming minority ministries would not be legal, the government ought to take recourse to Section 93 of the Government of India Act. Linlithgow had no intention of doing so, for he did not wish to give the Congress their badly needed escape clause, and that, too, through a British imposed measure.

Elections to provinces, as per the Government of India Act 1935 having been concluded, next on the reforms list came the question of a federation. On this front, proposals about the princely states generated apprehensions amongst them. However, in the five years between the First Round Table Conference of 1930 and the passing of the Act, the princes had perceptibly changed their attitudes, dropping more their initial approval of the idea and now stressing more their autonomy. Objections also got voiced to any infringement of their domestic sovereignty which the Act necessarily entailed, and they questioned even the minimum powers which would be required within the Indian states by the proposed federal authorities. They put the view that the princes' adherence to the federation would in effect constitute with the British government a bilateral agreement between allies and equals, and although the secretary of state firmly rejected this claim, it was clear that the princes, had concerns about sovereign status, and the precise nature of British paramountcy over them.

This was bound to be a slow and involved process, and it was not until early in 1939 that Linlithgow was able to formulate the terms on which the adherence of the princes to the Act was acceptable. For one, the Congress supported Praja Parishad agitations in some of the states had intensified, for another, some of the larger states whose accession to federation was vital, were now showing increasing anxiety about the future of their revenues to the federal treasury. Lord Lothian who had arrived in India in November 1937, on a kind of a reconnaissance mission reported that Nehru was determinedly opposed to the idea, as he just could not contemplate the responsibility of forming a government at the centre where most of the centre's revenue would be reserved for defence, leaving no money for carrying out reforms to which Nehru had committed the Congress. In addition, he would not accept participation by the princely states in government unless they had adopted representative institutions. Lothian thought that the Congress might, therefore, force a crisis over the federation proposal, if that idea was advanced determinedly.

Linlithgow, though, remained optimistic. He felt that if he could keep Congress in office for another year, they would not, rather could not then refuse to join the federation, how he arrived at such a conclusion remains obscure. However, the Muslims had by then decided that if they were to hold their ground, which they must as an organisation, then they had to act as an effective opposition to this Hindu Congress. In consequence, the chances of a united India emerging as the prize of independence were now beginning to recede, and all as a consequence of Congress' actions uptil now, the cumulative effect of their policies and misjudgements. Jawaharlal Nehru, having candidly voiced his opposition to a federation, went further when on a tour of North and North-West India in October 1937 and emphasised that the 'ultimate aim of (the) Congress was the overthrow of the present Constitution and its replacement by one based on severance of the British connection'.[30] Significantly, he also forecast that a European war was now inevitable, which, he said, would give an opportunity to Congress to fight for independence. 'The most important aspect of [our] struggle,'[31] he declared, 'was not the acceptance of office but the organizing of the masses and the instilling of 'mass revolutionary mentality' in them. Of equal importance, he said, was the recruiting of Muslims into the ranks of the Congress.'[32]

In contrast Gandhi's position was clear and not at all extreme. He had personally cancelled a proposal that Congress Ministries ought to resign if the proposed 'federation 'was implemented', though, he shared the objections voiced by Jawaharlal Nehru to Lord Lothian. Gandhi would also not oppose 'federation' because of Nehru's objections to the princely states' position, he was far more worried about the reservation of defence and external affairs, and he sought the assurance that these two subjects would cease to be reserved to the centre.

For the Muslims, yearning to have an all India figure lead them in these testing days found in Mohammad Ali Jinnah, as president of the Muslim League not just a 'sole spokesman,' but in reality also the 'sole saviour'. When he first met the viceroy, Linlithgow could not foresee the hold that Jinnah would eventually have over the Muslims. 'I do not frankly feel any deep confidence in him', the viceroy had then written 'and I suspect that he is one of those political leaders who can play a personal hand but no other, and whose permanent control on the allegiance of their followers is frequently open to question.'[33] This was 1937, the viceroy's assessment, superficial and hasty, took no account of how things were changing and at a pace faster than his assessments were. Jinnah was already then the central figure of Muslim politics at the national level.

Jinnah, too, like Gandhi, did not come out unequivocally against the federation proposal. Though, in the Legislature he had attacked the federal part of the 1935 Act as 'thoroughly rotten, fundamentally bad and totally unacceptable' as well as 'not workable', nevertheless, he had reaffirmed that he was not opposed to all-India federation as such, but merely to the scheme put forward by the British government (speech in the Legislative Assembly, 7 February 1935 on the report of the joint parliamentary committee on Indian constitutional reforms). Equally, like the Hindu leaders whom the viceroy, Lord Linlithgow had met, Jinnah, at his meeting thought they should start with a federated British India. The states could be admitted provided their representatives were elected on 'a wide franchise and on the basis of popular institutions'. Though, he did complain with some bitterness that Linlithgow had been 'unwise to see Gandhi', as by so doing he had 'greatly raised the stock of the Congress' and thereby set back the prospects of the Muslims. Linlithgow let Jinnah do most of the talking at this meeting, for him this first meeting between them was in the nature of a reconnaissance.[34]

In spite of the not-too-distant discomfiture of his party at the polls, Jinnah was arrogating to himself the right to speak on behalf of the hundred million Muslims of India: 'When I say hundred million I mean that 99 per cent of them are with us—leaving aside some who are traitors, cranks, supermen or lunatics'.

A few weeks later (October 1937, Lucknow Session), at a Muslim League meeting, Jinnah launched a strong indictment of the Congress for pursuing an exclusively 'Hindu policy'; a policy that would 'result in chaos, bitterness, communal war and the strengthening of the Imperial hold over India'.[35] 'The Muslims', said Jinnah, 'could expect neither justice nor fair play under Congress government and no settlement between them (League and the Congress) was possible'.[36] At the same meeting Sikandar Hayat Khan made what Linlithgow called 'a surprising and an important move'.[37] He (Sikandar) announced his decision to advise all Muslim members of his Unionist Party in the

Punjab to join the Muslim League. The premier of Bengal, Fazlul Haq, issued a statement, on similar lines, to the Muslims of Bengal. This Lucknow meeting also passed a resolution condemning the federal scheme and adopting 'independence' as the ultimate aim of the League. In its totality, this Lucknow meeting of the League became a great success for Jinnah. The league had gained significant strength and would now make rapid strides in extending its organisation. The premiers of the Punjab and Bengal had also clearly had their hands forced by Jinnah into decisions which, governing as each of them was with a coalition ministry, they could only have taken with very considerable reluctance.

In early February 1938, writing to the king, Linlithgow spoke of a significant increase in Hindu-Muslim tensions. He explained that Jinnah had become alarmed by the defection of a growing number of Muslims from the Muslim League to Congress. This was because they were seeing Ministers as being in a position 'to help their friends and to inconvenience their opponents;' really as purveyors of political patronage. Jinnah reacted by rousing the Muslims and calling out that this 'growing power of Congress threatened Muslim culture'.[38]

The viceroy saw Jinnah again on 6 April, 1938. This 'Muslim Leader' (for by now Jinnah was that) refused to support any scheme which would produce a Hindu majority in a federal India. His star was in the ascendant and he had moved away from the position that he had taken in his first meeting with the viceroy. His reorganisation of the Muslim League had brought about a marked stiffening of the communal attitudes, even in a province ordinarily so remote from communal disputes as Madras.

By then communal tensions began to rise also on account of each side's manoeuvring for position. The Muslim League held meetings in Calcutta at which Jinnah and Fazlul Haq made strong speeches, the latter not only criticised the viceroy for having seen Gandhi but also accused him of going out of his way to express to Gandhi his satisfaction with the manner of the Congress governments' functioning in seven provinces. In July 1938, Linlithgow saw Sikandar Hayat Khan who pleaded for a postponement of federation on the grounds that a Congress majority at the Centre, that would result from such an early implementation would immediately attack the reservation of defence and external affairs as a central subject. This, he argued, would undermine the privileged position which Punjab then enjoyed on army recruitment. He proposed instead a partitioning of India into six or seven regional groups, one of which could be Pakistan. On top of this he wanted a complicated system of central representation designed to prevent a Hindu majority in any all India legislature of the future. The viceroy listened patiently to even such patent illogic, for the British badly wanted the Muslims as allies, they could not have both the communities (Hindu and Muslim) alienated and working unitedly against the Raj. Eighteen fifty-seven continued to cast its long shadow over the British psyche for as long as they remained in India.

Linlithgow, had now to decide whether to continue to put pressure for an amendment of the 1935 Act or to wait. He had canvassed all the governors, inevitably their views varied but the sum of their advice was to leave things alone for fear of exacerbating a situation already bristling with unmarked mines of suspicions. There could, of course, be certain minor adjustments that the secretary of state needed to make, but that ought to be that. The viceroy's opinion, too, now veered to the view that the whole matter had better be postponed, and pressure from the states, also from British India to amend the Act of 1935, in their respective interests, would have to be deflected.

Early, in the second half of 1938, several rounds of talks took place between representatives of the two communities. Jinnah had by then begun to denounce the Congress in public, along with pronouncing a no compromise in what the League stood for policy. He suggested to the acting-viceroy (Lord Brabourne) that the Central Government should be kept as it was; that the British should protect the Muslims in the Congress provinces and that the Muslims, in turn, would protect the British Raj in New Delhi. He was far too intelligent to believe even for an instant that such a solution was at all possible but it suited his tactics at that point, to at least propose it.

Around then, Linlithgow had a long talk with Jinnah principally about the federation proposal. The Muslim leader said that he did not totally reject the federal idea, but the federation must be such as would ensure an adequate balance between Muslim and Hindu votes so that there existed a recognisable equipoise between the two communities. The viceroy enquired as to how this was to be attained? Jinnah had in mind the manipulation of territorial votes and an adjustment of territorial divisions, but upon being pressed about the implications of these suggestions 'was embarrassed, yet insisted that he preferred his ideas to any carving up of the country'. The viceroy then asked Jinnah if he thought that this equipoise could be maintained if the British left India, Jinnah said that it might be very difficult. Did he then want the British to stay? It is one of those rare occasions when Jinnah was left speechless.

Later the viceroy, as a record of this conversation wrote as follows to Lord Zetland, secretary of state: 'He (Jinnah) admitted with some reluctance that it looked very much as though that was the position which was going to emerge; but he added that many were losing faith in us (the British). It was perfectly clear that we had not yet made up our minds whether we were going to go or not; and the only possible course for the Muslims to take in these circumstances was to continue to abuse us as loudly as possible in public, partly because we were so clumsy in our handling of the situation, and partly because the Muslims must show the public that they were as good nationalists and as good Indians as any other community. Behind the scenes they might adopt a more co-operative attitude—so long, that is, as we did not intend to clear out'.[39]

'If, on the other hand, we really had it in mind to abandon control of this country then it was quite obvious that Muslims must bestir themselves and be ready to fight, and he felt quite sure that in doing so they could also look for the help of Congress'.[40]

So much for this 'British equipoise'. In March 1938, there was prolonged correspondence between Chaudhri Khaliquzzaman on the one side and Nehru, Azad, and Gandhi on the other. This led Khaliquzzaman to remark: 'It was a curious situation that when I had run after them begging to avoid a crisis, they had not listened and now they were thinking of re-opening the same sad chapter again, which had in the meanwhile become much more complex and difficult of solution.'[41]

Maulana Abul Kalam Azad too, was anxious about a settlement between the Congress and the League in the interest principally of Congress, but also his own position, because should this 'feud' with the League continue 'his own position in the community would…become anomalous'.[42]

At this stage Subhas Bose, who in 1938 was the president of the Congress now tried his hand at settling this communal question. After the Haripur Session of the Congress in February 1938, he initiated an exchange of letters with Jinnah, following which the two met at Bombay in May 1938. In the first letter dated 15 May 1938, after his meeting with Jinnah, Bose asked Jinnah to suggest a representative committee which would jointly settle terms and come to an understanding. In reply Jinnah assured him that the matter would be placed before the Working Committee of the All-India Muslim League which was due to meet in the first week of June 1938.[43] In course of his conversation with the new Congress president, Jinnah had also suggested that an agreement would have to be based on a clear understanding of the position of the Congress and that of the League. He (Jinnah) then proposed that their conversation should proceed on the lines that 'the All-India Muslim League as the authoritative and representative organisation of the India Muslims and the Congress as the authoritative organisation of the solid body of Hindu opinion, have hereby agreed to the following terms by way of a pact between the two major communities and as settlement of the Hindu-Muslim question'.[44] After further consideration, the suggested formula was modified by deleting any reference to the Congress as representing only Hindus. Thereafter it ran: 'The Congress and the All-India Muslim League as the authoritative and representative organisation of the Muslims of India have hereby agreed to the following terms of the Hindu-Muslim settlement by way of a pact'.[45]

Bose while agreeing that the Muslim League was an organisation representing a very large body of Muslim opinion expressed the view that the Congress would be bound to consult with existing Muslim organisations that had co-operated with it (the Congress) in the past. He added: 'In the event of other groups, or minority interests, being involved, it will be necessary to consult the representatives of such interests'.[46] The talks had then ended on this note. The Working Committee of the League thereafter held a meeting on 4 June 1938 at Bombay. A resolution, as a rejoinder to Subhas Bose's was drafted here, wherein, it was conveyed to be 'a very unfair act' on the part of Congress to secure favour with 'other minorities' at the cost of the Muslim League. Accordingly, Jinnah wrote to Bose the very next day, 5 June 1938:

> I am enclosing herewith unanimous opinion of the Executive Council of the All-India Muslim League as promised by me in my letter dated the 16th of May with reference to the note given to me by you on behalf of the Congress and your letter of the 15th of May, 1938.

Resolution No. 1

The Executive Council of the All-India Muslim League has considered the note handed over by the President Mr S. Bose on behalf of the Congress to Mr Jinnah the President of the All-India Muslim League on the 14th May and his letter of the 15th May 1938 and find that it is not possible for the All-India Muslim League to treat or negotiate with the Congress the question of Hindu-Muslim settlement except on the basis that the Muslim League is the authoritative and representative organisation of the Mussalmans of India.

Resolution No. 2

The Council have also considered the letter of Mr Gandhi dated the 22nd May 1938 and are of opinion that it is not desirable to include any Muslim in the personnel of the proposed Committee that may be appointed by the Congress.

Resolution No. 3

The Executive Council wishes to make it clear that it is the declared policy of the All-India Muslim League that all other minorities should have their rights and interest safeguarded so as to create a sense of security amongst them and win their confidence and the All-India Muslim League will consult the representatives of such minorities and any other interest as may involved, when necessary.'

Bose, who was then in Wardha responded after due consideration and consultations with his colleagues in the Congress Working Committee. His letter treated as each of the League resolutions worthy of detailed comment. He said:

The First Resolution

Though the resolution does not use the adjective 'only', the language of the resolution means that the adjective is understood. There are Muslim organisations which have been functioning independently of the Muslim League. Some of them are staunch supporters of the Congress. It is not only impossible, but improper for the Congress to make the admission which the first resolution of the League Council apparently desires the Congress to make. The Working Committee therefore hopes that the League Council will not ask the Congress to do the impossible.

As to the *second resolution* of the Council, I am afraid that it is not possible for the Working Committee to conform to the desire expressed therein.

The *third resolution*, the Working Committee is unable to understand.

Jinnah's response was prompt, acerbic and unambiguous both in tone and in its content, virtually bringing to an end the Congress president Subhas Bose's initiative. It asserted amongst other issues, 'the All-India Muslim League,...does not require any admission or recognition from the Congress and nor did the resolution of the Executive Council passed at Bombay. But in view of the fact that the position, in fact the very existence of the League had been questioned by Pandit Jawaharlal Nehru, the (former) President of the Congress, in one of his statements wherein he asserted that there were only "two parties in the country" viz., "the British Government and the Congress", it was considered necessary by the Executive Council to inform the Congress of the basis on which the negotiations between the two organisations could proceed'.

This was the end of Bose's solo run on this rather difficult course. However, there did occur now, almost synchronously, two other distinct exchanges of letters that Jinnah had with Gandhi, and with Nehru, aimed at reconciling divergent viewpoints. Let us first dwell on Jinnah's correspondence with Nehru. However, even before we do that a brief backgrounder: Nehru's private judgements about Jinnah, shaped by intensely personal and emotional factors and aversions, certainly intruded into all his dealings with Jinnah. The two men were in various respects similar: both from marginal social groups (Jinnah, a Khoja Muslim, Nehru, a Kashmiri Pandit), trained as lawyers, anglicised, fastidious, vain, and once colleagues in the Congress party until Jinnah's resignation from it in 1920. Yet their dislike for one another was personal, intense, and palpable. Already in 1929, Nehru for his part was writing 'I do not see exactly how Jinnah will fit in. I find there is not very much in common between him and me so far as outlooks are concerned'. Revisiting this correspondence and revisiting those years, even in hindsight illustrates better than any commentary how much these two disliked one another. Nehru questioning the very fundamentals of the League's existence, opened the innings aggressively on 25 February

1938 when writing from Bombay he, somewhat disingenuously feigned ignorance, He wrote, amongst other aspects: 'I am afraid I must confess that I do not yet know what the fundamental points of dispute are. It is for this reason that I had been requesting you to clarify them. So far I have not received any help in this direction'. And there then followed, a somewhat gratuitous homily: 'But when we meet (if we do) what are we to discuss? Responsible people with organisations behind them can hardly discuss anything in the air'.

Jinnah responded: 'When you say that "I am afraid I must confess that I do not know what fundamental points in dispute are", I am only amazed at your ignorance', However, Nehru would not let up and within days on 8 March, from Allahabad teasingly he (Nehru) complained—'I go on requesting you to tell us what exactly are the points of dispute and you go on insisting that this should not be done by correspondence'. Jinnah was now irritated and responded sharply, with barely concealed sarcasm: 'I am surprised when you say—but what are these matters which are germane. Perhaps you have heard of the fourteen points'. Yet in all this, however, a retrospective re-read of all this may sound as if there was a continuity in Nehru's stand. He had consistently, during these years, asserted that there existed no 'communal question'. It is that which led *New Times* of Lahore to comment on 1 March 1938—'In its last session at Haripur, Congress had passed a resolution assuring minorities of their religious and cultural rights. The resolution was moved by Nehru and carried. But while speaking on the resolution he had said—I have examined the so called communal question through the telescope (sic) and, if there is nothing that you can see, (then) it appears to us that it is the height of dishonesty to move a resolution with these premises. If there is no minority question, why proceed to pass a resolution? Why not stare that there is no minority question?'

This was not the first time that Nehru had expressed his complete inability to understand or see the communal question. Nehru had also said in his speech that the 'communal award was merely a problem created by the middle or upper classes for the sake of a few seats in the legislature or appointments in government service or for ministerial positions'.

Nehru did hold that many of the demands involved changes in the constitution 'which we are not in a position to bring about', adding that the '14 points were somewhat out of date', and that to 'describe the communal award as not being anti-national would be patently false'. To all this Nehru added, 'I do not understand what is meant by our recognition of the Muslim League as the one and only organisation of Indian Muslims. Obviously, the Muslim League is an important communal organisation and we deal with it as such. But we have to deal with all organisations and individuals that come within our ken. We do not determine the measure of importance or distinction they possess'. This was patently dismissive and Jinnah was prompt, angry and equally pointed in his reply. Replying from Bombay to Nehru's 6 April letter sent from Calcutta, Jinnah replied on 12 April:

> As to your letter it has been to me a most painful reading. It seems to me that you cannot even accurately understand my letter, as you very honestly say that your mind is obsessed with the international situation (context 1938) and the terrible sense of impending catastrophe that hangs over the world, so you are thinking in terms entirely diverse from realities which face us in India, I can only express my great regret at your turning and twisting what I wrote to you and putting entirely a wrong complexion upon the position I (had) placed at your request.
>
> Whether any constitutional changes are necessary, whether we should do it by convention, agreement and so forth are matters, I thought of discussion, but I am extremely sorry to find that you have in your letter (already) pronounced (your) judgment...Your tone and language again display the same arrogance and militant spirit as if the Congress is the sovereign power and, as an indication, you extend your patronage by saying that 'obviously the Muslim League is an important communal organisation and we deal with it as such, as we have to deal with all organisations and individuals that come within our ken'. Here I may add that in my opinion, as I have publicly stated so often that unless the Congress recognises the Muslim League on a footing of complete equality, and is prepared as such to negotiate for a Hindu-Muslim settlement, we shall have to wait and depend upon our inherent strength which will 'determine the measure of importance or distinction it possesses.' Having regard to your mentality it is really difficult for me to make you understand the position any further'.

Jinnah, then in this very letter added 'that he did not propose to discuss issues through correspondence', any further.

It is striking that though, Jinnah's centrality, hence of the Muslim League was implicitly recognised by all the principal actors on the stage in this rapidly evolving situation in India—the viceroy, the entire

Congress leadership, Gandhi, Subhas Bose, all other political organisations, yet, Nehru had difficulty, uptil almost the last minute, in accepting this reality. Even though Jinnah's correspondence with Subhas Bose and Jawaharlal Nehru ended inconclusively and rather abruptly there still was Gandhi.

> Dear Shri Jinnah,
>
> Kher has given me your message. I wish I could do something but I am utterly helpless. My faith in Unity is as bright as ever; only I see no daylight out of the impenetrable darkness, and in such distress, I cry to God for light.
>
> Yours sincerely
> M. K. Gandhi

Jinnah had sent B.G. Kher,[47] [a Bombay lawyer] with a special message to Gandhi seeking Hindu-Muslim unity so as to jointly work for independence of India. Kher saw Gandhi at Tithal, in south Gujarat. As a result of this conversation Gandhi addressed the above letter to Jinnah, a classic response from the Mahatma. Continuing he added: 'You complain of my silence. The reason for my silence is literally and truly in my note. Believe me, the moment I can do something that can bring the two communities together, nothing in the world can prevent me from so doing'.

As this correspondence continued, Jinnah opened up somewhat, recollecting ruefully on 15 February 1938 in his letter:

> You say that when in 1915 you returned from South Africa. Everybody spoke of me as one of staunchest of nationalists and the hope of both the Hindus and Muslims, and you ask me a question, 'Are you still the same Jinnah?' And proceed further to say, 'If you say you are in spite of your speeches, I shall accept your word'. And you say that in my speeches you miss the old nationalist. Do you think that you are justified in saying that? I would not like to say what people spoke of you in 1915 and what they speak and think of you today. Nationalism is not the monopoly of any single individual, and in these days, it is very difficult to define it; but I don't wish to pursue this line of controversy any further.
>
> As regards the formulation of proposals which would form the basis of unity, do you think that this can be done by correspondence?

Gandhi replied:

> So far as I am concerned, just as on the Hindu-Muslim question I was guided by Dr Ansari, now that he is no more in our midst, I have accepted Maulana Abul Kalam Azad as my guide. My suggestion, therefore, to you is that conversation should be opened in the first instance as between you and the Maulana Sahib. But in every case regard me as at your disposal.

This was clearly an error, suggesting Maulana Azad as Gandhi's alternative in the dialogue, he was clearly not the interlocutor that Jinnah would, or could work with. And that was Jinnah's response, sent within days on 3 March 1938 from New Delhi, saying:

> [I] find that there is no change in your attitude and mentality when you say you would be guided by Maulana Abul Kalam Azad as Dr Ansari is no more. If you pursue this line you will be repeating the same tragedy as you did when you expressed your helplessness because Dr Ansari, holding pronounced and die-hard views, did not agree, and you had to say that you were willing, but what could you do. This happened, as you know, before you went to the Round Table Conference.
>
> At the Round Table Conference the tragedy was repeated by you when you seemed to be willing to accept provisionally certain terms: but you, there also, expressed that you were helpless as the Hindus were unwilling and you, as a representative of the Congress, would have no objection if the Hindus and Muslims came to an agreement.
>
> We have reached a stage where no doubt should be left that you recognise the All-India Muslim League as the one authoritative and representative organisation of the Muslims of India and, on the other hand, you represent the Congress and other Hindus throughout the country. It is only on that basis that we can proceed further and devise a machinery of approach.
>
> Of course, I shall be glad to see you, although I shall be equally glad to see Pandit Jawaharlal or Mr Bose as you may desire, The matter, as you know, will not be clinched without reference again to you by either of them. Therefore, I will prefer to see you first.

This correspondence continued, Gandhi sending a note on 8 March from Segaon in which he sidestepped his responsibility, He wrote to Jinnah: 'Two questions arising from your letter demand a reply. You ask me whether I have now seen the light. Much to my regret, I have to say, 'No'. You expect me to be able to speak on behalf of 'the Congress and other Hindus throughout the country', I am afraid I cannot fulfil the test'.

This question of Maulana Sahib being the opening interlocutor with Gandhi insisting and Jinnah denouncing continued inconclusively for some time, and sadly, for it was precisely time that was at premium in the prevailing situation, Gandhi continued asserting with this request on the ground that as the Congress was not just a 'Hindu' party therefore, it had a right to depute a Muslim representative, and sure enough Jinnah persisted unchangingly till the last that he, Jinnah, was the 'sole spokesman' of all Muslims in India. The impasse continued with Gandhi pursuing with his aim, writing to Jinnah on 15 April from Delhi.

'In any event, could Maulana Abul Kalam Azad accompany me at the interview? Please write to Wardha which place I am reaching tomorrow'. To which Jinnah's reply was terse but not impolite (as yet). He responded immediately on 16 April from Calcutta: 'I would prefer to see you alone'—Jinnah.

It is remarkable what assiduous and persistent letter writers political leaders of those days were. There was, of course, the telegram and telephone, too, but recourse was almost always had to the format of a letter, of corresponding and all fully in the knowledge that the Imperial Raj was snooping, opening mail, copying, reading, recording it all and only then letting it go to the addressee. And yet the written letter remained that infinitely more civilised mode of corresponding.

To the main narrative, we must now return. While this correspondence between the principal players continued, several other strands were at work, simultaneously. As for example, in June 1938, Khaliquzzaman had met Maulana Azad in Calcutta and found the Maulana very worried over the turn of political events. He assessed that in the absence of a Congress-League settlement, his own personal position would suffer greatly in Muslim society. He asked Khaliquzzaman whether he could suggest any formula which could be acceptable to both the Congress and the League. Khaliquzzaman had then told Maulana Saheb that the Bose formula would have been acceptable to the Muslim League if he had not subsequently brought in the question of other Muslim organisations and the other minorities. Several rounds of talks, between Congress, Muslim League and the government having all floundered, this stalemate in the League-Congress talks began to trouble the Muslim mind, too, more particularly as no redeeming, clear ideology then existed as a supporting pillar. Was the League to suffer the same fate as that of the Khilafat Committee after the collapse of the movement, they wondered? Or that of the Congress after the Civil Disobedience Movement of 1932 had dissipated itself?

Under such very complex stalemates then prevailing, Khaliquzzaman made a trip to Cairo and London to participate in consultations on the Palestine issue. He reached London on 1 November 1938 and for months had not much to do except to wait for the Arab delegation to arrive. He met Chaudhuri Rahmat Ali one evening in London, the originator of the word 'Pakistan'. This is how Khaliquzzaman then describes the meeting and the subsequent events, which eventually also contributed to the Pakistan resolution of March 1940:

> We started talking about the scheme of Pakistan. I found that not only had he thought deeply over the question but was earnest about its realisation. It was very well known to us in India that the had placed this scheme before the Muslim leaders of the First Round Table Conference but no one took any notice of it...After some discussion I informed him that I was already a convert to the idea but I told him that I was not ready to use the word 'Pakistan' for partition of the country because that would make the British suspicious on the one hand and antagonise the Hindus on the other. Why should we not claim the right of self-determination for our areas instead of bringing in the name of 'Pakistan'? But this did not appeal to him. We had many other talks on the same subject later on. On one occasion I had asked him to send me details of his scheme which he did in a letter to me on 12 December 1938...I preferred the idea of having two Muslim Federations, one in the East comprising Bengal and Assam and the other in North-Western India composed of Sind, Punjab and the North-Western Frontier Province....[48]

Khaliquzzaman continues:

> ...After the breakdown of the Palestine conference there was no reason left for our staying on in London and near about 10 March 1939 we decided to go back to India. A few days later I read a news item in the press that the under-secretary of state for India had returned after a tour of the country. I, therefore, thought it might be helpful to see him to find out what impressions he had brought back of the Muslim League strength and our policy. I discussed it with Rahman and we asked for an interview with

Col. Muirhead, the under-secretary, which was fixed for 14 March 1939. As soon as we sat down (I) naturally inquired from him as to what impressions he had formed after meeting our leaders in India about our strength and policies. Here I give the conversation between Col. Muirhead and myself as accurately as I can. (I believe the name of the under-secretary was Col. Muirhead.)

Col. Muirhead: Yes, I have met your leaders and have heard their case. We have got great sympathy with you but we do not know how to help. You say that the British democracy does not suit you and I see that it does not, but we do not know of any other kind of democracy. We apply the same principles in India, which we apply in our own country, and you do not suggest any alternative.

As soon as he finished this sentence, I went up to the map of India which was hanging in his room, and pointed out the two areas, northwest and east, which were Muslim areas which might be separated from the rest of India. When I returned to occupy my chair, he said with a smile: 'Yes, that is an alternative. Have you talked about it to Lord Zetland?'

I: No. We have met the colonial secretary, Mr McDonald, but not Lord Zetland.

Col. Muirhead: Why don't you see him?

I: I am leaving on the 21st March for India, and I do not know whether he will have time to give us an interview.

Col. Muirhead: Oh, no, I shall see that he gives you time. You just write a letter to him and you will get time.

Thereafter, we left our chairs. He came to see us off to the door when I said to him, 'I do not know whether he (Lord Zetland) knows our credentials.'

'Don't worry about that,' he replied. 'He will have every thing before him.'

So my idea about the British attitude was coming true.

In reply to our letter for interview, we were informed that the secretary of state for India would receive us in the afternoon of 20 March, just one day before I was to leave England for India.

Lord Zetland was very cordial and after a few preliminary exchanges of views about the weather, I started by giving him a brief survey of the Muslim relationship with the British government extending over one hundred and fifty years and brought it down to the Government of India Act 1935. Thereafter I said, 'Now that you are transferring more powers to India, you are doing it in such a manner that one hundred million Muslims might find themselves the slaves of the majority when you have completed the task'. At this stage he interrupted me and made the same remark which was made by the under secretary, namely, 'But you do not suggest any alternative'. It did not require any searching of my brain for I had already suggested the alternative to Col. Muirhead. Therefore, as soon as Lord Zetland raised the question of an alternative, I immediately replied, 'You may partition the Muslim areas from the rest of India and proceed with your scheme of federation of Indian provinces without including the Muslim areas which should be independent from the rest'.

Lord Zetland: What would happen to the states?

I: They ought to follow their geographical situation. If they are in the Hindu zone, they must go with them and if they are in the Muslim zone they must go with that zone.

Lord Zetland: What about Defence?

I: For what period, my Lord? If you want to know for the period that you are associated, in some form or the other, with the administration of India there would be no difficulty in the defence of India, because you can use the armies of both these areas, according to your needs. But if you want to know for the period that you are not in any way connected with the administration of the country, then I beg of your Lordship not to put that question to me, for God only knows what would happen to us then.

Lord Zetland: Do you want an answer from me?

I: It would be presumptuous on my part to ask for an answer to this big question just after mentioning it to you. I have brought it to your notice that this is going to be the stand of the Muslims in the next session of the Muslim League. There is ample time for you to think about it.

We were with Lord Zetland for one and a half hours, and when he rose to take leave, he informed us that there was a very important Cabinet meeting which he had to attend. He thought that the world situation was very grave and nobody could say what would happen. There might be a war in the near future.

Khaliquzzaman returned to Bombay on 12 May 1939. The same evening he met Jinnah and narrated the whole talk, which he had had with the under secretary and the secretary of state.

CONGRESS MINISTRY—1937 TO 1939—THE CONSEQUENCES

For approximately two years while the Congress ministries remained preoccupied with office, and the wielding of not so much of power as dispensing patronage, the Muslim League worked towards mobilising and consolidating Muslim support in North India. This, in large part, was on account of the anger generated by communal riots during this period, all occurring during the tenure of the Congress ministry. Placing the responsibility for these riots solely upon the Congress was of course, neither justified nor fair but then the party was holding office, and it was the Congress alone who would have to answer and be held accountable for any disorder in UP.

By the time the Congress ministries resigned, they had had the misfortune of governing during a phase of heightened communal violence and tension. Because of the anger that these riots generated many more Muslims in the United Provinces now found it easy to put their trust in communal champions like the League. Also, given that this coming to power of the Congress, mainly Hindu in composition, had resulted in generating a predictable mood of belligerence among the Hindus, in consequence it became much less likely now that the UP Muslims were going to look towards the Congress for any relief or shelter. The Muslim League, by regularly speaking up for the Muslims in all such situations, also by relentlessly criticising the Congress ministry's handling of the communal riots, made the Muslims even more wary of the Congress and drew them into the League's fold.

It is this fact of holding office that had made the Congress so vulnerable, for they were now the '*sarkar*',[49] therefore, in a province as communally sensitive as UP it was not difficult to charge them (Congress) with culpability for the riots that occurred. In consequence, the most formidable weapon in the hands of the Muslim League became this very holding of office by the Congress, and a running of the administration. In a sharply divided two-party system, as in the UP of post-1937 elections where the opposition was overwhelmingly Muslim and the party of government overwhelmingly Hindu, implications of such accusations were very serious; they became tragically destructive, deepening an existing divide, which events, unseeing obduracy and the malevolence of the Raj was already encouraging.

If communal riots eroded what support the Congress had among the UP Muslims, on the rebound, they greatly strengthened the Muslim League's influence over the community. This happened in two ways: the riots helped negatively by scuttling Congress efforts at reaching out to the Muslim populace, the League playing an important part in the process by using the riots and the Congress' handling of them as a way of discrediting the Congress in the eyes of the Muslims. Then secondly, the riots helped the League to stand out as the champion of Muslims. The riots took place in villages and small towns and affected artisans and peasants, mostly Muslim. This gave the League a valuable opportunity to stand up and to speak exclusively for the Muslims, win their allegiance—an especially valuable opportunity considering that the League until then had been socially and programmatically a conservative body.

In retrospect, the misdemeanours of local Congressmen, the implications of Congress rhetoric on the riots, errors of administrative judgment, also instances of possible bias might not have strained Congress-Muslim relations as much had the Muslim League not been around to constantly scratch at these already sore vulnerabilities. The League's indictment of the Congress was almost always designed to help Muslims make just such connections, as would further inflame passions. It was also the Muslim League that widely publicised the failures of the government, which in any case was their job as the principal opposition. However, more than interventions in the Assembly, it was their (the League's) propaganda in the *qasbahs*[50] and villages of the UP that helped firm up Muslim attitudes against the Congress.

Such campaigns by the League, against the Congress' management of communal disputes ranged from straight, demagogic denunciations to the relatively temperate, quasi-documented indictments such as in the Pirpur Report.[51] This report was a minor landmark in the history of communal relations in the UP. In fact when it came into circulation in early 1939, the then chief secretary of UP thought it could well increase communal tension in the province. The League, by putting their indictment in print, in the form of a book and circulating it widely while the Congress held office, scored a propaganda success.

These communal riots, mark the beginning of large-scale Muslim alienation, not just in UP but elsewhere, too, correspondingly a simultaneous strengthening of the League's claim to speak for the Muslims. The reason these riots proved to be a decisive factor lay not so much in their spread or intensity, but also in the political context in which they had occurred. UP, though, not new to prolonged and widespread communal violence was not central now, what gave these riots of 1937-39 altogether a new dimension was the presence of a Congress government in the province, for the first time ever, and also when almost every elected Muslim was sitting in the opposition. Every incident of communal violence therefore, became an indictment of Congress, and its presumed bias. Decidedly, a coalition government would not have totally eliminated such communal rioting but it would then have saddled the Muslim League too, with responsibility besides a large and representative Muslim component, jointly in office, would certainly have made the government less vulnerable to charges of sectarian prejudice. As things stood, the political context in which Muslims in the United Provinces experienced this round of communal rioting made the prospects of a non-sectarian approach near impossible.

The Congress, partly in reaction and partly as a corrective, then launched a mass Muslim contact campaign. This was their last serious attempt to mobilize Muslims in a joint struggle against colonial rule. All this was based on Nehru's set of assumptions, but without adequately taking into account the presence of the Muslim League in opposition, also of the great complexity of the communal problem, which had by then come to prevail. Sadly, for the Congress this mass contact programme, too, resulted in a further accenting of Jinnah's Muslim support. No doubt, Jawaharlal Nehru and other protagonists of this programme faced numerous difficulties: amongst which stood the stout resistance of Jinnah; lukewarm support of their own party (the Congress) colleagues; and communal animosities manifest in the rioting. However, these problems were neither new nor insurmountable, as Nehru's own post-elections assessment of the communal situation had propounded earlier.

Despite all these unearned gains the Muslim League suffered from several shortcomings, it was divided and comparatively disorganised, and Jinnah did not still command the total allegiance of the powerful provincial groups of Punjab, the UP, and Bengal. These aspects, too, place Jinnah's outburst[52] against mass contact and the League's endeavours to arrest the progress of that programme in the correct perspective. The Congress soon lost heart, and whatever little steam and stamina the party had for this 'reach out to the Muslims' endeavour, the mass contact campaign finally petered out. This allowed Jinnah, yet again, to take advantage of the deteriorating communal relations and to rally Muslims around himself as the 'sole saviour' and hope for a 'separate Muslim homeland'.

In retrospect, it would seem as if this pre-condition for the recognition of the Muslim League as the one and only organisation of Muslims was asserted by Jinnah so as to avoid coming to the negotiating table. In

March 1938 when Nehru had urged the League leader to spell out the demands of the League, all that he could do was to refer Nehru to the 'Fourteen Points', and to an anonymous article in *The Statesman* dated 12 February 1938, along with another article in *The New Times* of 1 March 1938 plus also a statement by M.S. Aney, the Nationalist Party leader.[53]

THE SECOND WORLD WAR—THE CONGRESS—THE MUSLIM LEAGUE

At this critical juncture, the Second World War reached India. Lord Linlithgow on 4 September 1939, declared India as a combatant country and an ally, in a war that uptil then had largely been an Europe conflict. Protests flared instantly on this announcement. The viceroy's constitutional position was that as India was a subject country, with Britain at war it was then automatically at war. The viceroy was later criticised both in India and by elements in Britain for not asking the Legislative Assembly for their assent about India's entry into the war. However, when Linlithgow actually made his 'India at War' statement he was not criticised either by Gandhi or by any other responsible leader, all that came much later. On the merits of consulting the Assembly, quite apart from the constitutional position, Linlithgow later reasonably enquired of high representatives of the Crown 'where he would have been if Congress had refused his request (as they perhaps would have done)'.

On 4 September 1939, the viceroy saw Jinnah. Before the interview he had received a message from Sikandar Hayat Khan, who asked that nothing should be done to inflate Jinnah or make him more difficult to deal with. Sikandar Hayat Khan also repeated what he had already said in public 'that the Punjab and Bengal were wholly behind the government in the prosecution of the war whatever Jinnah and his friends might say'.[54]

The viceroy conveyed to Jinnah, as he had already to Gandhi, the need of suspending federal negotiations. Jinnah said he regretted that Sikandar Hayat Khan had rushed in front of his colleagues in the Muslim League to pledge co-operation. He had no feelings against Sikandar Hayat Khan, but as Sikandar alone could not deliver the goods, Jinnah asked the viceroy to strengthen his hands. He wanted something positive to take back to his followers, preferably a complete re-shaping of the constitution. Linlithgow asked if he wanted that the Congress ministries be turned out? 'Yes! Turn them out at once. Nothing else will bring them to their senses. Their object, though you may not believe it, and though I did not believe it till two years [back], is nothing less than to destroy both you British and us Muslims. They will never stand by you.'[55] The viceroy then asked Jinnah to explain a statement he had recently made in public that he no longer believed in democratic government for India. How was India to obtain self-government if not by democracy? Jinnah replied that the escape from this impasse lay in partition.

This was perhaps the first occasion where Jinnah mentioned a 'partition of India', formally. The viceroy saw Jinnah again, just a day later, on 5 October 1939, and found him more friendly and co-operative than earlier. Jinnah began by thanking Linlithgow for helping him (Jinnah) keep the Muslims together to which the viceroy, somewhat self-righteously responded that it 'was in public interest that the Muslim point of view be fully and competently expressed'. The viceroy then complained that he had not made much headway with the Congress, also that it would be difficult in any declaration to go beyond promising possible modifications in the existing constitutional scheme, and that, too, at the end of the war. There was little point in proclaiming the intention of granting dominion status on the coming of peace, if an essential preliminary like Federation, was not agreed to, at least in form,[56] by the two major communities. Jinnah did not like the idea of such a declaration as it would only increase communal tension. He saw no chance of unity unless Congress gave up the claim to speak on behalf of all parties and recognised the Muslim League as representing the Muslims, though he accepted that he had failed to move Nehru on this. Jinnah then pleaded for more protection for the Muslims. The viceroy replied that he had examined the position carefully but could find no specific instances of oppression. Jinnah said that the Hindus had 'a subtle intention'[57] to undermine the Muslim position, as for example in the instruction issued in the North-West Frontier Province for compulsory teaching of Hindi.

By the middle of November 1939, all the Congress ministries had resigned; several of them did so hesitantly and with real regret.

The outbreak of the war and subsequent resignations of the Congress ministries introduced a new element in India's politics; most significantly the Congress now lost its bargaining power, this strategic error of resigning office adding to an already long list of blunders that the Congress had already committed. *As* long as its ministries were in office, Linlithgow could not ignore the Congress, after all they (the Congress) were responsible for the governance of eight of the eleven British Indian provinces, and had within their power certainly the potential of obstructing, if not actually impairing, the government's war efforts. When however, the Congress ministries resigned, Linlithgow's attitude also changed, for there was now no urgent necessity to placate the Congress. Parliamentary governance had been suspended in the Congress held provinces and the administration resumed directly through Governor's rule, consequently the conduct of the war effort actually became so much easier. The British generally believed that in view of earlier commitments against fascism it was highly unlikely that the Congress would actually embark on a campaign of civil disobedience for no doubt international opinion would then roundly condemn any action thwarting the allied war effort. Besides, the viceroy was confident that the powers of the Raj were sufficient to deal with any Congress campaign of civil disobedience, should that at all be undertaken.

The Muslim League, late in 1939, did not come out openly in support of the government's war effort, but it did not also oppose it: the Muslim ministries of Bengal and the Punjab, in fact, announced and did render unconditional support. However, the Congress's insistence on a definition of Britain's war aims before it would agree to cooperate caused Linlithgow to suspect that Congress was manoeuvring to take advantage of Britain's difficulties. In order then to offset Congress hostility, and perhaps mindful of the dangers of Congress and the Muslims combining in their hostility against the British, as they had done during the Khilafat movement at the end of the First World War, (1857 again?) the viceroy sought support elsewhere. The obvious and only choice was Jinnah and his Muslim League. Linlithgow found it expedient to then befriend the Muslim League and encourage it to become a rival of the Congress on the all India scene. In the process, the government used the existence of 'internecine conflicts' between the Hindus and Muslims to consolidate its own position. Jinnah was not slow to recognise the changed situation. He remarked: 'After the war began...I was treated on the same basis as Mr Gandhi. I was wonderstruck why all of a sudden I was promoted and given a place side by side with Mr Gandhi'.[58]

In turning to Jinnah for support, Linlithgow knew that he could count on him. As early as August 1938, Jinnah had hinted to Lord Brabourne, then an acting viceroy, about the possibility of the Muslim League cooperating with the British, and had ended up with the startling suggestion that (Brabourne's description) British should 'keep the Centre as it is now, that we should make friends with the Muslims by protecting them in the Congress provinces and that if we did that, the Muslims would protect us at the Centre'.[59] Jinnah's disclosure had then not surprised Lord Zetland; it only confirmed his 'conviction that the dominating factor in India would prove to be the All-India Muslim League.'[60] He had long held the view that 'the solidarity of Islam is a hard fact against which it is futile to run one's head'.[61]

Later, in 1945, commenting upon the development following the outbreak of war, Jinnah remarked: 'There was going to be a deal between Mr Gandhi and Lord Linlithgow. Providence helped us. The war which nobody welcomes proved to be a blessing in disguise'.[62] Jinnah understood the benefits of collaborating with British and took full advantage of the situation and altered stance. However, he neither antagonised the British by attempting to extract too many concessions, nor adopted the opposite course of offering unconditional support in the war effort. He did not, therefore, reject the British offer outright but no sooner had one of his demands been met, then back he came promptly with another. By playing his cards adroitly he was able to secure for the League a status equal to that of the Congress. The Congress, on the other hand, displayed poverty of forethought, lack of statesmanship and absence of flexibility, in consequence it could simply not regain its earlier position of primacy. 'The League', wrote V.P. Menon, 'grew rapidly in [this] sunshine of [Imperial] favour'.[63]

There is a need to record here the contrast between the League's, really Jinnah's offer, and their more than implicit cooperation with the Raj in the war effort and what Mahatma Gandhi offered, it contrasts sharply. Through Viceroy Linlithgow Gandhi offered to the British government and the British people his assistance through non-violence. He suggested that they (the British) lay down their arms and practice 'ahimsa'. This was not anything other than a very seriously meant proposal. Towards the beginning of July 1940, Gandhi addressed an open letter to the British. It was published in the *Amrita Bazar Patrika* of 4 July 1940 under the, 'Method of non-violence—Mahatma Gandhi's appeal to every Briton'. It read, in parts to say:

> I appeal for cessation of hostilities...because war is bad in essence. You want to kill Nazism. Your soldiers are doing the same work of destruction as the Germans. The only difference is that perhaps yours are not as thorough as the Germans...I venture to present you with a nobler and a braver way, worthy of the bravest soldiers. I want you to fight Nazism without arms or...with non-violent arms. I would like you to lay down the arms you have as being useless for saving you or humanity...Invite Herr Hitler and Signor Mussolini to take what they want of the countries you call your possessions. Let them take possession of your beautiful island with your many beautiful buildings. You will give all these but not your souls nor your minds....

It is difficult to comment equably on this open letter. However, it does raise the query—What did the viceroy think upon getting this letter? Did he send this advice to London? And what did the soldiers, sailors and airmen think (it was after all an open, published letter)—British, Indian and of the dominions—those that were fighting and dying, or what their loved ones thought upon reading this appeal?

To revert to our examination—Jinnah was grateful to Linlithgow for his help in a consolidation of the League. In an interview Jinnah 'thanked Linlithgow with much graciousness for what he had done to assist him in keeping his party together and expressed gratitude for this'.[64] The Congress was 'non-cooperating', and in order to counter its demands the viceroy thought it necessary to have a powerful Muslim League as a counter-weight. The general consensus of opinion within the Government of India was against any settlement with the Congress, instead it inclined towards an accommodation of the Muslim League's demands. It should be remembered that Viceroy Linlithgow saw his primary responsibility as keeping the Indian Empire intact during the war, and to maximise India's war effort. That is why he favoured publicising the war, the irreconcilable demands of the minorities and insisted that agreement between the major parties (the Congress and the League) must be a precondition for any constitutional progress. In response to Linlithgow's advice Lord Zetland stated in the House of Lords that the British government felt the necessity for an agreement between the Hindus and the Muslims to be a precondition for any constitutional changes.

Early in November 1939, Linlithgow invited Gandhi, Rajendra Prasad and Jinnah to a joint discussion. He claimed that this 'lack of prior agreement between the major communities, such as would contribute to harmonious working in the Centre' was primarily responsible for delays in constitutional progress. He was, therefore, asking them to meet among themselves and submit agreed proposals 'which could be considered for some expansion of the Governor-General's Council at the Centre'. It seemed that Linlithgow was not prepared to allow the Congress to return to power save on his chosen terms. The Congress rejected the viceroy's proposals on the grounds that the crisis in India had been caused by the viceroy's declaration of India as a belligerent without the consent of the people. The Congress had not resigned because of any conflict with the League, for which reason there was no fresh necessity to work out any agreed proposals. The negotiations, the Congress claimed, failed because of the fundamental differences between the Congress and the British government.

Linlithgow did not, in his public statement on the failure of his talks, refer even once to the conflict between the British and the Congress, but only to that between the Congress and the League, thus giving ground for suspecting that his main objective in arranging these talks was to use them for advertising differences between the two and to claim that they persisted despite British efforts. An anti-British freedom movement had sadly now got centred on Hindu-Muslim rivalry. The focus against the British Raj had diffused, its core not centrally against the Empire any more.

The Congress leaders did meet Jinnah but no agreement could be reached as Jinnah's position was delicate. He could not openly refuse to be a party to the Congress demands for a declaration of war aims; if he did decline, he would promptly be branded as unpatriotic and 'pro-British'. At the same time, he could not very well support the Congress without first obtaining some concessions for the League, because were he to do so he would not only earn the disfavour of government but also strengthen the Congress, and that too, clearly at the expense of the League. He therefore side-stepped the main discussion by putting forward five conditions as his price for cooperating with the Congress: coalition ministries should be formed in the provinces; no measure should be passed by the legislatures if two-thirds of the Muslim members objected to it; the Congress flag should not be flown on public buildings; the singing of '*Vande Mataram*' should be abandoned; and the Congress should stop its campaign of mass contact of the Muslims. It was hardly likely that the Congress could concede even one of these but Jinnah did throw the onus of reaching a settlement or failing to, back on the Congress.

There is enough evidence in the preceding paragraphs to offer that Jinnah at this stage was working in collaboration with the viceroy. In an interview with Linlithgow, Jinnah admitted that Gandhi had enquired of him whether it was possible for the Congress and the Muslim League to jointly demand the declaration for which the Congress had been pressing the British government. Jinnah was thus placed in an embarrassing position and had difficulty in refusing to support Congress demands. The Congress leaders warned that unless Jinnah was prepared to join them in putting up a demand, he would be exposed before the public as the real obstacle to India's independence. In this situation Linlithgow decided to call off the idea of an all-parties conference, which he had planned to convene in order to expose the 'hollowness' of the Congress's claim to speak for the whole of India. The viceroy realised that while such a conference could perhaps, compromise the Congress' claim of representing all of India but it would then also confirm the Congress allegation that Jinnah was working for the British government. While reporting to Zetland the summary of his interview with Jinnah, Linlithgow candidly admitted:

> He [Jinnah] had given me very valuable help by standing against the Congress claims and I was duly grateful. It was clear that if he, Mr Jinnah had supported the Congress demand and confronted me with a joint demand, the strain upon me and His Majesty's Government would have been very great indeed. I thought therefore, I could claim to have a vested interest in his position.[65]

The above quote explains in plain terms the reason behind the British efforts to encourage the League; they were after all engaged in a war, a life and death effort for the British, and it would have been virtually impossible not to concede the Congress demands (which effectively amounted to independence) if they had the backing of the Muslim League, too. That is why for the Raj it was clearly a priority to somehow prevent the League from joining hands with the Congress, certainly for the duration of the war. And to reverse the calculations—it was equally necessary, therefore, for the Congress to not be duped by such an obvious British ploy. But all this now is no doubt hindsight.

The viceroy, though, gave a different version for public consumption. He said that he had 'begged' the leaders in 'most earnest manner to spare no endeavour to reach agreement',[66] and emphasized that it was essentially a question affecting Indians alone and on which agreement between the Indian themselves was essential. However, the India League, an organisation headed by Krishna Menon and representing the Congress in London, guessed what Linlithgow was up to. It issued a rejoinder denying that the talks between the Congress and the Muslim League had broken down on 'communal issues' and claimed that Jinnah had raised no such objections. It also claimed that the breakdown did not 'mean communal disagreement but rather the intensification of differences with British policy and a break with the British government which was refusing to make a satisfactory declaration'.[67]

India League's statement created some consternation in the India Office. Wanting to have it refuted, Zetland asked Linlithgow if it would be possible to persuade Jinnah to issue to Reuters a statement contradicting the India League's assertion. Such a reply would be given the widest publicity, both in Britain and the USA. Jinnah evinced interest and promised to give a befitting reply but on a 'suitable occasion'.[68]

There is no clear evidence, however, to show that Jinnah ever did give that 'befitting reply'. In the third week of December 1939, while corresponding with Nehru for exploring means for a detente between the Congress and the League, Jinnah did suddenly veer off uncharacteristically and called upon the Muslims to celebrate 'Deliverance Day'. This was supposed to be deliverance from the 'tyranny, oppression and injustice during the last two and a half years'[69] of Congress rule. Jinnah also urged the Government of India to enquire into the anti-Muslim policy of the Congress ministries. Attempts to persuade him to call off this 'Deliverance Day' failed, and his statement was construed as an open attack on the Congress. In consequence, negotiations between Nehru and Jinnah immediately came to an end. In the absence of any definite evidence it would be hasty to suggest that Jinnah's call was inspired by the government, but Linlithgow was inclined to regard it as a 'convincing reply'[70] to India League's statement. He claimed, in his correspondence with the secretary of state, that Jinnah by calling for 'Deliverance Day' had given sufficient evidence that the communal problem was a live issue. Meanwhile, so as to better explain to the British Cabinet and Parliament the Muslim position, Linlithgow proposed a Muslim delegation to Britain. Zetland demurred, considering the idea as somewhat 'misconceived', he felt instead that propaganda should not be confined solely to negative insistence that the Muslims could not be a party to self-government in India on the principle of unqualified majority. In order to be successful, the League ought to clarify the terms and conditions on which they would be prepared to accept self-government.

Linlithgow thereafter began to urge the Muslim League to put forward 'concrete proposals' to counteract the Congress's demand for independence, and a constituent assembly to frame a constitution for independent India. Linlithgow spoke to Jinnah on several occasions urging that it would be impossible to educate public opinion in Britain and 'more particularly' the 600-odd representative in the House of Commons by simply a submission of a formal memorandum to the British government. Reporting to Zetland on this subject Linlithgow wrote: 'I again put forward the familiar argument for formulating and publishing constructive policy and in the light of our discussion he said that he was disposed to think that it would be wise for his friends and himself to make public at any rate the outlines of their position in good time'.[71]

Still not very strong on the ground the League was probably not in a position at this stage to commit itself fully on the constitutional issue, but it could also not afford to postpone such a commitment indefinitely. Both the Congress and the Muslim League had rejected the British government's scheme, embodied in the 1935 Act, to establish an all-India federation. The Congress had countered it by an alternative plan of a constitution to be framed by a constituent assembly. The League while opposing both the British and the Congress proposals had no plans of its own. Previously it had subscribed nominally to the idea of a loose federation for India. The results of the 1937 elections had clearly shown that despite separate electorates and reservation of seats, the League could not hope to play a decisive role in the proposed federation, and that adherence to an all-India federation would leave them gravely disadvantaged. He suggested instead that the British government should revise India's future constitution de novo.

THE 'PAKISTAN' RESOLUTION—LAHORE 1940

It is in these circumstances that the fateful fourth decade of the twentieth century arrived. The year 1940 opened with two basic issues before the country: whether the viceroy's offer to expand his Council was acceptable to the main political parties; and, whether the formation of a Consultative Group of the Indian leaders for the prosecution of the war, would, in turn, be acceptable to the political parties concerned.

At a meeting of the League's Working Committee in February 1940, in Delhi, on the viceroy's suggestions a proposal was mooted to send a League delegation to London to plead its case before the prime minister and the secretary of state. Jinnah, in fact, suggested that Khaliquzzaman should form part of that delegation. Thereupon, a resolution on the subject was adopted. The members of this delegation were Fazlul Haq, Sikandar Hayat Khan, Khwaja Nazimuddin and Khaliquzzaman himself.

In the Working Committee meeting of the League of February 1940, while discussing the proposed delegation to London, guidance was sought from Jinnah on the matters to be placed before the British government. Khaliquzzaman had informed the Committee members of his meeting with Zetland and Col. Muirhead. The Working Committee had then discussed, an alternative to the 'Federal Objective'. Sir Sikandar's scheme proposing a division of India into seven different zones also then came up for discussion. He had pleaded for his confederal scheme but Jinnah opposed it. The scheme of 'Muslim zones' separated from the rest of India, discussed earlier with Zetland and Muirhead was finally approved. This was the first time that the Muslim League Working Committee had decided to claim a division of India. No one knew how, what provinces and where to 'partition' India, but inexorably the lines of fate were now getting etched deeper.

On 6 February 1940, Jinnah formally informed the viceroy that the Muslim League in its open session at Lahore, on 23 March, was going to ask for the partition of the country. Lord Zetland was, by then, also aware of these developments.

This 23 March 1940 session of the All-India Muslim League emphatically rejected the scheme of federation contained in the Government of India Act 1935. Its resolution asked for a federation of Punjab, Sind, NWFP and Baluchistan with complete autonomy and sovereign powers and of other states in the East[72] with similar powers. The resolution was moved by Fazlul Haq in the open session and Khaliquzzaman was asked by Jinnah to second it.

It was adopted by the midnight of 23 March 1940.[73] The next morning newspaper headlines everywhere claimed of a 'Pakistan Resolution' having been passed, though, this word had not been used by anyone in the speeches, nor was it in the main body of the Resolution. The press had supplied to the Muslim masses a slogan that instantly conveyed the idea of a state. It would have taken long for the Muslim leaders to explain the Lahore Resolution and to convey its real meaning and significance. This labour to propagate the full import of the Resolution amongst the citizens, was now greatly facilitated, also accelerated by the press in naming the resolution as the 'Pakistan Resolution'. Yet another inerasable line had got drawn by fate.

This Lahore resolution radically altered the dimensions of what was till then a communal problem. All solutions hitherto considered—separate electorates; composite cabinets; reservation of seats, parity—all suddenly became totally irrelevant. 'For the moment', wrote a British newspaper, 'Mr Jinnah has re-established the reign of chaos in India'.[74] This 'Pakistan resolution' added to the complexities of the constitutional controversy which the Congress leaders had earlier regarded as a simple issue between themselves and the British government.

Dr Latif observed later that 'The real Muslim problem does not concern so much the Muslims of those parts where they form a majority, and where they can look after themselves; in any constitution, as it concerns the Muslim minority from Delhi, Lucknow, Patna towns to Cape Comorin, who would be rendered eternal orphans under Mr Jinnah's plan....I have found Mr Jinnah incapable of conceiving the hundred million Muslims in India as an indivisible entity and that we can secure all the advantages of his Pakistan without having to labour under its inevitable disadvantages by setting the scheme against an all-India background.'

From Jinnah's point of view, the 'Pakistan resolution' was a part of his carefully planned strategy. He knew that the idea of a Muslim state, in or out of India, would prove to be a catch-all. He refused to spell the details of this 'Pakistan', principally because he had none, and his followers were thus left free to picture a Pakistan as their fancy led them to. The orthodox dreamt of a state representing the purity of a pristine Islam; those with a more 'secular outlook' (!) succumbed to the prospects of financial benefits from their 'own state'. Besides, this vision of a sovereign Muslim state was redolent with memories of the past glories of Muslim rule. Most Muslims therefore, took up the idea enthusiastically. Was this 'Pakistan' resolution, amongst other factors also the League's response to the viceroy's persistent request for a 'constructive proposal'?

Besides, once this 'Pakistan resolution' of 1940, had been adopted it became essential for the League to gain control of Muslim politics in that province, which was, as Jinnah said, 'the cornerstone of Pakistan'.[75] Jinnah later denied that he had promised not to interfere in provincial matters and asked how there could be a 'pact' between a leader (himself) and a follower (Sikandar Hayat).[76] He called upon Muslim leaders in the Punjab to abandon their 'sectional interests, jealousies, tribal notions and selfishness' and to substitute devotion to Islam and 'your nation'.[77] However, as late as 1944, Jinnah's negotiations with Khizr Hayat Khan, the then chief minister, failed and as a result, his prestige and that of the League suffered a setback in this vital province.[78]

In Bengal also there were constant clashes between Jinnah and the chief minister, Fazlul Haq, from 1937 until his defeat in 1943. 'In September 1941, long after the League, and by implication all Muslims, had officially adopted Pakistan as the goal, Fazlul Haq in a letter resigning from the Working Committee and Council of the League, protested in the strongest terms against the manner in which the interests of the Muslims of Bengal and the Punjab were being imperilled by the Muslim leaders of the minority provinces, and complained of the way in which the principles of democracy and autonomy were being subordinated to the arbitrary wishes of a single individual'.[79] When Fazlul Haq's ministry was defeated in 1943 Jinnah rejoiced at the fall of this 'curse to the politics of Bengal'.[80]

6

SUNSET OF THE EMPIRE— 'POST-DATED CHEQUE ON A COLLAPSING BANK'

THE LAHORE RESOLUTION (23 MARCH 1940)—A RETROSPECT

From a negative construct one can scarcely extract a positive product. The seeds of a vivisection of India having being sown, ceaselessly, year after year, as much by us (Hindus and Muslims) as by the post-Second World War enfeebled British; for they did of course divide to rule, but we also divided ourselves; what else could then follow but a destructive break-up?

M.R.A. Baig started working with Jinnah from 1934 on the latter's return from England till March 1940. Earlier he had met him several times in the company of people like Sarojini Naidu. As Baig stated himself that having known Jinnah in such circumstances as with Sarojini Naidu etc., he would not take him as seriously as Jinnah took himself. In consequence, unlike most of his followers, Baig was never in awe of him. He fell out with Jinnah over the Lahore Resolution which he felt to be communal. He, then became Jinnah's secretary and has recorded in his biographical memoir: 'Mr Jinnah left for Lahore', on this fateful journey and enterprise, 'about the middle of March 1940. I saw him the day before he left but neither by word nor manner did he give the slightest hint that the Pakistan Resolution was going to be moved'. However, the move it did, with or without the intent to actually divide. Baig goes onto then quote Penderel Moon: 'Privately, Jinnah told one or two people in Lahore that this Resolution was a "tactical move"; and the fact that six years later he was ready to accept something less than absolute partition suggests that in 1940 he was not really irrevocably committed to it. In part, therefore, it could well have been at this time [just] a tactical move, designed to [wrest] from Congress such concessions [as] would make [the] partnership, more tolerable. Certainly, the implications of the Resolution and even the composition of the proposed "Independent States" and their inter-relations had not at this stage [even] been thought out. Some of these matters were clarified later, but Jinnah was never keen to expound the exact nature of Pakistan, and right up till 1947 there was some doubt as to what he would accept'.

Gandhi, on the other hand, held that the Muslims must have the same right of self-determination that the rest of India has. 'We are at present a joint family. Any member may claim a division'. This view he frequently expressed. However, Nehru's response to Pakistan resolution had been 'if people wanted such things as suggested by the Muslim League at Lahore' how could they work with us. That being so it is somewhat startling to find the Congress, in April 1942, rejecting by a large majority C. Rajagopalachari's proposal that for the purpose of negotiation Congress should recognise Muslim separatism in some form, without closely defining what was implied.

Raja Sahib Mahmudabad in *Some Memories* (echoing what M.R.A. Baig said in his memoirs) that: 'My advocacy of an Islamic state brought me into conflict with Jinnah. He thoroughly disapproved of my ideas and dissuaded me from expressing them publicly from the League platform lest the people might be led to believe that Jinnah shared my view and that he was asking me to convey such ideas to the public. As I was convinced that I was right and did not want to compromise Jinnah's position, I decided to cut myself away and for nearly two years kept my distance from him, apart from seeing him during the working committee meetings and on other formal occasions'.[1]

With or without real intent this dice of united India's future had been rolled, and it kept rolling, fatefully, from one event to another for the next six event filled years: The Cripps Mission (1942); 'Quit India'—(April to September 1942); the Wavell Viceroyalty (June 1943); the Simla Conference (September 1944); the Second World War ends—the Cabinet Mission (July 1946); the Interim Government (July 1946); Wavell to Mountbatten—the fixing of a time limit—the final deconstruction of India. How could a positive outcome have emerged when all along we were set to dismember this 'one India', to actually deconstruct it?

It is in this event-filled short period that we now travel, along with those men and women who then held united India's future in their hands:

Must helpless man, in ignorance sedate,
Roll darkling down the torrent of his fate?
[Samuel Johnson—*The Vanity of Human Wishes* (1749)]

The Backdrop

The 'Cripps Mission', though, was still considered a possible opening despite all that had already happened. It is believed that amongst the various other factors that finally led to this mission was also a weekend at Filkins (Cripps' country house), to which Nehru had been invited while on a visit to England some years earlier, in the period June-October 1938. He went with Krishna Menon. Others on that weekend's guest list were Attlee, Aneurin Bevan and Harold Laski, apart from the host himself—Cripps,[2] amounting almost to a weekend meet of the India Conciliation Group sub-committee. Amongst the subjects discussed were the means by which the next Labour government would transfer power in India. The ideas considered included a constituent assembly composed on the basis of universal suffrage, subject to separate minority representation and the 'election' of members from princely states. Once this body had adopted a constitution, the Crown's treaties with the princes would lapse, so at least this 'sub-committee' had then surmised. In London, a fortnight later, Nehru therefore, told a meeting[3] that the idea of an all-India federation ought to be abandoned in favour of a constituent assembly.

During this period the dominion status debate was still alive, as was the phrase 'status', made clear by Lord Balfour in 1926, as 'complete self-government and absolute liberty to terminate partnership in the British Commonwealth of Nations'.[4] In November 1939, dissatisfaction with the official policy persuaded Cripps, to send Sir Stewart, then permanent under secretary for India, a scheme that promised India just that, dominion status. This scheme proposed an immediate implementation of Britain's promises and also a conceding of the right to India to frame its own constitution through a constituent assembly. As an Act of Parliament would be needed for this some delay was unavoidable, but His Majesty's Government affirmed that they would bind themselves to introducing a bill 'immediately after the war, or even before should a suitable opportunity arise'. Cripps then envisaged an 'assembly of some two thousand members, chosen on the basis of the existing provincial electorate, with adequate proportional representation of the citizens of the states, but he was open to such alternative ideas about the structure of the assembly as were agreeable to the Indian parties'. Britain would endorse decisions taken by the assembly on a three-fifths vote, provided only that the assembly agreed to enter into a fixed term treaty, (Cripps had suggested fifteen years), whereby Britain could discharge its obligations to the princes, the minorities, and the services, also for defence, finance, and commerce. For the present, Britain would 'do its utmost in association with the representatives of the Indian people to arrange such expedients as are possible under the existing constitution to give the Indian people a larger measure of self-government during the war.[5] All this is cited to underscore, how and why Cripps' bonafides in Jawaharlal Nehru's mind had got established, besides placing Cripps amongst the most forward-looking Labour leaders on the question of India's independence.

On a non-official visit to India, upon reaching Allahabad on 8 December 1939, Cripps had an occasion to again discuss this scheme with Nehru. From his first reactions, Nehru seemed to regard Cripps' proposal as offering some basis, though lacking the needed ballast of adult suffrage. Under the existing provincial franchise, the Muslim representatives in the envisaged constituent assembly would simply not agree with Congress on any revised constitution that failed to accommodate the Leagues' (class and community) interests. Nehru, on the other hand, continued to remain single-mindedly fixed upon undercutting the Muslim landlords and middle classes, through full adult franchise. If that were adopted, he argued, then the Congress would be willing to allow even special communal representation for the minorities, though, he continued to object to the words dominion status. This was a fixation with him. He also gravely doubted the need for the treaty period to be fifteen years, or for it to provide "minority rights in any other manner but through the constitution. Reporting to Mahadev Desai, Gandhi's secretary, Nehru had remarked that the scheme had some desirable features but also had two or three fatal defects. He (Nehru) was by now, in 1939, not going to intemperately pick a quarrel with Gandhi again on this score as he had in 1927. However, sadly dominion status as an option for India was perhaps already too late by now.

Cripps had also by now gradually begun to grasp the complexities of the Indian communal problem better, for even Congressmen like G.D. Birla admitted then that Congress may have been seriously at fault in excluding non-Congress Muslims from provincial cabinets in 1937.[6] In consequence Muslims, such as Liaquat Ali Khan in Uttar Pradesh, felt that they would be consigned to a permanent opposition in their own country—India. They wanted not merely cultural safeguards but an equal voice in politics, with power to veto legislation inimical to their (Muslim) interests. Here again unfortunately, events had outstripped ideas, perhaps the time for safeguards was over, Jinnah, now wanted a settlement of the communal question on constitutional lines, prior, that is, to any settlement of the issue of freedom from British rule. His experience of Congress provincial governments had convinced the rank and file of the League and, of course, Jinnah that unless constitutionally legislated safeguards, against the tyranny of majoritarianism, were mandated the Muslims would eventually lose all; implications of such a position being that as things stood, the Muslim League would not attend a constituent assembly functioning on the basis of a majority vote. There was an even greater, and strategically more significant, and saddening shift: The freedom movement against the Imperial British had by now become almost fixedly a Congress vs the Muslim League struggle, in consequence it became a direct Hindu-Muslim question. This suited the British Raj admirably. They could now concentrate undisturbed on meeting the many challenges of the Second World War, for as the principal Indian parties had divided themselves what else did the British have to do but rule.

On 11 December 1939, Cripps then undertook a journey to Lahore by train, pondering during that journey over some thoughts: 'A picture of a rather loose federation of provinces with few reserved subjects and with the right of the provinces to withdraw if they wish and new boundaries to make provinces either predominantly Muslim or Hindu—as the sort of lines of a possible settlement, with a constituent assembly to work out the scheme. It might be necessary to agree to the basis of the outcome of the constituent assembly in advance'.[7] The next day, 12 December 1939, at Lahore, which was then governed by a Unionist ministry, discussions with Premier Sikandar Hayat Khan, corroborated the trend of Cripp's thoughts: a settlement in terms of a 'loose federation as a prior condition of detailed constitution-making'.

On 15 December 1939, he met Jinnah in Bombay, where Jinnah again underlined the impossibility of 'western democracy' in India, with its inevitable permanent entrenchment of the majority community. Jinnah asserted that a Constituent Assembly was not the correct procedure until one had kicked out Great Britain, that 'the power factor had to be decided first'.[8] His immediate proposals were 'that Congress should accept the Muslim League as the negotiator on behalf of the Muslims; that Muslims should be represented in the provincial governments and that no bill should be proceeded with if two-thirds of the Muslim members of the legislature objected to it on communal grounds'.[9] Cripps questioned Jinnah on his recent call for Muslims to celebrate 22 December as a day of deliverance from Congress provincial governments. It is from this that a proposal of resuming dialogue between Jinnah and Nehru emerged, with Cripps deducting that Jinnah was willing. The difficulty of progress became clear the very next day when Cripps suggested to Nehru that he should meet Jinnah. Nehru insisted upon a prior abandoning of the proposed 'deliverance' day celebrations, a demand impossible for Jinnah to concede as the League was leading the celebration of 'deliverance' of the Muslims from Congress misrule. The Congress, anxious not to do anything to build up Jinnah, as a meeting with him could have done, plus, signifying a concession of his demand of being the sole spokesman of the Muslims did not, on their part, pursue the idea any further.

This tour of Cripps helped him to deduce that while the Congress was prepared to hold its hand for a limited period of time in the hope of a solution being arrived at, it could not indefinitely wait for Britain to grant the substance of its requests. The resignation of the Congress ministries made more likely an adoption of extra-constitutional campaigns to strengthen their support base amongst the masses. At the same time Jinnah's appeal for a day of deliverance had indisputable overtones of communal anger, thus again underscoring the need for prior negotiations between the League and Congress, these negotiations were now vital. However, in the path remained fixedly those old obstacles; the Congress would just not recognise the authority of the League to be the sole negotiator for the Muslims, and the League could scarcely stop claiming to be just that. His Majesty's Government would therefore, have to intervene and offer a constitutional prospect acceptable to both, as a pre-requisite of their co-operation and do all this quite early.

Here cropped up another obstacle, it was only the viceroy that could so bring the two together, though, Cripps concluded, among Indians and Englishmen alike, there existed serious doubts about Viceroy Linlithgow's negotiating skills. There then got added yet another debility. The viceroy's Executive until then was composed, on the basis of the 1919 India Act, comprised the viceroy himself, then the commander-in chief—India; three British officials with ten years' experience of India, and three non-official Indians. In Britain, Prime Minister Neville Chamberlain's Cabinet had stalwarts like Sir Samuel Hoare (Lord Privy Seal), Sir John Simon (chancellor of the exchequer), and Lord Halifax (foreign secretary), all of whom, Churchill, now First Lord of the Admiralty, despised as 'pygmies'; he held them as responsible for Britain's 'pusillanimous' Indian policy. Inevitably, thereafter, in a Cabinet discussion on Linlithgow's proposed move for an enlarged central executive, Churchill remained fixedly against 'yielding to the pressures of parties who were, after all, only exploiting the dangers with which Britain was faced'.[10] The Cabinet did finally agree, but subject to the viceroy being instructed that for any change, three tests must be satisfied: the supreme power of the viceroy must remain intact; Britain's freedom to deploy forces in India must not be affected; and there must be no constitutional legislation during the war, plus no such promises as would bind the British Parliament after the war.

When he got this directive, Linlithgow proceeded to sound Gandhi, Rajendra Prasad, and Jinnah on the possibility of the Congress and the League arriving at an agreed basis for sharing seats in an enlarged executive. The Congress demurred; it sought a prior declaration of India's right to frame its own independent constitution after the war. Jinnah's demand list was much longer: he would not concede to such a declaration until the Congress first recognised the Muslim League as the sole voice of India's Muslims, then redressed its (the League's) grievances, including the League's exclusion from the ministries in Congress led provinces. Immobility seized the situation, again, persuading Linlithgow to arrive at what had been obvious from the beginning, 'there is no basis for (any) agreement between the two communities'.[11] This was in early October of 1938.

On 10 January 1940 Linlithgow, in a speech at the Orient Club, Bombay, said that Britain's object was dominion status of the Westminster variety, and that he would be immediately enlarging his executive to include representatives of Congress, the League, and the princes. Gandhi, seeing some forward movement in this sought a meeting with Linlithgow, which was arranged for 5 February 1940. In the meantime Linlithgow met Jinnah to ascertain the League's minimum terms for agreement with the Congress, which got specified as: coalition ministries in the provinces; the right of the Muslim members to veto any bill brought before a provincial legislature if two-thirds of them opposed it; an abandoning of *Vande Mataram* and giving up the practice of flying the Congress flag from public buildings. These demands, inauspicious enough as starters, got added to by resistance from another front. Churchill and Simon were against any initiative at all, with Churchill advocating a firm stand against the Congress. Since the resumption of British control, he felt, that for the first time after several years the Congress provinces were again being properly administered, to which he added that '…he did not share (this) anxiety to encourage and promote unity between the Hindu and Muslim communities. Such unity was, in fact, almost out of the realm of practical politics, while, if it were to be brought about, the immediate result would be that the united communities would join in showing us the door. He regarded the Hindu-Muslim feud as the bulwark of British rule in India'.[12] (Why do we keep hearing echoes of the guns of 1857, and their continuing effect on the psyche of the British Raj?)

Sir John Simon, with fussy legalism added that 'there was every reason for not going any faster than we were obliged to'.[13] And Chamberlain, preoccupied as he was sought to look no farther then the present. Linlithgow, now left without any options, prudently fell in line and confirmed that it was best to 'refrain from action', also to avoid any 'running after the Congress'.[14]

The viceroy's talks with Gandhi ended on 6 February 1940, but were inconclusive, principally because Churchill and Simon were far more antagonistic to any initiative than even Linlithgow himself. Indeed, on 13 February 1940, Simon wrote to Chamberlain at some length to forestall any fresh approach. He quoted Jinnah's complaint that the viceroy 'never appeared to break with Gandhi and always left the impression that he was going to see him before long and that negotiations would be resumed'.[15]

'This', wrote Simon, 'is a perfectly well-founded criticism of our handling of Indian politics for...long time past and it is a course of conduct full of the gravest danger'.[16] Offering more and more to Congress produced 'the impression that we are in continuous retreat', and this could 'only end in our collapse'.[17] Churchill concurred, writing to Chamberlain that he was entirely in agreement with Simon: 'The policy of running[18] after Gandhi and the Congress, which the viceroy conceives his duty to pursue, is steadily wearing down every pillar of British authority. The secretary of state ought to send him clear instructions defining and correcting his course during the war'.

In the meantime, domestically, too, events were moving. The Ramgarh Session (19-20 March 1940) of the Congress passed a resolution calling for *purna swaraj* and the framing of a constitution by an assembly based on 'adult suffrage'. Similarly, the Muslim League, meeting at Lahore, had by then adopted the already cited 'Pakistan' resolution of 23 March 1940.

Despite the secretary of state's efforts, in the period November 1939 and March 1940, neither the viceroy nor the Cabinet was prepared to espouse Cripps' strategy of opening negotiations with representatives of the Congress and the League on the basis of India's right to frame its own constitution. It is futile speculating whether a more skilful personality, endowed with greater insight about India could have prevented a resort by the parties to such extreme demands as they had publicly espoused, as for example at Ramgarh, or at Lahore, respectively. However, in retrospect it does seem that the conclusions drawn by Cripps in December 1939, were in greater harmony with the existing political realities than the prevalent official British policy. In March 1940, Cripps, then in China, wrote to Nehru regretting that the British government was behaving 'so stupidly, as I had some hope after my talks with the viceroy that matters might improve'.[19]

THE AUGUST 1940 OFFER

On 10 May 1940, Winston Churchill was sworn in as the prime minister of a war challenged Britain; and that is where British thought and energy then got totally focused—in combating their principal adversary, Nazi Germany. In knowledge of developments Cripps then had a talk with Leopold Amery, the incoming secretary of state for India and shared with him his scheme, emphasising the need for deciding whether to coerce or conciliate the Congress, as the danger of civil disobedience in the midst of war now confronted the Raj. Personally, favouring conciliation, Cripps urged announcing that India would have the right to settle its own future, to assist which process HMG would send out a team of two or three negotiators to bring the parties together. Cripps emphasised that the existing divergence of Indian opinion only inflamed the situation, and reasoned the urgent necessity of finding 'a line of agreement and (to) work from that'.[20] This, for the moment remained Cripps' contribution to the Indian problem, for within days of becoming prime minister in May 1940 itself Cripps was sent to Moscow, and that is where he remained as ambassador until the January of 1942. Churchill wanted a left-wing conciliator to then be Britain's voice in Moscow, for Stalin was an invaluable war time ally; but did Churchill also want India and Cripps out of the way, at least while he fought a life and death war against Germany?

The course of events in Europe, disastrous to start with, were a convincing enough deterrent to provoking any additional problems or revolutionary movements in India, the goal instead became enlisting co-operation from that subcontinental signed country, and of course, of the Indian leadership, too, in the war effort. On 2 June 1940, Amery proposed to Linlithgow that Britain should concede India's right to frame its own constitution, subject of course, to suitable arrangements being made for the discharge of British responsibilities and provided the Indian parties agreed to the formulation that a constituent assembly could be set up after the war. Linlithgow had his doubts, but Amery persisted, possibly because perhaps he had a better feel of the war situation. This was despite his apprehension that convincing Churchill's war cabinet about yet another meaningful initiative for India, was not going to be at all easy. Amery was working for full dominion status, post the war, provided India's political leadership agreed upon a constitution, counting upon the support of some of the Labour members of the War Cabinet to overcome difficulties with Churchill and Simon. However, when the Cabinet met on 12 July 1940, Churchill opposed any new declaration of intent, and his colonial secretary, Lord Lloyd, abhorred any move that might bring together the Hindus and Muslims against

Britain. Churchill then took matters in his own hands cabling Linlithgow, direct—questioning the wisdom of any declaration when the invasion of Britain seemed imminent, rendering a parliamentary discussion of 'the issues involved in such a far reaching departure impossible'.[21] It is remarkable that even in such a war-stressed Britain, the Cabinet in London spent so much time and effort on India and kept high the aspect of parliamentary propriety, too.

Linlithgow now took yet another u-turn, replying rather abjectly to Churchill that he had been led by Amery's entreaties in asking for the Cabinet's support about a declaration that went beyond all past statements. Now that he knew of the Cabinet's reservations, he would 'send home a fresh draft'. It would still concede that Britain's object was dominion status within a year of the end of the war and that Indians should frame their own constitution but it would 'play down the change of approach, emphasise Britain's obligations, and omit any reference to a treaty'. That last point was the most serious loss, for it had, when first mooted, implied equality of status between Britain and an Indian dominion, as equal signatories to a treaty. On 25 July 1940, when Linlithgow's revised draft came before the Cabinet, Churchill remarked upon Amery misleading his colleagues into the belief that the initiative had come from the viceroy. There was another pointed jab: Churchill then called for all of Amery's correspondence with Linlithgow to be made available to the Cabinet ministers.

Five days later (30 July 1940) the war cabinet considered Churchill's suggested remodelling: 'Cabinet would not be able to promise in advance a 'body' which would frame the Constitution on which the Indian political leaders may agree'.[22] Also, that a future British Parliament must not feel restrained, in any way, by what could be construed as immediately binding upon it. Of course, all this could only be taken up after a conclusion of the war. Churchill then expunged reference to the time limit for dominion status and provided instead for Britain to assist the creation, with the least possible delay after the war, of a body to devise a constitution, which should primarily be the responsibility of the Indians themselves. India's right to frame its own constitution, a time limit for dominion status, and as a symbol of India's equality, the treaty, they were all now gone. So was the suggestion of a dominion as a partner-member of the Commonwealth.

This was then promulgated on 8 August 1940, the viceroy's offer emphasising continuity with past policy, (as had been expressed in October 1939), and that the future objective remained dominion status, also that the present offer was an enlargement of the Viceroy's Council to include party representatives and the establishment of a War Consultative Committee. Britain's obligations to the minorities were spelled out in a passage which the Muslims, hereafter, were to cling to as a pledge: 'It goes without saying that His Majesty's Government could not contemplate the transfer of their present responsibilities for the peace and welfare of India to any system of government whose authority is directly denied by large and powerful elements in India's national life'.[23] What was like a pledge to the League (being post Pakistan Resolution of 23 March 1940) was akin to a prior announcement of the break up of India to most other observers.

Not surprisingly, this offer was rejected by all the parties. The AICC concluded that Britain had 'no intention to recognise India's independence, and would, if they could, continue to hold this country indefinitely in bondage for British exploitation'. The viceroy thereupon advised, and the Cabinet agreed, that under these circumstances there was no need to proceed with any enlarging of the Viceroy's Council either.

The Working Committee of the Muslim League, however, took a contrary stand. It expressed its 'satisfaction with the viceroy's announcement' and gave a mandate to Jinnah to seek further details from Linlithgow. However, after his talk with the viceroy, Jinnah, too, rejected the offer, for he (Jinnah) wanted a Muslim League majority among the Indian members of the executive council, which the viceroy did not, rather could simply not agree to. Though Jinnah had legalistically queried that if the League was willing to assume the bulk of the responsibility in running the government, while the Congress was practicing civil disobedience, what would happen if the Congress reversed its stand and decided to join the Council again? Would not the cooperating party, the League, then find that the government had turned its back upon it and given more importance to the Congress? He asked, therefore, for a guarantee that after an agreement with the League there would be no agreement with the Congress, without the consent of the Muslim League. The viceroy conceded the need in such circumstances for consultation with members of the Council but could certainly not agree to hand Jinnah a veto over HMG's decisions. Consequently, the Muslim League on 26 December 1940 rejected both the offers with regard to the executive council and the defence advisory body.

Yet, during the war, Jinnah maintained a planned and balanced attitude on the question of assisting the war effort. He said that though the Muslim League could not take a fully positive stand without gaining an effective share in government, it would not hinder the war effort either. The Muslim League ministers in the provinces would be permitted to discharge their duties, but if the government took a position detrimental to the interests of the League, the ministers would resign and the League would take a stand against the government.

For the Congress their stand cost them politically. An acceptance of the August offer by them would have resulted in a return of their governments in the provinces. The only Congress leaders who took kindly to these proposals were Sardar Vallabhbhai Patel and C. Rajagopalachari. Patel had not been invited to meet the viceroy when he came to Bombay to discuss the proposals with the others. Appreciating fully the difficulties that the party would face from within, particularly from the socialist group dissenters, Patel was still not averse to the idea of facing up to the August offer in case the proposal was 'amended to some extent'. A meeting between Patel and the viceroy, in Bombay, at this juncture would have helped, it was also attempted. However, before that it was necessary to convey to the viceroy, Vallabhbhai's point of view about creating an atmosphere suitable for their meeting. Linlithgow in fact had not met C. Rajagopalachari either when he was in the south, and Patel, unfortunately, had not even been invited to meet him in Bombay. When an invitation to do so was about to be sent to Vallabhbhai Patel there arrived a telegram from Maulana Azad, who in his capacity as Congress president was to be included in the invitation, saying that he saw no basis for settlement in the 8 August proposals, and therefore, regretted coming to Bombay for talks with the viceroy. Laithwaite, private secretary to the viceroy, then concluded that it would not be fair to ask Vallabhbhai Patel alone to meet the viceroy, to which Vallabhbhai Patel's reaction was of disappointment, for, he felt that clearly another opportunity for consultations had been lost that this August offer, too, having failed; civil disobedience and the retaliations British policy of repression and detention, therefore, continued. However, as this could not have stood alone for too long, on 22 May 1941, in order to rally moderate support, Linlithgow offered another palliative; he proposed the setting up of the long-promised advisory National Defence Council and to increase its Indian membership. Churchill's response was prompt, and it was adverse: 'Such concessions of portfolios to Indians would neither advance the war effort nor buy off opposition, but it might engender fresh controversy,' he cautioned. Despite the caution on this occasion, Linlithgow persisted and carried his proposal through. Therefore, as reconstituted in the summer of 1941 the Viceroy's Executive included the commander-in-chief, the three official British members—for home, finance, and communications—and now eight Indians. For the first time Indians formed a majority in the Council, but this was an empty numerical satisfaction for the constitution of the government of India remained unaltered and no portfolio actually got transferred to any Indian. The viceroy retained his special responsibilities for peace and tranquillity, financial stability, the minorities, in respect of which he was required to act in accordance with his individual judgement. The National Defence Council remained essentially an advisory body 'to bring the war effort in the Provinces and the States as well as in the ranks of commerce, industry and labour into more direct and effective touch with the Central Government'.[24] It had twenty-two British Indians, mostly drawn from the provincial legislatures, and nine members from the states.

Though Churchill conceded the reconstruction of the executive, he was totally immovable when the question of Britain's aims in relation to India re-emerged. The occasion was his parliamentary speech on the Roosevelt-Churchill Atlantic Charter, signed at sea in August 1941. Article 3 of this Charter expressed 'the right of all peoples to choose the form of government under which they will live'.[25] It was significant that not even the advice of the US ambassador, Guy Winant[26] to whom he sent an advance copy of his proposed speech, could influence him. Winant believed that the passage denying the application of the article to India 'would simply intensify charges of Imperialism and leave Great Britain in the position of 'a do-nothing policy'.[27] Churchill refused to modify the passage. On 9 September 1941, he told the House of Commons that the article applied only to European nations under Nazi rule. It did not relate to 'the development of constitutional government in India, Burma or other parts of the Empire'.[28] The 'progressive evolution of self-governing institutions in the regions and peoples who owe allegiance to the British Crown'[29] was to be distinguished from the emancipation of Europe from Nazism, he affirmed. Paradoxically, this Atlantic Charter speech sharpened resentment and few could recall a wider gulf between Britain and India than that which now emerged.

The Cripps Mission

Yet no sooner had this offensive (to Indian sensibilities) Atlantic Charter been enunciated by Churchill in the Commons then suddenly events acquired a fateful momentum. Within weeks of that policy speech of 9 September 1941, USS *Arizona* was sunk in Pearl Harbour by Japanese aircrafts. From this one surprise action of daring, two consequences of great significance followed in rapid succession: the enormous industrial, technological, financial and military power of the US joined hands with the allies in the war effort, the US, too, was now at war; and secondly, the Second World War now having come to Asia, suddenly India's strategic centrality in this fight against Japanese forces got sharply focused.

The invading Japanese forces moved with startling speed, almost as a grim reminder of early advances of the German troops in Europe. One country after another fell against their relentless assaults; then a month and half after Pearl Harbour, on 15 February 1942, General Percival, commander-in-chief of British forces, in Singapore, surrendered to General Yamashita of the Japanese invading forces. Suddenly, Burma (now Myanmar) was now vulnerable, as was Rangoon, and then was it to be India? Could India, too, actually now face an invasion from the East? Field Marshal Lord Alanbrooke noted gloomily in his diary of that date (12 February 1942): 'We are paying very heavily now for failing to face the insurance premiums essential for security of an Empire! This has usually been the main cause for the loss of Empires in the past'. This presciently forecast a beginning of the end of the British Empire. Besides, this loss of Singapore was a crushing blow to the Allied morale; it was eventually regained, but at very heavy cost for the imperial spirit of old was never recaptured by the British after this.

Clearly, under such circumstances a 'do-nothing' policy was not an option. A fresh initiative based upon negotiations with the Indian parties had to be attempted and it was. As Stafford Cripps' was the only constructive approach to have been made during the first two years of the war that alternative now got revived, though, clearly the war remained the principal concern for Great Britain, and obviously India's political future a much lower priority; besides, in contrast to the towering political personality of a wartime Churchill, Sir Stafford Cripps was but a minor functionary of the imperial machinery. What helped, though, were the views of an all-party group of parliamentarians, who were impatient with the 'purely negative policy' of HMG as conveyed by Sir George Schuster[30] to Amery. The line of action suggested by this group resembled that of Cripps; send out a parliamentary mission to get the Indian party leaders down to the hard brain work of discussing the details of a new constitution, they urged Linlithgow who had, at first, rebuffed the idea, but following upon the Japanese attack on Pearl Harbour, on 7 December 1941, this representation got added ballast from several directions. India was now, suddenly, a vital base for operations in the Pacific and South-east Asia. In the course of just one month Churchill received recommendations from three important quarters: the Labour members of his Cabinet; the president of the United States of America; and Sir Tej Bahadur Sapru and his group of moderates from India. There was another factor—the Second World War had now reached the doorsteps of India. The imperatives, therefore, of this war and the need to confront the Japanese, had suddenly transformed the strategic relevance of India.

In early February 1941, Sir Tej Bahadur Sapru had attempted a rapprochement between Gandhi and Jinnah on the Hindu-Muslim question. However, that initiative floundered, as had several others, for Gandhi, quite appropriately, refused to meet Jinnah as a purely Hindu leader in contrast to Jinnah as the sole representative of the Muslims. Now, however, when the Japanese were on the borders of India, indeed had even lobbed the odd bomb or two on Kakinada, Vishakhapatnam and Calcutta, (spreading some needless panic), and when Japanese ships were sighted a few miles off the coast of Madras, the rationale of such a meeting became totally different.

The governor of Madras, Arthur Oswald James Hope, 2nd Baron Rankeillour had, in panic, then collected his British staff and fled to Ootacamund, (Singapore was fresh in his memory); but why only in the memory of this panicky peer? Lord Wavell, the then commander-in-chief, was sufficiently angered to send a strong wireless message 'upbraiding him [the 2nd Baron] for this unworthy and unbecoming abandonment of post'. Gandhi, no great military strategist, had also then written to Patel that an 'attack on Orissa seemed likely since the Government had massed troops there'.[31] Interesting how war focuses attention.

On 4 March 1942, Churchill cabled Roosevelt: 'We are earnestly considering whether a declaration of Dominion status after the war, carrying with it, if desired, the right to secede should be made at this critical juncture. We must not on any account break with the Muslims who represent a hundred million people and are the main army elements on which we rely for the immediate fighting'.[32] Churchill added that there were forty million untouchables and eighty million inhabitants of princely states who were not friendly to Congress, who had to be considered. Churchill continued: 'Naturally we do not want to throw India into chaos on the eve of invasion'.[33]

Roosevelt replied on 10 March 1942,[34] suggesting the setting up of what might be called a temporary government in India, headed by a small representative group to be recognised as a temporary dominion government. 'Some such method', Roosevelt advised, 'might give a new slant in India itself, and it might cause the people there to forget hard feelings, to become more loyal to the British Empire, and to stress the danger of Japanese domination, together with the advantage of peaceful evolution as against chaotic revolution'.[35] Churchill responded, his earlier resistance now replaced by an alert sense of the strategic centrality of an India totally involved with the war effort. The very next day, 11 March, Churchill announced in Parliament the appointment of the Cripps Mission. No doubt that pressure from the USA and from Roosevelt, had a marked influence on him and the British government, equally that he did not greatly welcome this 'interference'[36] but as a realist he let that be.

Sir Stafford Cripps reached New Delhi on 23 March 1942, as a representative of the war cabinet to discuss with Indian leaders their (war cabinet's) unanimous proposals. Patel had then reacted trenchantly: 'How could the Congress come to terms with the British government now, when in six months' time we might have other 'uncles' (the Japanese) to deal with?'[37] To Patel, (accurately) it was the American and Chinese pressure which had forced England to move on the Indian question and Cripps Mission was the result. Patel, at Ahmedabad, had said that Cripps was coming at a time when the sands of time were running out fast; when it might almost be 'impossible for the British government to give us anything or for us to take anything'.[38] This was in direct contrast to Patel's stance in August 1940, when he had conveyed openly that a section of the Congress wanted to arrive at some accord with the British government. Patel and Gandhi then worked to ensure that it would be Abul Kalam Azad that should see Cripps on behalf of the Congress and that Jawaharlal, Rajaji and Bhulabhai Desai must be kept in the background. Newspapers of that period report that Nehru continued to remain in Allahabad for three or four days after Cripps' arrival in New Delhi. However, as the talks progressed, inevitably Nehru began to play a part in the negotiations.

There was another consideration that then weighed with the Congress leadership. Gandhi, Patel and Mahadev Desai believed that as the British were losing the war, Japan was bound to invade India, why then come to any terms with the British through acceptance of the Cripps' proposals? Mahadev Desai had written in the *Harijan* of Sir Stafford Cripps' proposals as being 'stillborn'. It was only Bhulabhai Desai, and Nehru who assessed differently, but their views could not immediately influence, leave alone override those of the others. Indeed. Gandhi considered Cripps' proposals as a 'post-dated cheque'[39] on a collapsing bank. Gandhi wanted to return to Wardha immediately after his meeting with Cripps but was persuaded by the Working Committee to stay on in New Delhi. Abul Kalam Azad met Cripps on behalf of the Congress several times. The Congress Working Committee, on 29 March 1942, passed a resolution rejecting the Cripps offer. The resolution was communicated to Cripps but not made public until after the first week of April. During that week, Jawaharlal Nehru came on to the scene. There were further discussions about the powers and responsibilities of the Indian defence minister and Cripps arranged a meeting between the then commander-in-chief, Wavell, Azad and Nehru. Despite Gandhi's and Patel's opposition, the majority of the Congress Working Committee supported Nehru and would then have accepted the British government's proposals but for their sudden withdrawal by Churchill, just as they were about to be accepted. That those proposals were withdrawn was subsequently made clear in the House of Commons, in a debate an India. Churchill, making a speech in the House some years later, on 12 December 1946 had said:[40]

'I remember well when the Right Hon'ble and learned Gentleman went out as representative of the Government of which I was the Head, and how we had to pull him up because—(Interruption) I do not want to say anything.

'Sir S. Cripps: If the Rt. Hon. Gentleman intends to disclose what passed between me and the Cabinet on that occasion, I hope he will disclose it all'

'Mr Churchill: The Rt. Hon. and learned Gentleman is quite right in what he says and I shall not pursue the point...'

The fact that the failure of Cripps' mission is attributable to Churchill's attitude is further borne out in Colonel Louis Johnson's reactions:

Cripps is sincere; knows this matter should be solved. He and Nehru could solve it in five minutes if Cripps had any freedom or authority. To my amazement when a satisfactory solution seemed certain, with unimportant concessions, Cripps with embarrassment told me that he could not change the original draft declaration without Churchill's approval and that Churchill has cabled him that he will give no approval unless Wavell and the viceroy separately send their own coded cables, unqualifiedly endorsing any change Cripps wanted. I never lost confidence until then. London wanted a Congress refusal.[41]

On 11 April 1942,[42] Churchill informed Roosevelt of the failure. Roosevelt immediately cabled back suggesting that Cripps should continue to stay on in India until one more final effort had been made to prevent a breakdown in the negotiations. Churchill replied that Cripps had already left India. His Majesty's Government did not want a resolution of the problem in India, certainly not then, and certainly not when Churchill as the prime minister presided over the future of the British Empire.

Possibly those who drafted the proposals had assumed that they were putting forward an arrangement which would satisfy the Muslim League and also meet the views that Sir Sikandar Hayat Khan had directly put across to Prime Minister Churchill. Besides, the League, too, had noted significant drawbacks in these proposals, to illustrate: Assam could agree to join by a straight 60 per cent majority comprising only Hindus and this would put the Muslim majority, Sylhet district, in India. At the next stage, that is the referendum, whereas the vote in the Punjab might be in favour of separation but the situation in Bengal was still questionable, for political warfare had now broken out openly in that province between Fazlul Haq's Krishak Praja Party and the Muslim League. It could not be predicted what effect this would have on either the next election or a referendum. Considering all these factors the working committee of the Muslim League rejected the Cripps plan. The Congress, opposed to this after the war aspects of the plan also objected to the potential for a partitioning of the country contained in the scheme. Moreover, and importantly, the Congress leaders still thought Britain was losing the war.

At this point a prominent member of the Congress Working Committee, C. Rajagopalachari having declared that the path upon which the Congress was entering was wrong, took a new line. Rajaji said both the Congress' opposition to helping the war effort and its position that the Muslim League should be ignored were wrong. He held that if the Muslims were determined about a separate government in the areas in which they were a majority, well then, accept that there was no alternative to that and make a settlement on that basis. If there could be an agreement and cooperation on that premise, then make that choice, as that was greatly to be preferred over a situation in which neither was any agreement forthcoming nor was any forward movement being made possible.

Rajaji, therefore, gathered together Congress members of the suspended legislature of the Madras Presidency to convince them about his proposal. At their meeting on 23 April 1942, two resolutions were adopted. One recommended that the AICC accept the Muslim demand for partition; resume talks with the Muslim League on that basis; then through mutual understanding establish an interim national government so as to face this emergency of a war. The second proposed that the assembly and the ministry in Madras be restored and that the Muslim League be asked to join that cabinet. These two moves, particularly the first, were not liked by many in the Congress. Six days later, on 29 April, these recommendations were placed before the AICC meeting at Allahabad and were rejected by a large majority; the AICC also deciding that any 'proposal aimed at dividing the country was detrimental to the interests of the Indian people and harmful to the provinces, the princely states and the country as a whole'. Rajaji did not lose heart; he resigned from the Working Committee and from his seat in the Madras assembly and decided to propagate his views as an independent political worker. Seven other members of the assembly resigned with him.

Clearly, the Congress could not assert its position as an organisation that spoke for all; this vast geographical, social and political spread of India could simply not be contained in just one vessel, whatever be the claims.

The Politics of Provinces

The provinces in the meantime had also begun to be politically assertive. In Bengal, Maulvi Fazlul Haq's ministry was defeated after a series of complex events which began with the setting up of the viceroy's Defence Advisory Council in 1941. This council was part of the plan put forward by the viceroy on 8 August 1940, postponed then but implemented now, almost a year after announcement on July 1941. Pursuant to this, he invited the provincial premiers to become members of this Defence Advisory Council and they accepted, assuming they had been asked in their respective capacities as premiers, not as members of their party, the Muslim League. As they had blanket permission from the League to cooperate in the war effort in their ministerial role, they took it for granted that this would not be objected to by the League.

The viceroy then informed Jinnah about the intended steps, simultaneously assuring him that no injustice would be done to the Muslims in the matter of communal representation, listing the three Muslim premiers: Sir Sikandar Hayat Khan of the Punjab; Maulvi Fazlul Haq of Bengal; and Sir Muhammad Saadullah of Assam. The nature of their appointment immediately generated controversy, for Jinnah, legalistically interpreted their appointment as representatives of the Muslim community. Besides, receiving the letter through the governor of Bombay hurt his prickly pride as the 'sole spokesman'. Jinnah, therefore, ordered the Muslim League secretary to serve notice on the three premiers to 'explain their violation of discipline'. They were informed that formal action would be taken at a meeting of the Working Committee in Bombay on 24 August 1941.

Their hands thus forced, Sikandar Hayat and Saadullah of Assam agreed to step down from the Council, as did Fazlul Haq, but simultaneously he also quit the Working Committee and the League Council. In his letter, Fazlul Haq complained about the 'unconstitutional and dictatorial' attitude of the president of the League and said that Jinnah had framed the question in such a manner that a vote against it would have amounted to a no-confidence vote in Jinnah himself, as president of the League. Though this ended the crisis, it had hurt the self pride of Fazlul Haq who revolted against Jinnah by resigning. This was effected, cunningly on 28 March 1942 when the state budget had not yet been adopted by the Bengal Assembly and a new financial year was to begin in just three days time. This was Fazlul Haq's method of hitting back. The Punjab, though, remained apart from the tussles that were then witnessed in Bengal, Sindh and Assam.

However, even Fazlul Haq, Otherwise an extremely popular figure, 'had to experience black flags in almost every city of East Bengal when he left the Muslim League and formed a coalition government with the Mahasabha and the Congress, in the Shyama Prasad–Haq ministry (1941)'.[43]

Mahmud Husain further records that the years '1940 to 1947 may... be regarded as the most active, fruitful and significant years so far as Dacca University's contribution to the Pakistan movement is concerned. In the first place, the Muslim League found a stronghold among the students of this University. Then, Fazl-ul Rahman, a former student of the university helped the founding and publication of a fortnightly periodical called *Pakistan* which started coming out in Dacca from July 1942. Whereas several younger Muslim members of the staff worked for the journal as labour of love, even an 'eminent Hindu scholar wrote a new history of Bengali literature called "Islamic Literature" *(Islami Bangla Sahitya* by Sukumar Sen)'.

QUIT INDIA—19 APRIL 1942

Events now accelerated sharply, if 'Britain would not act India would', announced Gandhi. On 19 April 1942, he wrote in the *Harijan:* 'The safety and interest of both Britain and India lie in an orderly and timely British withdrawal from India'. This was the mild and understated launch of his Quit India agitation.

The Congress Working Committee and the AICC met thereafter in Allahabad, in the last week of April 1942. The AICC Resolution adopted at this meeting stated: 'The Committee repudiates the idea that freedom can come to India through interference or invasion by any foreign nation, whatever [its] professions...[and] invasion...it must be resisted. Such resistance can only take the form of non-violent, non-cooperation as the British Government has prevented the organisation of national defence by the people in any other way'.[44]

This was a departure, for the resolution made clear that Nehru had to give up his views of unconditional support to Britain, and violent resistance to the Japanese invaders had also been repudiated.

Allahabad was followed by the Wardha 'Quit India' Resolution of July 1942. This met with criticism, particularly from Sir Tej Bahadur Sapru, Dr Ambedkar, Sir Sikandar Hayat Khan, Jinnah, the British Labour Party, and also Rajaji. The Government of India, on the other hand, was nervous and decided to now take action against the Congress leaders on the basis of the Wardha Resolution of July 1942, which had asked for a British withdrawal in the middle of the war. As soon as the then governor of Bombay, Sir Roger Lumley informed the viceroy on the telephone that the 'Quit India' Resolution had been adopted, the Viceroy's Executive Council, which was then assumed as in continuous session, decided unanimously to arrest all the Congress Working Committee members and other Congress leaders, too, all over the country.

A month later, in August 1942, the Working Committee of the Muslim League met in Bombay. This meet followed the Congress' decision to launch the Quit India Movement. The leaders of the Congress had been arrested, just a few days prior to the meeting of the Working Committee of the Muslim League. When the Working Committee of the League met, some of its members held that an opportune moment to join hand with the Congress against the British had now arrived. Raja Sahib Mahmudabad, M.A.H. Ispahani and Jamaal Miya met Jinnah on the eve of the Working Committee to express just this view point, emphasising that such an opportunity for joining hands with the 'Hindus' against the British should not be allowed to go. Chaudhary Khaliquzzaman also expressed the same opinion, but Jinnah remained fixed in his view that the Muslim League should not join this battle against the British. When the resolution for supporting the Congress against the British was put to vote there were three abstentions—M.A.H. Ispahani, Raja Sahib Mahmudabad and Nawab Ismail Khan. G.M. Syed of Sindh refused to abstain. He cast his vote against the Resolution.

This decision of the Muslim League Working Committee, principally Jinnah's, kept the leaders of the Muslim League out of jail and enabled the Muslim League party to gain in strength, which it did significantly, between then (1942) and 1946. The Congress, on the other hand, suffered a severe setback, born of this voluntary absence from the political scene during these crucial years. With the Congress leaders in prison, no one could initiate any discussions on their behalf. This gave Jinnah time and a vacant space to dominate the political scene, to make use of this opportunity and to exploit official exasperation with the Congress. In reality, both the Congress and the government were now in a blind alley; neither could they easily turn nor was there any road ahead. The government held that unless the Congress categorically withdrew the Quit India Movement, they (the government) would neither release the leaders nor take any initiative for further talks about reforms. The Congress, in turn, demanded release first. In addition, a violent agitation launched just then by underground Congress Socialists, sharpened official animosities greatly deepening the impasse. The principal British concern then was the proper conduct of war, as much in Europe as in Asia. The country-wide disturbances that followed this adoption of the 'Quit India' resolve, naturally therefore, got interpreted by the British government, and significantly this time by America, too, as 'deliberate interference with the war effort', particularly when offensive operations against Japan were being organised with India as the main base and source of supply. This feeling deeply influenced world opinion for months and distanced even such elements as had earlier looked positively upon India's freedom movement. Jawaharlal Nehru's views about standing up with the 'Allies wholeheartedly' had been timely, the Congress Resolution ill-judged both in timing and in content.

LORD LINLITHGOW'S VICEROYALTY

The three great difficulties that Lord Linlithgow's successors had to contend with were: the establishment of parity between the minority and the majority; putting the *imprimatur* of the British government on this breaking of India's political unity; and conceding to the minority an indirect right to veto any political advance in India, or of India, except on terms that the League found as convenient. As a record of the sabotage of Indian nationalist struggles, Lord Linlithgow's term does, perhaps, excel that of any other viceroy, before or after.

The federal part of the Government of India Act of 1935, which would have introduced the principle of responsibility at the Centre, similar to that introduced in the provinces, had always worried Jinnah. Upon representation, Lord Linlithgow accepted the Muslim League's demand and on 11 September 1939, he announced that preparations in connection with the introduction of federation would remain in suspense until the end of the war. This was hailed by Jinnah and the Working Committee of the Muslim League which adopted a resolution, just a week later, on 18 September, appreciating this suspension, and expressing the hope that the federal scheme would be abandoned altogether.

The Congress party's stand about India's participation in the war had greatly exasperated the Conservative coalition government in Britain and also the bureaucracy in India headed by Lord Linlithgow. Consequently, the Raj then did everything possible to help and strengthen the Muslim League and offset the Congress, as for example in Bengal, in Sindh and also in Assam.

In Bengal, for example, Fazlul Haq, who was heading a coalition ministry commanding the confidence of the Legislature, was forced to resign in March 1943, on pain of dismissal, and a League Ministry under Nazimuddin was installed in its place. The governor allowed Nazimuddin to strengthen his position by raising the number of ministers to thirteen with an equal number of parliamentary secretaries, whereas Fazlul Haq had been denied permission to expand his Cabinet of eight by the addition of two scheduled caste members.

In Sindh, Allah Bux, a nationalist Muslim who was heading the provincial ministry, was dismissed by the governor in October 1942, for returning his title of 'Khan Bahadur' and 'OBE' as a protest against British refusal to meet nationalist India's demand for freedom. The League leader in the Assembly was invited and then actively helped by the governor to form the Ministry. In Assam, Rohini Kumar Chaudhury (Independent) claimed that he was in a position to form a ministry but was not invited to do so, though, and the League leader was asked instead by the governor to form a ministry in August 1942.

The Muslim League, too, had kept out of the Viceroy's Executive Council principally because their demands were not conceded immediately and they hesitated appearing as unreservedly pro-British. The League, did, however, cooperate with the war effort by opposing the 'Quit India' demand of the Congress which was denounced as an attempt to bypass the League.

Lord Linlithgow was foremost in forcefully pursuing the policy of helping the League to consolidate its power and form Muslim League ministries in the provinces where Congress had resigned from office. Whereas, at the beginning of the war there was not a single Muslim League ministry in any of the provinces, by the time Lord Linlithgow left office in November 1943, in all the four provinces of Bengal, Assam, the NWFP and Sindh, which were claimed by the League for Pakistan, Muslim League ministries had been established.

A further step in this direction was taken when after the commencement of Gandhi's fast in the Aga Khan Palace Detention Camp in February 1943, three of the Viceroy's Executive Councillors resigned in protest; Linlithgow filled the vacancies by making fresh nominations promptly. Commented *The New Statesman* and *Nation* on 8 May 1943: 'The newcomers are not an impressive team, but the most significant point about them is that the composition of the Council now realises Mr Jinnah's ideal of parity in numbers, between Muslims and Hindus. When once this precedent is established, it will be claimed by the minority community as a vested right. This seems a reckless innovation'.

A theory then began to be propounded by the British that the democratic principle of decisions by majority vote was not applicable to India as Hindus and Muslims were 'disparate elements', who were not agreed even on the 'fundamental rules of the game'. Therefore, the right of self-determination of the Muslims as a community should be recognised. A constitutional garb was thus provided to the 'Two-Nation' theory of the Muslim League. Top-ranking Conservatives like Winterton, Amery, Zetland and Churchill did their best through their speeches in Parliament and outside, to put their *imprimatur* on and give currency to this theory. Amery in his speech on 18 November 1941 explained: 'Rightly or wrongly, the experience of the Provincial self-Government on British Parliamentary lines has convinced the Moslems...that they cannot submit to any central Government for India in which the executive is directly dependent on a parliamentary majority, which if provincial experience is any guide would be an obedient mouthpiece of the Congress high command'. The British government also set the fashion of terming the Congress as 'Hindu'—even though the Congress had a large number of Muslims as members on its rolls, often a Muslim as its president, and routinely Muslims as members of its executive.

The League's propaganda, on the other hand, routinely underscored the negative. It refused to define the nature of Pakistan that was to be, and also never attempted to place the full picture of Pakistan either before the Muslims or those who were to concede it; it refused to define what Pakistan meant even geographically, for this could just not be done. No matter how the boundaries of Pakistan were drawn, Muslims being so distributed all over India that a substantial portion of them would still be left behind. The League was well aware that if Pakistan was defined: 'it would at once lose its attraction for the millions of Muslims who would then obviously be [geographically] left out of its benefits'. Ultimately when Pakistan did finally get defined it was only by the division of India, through a 'surgical operation'. This was entirely because the idea of Pakistan did not easily bear analysis, though it did become an excellent battle-cry, and that is how it had to be kept, a 'bright and undefined ideal'. And so, when Dr Rajendra Prasad in a statement on 16 April 1941, invited the League president to present the proposition in specific terms so that the Congress could discuss it, Jinnah contemptuously rejected the offer, saying that it is the 'principle' of a partitioning India that must first get accepted by the Congress. The League's intransigence was the trump card of the Raj. For so long as there existed a possibility of maintaining their power in India, the British encouraged but did not identify themselves with the League's Pakistan demand. It was to be used mainly as a threat against Congress nationalism. However, as the League became more and more conscious of its value to the British power, it insisted on having its pound of flesh which the British were unwilling, at that stage, to give. But for the time being each needed the other. 'The forces represented by the League needed British support for their continued existence [and] imperialism in India needed the support of those forces'. And so the tacit alliance between the two continued despite the divergence of their aims and the resulting occasional jolts.

Which is why Arthur Moore, then editor of the European-owned Calcutta daily, *The Statesman* commented: 'By insisting on the theoretical path of legal constitution-making by Indians themselves—and that, too, in war time of all times—His Majesty's Government has inevitably increased India's suspicion of its ultimate good faith'.

Field Marshal Lord Wavell's Viceroyalty

In October 1943 Lord Linlithgow's term ended. He left India even as Gandhi and other Congress leaders were still in jail. Field Marshal Lord Wavell was subsequently appointed viceroy. Of all the viceroys of India Wavell brought to this post more experience and understanding of India, along with his commitment to the country, the British Indian Army and the Indian soldiers than any other. He had served for long in India with Indian soldiers, had commanded them, through different ranks, then as a general in various theatres in both the wars. By the time Wavell took office as the viceroy the war situation had also greatly changed—signals of an eventual allied victory were coming clearly across, even to lay observers.

Pyarelal, a disciple of Gandhi and his biographer has conceded that Wavell was 'a man of great dignity—tight-lipped, straightforward, warm hearted—'guinea-a-word Wavell', as he was affectionately nicknamed.... His sincerity was beyond question. No doubt he, too, wanted in his own way to help India on the road to freedom. He had a wonderful [sense of] loyalty which on more than one occasion made him take upon his shoulders other people's blame, and a blunt soldierly manner...But...his soldier's single-track mind understood little and cared less for legal and constitutional proprieties. They appeared to confuse and sometimes even to irritate him. The British officials in India made the fullest use of his goodness as well as his limitations to further their own plans. The result was a tragedy'.[45]

On 6 May 1944, Gandhi was released from jail; he had been ailing and the British wanted to have no responsibility for any possible complications. Gandhi, though, had hardly had any direct contact with what was going on in the country for the period of his detention. Yet, after his release on 17 July 1944, he wrote to Jinnah and offered to meet him, adding that he was not an enemy of the Muslims but rather a friend to Jinnah, indeed of all mankind. He asked Jinnah not to disappoint him. Gandhi had written to Jinnah in Gujarati, reminding him that both their families belonged to Gujarat and he was trying to find a new basis for fraternity, their common homeland. Jinnah, the constitutionalist, sent his reply in English, explaining that this was the language in which the possibility of his erring in the expression of his views was the least. Jinnah informed Gandhi that he was going to Kashmir but that he would be greatly honoured if Gandhi could visit his home when he (Jinnah) had returned. Gandhi, at his own ashram would seldom be permitted to talk to his visitors without being disturbed by his followers and this was the principal reason why Jinnah had said openly to Gandhi that he never went to meet him at his residence.

Gandhi–Jinnah Talks (Part I)

Since the arrest of the Congress leaders in August 1942, (C. Rajagopalachari was not arrested because of his known opposition to 'Quit India'), Rajaji had been striving to bring about a rapprochement between the Congress and the Muslim League. He was convinced that the League would join hands with Congress only when assured of their right of self-determination for the Muslim majority areas, but the British would not transfer power, come what may, during the pendency of the war. Rajaji's opportunity to put before Gandhi his formula came when with the Mahatma's temporary release. The main features of these proposals, later known eponymously as the 'Rajaji formula' were: (1) The Muslim League should endorse India's demand for independence and cooperate with the Congress in the formation of a provisional interim government for the transitional period; (2) the Congress would agree, after the termination of war, to the appointment of a commission for demarcating contiguous districts in the north-west and north-east of India, wherein the Muslims were in absolute majority; (3) in the areas thus demarcated a plebiscite of all the inhabitants held on the basis of adult franchise, or some equivalent device, would decide the issue of separation from India. If the majority decided in favour of forming a sovereign state separate from India, such decision would be given effect to; (4) in the event of separation, mutual agreement would be entered into for safeguarding defence, commerce, communications, and other essential matters; and finally (5) these terms would be binding only in case of transfer by Britain of full power and responsibility for the governance of India.

Gandhi needed hardly a moment's consideration to give his assent. Armed with that Rajaji then met Jinnah who expressed his inability to 'approve' the formula as it did not meet the League's demand for Pakistan. In a speech before the Muslim League Council he later characterised [the formula] as 'a shadow and [a] husk, maimed, mutilated, and moth-eaten Pakistan'. He, however, offered to put the formula before the Muslim League Council if Rajaji so desired. Knowing full well that no useful purpose would be served by doing so without Jinnah's own approval, and viewing it as unfair to the public and an injustice to the scheme if it were disposed of in that manner, Rajaji released his formula, along with his correspondence with Jinnah, to the press. To Jinnah he finally wrote: 'With it (our) private negotiations end. It is necessary to take the public into confidence now'.

Four days before the Quit India Resolution had been adopted by the All-India Congress Committee, on 4 August 1942, Gandhi had made an important advance for a Congress–League settlement with Jinnah, this time through a common Muslim friend—Meklai, on the following lines:

> Provided the Muslim League co-operated fully with the Congress' demand for immediate independence without the slightest reservation, subject of course to the provision that independent India will permit the operations of the Allied armies in order to check Axis aggression and thus to help both China and Russia, the Congress will have no objection to the British government transferring all the power it today exercises to the Muslim League on behalf of the whole of India, including the so-called Indian India. And the Congress will not only not obstruct any government that the Muslim League may form on behalf of the people, but will even join the government in running the machinery of the free state.

Jinnah's response was that he could not take note of an offer or a proposition that had not directly been made to him. Gandhi, at this stage, would have met Jinnah had he not, a few days later, been all of a sudden put into jail again.

In April 1943, during Gandhi detention, speaking before the open session of the Muslim League at Delhi, Jinnah had declared that nobody would welcome it more than he if Gandhi was really willing to come to a settlement with the Muslim League: 'If that is Mr Gandhi's desire, what is there to prevent him from writing directly to me?...Strong as this government may be in this country, I cannot believe that it would have the daring to stop such a letter if it were sent to me. It would be a very serious thing indeed if such a letter were stopped…If there is any change of heart…he has only to drop a few lines to me. Then the Muslim League will not fail'.

As response Gandhi wrote to Jinnah expressing his willingness to meet him: 'There seems to be an "if" about your invitation. Do you say I should write only if I have changed my heart? God alone knows men's hearts. I would like you to take me as I am. Why should not both you and I approach the great question of communal unity as men determined on finding a common solution and work together to make our solution acceptable to all who are concerned with it or interested in it?'

Notwithstanding Jinnah's opinion about HMG's intentions, the government did stop this letter from reaching Jinnah, but made the 'substance' of it available to him. Thereupon, Jinnah responded that this was not what he sought; he wanted Gandhi to first agree to the Muslim League's demand for Pakistan and then write to him. 'This (present) letter of Mr Gandhi can only be construed as a move on his part to embroil the Muslim League to come into dash with the British government solely for the purpose of his release'. However, Jinnah had, at this prompt demonstration of British censorship, chosen to overlook their misdemeanour, however 'serious' he might have earlier considered it to be.

This was principally because revealing the substance of it, while withholding the letter proper eminently suited the parties in this tacit conspiracy, (Jinnah and the British). However, when the next time during the Cabinet Mission's negotiations, Jinnah settled again for the 'substance' of a Congress letter at Lord Wavell's hands, without waiting for the text, then that cost him dear. But that would amount to outstripping events again, all this will follow in a subsequent chapter.

In the small hours of the night of 17 July 1944, Gandhi wrote to Jinnah addressing him as 'Brother Jinnah' and signing the letter as 'Your brother, Gandhi'. He wrote in Gujarati to say:

There was a time when I was able to induce you to speak in the mother tongue. Today I venture to write to you in the mother tongue. I have already suggested a meeting between you and me in my invitation from jail. I have not yet written to you since my release. Today I feel prompted to do so. Let us meet whenever you wish. Do not regard me as an enemy of Islam or of Indian Muslims. I have always been a servant and friend to you and mankind. Do not disappoint me.

This letter was written in Gujarati deliberately—the common mother tongue (whose very existence was subsequently denied in the philosophy of Pakistan) of the Hindus, Parsis and the Muslim community to which Jinnah belonged. Promptly came the reply from 'Brother Jinnah', in English, from the house boat *Queen Elizabeth* in Srinagar to 'Dear Mr Gandhi', informing him that he would be 'glad to receive' Gandhi at his house in Bombay on his return from Kashmir some time in the middle of August 1944. Sir Tej Bahadur Sapru, the Liberal leader, then remarked to Gandhi: 'I have no doubt that a...man like you can afford to be "received"!'

GANDHI–JINNAH TALKS (PART II)

As things stood in 1944, inside the British system the problem posed by the communal triangle of the Raj, the Muslim League and the Congress seemingly defied solution. And yet, we need to recognise that outside of the British Raj, the problem would have had no existence in this form, the two communities would have found answers, in one manner or another, to their contention. The political and historical background in which the Gandhi–Jinnah talks of 1944 were held, generated pressure on Jinnah, inside the League and also outside, to come to a settlement with the Congress so as to clear the way for India's independence. There were widespread expectations in the country that something tangible would result from these talks. In an extraordinary departure from his standard practice, Jinnah called Gandhi 'Mahatma' and appealed for a period of political truce. 'It has been the universal desire that we should meet. Now that we are going to meet, help us. We are coming to grips. Bury the past'.

If there was a party in this triangle that wanted no settlement, it was the British; they were greatly troubled by all this for they continued to seriously apprehend any prospects of a Hindu-Muslim settlement. The viceroy made his position known on the eve of the meeting that 'there must be...agreement in principle between Hindus and Muslims and all important elements' before HMG could think of even a transitional national Government with limited powers. This was followed by a leading article in the London *Times*: 'No agreement between Mr Gandhi and Mr Jinnah, however satisfactory to their adherents, can materially advance political progress in India unless it takes into account wider interests...the anxiety of the depressed classes...the claims of the Princes...' All these not so subtle propaganda points, insinuations or suggestions were not to assist the talks, rather to make clear that there was a third party to all this—the Raj—and it is the Raj that had the trump card in their hand.

The announcement of the impending meeting also angered the members of the Hindu Mahasabha. Similarly a batch of Khaksars, a paramilitary Muslim organisation, had swarmed into Bombay and was holding parades to create the proper atmosphere to stimulate a Congress–League settlement. The Communists were holding mass meetings which would compel the two leaders to unite in the defence of democracy as symbolised by Russian resistance to the Nazi aggression. Fearing that Gandhi was going to accept the League's demand for Pakistan, the Sikhs had come out with their demand for 'Sikhistan'—a self-determining state in the Punjab—formed on property basis, meaning obviously that areas where they had by their toil turned waste land into rich agricultural farms, and in which the bulk of their landed property was located, should be constituted into a separate Sikh state. The Bombay police by way of precaution promulgated an order that prohibited the use of 'a certain number of roads and public places except by those persons who are resident in the locality surrounding those roads and by persons who genuinely need to visit those persons'. To it Quaid-i-Azam Jinnah had added a characteristic announcement of his own: 'Press representatives, I hope, will understand that obviously the meeting is not open to the press and, therefore, I would request them not to take the trouble of coming to my house...Photographers and film companies are at liberty to take photos and shots on the arrival of Mr Gandhi'.

The talks with Jinnah began on 9 September 1944, and continued for eighteen days at Jinnah's residence at 10, Mount Pleasant Road, Bombay. Gandhi sent Jinnah special wheaten wafers that had been prepared for himself on Id, which fell during the talks. He also sent Jinnah his nature-cure doctor during the talks to give him curative massages.

As Pyarelal has recorded in *The Final Phase:* 'They met, they shook hands, they embraced each other. There seemed to be a genuine human touch in their first meeting. Jinnah came out into his porch to receive the Mahatma and to escort him back at the time of leaving and even posed with him to be photographed. Observers fancied they noticed in

Jinnah's parting warm handshake more than a mere histrionic gesture. But that was all. At the very outset Jinnah questioned the representative capacity of the Mahatma but ultimately relented and agreed to continue the talks'. As the talks progressed truth began to emerge that there was going to be 'no give but only take'. The Quaid-i-Azam had come not to be convinced or even to discuss: 'the objection had been waived only to give the seeker a chance to receive the light and join the band of the faithful'. 'Have you brought anything from Jinnah?' Gandhiji was asked on his return. 'Only flowers,' was the Mahatmas laconic reply.

Later he gave Rajaji the full story of their three-and-a-quarter hours' talk. It was 'most disappointing': It was a test of my patience…I am amazed at my own patience'. However, it was a friendly talk. As per Pyarelal Gandhi continued: 'His (Jinnah's) contempt for your formula (Rajaji formula) and his contempt for you is staggering. You rose in my estimation that you could have talked to him for all those hours and that you should have taken the trouble to draw up that formula. He says you have accepted his demand and so should I. I said, "I endorse Rajaji's formula and you can call it Pakistan if you like. He talked of the Lahore resolution. I said, I have not studied it and I do not want to talk about it. Let us talk about Rajaji's formula and you can point out any flaws that you find there".

'In the middle of the talk he came back to the old ghost: "I thought you had come here as a Hindu, as a representative of the Hindu Congress". I said, "No, I have come here neither as a Hindu nor as a representative of the Congress. I have come here as an individual. You can talk to me as an individual or as the president of the League, whichever way you prefer. If you had agreed with Rajaji and accepted his formula, you and he would have gone before your respective organisations and pleaded with them to accept it. That is why Rajaji came to you. You would then have placed it before other parties, too, in the same way. Now you and I have to do it". He said he was the president of the League. 'Where was the basis for a talk if I was there representing nobody except myself? Who was to deliver the goods? I was the same man as he had found me in 1939. There was no change in me. I almost felt like saying, "Yes, I am the same man and since you think it is no use talking to me, I will go away." But I resisted the temptation. I told him, "Is not it worth your while to convert an individual? I am the same man no doubt. You can change my views if you can and I will support you wholeheartedly". "Yes, I know, if I can convert you, you will be my Ali", he said'.

'It was a most revealing remark,' Gandhi observed afterwards. 'I was meeting the prophet of Pakistan looking for his Ali!'

To continue with Gandhi's narrative as recorded by Pyarelal:

'He said I should concede Pakistan and he would go the whole length with me. He would go to jail, he would even face bullets. I said, "I will stand by your side to face them". "You may not", he said. "Try me", I replied'.

'We came back to the formula. He wants Pakistan now, not after independence. "We will have independence for Pakistan and Hindustan", he said. "We should come to an agreement and then go to the Government and ask them to accept it, force them to accept our solution". I said I could never be a party to that. I could never ask the Britishers to impose partition on India. "If you all want to separate, I can't stop you. I have not got the power to compel you and I would not use it if I had". He said, "The Muslims want Pakistan. The League represents the Muslims and it wants separation". I said, "I agree the League is the most powerful Muslim organisation. I might even concede that you as—its president represents the Muslims of India, but that does not mean that all Muslims want Pakistan. Put it to the vote of all the inhabitants of the area and see". He said, "Why should you ask non-Muslims?" I said, "You cannot possibly deprive a section of the population of its vote. You must carry them with you, and if you are in the majority why should you be afraid?" I told him of what Kiron Shankar Roy had said to me: "If the worst comes to the worst, we in Bengal will all go in Pakistan, but for goodness' sake do not partition Bengal. Do not vivisect it".

"If you are in majority", I said, "you will have your choice. I know it is a bad thing for you, but if you want it all the same, you will have it. But that will be an adjustment between you and me. It cannot occur while the Britishers are here".

'He began to cross examine me on the various clauses of the formula. I said to him, "If you want clarification of those things, is not it better to have it from the author of the formula?" "Oh, no". He did not want that. I said, "What is the use of your cross-examining me?" He checked himself. "Oh, no. I am not cross-examining you", and then added, "I have been a lawyer all my life and my manner may have suggested that

I was cross-examining you". I asked him to reduce to writing his objections to the formula. He was disinclined. "Must I do so?" he asked. "Yes, I would like you to". He agreed.

'In the end he said, "I would like to come to an agreement with you". I answered, "You remember what I have said, that we should meet not to separate till we had come to an agreement". He said, yes, he agreed. I suggested, "Should we put that also in our statement?" He said, "No, better not. Nevertheless that will be the understanding between us and the cordiality and friendliness of our talk will be reflected in our public utterances, too".

'Rajaji: Do you think he wants a settlement?

'Gandhi: I am not certain. He thought he probably did.

'Rajaji: Then you will get it through.

'Gandhi: Yes...If the right word comes to me.'

The next day they did not meet. Jinnah said it was 'the twenty-first day of Ramzan, a very important day for all Muslims'. A former colleague of Jinnah remarked: 'Why did he not say it was Sunday and he wanted a holiday? He understands Sunday better than Ramzan!'

The talks were resumed in the evening on 11 September. The Mahatma had his evening meal in the middle of their conversation at Jinnah's residence. A bottle of boiled water was included in his tiffin basket. Lest anyone should think that the Mahatma was using holy Ganges water or something like that when dining in a Muslim house, Gandhi gave instructions that the water bottle was not to be sent along thereafter any more.

The wooing on the part of Quaid-i-Azam continued on 12 September. In Gandhi's own words from Pyarelal:

'He drew a very alluring picture of the government of Pakistan. It would be a perfect democracy. I asked him if he had not told me that democracy did not suit Indian conditions. He did not remember it. He asked me to tell him what he had said. So I told him all that and said that I might have misunderstood him. In that case he should correct me. But when I repeated in detail what he had said, he could not say no. He said, yes, he had said that, but that was with regard to imposed democracy.

'Then he said, "Do you think it is a question of religious minority with us?" I said, "Yes". If not, he should tell me what it was. He harangued. I won't repeat all that here. I asked him what would happen to other minorities in Pakistan: Sikhs, Christians, Depressed Classes etc. He said they would be part of Pakistan. I asked him if he meant joint electorates. He knew I was coming to it. He said, yes, he would like them to be a part of the whole. He would explain the advantages of joint electorates, but if they wanted separate electorates they would have it. Sikhs would have Gurumukhi if they wanted and the Pakistan government would give them financial aid. I asked, "What about Jats?" At first he pooh-poohed the idea. Then he said, "If they want it, they will also have it. They will have separate existence if they want it". I said, "What about Christians? They also want some place where they are in a majority and where they can rule, as for instance in Travancore?" He said that was a problem for the Hindus. I said supposing Travancore was in Pakistan? He said he would give it to them. He cited the instance of Newfoundland. The rest of the talk was nothing. I am to continue exploring his mind.

'Rajaji: Find out what he wants.'

'Gandhi: Yes, that is what I am doing. I am to prove from his own mouth that the whole of the Pakistan proposition is absurd. I think he does not want to break. On my part I am not going to be in a hurry. But he can't expect me to endorse an undefined Pakistan.'

'Rajaji: Do you think he will give up the claim?'

'Gandhi: He has to, if there is to be a settlement. He wants a settlement, but what he wants he does not know. I want to show him that your formula is the only thing that he can reasonably ask for.'

From 9 to 13 September was the period of subdued optimism, so far as the outside world was concerned. Then hope began to wilt. From the 14th to the 19th—when Quaid-i-Azam in his Id day message dwelt on the advance of the Muslims 'as a nation' and instead of striking a note of friendship or goodwill indulged in a tirade against 'renegades of the Millat, who are blocking our progress'—covered the phase of growing pessimism. From then onward it was a steep decline, culminating in the complete breakdown on 27 September.

The whole period was marked by an exchange of letters—the queerest correspondence that perhaps ever covered a period of friendly negotiations. The correspondence and the talks never converged but ran a parallel course and were conducted, as it were, in different tongues. 'The talks are to get round you and the correspondence is in anticipation of the failure,' was Rajaji's shrewd comment.

Gandhi had started from the position that his life's mission was Hindu-Muslim unity. Which is why he was prepared to accept, if the Muslims so desired, the substance of the Muslim League's demand as put forth in the Lahore resolution: 'self-determination for areas where the Muslims were in a majority'. However, it was obvious that 'self-determination could not be exercised in the absence of freedom'. Therefore, the League and all other groups composing India should agree to combine, in the first instance, to achieve independence through a joint effort.

To Jinnah this was like putting the cart before the horse. Joint action, he maintained, for achieving independence could follow, not precede a settlement with the League. Gandhi, on the other hand stressed that unless they 'ousted the third party, they could not live at peace with one another'. However, he was ever ready to make an effort 'to find ways and means of establishing a living peace between us'. That was why he had given his approval to the Rajaji formula. It embodied the substance of the demand put forth in the Lahore resolution, and gave it shape. Jinnah objected. The Rajaji formula required the Muslim League to endorse the demand for independence on the basis of a united India. 'If we come to a settlement...we reach by joint effort independence for India as it stands. India, becomes free, we will proceed to demarcation, plebiscite and partition, if the people concerned vote for partition.' Was that not the substance of self-determination? Gandhi had enquired.

Jinnah, legalistically then proceeded to show where the Rajaji formula fell short: Who, for instance, would appoint the Commission for demarcating areas and who would decide the form of the plebiscite and franchise contemplated by the formula? Who would give effect to the verdict of the plebiscite? To which Gandhi had responded by saying the: provisional interim government, unless they decided that very moment.

Jinnah asked: 'What was the basis on which the provisional national government was to be formed?'

Gandhi replied that would have to be agreed to between the League and the Congress. Naturally, if they could agree on some basis, it would be for them to consult other parties. That did not satisfy Jinnah. He wanted a definite outline if Gandhi had any. Since it was the Gandhi formula, he said, he must have thought it out. Gandhi explained that he had not come with any, but if Jinnah had one in connection with the Lahore resolution 'which also I presume requires an Interim Government' they could discuss it. That led them to the Lahore resolution.

Why did not Gandhi accept the Lahore resolution since he (Gandhi) had said that the Rajaji formula conceded in substance the demand embodied in the Lahore Resolution?

To which Gandhi put forth his difficulty: 'The Lahore resolution was vague and indefinite. The 'Pakistan' word was not even in it, nor did it contain any reference to the Two-Nation theory. If the basis of the League's Pakistan demand was religious, then was Pan-Islam its ultimate goal since all the Muslims of the world constituted one community? If, on the other hand, Pakistan was to be confined to Indian Muslims alone, would Jinnah explain what it was that distinguished an Indian Muslim from every other Indian, if not his religion? Was he different from a Turk or an Arab?'

Jinnah replied that pan-Islam was a mere bogey. The word 'Pakistan', he admitted, did not occur in the Lahore resolution, nor was it used by him or the League in its original sense. 'The word has now become synonymous with the Lahore resolution…We maintain and hold that Muslims and Hindus are two major nations by any definition or test of a nation.' Muslims were a separate nation by virtue of their 'distinctive culture and civilisation, language and literature, art and architecture, names and nomenclature, sense of value and proportion, legal laws and moral codes, customs and calendar, history and tradition', and, therefore, they were entitled to a separate, sovereign existence in a homeland of their own.

'Mere assertion is no proof,' Gandhi had protested.

Gandhi had then pleaded with Jinnah to consider how the independent states envisaged by him would be benefited by being split and whether independent states would not become a menace to themselves and to the rest of India? Jinnah's inflexible reply was that this was the only solution of the Indian problem and the 'price India must pay for its independence'.

Pakistan had hitherto appeared before them heavily veiled. Now for the first time its lineaments were exposed to view. 'The more our argument progresses, the more alarming your picture appears to me', wrote Gandhi to Jinnah on 15 September, at the end of the first week of their talks. 'As I...imagine the working of the (Lahore) resolution in practice, I see nothing but ruin for the whole of India'.

The discussion thereafter, entered an acrimonious phase. Jinnah took exception even to Gandhi saying that though he represented nobody, he aspired 'to represent all the inhabitants of India', because he realised in his own person 'their misery and degradation which is their common lot irrespective of class, caste or creed.' This was too much for the future Quaid-i-Azam. Although he had accepted that Gandhi was 'a great man', who was exercising enormous influence over the Hindus, 'particularly the masses', he could not accept his statement that he aspired to represent all inhabitants.

'It is quite clear that you represent nobody but the Hindus, and as long as you do not realise your true position...it is very difficult for me to argue with you,' Jinnah had said.

'Why can you not accept that I aspire to represent all the sections that comprise the people of India?' pleaded Gandhi. 'Do you not aspire? Should not every Indian? That the aspiration may never be realised is beside the point.'

Jinnah insisted that Gandhi should accept the 'basis and fundamental principles' adumbrated in the Lahore resolution. Gandhi pleaded with him that, that was not unnecessary since he had accepted 'the concrete consequence' that would follow from such acceptance in as far as it was reasonable and practicable? 'I cannot accept the Lahore resolution as you want me to, especially when you seek to introduce into its interpretation theories and claims which I cannot accept and which I cannot ever hope to induce India to accept.'

'Can we not agree,' Gandhi finally pleaded, 'to differ on the question of 'two-nations' and yet solve the problem on the basis of self-determination?'

The basis of this offer of Gandhi was that India was not to be regarded as the home of two or more nations, but as one family, consisting of many members, of whom one, the Muslims, living in certain parts in absolute majority, desired to live in separation from the rest of India. 'If the regions holding Muslim majorities have to be separated according to the Lahore resolution, this grave step of separation should specifically be placed before and approved by the people in that area'. Differing from the general basis proposed by the Muslim League of the Two-Nation Theory, Gandhi had said, he could yet recommend to the Congress and the country acceptance of the claim for separation of those parts. If the majority of all the adult population of those parts voted in favour of a separation, then those areas would be formed into a separate state as soon as India was free.

This he called 'division as between two brothers'. Children of the same family, dissatisfied with one another by reason of change of religion, if they wished, could separate, but then the separation would be within themselves and not separation in the face of the whole world, 'When two brothers separate, they do not become enemies...in the eyes of the world. The world would still recognise them as brothers.'

Whilst, therefore, the two parts might agree to live separately, Gandhi proposed that the treaty of separation should also provide for the efficient and satisfactory administration of matters of common concern like defence, foreign affairs, internal communications, customs, commerce and others plus terms for fully safeguarding the rights of minorities in the two states. Immediately on the acceptance of this agreement by the Congress and the League the two would decide on a common course of action for the attainment of independence. The League would, however, be free to remain out of any direct action to which the Congress might resort and in which the League might not be willing to participate.

However, Jinnah did not want separation on the basis of a plebiscite in which all the inhabitants affected by it could participate; he wanted the issue to be decided on the basis of 'self-determination' confined to the Muslims alone. 'We claim the right of self-determination as a nation...You are labouring under the wrong idea that "self-determination" means only that of "a territorial unit"...Ours is a case of division and carving out two independent, sovereign States by way of settlement between two major nations, Hindus and Muslims, and not of severance or secession *from any existing union*, which is *non est* in India.'

'I find no parallel in history for a body of converts and their descendants claiming to be a nation apart from the parent stock', wrote Gandhi to Jinnah on 15 September. 'If India was one nation before the advent of Islam, it must remain one in spite of the change of faith of a very large body of her children...You seem to have introduced a new test of nationhood. If I accept it, I would have to subscribe to many more claims and face an insoluble problem.'

In reply to Gandhi's question as to what provision for defence and similar matters of common concern he contemplated under the Lahore resolution, he replied: 'There cannot be defence and similar matters of 'common concern' when it is accepted that Pakistan and Hindustan will be two separate, independent sovereign states, except by treaty between the two.'

While Gandhi was prepared to let the Muslim majority areas separate if they wanted to provide a treaty for the satisfactory administration of defence and other matters of 'common concern' to both the parts. Jinnah wanted separation to come first and a treaty for the safeguarding of 'common interest' to India afterwards, on such terms as the two parts might agree to, that is if they could so agree. This, as the then Congress president, Maulana Azad put it, was like 'divorce before marriage'!

What would happen if one or the other broke the treaty, if there was nothing left as of 'joint' concern? The reply was that the 'consequence would be what has happened throughout the world all along up till now, i.e., war.' In other words, Jinnah wanted recognition of the freedom of the Pakistan areas to enter into a combination hostile to India or even to make war upon her. Such a freedom, Gandhi pointed out, could not be had by agreement. He had agreed to separation on the basis of members of a family desiring severance of the family ties in matters of conflict, wrote Gandhi to Sir Tej Bahadur Sapru afterwards, explaining his talks with Jinnah, 'but not in all matters so as to become enemies one of the other, as if there was nothing common between the two except enmity'.

'We seem to be moving in a circle', he wrote to Jinnah on 22 September, and the next day, 23 September, marked a crucial point in the talks.

In a note to Jinnah that day, Gandhi wrote: 'Last evening's talk has left a bad taste in the mouth.' And again on 26 September: 'You keep on saying that I should accept certain theses which you call the basis and fundamental principles of the Lahore resolution, while I have been contending that the best way for us who differ in our approach to the problem is to give body to the demand as it stands in the resolution and work it out to our mutual satisfaction'.

However, Jinnah refused even to discuss Gandhi's proposal. 'You repeat that if you and I can agree upon a common course of action, you may use what influence you possess for its acceptance by the Congress and the country. I have already stated from the very beginning that that is not enough.'

He had agreed to receive the Mahatma because, as the Mahatma had said, he had come as a seeker of light and knowledge and, 'if I can convert you, exercising as you do tremendous influence over Hindu India, it will be of no small assistance to me'. But he was not prepared to discuss counter proposals for an agreement with one who was not an accredited representative armed with full authority. '(While)...we confined ourselves to the Lahore resolution...the question of your representative capacity did not arise...Now you have...made a new proposal of your own on your own basis...and it is difficult to deal with it any further unless it comes from you in your representative capacity'.

'Your constant references to my not being clothed with representative authority are really irrelevant', replied Gandhi, 'If you break, it cannot be because I have no representative capacity or because I have been unwilling to give you satisfaction in regard to the claim embodied in the Lahore resolution'.

When the matter had reached breaking point, Gandhi finally suggested that he should be allowed to meet the Muslim League Council to make them see the reasonableness of his proposals. 'Do not take, I pray, the responsibility of rejecting the offer. Throw it on your Council. Give me an opportunity of addressing them. If they feel like rejecting it I would like you to advise the Council to put it before the open session of the League. If you will accept my advice and permit me I would attend the open session and address it'.

As an alternative, he suggested that the issue might be put to arbitration. 'Is it irrelevant or inadmissible to supplement our efforts to convince each other with outside help, guidance, advice or even arbitration?' he asked. If they were bent on reaching an agreement, all these approaches were there to make use of.

However, none of these suggestions were acceptable to Jinnah. 'It is a most extraordinary and unprecedented suggestion to make. Only a member or delegate is entitled to participate in the deliberations of the meeting of the Council or in the open session'.

The following from Pyarelal's diary under the date 24 September 1944, gives an account of the final breakdown of the talks:

'On his return at 7.10 p.m. Bapu spoke to Rajaji and then again after prayers. Jinnah had refused even to discuss Bapu's proposal, as he (Bapu) was not vested with authority; he represented nobody. "If you want defence and so many things in common, that means that you visualise a centre?" "No, but I must say, in practice there will have to be a body selected by both parties to regulate these things."

'Then he came to the August (1942) resolution. He said, it was inimical to Muslims. "But don't you see that it is absolutely a baseless charge? With all the legal acumen that is attributed to you, why cannot you see that it deals with only India and the British rule? It has nothing to do with the Muslims. You can refer the matter to a lawyer of eminence impersonally and take his opinion whether there is anything in it which could be considered inimical to the Muslim League or the Muslims."

'He said he did not need to do so. "Why should I want another's opinion when I know it for myself?" "I broached the subject that I had fixed up to be at Sevagram on the 2 October. I would like to leave on the 30th and would be back in 4 or 5 days." He said, "Why must we take so long? We had better close up now. I will have everything ready (the reference was to their correspondence) on Tuesday. You will examine the copies and I will do so." He had the introduction also ready and read it out. "I said, I had nothing to say against it, but if I had a copy I could examine it. He said I could do so on Tuesday. I said, all right. He would not have a third party, nor would he produce his own scheme. He condemned the August resolution. He suggested in so many words that amends should be made, i.e., it should be retracted"'.

'Reporting the failure of the talks at a largely attended evening prayer meeting, on 27 September, Gandhi said that although the result he was hoping for had not materialised, he had no sense of disappointment or despondency. He was convinced that even out of that breakdown good would result. He had tried his best, he went on to explain, to go as far as he could to meet Jinnah's viewpoint for the common good of all. He had knocked at the Quaid-i-Azam's door, but he had failed.

"I believe Mr Jinnah is sincere, but I think he is suffering from hallucination when he imagines that an unnatural division of India could bring either happiness or prosperity to the people concerned", Gandhi remarked in an interview to Mr Gelder of the *News Chronicle*.

'Their talks had only been adjourned *sine die*, Gandhi explained to another group of pressmen. "I am convinced that Mr Jinnah is a good man. I hope we shall meet again....In the meantime it is the duty of the public to digest the situation and bring the pressure of their opinion upon us."'

Gandhi had sought a reconciliation, a last attempt to gather some grains from the dust of a destructive partition, but it was not to be.

Besides, the risk of bad faith had to be taken; it was inseparable from a completely independent existence. And in any event, the great edifice of independence could not be raised on a foundation of fear.

The Rajaji formula conceded the essence of the League's demand, in so far as it was reasonable, said Gandhi. He did not mind if it was given the name 'Pakistan'. But since Jinnah had characterised it as 'a parody or negation' and an attempt to torpedo the Muslim League's Lahore resolution of March 1940, he felt it necessary to understand the basis of Jinnah's objection. If the League's demand, which it called Pakistan, was not full sovereignty minus only the agreement to wage war, or avoidance of measures detrimental to both parts regarded as a whole, then what was Pakistan? If the object was to create a unit where there would be the fullest scope for the development of Muslim religion and culture and for the expression of the talents and personality of the leaders of the Muslim community, without being overshadowed by more outstanding talent which they feared in an undivided India, his formula, Gandhi felt should give full satisfaction. If, on the other hand, the plan was to use 'Pakistan' as a fulcrum for employing Sudetenland tactics against India, it would not lend itself to that use.

Gandhi continued to have the highest regard for Jinnah's single-mindedness, his great ability and integrity which nothing could buy. Surely, Jinnah—the patriot—would not insist on freedom to engage in a fratricidal war or to do things that would weaken the two parts taken as a whole economically or in regard to defence. That was why Gandhi had knocked on his door, presented his cards to him for examination and entreated him to produce his without any mental reservation.

However, he had to contend against loaded dice. 'The correspondence makes clear', wrote Dr M.R. Jayakar, the eminent jurist and liberal leader from Maharashtra, to Gandhi, 'that any day, Mr Jinnah would prefer a settlement with the British rather than with his own countrymen...He will use this formula as a bargaining counter with the British Government and also as the starting point in future negotiations with Indian leaders'.

This was virtually the last, sustained effort that Gandhi made to somehow, any reasonable how avoid a partition (which he consistently termed as vivisection) of the country. On the borders of India a war raged, he and Jinnah both were no longer young men; time was fast running out for all the principal actors. The choice was stark, to make an effort knowing it might come to naught or let matters drift. For a united India Gandhi tried, but did not succeed, public expectations having been raised, filled with hope, were shattered. In consequence this last effort by Gandhi is often criticised, but for him it was his 'dharma' to try.

Desai–Liaquat Pact: A Premature Delivery

It was at this stage, when everything looked so hopeless and bleak, that Bhulabhai Desai, a lawyer and a prominent Congress member of the Assembly made his efforts at finding a solution to the political impasse.

In view of the vastly changed war situation and also of politics in India, Bhulabhai and the Congress party had given up their boycott of the Central Legislature and resumed their seats. Here Bhulabhai came to terms with Liaquat Ali Khan, deputy leader of the Muslim League in the Legislative Assembly, and often defeated the government in the period February/March 1945. It was understood that Bhulabhai and Liaquat Ali had arrived at an agreement, or a plan, the basis of which was that Jinnah and Desai, the leaders of the two opposition parties in the Assembly, should form an interim government at the Centre, within the present constitutional framework and appoint all the members of the Executive Council, all of whom, except the governor-general and the commander-in-chief, should be Indian. Also, that there was to be parity between the Hindus and Muslims in the Executive Council. To quote Motilal Setalvad who knew Bhulabhai Desai very well:[46] 'Though Gandhi had been released, the members of the Working Committee of the Congress and other leaders had remained in jail. Bhulabhai had, towards the end of 1944 and at the beginning of 1945, held conversations with the viceroy on the possibility of forming an interim government with the consensus of both the Hindus and the Muslims. Evidently, his relations with Liaquat Ali Khan who was a member of the Muslim League group in the Assembly and the right-hand man of Jinnah were very cordial'. Some of these conversations appear to have taken place in January 1945, when proposals for the formation of an interim government were discussed. The first act of the interim government was to be the release of the imprisoned leaders. Bhulabhai, in whom Gandhi had great confidence, consulted Gandhi about these proposals on more than one occasion, visiting him at Wardha, where Gandhi was then living. A draft of the proposals in Bhulabhai's handwriting was also shown him which Gandhi approved, making some alterations, in his own hand. Eventually, two copies of these proposals, as finalised, were made and signed by Bhulabhai and Liaquat Ali Khan. The contents of the signed documents, which later came to be called the Desai–Liaquat Ali Pact, clearly indicated that Jinnah must have been consulted by Liaquat Ali Khan before agreeing to sign. All kind of rumours, also various accounts of these proposals had begun to appear, from time to time in the Indian press but nothing authoritative was (till then) known to the public.

In June 1945, the members of the Working Committee of the Congress were finally released. Soon thereafter, a storm burst in the Congress camp over this Pact. Bhulabhai was accused of having acted behind Gandhi's back and betrayed the Congress. These charges were made in public and in press by important persons, whereupon Gandhi came out with a statement, in which, in substance, he stated that Bhulabhai had acted after consulting him and with his authority. Notwithstanding these statements of Gandhi and some other Congress leaders supporting Bhulabhai, others took a very hostile attitude, and despite the expressed views of Gandhi and Maulana Abul Kalam Azad, other important members of the Working Committee decided to repudiate the Pact and disown Bhulabhai for having acted without due authority. It was alleged that Bhulabhai had exceeded his brief and attempted to promote a compromise which was not in the interests of the Congress. To this Setalvad adds: 'I am certain that Bhulabhai acted honourably and in good faith and under the full authority of Gandhi. Clearly, for personal or other reasons, Bhulabhai was not acceptable to some of the members of the Working Committee, who appeared to have taken this opportunity to destroy his reputation...Setalvad goes on to clarify: 'Though the Congress was intending to contest the elections to the Central Legislature that were soon to take place, those in power in the Congress unscrupulously decided not to select Bhulabhai as a candidate for the Congress in the Central Legislature.' Such malice was at whose behest? And why did Gandhi not accept responsibility or at least share it? Motilal Setalvad preserved the original note in Desai's handwriting, the one which Desai had showed to Gandhi between 3 and 5 January 1945. This note contains corrections, alterations and additions, all in Gandhi's handwriting, Seralvad had also affirmed the note.

Liaquat Ali Khan survived this crisis but only just, for Sir Sultan Ahmed, Fazlul Haq and Begum Shah Nawaz had all been expelled from the Muslim League for having joined the National Defence Council. Liaquat's was a much more serious matter, about forming a coalition government, for which Jinnah would certainly have reacted equally strongly if he had not been consulted. It is relevant that Bhulabhai Desai and Liaquat Ali Khan had been personal friends for sometime. Desai's scholarship of Persian and his penchant for Urdu poetry were amongst the several factors bringing these two leaders together and they had not come together for the first time over these proposals. Liaquat Ali went off on his south Indian tour the day he had initialled the draft and Desai made it public before Liaquat Ali could brief Jinnah, personally. Jinnah assessed that there were grounds for aggrievement; but he also realised that there were no grounds for impeachment. Perhaps he (Jinnah) also wanted to act differently from what the Congress had done.

This defeat of the 'Desai proposals' was on account of not having the whole hearted support of the Congress, and possibly the best requiem for this whole episode was written by Jamna Das Mehta when he later said, in a statement that the 'Simla Conference failed because the Congress had refused to abide by the Liaquat–Desai formula'. According to Mehta, Jinnah had adopted the only course left to him after the Pakistan Resolution, but if there had been parity between the Congress and the Muslim League, then Jinnah would have backed the move. Parity, then, emerges here as the elusive prize, a condition which made all the difference between the interim government which Desai had proposed and the interim government that eventually got formed.

It is fascinating that even as the options narrowed, the end-game became ever more tense, more complex, the British tired visibly and the communal tangles worsened, the debate remained fixed, points of discord remained the same, the quest was unaltered: how to safeguard against the weight of majoritarianism; how to create such political space as would enable the Muslims of India to be the full, unfettered arbiters of their own social, religious and political destinies? What was sought by them (the Muslims) was just this convincing enough space and a reassuring system, ideally (still) in India, but outside, if inevitable. Did the answer lie in devising such a system, through the agreement of all as would provide the needed assurance, or was the problem really of attitudes? This last, 'attitudes', born of the many centuries of historical experiences had by now got embedded as the societal characteristics of the various communities, Hindu, Sikh, Muslim—whatever. No governmental executive order can possibly change attitudes; it is only the comfort and ultimate conviction of societies, born of altered circumstances which bring about the needed mutual confidence and assurance. This India had to do on its own; Indian society's internal cleansing mechanisms could do it, an evolution of sensibilities alone could (had to) do it; only this could (would) keep India unbreakably united. The viceroy, Wavell or any other could only either externally enforce or help evolve, or devise a system of cooperative, executive functioning, but only of governance, not of the other integrals of societies like attitudes. Communal amity and accord and mutual regard was India's responsibility, of the undivided Indians alone, not of that alien, imperial authority. Why did we at all ask them for it? This reflection and question invades our thoughts as we move unstoppably (?) towards that awesome human tragedy, that hasty vivisection, that deconstruction of India.

'Trail all your pikes, dispirit every drum, March in slow procession from afar'

(*The Soldier's Deaths*—Anne Finch)

For, in this tearing apart of a united India, what do we rejoice? How to do that?

7

A WAR OF SUCCESSION—DIVERGING PATHS

WAVELL—THE SOLDIER-VICEROY—OCTOBER 1943 TO MARCH 1947

Field Marshal Wavell's appointment as the viceroy of India in succession to Linlithgow, and his tenure as the penultimate holder of that high office was turbulent from appointment to departure. For one, Wavell had never been on the most cordial of terms with Prime Minister Churchill, from whom he got little real cooperation but sadly, he did not get that even from the successor prime minister, Clement Attlee. When Wavell became the viceroy of India, Britain faced the complex challenges of the Second World War, India could scarcely be the priority then, but when Germany surrendered then, too, he did not get the needed consideration from the successor Labour government. Wavell (had) wanted primarily to remain in uniform though, he did not mind being 'put on the shelf', should such a national need ever arise. His diary of 24 June 1943 records his dilemma and the many issues that then confronted him:

> I accepted the Viceroyalty in the spirit of a military appointment—one goes where one is told in time of war without making conditions or asking questions. I think I ought to have treated it in a political spirit and found out what the policy to India really was to be and I think I could have made my own conditions, for I think Winston was really hard put to it to find someone. However, here I am and I must do my best, though I am frankly appalled at the prospect of five years—hard to the mind and soft to the body.
>
> I certainly do not look forward to 1944 and its problems. The food, coal and inflation problems do not look any lighter; there seems likely to be little

progress in the war on the Burma front; and I see no prospect of any advancement in the political field.[1]

Wavell's qualifications for this appointment are justly described by Penderel Moon in his work, *Wavell—The Viceroy's Journal*. 'Wavell', he writes, 'was the only soldier to hold the office of Viceroy after the Crown took over control of India from the East India Company in 1858; and not from the aristocracy, but from an upper-middle-class family...the mainstay of the British Raj...He typified the best qualities of this class....First and foremost was his deep sense of public duty and public service; next his straightforwardness and complete integrity; and next his energy and capacity for hard work. But he also possessed some rarer qualities to which the younger of Nehru's two sisters, Krishna Nehru Hutheesing, has drawn attention. 'He was a good Viceroy', she has written, and besides being conscientious was 'understanding and humane'.... Lord Wavell was in the tradition of the greatest line of British administrators in India, Warren Hastings, Munro, Malcolm, Sleeman, and Henry Lawrence, all of whom respected the people... sympathized with their feelings, and tried to understand them'. This was in reality a stop-gap, war time appointment, as Churchill himself put it, though other names like Anthony Eden's had also been considered at that stage. As it transpired, Field Marshal Lord Wavell's viceroyalty, the penultimate before a final British withdrawal turned out far different to what Churchill had wanted, neither stop-gap nor rubber stamp.

Wavell brought to his responsibilities many extra burdens; the principal amongst them was this antipathy that Churchill carried about India, the Indian Army and Indians in general. There are, of course, innumerable instances that could be cited here of Churchill's intransigent, truculent attitude to things and matters Indian but just a few before we commence travelling with Field Marshal Wavell on his viceregal journey of India ought to suffice, and they are really best recounted in Wavell's own words.[2] Churchill really did 'hate India and everything to do with it'[3] and as Amery had observed then that he (Churchill) knew 'as much of the Indian problem as George III did of the American colonies'. On another occasion, Wavell had commented that Churchill's views about India are like those of 'a cavalry subaltern of old and his military thinking is of Boer War vintage'. However, he (Wavell) had not been prepared for what was the Cabinet's obvious lack of interest in India. 'I have discovered that the Cabinet is not honest in its expressed desire to make progress in India; and that very few of them have any foresight or political courage'.[4] Wavell surmised, accurately that Churchill feared a division among the Conservatives over the India question and also that such a split would destroy his government by irreparably damaging the war-time coalition. This certainly was not any part of Churchill's agenda then. Besides, Churchill's opponents on Indian policy had good reason to defer to his prejudices but only for the duration of the war, for, quite unexceptionably, winning the war was then the principal objective, which is why war-time unity at home always took precedence over initiatives on India's independence. In this sense, Wavell came to his new responsibilities when openings for settlement in India were possibly the lowest priority. That is why it was not until after a full year in office that Wavell took up India's constitutional problems. However, when he finally did, he stressed the inevitability of negotiations with both the Congress and the Muslim League. Unlike Churchill or the Cabinet, Wavell judged the 'present as a propitious moment', for after the war, he reasoned there was bound to be 'a fertile field for agitation(s),[5] with the release of political prisoners, the demobilisation of troops, and the closure of munitions factories'.

Wavell pursued his ideas proposing 'a provisional political government, of the type suggested in the Cripps declaration, within the present constitution', coupled with an attempt to reach a constitutional settlement. Outlining his scheme, he explained that he would begin by calling a small conference of political leaders to frame agreed proposals for the composition of a transitional government and consider the re-establishment of popular governments in the provinces, which were then under governor's rule. Churchill's response was standard: that 'these very large problems required to be considered at leisure and in victorious peace'. Wavell persisted, asserting 'that present time is the most favourable opportunity we have had for some years to make progress with Indian problem',[6] and he conveyed to Amery that unless his recommendations received urgent attention from the Cabinet he would seek permission to fly home to state his case in person.

Bhulabhai Desai had in the meantime come to meet Wavell; this was on 15 November 1944. Desai then suggested the formation of a national government, under the 1935 constitution, with members drawn from the existing legislature. A precondition, of course, was the release of the imprisoned members of the Congress Working Committee and 'replacement of Section 93 Governments' that is end of Governor's rule. In Desai's next meeting with the private secretary to the viceroy, Sir George Abell, on 12 January 1945, he conveyed he had the agreement of both Gandhi and Jinnah on this proposal of coalition governments. As this sounded encouraging the viceroy informed the government back home about it. He also invited Desai to elaborate his proposals in person, recording 'I think it may be an advantage in some ways that the approach has come from the Indian side'. A week later on 20 January 1945, Wavell met Desai to assess the proposals as well as to ascertain for himself the support that Desai had, for he was not convinced of the backing that these proposals had, but he was curious enough to cable London that he proposed to see Jinnah also in this connection, if the government so agreed. The government in London agreed but raised some routine queries. There upon, the viceroy in a personal message responded that 'this was the best chance they have had for a long time, or were likely to have, to make a moderate advance on the Indian problem and that they had better take it at once and not worry too much about details and comparisons with Cripps offer and such like.'[7] The government gave its assent but as Jinnah was too busy then to come to Delhi, Wavell authorised the governor of Bombay, Sir John Colville, to see him in Bombay itself and ascertain his views on the 'Desai proposals'. At this meeting, Jinnah, astonishingly disclaimed all knowledge of Liaquat's talk with Desai. Wavell felt this was a falsehood on part of Jinnah, though, Jinnah did convey that he was prepared to consider such an offer, that he would be in Delhi on 6 March 1945, and would then also be available for a discussion.[8]

Accordingly, Jinnah was to have met Wavell on 7 March 1945 but having again taken ill, could not. The importance attached to this meeting by the British government can be gauged by Wavell's frustration with HMG's reluctance to call him to London for immediate consultations: 'I don't intend to let them use Desai and Jinnah as reasons for delay. After all, the principal of my going home for a discussion was accepted long before Desai's proposals came up; and it is the mind of HMG that I want to know rather than the minds of Desai and Jinnah'.[9] Desai's approach was, in reality, 'irksome to the soldier viceroy', for he (Desai) along with Liaquat had regularly cooperated in the Assembly to almost routinely defeat the government. Wavell observes in his *Journal*—

'Desai and Liaquat are obviously out to show me that I had better get rid of my Executive Council and give them the loaves and the fishes. I am told that Desai has been offering portfolios to his friends. I have made up my mind not to see Desai again before I go home'.[10] About an official announcement of his visit to London for consultations, Wavell was chary, apprehending that it could appear as a sudden decision and that too, because of the 'Desai' proposals. In any event Wavell had his own plans as well as a copy of the Desai–Liaquat agreement when he left for London on 22 March 1945.

Meanwhile, two Muslim League ministries lost their majorities in the provinces: Sardar Aurangzeb Khan's cabinet in the Frontier fell on 12 March 1945 and Khwaja Sir Nazimuddin's, in Bengal, on 28 March 1945. The order of the Congress high command under which the Congress ministries had resigned in October 1939 had not yet been rescinded, though for the Frontier, special permission was given to Dr Khan Sahib to attempt an alternative ministry. In Bengal no ministry could be formed as elections were due some nine months later.

Wavell's visit dragged on fruitlessly for nine weeks, principally because the prime minister kept avoiding meeting him fearing Wavell would present him with demands about India that he (the prime minister) would find disagreeable. However, Wavell's dour persistence, finally broke through Churchill's barricades of hesitation. For the first time since August 1942 the viceroy of India had reached out to the citizens of India, and 'negotiations and compromise were back on the agenda', Wavell had still to overcome a host of other objections to this revival of the short-term aspect of the Cripps offer before the Cabinet finally assented. At best, this agreement was a kind of a stop-gap consent so as to keep the problem of India out of the British election campaign due in June 1945, and also because the British Cabinet estimated as remote Wavell's prospects of obtaining the support of both the Congress and the League. Even those who were sympathetic feared that any reconstitution of the executive, which was one of the proposals would erode the viceroy's position and could place power in the hands of 'undemocratic, non-representative party oligarchies'. Attlee wanted a panel of politicians elected by the Central and provincial legislatures, from which Wavell could choose his council. Cripps, with some support from other members of the India Committee felt that as reconstructing the executive would necessarily reduce the viceroy's powers, limits to the reduction could be fixed by statute. However, Wavell resisted all such pressures and obtained from the Cabinet freedom to select his council, while simultaneously retaining the power to override it.

Unfortunately, two events then further delayed Wavell's return. The first was President Roosevelt's death on 13 April 1945. This upset all schedules for over a fortnight; where after, a rush of events in Europe following Nazi Germany's sudden collapse further delayed matters. Attending to that naturally then became the priority. This unavoidable delay in addressing the Indian problem generated distrust and impatience back in the country. Had the leaders been released in April 1945, before say, the collapse of Germany, and thereafter the viceroy's conference convened, chances of 'success' might have been brighter, but this kind of speculation now has no relevance. By the time Lord Wavell returned, (after almost two and a half months) there were just two provinces left under Muslim League ministries—Sindh and Assam. Jinnah's self-confidence though, remained unshaken, rather he now affirmed even more emphatically, more than ever before his exclusive right to represent the Muslims of India.

THE FIRST SIMLA CONFERENCE

Wavell returned on 4 June 1945, and on 14 June broadcast his proposals for a conference of the kind that he had intended to convene from the very beginning. The main features announced were: A political conference of twenty-one leaders representing all parties, to meet at Simla on 25 June 1945, to discuss the composition of a new Executive Council, to which but for the viceroy and the commander-in-chief, who would hold charge of the war portfolio, it would be a totally Indian Council. The subject of external affairs, till now administered by the viceroy, would also be placed in the charge of an Indian member of the new Council. This new Council would work under the existing constitution. It was proposed then to appoint a British high commissioner in India, as in other dominions, to represent Britain's commercial and other interests. Lord Wavell also clarified that this formation of an interim government in no way prejudiced the final constitutional settlement. The main task of the new Executive Council would be to first, prosecute the war against Japan; second, to carry on the government of British India until a new, permanent constitution could be agreed upon and for it to enter into force; and third, to consider the means by which such an agreement could be achieved expeditiously.

Gandhi was at Panchgani, a hill-station near Poona, still weak from his recent illness when the text of the viceregal broadcast, inviting him to Simla, was put into his hands by a press correspondent. He immediately wired to the viceroy that he (Gandhi) represented no institution; having ceased to be even a primary member of the Congress since 1934. The viceroy recognised the force of his argument and rectified the situation by sending an invitation to the Congress president to attend the conference. Gandhi nevertheless, agreed to go to Simla, to meet the viceroy and stay there for as long as the viceroy wanted.

The viceroy's broadcast had not only avoided the word 'independence' but had also introduced a new notion, that of 'caste-Hindu-Muslim parity', in the proposed national government as a basic condition. Drawing the viceroy's attention to this point, Gandhi wired: 'Personally I can never subscribe to it (caste-Hindu-Muslim parity) nor the Congress, if I know its mind. In spite of having overwhelming Hindu membership the Congress has striven to be purely political. I am quite capable of advising the Congress to nominate all non-Hindus and most decidedly non-caste Hindus'. And again: '(The) Congress has never identified (itself) with caste or non-caste Hindus and never can, even to gain independence, which will be one-sided, untrue and suicidal'. The viceroy in reply assured Gandhi that acceptance of the invitation did not 'commit the parties' to anything. The members would be free to discuss the pros and cons of the proposals at the conference and to accept or reject them as they chose. That cleared the ground for the Congress participation in the conference.

The Congress Working Committee now met at Bombay; it was doing so after a period of three years and drew up an 'instrument of instructions' for its nine representatives invited to the conference. Among other issues it took note of the fact that the All-India Congress Committee and other Congress Committees were still banned and that was an obstacle in [the] way and must be regarded as coercion. Further, large numbers of Congress prisoners must interfere with the progress of the conference. Most of the Congress leaders had come out of prison with shattered health. A friend described the Working Committee meeting as a 'sick parade'. However, they decided that 'Congress as an organisation should participate in the forthcoming conference. 'The

Working Committee then charged its representatives at the conference to bear in mind that, Allied victory in South-East Asia must mean freedom of the countries concerned from all Imperialist control, British or other....Prohibition of the Use of Indian resources for the deprivation of freedom of any other countries must be an accepted fact'.

As the Congress members journeyed, they were hailed by delirious crowds at various stations all along the 1,100 miles route between Bombay and Simla. It was also a welcome to the members of the Congress Working Committee on their release after thirty-four months of incarceration.

June being the hottest month of the year in peninsular India, the viceroy had thoughtfully instructed that suitable air-cooled (no air conditioning then) coaches be reserved for Gandhi and other Congress leaders headed for Simla. Gandhi, however, declined to use such a facility.

Preston Grover of the United Press of America was travelling with Gandhi on the same train. Solicitous about Gandhi's health, he handed him a short note at one of the halts on the way: 'Would not it be wise for you to go into the cooler Congress car for the afternoon, so you could stretch yourself a while? You have not had any sleep for twenty-four hours. It is not going to help much if you arrive at Simla tired out from the interruptions in your sleep at wayside stations. As we say in America, "Give yourself a break".

Preston Grover received the following reply: 'Many thanks for your considerate note. But let me melt myself in this natural heat. As sure as fate, this heat will be followed by refreshing coolness which I shall enjoy. Let me feel just a touch of real India'.

After a hurried bath and meal on arrival at Simla, Gandhi went straight to the Viceregal Lodge for his first meeting with the viceroy. Wavell, very keen on Gandhi attending the conference as a delegate, could not persuade the Mahatma to do so, who continued to maintain that in a representative conference like the present no individual, however eminent, should have a place if not a delegate. Constitutional correctness required that, but if his advice was wanted he would stay in Simla during the conference and even attend it as a visitor. The viceroy said he would like him to stay, to which Gandhi agreed. It transpired later that Jinnah had voiced it as a grievance saying that Gandhi had 'withdrawn' from the conference. 'If Mr Jinnah wants me there', said

Gandhi in an interview with Preston Grover, 'he can take me there. Such a gesture on Jinnah's part would mean that he wants a settlement even in the teeth of differences and obstacles that face the conference'.

By all accounts, Lord Wavell began well, guiding the deliberations of the conference with great tact, delicacy and quiet wisdom: 'I said in my broadcast that on all sides there was something to forgive and forget... You must accept my leadership for the present...I will endeavour to guide the discussion of this conference in what I believe to be the best interests of the country'. Referring to this part of the viceroy's speech Gandhi commented: 'It is a good and dignified expression that Lord Wavell has used. He thus acts in the conference as its leader and not as the agent of Whitehall.'

The viceroy deftly bypassed thorny points when they threatened to hold up progress. He was trying to explain that he had nowhere suggested that the Congress was a Hindu body when Jinnah launched forth on one of his usual diatribes against the Congress, characterising it as a 'Hindu' body. A passage at arms followed:

Viceroy: 'There is nothing in my proposals which characterises Congress as a communal body.'

Jinnah: 'We have met here as communities and Congress does not represent anybody but the Hindus.'

Viceroy: 'Congress represents its members.'

Dr Khan Saheb: 'What does he mean? I am a Congressman. Am I a Hindu or a Muslim?'

Viceroy: 'Leave it at that. The Congress represents its members.'

Gandhi argued with the Congress leaders that he took the viceregal announcement in regard to parity to mean that neither community could ask for more representation than the other but 'was free to accept less if it chose'. Congress should accept the position that the non-scheduled Hindus would in no case exceed Muslims and break the parity by nominating the best Indians drawn from all minority groups, including one representative each of Anglo-Indians, Englishmen, Parsis, Sikhs, Jews (if available), Indian Christians, Scheduled Castes and women, and to do so irrespective of whether they were Congress members or not.

There need not thus be more than one or two Hindus apart from the Scheduled Castes, Gandhi reasoned, and even they should be present not as caste representatives but because they were the 'best Indians' available. By refusing to exercise the right of parity on behalf of the Hindus, Gandhi reasoned, they would cut across sectional complications and lay a solid and safe foundation for independent India, (and all this) on a purely nationalist basis. If they accepted the (suggested) parity formula, it would inevitably give rise to a gladiatorial duel between the Hindus and Muslims in the Viceroy's Executive Council and bring into play the viceroy's veto. But they could render nugatory the parity part of the viceregal proposal if they voluntarily chose sub-parity for the Hindus by selecting the bulk of their nominees from among the minorities. With five Muslim members pitted against five 'caste Hindus', the Muslim League, with the help of the viceroy and commander-in-chief, could any time create a tie in the Cabinet. If, on the other hand, the Cabinet was largely composed of patriotic nationalist-minded minority group representatives with only one, two or even three 'caste Hindus', there would be no communal alignment in the Cabinet and the League would be beating empty air if it tried to raise the bogey of the Hindu majority rule.

This was such a characteristically Gandhi touch, on the surface impractical and yet, it dexterously eliminated contention by simply side-stepping it. Unfortunately, the Congress Working Committee would not be persuaded to adopt Gandhi's proposal, though several members of the Working Committee and Congress leaders individually, were convinced of the wisdom of his stand. 'It appeals to me; Gandhi is right,' remarked the ex-chief minister of a province to one of his colleagues. 'But do you expect to be able to face the electorate after accepting sub-parity for the Hindus?'

When the conference met on 29 June, the viceroy announced that since the parties were unable to come to an agreement about the composition and strength of the government, he would use his personal offices to resolve the difficulty. He asked all interests represented in the conference to send him lists of persons they would like to be selected for joining the national government. He would add to them some names himself and after scrutinizing all the names, and after consulting with the parties concerned, he would try to arrive at a list generally acceptable to the conference.

Jinnah would not agree; he wanted first to know whether, if the League sent a list, the viceroy would accept the League panel en bloc. The viceroy replied that he could give no such guarantee beforehand; it was his function to do the final selection. However, the conference would be given the opportunity to discuss and finally accept or reject the names recommended by him. Jinnah then asked whether the viceroy would still proceed with his proposal if one of the parties finally rejected it, to which again the viceroy replied that he could not commit himself 'in advance as to what he would do in the contingency envisaged'. Finally, when the viceroy asked him point blank whether the League would submit the list of names or not, Jinnah answered that he was there only in his individual capacity; he would need the viceroy's proposal in writing to place before the Working Committee of the League before he could give a definite reply. He was told he would have it.

The conference then adjourned for a fortnight.

During this adjourned period, all parties except the Muslim League submitted their list of names to the viceroy. The European group decided not to submit any separate list on behalf of their group. The Congress submitted a panel of fifteen names for the proposed Executive Council, holding that in order to give representation to as many minority communities as possible, the strength of the Executive Council—besides the viceroy and the commander-in-chief—should be fifteen. The Congress list of names is at Appendix XI.

On the other hand, Jinnah, in the matter of submitting names conveyed to Lord Wavell: 'With regard to your suggestion for submitting a panel of names...the Working Committee (of the Muslim League) desires to point out that when a similar proposal was made by your Excellency's predecessor, Lord Linlithgow...the Working Committee opposed it and, when its objections were brought to the notice of Lord Linlithgow, he dropped the proposal and suggested another alternative'. Lord Linlithgow's alternative was contained in this letter that the Lord had written to Jinnah on 25 September 1940: 'I am content that the selection of representatives, while resting with the Governor-General, be based in the case of the Muslim League...not on a panel formally submitted but on confidential discussion between the leader of the party concerned and myself (the viceroy)'. Concluding his letter to Wavell, Jinnah wrote: 'The Working Committee is of the opinion...that the procedure settled on the precious occasion should be followed in the present case so far as the Muslim League is concerned'.

This suggestion, obviously, did not find merit in Wavell's views, whereupon Jinnah again wrote: 'The Committee...desires me to state that it regrets very much to note that your Excellency is not able to give the assurance that all the Muslim members of the proposed Executive Council will be selected from the Muslim League...and, in the circumstances, I regret, I am not in a position to send the names on behalf of the Muslim League for inclusion in the proposed Executive Council'.

In the final meeting of the conference on 14 July, the viceroy revealed that even without receiving any list from the Muslim League he had formed an Executive Council on paper which he thought would be acceptable to the conference. However, the Muslim names which he then proposed were not acceptable to Jinnah. The viceroy, however, did not show his list to the Congress president even when it was asked for, or to anyone else. Nor did the viceroy place his list before the conference. He simply announced that the conference had failed to achieve its objective and he took upon himself the entire responsibility for this failure.

'It grieves me to think', wrote Gandhi then, in his letter to the viceroy, 'that the conference which began so happily and so hopefully should have ended in apparent failure due exactly, as it would seem, to the same cause as before. This time you have taken the blame on your own shoulders. But the world will think otherwise. India certainly does'. Probing into the cause of the failure he continued: 'I must not hide from me the suspicion, that the deeper cause is perhaps the reluctance of the official world to part with power, which the passing of virtual control into the hands of their erstwhile prisoners would have meant'.

It was a pity that the attempt to resolve the deadlock should have thus foundered upon the old rocks of prejudice, and yet again. Never was the country more prepared to accept a British offer for a settlement on its face value. The earlier declarations of the viceroy had led the people to hope that a new beginning would be made this time. Where was the need for summoning an all-party conference, they asked, if a Congress-League agreement was to be made a necessary condition for any advance, or if the viceroy was not to go ahead with his plans if the League refused to cooperate? Why should not, in that case, the presidents of the Congress and the League alone have been called and the rest spared the bother of a dummy show? This, too, was a question that got voiced repeatedly.

Jinnah, in a statement, characterized the Wavell plan as 'a snare' and 'a death warrant' for the Muslim League because, even if all the Muslims in the government were to be the Muslim Leaguers, they would still be in a minority of one-third in the Cabinet. The representatives of 'all the minorities,' Jinnah said, would 'in actual practice, invariably...vote... against us' in the government. Previously Jinnah used to say that the Muslim League was the champion and protector of all the minorities in India, and the Congress represented not even 'Hindus' but 'caste Hindus' only. However, he now said: 'All other minorities, such as Scheduled Castes, Sikhs and the Christians have the same goal as the Congress... Their goal and ideology is '...of a united India. Ethnically and culturally, they are very closely knitted to Hindu society'. Surely, both these assertions could not be simultaneously correct, besides, it was asked as to how the Wavell plan would have ceased to be 'a snare' and 'a death warrant' even if the League's demand for nominating all the Muslims in the Cabinet from the Muslim League had been conceded.

In a penetrating analysis of the Quaid-i-Azam's attitude at the conference, Dr Jayakar wrote to Gandhi:

As I read this speech, where he called the Wavell arrangement a snare, it was clear to me that his apprehension (was) that...if he accepted the interim arrangement...in the day to day harmony of working the acerbities and animosities, out of which Pakistan is (to be) born and fed, would be gradually smoothened and Muslims would lose the zest for separate existence on discovering that its basis rests not in realities but only in long cherished suspicion...He puts two conditions as precedent to his assent, which he must realize are impossible, viz. (1) assurance about Pakistan and (2) equality of the Muslim vote with all the other interests in India. True to his habit, intensified by frequent successes, he swallows the concessions Muslims have received, viz., parity between caste Hindus and Muslims and now wants parity between Muslims and all other interests put together, i.e., 50 for Muslims, 50 for all the rest of India—a mathematical monstrosity that 27 equals seventy-three...He is in no hurry to attain freedom and would demand for its attainment a price which would almost render it nugatory.

The net result of the conference was to introduce the formula of 'caste-Hindu-Muslim parity' into practical politics and to stereotype officially the principle of religious division and this sadly, on the eve of independence. The conference also marked the beginning of an essay, which became so prominent during the Cabinet Mission's negotiations later, in double-speak in which the intentions of British were belied by the text of their declarations and what was repudiated in profession was pursued in practice through the device of the ambiguous middle.

'You will admit,' remarked Francis Sayer of the United Nations Relief and Rehabilitation Administration in the course of an interview with Gandhi, 'that Wavell did make an honest attempt to break the deadlock.'

An honest attempt should have ended honestly,' Gandhi responded.

What was it that then happened between 29 June, when the conference had adjourned for a fortnight and 14 July when it reconvened? What made Wavell confess at this 14 July meet that he had failed in his attempts? Confirmation followed a fortnight later in a letter received by Pandit Nehru from London: 'It is now known that the Wavell offer was maintained in being as part of election necessities. Also, that the final termination of the talks by Wavell, without taking the obvious course of forming a government without Jinnah, was dictated from London'. Amery had also sent a cable to Wavell[11] at the last minute, advising him to not proceed any further as the Muslim League was refusing cooperation in the formation of the new Executive Council. Amery is believed to have also said, reasonably, that since the results of the parliamentary elections in Britain were expected on 25 July, it was not possible for Churchill, Amery and the British Cabinet to give any definite instructions, best therefore, he advised that the status quo be maintained in India. This meant a failure of the conference, for the viceroy could scarcely take major decisions with London just standing by.

That is why Wavell in his final address, announcing the failure of the Conference had, like a military commander, which is what he essentially was and remained said: 'I wish to make it clear that the responsibility for this failure is mine. The main idea underlying the conference was mine. If it had succeeded, its success would have been attributed to me, and I cannot place the blame for its failure on any of the parties. I ask the party leaders...to ensure that there are no recriminations'. This, of course, was a vain hope for mutual recriminations resumed and energetically, very soon thereafter. Whatever the other reasons, the root cause of the failure was doubtless Jinnah's intransigence about Muslim representation, and Wavell could scarcely have constituted a new council with only Congress nominees in it, certainly not then, though ironically, later this is precisely what he was compelled to do.

However, there were other factors, too, more fundamental, arising principally from the changes that had occurred in Indian politics since the Cripps Mission. Wavell's scheme was an eminently commendable initiative both in its positive contents and its timing, but Jinnah's obstruction of it was also a clear demonstration of the post-Cripps-Mission changes that we speak of Cripps' concession of parity of representation between Hindus and Muslims had resulted in totally unexpected consequence; it conferred a kind of a functional legitimacy to Jinnah's claims about India being two nations. Thereafter, his demand that the League alone could and must therefore, nominate all Muslim members of the proposed new Council flowed from his argument that the League alone was the authentic, and the sole voice of this Muslim 'nation'. However, this was clearly an overstated demand, it went too far and placed an unbearable load on the existing political platform of India, diminishing, in the process the standing of the Congress party. Besides, all else having already been conceded how could, and why should Jinnah then acquire a veto over Congress' right to nominate their representatives? That is why to the governor of Punjab, Sir Bertrand Glancy, Jinnah's demand was 'quite preposterous', as only Sindh and Assam (with a shaky coalition) then had League ministries.

On the other hand, to the Unionists, who were then in office in Punjab, it was equally unclear as to how and why ought the Congress to enjoy 'such instant transition from the goal to political eminence?' This query was just as trenchant as was the Muslim League's claim of being the sole spokesman of all the Muslims. Jinnah's claim was of course, untenable and was challenged consistently, just as the Congress' claim to represent all, in the whole of India, could simply not be upheld, for surely how could they have that status in the absence of Muslim support? Nonetheless, it was also not possible for Wavell to reconstruct his Executive and do so totally without the League. His Simla initiative had secured the assent of Churchill's government on the assurance that the proposed reconstruction would proceed only upon the full agreement of all, its rationale centred upon securing an accommodation of communal differences. Even if Attlee had then been in office his suspicions of the un-representativeness, or rather the fractured representative status of the parties would have led him to reject an

Executive (hence ministry) that was predominantly of a Hindu Congress. If the party leaders could not or would not, agree on an interim coalition then their respective claims will have to be tested against the litmus of electoral support. This meant elections and they followed soon enough.

During the unreal years of the Congress' absence from politics the League had benefited by being catapulted as a major all-India party; besides it then enjoyed office, too, in some provinces. Its main achievements since the 1937 elections were to create a fairly effective party machine, with strong provincial organisational units, to launch an English language daily, create a disciplined cadre of national guards, and to set up bodies for co-coordinating plans for the education and economic development of the possible 'Pakistan areas'. These, by any reckoning, were significant gains. It was Jinnah's persistent demand for a Muslim nation, and his capacity to block progress unless this was conceded that Wavell had striven to dilute, unsuccessfully as it transpired. However, by then through persisting skillfully with his use of this 'Two-Nation' theory in negotiations, Jinnah had succeeded in almost totally polarizing the political situation in India, between the Congress and the Muslim League, thus adding ballast to existing British prejudices; and he obtained for the Muslims a voice in Indian politics which the straight arithmetic of numbers could never have given them.

At the time of the Cripps mission, Jinnah had been prepared to commit the League to participating in the Central Government, though, it was then purely a party of opposition, governing none of the Muslim majority provinces which it later claimed for Pakistan. At that time Jinnah had not any confidence that these Muslim majority provinces would actually choose to opt out of the Union of India, but just the offer of a Pakistan, simply the principle of it, not any different land on offer, became a powerful enough magnet to obtain the needed support and co-operation of the community. The constitutional deadlock that followed the failure of the Cripps mission gave Jinnah and the League three invaluable years in which to strengthen their organisation, to extend their communal spread, and to deepen the League's influence. The political situation in India also got transformed between 1942 and 1945, as in those three years the League become the party of government in Sindh, Bengal, the NWFP, and even in the Hindu-majority province of Assam; besides the NWFP and Assam were the provinces where the

Congress had earlier governed. Of the provinces, that Jinnah claimed for Pakistan only the Punjab now stood defiantly apart. Had he secured power there, perhaps he would have accepted Wavell's scheme, but even so, he would surely have sought more than just a restatement of the Cripps offer of local options. Jinnah now hoped, with some reason, for a Pakistan that included all of the Muslim majority provinces, and that also only if absolutely necessary through plebiscites.

The total immobilization of the Congress leadership, by being jailed and their consequent political subjection for three years, without doubt effected the functioning of the Congress party during that period, throughout the country, but much more significantly it also greatly distorted the future course of India's politics, contributing markedly to enhancing Jinnah's unreal sense of the relative political and social importance of the League.

This illusory 'success' had another consequence: it ensured that claims for a separate and sovereign 'Muslim nation' could now not be lightly brushed aside. However, once the constitutional dialogue was reopened by the Labour's Cabinet Mission in 1946, the League's exaggerated demands did get exposed, for their claims of a separate land were found to be sustainable in only the Muslim majority areas of the two largest Muslim majority provinces of undivided India, Punjab and Bengal. That being so an eventual partition of these two provinces, (Bengal and Punjab) also became the logical and inevitable consequence of this arrival of the League as a Muslim party. This was that unreal political world of the forties, particularly so after the failure of the Cripps mission.

The rejection of the Cripps offer by India's political parties, in 1942 was an error, for without doubt it contributed significantly to an eventual partitioning of India. That the Cripps Mission had been Labour's initiative to attend to the challenge of India's freedom movement, but for a united India is clear; the Conservatives (and Indians, too, Hindus and Muslims both) defeated that initiative resulting in an indefinite postponement of a national government at the Centre in India; a brushing away of the Congress from competition in provincial politics; and a *de-facto* recognition of Jinnah as the sole Muslim spokesman on the all-India canvas. It also greatly emboldened the League to then capture, by constitutional processes, all but one of the component provinces of a till then putative Pakistan. Cripps' offer was a wartime attempt which could have arrested this trend, as Wavell subsequently came to appreciate, by using the Central Government as a means of encouraging a Congress-League cooperation. The great irony is that by the time the Labour Party finally achieved office, that original scheme for a transfer of power was no longer feasible. By July 1945, the initiative that had, in a fashion, originated in discussions with Nehru at Cripps' country house seven years earlier had now exhausted its relevance. Attlee needed a different solution to India's problem, or more accurately the many problems of India.

The Labour Party won the elections in Britain in 1945; Clement Attlee was sworn in as the prime minister, raising hopes in India of an early settlement. Whereafter, Japan's surrender in August 1945 added weight to such hopes, but the accompanying developments were not so encouraging. The next few months became a record of neglected opportunities and bushel loads of wrong decisions, yet again dropped upon the hapless citizens of undivided India.

Jinnah did not show any special recognition of this political change in Britain, though he did call a meeting of the League working committee and had it adopt a resolution calling for new elections in India as soon as possible. From his point of view, the uppermost need now was to prove, through elections, that the entire Muslim community stood solidly behind the League. This was important because based on the then existing representation in the legislatures of the provinces, Jinnah's numbers were not consonant with his claims, as opponents of the League had constantly challenged, in almost every debate of the Assembly, his assertion of being the only representative of all the Muslims.

After the Simla conference, no progress by way of further consultations between the government and Congress, or even amongst the Congress members themselves took place for the next two months. The Congress did want to return to office in the provinces but hesitated from asking, hoping that Wavell would take up this matter himself soon after the Simla Conference. However, as no contacts, formal or informal, had been kept with Wavell, the viceroy, neither disclosed his mind to the Congress leaders nor did he initiate any action. Thereafter, in late August 1945 Wavell went to England for consultations with the new government, to return only a month later, in September. Fresh elections for the Central and Provincial Legislatures were announced soon after, and it was also then announced that steps towards self-government and the creation of a constitution making body will follow these elections. For the Congress, resuming office in the provinces was now not at all a possibility, certainly not under the circumstance of pending elections, and this became yet another lost opportunity. Had the Congress president, immediately after the Simla Conference, met or written to the viceroy and stated that the Congress wished to return to office in the provinces, where they had earlier won the elections and held office until dismissed by the respective governors, and jailed, Wavell would not have found it easy to refuse, in fact Wavell and Governor Colville[12] might well have found this a welcome request. However, Congress leaders, post Simla, reverted, without loss of much time, to that which they found easy and were most familiar with, the path of protests and agitations, not recognising India's greatly altered circumstances. Wavell, somewhat perturbed by the conduct of most of the prominent Congress leaders, termed these agitations as bordering on the 'seditious'.[13] Then followed the decision to dissolve the Provincial Legislatures taken at the Governors' Conference of August 1945. Elections, fateful in consequence, not so much in their bland announcement followed soon after.

The Elections of 1946

From about October 1945 until the arrival of the Cabinet Mission towards the end of March 1946 there was little forward movement in the realm of Indo-British political initiatives. India, marked time and waited, but the country's political community was certainly not somnolent, for the very announcement of elections had generated great internal debate and churning. The future, to a significant extent, now depended on the results of these elections, the Muslim League declared that they would contest on just one single plank, that of 'Pakistan', with Jinnah personally appealing to all the Muslim voters to disregard individual candidates and to vote for all of them as representatives of the Muslim League, also that a vote in their (Muslim candidate's) favour would be vote for the creation of Pakistan.

The first poll was for to the Central Legislative Assembly. By the end of December 1945, its results were announced. The Muslim League won all the Muslim seats, polling ninety per cent of that vote. The Congress successes were in the Hindu (i.e., 'general') seats, of these it won fifty-seven of the sixty-two. This battle of Muslim allegiance, to sustain Jinnah's assertions of being the 'sole spokesman' had been won by the Muslim league decisively. Thereafter, upon Jinnah's call, Muslims observed 11 January 1946 as a victory day throughout the country.

Elections to the provincial assemblies' followed.[14] The Muslim League once again came out successful in every province except the NWFP. The tabulated results at Appendix XII, are telling in the message they transmit; the Muslim League commands the allegiance of the Muslim voter was beyond any questioning now. In Punjab, four of the members elected on different platforms joined the League after the results had been announced. The Muslim League demonstrated incontrovertible electoral proof that it had an overwhelming support in what it claimed as its 'sole preserve': the Muslim electorate of India. Elections having been completed the political tussle for Pakistan now resumed, with renewed vigor and added bitterness.

Formation of ministries followed as the logical and essential next step, this obligation, generating an entirely new set of problem that of 'sharing office'; how was this to be done? Such queries could scarcely be brushed aside.

The central paradox of the outcome and its electoral arithmetic was stark, it was also brutal: Even where the League had won 90 per cent of the seats reserved for the Muslims, it had still failed to get an absolute majority in the Assembly; there just were not enough numbers in the 'reserved quota' for the Muslims to gain office on their reserved strength alone. This was galling; once again the League was relegated to the status of the Opposition. In Sindh and Bengal, the governors invited the leaders of the largest parties to form their respective ministries, the Muslim League being in that category duly got invited in both the provinces and coalition ministries were also soon sworn in. In Punjab, Governor Sir Bertram Glancy, deviating from the principle of the 'largest single party', at first, delayed extending his invitation, then instead of inviting the largest single party, that is the leader of the Muslim League to form a ministry, he expressed his doubts about the non-Muslim parties' willingness to join a coalition with the League. Instead, the governor first encouraged and then paved the way for a coalition of the Unionists, the Akalis, and the Congress which commanded the support of a total of eighty-four Hindu and Sikh members, with the Unionist Muslim, comprising only twelve members joining in, thus leaving themselves open and vulnerable to charges of being 'betrayers' of the 'Muslim cause';[15] and this was when the total strength of the Punjab Assembly was 175.

Glancy had committed a serious tactical and constitutional error in failing to first invite Nawab Iftikhar Hussain Khan of Mamdot,[16] the leader of the Muslim League, the largest single party, to form the government. It is not much good now speculating as to all that might have happened had he invited Mamdot, for power is a potent glue and sticking to it an universal characteristic amongst politicians. This stumble by Glancy provided added ammunition to the suspicious and to such others as in any event always believed that the rest of the world was constantly plotting against them. The crisis deepened, many naïve assumptions, principally about this transplant of first past the post system of elective democracy sinking roots immediately in India's alien soil, and thereafter, also taking adequate care of all minority interests got eroded. All this left a bitter after taste. In consequence, the League's Pakistan plank and Jinnah's hand got further strengthened; the bile of failure poured added bitterness, separating the two communities and parties even more.

The Congress and the Muslims in Uttar Pradesh (1945-46)

Post-1946 elections in UP, and despite the Congress having got less than one per cent of the urban Muslim vote there, (though, it did get more of the rural Muslim vote) no change in the assertive and insensitive attitude of the Congress was witnessed. It had been a decisive defeat for the Congress in UP's Muslim constituencies, yet, the policies of UP Congress did not change, and this despite the additional factor of communal riots, like in Garhmukteshwar. The significance of the Garhmukteshwar riots lay more in its timing than in its actual occurrence. This riot had occurred immediately after the major communal riots of Noakhali and Bihar. Gandhi, greatly distressed had then commented on the damage that the riots did to the Congress party's image: 'The misdeeds of Bihari Hindus may justify Quaid-i-Azam Jinnah's taunt that the Congress is a Hindu organisation in spite of its boast that it has in its ranks a few Sikhs, Muslims, Christians and others'. Garhmukteshwar, for the Congress, was also important for it brought into focus the public conduct of Congress MLAs, local Congressmen and even the pro-Congress press during and after the tragedy. The official Congress organ, the *National Herald,* had then chosen to rationalise that the 'provocation' of the Noakhali killings, had in a fashion, mitigated the violence done to Muslims in Garhmukteshwar.

We need to dwell a little longer on the aspect of this separation of the two communities, as this was the central political question facing India then. As H.M. Seervai has commented; 'Democracy is not merely government by the majority, but government with the broad consent or acquiescence of the people. Any theory which merely relie[s] on counting heads'[17] offers no safeguards against both the tyranny of majoritarianism and of providing a space, a voice and a reassuring share to the minorities in government. And, here by 'minorities' is not meant merely the religious minorities but political, too. Let us therefore go back to Delhi, where Maulana Azad had offered a personal solution of this complex situation to Gandhi in a letter of 2 August 1945.

Both this letter and Gandhi's reply were intercepted, and subsequently forwarded by Evan Jenkins to Abell, the viceroy's secretary, on 25 and 28 August 1945. As this letter is best read in full, I reproduce the text of it as contained in the *Transfer of Power,* Vol. VI, pp.155-57.

68

Sir E. Jenkins to Mr Abell Telegram, Wavell Papers. Political Series, July-September 1945.

IMPORTANT   *25 August 1945*

SECRET

No. 1394-S. For Abell from Jenkins. I have just seen copy of intercepted scheme...Azad says all the Muslim organisations that are outside the Muslim League should fully organise themselves and come to a decision about the future constitution. The Congress should then accept this decision and with these Muslim organisations should stand firmly by it...
2. ...The Muslims are afraid and their fears can be removed only by devising a scheme under which they will feel secure. Any attempt to form a unitary government will fail. Partition will also fail and is against the interests of the Muslims themselves. As an Indian Muslim, Azad regards partition as a defeatist policy and cannot accept it.

3. Memorandum then gives following 'rough outline':-
Begins, (a) The future constitution of India must be federal with fully autonomous units in which the Central subjects must be only of an all-India nature and agreed upon by the constituent units.
(b) The units must be given the right of secession.
(c) There must be joint electorates in both the Centre and the Provinces with reservation of seats and such differential franchise as may be needed to make the electorates reflect the strength of population of the communities.
(d) There must be parity of Hindus and Muslims in the Central Legislature and the Central Executive till such time as communal suspicion disappears and parties are formed on economic and political lines.
(e) There should be a convention by which the Head of the Indian Federation should in the initial period be Hindu and Muslim by turn. Ends.
4. ....
5. Memorandum ends with appeal to Azad's Hindu friends 'to leave entirely to Muslims the questions of their status in the future constitution of India'.
6. ....

76

Sir E. Jenkins to Mr Abell Telegram, Wavell Papers. Political Series, July–September 1945, p. 67

IMPORTANT   *28 August 1945*
PRIVATE
SECRET

No. 1420-S. For Abell from Jenkins. My telegram No. 1394-S[1] of August 25th. Following is text of intercepted letter dated August 16th from Gandhi to Azad.
Begins. On receipt of your letter today I sent you the following wire: 'Your letter I think should not be published. Writing fully'.

I do not infer from your letter that you are writing about my Hindus. Whatever you have in your heart has not appeared in your writing. But don't worry, we will talk the matter over when next we meet, if you so desire. Whatever you want to say about the communal problems should not be said without consulting the Working Committee. I also am of the opinion that it would be better to keep quiet. The Party can give its opinion after consultations with you. They have the right to do so. Besides it is their duty.

My opinion differs from your [sic]. ....All this needs careful pondering over. I do not feel the urge to do anything hastily. *Ends.*
(Copy follows by bag. This is not very encouraging for Azad. Sir John Colville has seen.)[18]

The Maulana had clearly written in pain, rejecting Pakistan as being 'inimical to Muslim interests'; he had also held that 'to concede Pakistan was wrong, it was defeatist', adding that it was necessary though, to 'assuage Muslim fears and apprehensions, for they were genuine'. Therefore, the Maulana proposed: 'A federal India with the Centre looking after only the central subjects; the constituent units having a right to secede, (in that context); joint electorates with reservation of seats and 'parity' between the 'Hindus and Muslims in both the Central legislature and the Central executive'.[19] As contained in the documents, Gandhi had then telegraphed to Maulana Sahib to not make public these views, not until 'we have a chance to discuss' [them]. To this episode we will have occasion to revert later but clearly a new initiative was now called for, it came soon, termed, appropriately, I reckon as the Cabinet Mission.

THE CABINET MISSION

To avoid being immobilised by the prevailing social and political impasse, also to try and find a bridge between the two communities and, even at this late stage attempt to arrive at an agreed solution, a mission comprising Cabinet members of the British government, with Lord Pethick-Lawrence, then the secretary of state for India as its leader, Sir Stafford Cripps, president of the Board of Trade and A.V. Alexander, the First Lord of the Admiralty, as Members, was announced in the House of Commons by Prime Minister Attlee on 19 February 1946. This Mission was the highest level group ever sent by Britain to India, it was in India for three and a half months at a stretch; it had plenipotentiary powers to negotiate and had the complete backing of His Majesty's Government. It (the Mission) was also tasked to try and obtain an agreement amongst the leaders of India on the principles and procedure to be followed in 'framing a new constitution for an independent India'.

On 24 March 1946, the Mission reached New Delhi. To quote Sir Tej Bahadur Sapru: '...as regards Jinnah's demand that there should be two Constitution-making bodies, I was strongly opposed to it and urged on them the appointment of a single Constitution-making body'. Sir Stafford Cripps, (on this occasion as a member of the Mission) suggested that it did, at times, become necessary to devise face-saving formulae, and he frankly admitted in reply to a question that he wanted to 'save the face of Jinnah'. His proposal was that there should be a single Constitution-making body divided into two compartments, one dealing with Hindustan and providing a centre for it, and the other with Pakistan and providing a centre for that; and then they should meet together and provide a super-centre for both, which dealt with defence, foreign affairs and other cognate matters. 'I pointed out to them that if the two separate centres came to a conflict there would be no power left to bring about a reconciliation and this would certainly not be done by the so-called super-centre...'. Clearly the Cabinet delegation's task was not going to be easy, that of seeking a reconciliation between the Congress and the Muslim League specially when even the Liberals (Sir Tej Bahadur Sapru) would not settle for a truly federal set up.

The League was now demanding that the Muslim majority provinces should have full autonomy. The Cabinet Mission informed Jinnah, in the course of their talk with him, that as power could be transferred only to one body, therefore, the establishment of two centers in India could not be conceived under 'Constitutional law and practice'. The Mission also drew his attention to the need for a single centre being vital for security reasons. To the Cabinet Mission, when interviewed for the second time on 16 April 1946, Jinnah declared that the unity of India was a myth. Earlier he had told Sir Stafford Cripps that the Muslims had a different conception of life from division of India.

Amidst such consultations, Jinnah convened a meeting of the Muslim League legislators on 10 April 1946, and got them to adopt a resolution demanding the 'independent State of Pakistan'. Though the Congress was not agreeable to an all India union based on a three-tier grouping, they did recognise (now) that the Central Government had to be federal and that the provincial units ought also to have a larger measure of autonomy. The Muslim League, on the other hand, stood for a totally separate, sovereign state of Pakistan and demanded a prior recognition of this principle, in consequence, therefore, starting with two separate constitution-making bodies. This multiplicity of conflicting objectives was the principal obstacle that the Cabinet Mission had now to cross without taking a fall; Cripps, not exactly renowned for his skill in the saddle, cautioned.

When the Mission returned on 24 April to Delhi from a short trip to Srinagar (Jammu & Kashmir) and still no award was announced as spreading rumours had informed the Mission would, impatience and tempers rose in tandem, with the heat. In this deteriorating atmosphere, invitations were sent out to the League and Congress to come to conference in Simla where the Mission's thinking could be paraded for inspection and then straightened into an agreement. Four representatives each, from the League and the Congress it was to be.

Maulana Azad and Badshah Khan were amongst the four who represented the Congress at Simla. Their inclusion was deliberate, to emphasise that Jinnah could not presume to represent all the Muslims of India, and also a clear signal that the Congress would not compromise on this issue.

On 5 May 1946, the visiting Cabinet delegation, at the Second Simla Conference through an innovatory scheme recommended that the proposed Indian constitution ought to have a system which, for want of a more elegant phase got called 'Groupings'. This proposal was, in essence the brain-child of the legalistic mind of Sir Stafford Cripps. Even when shorn down to its bare essentials it was a scheme of great complexity, full of unchartered trap. That this proposed theme of 'Groupings' ought to have gone unresolved all the way, from when proposed in 5 May 1946 to That final conference in London under Attlee's chairmanship, on 6 December 1940, and still remain obstinately an obstacle testifies to the impractical nature of it. Its essentials were:

1. That there will be an All-India Union embracing both, British India and the Indian States dealing with Foreign Affairs, Defence and Communications; (the qualifying 'at least' is per the Transfer of Power documents).
2. That the Provinces of British India will be divided into three groups, numbered alphabetically, as under, comprising the Provinces mentioned against each:

(Group-A)—Madras, Bombay, United Provinces, Bihar, Central Provinces and Orissa;

(Group-B)—Punjab, North-West Frontier Province, Sindh and Baluchistan
(Group-C)—Bengal and Assam

3. The composition of the Groups would be subject to a Province having the right to change its group immediately upon the new constitution being adopted. Whereafter only upon the expiry of ten years. Each group would settle the subjects it desired to adopt as group subjects; these would then be an obligatory responsibility of all the members of that group. The remaining subjects, and all residuary powers would vest in the relevant Province.
4. For these three groups (A, B and C), separate Constituent Assemblies would then be established, the provincial legislatures of each group sending their elected representatives to their Group's Constituent Assembly.
5. Only when the Provincial and Group Constitutions had been settled by the Group Constituent Assemblies, was it to be open to a Province to change its Group, through a majority decision of its Provincial Legislative Assembly.
6. After having settled the Provincial and Group Constitutions, the three Group Constituent Assemblies were to meet together, with 32 representatives of the Indian States, to settle the All India Union Constitution, in which would be incorporated national aspects like: fundamental rights, minority protection clauses etc., and these would be applicable to all of India.
7. It was also mandated that decision in the Union Constituent Assembly would have to be by a majority of 2/3rd of the present and voting.

This Conference brought into open the intentions and aims of the participants. Congress had no intention of compromising or admitting that Jinnah alone represented the Muslims and he (Jinnah), in turn, remained fixed and inflexible about that. He did though agree to a Federal Union government concept. This was a major concession as it implied Jinnah, if not entirely giving up, then certainly diluting his demand for a sovereign Pakistan. Soon, however, he found that the Cabinet Mission had not sufficiently recognised the significance of this gesture. In return, Jinnah had expected the Congress to shed their policy of 'grouping', which they would not; and here Jinnah, quite reasonably relied upon the Cabinet Mission to find a reasonable via media. This was that critical stage in the Simla Conference when Nehru and Jinnah had come so close to an agreement that they were left alone to talk. They met again, one to one, but got nowhere. Jinnah would agree to a Union Government but not just one Central legislature that the Congress wanted; the Congress on its part was not prepared to agree to each of the 'groups' having a separate executive and a legislature of their own, as a group which Jinnah regarded as vital.

However, there were, in addition, three communications exchanged that also call for our attention; Maulana Azad's letter of 6 May 1946 addressed to Pethick-Lawrence, on his own and his colleague's behalf. The concluding paragraph of this letter totally repudiates what the Maulana had written to Gandhi on 2 August 1945, and which the latter had urgently advised the Maulana to not make public. In the present communication to Pethick-Lawrence, Maulana now totally reversed his earlier stand by stating that the way to remove fears and suspicions from the mind of every group and community cannot be through 'unreal methods which go against the basic principles of democracy'.[20] This was a clear and categorical rejection of both reserved seats and parity for the Muslims. Writing three days later, again to Pethick-Lawrence, this time on behalf of the Congress, Maulana repeated the party's objections saying: 'We are entirely opposed to the proposed parity, both in the Executive and in the Legislature, as between wholly unequal Groups. This is unfair and will lead to trouble. Such a provision contains in itself the seed of conflict and the destruction of free growth. If there is no agreement on this or any similar matter, we are prepared to leave it to arbitration'.[21] A day earlier, on 8 May 1946 in a letter addressed to Stafford Cripps, Gandhi had raised his objection to parity in telling words: 'As to merits the difficulty about parity between six Hindu majority Provinces and five Muslim majority Provinces is insurmountable'. How can 'over nine crores of [Muslims] be treated on parity with nineteen crores of Hindu majority Province. This is really worse than Pakistan. 'What is suggested in its place is that the Central Legislature should be formed on the population basis. And so too the Executive'.[22]

Nothing, therefore, came of this, and Simla II also ended inconclusively. Whereafter, on 16 May 1946 the Cabinet Mission issued a White Paper, which they considered as 'the best arrangement to ensure the speedy setting up of a Constitution for India'.[23] Both the Cabinet Mission and the viceroy recommended that this future constitution of India should adopt certain basic principals. About Pakistan, the above cited White Paper held: 'We are unable to advise the British Government that the power which at present resides in British hands should be handed over two entirely separate Sovereign States. The Delegation and the Viceroy have been forced to the conclusion that neither a large nor a smaller Sovereign State of Pakistan would provide an acceptable solution for the communal problem'.[24]

Built in the Cabinet Mission's statement of 16 May 1946 were two plans—a long- and a short-term scheme. Through these plans the Mission had rejected the Pakistan demand and put forth a scheme of loose federation with one Constituent Assembly for framing a constitution for the proposed Indian Union. The long-term scheme visualised three groupings of provinces; those of Hindu majority, one of Muslim majority and the third group of provinces of the East and North-east, i.e., Bengal and Assam. Each grouping was to have its own legislature and an executive with each province, or a grouping of provinces, having the right to opt out from the proposed Indian Union. The short-term scheme proposed an interim government, to be formed immediately.

Differences existed between the Congress and the Muslim League on the status of the proposed Constituent Assembly; on the nature and functions of this three-tier grouping; and also on representation in the interim government. For the Congress, the Constituent Assembly was to be a sovereign entity to which proposal the Muslim League would not agree. To the Congress, these 'groupings' under the three-tier arrangement were unacceptable, if they were made compulsory for the Muslim League that was an essential condition. The Congress would not accept parity as a precondition to entering the interim government; the League insisted upon it.

The Cabinet delegation had been in India since March 1946. Its plan had been built up gradually and Jinnah now had two stark choices confronting him: one, if he wanted the whole of the Punjab, Bengal and Assam for his Muslim sub-federations, then he must accept a federal centre, however limited its strength and powers; should he instead, persist with a division of India and also demand a sovereign, independent entity then he must make do with a truncated Pakistan.

To the statement of 16 May some important revisions had been made before it was finally issued. The most significant being the one suggested by the Bengal governor, Sir Fredrick Burrows, to paragraph 19 on the 'Right to opt out of the Groups'. It was this which made the Congress apprehensive, that this amendment would result in preempting Assam's choice. In his letter to Wavell, Fredrick Burrows on 9 May 1946 had suggested:

> While I realize that power to contract out of original group into another as soon as group and provincial constitutions are framed is intended to safeguard smaller provinces during the drafting period, there is no doubt, omission of this immediate power to contract out would help Bengal Muslims to reconcile themselves to proposals as a whole and for geographical reasons it is difficult to believe Assam would ever be able to avail herself of the right. I would therefore omit last four lines of paragraph 19.

It was at the instance of Governor Burrows of Bengal that the provision was modified and the right to opt out was made exercisable only after the first election under the new Constitution had been completed. Assam had in any event, apprehended just such a manipulation of franchise and electorates by the dominant Muslim majority in the Eastern Group. It was in the meeting of the Cabinet Delegation of Friday, 10 May 1946, that Burrows suggestion was accepted, even though the governor of Assam had not been consulted on the issue. The record of the meeting simply says: 'Paragraph 19(vi) amended. It was agreed that the decision to opt out of a Group must be taken by the new Legislature under the new Constitution and it was not necessary to specify that a Province could opt into another. This should be left for negotiation'. This change, made paragraph 19, of the 16 May statement as totally unacceptable to the Congress, and subsequently it became the principal issue of contention between the parties.[25]

Woodrow Wyatt, then a young British Labour MP on Cripps' staff, travelled to Simla in late May 1946 to meet Jinnah. Wyatt found 'Jinnah nervous, edgy, and less in command of himself'. Jinnah had then appeared, to Wyatt as 'quite hesitant of meeting the Muslim League Working Committee and its all India Council'. As Wyatt inferred from his discussions, Jinnah found the outlined scheme (in the 16 May Statement) impracticable. However, in order to show that he would give it a trial he was ready to accept the statement, as a first step on the road to Pakistan. That is exactly what he made the Muslim League do on 6 June 1946.

Well before the 16 May statement, Wavell had sounded Jinnah on the interim government. He (Wavell) had in mind a Council of twelve to begin with...five from the Muslim League, 'five from the Congress, including a schedule caste, one Sikh and another'.[26] From now on, as the story of these negotiations unfolds, clearly discernible is the trend which eventually weakened Jinnah's stand; that of a gradual dilution of his parity formula. This happened with each passing letter, with each meeting, and ended with an eventual rejection of the 16 May statement by the Muslim League by their calamitous Resolutions of 29 July 1946. Could anyone then have foreseen the consequence that lay just a fortnight away—the Direct Action Day in Calcutta, of 16 August 1946?

On 3 June 1946, Wavell met Jinnah twice over the issue of the Cabinet Mission Plan. Here are the records of the first meeting which Jinnah had with Wavell and the Cabinet delegation at 10 a.m.:

> ...Jinnah had said that he would give his list of names on the 7th June if all went well. The general impression which the Viceroy had received was that Jinnah would try to get his people to come in on the Delegation's proposals....Jinnah had said that the question of absence of parity at the Centre in a Union Government was a very difficult point for the Muslim League to accept. The Viceroy had pointed to the alternative safeguards provided and had urged that the Muslim League could hardly expect to receive parity in an Indian Union.
>
> Jinnah had asked what would happen if Congress rejected the proposals and the Muslim League accepted them. The Viceroy had said he could not give any guarantee but speaking personally he thought that if the Muslim League accepted them they would not lose by it...Jinnah had asked whether the Muslim League would in these circumstances be invited to join the Interim Government and be given their due proportion of the portfolios. The Viceroy had said that he thought that he could guarantee that the Muslim League would have a share in it. Mr Jinnah had asked whether he could have an assurance to this effect in writing as it would help him with his Working Committee. It was agreed that the Viceroy should draft a letter to Mr Jinnah which should be considered by the Delegation after lunch.[27]
>
> (Sir Stafford Cripps appears not to have been present)

When Wavell saw Jinnah again at 4 p.m. on 3 June 1946, for the second time, his discussions centered mainly around the 'assurances'. During this meeting Wavell showed these 'assurances' to Jinnah. What is recorded on it in the official documents is as follows:

Field Marshal Viscount Wavell to Mr Abell

3 June
Private Secretary to Viceroy

We had better keep these on a file. I showed them both to Jinnah, and he seemed satisfied.

Wavell (Sd.).

TOP SECRET
VERBAL ASSURANCE GIVEN TO MR JINNAH 3-6-1946

I have discussed with the Cabinet Delegation the point about which you spoke to me this morning.
The Delegation cannot give you a written assurance of what its action will be in the event of the breakdown of the present negotiations; but I can give you, on behalf of the Delegation, my personal assurance that we do not propose to make any discrimination in the treatment of either party; and that we shall go ahead with the plan laid down in our statement so far as circumstances permit, if either party accepts; but we hope that both will.
As I know I can trust you, I will ask you not to make this assurance public, and simply to say to your Working Committee, if necessary, that you are satisfied on this point.

Enclosure 2 to No. 440
OFFICE OF CABINET DELEGATION,
THE VICEROY'S HOUSE, NEW DELHI

It is our intention to stick to the scheme as far as possible if either party are prepared to come in and work it. We may have to make some variations in view of the actual circumstances at the time but our intention will be to follow out the scheme as far as we can.

[This note is undated unsigned but appears to be in the hand of Sir S. Cripps.][28]

The Muslim League Working Committee had then met on 4 June 1946, at which one of the members, Ispahani, had voiced an apprehension, quite justified, as to what would happen if the Muslim League accepted and the Congress rejected the 16 May statement? The Muslim League would then be severely criticised for having accepted something less than a Pakistan, were the British 'to let them down'. It was on this that Jinnah had wanted an assurance in writing but was yet to receive it from the viceroy. Wavell's team, of course, was apprehensive of incurring the Congress' ire if such a written assurance was given, in the sought manner, to the League.

A meeting of the Council of the All-India Muslim League followed on 6 June 1946 to consider this very 16 May statement of the Cabinet Mission. After discussion, it authorised Jinnah, to negotiate with the viceroy and take such decisions (and subsequent actions) as the president (Jinnah) deemed fit. In the same meeting, Jinnah had emphatically declared; 'I advised you to reject the Cripps' Proposal. I advised you to reject the last Simla Conference Formula. But I cannot advise you to reject the British Cabinet Mission's Proposal. I advise you to accept it.' Of course, the League Council did just what Jinnah wanted them to.

After having accepted the Cabinet Mission proposals, just to further reassure himself, Jinnah in a letter to Wavell on 8 June 1946 reiterated a demand for those very assurances. The issue again was that of 'parity'. This is what Jinnah wrote: 'that with your previous permission I informed the Working Committee of this assurance and this was one of the most important considerations which weighed with them together with the Statement of the Cabinet Mission. These two together formed one whole and, as such, the Council of the All-India Muslim League has given its final decision on the 6th of June 1946. And we further inform you that similarly I had to repeat the assurance to the Council before they finally gave their approval'.

Jinnah firmly stood for parity in the formation of the interim government, i.e., five from League and five from Congress. However, Wavell was of the opinion that Jinnah may ultimately have to yield for the sake of the chief ministers of Assam and Bengal as Saadullah and Nazimuddin, respectively, had then appeared to be dependent in office, on Congress goodwill. Besides, Liaquat Ali too, seemed anxious to take office. Wavell, therefore, felt inclined that Jinnah, under pressure, was likely to send his list of names. However, that letter did not come.

Instead, Jinnah informed Wavell: 'I understand the Congress have not yet given their decision and it seems to me that until they decide it is not advisable to discuss how best either the personnel or the portfolios should be adjusted'.[29]

The issue of parity which the viceroy was negotiating with the Congress lay unresolved. On 15 June 1946, Wavell informed Jinnah that his discussions with Congress to negotiate an agreement on the composition of the Interim Government, as had been earlier suggested to Jinnah, had failed. The Cabinet delegation and the viceroy had therefore decided to issue a statement on the action to be taken in future.[30]

This future action, the statement of 16 June 1946 elaborated, extending an invitation to fourteen persons to serve on the interim government, two more instead of the twelve originally discussed. If this proposal was accepted, the viceroy would then aim at inaugurating the new government about 26 June 1946 or so. However, in the event of either of the two major parties found as unwilling to join, the intention of the viceroy remained firm on proceeding with the formation of an interim government.[31] The 16 June statement did speak of the formation of the interim government on such a basis as would remain in essential accord with the statement of principles of a month earlier, i.e., of 16 May, but nowhere did it stipulate that the two major parties must necessarily be in agreement with that before the interim government could be formed. Why then did the Cabinet delegation in its meeting with Jinnah on 25 June, (the records of which have been cited) make this into an issue, refusing to accept the Muslim League alone in the interim government? For a perfectly obvious reason, for had they done so, it would have further inflamed an already aggrieved majority; and clearly it was difficult for Wavell to say so explicitly.

On 18 June 1946 there then arose another issue, that of the substitution of a name from the Congress side, of Dr Zakir Hussain in place of a Hindu invited by Wavell to join the interim government. Of his meeting with Jinnah on this issue, Wavell records: 'I began by telling him about my interview with Azad and Nehru this morning. He accepted the substitution of Bose for Mahtab without comment; but when I told him that they might propose Zakir Hussain instead of a Congress Hindu, he said that this was absolutely and entirely unacceptable. He turned to this at intervals throughout the discussion, characterising Zakir Hussain as a quisling and saying that if he accepted this he would be unable to show his face anywhere'. This too, then became a major hurdle between Jinnah and the Cabinet Delegation when they met for that fateful meeting of 25 June 1946.[32]

Jinnah kept reiterating the issue of 'parity'. On 19 June 1946, he raised this issue again with Wavell: that of five Muslims, five Congress, one Sikh and one Indian Christian. Jinnah in the letter had recalled the assurance given to him earlier, at New Delhi, and said that accordingly he had made a statement before the League Council. To him this was one of the most important considerations which weighed with the Council, 'Why [then] had the basis of it been altered to five Congress, five Muslim League and three others? Had he not kept Wavell informed that if any such change was proposed, Jinnah would have to place the matter before the Working Committee again and may also have to call another meeting of the Council?' He was also surprised, and so was the League Working Committee, 'by these invitations which had been sent directly to the five Muslim Leaguers to join the Interim Government without consulting the Muslim League'... 'Also why the parity between Congress and the Muslim League had been abandoned and substituted with parity between the Muslim League and 'caste Hindus'? Why, to further disturb this parity, Mr Jagjivan Ram's name was proposed as a representative of the scheduled caste since he was already a Congressman?' To Jinnah these modifications adversely effected the ratio of Muslims in the interim government as a whole and also as against Congress as a single group. However, even at this stage Jinnah did not refuse to participate in the interim government. In his letter to Wavell of 19 June 1946, he was still discussing the question of distribution of portfolios in the government.[33]

Indisputably, events were now becoming difficult for Jinnah to handle, 'I am sure you will appreciate' he was informed by Wavell, 'that negotiations designed to secure acceptance by two parties with conflicting interests may not always end on the same basis as that on which they began; and as you know, I never gave you any guarantee that they would necessarily be concluded on any particular basis,' was Wavell's reply to Jinnah's letter.[34] To an earlier query, Wavell still reassured Jinnah saying that 'no decision on major communal issue could be taken by the Interim Government if the majority of either of the main parties were opposed to it.' Wavell also said that he had pointed this out to the

Congress president, Maulana Azad, who expressed that the Congress appreciated this point.

And then came the letter of the Congress president to the viceroy, followed by the resolution of the Congress Working Committee, both of 25 June 1946; these now really confounded matters. This game of one-upmanship had by now become destructive. Reproduced are some excerpts from this letter as well as from the Congress Resolution; these are cited in the original language as paraphrasing them or making a précis of them would be full of untold peril, even now, in the twenty-first century, decades after those obtuse disputations.

Maulana Azad to Field Marshal Viscount Wavell

25 June 1946

'We could not accept anything in the nature of "parity" even as a temporary expedient the Provisional Government should consist of fifteen members.

'One outstanding feature of this list [to form the provisional national government] was the non-inclusion of any nationalist Muslim. We felt that this was a grave omission. We wanted to suggest the name of a Muslim to take the place of one of the Congress names on the list. We felt that no one could possibly object to our changing the name of one of our own men. Indeed when I had drawn your attention to the fact that among the Muslim League nominees was included the name of a person who had actually lost in the recent elections in the Frontier Province and whose name we felt had been placed there for political reasons, you wrote to me as follows: "I am afraid that I cannot accept the right of the Congress to object to names put forward by the Muslim League, any more than I would accept similar objections from the other side. The test must be that of ability". But before we could make our suggestion I received your letter of the 22 June which surprised us greatly. You had written this letter on the basis of some Press reports. You told us that the Cabinet Mission and you were not prepared to accept a request for the inclusion of a Muslim chosen by the Congress among the representatives of the Congress in the Interim Government. This seemed to us an extraordinary decision. It was in direct opposition to your own statement quoted above. It meant that the Congress could not freely choose even its own nominees.

'Mr Jinnah has thus included the Scheduled Castes among the minorities and presumably you have agreed with this view. So far as we are concerned, we repudiate this view and consider the Scheduled Castes as integral parts of Hindu Society.

'Finally, you state in answer to question 5 that 'No decision of a major communal issue could be taken by the Interim Government if the majority of either of the main parties were opposed to it'. You further say that you had pointed this out to the Congress President and he had agreed that the Congress appreciated this point. In this connection I desire to point out that we had accepted this principle for the long-term arrangement in the Union Legislature and it could possibly be applied to the Provisional Government if it was responsible to the Legislature and was composed of representatives on the population basis of major communities. It could not be applied to the Provisional Government formed on a different basis altogether.

'My Committee have, therefore, reluctantly come to the conclusion that they are unable to assist you in forming a Provisional Government as proposed in your statement of 16 June 1946.

'With regard to the proposals made in the statement of 16 May 1946, relating to the formation and functioning of the constitution making body, the Working Committee of the Congress passed a resolution on the 24 May 1946, and conversations and correspondence have taken place we have pointed out what in our opinion were the defects in the proposals. We also gave our interpretation of some of the provisions of the statement. 'While adhering to our views, we accept your proposals and are prepared to work them with a view to achieve our objective. We would add, however, that the successful working of the Constituent Assembly will largely depend on the formation of a satisfactory Provisional Government'.[35]

Enclosure to No. 603
RESOLUTION OF THE CONGRESS WORKING COMMITTEE, DATED 25TH JUNE 1946

'The kind of independence which Congress has aimed at is the establishment of a united democratic Indian Federation with a Central authority which would command respect from the nations of the world, maximum provincial autonomy and equal rights for all men and women in the country. The limitation of the Central authority, as contained in the proposals, as well as the system of grouping of Provinces, weakened the whole structure and was unfair to some Provinces, such as the North-West Frontier Province, and Assam, and to some of the minorities, notably the Sikhs. The Committee disapproved of this.

'In the proposals for an Interim Government contained in the Statement of 16 June, the defects related to matters of vital concern to the Congress. Some of these have been pointed out in a letter of 25 June, from the Congress President to the Viceroy. The Provisional Government must have power and authority and responsibility and should function, in fact if not

An elegant Mohammad Ali Jinnah.

A rare photograph of Jinnah relaxing.

Barrister Jinnah in his chambers.

Jinnah on a car ride with Pestonjee H.J. Rustomjee with Homi Rustomjee on the backseat.

Jinnah presiding over a joint meeting of the Indian National Congress and All-India Muslim League in 1916.

A dapper and elegantly graying house holder: Jinnah with his pets—a Black Doberman and West Highland Terrier, in Bombay, in the 1940s.

The father with daughter.

Jinnah with his sister Fatima and his daughter Dina.

Muslim League leaders after dinner at the residence of Mian Bashir Ahmed.

Round Table Conference, London 1931, with Ramsay MacDonald presiding over the Indian leaders; to his left are: Mohandas Karamchand Gandhi, Madan Mohan Malaviya, Srinivas Sastri Iyenger and Tej Bahadur Sapru.

Shared aversion for Gandhi—Subhas Chandra Bose with Jinnah.

All-India Muslim League, 26th Session at Patna, 26–29 December 1938.

Jinnah at 10 Aurangzeb Road, New Delhi, 1944–45.

Reception at India House, 6 December 1946, during the London Conference.
L to R: Liaquat Ali Khan, Sir S. Raghunathan, Mr Jinnah with others.

Jinnah arrives at Karachi as governor-general designate of the country he founded,
7 August 1947.

Quaid-i-Azam Jinnah and Fatima Jinnah at the opening ceremony of the State Bank of Pakistan, 1 July 1948. The governor of the bank, Zahid Hussain addresses the audience; a visibly fatigued Jinnah.

Jinnah meeting supporters at Quetta Railway Station in 1945.

Jinnah and Louis Fischer of *Time* magazine in 1945. A man of substance combined with sartorial elegance.

Jinnah with the Muslim League Women's Guard.

Jinnah and his sister Fatima in later years.

Jinnah in his study in India.

Jinnah in Jodhpur breeches.

Above and below: As Barrister-at-Law.

Jinnah on holiday-I.

On holiday-II.

Quaid-i-Azam Governor-General Mohammad Ali Jinnah.

in law, as a *de facto* independent Government leading to the full independence to come. The Members of such a Government can only hold themselves responsible to the people and not to any external authority. In the formation of a Provisional or other Government, Congressmen can never give up the national character of Congress or accept an artificial and unjust parity, or agree to a veto of a communal group. The Committee are unable to accept the proposals for the formation of an Interim Government as contained in the Statement of 16 June.

'The Committee have, however, decided that the Congress should join the proposed Constituent Assembly with a view to framing the Constitution of a free, united, and democratic India.

'While the Committee have agreed to Congress participation in the Constituent Assembly, it is, in their opinion, essential that a representative and responsible Provisional National Government be formed at the earliest possible date'.[36]

The fall out of all this was a meeting that Jinnah then had with the Cabinet delegation and Wavell, jointly, on 25 June itself. This meeting did not go well. It began with Jinnah questioning the genuineness of the Congress acceptance of the 16 May statement. The secretary of state then accused Jinnah of sabotaging the prospects for an interim government, laying the blame on Jinnah for publishing his letter to Wavell of 19 June. This important and fateful meeting of 25 June yielded no results. The Cabinet Mission and the viceroy there after issued a public statement on 26 June that the formation of an interim government stood postponed for now.

Simultaneously, Wavell and the Cabinet delegation made clear to Jinnah their resolve to go ahead with the election to the Constituent Assembly, in the face of Jinnah having strongly urged their postponement. To Jinnah both, the long-term plan of constitution-making and the short term plan of interim government constituted an integral whole. He held that it would be undesirable to proceed with one, elections to the Constituent Assembly and postpone the other, the formation of the Interim Government.[37] This suggestion of Jinnah's, too, the viceroy did not accept.

In this saga of the Cabinet Mission it was Wavell, the viceroy, who paradoxically had now to gather the pieces of their failed visit. Even before the 16 May statement had been issued, Wavell had suggested a discussion on the action to be taken in case one or both the parties turned down the proposals. Simultaneously, he had also done some loud thinking on this issue with George Abell, his private secretary. Wavell correctly predicted a crisis in case the delegation went along with the Congress, in the event of the Muslim League declining to be part of the interim government. Wavell anticipated that 'parity' in the government will be the main issue between the Congress and the Muslim League, and he was unclear of the stand that Cripps and Pethick-Lawrence would take. To Wavell these two appeared so committed to the Congress that it was impossible for them to take a firm stand with that party. He, (Wavell) in no uncertain terms accuses them of a strong Congress bias in his diaries.

On 25 June, before that fateful meeting with Jinnah, Cripps categorically informed Wavell of the Congress not accepting the 16 May statement, but he then (Cripps) went on to do exactly the opposite, he urged the Congress to accept it, pointing out to them the tactical advantages. Pethick-Lawrence also acquiesced, sadly leaving Wavell in an impossible situation with Jinnah. It redounds greatly to Wavell's objectivity to have termed the Congress acquiescence as a dishonest acceptance.

But Wavell persisted, on 26 June, when meeting the Congress leaders along with the Cabinet delegation, he still insisted on not accepting the Congress interpretation. His disappointment of that morning reached such proportions that he contemplated being relieved of his appointment. To him, it was difficult to accept that some of the members of the Cabinet Mission had themselves not played straight. Cripps, in fact, did not see him (not even out of courtesy) before leaving for Britain on 29 June.

Following the Cabinet Mission's refusal to invite the Muslim League alone to form the interim government, communal rioting in an ugly form had again broken out in Ahmedabad. Gandhi's advice to Morarji Desai, the Bombay Home Minister, who came to consult him before proceeding to the site of the trouble, was that he 'must go to meet the flames under the sole protection of God, not that of the police or the military'. If need be, he must 'perish in the flames' in the attempt to quell them as had been done by the late Ganesh Shankar Vidyarthi, the young editor of the Kanpur nationalist daily *Pratap,* who was killed during the Kanpur Hindu-Muslim riots of 1931 while engaged in a mission of peace.

The Congress President Elect's Interview

The prospects of an agreement, following complications of the post-16 June 1946 statement had become dim. The resolution of the Congress Working Committee (of 25 June) and the decision of the Cabinet delegation to defer formation of the interim government had further complicated matters. Under such complex circumstances, the press conference of Jawaharlal Nehru, of 10 July 1946, could not have come at a worse time. It is difficult to give the benefit of doubt to Nehru for not having known, in advance, what the fallout of such conferences or his interviews could be. This is why it is necessary that some excerpts of this interview be reproduced verbatim:

> Interview to the press, Bombay, 10 July 1946, from *The Hindu* of 11 July 1946
>
> Jawahar Lal Nehru, responding to a question answered, in part: 'It is true that in going into the constituent assembly we have inevitably to agree to a certain procedure in advance, that is, the election of the candidates to the constituent assembly. What we do there, we are entirely and absolutely free to determine. We have not committed ourselves on any single matter to anybody. Naturally, even though one might not agree to commit oneself, there is certain compulsion of facts which makes one accept this thing or that thing.
>
> The big probability is that, from any approach to the grouping question, there will be no grouping. Obviously, Section A will decide against grouping. Speaking in betting language, there is a four-to-one chance of the North West Frontier Province deciding against grouping, Then Group B collapses. It is highly likely that Assam will decide against grouping with Bengal, although I would not like to say what the initial decision may be, since it is evenly balanced. But I can say, with every assurance and conviction, that there is going to be, finally, no grouping there, because Assam will not tolerate it under any circumstances whatever. Thus you see this grouping business, approached from any point of view, does not get on at all.
>
> Q. How would be provincial jealousies work against grouping?
>
> JN: First, but for the Muslim League, the entire country is opposed to the grouping of provinces. The Muslim League thus stands by itself, isolated on this question...there is a good deal of feeling against grouping with (sic) the Punjab, both in the North West Frontier Province and Sind, for economic

and other reasons. That is to say, even the Muslims in Sindh dislike the idea of grouping with the Punjab, both these provinces (Sind/NWFP) are afraid of being swamped by the Punjab.

Q. When will the provisional national government be formed at the Centre?

For the moment, we are somewhat engaged in the constituent assembly elections.

Q. What do you expect from the forthcoming meeting of the All-India Muslim League Council at Bombay

Whatever the Congress does, it is always intended to create new situations. We do not follow other people's situations. I am glad that the Muslim League has realized that we have created a new situation. We propose to create many further new situations. We are sometimes asked what we would do if the League decides to do this or that. We shall see what the conditions then are and decide accordingly.

Such assertions, and made at this critical juncture, completely reversed the gains of the 16 May proposals and their acceptance by all. Predictably, this made Jinnah even more suspicious of Congress' real intentions, in consequence more obstinate in his opposition to any effort for cooperation with the Congress. Jinnah had altered the League's stand, he had supported the proposed scheme, in the process virtually abandoning a sovereign Pakistan but insisting upon the grouping of Provinces with residuary powers. On the other hand, Nehru's statements went directly and totally against the letter and spirit of the Cabinet Mission's plan. To further compound difficulties, Nehru even then did not recognise his error, or that there was much to be gained by silence, or that this statement had greatly upset prospects of a settlement. Besides, it was not within Nehru's remit to alter unilaterally that which the Congress Working Committee had accepted; and to do so in this manner, especially when the possibility of real rapprochement appeared within reach was beyond reason, it was eventually to lead to yet another crisis.

Maulana Azad, the retiring Congress president referred then to Nehru's press conference as 'one of those unfortunate events which changed the course of history,'[38] adding that 'it was not correct to say, as Nehru did, that Congress was free to modify the Cabinet Mission

Plan as it pleased'. Azad further said: 'Jinnah had accepted the Cabinet Mission Plan as there was no alternative'. In response to Nehru's reaction, Jinnah issued a statement that it was for the British parliament and His Majesty's Government to make it clear beyond doubt and remove the impression that the Congress had accepted the long-term scheme of the Cabinet Mission, as was being conveyed abroad by the timid efforts of the Cabinet Mission's delegates and the viceroy. Jinnah also added that Nehru's statement was a complete repudiation of the basic form upon which the long-term scheme rested. Jinnah also threatened to reconsider the whole situation when the League Working Committee and the Council met at the end of July 1946.[39] There were now enough indications that Congress and the League were heading towards an impending conflict. Even Vallabhbhai Patel had then commented that Nehru's remarks were a consequence of his emotional immaturity.

Efforts at forming an interim government having failed, issues like parity and Muslim representation by Congress in the government remained, as hurdles. In his interview of 10 July 1946, Nehru had stated clearly that the Congress did not accept the grouping scheme on the lines that Jinnah understood, or rather on the lines put forth by the 16 May statement. After this rejection by the Congress and an acceptance by the League, was the viceroy not bound (by 16 May) to form the government with the nominees of the Muslim League alone? This became the issue; also under such circumstances to defer forming the government for an 'interval' became very contentious. These questions rankled greatly, then.

After an interval of more than three weeks, Wavell informed Jinnah of his intention to replace the caretaker government of officials by an interim coalition government 'as soon as possible'. He sought Jinnah's cooperation in a negotiation, on strictly personal and secret basis between himself and the two presidents, that of the Congress and the Muslim League. While suggesting that this interim government will consist of fourteen members, six including one scheduled caste representative to be nominated by the Congress; five to be nominated by the Muslim League; and three representatives of the minorities to be nominated by the viceroy, of which one will be reserved for a Sikh, he clarified that it was not open either to the Congress or to the Muslim League to object to names submitted by the other parties, only the viceroy having the prerogative to reject. This ratio of 6:5:3 representatives in the interim government amounted to an abandoning of 'parity'. It also negated the stand which the Muslim League had taken, of course, insupportably about holding an exclusive right over Muslim nomination in the interim government. With parity gone, with groupings rejected by the Congress and with no exclusive right left with Jinnah, he could hardly then accept the viceroy's invitation to join the interim government.[40] The Muslim League Council therefore, adopted a resolution rejecting the Cabinet Mission Plan.

Despite these negative developments, events could of course, not wait. On instructions from the secretary of state, the viceroy then invited Nehru to form a government at the Centre, and he readily accepted. On 24 August, a communiqué was issued from Delhi announcing the appointment of a new Executive Council, which would take office on 2 September 1946.[41] The entry of only the Congress in the interim government, something which the Muslim League had asked for itself at one time, and which was then denied them, greatly disturbed the Muslim sentiment, with Jinnah strongly criticising the viceroy's action. The day the Congress took office, Muslims throughout the country flew black flags on their houses and shops.[42]

On 18 July 1946, Pethick-Lawrence and Cripps had, in the British parliament, again assured that HMG would adhere to the Cabinet Mission plan of 16 May as it stood. Jinnah, remained unconvinced and sought assurances about the status of minorities after the British left: 'Would not the Congress change tack again and go back to the position taken in Nehru's statement'?, was his enquiry. Jinnah was bitter in his opening speech at the meeting of the Muslim League Council in Bombay, on 27 July 1946,[43] reiterating the demand for Pakistan. It was at this Council meeting that the Cabinet Mission Plan was formally rejected by the Muslim League and a decision to resort to 'Direct Action', as a means of achieving Pakistan, was announced.[44]

This was a very significant and consequential departure, for Jinnah and for the future. It is possible that some of his earlier adherence to constitutionalism was tactical as the political space of public agitations having almost totally been taken over by Gandhi and the Congress. That era of Jinnah's constitutional politics was now over, demonstrating exasperation with frequent shifts of the Congress positions on issues of central importance to him and the League. The end of the Second World

War and mounting impatience with this tardy progress towards gaining his goal of an independent Pakistan, all these in small or large measure contributed to this transformation, and resulted in Jinnah's announcement of 'direct action'. Jinnah then accepted publicly that this was 'unconstitutional', but he denied suggestions of it being 'violent'. Though, this 'Direct Action Resolution' was aimed at the imperial British, in those surcharged days of explosive emotionalism, Jinnah knew well enough that it would result in generating great violence and an extreme anti-Hindu sentiment. Sadly, that is just what happened. This 'Direct Action' day of 16 August 1946, resulted in the killing of over 6000 humans in Calcutta alone, over 15,000 were injured. It had an immediate and cascading effect all around, death now began to stalk India; and many other equally serious consequences followed in Bihar, in Orissa, in UP, in Bombay and in many other areas.

DIRECT ACTION DAY—16 AUGUST 1946: THE CALCUTTA RIOTS

The Calcutta killings, in one form or another, lasted a full year, from August 1946 until independence. Portents of this had actually begun to manifest themselves, in Calcutta, from well before Jinnah's announcement of Direct Action, trouble having started to simmer from around November 1945. Though these earlier protests were not at all communal in nature, collectively they created a climate of discontent and prepared the ground for just that, a communal riot. For example, a procession of five hundred students on 21 November 1945 demonstrated in Calcutta, responding to an appeal from their political leaders to observe the day as 'I.N.A. Day'. Almost predictably and as if following an established pattern the ensuing procession (deliberately, defiantly,) entered a prohibited area, clashed with the police and in consequence one student was killed; by the following day mob violence swept throughout the city. Simultaneously, a municipal strike was also then called converting the existing overcrowding of the city to utter and absolute chaos. Nonetheless, these, as all such incidents tend to, passed.

Then early in 1946, increasing communal tension was observed in the city. On 11 February 1946, the students demonstrated again, as they had done in November 1945, this time in protest against the INA trials, but now around this complex issue had got wound with the case of a

Former Muslim officer of the INA who had been court-martialled. The demonstrators, this time mostly Muslim, protested against the relative severity of his punishment, alleging that in comparison Hindu INA officers had been awarded lighter sentences. This was clearly an instigated protest. Muslim shops closed in sympathetic protest and Muslims carrying League flags demonstrated through Calcutta. Once again these demonstrations deteriorated rapidly into mob violence, with a larger number of casualties, besides this round of rioting lasted far longer than that of November last. Leaders of the Congress and the Muslim League interpreted these riots in their own fashion; for the Congressmen it was the *goonda* and irresponsible elements of this city who had gained an upper hand. For the League, it became a show of strength. H.S. Suhrawardy, then the prominent League leader in Bengal, and soon to become its chief minister, had, it was alleged, first instigated then egged on the demonstrators.

Even as the League was adopting its resolution, Calcutta was preoccupied with quite another matter. On the day (29 July 1946) that the Direct Action Resolution was adopted, entirely through coincidence, a one-day general strike of transport, industrial and government employees had paralysed Calcutta. This general strike had also then coincided with the postal strike (of 16,000 employees), who had struck work throughout Bengal from 21 July. As if all these protests were not enough for Bengal, yet another strike, that of the Imperial Bank employees was then announced. The affect of each of these strikes overlapped the other compounding their collective consequence, and all such elements and forces as revealed in unrest and violent disorder in the city now held Calcutta to ransom.

At the 'Raj end' of this fast spiralling out of control India, in Delhi, by 14 August 1946, Nehru had accepted the viceroy's invitation to form an interim government. Thereafter, he met Jinnah in Bombay, on 15 August on the issue of interim government and the general Hindu-Muslim question. The far more important issue of the impending fallout of the 'Direct Action' day appears not to have figured at all, neither in the Nehru–Jinnah correspondence, nor in their meeting.[45] Separate events seem to have then all come together in time and in collective consequence, as if some malevolent force was then deliberately arranging the setting for 16 August: with Jinnah announcing a 'Direct Action Day'; Nehru was totally preoccupied with the formation of his interim government; the viceroy hoping for a reconciliation and Gandhi, in Sevagram, in the 'final phase' of his epic life. He was, alas, now increasingly isolated and ignored by that very Congress which he had, patiently and laboriously, decade after decade, built from obscurity to governance, also developing a leadership (Nehru–Patel) from virtually nothing. No one, not the viceroy, the government, the opposition or the press had anticipated the magnitude of this looming tragedy; the molten lava of accumulated discontents was pushing unstoppably against this veneer of order in front of their very eyes; they could hear the great, subterranean rumblings but stood rooted and immobile, as if mesmerised into inaction. It is they who had uncapped the volcanoes of national disorder, now they could scarcely cap it again.

It was not the massacres alone but the response to it of the Indian politicians, of all those who were then engaged in fighting this 'war of succession' in India, that was so inexpressibly tragic, also so unforgivable. Nehru was too preoccupied by this idea of forming the first independent, even if interim, government of India and remained largely oblivious to these rumblings in Calcutta. When asked by the press (on early reports of the riots) whether Calcutta's disturbances would affect his plans, Nehru replied, 'Our programme will certainly not be upset because a few persons misbehave in Calcutta'.[46] Once the scale of the tragedy struck the Congress, no time was lost in placing the responsibility for it squarely on the League ministry's head in Bengal, this time with ample justification, though. Then that sad, crud, and empty blame game began, each blaming the other, even as death and communal fear haunted the streets, lanes and alleys of Calcutta. August 1946 was followed by that major communal riot of 1947, in Calcutta in late March. Thereafter, rioting became endemic, a chronic ailment afflicting this great metropolis. And the disease being highly contagious spread at the speed of a forest fire, jumping from one area to another, province to province, one riot being but the forerunner of another and thus seemingly an endless contagion.

Could one have foreseen all these ominous portents? With the Cabinet delegation returning to Britain, the Muslim League felt it had been out-manoeuvred, also let down and then deceived. Since the formation of an interim government had been shelved, Jinnah demanded that the election to the Constituent Assembly be also postponed, and when even that demand was turned down he accused the Cabinet

Mission's interpretation of para 8 as 'most fantastic and dishonest'. All this was perhaps foreseeable, and yet Jinnah's discomfiture evoked little sympathy, the general verdict being that he had been hoist with his own petard. It was only Gandhi that then stood up for him: 'They (The Cabinet Mission) should not have dealt with him (Jinnah) in that legalistic manner,' he said. 'He is a great Indian and the recognised leader of a great organisation.'

As already mentioned, in consequence of their request having been denied the League Council met on 29 July and withdrew its previous acceptance of the 16 May plan of the Cabinet Mission plan. And this is when the League further decided to launch 'Direct Action' to achieve Pakistan and 'to organise the Muslims for the coming struggle to be launched as and when necessary'. This is also when 16 August was declared as the Direct Action day, to be observed all over India as a day of protest. Immediately after this Direct Action resolution had been adopted Jinnah, in the concluding session of the Council of the Muslim League, declared amidst loud applause, 'Today we bid good-bye to the constitutional methods.' And again: 'We have also forged a pistol and are in a position to use it.'

Elucidating his meaning further in a press conference on 31 July, Jinnah said that while both the British and the Congress were armed in their own way, one with weapons and the other with the threat of mass struggle, the Muslim League felt the need to forge its own methods and be prepared for a struggle to enforce its demand for Pakistan. He declined to discuss the details of the proposed Direct Action saying, 'I am not prepared to tell you that now.' Questioned as to whether it would be violent or non-violent, he replied, 'I am not going to discuss ethics.'

Thereafter, in pursuance of their resolution of 29 July, the Muslim League set up a Council of Action. It met behind closed doors but the programme of action which it drew up and which was subsequently elaborated and broadcast by the Muslim League press was not clear enough. The Muslims were reminded that it was in the month of Ramzan that the first open conflict between Islam and Heathenism had been fought and won by 313 Muslims in Arabia. A leaflet containing a special prayer for this Direct Action announced that ten crores of Indian Muslims 'who through bad luck had become slaves of Hindus and the British' would be starting 'a Jehad in this very month of Ramzan'.

Another leaflet bearing a picture of Jinnah with sword in hand, said: 'We Muslims have had the crown and have ruled. Be ready and take your swords...O Kafer!...your doom is not far and the general massacre will come!'

A Muslim League government with Shaheed Suhrawardy as the chief minister was then in power in Bengal. After this rupture between the League and the Cabinet Mission, Suhrawardy had declared that if the Congress were put in power at the Centre, Bengal would raise the standard of rebellion. No part of the provincial revenues would be paid to the Centre and Bengal would set up an independent state owning no allegiance to the Central Government.

This Direct Action programme reached its culmination in the great Calcutta killing on 16, 17 and 18 August. From the midnight of 15 August 1946, organised bands of Muslims variously armed were seen moving about the streets rending the silence of the night by their cries and slogans. The dawn of 16 August broke under a cloudy sky but the rain held off till the evening. Muslim hooligans got busy from early morning on the 16th and by mid-day, almost all normal activities had been paralysed in many parts of the city. A huge procession of Muslims armed with lathis, spears and daggers started from Howrah from Calcutta to attend the mass rally. It was stopped by an army sergeant at the Howrah Bridge. The processionists were disarmed, the lethal weapons and incendiary material recovered from them making two-truck-loads.

All this, to little avail, however, for the conflagration became general towards the evening and near total chaos reigned all over the city when swelling, unruly mobs returning from the maidan after the grand rally, presided over by Suhrawardy, began to interfere with those who did not join the hartal. Their shops were looted, and the contents of the shops thrown on to the streets; private cars and trams were burnt; stray pedestrians were assaulted and stabbed. All vehicular traffic and essential services were brought to a standstill. The only vehicles seen on the streets were the Muslim League lorries and jeeps loaded with hooligans, shouting pro-Pakistan slogans and inciting the mob to violence.

These communal riots that started in Calcutta on 16 August with the observance of Direct Action day, spread like a chain-reaction, a rapidly transferring contagion from Calcutta to the rest of East Bengal, Noakhali became the word best describing it all, then to Bihar, and from Bihar eastwards the contagion spread to Punjab. Unfortunately the League as indeed the Congress leaders viewed these riots with a jaundiced political eye—not even humanist concern leave alone vision. It was only Gandhi that then stood out and apart.

Kim Christen caught the tragedy graphically when he wrote in *The Statesman*: 'I have a stomach made strong the experience of a war hospital, but war was never like this'. 'This is not a riot,' commented *The Statesman* editorially. 'It needs a word found in medieval history, a fury. Yet "fury" sounds spontaneous and there must have been some deliberation and organisation to set this fury on the way. Hordes who ran about battering and killing with eight-foot lathis may have found them lying about or bough them out of their own pockets, but that is hard to believe. We have already commented on the bands who found it easy to get petrol and vehicles when no others were permitted on the streets. It is not mere supposition that men were imported into Calcutta to help in making an impression'. In the same issue, in a leading article entitle 'Disgrace Abounding', the paper commented:

> The origin of the appalling carnage and loss in the capital of a great Province—we believe the worst communal riot in India's history—was a political demonstration by the Muslim League...In retrospect its conduct before the riots stands open to the inference—not only by political opponents—that it was divided in mind on whether rioting of some sort would be good or bad....The bloody shambles to which this country's largest city has been reduced is an abounding disgrace, which, owing to the Bengal Ministry's pre-eminence as a League Ministry, has inevitably tarnished seriously the all-India reputation of the League itself.

Soon after his return from Calcutta, Wavell met Gandhi and Nehru on 27 August 1946. 'I have just come back from Calcutta.' He said, 'and I am appalled at what I have seen.'[47] He then elaborated on the enormity of the killings, accepting that, 'as an Englishman, he had no right to judge the actions of the Indian political parties, even though he totally condemned and was cast down by the barbarities which had been committed in their name'. But so long as 'he was Viceroy of India', he went on, he felt it necessary 'to do all in his power to prevent any more massacres of this kind...Neither as an Englishman nor as a human being could he stomach such savagery and bestiality. He would be abdicating his responsibilities if he did not make a supreme effort to bring the two communities, Hindu and Muslim, together and persuade them that working together was the only sure way to freedom.'[48]

Leonard Mosley's account of this meeting and the verbatim test, as he reports it, is at Appendix VII. Wavell, too, though in much more sober but palpably anguished words records this meeting in his Diary. Penderel Moon's (the editor of the viceroy's journal) comments precede the main text:

> According to V.P. Menon a definite change in Lord Wavell's attitude and policy was noticeable after his return from Calcutta. He had become convinced that unless some agreement was effected soon between the Congress and the League, the fearful Calcutta disorders would be repeated in other parts of India. He was also much struck by what Nazimuddin had told him about the attitude of the League towards participation in the Constituent Assembly. These factors account for his abortive attempt (recorded in the next entry) to induce Nehru and Gandhi to make a statement about the Constituent Assembly that would really satisfy the League'. Wavell's Diary notes merit quoting in full because the great killings that followed the 'Direct Action' day hastened India's eventual partition:

> **27 August**—'I determined to make an attempt to induce the Congress to state clearly their intentions about Grouping in the Constituent Assembly, since this was obviously one of the main obstacles to cooperation by the League. I therefore, asked Gandhi and Nehru to come and see me in the evening...The meeting was not a great success. The old man [Gandhi] was in a legalistic and malevolent mood, and Nehru was full of hate against the League. I told them what I thought the only chance of a peaceful transfer of power in India was if the Congress made a categorical statement that they would accept the position that the Provinces must remain in their Sections, as intended by the Mission, until after the first elections under the new Constitution. I said that I could not undertake the responsibility of calling together the Constituent Assembly until this point was settled. I handed them the draft of a statement which I asked them to make. [It read] 'The Congress are prepared in the interest of communal harmony to accept the intention of the Statement of 16 May that Provinces cannot exercise any option affecting their part of the Section or the Groups, if formed, until the decision contemplated in para 19 (viii) of the Statement of 16 May is taken by the new Legislature, after the new constitutional arrangements have come into operation and the first general elections have been held.[49]

> 'Gandhi went off into long legalistic arguments about the interpretation of the Mission's statement. I said that I was a plain man and not a lawyer,

and that I knew perfectly well what the Mission meant, and that compulsory Grouping was the whole crux of the Plan.

'The argument went on for some time, and Nehru got very heated. Gandhi said that if a blood bath was necessary, it would come about in spite of non-violence I said that I was very shocked to hear such words from him. In the end they took away the formula, but I do not think there is much hope of their accepting it'.

'28 August: 'During the morning I received an abusive and vindictive letter from Gandhi, which he asked should be telegraphed home. Evidently my rebuke to him on his 'blood-bath' remark had gone home. It confirmed the view I have always held of G., that his professions of non-violence and saintliness are political weapons against the British rather than natural attributions. It looked like a declaration of war, and I wondered whether I really had held the last meeting of my Caretaker Council. However, I received later a letter from Nehru about nominations to the Peace Conference and U.N.O Assembly, which seemed to show that Congress still intended to come into the Government.

Gandhi's letter was as follows:

28 August, 1946

Dear Friend,

I write this as a friend and after deep though. Several times last evening you repeated that you were a 'plain man and a soldier' and that you did not know the law. We are all plain men though we may not all be soldiers and even though some of us may know the law. It is our purpose, I take it, to devise methods to prevent a repetition of the recent terrible happenings in Calcutta. The question before us is how best to do it.

Your language last evening was minatory. As representative of the King you cannot afford to be a military man only, nor to ignore the law, much less the law of your own making. You should be assisted, if necessary, by a legal mind enjoying your full confidence. You threatened not to convene the Constituent Assembly if the formula you placed before Pandit Nehru and me was not acted upon by the Congress. If such be really the case, then you should not have made the announcement you did on 12 August. But having made it you should recall the action and form another ministry enjoying your full confidence. If British arms are kept here for internal peace and order your Interim Government would be reduced to a farce. The Congress cannot afford to impose its will on warring elements in India through the use of British arms. Nor can the Congress be expected to bend itself and adopt what it considers a wrong course because of the brutal exhibition recently witnessed in Bengal. Such submissions would itself lead to an encouragement and repetition of such tragedies. The vindictive spirit on either side would go deeper, biding for an opportunity to exhibit itself more fiercely and more disgracefully when occasion occurs. And all this will be chiefly due to the continued presence in India of a foreign power strong and proud of its arms.

I say this neither as a Hindu nor as a Muslim. I write only as an Indian. Insofar as I am aware, the Congress claims to know both the Hindu and Muslim mind more than you or any Britisher can do. Unless, therefore, you can wholly trust the Congress Government which you have announced, you should reconsider your decision, as I have already suggested.

You will please convey the whole letter to the British Cabinet.
I am yours Sincerely,
Sd/- M.K. Gandhi

Just before going to bed, I received a letter from Nehru but as it might have spoilt my sleep I left it unread.

'**29 August:** Nehru's letter might have been worse, and it seems clear that the Congress will come into the Government all right, whatever I say about the Constituent Assembly. I answered it and said it was not a matter of legal interpretation but of practical politics. I had an almost panic-stricken telegram from the S. of S. (Secretary of State) asking me to do nothing rash with Congress.'

Editorial comment by Penderel Moon added: 'Nehru in his letter conveyed the refusal of the Working Committee to make an unambiguous statement about Grouping such as Wavell had requested. He said that the Congress had accepted the Cabinet Mission's scheme in its entirety, but 'they interpreted it so as to resolve the inconsistencies contained in it.... They hold that Provincial autonomy is a basic provision and each Provision has the right to decide whether to form or join a Group or not'. Questions of interpretation could be referred to the Federal Court'.

These efforts by Wavell led nowhere, it was perhaps already too late and neither the Congress nor the Muslim League would shift from their adopted positions. Events now led men, not the other way around.

8

STYMIED NEGOTIATIONS?

An intransigent Jinnah had always been difficult to deal with. However, for the Muslim League lately it had become a one-man show, Jinnah alone counted. Attempts therefore, to persuade him into negotiations with the nationalist Muslims (e.g. Azad or Ghaffar Khan), men of far lesser influence in Congress, would always irritate him, perhaps justifiably, for he suspected such ploys were meant to denigrate him deliberately. Then there was the Congress trio of Gandhi, Nehru, and Patel. For the Cabinet Mission, it was always Jinnah alone on the one side and a host of Congress leaders on the other. To obtain a response from the Congress was always more taxing. In the Viceroy's Journal, there are several such instances where the Cabinet delegation appears to have jumped the gun in assessing the Congress leaders' response without having consulted/discussed with all. From amongst the Congress leaders, Gandhi proved the most unpredictable, persuading Wavell to note repeatedly in his diary, of his exasperation. These compel us to reflect and question Gandhi's role in the formation of a single Constituent Assembly, also the establishing of an Interim Government.

Wavell records in his diary:

> *6 May 1946*—'He [Gandhi] came at 7.30 p.m..... The result was a shock to them (Cabinet delegation). Gandhi, who had been living with Ghaffar Khan and Patel, the two malcontents, had adopted entirely their point of view.... We must either adopt entirely the Congress point of view or Jinnah's point of view; but there was no half way house. Gandhi seemed quite unmoved at the prospect of civil war, I think he had adopted Patel's thesis that if we are firm the Muslims will not fight'.

Almost a fortnight later is recorded the following entry:

19 May 1946—Cripps then told me very briefly the result of seven hours talk with Gandhi....They (the Cabinet delegation) then produced a letter from Gandhi, the first of the Congress efforts to wreck the groups of Provinces. This is what the Delegation has let itself in for by not standing firm and definite on our statement (of 16 May); they have had seven hours with Gandhi, and this is the result, the clever attempt of an able and unscrupulous politician to torpedo the whole plan.

20 May 1946—Just then he [Lord Pethick-Lawrence] was handed another letter from Gandhi and read it out. I have never seen three men [the Cabinet delegation] taken more aback by this revelation of Gandhi in his true colours. Cripps and the Secretary of State were shaken to the core while Alexander's reactions were pure John Bull at his most patriotic and insular.

Then follow explanatory comments by Penderel Moon, the editor of Viceroy's Journal: 'In this second letter Gandhi discussed at some length the other points that he had raised in his talks with Cripps and the Secretary of State and on which Cripps claimed to have satisfied him. It was very clear that Gandhi was far from satisfied. The Secretary of State said that this letter greatly misrepresented what had passed in their interview with him and he was now convinced that nobody should see Gandhi apart from other members of the Delegation and without a note being taken. Alexander said that Gandhi clearly did not want a settlement on the basis of the Statement and that his [Gandhi's] letter grossly misrepresented the Delegation's position.'

As I have mentioned earlier in this chapter, Gandhi, on 8 May 1946, in a letter to Sir Stafford Cripps had expressed an emphatic rejection of the 'grouping scheme'. He wanted the formation of the Central Legislature, as well as the Executive, instead, on a population basis.

The entries continue:

11 June 1946—Pethick-Lawrence was all for seeing Gandhi. Alexander was bitterly opposed and went so far as to threaten to go straight home if Pethick-Lawrence insisted...George Abell came in with a message that Gandhi really wanted to see me, and Alexander said he had no objection to this.... He [Gandhi] said he was thoroughly anxious for a settlement and agreed that a coalition was necessary. He said parity was of no account nor whether the members belonged to the Congress or to the League, provided they were the best men available.

'Ironically early on 13 June 1946, Patel informed the Cabinet Delegation and the viceroy that the Congress Working Committee had not even taken five minutes to turn down the proposal for interim government formation. The letter which Gandhi then sent to the viceroy on 13 June 1946 unexpectedly sang an entirely different tune: 'You must make the choice of one horse or the other. So far as I can see, you will never succeed in riding two at the same time. Choose the names either submitted by the Congress or the League. For God's sake do not make an incompatible mixture and in trying to do so produce a fearful explosion'.

19 June 1946—The information from Sudhir Ghosh and Rajagopalachari was to the effect that the Congress Working Committee had decided, against the advise of Gandhi, not to put forward a Nationalist Muslim for the Interim Government. Things looked hopeful....Vallabhbhai was reported to have opposed Gandhi on the Nationalist Muslim issue. Nehru had gone off to Kashmir.

20 June 1946—The situation seems to have gone all haywire again, thanks to Gandhi...then Woodrow Wyatt appeared with a message....

He said Rajagopalachari had told him that Congress had gone back on yesterday's decision, upon the instance of Gandhi, and were going to insist on the removal of Engineer's name since he was an official and place Azad in the government. I said at once that both conditions were utterly unacceptable and that putting Azad forward was simply a manoeuvre to ensure Jinnah's refusal.

[Sir N.P. Engineer was not an official, but he held at that time an official position, that of an advocate general to the Indian Army].

The Cabinet Mission Plan floundered as differing interpretations of the 16 May statement by the Congress and the League divided them irretrievably. The Viceroy's Journal brings out vividly the seriousness Wavell attached to the attempts he made with Gandhi and Nehru for a rapprochement with the Muslim League. Wavell had to pay a price for failing to achieve what he had set out to. I feel compelled, therefore, to quote from Wavell's note for the Cabinet Mission. Wavell, an author, was doubtless imbued with a marked sense of history. What I reproduce here from his notes amply justifies where he and the Cabinet Mission stood, morally.

This is what Wavell, in part wrote on 25 June 1946:

The Cabinet Mission will remember that I raised the point of what would happen in the event of Congress attempting to obtain a legal decision in favour of their own interpretation of our Statement of May 16th. My point was that the 'Statement' is not a legal document and that its interpretation must depend on the intentions of those who framed it. I therefore suggested to Sir Stafford Cripps that the Cabinet Mission, before leaving India, should draw up a paper stating clearly what the intentions of those who framed the document were in this respect; so that I could produce it as evidence of our intentions if the document were challenged in court, or elsewhere.

'I do not quite understand the paper which has been drawn up by Sir Stafford Cripps; but I gather from it that he considers that the document may be challenged legally, and that its interpretation is open to question; and he proposes that a tribunal should be set up by the Constituent Assembly to interpret the document. As a layman, I do not understand this; and I cannot accept that our clear intentions should be open to interpretation by another body'.

THE AUTUMN OF PEACE PARLEYS

The Calcutta killings were followed by a vicious chain reaction of continuing inhumanity: names that have now become etched on our collective memory were the places of barbaric inhumanity: Noakhali, Bihar, Garhmukteshwar; a spiral of communal violence, continued, unabated. At such a stage, even as the tragedy of partition loomed, another effort at reconciling positions seemed an exercise in futility yet Gandhi and Jinnah met once again, to devise a formula for a Congress–League settlement. It was left to Nehru and Jinnah to work out details; a fortnight long initiative of Nawab Saheb of Bhopal had borne at least this result. Reminiscent then of May 1938, when Subhas Bose had made an effort and of August 1945 when Maulana Azad came close to recognizing the League's right to exclusively represent the Muslims of India, it was Gandhi's turn now to recognize an electorally proven reality: the League held the allegiance of a predominant majority of Muslims in India. It was only after Gandhi had conceded this essential point that Jinnah agreed to meet Nehru on 5 October 1946. The basis of this meeting, in the slang of political reportage was the Gandhi–Jinnah 'formula' stating the following:

The Congress does not challenge and accepts that the Muslim League is now the authoritative representative of an overwhelming majority of the Muslims of India. As such, and in accordance with democratic principles, they alone have an unquestionable right to represent the Muslims of India. But the Congress cannot agree that any restriction or limitation should be put upon the Congress to choose such representatives as they think proper from amongst the members of the Congress as their representatives.[1]

The two (Nehru and Jinnah) met again on 7 October. A week later, by 14 October the talks had failed; the story had an all too familiar a ring. The bigger picture of a 'settlement' was lost in the fog of those peripherals. Nehru had himself summarized them:

1. The 'formula' suggested by Gandhiji.
2. The League not being responsible for the Members at present representing the Scheduled Castes and minorities.
3. What should be done in case any vacancy should arise among the Members representing the minorities other than the Scheduled Castes?
4. The procedure to be adopted over what may be called major communal issues? and,
5. Alternating Vice-Presidentship.[2]

Nehru 'was not comfortable with the way the 'formula' had been worded. To him this 'formula' was not even necessary, though he would not question its underlying purpose. The issues, in reality, were not insurmountable; nothing earthshaking would have happened if for a larger purpose greater accommodation had been demonstrated.

To Jinnah, the 'formula' agreed to with Gandhi could not change, it was the foundation of the settlement, it had been signed by Gandhi and accepted by Jinnah. While reiterating this in his letter to Nehru of 7 October, Jinnah mentioned something central, that the Congress should not include, in the remaining five members of their quota, a Muslim of their choice in case the League joined the interim government.[3] According to the accepted 'formula', Congress could 'choose such representatives as they thought proper from amongst the members of the Congress.' Why did Jinnah then choose to mention this in his letter? Was it because Nehru had begun to dilute the agreed-to formula? In the enclosure attached to his letter, there were eight other points for Nehru to reflect upon: the what may be called major focus of the formula was now getting blurred, or was it getting confused beyond redemption?

Fortunately, they met again on the very day that Jinnah had written to Nehru, 7 October. But this meeting too, did not yield any result. To Nehru and his colleagues in the Congress, the whole scheme was now entirely wrong. Referring to his meeting with Jinnah of 5 October, Nehru said that he was unaware that their meeting was a consequence of any 'agreed formula'. As was to be expected, Nehru, too, wanted it clearly understood that the Congress had the right to appoint a Muslim out of its quota. In his letter of 8 October addressed to Jinnah, he alluded to another paragraph, which the formula contained and to which Jinnah had not even referred.[4] Jinnah responded promptly stating that the paragraph was not part of the agreed formula. And that this was a matter of record.[5] On the important issue of nomination of Muslims from the Congress quota, he stated in writing that it was discussed between him and Nehru in their last meeting of 7 October. He also said that 'this again was a serious departure from the agreed formula'.[6] Nehru responded observing that Jinnah's letter contained 'several mis-statements'.

Nehru and the Congress leadership had rejected the formula to which Gandhi had put his signature. When the Jinnah–Nehru talks failed and the correspondence was made public, Gandhi refrained from commenting on it. For it was only he, by now an old man, what were words now, he must have reflected: Mohandas Karamchand Gandhi, born of the soil of India and with that soil permeating every cell of his body; who saw what great tragedy now loomed over us; none else did, little wonder, therefore, that he remained silent. This was, in a sense, Gandhi's last attempt with Jinnah to save India from a partition. He failed and with that a great chapter in his life and our annals come to an end. There remains just one single note which metronome like keeps striking the same chord: Why was there such desperate hurry to destroy? And why do we ponder now upon all this if it was as clear-cut then as Nehru would have us believe?

The Attlee – Wavell – Jinnah – Nehru Conference

London, 3-6 December 1946

There did not arise another opportunity, for the Congress and the Muslim League to resolve the issues that divided them. Prime Minister Attlee convened a Conference in London, on 6 December 1946. This in reality was the final attempt by the British premier and his Cabinet to find a solution. There were principally two reasons for this initiative, they were both operational, not tied to the imperative of keeping India united, more to making as early as orderly, (at least in appearance) a withdrawal of the British Empire from India.

The first was the worry arising from the rapidly deteriorating law and order situation in India just when a transfer of power, from the British point of view, was urgently needed. Besides, it had yet to be, officially, legally and legislatively determined as to which authority, or authorities, this 'power' was to be transferred. This led to the second reason.

The provision for provinces opting out of the groups was continuing as the focal point of controversy between the Congress and the League. The Congress now, in contrast to the League's position had accepted the Cabinet Mission Plan, subject to the 'interpretation' that a province could decline to go into its group from the very beginning. This interpretation, placed by the Congress nullified the Plan according to the League and could only mean rejection of the entire long-term scheme. The League argued that if, for example, Dr Khan Sahib's Congress government in the NWFP refused to join Group A; and Assam, with its Congress Ministry, opted out of Group C, from the very start, what possible attraction would then be left for the League in the Mission Plan? The League feared that were it to go into the Constituent Assembly under these circumstances it would have no chance at all against the majoritarianism of the Congress for the adopting of an appropriate (to the League) Constitution.

The Congress' 'interpretation' of the Plan, in practical terms required a restatement of intentions from its authors. This came on 6 December 1946, as an announcement by HMG's government, in London. While implying a vindication of the Muslim League stand on this issue, it had yet to be convened to an agreement; the London meet was an attempt in just that direction. This meeting was chaired by Prime Minister

Attlee, and the attendees were Sir Pethick-Lawrence, Sir Stafford Cripps, Nehru, Jinnah, Liaquat Ali Khan and Sardar Baldev Singh. The statement as well as what transpired in those meetings are matters of record, only excerpts are given here, for they eventually went towards shaping India's future as a united country. Two meetings, one of 4 December and the other of 6 December are relevant to our concerns.

Indian Conference in London. Paper I.C.L (46)2
L/P &J/10/111: ff 77-81
Record of Meeting held in the Secretary of State's Room
at the India Office on 4 December 1946 at 10.30 am

SECRET

Those present were: Lord Pethick-Lawrence (in the Chair), Sir S. Cripps, Mr Alexander, Field Marshal Viscount Wavell, Pandit Nehru, Mr Turnbull, Mr Abell (Secretaries).

The Viceroy said that there had been no conflict at Cabinet meetings of the Interim Government. Pandit Nehru said that the Muslim Members refused to meet him. The Viceroy pointed out that Pandit Nehru had declined to see Mr Liaqat Ali Khan on two occasions when he had been asked to do so, to which Pandit Nehru replied that Mr Liaqat Ali Khan insulted him and he saw no reason why he should meet him. On the very first day of the Interim Government he (Nehru) had been insulted and almost assaulted by Muslims outside the Viceroy's House. The Interim Government could not function as two groups. If it did, the Muslim League would be outvoted, but everything could not go to Cabinet. Even recently two Muslim League representatives, with the help of the India Office had gone to the United States and had made virulent speeches at the New York Herald Forum.

The Minister without Portfolio said that in the War Coalition in this country, Ministers did not work as Party Groups. The work was all done in formal sub-committees of the Cabinet in which Pandit Nehru said he did not ask the Muslim League to give up what it stood for, but there was an absence of any desire to find a way out.

There then followed some discussion focussed almost entirely on the vexatious question of Grouping. Pandit Nehru also complained that the League newspapers were full of irresponsible abuse of the Government in which the League itself was serving. Sir Stafford Cripps thereupon asked whether, in Pandit Nehru's view, it would help if some sort of guarantee of the emergence of a three-tier system were given. Nehru replied that the Statement of May 16th did not please the Congress, but they accepted it, partly because it was flexible and left the Constituent Assembly a fairly free field. The major limitation on its freedom was an internal one of being able to carry on with the support of enough people. The three-tier system was laid down only as something that may emerge if the provinces and people concerned want it. If they want to make a Group the Congress will accept their decision completely, but the Congress hopes to convince others that there should not be Groups. Nevertheless they would accept the decision of the Federal Court. But this was clearly not getting any where though, there was some more desultory discussion on it.

There then followed the concluding session of which the record is both relevant and highly informative.

Record of Meeting at 10 Downing Street on 6 December 1946 at 4.0 pm

SECRET

Those present were: Mr Attlee (in the Chair), Lord Pethick-Lawrence, Sir S. Cripps, Mr Alexander, Field Marshal Viscount Wavell; Mr Turnbull (Secretary)

STATEMENT BY HIS MAJESTY'S GOVERNMENT

The conversations held by His Majesty's Government with Pandit Nehru, Mr Jinnah, Mr Liaquat Ali Khan and Sardar Baldev Singh came to an end this evening, as Pandit Nehru and Sardar Baldev Singh are returning to India tomorrow morning.

The object of the conversations has been to obtain the participation and co-operation of all parties in the Constituent Assembly. It was not expected that any final settlement could be arrived at since the Indian representatives must consult their colleagues before any final decision is reached.

The main difficulty that has arisen has been over the interpretation of paragraph 19(v) and (viii) of the Cabinet Mission's Statement of May 16th relating to the Meetings in Sections which run as follows:—

Paragraph 19(v) 'These Sections shall proceed to settle provincial constitutions for the Provinces included in each Section and shall also decide whether any group constitution shall be set up for those Provinces and if so with what provincial subjects the group should deal. Provinces should have power to opt out of groups in accordance with the provisions of sub-clause (viii) below.'

Paragraph 19(viii) 'As soon as the new constitutional arrangements have come into operation it shall be open to any Province to elect to come out of any group in which it has been placed. Such a decision shall be taken by the legislature of the Province after the first General Election under the new constitution.'

The Cabinet Mission have throughout maintained the view that the decisions of the Sections should, in the absence of agreement to the contrary, be taken by simple majority vote of the representatives in the Sections. This view has been accepted by the Muslim League, but the Congress have put forward a different view. They have asserted that the true meaning of the Statement, read as a whole, is that the Provinces have a right to decide both as to grouping and as to their own constitutions.

His Majesty's Government have had legal advice which confirms that the Statement of May 16th means what the Cabinet Mission have always stated was their intention. This part of the Statement, as so interpreted, must therefore, be considered an essential part of the scheme of May 16th, for enabling the Indian people to formulate a constitution which His Majesty's Government would be prepared to submit to Parliament. It should, therefore, be accepted by all parties in the Constituent Assembly.

It is however clear that other questions of interpretation of the Statement of May 16th may arise, and His Majesty's Government hope that if the Council of the Muslim League are able to agree to participate in the Constituent Assembly they will also agree, as have the Congress, that the Federal Court should be asked to decide matters of interpretation that may be referred to them by either side and will accept such decision, so that the procedure both in the Union Constituent Assembly and in the Sections may accord with the Cabinet Mission's Plan.

On the matter immediately in dispute His Majesty's Government urge the Congress to accept the view of the Cabinet Mission in order that the way may be open for the Muslim League to reconsider their attitude. If, in spite of this re-affirmation of the intention of the Cabinet Mission, the Constituent Assembly desires that this fundamental point should be referred for the decision of the Federal Court, such reference should be made at a very early date. It will then be reasonable that the meetings of the Sections of the Constituent Assembly should be postponed until the decision of the Federal Court is known.

There has never been any prospect of success for the Constituent Assembly, except upon the basis of an agreed procedure. Should a Constitution come to be framed by a Constituent Assembly in which a large section of the Indian population had not been represented, His Majesty's Government could not, of course, contemplate—as the Congress have stated they would not contemplate—forcing such a Constitution upon any unwilling parts of the country.

After the Statement had been read, Mr Jinnah asked what the position would be if the Federal Court took a different view of the interpretation of the document from that held by H.M.G. The Minister without Portfolio said that H.M.G. would then have to consider the position. Mr Jinnah said that he must make it clear that a decision by the Federal Court would not be binding on the Muslim League. It seemed to him that the Constituent Assembly would decide by a large Hindu majority to refer the matter to the Federal Court and would be bound by the Federal Court's ruling. The Muslim League could not, therefore, be a party to such a reference as they were not prepared to be bound by it. Apart from this he was not in a position to say anything on behalf of the Muslim League: but he would certainly consider the position with his Council. He thanked the British Government for doing their best to secure an agreement.

Pandit Nehru said that the Congress would, of course, require time to consider the Statement which had been read and he could not give any answer, though there were certain things he would wish to say.

The Statement was, he considered an amendment of the Statement of May 16th and went beyond it. The Congress had proceeded on the basis of that Statement throughout. The Cabinet Mission and the Viceroy would bear out his statement that Congress had from the very beginning pointed out that they discussed it on a certain basis. Subsequently they were told that no amendment or change would be made. Now this elucidation took the Statement a stage further. Clearly it created a new situation for the Congress. He did not know what their response would have been if this Statement had been made originally.

The new Statement quoted paragraphs 19(v) and 19(viii), but not paragraph 15 of the Statement of May 16th. Taken together these paragraphs might bear a different interpretation from that which paragraph 19 would bear by itself.

The Prime Minister said that it was not at all clear to him on what grounds that view was advanced. Paragraph 15 dealt with fundamental principles to be embodied in the constitution. Paragraph 19 dealt with the methods of arriving at decisions about the constitution. These appeared to be quite different and separate things, and the principles laid down for one need not be the same as those for the other. Pandit Nehru said that the view of Congress was that, taken together, these two sections might mean something different. Any statement by H.M.G. must obviously be carefully considered by the Congress. The Prime Minister observed that the present Statement dealt only with the interpretation of the document of May 16th. The Congress themselves had placed an interpretation on it. He could not see why an interpretation by H.M.G. extended the document if an interpretation by Congress did not do so. Pandit Nehru replied that H.M.G. as the authors of the document were capable of extending it while the Congress could not do so.

Pandit Nehru said that he did not know what the reaction of the Constituent Assembly would be. Normally speaking, a body such as that resented outside pressure and reacted from it. Compulsion destroyed cooperation. The attitude of various groups and Provinces had been strongly expressed. The Sikhs, for example, had held strong views and the Congress were personally involved in this question of interpretation. He could assure Mr Jinnah and Mr Liaquat Ali Khan that all on the Congress side were anxious to find ways out honourable for both parties because they did not wish to waste the rest of their lives in conflict. They could not conceive of any constitution imposed over one part of the country by another. It was not surprising that they had to face difficulties. He did not take a dismal view of the past or the future and he thought that an unnecessarily dismal view had been taken. There was great danger of solving one difficulty and raising others of vaster dimensions in the process. To some extent it was true that this was a conflict between Indian points of view but he was convinced that, unless Indians had a free hand, other difficulties would arise. Indians must have the burden of deciding and bearing the consequences themselves.

Pandit Nehru concluded by thanking H.M.G. for their courtesy in asking him to this country.

The Prime Minister said that he would like to make three comments on what Pandit Nehru had said. Firstly, he could not admit that any addition had been made to the Statement of May 16th. Secondly, the present Statement could not be termed 'pressure from outside' on the Constituent Assembly. The British Government were throughout in the position of persons who were trying to assist an agreement between Indians. Thirdly, he could not agree that there was any sort of coercion on the Constituent Assembly except that of working within an agreed framework. There always had to be a framework within which such a body would work. Sardar Baldev Singh said that the new Statement would worsen the position of the Sikh Community. If there was majority voting in Group B and not voting by Provinces, the four Sikh representatives would be in an even less influential position. This would have a bad reaction on the Sikhs who had only been persuaded to join the Interim Government and accept the Cabinet Mission's Statement with great difficulty. He feared that the Federal Court was now likely to take the same view as H.M.G. and that the Sikhs might take steps which would be very embarrassing for him personally and for his other colleagues. He would, however, try his best to persuade his people to give the Constituent Assembly a trial.

The President of the Board of Trade said that the Statement did not, of course, in any way prohibit some special arrangement being made by general agreement. He had always understood that the other parties were ready to deal generously with the Sikh position.

Mr Liaquat Ali Khan said that he endorsed everything said by his leader, Mr Jinnah. There had always been a desire in the Muslim League to solve the communal problem in a cooperative spirit. He was grateful for the patience and courtesy shown by the British Ministers and it was his earnest desire that India should attain independence peacefully.

The Secretary of State said that he hoped that the Indian leaders would look at this new Statement with an open mind. It was not designed to take a partial view and was framed with goodwill towards all parties. There was no change in it from what the Cabinet Mission had said all along.

The Minister without Portfolio thanked the Indian representatives for coming to this country and said that there was nothing in the Statement which had been read which went beyond what was contained in the Statements of May 16th and May 25th.

The President of the Board of Trade said that if the desire for cooperation which all present had expressed could only be translated into some actual form of deeds, the difficulties would be overcome. Basically, he felt that the trouble was suspicion which had grown up over past years. If the oppositional attitude could be changed to coalitional attitude these difficulties could be ironed out. His Excellency the Viceroy said that ever since he had held his present office he had tried to bring the parties together and he would continue to do his best to this end. He sincerely trusted that they might be able to arrive at a solution to the present difficulties.

After the usual courtesies this meeting, the final effort to save the Cabinet Mission Plan was then abandoned.

This statement of 6 December 1946 by HMG was based on a legal advice; it was an attempt at conferring an authoritative meaning to the Plan. To this Nehru had responded by commenting that as this amounted to an addition to the 16 May Plan, it was coercive and amounted to telling the Constituent Assembly what its sign posts were, therefore, he could not accept the statement of HMG. Attlee had responded but fruitlessly and Nehru returned to Delhi to proceed unilaterally with the process of constitution making. The Muslim League, in reaction, declined to join this assembly demanding a separate Constituent Assembly of their own. The Cabinet Mission Plan had now been rendered as brain-dead, what was really not inevitable sadly became so; Pakistan became a reality. There is need here, not as a post-script, but as perhaps an elaboration, or giving due space to other views in the Congress to shed some light on the thinking of senior Congress leaders then that some portions of a letter written by Sardar Patel to Sir Stafford Cripps on 15 December 1946 are reproduced here:

'...you called the League delegation there to (London, December 1946) at a time when there was some realization that violence is a game at which both parties can play and the mild Hindu also, when driven to desperation can retaliate as brutally as a fanatic Muslim. Just when the time for settlement was reached Jinnah got the invitation, and he was able to convince the Muslims once again that he had...[got] more concessions by creating trouble and violence.

'...but I will only say that if strong action had been taken, or had been allowed to be taken here, when 'Direct Action Day' was fixed by the Muslim League and when 16 August was fixed as the day of demonstration in Calcutta, all this colossal loss of life and property and bloodcurdling events would not have happened. The Viceroy here took the contrary view, and every action of his since the great Calcutta killings has been in the direction of encouraging the Muslim League and putting pressure on us towards appeasement.'

'Your interpretation means that Bengal Muslims can draft the Constitution of Assam. It is amazing. Do you think that such a monstrous proposition can be accepted by the Hindus of Assam, particularly after the sad experience of wholesale forcible conversions, arson, looting, rape and forcible marriages? You can have no idea of resentment and anger caused by your emphasis on this interpretation. If you think that Assam can be coerced to accept the domination of Bengal, the sooner you are rid of that illusion the better. What can we do to satisfy the Sikhs who have admittedly been unjustly treated? If they frame the Constitution of Assam in such a way as to make Assam's opting out impossible, what is the remedy in your statement?[7]

Nehru returned to India on 7 December 1946 to attend the opening session of the Constituent Assembly, due on 9 December. This Session, indeed the Assembly itself, remained boycotted by the Muslim League. Patel, towards the end of the December 1946, did relent and finally admit that the 'Congress had made a mistake in distrusting Attlee and not accepting his suggestion for a compromise'.[8]

On 9 December 1946, the Constituent Assembly met, but an atmosphere of near total unreality pervaded this gathering. It was a great and, a historic occasion. It was a meeting to determine an Independent and hopefully, a united India's constitution, but tellingly, as a portend of the future, the Muslim League was represented only by empty chairs. After a short session, the Assembly adjourned without achieving any results except adopting a declaration of independence, moved by Nehru. This was not put to vote.

Lord Pethick-Lawrence had then wanted to send a cable to congratulate Nehru on the formation of the Constituent Assembly but refrained apprehending that such a gesture might well elicit 'howls of protest from Jinnah to which...Nehru would then, in turn reply, by making still more speeches and there would be more trouble than ever before'. 'Could not someone tell Nehru not to make speeches in reply to Jinnah and Churchill? They were out for trouble and mischief and Nehru was playing into their hands by taking serious notice of [all of] them'. So Pethick-Lawrence had commented asking in exasperation: 'Why do the Congress people worry about groupings? Why can't they set about the task quickly without worrying about what would happen to Assam? Those things would adjust themselves in course of time. It was foolish to waste time and energy on these little matters when so much had to be done'.[9]

Was there some substance in this observation? Were we missing something important by constantly harping on the small detail? This comment was not so much a woolly sentiment expressed by an elderly and a pacific man, rather it was the voice of concern of a friend of India, though sadly, neither dynamic nor effective enough for the complex challenges of those times.

Bevan, an important Labour Cabinet member had echoed somewhat similar sentiments but much more forcefully: 'It is true that we the British have created[10] communal discord in your country in the past. We have taken full advantage of the troubles between the Hindus and the Muslims. We have exploited these troubles, but that is all a matter of the past. Now the Labour government has come and has offered you self-government and you won't take it. Don't be stupid, go ahead and take it. Settle with Jinnah and we shall have enough work to do after that.' On being asked whether Bevan had expressed these sentiments to Nehru when he was in London, Bevan retorted, 'How could I have met him? From the moment Nehru came, he was in hurry to go back.'[11] This is how 1946 ended and the fateful 1947 knocked on our door.

That Bitter End Game of 1947

When the fateful 1947 arrived, what clouded India's political skies more than anything else was this implacable and mounting hostility between the two communities and the leading political parties, the Congress and the Muslim League. No one knew or could then have prophesied what the year would bring, or how this fateful year would end, though, all were filled with uncertainty, apprehension and undefined forebodings.

On 31 January 1947, the Working Committee of the Muslim League met at Karachi and adopted a Resolution denouncing the composition and procedure of the Constituent Assembly. It called upon the British government to announce a formal failure of the Cabinet Mission Plan because the Congress had not accepted it, as had not the Sikhs or the Scheduled castes. The Congress reacted by demanding the resignation of the League Members from the government. To drive home the point, on 15 February, in a press statement, Sardar Patel warned of retaliatory actions by the Congress if the Muslim League did not resign. Were that to happen, the Sardar cautioned it would[12] 'result in serious communal conflict and may (even) be a civil war.'

We need, however, to go back by just a few days, for then took place a rather momentous development. On 4 February 1947, Field Marshal Lord Wavell recorded in his diary: 'Just after lunch, I had a letter from the P.M. by special messenger, dismissing me from my post, at a month's notice. Not very courteously done'. That was all that Wavell recorded in a personal journal about his leaving the viceroy's position, a major development vitally affecting his future; Wavell's reaction is that of a soldier; stoic, almost dour, taking good with the bad without breaking stride. (For a text of this letter from Attlee and Wavell's reply, please see Appendix VIII.)

On 20 February 1947, the British government's White Paper on the constitutional future of India was presented by the prime minister in the House of Commons. Introducing it in the House, Attlee said: 'His Majesty's Government desire to hand over their responsibility to authorities established by a Constitution, approved by all parties in India in accordance with the Cabinet Mission's Plan, but unfortunately there

PARTITION BOUNDARIES IN THE PUNJAB

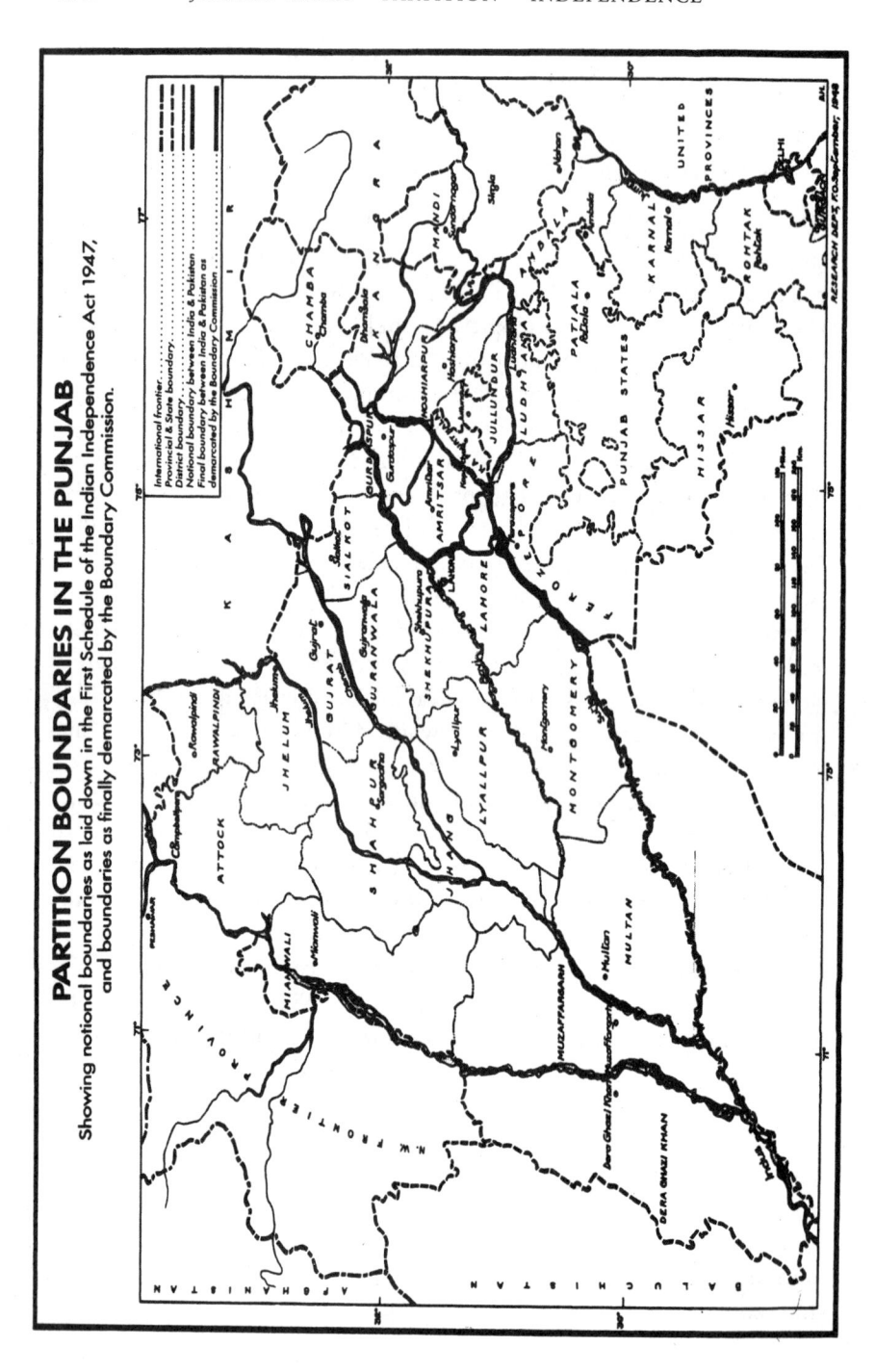

Showing notional boundaries as laid down in the First Schedule of the Indian Independence Act 1947, and boundaries as finally demarcated by the Boundary Commission.

PARTITION BOUNDARIES IN BENGAL AND ASSAM

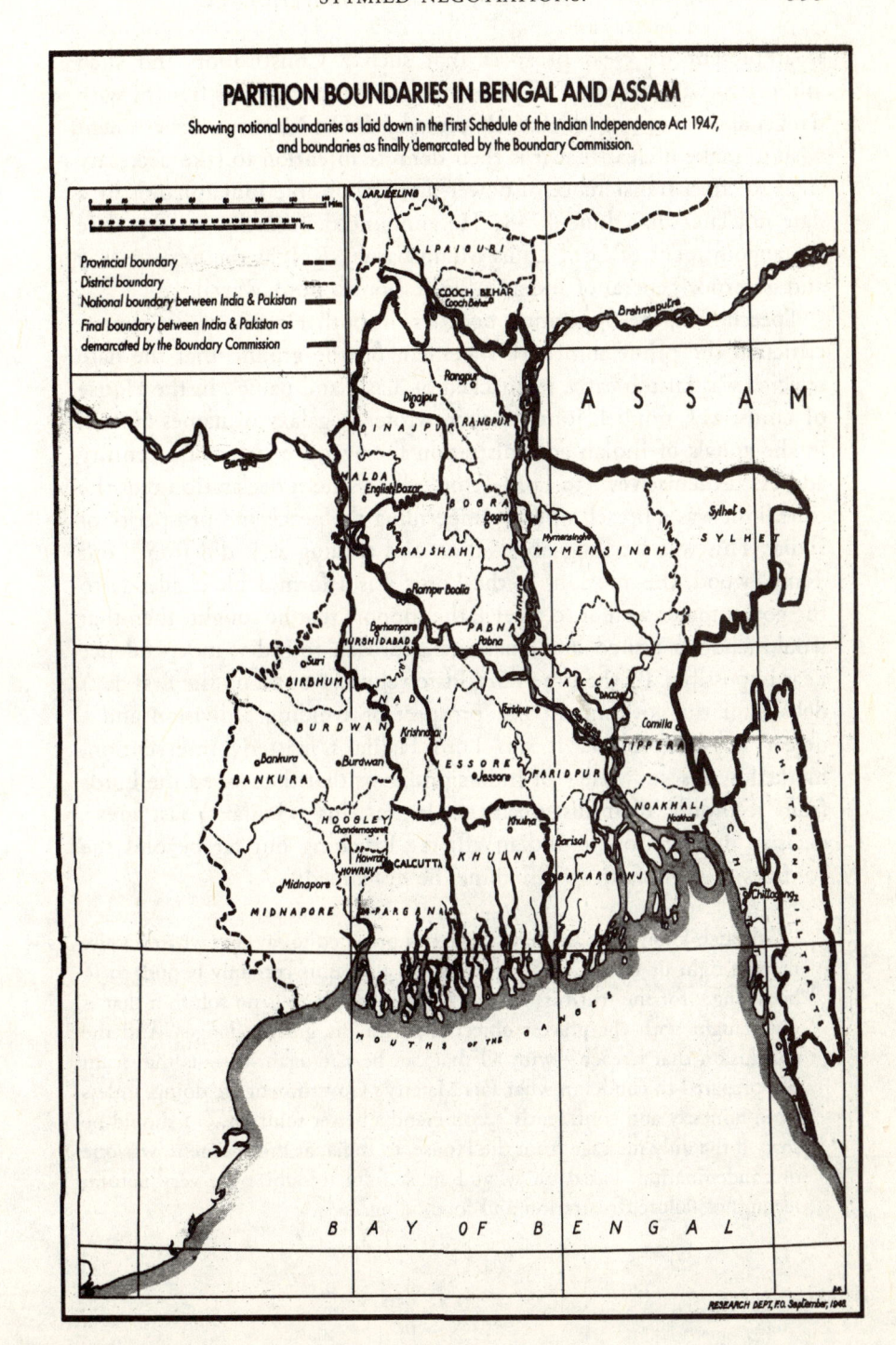

Showing notional boundaries as laid down in the First Schedule of the Indian Independence Act 1947, and boundaries as finally demarcated by the Boundary Commission.

is at present no clear prospect that such a Constitution and such authorities will emerge. The present state of uncertainty is fraught with danger and cannot be indefinitely prolonged. His Majesty's Government wish to make it clear that it is their definite intention to take necessary steps to effect transference of power into responsible Indian hands by a date not later than June 1948.' He announced, formally, on this date the appointment of Lord Louis Mountbatten, RN, as the next viceroy and governor-general of India, in succession to Lord Wavell.

Speeches by the opposition benches, in both Houses of Parliament criticized the prime minister's statement on the ground that the date selected was far too early, it smacked of 'haste and panic'. In the House of Lords, as Campbell Johnson then wrote: 'A galaxy of names famous in the annals of Indian administration for over a quarter of a century addressed themselves...to Lord Templewood's stern declaration that the time limit was a breach of faith imperilling the peace and prosperity of India'. This was a telling observation and coming as it did from Lord Templewood, this motion, in the Lords was a formidable challenge to the government; were it to receive the support that he sought, then that would render a 'united, and a national approach' to India's independence near impossible. By the time Lord Listowel had wound up the first day's debate for the government the 'prospect of avoiding a division and a defeat' appeared bleak. It was Lord Halifax's masterly intervention, marked by his knowledge of India's problems that then saved the Lords from recording their disagreement. It was 'his (Halifax's) last great, decisive intervention in Indian affairs'. Reaching out far beyond the confines of party faith or discipline, he declaimed:

'With such knowledge as I have, I am not prepared to say that whatever else may be right or wrong, this step must on all counts certainly be judged to be wrong...for the truth is that for India today there is no solution that is not fraught with the gravest objection, with the gravest danger. And the conclusion that I reach—with all that can be said against it—is that I am not prepared to condemn what His Majesty's Government are doing, unless I can honestly and confidently recommend a better solution.... I should be sorry if the only message from the House, to India, at this moment, was one of condemnation, based on what I must fully recognize are very natural feelings of failure, frustration and foreboding.'

Alan Campbell Johnson thereafter records how 'Lord Samuel told me afterwards that it was the most persuasive speech he had ever heard delivered in the House of Lords, and that its impact was such that many Conservative Peers who, before he rose, had firmly decided to vote against the Government, changed their minds while he was speaking and fell in with his appeal to Templewood to spare the House the necessity of going to a Division'. The rest of the debate was an anti-climax. The tide of opinion had turned, and Templewood, while maintaining his criticisms, duly withdrew his motion.

Thereafter on 5 March 1947, the Commons debated the issue. Records are almost elegiac when describing the debate '...the opening of the two-day Debate in the House of Commons was obviously a great Parliamentary occasion...Cripps' speeches always so closely reasoned, were on this occasion delivered with great authority and emphasis.

'...He [Cripps] was at pains to stress that it was administratively and militarily out of the question to stay on beyond 1948. Otherwise, he laid no special emphasis on the time limit, and he made no reference whatever to Lord Wavell. This last omission was undoubtedly a pity, as it tended to confirm the ill-disposed gossip about serious differences of opinion between the Government and the returning Viceroy.

'When Churchill resumed the Debate on Thursday, 6th March,' 1947 recorded Campbell Johnson, 'we were regaled with the long-awaited firework display. Over the years Churchill has remained very loyal to his pet aversions, and what may perhaps best be termed his Indian invective, proclaims probably the most rigid and unbending of all his opinions upon the public issues of our time.'

'He started off by taking his stand on the Cripps' Mission of 1942. Although the offer had not been accepted at the time, both sides of the House were still bound by it. He denounced the present plan as involving grave departures from the "scope and integrity" of its principles.' There was at last a reference in this debate to Wavell, but it was far from cordial. 'The Viceroy, Lord Wavell, has been dismissed, I hold no brief for Lord Wavell. He has been the willing or unwilling agent of the Government in all the errors and mistakes into which they have been led.' But Churchill continued to assert that he did not know 'why Wavell had been cast aside at this juncture, and to press for a personal statement from him on his return'.

As for the new viceroy, Churchill enquired with biting sarcasm. 'Is he to make a new effort to restore the situation, or is it merely Operation Scuttle, on which he and other distinguished officers have been dispatched?...I am bound to say the whole thing wears the aspect of an attempt by the Government to make use of brilliant war figures in order to cover up a melancholy and disastrous transaction.'

Churchill then entered the field of prophecy. 'India is to be subjected not merely to partition but to fragmentation and to haphazard fragmentation. ...In handing over the Government of India to these so-called political classes, we are handing over to men of straw, of whom in a few years no trace will remain. This Government by their latest action, this fifteen months' limitation, cripple the new Viceroy and destroy the prospect of even going through the business on the agenda which has to be settled.' And then that funereal conclusion: 'Many have defended Britain against her foes, none can defend her against herself.... But, at least, let us not add—by shameful flight, by a premature hurried scuttle—at least, let us not add to the pangs of sorrow so many of us feel, the taint and smear of shame.' Marvellous, resonant, Gibbonesque elocution, but alas so greatly in error.

Prime Minister Attlee's reasoned reply and Labour's staunch, unwavering support for the Motion carried it in the House of Commons, too. The Independence of India Act of 1947 was adopted on 18 July 1947.

Events now began to roll faster, unstoppably tragic in consequence and weighted, as they were, by human folly; therefore, relentless in their momentum towards a destructive and death-filled partition. Even the most ardent supporters of an undivided India had begun to now seek partition for they sought relief from the torments of the past many years; in the process offering many gratuitous suggestions, impractical and unrealistic assessments. Sardar Patel on 4 March 1947 wrote to Kanji Dwarkadas, giving voice to his ideas:[13] '...I am not, however, taking such a gloomy view...as you....Before next June, the Constitution must be ready and if the League insists on Pakistan, the only alternative is the division of the Punjab and Bengal. They cannot have Punjab as a whole or Bengal without civil war. I do not think that the British Government will agree to division. In the end, they will see the wisdom of handing over the reins of government to the strongest party. Even if they do not do so, they will not help the minority in securing or maintaining division and a strong centre with the whole of India except Eastern Bengal and a part of the Punjab, Sindh and Baluchistan, enjoying full autonomy under that Centre, will be so powerful that the remaining portions will eventually come in'.

This is a revealing letter for quite apart from how far off from the mark Patel was in respect of so many of his projections about the future, he was also for the first time, even if by implication, accepting partition on condition of a division of the Punjab and Bengal. This letter was written just three weeks before Mountbatten arrived in India and Patel foresaw, (rather futilely, in retrospect) that the 'British would not want a division of the country'. Four days later, on 8 March 1947, the Congress Working Committee adopted a Resolution, with the full support of Jawaharlal Nehru and Vallabhbhai Patel, which among other things said:

'...These tragic events [in Punjab} have demonstrated that there can be no settlement of the problems in the Punjab by violence and coercion and that no agreement based on coercion can last. Therefore, it is necessary to find a way out which involves the least amount of compulsion. This would necessitate a division of the Punjab into two provinces, so that the predominantly Muslim part may be separated from the predominantly non-Muslim part. The Working Committee commend this solution which should work to the advantage of all the communities concerned, and lessen friction and fear and suspicion of each other. The Committee earnestly appeal to the people of the Punjab to put an end to the killing and brutality that are going on, and to face the tragic situation, determined to find a solution which does not involve compulsion of any major group and which will effectively remove the causes of friction.'[14]

Earlier Nehru had gone to the extent of recommending a trifurcation of Punjab into: 'A Muslim majority area; a Sikh dominated area; and, an area of rather mixed population.' It is difficult to accept that Nehru had offered this solution seriously or was it more an insidious design to further narrow the funnel of Jinnah's options?

The date of the adoption of this Resolution by the Congress was unfortunate for it was when Gandhi was away on his great healing mission in Bihar, Maulana Azad was also absent. Patel and Nehru had both known, all along, that the two absentees would oppose the Resolution. It was, in fact, about three weeks later that Gandhi finally through a letter, asked Nehru the reason for this Resolution.[15] He wrote simultaneously to Patel asking him to explain the Resolution. Patel was the first to reply: 'It has been difficult to explain to you the Resolution about the Punjab. It was adopted after the deepest deliberation. Nothing has been done in a hurry or without full thought. That you had expressed your views against it, we learnt only through the papers. But you are of course entitled to say what you feel right.' Nehru's reply, which followed a day later was even more lame. 'About our proposal to divide Punjab, this flows naturally from our previous discussions'.[16]

This Resolution was a fundamental change in the Congress party's stand and strategy. Mountbatten, who had by then assumed charge as viceroy, sent for Patel at once, jubilantly assessing that Patel by accepting the division of Punjab had implicitly recognized the principle of India's partition, too. Jawaharlal Nehru's opposition to partition had also been whittled down by now. Within a month of Lord Mountbatten's arrival in India, on 20 March 1947, Jawaharlal Nehru, until then a vocal opponent of partition had become a committed advocate of it.

This Resolution amounted to an acceptance of Jinnah's Two-Nation Theory, that destructive basis of fracturing India's geography, society, and polity. It was also a sad comment on the Congress party, an organisation that had just a little over thirty years back, opposed even the partition of Bengal; that very Congress was now proposing a partition, effectively of India. Another resolution, however, invited the Muslim League to nominate its representatives to meet the representatives of the Congress 'in order to consider the situation that has arisen and to devise means to meet it.'[17] This second resolution appeared, therefore, as really an ironic afterthought to the first. Though one dearly wishes that even at this late stage Jinnah had accepted this Congress invitation, but a nagging question surfaces: 'to what purpose? Besides, Jinnah was by now so embittered by the Congress' double-talk on the grouping formula of the Cabinet Mission's Plan that he just ignored the Congress invitation for consultations. On 21 April 1947,[18] Nehru then openly declared that those 'who demanded Pakistan could have it', but on the condition that they did not coerce other unwilling parts of India to join such a Pakistan. This was rather an incomprehensible and an unreal caveat; why did Nehru do this? Unless his fears of 'groupings' had so persuaded him of the coercive potential of that measure that he felt compelled to place all possible hurdles on the path of it.

For, from here onwards, the partition of India, already a forgone conclusion became an objective reality, only the detail of it remained—when, where and how will this partition be carried out? And where will the dividing line run, this no one knew, and none could explain. Addressing the Constituent Assembly its president, Dr Rajendra Prasad, on 28 April 1947, said that the 'House should be prepared not only for a division of India, but also for a division of some Provinces as well.'[19]

On 2 May 1947, Lord Ismay and George Abell left for London with the first Mountbatten plan for India's independence. This Draft Plan was in fact an adaptation of the Cabinet Mission Plan—to transfer power unilaterally, without the willing consent of the party leaders, and with a federal rather than a strong central government.

What followed thereafter was sadly like comic opera: India's independence was being reduced to farcical casualness. Even while Ismay and Abell were in London, V.P. Menon, the reforms commissioner and advisor to the viceroy recapitulated a talk he had had with Patel, in the Viceregal Lodge, in Simla,[20] it was about the un-workability of the Cabinet Mission Plan. 'I told Patel that he had better face the fact that Jinnah had the support of influential British opinion in his claim for Pakistan, and more importantly, he was supported by most of the high officers of the Army in India'.[21] 'He assured me,' Menon later told the viceroy, 'that if power could be transferred at once on the basis of Dominion Status, he would use his influence to see that Congress accepted it.' Menon, in Patel's presence had then dictated an outline of the plan and sent it by special messenger to the secretary of state for India—omitting only that Patel had seen and approved it. Patel never heard anything further about this afterwards, but Mountbatten was 'ecstatic after hearing of the episode from Menon'.[22] On 10 May 1947, while Nehru was at Simla, Mountbatten had an occasion of discussing V.P. Menon's partition plan with him. The viceroy underlined the simplicity and the importance of it by pointing out that with such straightforward arrangements there would be no need to wait until June 1948, to hand over power. It could be passed on the moment the Cabinet in Britain agreed to the scheme. It is not clear as to whether Nehru actually agreed or only 'seemed' to agree.

The next logical step would then have been a formal adoption of this, as the accepted formula for transferring power. However, that could not be, for there already was another Plan in existence, which was then already in London, taken there by Ismay for the approval of the British Cabinet. It was upon this that the viceroy was resting his hopes for a settlement of the deadlock and the final handing over of power. 'Why then did Mountbatten allow this rather ad hoc Menon plan, as an additionality, to be put out, on a semi-official basis for a formal discussion, and also to be recorded so in the Viceregal Minutes with Nehru? This was immature, clearly asking for trouble, and that is exactly what followed.

Mountbatten's own Plan, the one which Ismay had carried, had also been cabled back from London on 10 May 1947, containing some minor amendments suggested by the Cabinet, without having any of the principles altered. That same evening at an after-dinner session, Mountbatten on an impulse shared this cable with Nehru, who upon going through the papers was aghast and would simply not accept this 'half approved' Plan. Things thereafter, moved at a rather dramatic speed between Simla and London. One of the cables sent by Mountbatten to Attlee said, in effect: 'the Draft Plan which you have approved is hereby cancelled. Please standby for the revised Plan'.[23] By 6 p.m. on 11 May 1947, Menon had finished the last sentence of his Draft Plan and was subsequently informed the same evening that Nehru had accepted. It had taken Menon exactly four hours to draw up the Plan changing the face of India, also that of the world. It is deeply troubling to even acknowledge the question(s) that surface: Is that all it took to break the ancient unities of India?

On 18 May 1947, Mountbatten and Menon left for London, Ismay and Abell already there, fought long and hard against this Menon Plan; they still preferred their own, but Attlee and his Cabinet, accepted the Menon Plan.[24]

Gandhi–Jinnah Meet

For almost the last time Gandhi and Jinnah met in New Delhi on 6 May 1947, and as had happened so often earlier, parted in disagreement. A communiqué issued by Jinnah, with Gandhi's approval, amongst other things read: 'We discussed two matters. One was the question of division of India into Pakistan and Hindustan. Mr Gandhi does not accept the principle of division. He thinks that division is not inevitable, whereas in my opinion not only is Pakistan inevitable but it is the only practical solution of India's political problem. The second matter which we discussed was a letter which we both had signed jointly appealing to the people to maintain peace and we both have come to the conclusion that we must do our best in our respective spheres so that, that appeal of ours is carried out and we will make every effort for this purpose'.[25]

A strategic step-by-step withdrawal would certainly had reduced, if not totally eliminated, the possibility of large-scale violence, the kind that India eventually went through before, during and after partition. But that was not to be, for within weeks of Mountbatten's arrival, serious talks had commenced on how to partition India. By 3 June 1947, the Muslim League, the Congress and the Akalis all had agreed that India was to be cut into pieces. On the prospects that India then faced Sir Chimanlal Setalvad predicted: 'This division of India [has]…laid the foundations of interminable quarrels and chaos which would bring untold suffering to generations yet unborn'.[26] Sir Chimanlal, however, put the principal blame for partition on the Congress double-talk on the grouping formula of the Cabinet Mission.

The end game, too, of the Cabinet Mission was now finally over, all played out, the pieces dispersed, the board, finally packed. Now only the curtain on a united and independent India remained to be formally rung down. Problems of the departing British, their collapsing Empire became predominant; partition became just an internalized detail to rapidly be got over with. British withdrawal now focused almost entirely on self-preservation, a quick getaway, orderly if possible, but any how, even disorderly if that is what it was to be; but 'exit quickly before total chaos' overtook the occupiers; that was all that mattered. The mood was panicky, predominantly of retreating quickly as in a badly planned and led withdrawal after defeat in battle. Future pensions, where to live in a war ravaged Britain, and how? The present, in an India that was tearing itself apart looked uninviting, but then so did the prospects of bleak and cold retirement in distant *vilayat*;[27] that war ravaged home. The Koh-i-noor[28] did still remain adoring the crown of their majesties, but its lustre was now no more, the flawless purity of its water had drained. The Empire itself now became a redundancy, an anachronism. The British withdrawal from India announced the end of the Imperial Age, the twentieth century brought it about.

For Mohammad Ali Jinnah, now the *Quaid-i-Azam* of a shortly to emerge Pakistan, his political journey from being an ambassador of

Hindu-Muslim unity to the principal architect of Pakistan had also reached its last terminal; Jinnah was at the final junction of his life. We travel with him now, on that final lap, in the concluding part: 'In Retrospect', but before that we are yet to witness the conclusion, in this stadium of time, of Viceroy Mountbatten's 'last *chukkah*', this had yet to be played to its finish. That, too, in the succeeding chapter. It is time now to bid farewell to Field Marshal Lord Wavell, the departing soldier-viceroy of India.

THE DISMISSAL OF LORD WAVELL

Penderel Moon in his biography of Wavell wrote in 1973:

'Wavell...urged the British Government to fix a date for withdrawal and to make timely arrangements [for] an orderly retreat, and when he found that they preferred...to hope for the best and scuttle if these hopes were not realized, he pressed his advice with a blunt insistence that was, no doubt, partly responsible for his dismissal. In the end the British Government agreed to fix a date, and took credit for "this bold and courageous move" that he had for months been vainly advocating'.

And so, the wheel had come full circle. Attlee and his Cabinet were the real defeatists and were guilty of the 'shameful and ignoble scuttle' with which Attlee had unfairly charged Wavell, a scuttle which Wavell had done his best to avoid. For as far back as 30 May 1946, Wavell had advised HMG that: 'A policy of immediate withdrawal of our authority, influence and power from India, unconditionally would, to my mind be disastrous and even more fatal to the tradition and morale of our people and to our position in the world than a policy of repression. I could not consent to carry out such a policy. It remains to examine whether any middle course between "repression" and "scuttle" can be found, if we are unable to persuade Indians to agree to a peaceful settlement of their Constitution'.[29]

That middle course was his Breakdown Plan. Again, in a note dated 2 December 1946, for discussion with the prime minister and other ministries in England, Wavell set out four courses open to the government: (A) 'repression', which he had himself ruled out; (B) fresh negotiations which was not [now] a practical policy; (C) to surrender to Congress as a majority party. 'I do not think this honourable or a wise policy; it will end British rule in India in discredit and eventually an ignominious scuttle or dismissal by the Congress. There is no statesmanship or generosity in the Congress'; and (D) to announce a withdrawal from India—as proposed in the Breakdown Plans and reproduced in full in Appendix X.

But it was too late. The Labour government had neither the stomach nor the will to stay with the logic of Wavell's gradualism as proposed in his Breakdown Plan, a plan that would certainly have minimized the killings that followed the scuttle. Attlee's justification for that rather graceless 'withdrawal of a Viceroy of India' is not tenable. Besides, the Labour government too, wanted to exit India quickly, ironically exactly what Mountbatten later proposed.

Amongst the concluding acts of Wavell's viceroyalty were to send his final report to HM the king; which he submitted on 24 February 1947. He then also broadcast his farewell message to India over All-India Radio on 21 March 1947. Both these are worthy of being reproduced in full. The first, an objective and analytical summation of his term as viceroy; the broadcast a moving farewell to a land, its people and its soldiers, to all of whom he had given so much affection.

To His Majesty the King, the Viceroy's House, New Delhi, 24 February 1947: The Final Report

'Our power in India has always depended on prestige rather than on numbers; and it is the decline in our prestige rather than the lack of numbers that has reduced our control in India to its present state of something approaching impotence. The damage to our prestige was begun in the First World War and the years that followed it. In this last war it has had of course still ruder shocks by our loss of Singapore and of Burma; and our subsequent recapture of these did little really to re-establish it.

'Politically, the Cripps Mission in 1942 marked a stage in our retrocession from power which it was never possible to retrace. Our repression of the 1942 Rebellion showed that our prestige and power were still high, when we chose to exercise them; but they were definitely in danger, since events showed how easy it was for agitators to inflame the mobs and to make ordered government impossible over large parts of the country. It seems remarkable to me how even at the present time, when our power has been so greatly reduced, the momentum of our prestige still enables us to influence events to the extent that we do'.[30]

TEXT OF LORD WAVELL'S BROADCAST FROM ALL-INDIA RADIO, NEW DELHI, 2 MARCH

'This is a short personal message to the people of India to say good-bye and farewell—God be with you and fare you well—as those words mean. They come from my heart for I owe much to India where I have spent more than thirteen years of my life. As a child I played and grew up for two and a half years in the Nilgiri Hills where the sun and air of a fine climate gave my body a good start in life. As a young subaltern I spent five years in Northern India and they were certainly some of the best years of my life. They were devoted perhaps more to sport than to hard work or to hard thinking but you learn the elements of my profession of soldiering in a land which has always bred fine soldiers. In those years I came closest to knowledge of the common Indian people. I learnt enough of the language to speak with the villagers where I camped and shot, with my Shikaris in the hills of Kashmir where I was several times alone with them for many weeks, and with the soldiers of India with whom I served. My first independent command on active service was a detachment of 33 Indian soldiers: a V.C.O., 8 Sikhs, 8 Punjabi Mussalmans, 8 Dogras and 8 Pathans—all magnificent men. I also acted as transport officer to an Indian mountain battery for several weeks' march, and a friend in the Royal Engineers used to allow me to come out sometimes with his company of Madras Sappers and Miners. So that I left India with some knowledge of and a great affection for Indian soldiers and Indian peasants.

'During two world wars it was my fortune to see much of the prowess of the Indian soldier and to profit by it.

'My last service in India has been the longest, two years as Commander-in-Chief and nearly three and a half years as Viceroy. They have been years of hard work and heavy responsibility. I shall be glad if I have during them done anything to repay India my debt for the five years I enjoyed as a young man and for the skill and gallantry of the Indian Army, which served under me through a number of campaigns, in success or failure, in good times or bad, but always with the value and endurance of true warriors.

'I am conscious of the mistakes I have made in these years, but I hope you will know that I have always tried to work for the welfare of India's inhabitants and for the advancement of India towards self rule.

'I am a soldier and my first words of farewell must be to the soldiers of India, in admiration and in gratitude. I believe that the stability of the Indian Army may perhaps be a deciding factor in the future of India. It has shown how all communities may work together to meet a common danger with comradeship and self-devotion. To all those with whom I have worked in these last years, within or without—Rulers of States, Ministers, officials and non-officials—I give deep-felt thanks for their kindness, friendship and support. I would say a special word of gratitude and encouragement to the men of the Service, at the centre and in the Provinces. I know and sympathize with their difficulty in these times of stress. I know to what strains they have been subjected and I know with what courage and hard work they have met them. They have been very devoted servants of India.

'My successor is known to many of you personally and to all by reputation as a great leader in war and an ardent supporter of progress. I can assure you of his goodwill towards India and of his vigour in showing it.

'You have hard, dangerous and difficult years ahead, but you will overcome them. I have always believed steadfastly in the future of India. I thank you and wish you good fortune. Goodbye, and may the world go well with you.'

9

MOUNTBATTEN VICEROYALTY: THE END OF THE RAJ

23 March 1947–15 August 1947

Field Marshal Lord Alanbrooke, Churchill's chief of the Imperial General Staff during the challenging years of the Second World War has, in his *War Diaries 1939-45*, given fascinating sketches of the principal cast of those years. His rendering of Mountbatten's character is masterly, in concision, acuity of observation and wit: 'Mountbatten as a great grandson of Queen Victoria...rose to command his own ship (the appropriately named *Daring*) in 1934. The outbreak of war saw him Captain of the Kelly. During eighteen months in command he almost capsized in high seas, collided with another destroyer, was mined once, torpedoed twice, and finally sunk by enemy aircraft.... His time as Chief of Combined Operations (CCO) was marred by the wasteful disaster of the Dieppe raid, for which he must shoulder some of the blame.... He was appointed to South East Asia Command (SEAC). There, thanks to a number of talented subordinates, he was able to preside over the eventual triumph of the Imperial Armies. In the opposed seaborne invasion of the Malayan peninsula, which could have been the culmination of his career thus far—the invading troops sank to their waists in wet sand—[their total loss] was prevented by the end of war....

'His time as last Viceroy of India...was fully as dramatic;' and as the quote goes on to say, 'With the possible exception of Montgomery, he was [the] most talented self publicist among the Senior British Commanders, with an instinctive grasp of how to enhance his popularity. This was most clearly seen in the film version of the sinking of the *Kelly, In Which We Serve,* featuring Noel Coward as Mountbatten, which he watched twelve times on its first release.'[1] In this same work by

Alanbrooke, Wavell is described as an '...extremely, possibly overly intelligent General...in terms of his taciturnity, Wavell was a Commander in the Douglas Haig mould'. Woodrow Wyatt reminisced in *Confessions of an Optimist* about seeing Mountbatten before he left for India, and found him chiefly concerned with what he 'should wear on arrival'? Writes Wyatt: 'They're all a bit left wing, aren't they? Hadn't I better land in ordinary day clothes?' Mountbatten enquired, and was delighted when I said, 'No, no, you are the last Viceroy. You are a royal. You must wear your grandest uniform and all your decorations and be met in full panoply and with all the works. Otherwise they will feel slighted.' And that is what he did, to everyone's pleasure.'[2]

H.V. Hodson has left comments on this viceroyalty, amongst which are: 'The first point to make about Mountbatten's viceroyalty is that he wrote his own ticket. The announcement of 20 February 1947 was not dictated by him, but it was agreed word by word with him and it arose out of the conversations that he had with Mr Atlee when the latter invited him at the end of 1946, to go out to India and, in effect end the British Raj.'

Equally important, Mountbatten caused to be written into his mandate that if no constitution had been worked by June 1948: 'H.M.G. would have to consider whether to hand over power as a whole to some form of central Government for British India, or in some areas to the existing provincial Governments, or in such other way as may seem most reasonable and in the best interests of the Indian people'. Such a comprehensive list of alternatives covering nearly all contingencies was without doubt the logical corollary of having a fixed date of departure. More, by so spelling out the contingencies, a public and an open license for the creation of Pakistan had also been announced by HMG.

Philip Ziegler recounts Mountbatten's arrival in India and Nehru's reaction to it. 'There is a legend that Nehru was so struck by the air of authority with which Mountbatten spoke that a few days after his arrival in India Nehru asked him: "Have you by some miracle got plenipotentiary powers?" "Suppose I have", Mountbatten [responded] "What difference would it make?" to which Nehru answered: "Why then, you will succeed where all others have failed". Whatever Mountbatten may or may not have said to Nehru about "plenipotentiary" powers, it is quite clear that no such powers had been conferred on him'. As Ziegler has himself, pointed out: 'Nor, if by... "plenipotentiary powers" is meant the liberty to act at one's discretion without referring to a home government (there is nothing else it can mean, if it is to have any real significance), did Mountbatten avail himself of such freedom. On the contrary, not only did he submit to London his draft plan for a settlement but when he needed to modify it he himself flew to London to present his case'.

Mountbatten had been given freedom to act on his initiative, as the man on the spot, which had consistently been denied to Wavell. The Attlee government, broadly speaking, gave 'Mountbatten whatever he wanted', and only because they desperately wanted out; India had to be 'vacated'—was their highest priority then.

Ziegler, Mountbatten's admiring biographer has also painted a word picture of the last viceroy: 'His faults were on the grandest scale. His vanity, though child-like, was monstrous, his ambition unbridled. The truth, in his hands, was swiftly converted from what it was to what it should have been. He sought to rewrite history with cavalier indifference to the facts to magnify his own achievements.'

Sadly, India's last viceroy did prefer modifying truth in order to magnify his own achievements. Ziegler's picture of Mountbatten as viceroy of India is very disturbing, for as the last viceroy upon him devolved the power to decide the future of the millions of an undivided India; that is also why it is so profoundly unsettling to recognize that India's future then lay in the hands of a person who failed to distinguish between truth and untruth. 'Open diplomacy was, so far as possible, the order of the day yet openness did not exclude *a degree of manipulation, even chicanery,* which would have been inconceivable to either of his immediate predecessors. Mountbatten was well aware that certain of his advisers felt that his tactics sometimes verged on the unethical, but he believed that *sleight of hand* was justifiable....; *the lie direct was to be avoided, the lie circumstantial...acceptable.* Ian Scott, his deputy private secretary, remembered the viceroy looking up after proposing a certain course of action and catching the expression on his and Abell's faces: 'I know what you're thinking. Wavell would never have done it. Well, I'm not Wavell, and I will!".'[3] (Emphasis added)

But once we accept, as the candid passages quoted above from Alanbrooke to Zeigler persuade us to, that Mountbatten as viceroy preferred 'falsehood to truth for his own glorification', his credibility as a witness to the part he played in the transfer of power is gravely impaired. His statements about what he and others said and did become suspect, and cannot be accepted without independent 'corroboration and scrutiny'.[4] I cannot then easily accept the last viceroy's views, given his own 'monstrous vanity', when he or the other members of his staff speak or write, for example of Jinnah's vanity.

The last viceroy, modestly describing his working style informs that he 'went into them', he surely means his work but being Mountbatten he is informing us about the principal Indian personalities of those times; in his own modest words, 'with the most enormous confidence in my ability to persuade people to do the right thing, not because I am persuasive so much as because I have the knack of being able to present things in the most favourable light'. All this leaves us speechless in wonderment until Mountbatten later recalls: 'I tried every trick I could play, I used every appeal I could imagine, to shake Jinnah's resolve.... Nothing would. There was no argument that could move him from his consuming determination to realize the dream of Pakistan'. Mohammad Ali Jinnah was probably the only man he [did] not succeed in 'tricking', but he fully appreciated Jinnah's near unique 'importance for the future of India'. He wrote home: 'It was clear that he was the man who held the key to the whole situation....' Yet, as we go through the records of those confidential talks there is little evidence of the skill of persuasion that Mountbatten self-extolls as his special attribute, and which he might have been expected to exercise with special care upon, admittedly, so crucial a figure. The first interview left an impression that was not dispelled by subsequent meetings. Mountbatten found Jinnah 'frigid, haughty and disdainful'.[5] One wonders what else the Quaid-i-Azam could have been in the presence of this great-grandson or whatever of *mallika* Victoria?

Mountbatten's meeting with Churchill cited in the *Transfer of Power*[6] merits our attention somewhat out of turn as this took place on 27 May 1947. To start with, Churchill enquired of Mountbatten 'whether [he] had received a letter from Nehru accepting Dominion status if power was transferred this year'. Mountbatten recalling the interview, records: 'I replied in the affirmative and added that I had given a copy to the Prime Minister. I pointed out that I had been unable to obtain a similar written assurance from Mr Jinnah. [To which] Mr Churchill expressed great surprise: "By God", he said, "he is the one man who cannot do without British help". I pointed out that Mr Jinnah's methods of procedure could not be predicted by logic, and I told him that I must have a definite line of action to pursue in the event of his refusing to make up his mind about Dominion status. I told him that I proposed to inform Mr Jinnah that in that case we could go ahead with the transfer of power this year on a Dominion status basis for Hindustan, with an option for Dominion status to be taken up [later] at any time by Pakistan. He told me that the Conservative Party might not agree to the passing of legislation under those terms, and that he might, in fact, have to oppose this. I then asked him if he would advise me how I should proceed if Jinnah was intransigent'. According to Mountbatten, Churchill reflected upon this 'for a long time and finally said: "To begin with you must threaten. Take away all British officers. Give them military units without British officers. Make it clear to them how impossible it would be to run Pakistan without British help".'7

This account, certainly questions two myths, and as Seervai comments with impeccable logic: First, that it was a benevolent Labour government which, out of the goodness of its heart and its love of freedom, transferred power to India; secondly, that Wavell, who had persisted in asking HMG to make a declaration about the withdrawal from India by a specified date, was a 'defeatist'. As we have seen, when it became known that Wavell was leaving India, Azad issued a statement paying glowing tributes to Wavell's services to India, and castigating Attlee's government lacking courage, for which India paid the 'price of partition, or, at any rate, the price of more than 6,00,000 people massacred and about 1,50,00,000 uprooted from their homes and compelled to migrate in disorder and great distress'.

Wavell and Mountbatten 'were in reality different in temperament and style as if they were almost beings of different species....Mountbatten was flamboyant; Wavell, reserved, reflective and an introvert as candidly in his *Diary* he admits "I have not that convinced certainly of my wisdom that Monty (Field Marshal Montgomery) has, for instance...." [31 December 1946] Wavell was innately modest, courteous and fair. Recording his views about Mountbatten's appointment he had written, "no doubt he would be more able in this job than I have been". Wavell was an author, a biographer, a historian, attributes that one simply cannot adorn Mountbatten with. Wavell has a characteristically amusing entry in his *Journal,* bringing out a fundamental difference between them.

'December 7, 1943, M.B. (Mountbatten) dined and we had a cinema—*Casablanca,* a typical film story of the sentimental-thriller type. The others seemed to like it but I was neither touched nor thrilled and said so to M.B. afterwards. He is a great film fan and was horrified. He apparently has one most nights—"so much easier and quicker than reading a novel" he urged: "But I seldom read novels", I said. "But what do you read then for relaxation, from your writing it is obvious that you do read sometimes". [!] I replied that I read biographies and poetry rather than novels. "But don't you like musical films?" "I fear I am not musical", "But you don't need to be musical to enjoy musical films, with just cheerful songs and dancing". He is still youthful and I am afraid received the impression that I was a cheerless kill-joy not to like films'.

Wavell looked upon art and poetry and thought them as the real mainsprings of life, his character, personality and actions were deeply rooted here, commanding admiration and respect from all. Mountbatten had no such roots. Even when he took part in great events, he was rooted only in himself, his own real or imagined glory and his royal descent. But these are short-lived assets. Few would say of Mountbatten what Attlee said about Wavell: 'It (your telegram) is in keeping with the high principles on which you have always acted....'[8]

Soon after he had assumed office, Mountbatten began meeting the principal Indian leaders. The first, on 1 April 1947 was Mahatma Gandhi, who started by giving the new viceroy his views on the origin of Hindu-Muslim animosity, and though, 'he did not hold the British responsible for its origin, he said their policy of Divide and Rule had kept the tension very much alive, and that the Viceroy should now reap what his predecessors had deliberately sown'. 'He urged me', Mountbatten records 'whatever happened to have the courage to see the truth and act by it'.

It is in this meeting that Gandhi made his startling proposal of letting Jinnah be the prime minister and form the government of a United India. This is how it has been recorded in the Mountbatten Papers. 'Finally, he gave me the first brief summary of the solution which he wishes me to adopt: "Mr Jinnah should forthwith be invited to form the Central Interim Government with members of the Muslim League. This Government [should] operate under the Viceroy in the way the present Interim Government [does]...Any difficulty experienced through Congress having a majority in the Assembly to be overcome by their able advocacy of the measures they wished to introduce". I need not say that this solution coming at this time staggered me. I asked "What would Mr Jinnah say to such a proposal"? The reply was "If you tell him I am the author he will reply 'Wily Gandhi'." I then remarked "And I presume Mr Jinnah will be right"? To which he replied with great fervour: "No, I am entirely sincere in my suggestion." I did however obtain Mr Gandhi's permission to discuss the matter with Pandit Nehru and Maulana Azad, in strict confidence, the next time they came to see me'. This talk with Gandhi did not end here, it continued the next day, 2 April 1947, and lasted for a clear two hours or so. About which Mountbatten has recorded how he 'twitted him [Gandhi] that he really desired me to form a Central Government run by Congress, to whom I would turn over power, and that the preliminary offer to Jinnah was merely a manoeuvre. He assured me [again] with burning sincerity that this was so far from being the case that he then and there volunteered to place his whole services at my disposal in trying to get the Jinnah Government through first, by exercising his influence with Congress to accept it, and secondly by touring the length and breadth of the country getting all the peoples of India to accept the decision. He convinced me of his sincerity, and I told him so. He [also] agreed that I should discuss this plan with Maulana Azad and Nehru'. And so this continued until 'Finally, he said that he proposed also to discuss it with those two and with Mr Kripalani. He agreed as to the supreme importance of complete secrecy, particularly as far as the Press were concerned. He asked if he might quote me as being in favour of this plan, to which I replied that the most he could say was that I was very interested by it, but that I would require an assurance from some of the other leaders that they considered it capable of being implemented before I would commit myself to its support'.

Having 'gone into' Gandhi, as Mountbatten inelegantly records, it was now time for the viceroy to attend to his meeting with the man who held the key to the whole situation, whom Mountbatten's memoirs recount as 'frigid, haughty and disdainful', the man with matching vanity, Mohammad Ali Jinnah. The flair, but not entirely the charm, failed him here with Jinnah. The latter did regard the viceroy, but he never got on any terms of understanding and accommodation with him. After all, Jinnah was an advocate of the first order, and he could and did use 'sharp points of constitutional law to back his case but also knew superbly well how to win a case on a weak brief by tactical procedures'.[9]

'It is open to speculation whether events would have gone differently had the viceroy accepted, from the start, Jinnah's purpose of Pakistan as no less valid and right than Nehru's purpose of independence; for, after all, both ends were equally implicit in his mandate'. In other words, had Mountbatten endeavoured to 'disarm rather than confront the champion of the Muslim League'.

This took place on 5 and 6 April, (a month before his earlier recounted meeting with Churchill) Mountbatten was doubtless moving with great energy and dispatch, he was devoting considerable time ascertaining the views, at first hand of the principal personalities who were then active on the Indian scene. Mountbatten's papers record this meeting, starting with a somewhat tart observation: 'After having acted for some time in a gracious tea-party hostess manner, he eventually said that he had come to tell me exactly what he was prepared to accept'. To this Mountbatten demurred saying 'that I did not want to hear that at this stage—the object of this first interview was that we should make each other's acquaintance. For half an hour more he made monosyllabic replies to my attempts at conversation—but one and a half hours after the interview started he was joking, and by the end of our talk last night (6 April, when he came to dinner and stayed until half an hour past midnight) the ice was really broken.

'Our talks covered all subjects. I made it clear to him that I had not yet made up my mind what solution to recommend to His Majesty's Government, and that at the present I was utterly impartial. But I explained that it was my policy to make a decision as soon as possible after seeing all concerned. He agreed about not forcing the pace, but assenting that, whereas the whole of India was awaiting a quick decision, that decision must be the right one. I added that the problem, as I saw it at the moment, was not so much what to do, but how to do it in the time. [A very curious and somewhat alarming definition of his aim: outcome not important; speed of execution is all].

'Mr Jinnah claimed that there was only one solution—a "surgical operation" on India, otherwise India would perish altogether. I replied by reiterating that I had not yet made up my mind, and pointed out that an "anaesthetic" must precede any "surgical operation".'

The record continues giving a variety of detail not all of it relevant to our purpose. Though, record does have Jinnah's views 'about his previous negotiations with Mr Gandhi, including his version of the

Gandhi/Jinnah correspondence in September 1944'. There was an important aspect which Jinnah emphasized 'that on the Muslim side' he was the 'sole spokesman', adding 'If he took a decision it would be enforced—or, if the Muslim League refused to ratify it, he would resign and that would be the end of the Muslim League. But the same was not true of the representatives of Congress—there was no one man to deal with on their side. Mr Gandhi had openly confessed that he represented nobody—he only agreed to 'endeavour to use his influence'—he had enormous authority with no responsibility. Nehru and Patel represented different points of view within the Congress—neither could give a categorical answer on behalf of the party as a whole. Jinnah also related that when the impasse in the formation of the interim government occurred, he had refused to let the Muslim League join 'if Congress insisted on including a Congress Muslim'; Jinnah's suspicion being that Congress's only 'object in this insistence was to show that the Muslims were not united. After he had had forty-eight hours' negotiations with Gandhi, a formula had been devised whereby the Congress would agree publicly that the vast majority of Indian Muslims were represented by the Muslim League, and he (Jinnah) would then agree to them nominating a Congress Muslim to the government. Gandhi had agreed to this formula, but the Congress party had rejected it. Gandhi had thereupon withdrawn his agreement and stated that he had made 'a Himalayan mistake'.* This went to show, Mr Jinnah emphasized, that 'not only Gandhi's word but also his signatures were valueless'. Jinnah also spoke of the 'emotionalism of the Congress leaders, pointing out that they had every reason for this when it was a question of getting rid of the British, but this reason [now] no longer held good'. Jinnah also 'accused the Congress leaders of constantly shifting their front. They were determined, he said, to inherit to the full, all the powers now exercised by the British in India. They would stoop to anything to gain this object—even to acceptance of dominion status—rather than that any part of India should be handed over to the Muslims'.

We examine next, and in some detail the Radcliffe Award, for all else about this period of independent India's history, an account of those last few remaining months of an united India in which occurred the terrible

---

* The 'Himalayan mistake' to which Jinnah refers is given an interpretation by Jinnah. Gandhi's blunder was not in making the offer but in assuming that his chief lieutenants in the Congress, Nehru and Patel would stand by what he had said. They did not.

riots, the great migrations and the uprootings have all been written about extensively; why make the subcontinent relive again that great betrayal, that ignoble British scuttle out of India—and the horror of those millions killed, the great laments that then filled the air. We examine the Radcliffe award because the consequences of it stay with us and continue to cast their shadow on these sixty years of India and Pakistan's journeys as independent countries. For after all Radcliffe was a consequence of Jinnah insisting upon a separate land, also of course, of the Congress conceding it.

THE RADCLIFFE COMMISSIONS AND AWARDS

The man assigned this responsibility of delineating the new boundary, Sir (later Viscount) Cyril John Radcliffe (1899-1977), was an illustrious and eminent citizen of Great Britain. However, as the author of the Boundary Award, prepared in almost irresponsible haste, and then announced with unforgivable delay on 17 August 1947, he became a highly controversial figure.

He was a total stranger to India; an otherwise outstanding figure at the Chancery Bar. His legal career was of uninterrupted success and brilliance, but only in Britain. During the Second World War, in 1941, when deputed as a director general in the ministry of information he acquired his 'only experience of administration'.

If Radcliffe's appointment to the position of chairman of the Boundary Commissions did not generate any great controversy, it was also because of an established tradition in British Indian Civil Administration to offer responsible and prestigious jobs to a confident amateur rather than just a narrow technocrat, though, clearly the drawing of boundaries in a totally alien land, was not at all a generalist's assignment. Radcliffe's name was recommended to Mountbatten by Lord Listowel, who considered him 'as a man of high integrity, legal reputation and wide experience'; which doubtless Radcliffe was, but for him India was a totally alien land, he had not visited it ever, even casually, and had no knowledge of its complex sociology, or geography of the land, or any of the languages. Yet, it was he, who with Mountbatten vivisected this great land of such great diversity. The suggestion that Radcliffe should chair both commissions, one for the East of India the other for the West, had come from Jinnah.[10] Mountbatten was quick to take up the suggestion, adding that one chairman could usefully make adjustments of 'losses and gains' (sic) between the two borders.[11] This thought, as a bargaining chip—of 'losses and gains', a very typical Mountbatten device—is a startling give away. Either the Boundary Commission had unalterable principles, and criteria to work upon, or it was a negotiating, political body, malleable enough to make adjustments by balancing pluses and minuses. But that it clearly was not, it was just not a political body assigned the task of negotiating an award through discussion and compromise, a give and take approach; and Mountbatten was unacceptably offhand in his attitude, also entirely wrong to start with such an assumption. It is this kind of thinking that later caused so many cruel and intractable problems to remain; they persist till today.

Besides, the actual business of partition was not like the administrative implementation of a recently concluded, or even a prior political agreement. It was also not as if the rumoured non-partisan administrators of British-India had used apolitical and neutral processes to work out this partitioning of India. That would be a gross over simplification of the relationship between politics and administration, for these two domains can simply never be mutually exclusive, however much we falsely always so assume and, tend occasionally to also proclaim.

Jinnah also favoured a commission composed of three impartial non-Indians, appointed on the recommendation of the United Nations. However, this did not find favour with the Earl of Listowel, secretary of state for India, who apprehended international interference, besides being also concerned that an appeal to the UN might actually suggest British incapacity. The Congress had also opposed Jinnah's proposals, Nehru fearing that going to the United Nations would cause an unacceptable delay. [Ironical that this very same Nehru, in haste, through ill-judgment and upon Mountbatten's urgings, later as prime minister of India volunteered a reference of the J&K issue to the UN]. He [Nehru] suggested instead that 'each commission should consist of an independent chairman and four other persons of whom two would be nominated by the League and two by the Congress; that they should all be of high judicial standing and elect their own chairman'. Mountbatten had initially agreed with Jinnah, telling Listowel that personally, he 'could think of no better proposal' than reference the UN[12] but he performed a volte-face, as he frequently did, no sooner had Nehru made his objections known. It suited Mountbatten's strategy better, for that would be akin to an Indian gloss to the Commission while the reality of an effective deciding voice remained with a non-Indian chairman, whose appointment was solely a viceregal prerogative.

The members of the Boundary Commission being nominated by political parties, made party considerations dominate its (the commission's) findings. The Congress had initially objected to Radcliffe's appointment, but later muted its objections and accepted both the principle of it as also the composition. In this context, a letter from one Major Short[13] to Stafford Cripps of 3 August 1947 is interesting: 'the most delicate factor' he wrote then 'is the obstinate popular belief that Radcliffe will award as H.E. [Mountbatten] dictates. And this is a truly popular belief. Whatever any Indian may say to H.E., I, living here with Indians, am all too aware that nothing will shake their conviction that this is so. Which means—well, you will draw all the conclusions'.[14] There are grounds now to confirm that this fear was not unfounded, Mountbatten may not have influenced the fineprint of the award on any regular basis, but he undoubtedly did inspire some of its vital features.

Consider then this letter of 12 June from Nehru to Mountbatten.[15] Enclosing the terms of reference suggested for the Boundary Commissions in Punjab and Bengal, Nehru had said: 'you will notice that they are very simple and brief...it is better to leave the matter to the Boundary Commission....The work of the Boundary Commissions is meant to be done fairly rapidly. [Why? I cannot resist interjecting 'why rapidly'?] If we complicate the issue at this stage', continued Nehru, 'the work will be prolonged and final decision will be delayed. [Which is worse 'delay' or preventable death and suffering?] I imagine that if and when two States have been formed, those States will mutually consider modifications and variations of their frontiers so that a satisfactory arrangement may be arrived at.'

This is so totally impractical and naïve as to almost be beyond belief. The country was getting divided on account of unbridgeable differences, and problems of such complexity that they fester till today; from where therefore, and how were 'modifications and variations' to be carried out 'mutually'? Nehru also apprehended that this was likely to be a fairly lengthy process involving the ascertaining of the wishes of the people concerned in areas affected. 'If all this work is entrusted to the Boundary Commissions, their work', Nehru felt 'will be rendered heavy and prolonged. Hence our desire to leave the issues as clear and simple as possible.'

Two particular areas, however, have been mentioned. 'The Tharparkar District in Sindh and some parts of Purnea District in Bihar....It would produce confusion if a new province like Bihar was affected....In any event no such division could take place without some kind of a referendum. All this would involve complications and delay....So far as Tharparkar is concerned, it is a district of Sindh and can be dealt with as a unit [A hasty, unwise and a thoughtless decision, leaving millions of 'Hindu Rajputs' out of India'...] we think that this question should also not be raised at this stage and in this manner. I have, therefore, not mentioned Tharparkar [A great and a signal error] or Purnea in the terms of reference of the Boundary Commission'.

Nehru was working on hopelessly impractical assumptions: that the work of the Boundary Commissions was to be done in the shortest possible time so as to hasten the transfer of power; this was his priority, an early transfer, not a viable, trouble free, just border. Most unthinkingly, he actually commented, in words to the effect that a temporary, makeshift border, to be 'mutually adjusted later between the two parties' would do. This was so totally lacking in foresight as to beggar belief. Mountbatten, though, not surprisingly agreed with Nehru, for he too, was in a hurry. To them 'people', it seems did not really matter, only speed and 'power'. Nehru suggested that the Boundary Commission be instructed only 'to demarcate the boundaries of the two parts of Bengal on the basis of ascertaining contiguous majority areas of Muslims and non-Muslims', Mountbatten again accepted Nehru's proposal. The fact that the border was never intended to be anything other than a 'rough and ready improvisation' was impressed upon Radcliffe, and the result of the labours of this eponymous Commission bear all the marks of the rush job that they finally produced. This was also as close as Nehru would come to recognizing that the way in which the peoples' wishes had been ascertained, under the terms of the Plan, had been far from satisfactory. Despite this, it was to be the last time that Nehru would even refer to the need of further investigation into peoples' wishes. What is cited here is an extract from another letter of Jawaharlal Nehru to Lord Mountbatten, in a context that is similar:

'....5. As previously pointed out, a small change would be necessary in regard to a predominantly Hindu Rajput area in Sindh.
6. I take it that decisions in regard to Sylhet and Baluchistan would be taken after the main decisions in Bengal and Punjab had been taken. They would partly be influenced by the latter decisions'.[16]

What Nehru is indicating on the issue of Sindh in the month of May 1947 and then again subsequently (in his letter of 12 June quoted in preceding paragraphs) are widely differing interpretations; not that his policy on Sylhet too, acquired any subsequent clarity. This is a very great pity as haste, misplaced priorities, insufficient geographical knowledge, and not even a rudimentary understanding of the social spread, intermix and realities of this vast land, resulted in a 'hasty' division. This was done in a manner that actually multiplied our problems, and without solving any communal issue. If the 'communal', the principle issue remains and in an even more exacerbated form than it ever was before this partition, then why did we at all divide? This is not a rhetorical query; it is the central question.

Though Mountbatten had left Radcliffe to interpret his own terms of reference, in reality they had been set out by the viceroy himself. There had arisen, for example, a difference of opinion among the members of the Bengal Boundary Commission as to the scope of their duty in respect of Sylhet.[17] Two members of the Commission took the view that the adjoining districts included all such parts of Assam as joined with Bengal, even if they did not adjoin Sylhet and, therefore, the Commission must ascertain contiguous Muslim areas of all such districts and then transfer them to East Bengal. The other two members took the view that the only districts of Assam that the Commission ought to consider are those which, in fact, adjoined Sylhet, and that too, only the contiguous Muslim majority areas of those districts that should go with the Muslim areas of Sylhet to East Bengal. The ruling which Radcliffe sought from Mountbatten were on the questions that 'If I have to decide between these two views I should, with some hesitation, adopt the latter, I think that it accords better with the natural meaning of the words used in our Terms of Reference, and with paragraph 13 of the statement of the 3rd June, 1947. I think also that it would be to some extent anomalous that a referendum in Sylhet in favour of amalgamation with East Bengal should occasion the transfer to East Bengal of parts of other districts that have had no hand in the Sylhet decision, and are not even its neighbours geographically. The question is, however, an open one, and as the Commission only wish to carry out whatever duty was intended to be entrusted to it, I think I ought to ask whether any further instructions can be given to me on this point so as to put the matter beyond dispute. It does not seem to me that there would be anything to object to in the Terms of Reference being supplemented in this way, but I would be grateful if any instructions that are to be given should be given at the earliest possible date, as the Sylhet sittings of the Commission begin on Monday, 4th August, and I shall have to give them a decision one way or the other by Monday, the 4th August'.

What has also been revealed by Christopher Beaumont, Radcliffe's private secretary subsequently, is that Mountbatten persuaded Radcliffe to change the Punjab borderline and the award of Ferozepur tehsil to India. Though it is difficult to judge authoritatively on this now, so much time having elapsed, yet Beaumont even mentioning it colours the Commission's assumed impartiality.[18]

The Commission's powers were not delegated to its members and the report was to be made to the viceroy as that of the chairman's. No report of, or from the members was to be sent. Justice Mohammad Munir (a member of the Boundary Commission) contended that this was contrary to the terms of their appointment. An amendment was, therefore, brought to the India Independence Bill to convert the report of the chairman into the report of the Commission. This, Justice Munir felt, reduced the members of the Commission to a position of being 'just advocates of a party concerned.' A consequence of this limitation was that a member could not question the chairman, or check his ruling. The chairman being the sole determinant of this fateful boundary ended by becoming vulnerable to a variety of pressures, and all this lay outside of the knowledge of those whose lives were to be altered for always, the citizens of an undivided India.

The insistence on 'speed' was against all advice from the administrators. The clearest warning about it had come from Sir Evan Jenkins, then governor of the Punjab, for he feared the worst. In the Governor's Appreciation Report of 11 July 1947[19] he had warned clearly and unambiguously that:

- The higher Services have virtually disintegrated. They were given the final blow by the partition policy, which turned professional

civil servants into subordinate politicians. In the I.C.S. not one non-Muslim Indian is prepared to serve in West Punjab, and only one Muslim is prepared to serve in East Punjab. Hatred and suspicion are entirely undisguised.
- Partition goes very slowly indeed. Meetings of the Partition Committee resemble a Peace Conference with a new war in sight. In the time available: it will be quite impossible to make a clean job of partition, and even if we can check disorder up to 15th August, and the new Governments can maintain themselves thereafter, there will be appalling confusion. In civil administration certain things cannot be done properly in a matter of days or weeks, and 'standstill' orders (most of which will be accepted very grudgingly by the Parties) do not really solve the administrative problem.
- The Chairman of the Boundary Commission does not arrive until 14th July. His colleagues have given the Punjab Government an enormous questionnaire, the replies to which cannot, at the earliest, be ready before about 20th July. Thereafter, if all the information collected is to be studied and transferred to special maps and if the parties are to be heard at any length (they have engaged very eminent counsels), it is difficult to see how the Commission can report by 15th August.
- If the Commission does report by 15th August, there will in all probability be a row because the Muslims or the Sikhs are not satisfied with the report.
- If the Commission does not report by 15th August, there will be a row because the Sikhs do not like the 'notional boundary'.
- The prospect is, in short, far from encouraging, but we can only go ahead and see what happens.'

This appreciation was a pointed reference to Mountbatten's ignorance of civilian, as also his rather limited grasp of military matters, other than the strictly naval, which even if not as total as the former was certainly evident through its misapplication. These messages, of which only a small portion of just one is cited, are outstanding examples of upright and clear advice against ill judged decisions of the viceroy, but all these too, were of little avail.

Counsels, such as that of the governor of Punjab, Evan Jenkins, were not heeded. Mountbatten's entire strategy for partition was to rush it through without giving anyone a moment to pause and reflect. The Congress leaders were tempted by illusory hopes of short-term gains which they assumed a speedy settlement offered, and they went blindly along. Commenting on the extreme haste with which the partition plan was settled and then executed, Maulana Azad writes, 'Why was there such hurry in taking a decision which almost everybody regarded as wrong? If the right solution to the Indian problem could not be found by 15 August, why take a wrong decision and then sorrow over it? [for always] I had again and again said that it was better to wait until a correct solution was found. I had done my best but my friends and colleagues did not support me. The only explanation I can find for their strange blindness to facts is that anger or despair had clouded their vision. Perhaps also the fixation of a date—15 August acted like a charm and hypnotized them into accepting whatever Mountbatten said....'[20]

Radcliffe's awards were ready on 12 August 1947, well in time for the transfer of power in Pakistan on 14 August. But Mountbatten brought his influence to bear upon Radcliffe to hold the Award until 13 August 1947, by which time he had already left for Karachi. Pakistan came into being on 14 August, as did India on the 15th. Neither of these new born countries knew where their borders ran, where was that dividing line across which Hindus and Muslims must now separate? Ultimately, this Award was published only on 17 August, and as feared (also predicted) with disastrous consequences. Mountbatten had ignored even the experienced administrative advice from his commander-in-chief, Auchinleck, who warned that 'delay, after it becomes common knowledge that the Award was ready would lead to wild rumours and very harmful consequences'.[21] Again to no avail, for power was transferred on the basis of entirely notional boundaries and the hurry with which the Radcliffe line was drawn, turned out to be so completely and tragically wrong as to leave behind not settled boundaries but unending, fixed troubles.

In accord with Mountbatten, Nehru and Jinnah's collective requirement that his work be completed before 15 August, Radcliffe submitted his Award on 12 August. Then Mountbatten, as an afterthought, asked Radcliffe to delay the Award until after 15 August. Radcliffe, by now fatigued, feeling trapped and wanting to escape from India, 'flatly refused'. Mountbatten, nevertheless, chose not to release the Award until 16 August, which is when he discussed it formally with the Indian and Pakistani leaders, though he had shared it informally with Nehru, much earlier. It was only on 17 August that this Award was finally gazetted. When it ultimately trickled down to the districts and below, where it actually counted on the ground, is impossible to judge. But India, in effect, had already been partitioned. Days prior to the Award vast columns of displaced humanity were already on the move. This hasty 'Award' resulted in so many indescribable crimes, caused such incurable ills: 'Who is this cruel person who has with burning pen "Cut a deep line of innocent blood across my motherland's breast"...' lamented poets in despair.[22]

THE CONGRESS AND PARTITION PLAN

R.C. Majumdar, in *Struggle for Freedom* has expressed that in the 'course of his talks with party leaders Mountbatten was convinced that there was absolutely no prospect of an agreed solution on the basis of the Cabinet Mission plan, and that the partition of India on 'communal lines was inevitable.' He succeeded in convincing both Patel and Nehru and gradually Congress leaders veered round to it. Azad, Mosley, and many others have condemned both Nehru and Patel on this account, and held them up as the real authors of the ill-fated Partition of India. But before denouncing Patel or Nehru and describing them as mere dupes of 'wily Mountbatten's clever manoeuering', it is only fair to remember that the Congress had unanimously [also] passed resolutions, directly or indirectly conceding Pakistan, in 1934, 1942, 1945, and March 1947. Gandhi and Nehru had also referred to the partition contingency as a very possible one.

It was in this backdrop that a 'partition' of India was announced by HMG on 3 June 1947, and Nehru, impressed by the statement had described a decision to fix the date for the final transfer of power 'a wise and courageous one' which would have far-reaching consequences.[23] Thus all the strenuous efforts of Wavell and the Cabinet Mission to preserve the unity of India, in which the British Empire had had a role to play, were now coming to be recognized as futile and as Penderel Moon remarked caustically, 'Pakistan...the moth-eaten variety, had become a certainty,' adding, ...'This afforded Jinnah only moderate satisfaction; he still hankered after a Pakistan of six whole Provinces. Yet to get Pakistan at all, a completely sovereign, if truncated, Muslim State, was for Jinnah an amazing triumph, the outcome not of some ineluctable historic trend, but of the determination of a single individual. Only Jinnah could have mastered Fazlul Haq, Sir Sikandar and Khizar and, despite their opposition to Pakistan, (Jinnah) united the Muslims of Bengal and the Punjab in demanding it. There was no other Muslim leader who could have even attempted to do so, much less achieved success. Pakistan was coming into being as a result of Jinnah's individual pertinacity'.

Mangat Ram's assessment, formerly of the ICS, has a very different ring: 'It is essential to add, however, that Indians, without exception, admired, and still admire, the sincerity of the post-war British government—of men such as Cripps, Pethick-Lawrence, Attlee—in their aim of achieving a united India. In the creation of Pakistan they were hoisted on the petard of history, part of which had been created by their own forebears. The Muslims and the "Native States" had become "breakwaters" sustaining British power. It is difficult, therefore, to accept [in its entirety] Moon's insistence of 'a striking example of a single individual influencing the broad course of history; for without Jinnah there would have been no Pakistan. I dissent from these judgements. My own hypothesis is rather different; namely, that the product-mix of British, Muslim and non-Muslim Indians (both Hindu and others), and not Jinnah alone, created Pakistan.'[24] The question: 'Who actually did it?' remains.

In a very perceptive essay upon those events then written, was by the Liberal jurist Sir Chimanlal Setalvad, who deplored that the partition of India had not been reached as a result of 'mutual goodwill and understanding,' and his opinion 'All the parties concerned were to blame for this.' The Cabinet Mission's scheme 'had been killed by the wobbling and vacillating attitude of one party' (the Congress). He added, 'The cherished boon of a united India had fallen into their (Congress) lap, but they by their own want of political wisdom threw it out and made it beyond their reach.'

'No one studying the swift movement of India towards partition in the years preceding the 1947 can fail to be surprised at the tame manner in which the Indian National Congress in 1939 yielded the political initiative and position of power which it had so manfully and deservedly won for itself in the previous two decades. Almost equally surprising was its subsequent failure to restore its fortune and reassert itself. It was this breakdown of Congress which opened the way for the Muslim League and Pakistan'....Against this record of achievement and potential by 1939, the acceptance of partition less than ten years later, along with the recognition that the Muslim League under Jinnah had become the representative Muslim party, was a terrible defeat, mortifying and almost incomprehensible and unacceptable. Yet the fact was that within those ten years India was split and Pakistan was born. Even the most confirmed Congressman cannot fail to ask what went wrong'...he continues, his palpable anguish marked by irrefutable logic, in the same vein recording that 'Nehru after the frustrating experience of the working of the interim government noticed a "mental alliance" between British officials and the League members'.

B.R. Nanda in his essay, *'Nehru, the Indian National Congress and the Partition of India, 1935-47'* had mentioned that Nehru and Patel had agreed to the partition of India because they were avid for power. The immediate problem, as Nehru saw it was 'to arrest the swift drift to anarchy and chaos.' In retrospect, it appears the Congress acceptance of partition was not such a development as may have seemed at that time. 'It was the culmination of a process which had begun immediately after the passage of the Pakistan resolution by the Lahore session of the All-India Muslim League. Gandhi had opposed the two-nation theory and "vivisection" of India, but he had nevertheless written as early as April 1940: "I know no non-violent method of compelling the obedience of eight crores of Muslims to the will of the rest of India, however powerful the majority the rest may represent. The Muslims must have the same right of self-determination that the rest of India has. We are at present a joint family. Any member may claim division".'

Two years later, the Congress Working Committee in its resolution on the Cripps proposals voiced the same sentiment when it affirmed that 'it cannot think in terms of compelling the people of any territorial unit to remain in the Indian Union against their declared and established will.' Under the impact of the League propaganda and the political deadlock with the government, the Congress position on the question of partition was gradually softening. In 1944, Gandhi in his talks with Jinnah not only accepted the principle of partition, but also discussed the mechanism for the demarcation of boundaries. In 1946, the Congress, after much heart searching, accepted the Cabinet Mission Plan with its loose three-tier structure, and a Central Government which was unlikely to have the powers or the resources to maintain the unity of the subcontinent.

In this fashion the Congress Party engineered the partition of India; none amongst them then stood up to say: 'There will be no compromise on the geographical oneness of India'!

THE AICC MEET OF 14-15 JUNE 1947

A special meeting of the AICC was then called in Delhi, on 14 and 15 June 1947 to adopt a resolution accepting the Mountbatten Plan of Partition, as announced on 3 June. At this meeting, there were several voices of dissent raised against this proposed Partition. Amongst such speakers was Chothram Gidwani from Sindh who bitterly criticized the resolution as a total and abject surrender to the 'blackmailing tactics of violence resorted to by the Muslim League under Jinnah'. Amongst others of the Congress leadership that spoke were for example Purushotamdas Tandon, who firmly stood out against the resolution till the very end. In a voice charged with emotion, he shared his anguish with the delegates: This 'Resolution is a counsel of weakness and despair. The Nehru government has been unnerved by the terror tactics of the Muslim League and an acceptance of Partition would be an act of betrayal and surrender. Let us rather suffer the continuation of the British Rule a little longer than sacrifice our cherished goal of a United India. Let us gird up our loins to fight, if need be both the British and the Muslim League, and safeguard the integrity of the country'. The loud applause that greeted Tandon's speech gave a note of warning to the Congress leadership. Of all the other interventions in this fateful meet, remarkable were those by Lohia, and Jayaprakash Narayan. In Lohia's own words, 'barring us two [himself and Jayaprakash Narayan], Mahatma Gandhi and Abdul Ghaffar Khan none spoke a single word in opposition to partition'.

Maulana Azad sat in a chair through the two days of this meeting, 'in a corner of my very small room which packed us all, puffed away at his endless cigarettes, and spoke not a word. He may have been pained', commented Lohia 'but it is silly of him to try to make out as though he were the only one opposed to partition. Not only did he keep unbrokenly silent at this meeting, he also continued in office as a minister of partitioned India for an entire decade and more. I may concede.' Lohia continues, 'and even understand, that he was unhappy at the partition and tried to oppose it in his own way at informal or tête-à-tête meetings. But this was an opposition that did not object to the service of the thing opposed—a strange combination of opposition and service, in a conscience which was either greatly wise or equally elastic. It might be interesting to explore Maulana Azad's conscience, for I sometimes suspect that wisdom and elasticity go together.' It was not Maulana alone that got such ex post-facto whiplashes of comments from Lohia and others, too, came in his sight. He continued next with the Congress president.

'Acharya Kripalani was a pathetic figure at these meetings. He was president of the Congress party at that time. He sat drowsily and reclined at this meeting. At some point in the debate, Mahatma Gandhi referred to the exhausted Congress president and shook his arm in deep annoyance. He volunteered the information that he was suffering from a bad headache. His opposition to partition must have been sincere, for it was also personal. But the disease of old age and exhaustion had come over this fighting organisation of freedom [the Congress party] in its moment of greatest distress.'

'Khan Abdul Ghaffar Khan spoke a bare two sentences. He expressed his sorrow over the fact that his colleagues had accepted the scheme of partition. As a small mercy, he wanted them to find out if the proposed plebiscite in the north-west frontier could include the alternative of independence alongside of the two other choices of accession to India or Pakistan. He spoke not a word more at any stage; for he must have been so pained'. Unsparing of even his socialist colleagues Lohia ploughs relentlessly on.

'Mr Jayaprakash Narayan spoke some brief but definitive remarks against partition in a single stretch and was silent for the rest of the meeting. What made him do that? Was he disgusted at the way the working committee was going about the business of partitioning the country? Or, did he consider it prudent to keep quiet in the face of a leadership so stubbornly united for the acceptance of the partition? His character is probably a mixture of healthful responses at some stage and prudence for most of the time, a very irritating mixture, no doubt, which has often made me very angry with him.' But Lohia is sharp in self-introspection, too.

'My own opposition to partition was persistent and vocal, but it could not have been serious enough and I now recollect some false notes. In any event, my opposition could not have moved mountains, it could only have been on record as the healthful opposition of a fighter for freedom without much influence. Nevertheless, the absence of serious opposition to partition even from a man like me, who had absolutely no selfish axes to grind showed the depths of weakness and fear to which our people and I, as an ordinary one among them, had fallen. I may have occasion to reveal some of the aspects of my opposition. What is of significance is Mahatma Gandhi's intervention at this meeting.' Lohia proceeds with details of this great man's virtual parting words to a party that he had actually created, given shape and country-wide organisation to, and above all infused it with the spirit of freedom. He recounts: 'I should like especially to bring out two points that Gandhiji made at this meeting. He turned to Mr Nehru and Sardar Patel in mild complaint that they had not informed him of the scheme of partition before committing themselves to it.' Before Gandhiji could make out his point fully, Mr Nehru intervened with some passion to say that he had kept him fully informed. 'On Mahatma Gandhi's repeating that he did not know of the scheme of partition, Mr Nehru slightly altered his earlier observation. He said that Noakhali was so far away and that, while he may not have described the details of the scheme, he had broadly written of partition to Gandhiji.'

Lohia then goes on to judge: 'I will accept Mahatma Gandhi's version of the case, and not Mr Nehru's, and who will not? One does not have to dismiss Mr Nehru as a liar. All that is at issue here is whether Mahatma Gandhi knew of the scheme of partition before Mr Nehru and Sardar Patel had committed themselves to it. It would not do for Mr Nehru to publish vague letters which he might have written to Mahatma Gandhi doling out hypothetical and insubstantial information. There was definitely a hole-and-corner aspect to this business. Mr Nehru and Sardar Patel had obviously between themselves decided that it would be best not to scare Gandhiji away before the deed was definitely resolved upon.'

Staying turned towards Nehru and Patel, and facing them Gandhi made his second point. 'He wanted the Congress party to honour the commitments made by its leaders. He would, therefore, ask the Congress to accept the principle of partition. After accepting the principle, the

Congress should make a declaration concerning its execution. It should ask the British government and the Viceroy to step aside, once the Congress and the Muslim League had signified their acceptance of partition. The partitioning of the country should be carried out jointly, by the Congress party and the Muslim League, without the intervention of a third party.'

This was, in Lohia's view 'a grand tactical stroke'. Much has been said about the saint having simultaneously been a tactician, but this fine and cunning proposal has, to my knowledge, not so far been put on record.

'Dr Khan Saheb, the elder brother of the Frontier Gandhi, was the first and the only one to shout the proposal down as utterly impracticable. There was no need for anyone else to oppose the proposal. It was not [therefore] considered, I remonstrated with Dr Khan Saheb that the beauty of the proposal lay precisely in its impracticability and that India would not lose if Mr Jinnah and the Congress representatives failed to agree on how to partition the country without British assistance. Who listened to such remonstrances? The proposal was in itself cunning, but, in view of the determination of the Congress leadership to buy freedom at the price of unity, it made no practical meaning. It would have made meaning if Gandhiji had backed his proposal up with the prospect of action'.

Turning then to the triad of the Congress, Lohia writes: 'Messrs Nehru and Patel were offensively aggressive to Gandhiji at this meeting. I had a few sharp exchanges with both of them, some of which I shall [now] relate. What appeared to be astonishing then, as now, though I can today understand it somewhat better, was the exceedingly rough behaviour of two chosen disciples towards their master. There was something psychopathic about it. They seemed to have set their heart on something and, whenever they scented that Gandhiji was preparing to obstruct them, they barked violently'.

Lohia had some sharp exchanges in this AICC meeting with Nehru and Patel. Patel asked Lohia to forget all this talk about what would happen to India after the Partition. He would talk to Jinnah in the language of 'danda'.* To which, Lohia retorted that he had been listening to Sardar's language of sword for years; now in future he would have to

---

* In the Devanagari script, the *danda* (lit. *stick*) is a punctuation character. The glyph consists of a single vertical stroke.

listen to the language of 'danda'. Adding 'if you have fought for the freedom of India as Generals, so have we as soldiers'.

On the resolution proper on Mountbatten's proposals, a view was expressed that negative mention be made in it of the 'Two-Nation' Theory. In the original draft which Nehru had brought there was no such mention. Lohia, therefore, suggested an amendment to the resolution; this was backed by Gandhi. The amendment eloquently said: 'Geography and the mountains and the seas fashioned India as she is and no human agency can change that shape or come in the way of her final destiny. The picture of India we have learnt to cherish will remain in our minds and hearts and the false doctrine of the two nations in India will be discredited and discarded by all'.

[*This resolution, as amended was passed by the Working Committee.*] But when this amendment was moved by Lohia and backed up by Gandhi, Nehru in anger had said that they were obsessed by the views of Jinnah and were arguing with him all the time. 'What is the cause of calling the people who are flaying at each other's throat, brothers?' he asked. To which Lohia replied that the 'Americans had their Civil War; 300 to 400 thousand Americans were killed or may be more on both the sides; they did not cease to be brothers'. It was at this crucial moment that Gandhi intervened, again effectively, and got the Partition Resolution passed by the AICC. Gandhi spoke from the heart, and in despair, when he said: 'If at this stage, the AICC were to reject (the) Congress Working Committee's decision to accept the Mountbatten Partition Plan, what would the world think of it? The consequences of rejection will entail the finding of a new set of leaders who will have to constitute a new Working Committee and also be capable of running the government. Maintaining peace in the country is very essential at the present juncture. Congress has been all along opposed to Pakistan; and I too have steadfastly opposed it. Yet I have now to urge for its acceptance. Sometimes certain decisions, however unpalatable have to be taken'.[25]

Rajendra Prasad's motive in accepting Partition may be understood from the following passage: 'It is necessary to mention here that it was the Working Committee and particularly such of its members as were represented on the Central Cabinet, which had agreed to the scheme of partition. ... (They) did so because they become disgusted with the situation then obtaining in the country. They saw that riots had become a thing of everyday occurrence and would continue to be so; and that the Government...was incapable of preventing them because the Muslim League Ministers would cause obstruction everywhere....It had thus become impossible to carry on the administration. We thought that, by accepting partition, we could at least govern the portion which remained with us in accordance with our views, preserve law and order in a greater part of the country and organise it in such a way that we might be of the greatest service to it. We had, accordingly, no alternative but to accept partition.'

As regards the reasons which finally persuaded Nehru to accept the partition scheme, we have his own testimony as recorded by Leonard Mosley:

> Pandit Nehru told Michael Brecher, his biographer, (in 1956, the reasons for accepting the Partition of India): Well, I suppose it was the compulsion of events and the feeling that we wouldn't get out of that deadlock or morass by pursuing the way we had done; it became worse and worse. Further a feeling that even if we got freedom for India with that background, it would be very weak India; that is a federal India with far too much power in the federating units. A larger India would have constant troubles, constant disintegrating pulls. And also the fact that we saw no other way of getting our freedom—in the near future, I mean. And so we accepted it and said, let us build up a strong India. And if others do not want to do it, well then how can we and why should we force them to be in it? However, R.C. Majumdar comments Pandit Nehru came nearer the truth in conversation with Mosley in 1960, when he said: 'The truth is that we were tired men, and we were getting on in years too. Few of us could stand the prospect of going to prison again—and if we had stood out for a united India as we wished it, prison obviously awaited us. We saw the fires burning in Punjab and heard every day of the killings. The plan for partition offered a way out and we took it.

Nehru then added: 'But if Gandhi had told us not to, we would have gone on fighting, and waiting. But we accepted. We expected that partition would be temporary, that Pakistan was bound to come back to us. None of us guessed how much the killing and the crisis in Kashmir would embitter relations.' These statements, slightly different, are not self-contradictory, and have 'great deal of truth' in them.

Like Nehru, Gandhi too finally admitted not only to the possibility, but almost the inevitability, of Pakistan. He wrote in *Harijan* in 1942 that if the vast majority of Muslims want to partition India they 'must have the partition,' and in 1944 he actually carried on negotiations with Jinnah on this very basis. And yet, when the crucial moment for the final decision arrived, he told Azad on 3 March 1947, before he met Mountbatten: 'If the Congress wishes to accept partition, it will be over my dead body. So long as I am alive, I will never agree to the partition of India. Nor will I, if I can help it, allow Congress to accept it.' According to Azad, a great change came over Gandhi after he had interviewed Mountbatten. Gandhi 'no longer spoke so vehemently against it (partition) and began to repeat the arguments which Sardar Patel had already used. For over two hours I pleaded with him but could make no impression on him.'

According to Rajendra Prasad, 'Mahatmaji feared that the results of the acceptance (of Partition) would be disastrous....But when he realized that those who were entrusted with the responsibility of administration found that it was not possible to carry on and that there must either be partition or open war with the League, he decided to keep quiet and not to oppose partition in any way.'

Nehru, who spoke on the second day, asserted 'that the most urgent task at present was to arrest the swift drift towards anarchy and chaos by the establishment of a strong Central Government'. He said that there was no question of any surrender to the Muslim League. The Congress had all along been against coercing any unit to remain under the Indian Union. It was wrong to suggest that the Congress Working Committee had taken fright and therefore surrendered, though it was correct to say that they were very much disturbed at the prevailing madness. Partition was better than murder of innocent citizens. Following Nehru, Sardar Vallabhbhai Patel in a vigorous speech extended his full support to the 3 June Plan. He entirely disagreed with the view of Azad that the Cabinet Mission's Plan was better, and said 'that, looking at the Cabinet Mission's proposals today in the light of his experience in the Interim Government during the past nine months, he was not at all sorry that the Statement of 16 May had gone. Had they accepted it, the whole of India would have gone the Pakistan way. Today they had 75 to 80 per cent, of India, which they could develop and make strong according to their genius. The League could develop the rest of the country'.

Acharya Kripalani, the Congress president, concluded:

'The Hindu and Moslem communities have vied with each other in the worst orgies of violence...I have seen a well where women with their children, 107 in all, threw themselves to save their honour. In another place, a place of worship, fifty young women were killed by their menfolk for the same reason. I have seen heaps of bones in a house where 307 persons, mainly women and children, were driven, locked up and then burnt alive by the invading mob. These ghastly experiences have no doubt affected my approach to the question. Some members have accused us that we have taken this decision out of fear. I must admit the truth of this charge, but not in the sense that it is made. The fear is not for the lives lost, or of the widows' wail, or the orphan's cry, or of the many houses burned. The fear is that if we go on like this, retaliating and heaping indignities on each other, we shall progressively reduce ourselves to a stage of cannibalism and worse. In every fresh communal fight the most brutal and degraded acts of the previous fight becomes the norm.'

Even at this stage, no one knew how this ancient land stood divided, or where the boundary actually ran, not even where it might finally get delineated. Many million laments then filled the air, hauntingly, in India and in Pakistan. Individual pain got a voice (and it still continues to) in poetry and drama and memoirs. This loss was not just individual, nor in Punjab and Bengal alone. Established geographically and economic entities, ancient cultural unities, having evolved over millennia into a distinct and unique oneness, got fragmented; this historical synthesis of an ancient land, its people, its culture and its civilization was deliberately broken into pieces.

The Governor-General of Pakistan

On 4 July 1947 Liaquat Ali Khan, in a letter to Mountbatten, conveyed that Jinnah had made up his mind, and requested Mountbatten 'formally to recommend to the king the appointment of Mohammad Ali Jinnah as the governor-general of Pakistan'. This letter also expressed the hope that Mountbatten would remain as governor-general of India.

This episode in its totality is telling, it is unfortunate, and should not have ever occurred, however incredible it might be that Mountbatten actually sought to be, simultaneously, the constitutional governor-general of two countries, both in the process of being 'born'. It is self-evident that the constitutional head of a dominion is bound to act upon the advice of the ministry of that dominion where his office and seal lie. As independent dominions pursue their own independent policies and programmes, they could conflict with the other. In that even a constitutional head, who is simultaneously the head of two dominions, would unquestionably be placed in an impossible position, for his two governments could very well give conflicting advice. On this count jurists have commented: '[An] explanation that the only way of giving effect to Jinnah's suggestion of a "super-governor-general" was to provide for a common governor-general of the two countries in specious pleading.' Mountbatten, thereupon, records in a letter to Cripps: 'My private information is that Mr Jinnah's immediate followers and advisers are horrified at the line he has taken; and it seems almost incredible that a man's megalomania should be so chronic as to cause him to throw away such material advantages to his own future Dominion for the sake of becoming "His Excellency", some eight months earlier than he would in any case have assumed that title. Jawaharlal Nehru is convinced of this view; but Vallabhbhai Patel ascribes more sinister motives to Mr Jinnah and thinks that he wishes to set up a form of Fascist dictatorship with ultimate designs against the Dominion of India. The one satisfactory feature is that Mr Jinnah has not only pressed me to be the Chairman of the Joint Defence Council, but assured me that the Muslim League Press would welcome the new arrangement.'

It is near impossible to separate facts from biased expression of views. It is also facile to quote V.P. Menon's view to counter Jinnah's opinion on the subject. And as for megalomania, who, in reality, suffered a more serious version of it, Jinnah or Mountbatten, is difficult to tell. The talk that followed on the subject of the 'governor-general' between Lord Ismay and Jinnah on 24 July 1947, and in turn conveyed to Mountbatten by his chief of staff is quite telling:[26]

'First there was the eleventh hour announcement by Mr Jinnah that he intended himself to assume the appointment of Governor-General, Pakistan. This had put the Viceroy in an extremely awkward position and, incidentally, had lost Mr Jinnah a lot of ground in England amongst all shades of opinion. Secondly, the Viceroy had particularly asked Mr Jinnah to restrain his Press from chortling over the fact that Congress were to have a European Governor-General, while Pakistan was to have one of its own nationals. Mr Jinnah had undertaken to do this, but the undertaking had not been fulfilled. *Dawn* had done precisely what Lord Mountbatten had wished them not to do.

'As regards the first point, he [Jinnah] protested that he had from the start dissented....He had always been sure—and he was still sure—that it would not have worked. I intervened to remark that our grievance was not so much the substance of Mr Jinnah's decision, but the fact that he had waited until the eleventh hour to announce it. I reminded him that Sir Eric Mieville and I had asked Mr Liaquat Ali Khan in the very early days of June to persuade Mr Jinnah to nominate the Governor-General of Pakistan as soon as possible, and that if he had only said frankly and finally at that time that he proposed to be Governor-General himself, a great deal of misunderstanding and trouble would have been saved. Mr Jinnah kept on reiterating that he had never given the Viceroy the slightest grounds for believing that he would agree to a common Governor-General and there seemed to be no object [therefore] in pursuing the argument.'

'He then turned to the question of the Muslim League press. He said that he had kept his undertaking and that the Muslim press had done no chortling until the Congress press had attacked Mr Jinnah for having, in the first place, agreed to a common governor-general and of subsequently having broken his word. This was intolerable and untrue accusation which had to be countered. I observed that I had been away in London and had not seen the articles in question. I was not, therefore, in a position to continue the argument.

'Considering the somewhat embarrassing character of our talk, the atmosphere throughout our meeting was cordial.'

'As Mr Jinnah was leaving the house, he stopped, put his hand on my shoulder and said with great sincerity: "I beg you to assure the Viceroy that I am his friend and yours for now and always. I beg that he should judge me by deeds and not by words".'[27]

So some portions of the account, of a great and momentous happening which troubled Mountbatten so profoundly that in the midst of all other terrible events occurring in India, the viceroy assigned his principal staff officer for 'straightening' out issues of such great significance as the 'white ensign'. Though over sixty years have since passed, still, upon re-reading of those documents, as a part of Mountbatten's legacy to India and Pakistan, it is dismaying that such utter trivia, a consuming passion with form dominated Mountbatten's thoughts, above all other concerns; even as inhuman tragedies paralyzed the land, death then relentlessly stalking the villages and towns and haunting the people.

And in this fashion Mohammad Ali Jinnah finally departed from the land that had nurtured him. '... on 7 August, with Ahsan, the Naval ADC, Ms Jinnah, and the Quaid, we flew from Delhi to Karachi, in Mountbatten's white Dakota. There were only a handful of people to see him off', records Hector Bolitho in his *In Quest of Jinnah*. Before leaving the house Jinnah had given me a cane basket full of documents to take to the aircraft. Before we took off, he went out to be photographed, but he did not speak. As we taxied out he made only one remark; he murmured, "That's the end of that," meaning I supposed, the end of the struggle on Indian soil.

'He was perfectly dressed, as ever, in a white *sherwani,* and his Jinnah cap. Dark glasses. Miss Jinnah sat in the front and I sat opposite the Quaid. He had an immense bundle of newspapers which he read immediately and during the entire flight. Only once, he spoke. He handed me some of the newspapers and said, "Would you like to read these?"

'This was his only remark during a journey of 4 hours—all he said in what one might describe as the greatest hours of his life....We reached Karachi in the evening, and as we flew over Mauripur, Jinnah looked down and saw thousands of people waiting for him, including many women—waiting on the sand, to greet him....Even then there was no change in his expression and he did not say a word. He was the first to emerge from the aircraft, followed by Miss Jinnah. All the Muslim big guns were waiting for him. He shook hands with a few of them, and then got into the motor-car.

'The thousands of people were cheering, "Pakistan Zindabad!" "Quaid-i-Azam Zindabad", still he showed no signs of pleasure. He was very tired and he entered Government House, for the first time, without a word. After two or three days he changed his apartment from the left to the right side of the house'.

Mohammad Ali Jinnah had left Delhi for Karachi and for the putative Pakistan on 7 August 1947. Thereafter, he was never to return to India. The next day, Patel then said in the Constituent Assembly in Delhi: 'The poison has been removed from the body of India. We are now one and indivisible. You cannot divide the sea or the waters of the river. As for the Muslims they have their roots, their sacred places and their centres here. I do not know what they can possibly do in Pakistan. It will not be long before they return....'[28]

This voicing of a 'returning' to India, through constant repetition then became a kind of a challenge for Pakistan; to stay, to remain as Pakistan became the overriding objective, and 'success' began to be measured by just this limited test of 'still being there'. Later, reflecting on this in a conversation with his nephew B.K. Nehru, Prime Minister Nehru, too, had remarked rather wistfully, 'Let us see for how long they remain separate'. Such expressions then got picked up by watchful observers in Pakistan, and just remaining as Pakistan, despite what Indian leaders like Nehru and Patel might say became the critical index, at times the only criteria of Pakistan's 'success as a state'.

As the scenario of partition is replayed we find that parity had been rejected, and no doubt with reason; yet a little objective reflection would have demonstrated that once India and Pakistan did finally become separate countries, (and this ultimately did became a reality) then their very emergence as different countries, as two sovereigns, stood them on equal footing in the comity of nations. It conferred a *parity of status between them*; (emphasis added) for then Pakistan must, as a sovereign, with a separate existence, have an equal standing as India. But this, though, correct in theory is not entirely tenable in practice, which is why post-partition, this disparity (as against parity) in itself, became a divisive issue. V.P. Menon commented: 'Even the safeguards and protection demanded for their community by Nationalist Muslims went so far that they (Muslims) would have prevented for all time the growth of a united nation.'[29] Once parity had been rejected by the Congress in a United India, it began to be apprehended that it would be rejected in practice, too. That held as an axiomatic extension of a reality, of course not a legally or constitutionally enforceable point, but as the undeniable reality of post-partition relations between India and Pakistan.

Another cause that led the Congress to accept partition must be noted here. It was said that the Interim Government did not act harmoniously and did not act as a Cabinet with Nehru, though the head of only an interim government, conducting himself, functionally, as prime minister. This situation was, of course, aggravated by Liaquat Ali Khan's rather negative term as Finance minister, for he knowingly sabotaged schemes. The interim government failed to act harmoniously, for above all else,

Nehru wanted to be treated as 'the *de facto* Prime Minister of a Dominion Cabinet, a claim which the Muslim League strenuously opposed and His Majesty's Government [had] never [really] conceded.'

15 August 1947[30]

Assuming that partition had become inevitable and had been accepted by the Congress and the Muslim League, was there then any justification whatsoever, for the destructive haste with which the date of transfer of power was brought forward from June 1948, first to October 1947, and then to 15 August 1947? Why did Mountbatten choose 15 August? I find the reply given by the outgoing viceroy casual and insulting. A book[31] on Mountbatten reports him as having told his authors: 'The date I chose came out of the blue. I chose it in reply to a question. *I was determined to show I was master of the whole event.* When they asked: had we set a date, I knew it had to be soon. I hadn't worked it out exactly then—I thought it had to be August or September and I then went to the 15th of August. Why? Because it was the second anniversary of Japan's surrender.[32] This is paralyzing in its insensitivity, the sheer horror of Mountbatten's casual untruthfulness, in how trivial this last viceroy's approach was to a grim and unprecedented tragedy.

This statement cannot be simply brushed aside, as this was not on account of any failing memory about events that had taken place some twenty-five years earlier. For, on 15 August 1947 as Independence Day was broadcast to the United States of America *to celebrate the second anniversary of Allied Victory over Japan.* (He) said: 'Two years ago today, I had just returned from the Potsdam Conference and was in the Prime Minister's room in 10 Downing Street, when the news of Japanese surrender came through. Here, as I speak to you tonight in Delhi, we are celebrating an event no less momentous for the future of the world—India's Independence Day.'

That 15 August 1947 was the second anniversary of the surrender of Japan could have had a personal association for Mountbatten. But that was entirely extraneous and totally irrelevant to his present responsibility, which spelt 'to transfer power with the least amount of bloodshed and misery.' Mountbatten realized that the date fixed by him, had exposed him to criticism of just this: 'bloodshed and misery, and in plenty.' In paragraph 17 of the conclusions appended to an Official Report which he made in September 1948 he summarizes five reasons for selecting 15 August, *none of those reasons make any reference to the second anniversary of the Japanese surrender.*[33] Where then was Mountbatten prevaricating? Rather, when was he not so engaged? Which is why we are seized by this awful question: 'Did Mountbatten then turn India's partition also into an exercise in disingenuity?'

10

PAKISTAN: BIRTH–INDEPENDENCE: THE QUAID-I-AZAM'S LAST JOURNEY

Let us now travel to an about-to-be-born Pakistan with the Quaid-i-Azam, the founder. Jinnah left India, finally, for Karachi on 7 August 1947, he did so with an appeal to both Hindus and Muslims to 'bury the past', and wished India success and prosperity. (See Appendix for his message).

In Pakistan, all then assumed the Quaid-i-Azam had reached his destination the 'terminal station' of his life's journey. Questions, though, had already begun to be raised: 'Was this the Pakistan that we had sought'? A few cameos of those early days recapture some of the perplexity. Maj.-Gen. Shahid Hamid, then military secretary to Governor-General Mohammad Ali Jinnah has left a record of this day in his memoirs *Disastrous Twilight—A Personal Record of the Partition of India*.[1] He wrote:

13 August 1947

'Karachi is in a festive mood but there is inadequate accommodation for the hundreds of correspondents and visitors who have gathered to see the State of Pakistan being born. My brother-in-law, Colonel Majid Malik, Director of Public Relations in General Headquarters, India, is now the Principal Information Officer to the Government of Pakistan; he is being greatly harassed. All the correspondents expect the impossible. There is no Government of Pakistan but it is being created overnight. There are no Government officials, no Ministries, and no office furniture or stationary. Typewriters are a luxury. It is utter chaos....The Viceroy expected that by 13th August Karachi would emerge as a fully fledged working state capital and would be in a position to receive him, the King's representative.

'The first function was the banquet at the Governor-General's House where some fifty guests were invited. The atmosphere was tense. Quaid-i-

Azam made a short speech. I think it was the only time when he proposed a toast to His Majesty the King. On the contrary Mountbatten, after conveying the good wishes of the King, indulged in a long oration which was not in keeping with such an occasion. Among other things he mentioned that people often wonder why he brought the date of the transfer of power forward. He drew a childish simile by saying that the best way to teach a youngster to cycle was to take him on top of a hill, put him on the seat and then push him down the hill. By the time he arrived on the flat ground below he would have learnt to cycle. After the banquet, which lasted longer than anticipated, there was a reception outside in the garden. It was attended by over a thousand guests.

'Quaid-i-Azam was quiet and aloof. I went to him and stood close by him without saying a word. He looked at me and smiled...physically he looked frail, tired and pre-occupied. Somehow I could sense that he wanted the reception terminated as soon as possible. Mountbatten did not seem in a mood to go, trying his level best to charm the guests...' Obviously Quaid-i-Azam could not leave until the representative of the King had left.

'I was not far from the Quaid when he called his ADC and told him to tell Mountbatten to go home and that he has had enough of him. The poor ADC did not know what to do. He came to me for advice. I told him to go and tell Mountbatten exactly what the Quaid had said. To give him moral support I told him that I would accompany him. We walked up to Mountbatten and gave him the message verbatim. He was taken aback and said, 'Of course, I should have realized how late it was and that Mr Jinnah was getting tired.' He walked up to the Quaid, apologized and left! What a day it had been.'

14 August 1947

'This morning there was so much happening, in the middle of which Mountbatten tried to pull a fast one. He had it conveyed to the Quaid that, according to Intelligence sources in Delhi, a plot has been unearthed. A bomb would be thrown at the carriage carrying the Quaid during his State drive through Karachi. He asked the Quaid to cancel the drive. Quaid refused to do so, whereupon Mountbatten suggested that they travel in a closed car. Once again the Quaid declined.

'All along the route there was great enthusiasm and wild cheering. It was a sight for sore eyes and very difficult to describe. A dream was coming true and a State was being born. The name of the Quaid-i-Azam was on everyone's lips as well as their thanks to the Almighty. On their return Mountbatten told his staff that Jinnah was tense and pathetic and held his knees and broke down. He also said that Miss Jinnah is a 'funny woman'.'

It is impossible to comment on all this, also on the accuracy of what Maj.-Gen. Shahid Hamid has written, but it does say a great deal about Mountbatten. In a film on Jinnah by Christopher Mitchell, there is a telling scene. Governor-General Jinnah and Mountbatten rode the celebrations in the same limousine, the latter jaunty and bemedalled in the uniform of the Royal Navy, the Quaid-i-Azam, in his by now hallmark attire, tired, withdrawn, sitting somewhat aloof even as Mountbatten waved and acknowledged all greetings proprietarily. Jinnah seeing all this, suddenly and despite all his fatigue of the past many days, his illness, the heat and humidity of the day pulls himself. It is he, the Quaid-i-Azam, who represents Pakistan now, not Mountbatten, was the signal.

Within just thirteen months of having helped create Pakistan, Quaid-i-Azam Mohammad Ali Jinnah, the first governor-general of an independent Pakistan, died. With his death the inspiration too, behind the country was lost. So soon after birth, this infant country was left a conceptual and moral orphan, a grievous and an irreplaceable loss, from which Pakistan has not been able to recover, yet. There is a vivid and a very moving description then of that last journey of the Quaid-i-Azam written by Dr Ilahi Bux. It would be unjust to shorten it or to omit any portion of the author's description of it, so full of pathos and looming tragedy.

Dr Ilahi Bux, personal physician to Jinnah, in his work, *With Quaid-i-Azam During his Last Days* has written movingly. He recounts that 'last journey' from Ziarat,[2] where Jinnah had gone to rest and recuperates, as much as he could, from the ravages of the tuberculosis that was now galloping through his already frail body. Dr Ilahi Bux shares

> '...assured...that all arrangements had been made—an ambulance with a nurse would meet us at Mauripur Aerodrome where we were to land....It was 12.30 but there were no signs of our being able to move by 1 o'clock.... The packing...complete by 1.20. I...proceeded to [inform] the Quaid-i-Azam with which duty Miss Jinnah had entrusted me. As I entered his room and greeted him, he looked at me and gave a faint smile. He appeared very weak and exhausted and had a toxic look in his eyes. As I was standing he indicated a chair, which I took. The following conversation then took place:
> "Sir, would you like to go to Karachi?" "Yes."
> "Sir, would you like to leave today?"

"I don't mind."

"We are ready to move by plane, would you like few minutes?"

The Quaid-i-Azam nodded and said in a weak tone, "All right."

'I was greatly relieved, but could not help wondering what had made him give up so easily his old objection to go to Karachi. Since we had not told him how critical his condition was, it could only be that, having himself lost all hope, he had made up his mind to return to the place of his birth. I went and told Miss Jinnah that the Quaid-i-Azam had agreed to leave immediately. Within a few minutes we had him shifted to the ambulance. Miss Jinnah and the nurse sat on the opposite seat, I was in front with Lt. Mazhar, next to the driver.

'As the ambulance started to move I realized what a grave decision we had taken. With many unnerving thoughts in my mind I began to pray to God to vouchsafe the Quaid-i-Azam a comfortable journey. I was fortified by the prayer, and then attended to the various needs likely to arise in the course of the journey. From a distance we could see the Governor-General's Viking glittering like a silver bird in the sun. We were at the Aerodrome at two. As the Quaid-i-Azam was being taken on a stretcher to the plane, the crew gave him a salute. To our astonishment, he returned it promptly.

'It was September, the weather pattern—of a withdrawing monsoon, the time of the day—2 p.m.—possibly the worst for thermal turbulence.... It was fairly warm in the plane. Miss Jinnah, Dr Mistry and the nurse were in the front cabin and I, together with Mr Amin and Lt. Mazhar, was in the next cabin. A few minutes after the plane had taken off, I saw Dr Mistry coming out of the cabin, and my heart sank, but he relieved my anxiety by telling me that Miss Jinnah had sent him away and would call for him if necessary. He occupied a chair in front of me and did not take long to doze off. Soon we were flying at a height of 7,000 feet and I was looking through the glass window at the rugged scenery of the Quetta hills, when the communicating door opened and Miss Jinnah came in and told me that the nurse had been incapacitated by air sickness and her brother Jinnah was not taking the oxygen from her. I went into his cabin, counted his pulse, which was regular and of good volume, and examined his nails for cyanosis. After reassuring myself I began to administer the oxygen. When I brought the mask near his mouth he pushed my hand away but when I quietly explained that it was necessary to prevent any damage to his system he looked at me, smiled, and allowed me to adjust the mask. There was no place for me to sit, but I made myself as comfortable as I could on the stairs between the two cabins with my back towards the door. The Quaid-i-Azam would take the oxygen for about five minutes and then try to remove the mask, but each time I spoke to him he would look at me, smile and allow me to readjust it. Every few minutes I would count his pulse and compare the colour of his nails with that of mine. He would become restless and try to push away the blanket, but Miss Jinnah would quickly cover him again. After sitting for 20 minutes in that cramped posture, I felt the need of relaxing for a few minutes. Miss Jinnah noticed my discomfort and asked me to rest a little, while she would give the oxygen herself. She had been doing it at Quetta quite satisfactorily, so I went back into my cabin. Everybody was fast asleep and snoring, except Lt. Mazhar who looked very pale and air-sick.

'I had not been away for more than a couple of minutes when Miss Jinnah came and asked me to administer the oxygen again as her brother was not taking it from her. I went in and gave the oxygen for about 20 minutes more. By that time we had left the hills and were flying at a height of 4 to 5 thousand feet. I did not consider it necessary to give any more oxygen, and went back to my cabin. The most difficult and risky part of the journey was over....I looked through the window at the flooded areas of Sindh below, and mused over Nature's hostility to our infant State.' Then followed yet more agony.

At Karachi

'We landed at the Mauripur Aerodrome at 4.15 p.m. and a great load was taken off my mind. As I got out of the plane, I saw the Military Secretary to the Governor-General, Colonel Knowles, standing by an ambulance but could see no nurse. It was rather warm at Karachi but not uncomfortable as there was a strong breeze...We lost no time in shifting the Quaid-i-Azam to the ambulance. Miss Jinnah and the nurse from Quetta sat in the ambulance, while the Military Secretary, Dr Mistry and I followed in the Governor-General's Cadillac. The luggage and the servants were in the truck behind us. We moved from the Aerodrome [towards] the Governor-General's House, a distance of about 9 to 10 miles, at very slow speed. We had hardly gone four miles when the ambulance stopped. Wondering what had happened, I got out and found that there [was] a breakdown due to engine trouble. The driver assured us that he would soon put it right, but he fiddled with the engine for about twenty minutes, and [yet] the ambulance would not start. Miss Jinnah sent the Military Secretary to fetch another ambulance. Dr Mistry went with him. It was very oppressive in the ambulance, and the Quaid-i-Azam was perspiring in spite of continued fanning by the nurse and the servants. We thought of removing him to the big car but the stretcher could not be taken in and he was too weak to be popped up in the back seat. Besides, his clothes were wet with perspiration, and with a fairly strong breeze blowing there was risk of an exposure. I examined him and was horrified to find his pulse becoming weak and irregular. I ran to the truck and brought back a thermos flask containing hot tea. Miss Jinnah quickly gave him a cup, and observed that it was the first time in the day that he had taken any nourishment, having so far refused everything except a few sips of fruit juice. I told her this was an encouraging sign. Except for the most distressing breakdown of the ambulance, everything had been going in the patient's favour. What a catastrophe if, having survived the air journey, he were to die by the road-side. With mounting anxiety I examined his pulse again: the cup of tea having revived him, it was luckily stronger and more regular. I kept on looking distractedly towards the town, but there was no sign of an ambulance. Many trucks and buses were passing up and down, but none of them could be safely used. I felt utterly forlorn and helpless. After an excruciatingly prolonged interval the ambulance appeared at last. We quickly-shined the Quaid-i-Azam into the new ambulance and resumed our unhappily interrupted journey. The ambulance did not fly the Governor-General's flag, so nobody knew that the Quaid-i-Azam was being taken in a critical condition through the streets of Karachi.'

This is a deeply troubling account by the governor-general's personal physician. Jinnah was the first governor-general of a newly created and independent Pakistan; he was by then very frail and terminally ill, and as the Quaid-i-Azam, he was flying back to the first capital of Pakistan.

His rather indifferent reception at the airport upon return, this patently casual air of unconcern, the ambulance that failed en-route; the Quaid-i-Azam on that road virtually alone, for over half an hour with trucks and buses passing by unconcernedly—there is something deeply troubling in this account, and extremely painful, too.

Dr Bux continues: 'We reached our destination at 6.10, almost two hours after we had landed at the Mauripur Aerodrome It is difficult to exaggerate our relief at the safe conclusion of a journey, which might have proved calamitous'.

The Quaid-i-Azam of Pakistan, Mohammad Ali Jinnah died in Karachi, that very night, some time after 10 p.m. on 11 September 1948.

The two great figures of India's freedom struggle, the two great sons of Kathiawar, both products of a nineteenth century education in Britain, and law in the Inns of Court, both leaders of their respective political parties and communities, Hindu and Muslim, died within months of each other in 1948; Gandhi, on 30 January 1948, Jinnah on 11 September 1948.

With their death an era of a distinctive kind of politics in India came to an end. With Jinnah's death Pakistan lost its moorings. In India there will not easily arrive another Gandhi, nor in Pakistan another Jinnah. The Indian subcontinent is the poorer for that. An *Extraordinary Gazette* issued then announced: 'The government of Pakistan regrets to announce the death of Quaid-i-Azam Mohammad Ali Jinnah from heart failure at 10:25 p.m. on Saturday, September 11.

'The Funeral procession will start at 3 p.m. on Sunday from the Governor-General's House. The Namaz-i-Janaza (funeral prayer) will be held at Exhibition Grounds in Karachi. Maulana Shabbir Ahmad Osmani will lead the prayer. The Quaid will be buried within the compound of the proposed Jumma Mosque near Exhibition grounds.'

The succession in Pakistan was orderly and peaceful; Khwaja Nazimuddin succeeded Jinnah. State mourning was announced in Delhi and flags flew at half-mast on all official buildings. The governor-general of India, C. Rajagopalachari cancelled an official reception on that day as a mark of respect to Jinnah.

On 13 September 1948, most newspapers carried their obituaries on Jinnah in their edit pages, mostly as lead editorials. Two of the then prominent English language papers, *Hindustan Times* and the *Times of India,* carried lengthy obituaries analyzing Jinnah's role. *The London Times,* on the other hand, was more fulsome in its praise observing: 'Mr Jinnah was something more than Quaid-i-Azam, supreme head of the State, to the people who followed him; he was more even than the architect of the Islamic nation he personally called into being. He commanded their imagination as well as their confidence. In the face of difficulties which might have overwhelmed him, it was given to him to fulfil the hope foreshadowed in the inspired vision of the great Iqbal by creating for the Muslims of India a homeland where the old glory of Islam could grow afresh into a modern state, worthy of its place in the community of nations. Few statesmen have shaped events to their policy more surely than Mr Jinnah. He was a legend even in his lifetime'.

Hindustan Times, the voice then, (as now?) in reality, of the Congress party held that: 'He [Jinnah] did not create: Pakistan in the sense that Gandhiji created free India. Mr Jinnah had neither the gift nor the desire to mould the outlook of his people, put them through severe ordeals, set before them difficult goals and fashion for them an organisation and leadership which had stood the test of time and trial. He was a master political tactician who seized the opportune moment...India may not forget that he began his political career as a nationalist...Mr Jinnah of recent years...was the victim of circumstances and was...not great enough to resist the temptation which history placed before him...It would be foolish on the part of any Indian to think that it must now lead quickly to the reunion of India and Pakistan'.

The *Times of India,* on the other hand, expanded the theme of comparisons between Jinnah and Gandhi: 'No spiritual parallel can be drawn between Mahatma Gandhi and the Quaid...As figures in the long scroll of history the two leaders were in sharp contrast. For a period their career appeared to move in parallel groove—from the English legal training...but while one dealt in spiritual values and concepts, the other was confined by nature of a strong rigid character, to ruthless legalism, technically constitutional to coldly uncompromising [stand] which yet demanded without fear of the consequences, its full pound of flesh. Did Jinnah have Napoleonic illusions? Whether he did or not the consequences of his death were fateful for his own creation—Pakistan; it lost its focus'.

Nehru, on hearing the news of Jinnah's death, acknowledged though, sadly, still not free of his customary condescension: 'Jinnah did mould history in India, in the wrong way it is true, and let loose forces which have done so much evil...How shall we judge him? I have been very angry with him often during the past years. But now there is no bitterness in my thought of him, only a great sadness for all that has been...Outwardly, he succeeded in his quest and gained his objective, but at what a cost and with what a difference from what he had imagined. What must he have thought of all this, did he feel sorry or regret for any past action? Probably not, for he wrapped himself in a cloak of hatred and every evil seemed to flow from those whom he hated. Hatred is poor nourishment for any person'.

With the editorials and the obituaries done we are left with Jinnah's legacy, his thoughts, his concepts, and what he bequeathed to Pakistan.

11

IN RETROSPECT

> They paid the price....
> Across a world in flames
> But their own hate slew
> their own soul
> Before [any] victory came
>
> RUDYARD KIPLING—The Outlaws; 1914[1]

Our 'journey of understanding', at least attempting to grasp the reasoning that underlay our traumatic partition in 1947, ends here. We began with the advent of Islam in Hindustan in the seventh century, then skipping many centuries we had come to that great divide, the uprising of 1857. It was here, in the middle of the nineteenth century that the symbol of our sovereignty was finally seized and trampled underfoot by British boots. An entirely commerce-driven and destructive impulse of that distant land with wholly alien civilizational notions, conduct, and a totally different value system, now became the arbiter of our political, economic, and even social fate. It was their will, their judgment, even folly that hereafter determined India's geographical shape, our historical evolution, even how to socially relate to one another, and all this in our own land.

The British that then served in India, certainly most of them whether for the East India Company or post-1857, the Crown, did not really know the land, the people, their many languages, diverse customs, multiple shades of faith and beliefs, or their persuasions, passions, instincts and commitments. It was only a small fragment of this vast civilizational entity that they grasped, just a very small part. The British ruled from vast distances away—Calcutta, Delhi, Simla to White Hall and then back to this great spread of India, larger than today's entire

European Union, in size and in the number of humans that inhabited it even then. For so long as Indians alone were the arbiters of their own fortunes (or misfortunes) then whether they fought or struggled or squabbled, cooperated or occasionally (even frequently) killed one another, that was their concern, it was an internal matter, entirely India's choice; solely of those that lived here, of whatever faith, belief or persuasion. Not so after the declaration of the Empire, for we then became 'subjects', living in a 'subject territory'. This particular humiliation, for there were others too, lasted just under one hundred years: 1857 to 1947. However, sadly, our fate, post-1947 also did not remain entirely ours to determine, solely by ourselves; it became subject to the consequences of so many factors, most of which were, in turn, the residual detritus of India's subjugation by European thought, language and power, principally British. Yes, the British did leave India, and left behind many legacies that benefit but also left behind many great divides, too, and an anglophile leadership, that further deepened these divides turning them into yawning chasms. While leaving the British fractured our freedom, but we went beyond, denying our citizens the essence of it.

Gandhi understood this world and the many paradoxes, contradictions that came with 1947, for he knew the essence of India. Though exposed to education in the West, Gandhi's instincts, his roots his groundings and his responses always remained entirely Indian. Unfortunately, not so in the case of Jinnah or Nehru, they were both so totally imbued with the colours and teachings of the West that in their thinking they were, and remained totally English, all through their respective political lives. Both thought in terms of carving out successor 'states': the state of India, and the state of Pakistan, but entirely in the European sense of the phrase; centralized, defined territorial units inheriting all the occidental clutter of ersatz modernity. This was damaging (perhaps more, it was destructive) in many ways, the most telling and significant being Jinnah's call of 'Muslims are a separate nation'. From this notion, buttressed by imperial aims, finally emerged Pakistan, even if 'moth-eaten'. And that is also how, rather why, a post-1947, residual India began to look both conceptually questionable and even incomplete, an aspect which, in reality, is the post-independence challenge but which India has not yet responded to convincingly, indeed shies away from.

Why? Because acceptance of partition on grounds of faith, particularly when that is demanded on grounds of 'Muslims (being) a separate nation', spawned such vast shoals of ravenous political piranha as to totally eliminate all reason from our midst. For one, such an assertion, though entirely illogical, is fundamentally of an insatiable nature, it will always remain so, forever, as it never can be quenched being born of a peculiar Indian phenomenon 'minoritism', endlessly it will continue to give birth to more destructive minoritism, being politically contagious for, Pakistan is doubtless Muslim, but 'theocentrically', it is not a 'theocratic' state, indeed there is no such state other perhaps than the Vatican, but then who, other than Gandhi and a few others was to advise caution as we rushed headlong (and unheeding?) down this destructive path.

For India, tragically the birth of Pakistan does not end this debate—about the status of minorities, particularly Muslims. I question seriously whether it does so, in Pakistan either. But in India our having once accepted this principal of reservations, *circa* 1909, then of partition, how can we now deny it to others, even such Muslims as have had to or chosen to live in India? Which is why some voices of Muslim protest now go to the extent of speaking of a 'Third Partition', the second being the birth of Bangladesh.

This, in reality, is amongst the mound of residues of our 'fractured freedom'; the vivisection of 1947 has left us no peace, and it has not left behind any settled peace in the separated portions either; primarily because the central problem of relations between Hindus and Muslims remains, as partition had come escorting a permanent divide between our people. It is the land, (admittedly) that we had accepted to partition, but in the process had we not also agreed to a simultaneous cutting up of human societies too? How could 'they' have consigned this as a legacy to us, the future generations of our entire subcontinent? What gall, what a legacy. Those Muslims who remained or were left behind in India now and themselves as almost abandoned, bereft of a sense of real kinship of not being 'one', in their entirety with the rest. This robs them of the essence of psychological security; as indeed the remaining Hindus suffer in Pakistan and/or Bangladesh; even as they are slowly, silently but continuously driven out.

Our other, post-independence challenge, rather the responsibility, was of organizing ourselves into a truly democratic and republican framework, but this within the context of our complex society has not really worked, certainly not satisfactorily, at least not yet, principally and perhaps only because one of the unintended (perhaps also not initially appreciated), consequence, of this partition has been the de-facto creation of different categories (classes) of citizens, even if we shy away from recognizing this as a fact. At the upper end of this problem, it is truly Orwellian, 'some people are just more people', than the others. At the other end we frequently take recourse to a whole variety of short term palliatives, these, at best, work for a while but only as empty, placatory gestures; for that is just what they are, not the needed solutions. For, underlying these gestures is no honesty of purpose, consequently, they are not accompanied by the needed efficiency of delivery, therefore, they too, after a while grind to a halt. Thus further damage is caused, for all such measures seal our societal divisions into water-tight compartments but only of demands; the challenge lies in our addressing these fundamentals honestly, but that 'challenge' we shy away from, it intimidates us, questioning the very bona fides of our vote obsessed policy.

Muslims in India had got habituated for about a millennium to being rulers, certainly in large parts of North India; whereafter they acclimatized their psyche to being subjects of the British; but now, post-1947, in India they are, at least in theory, only equal citizens; primarily because the Indian Constitution's basic premise is the individual citizen, that is the first building block of our Republic. Having adopted that Constitution we started, straightaway, granting special rights, but this favour was granted selectively; inevitably therefore, Muslim citizens of India have also eventually now begun demanding a share. This invites a rejoinder, woundingly voiced, almost always tauntingly asking: 'Special rights? Still? Even after Pakistan? Why?' That is why this question of the 'unfinished agenda of partition' keeps resurfacing. Have we resolved this and many other similar questions posed to us during the freedom movement, or even after, or have we not, yet? Then how can we satisfactorily address them now, for the break-up of the country has rendered them as so much more complex, so infinitely intimidating.

This partition has unfortunately also put paid to that great formulation of Wilfred Cantwell Smith's,* that 'if there is any chance of an ideological break-through in Islam, it will be in India.'** Does this still hold as valid, even now? Pakistan has been born, and Jinnah had asserted that 'only he represented the Muslims in (undivided) India', therefore, has that right and status now got transferred to Pakistan? But to whom? Then what of Bangladesh, or where do Indian Muslim citizens stand? And what are the Muslims in India to do? Lacking both sufficient electoral numbers and a leadership that can lead them out of this morass, they take recourse to soul sapping shortcuts of 'benefit seeking' (understandable, yes, but only up to a point) in these seemingly unending 'electoral auctions' of India, even as the current political anomie in the country spreads wider and our deep distress sinks deeper. This then widens the existing gap and again keeps alive this notion of the 'unfinished agenda of partition'. 'What is broken up [soon] becomes confused' Seneca† had counselled many centuries ago. In our case—India, Pakistan, Bangladesh—why did we fracture history? For with us history is not just a collection of facts, it is what we begin saying, then believing and accepting it to be. That is why, for us, history is the repository of all our collective experiences, and the distilled learning of our people, but that is so only if we are able to first accept the relevance of that resource and then mine it diligently, with reverence, understanding and with honest restraint.

Modern Indian historiography has not sufficiently analyzed the role of such Muslim parties as the Khaksars, Ahrars, Khudai Khidmatgars, Momins and such others who opposed the Partition of India. Consequently, the role of the Muslim League, in events leading up to India's Partition has got accepted, but raising questions that must be answered. Also, whereas Jinnah and the Muslim League, from about

---

* Wilfred Cantwell Smith graduated in 1938 with his undergraduate degree at the University of Toronto, studying Oriental languages. He carried out theological studies in England working with, among others, the famous Islamicist H.A.R. Gibb (1895-1971), one of the editors of the famous *Encyclopedia of Islam*.
Source: http://www.as.ua.edu/rel/aboutrelbiowcsmith.html
** Mentioned by Bashiruddin Ahmed, vice-chancellor of Jamia Millia Islamic in a seminar 'Our Republic Post 6 December: A Dialogue', organised by the author on 6 March 1993.
† Lucus Annaeus Seneca was a Roman stoic philosopher, statesman, dramatist. He was tutor and advisor to Emperor Nero.

1937 onwards, contested only the Congress; the Congress, in turn was meeting the challenge on two fronts—against the British and against the Muslim League. Had Muslim parties like Khaksars and Ahrars, who stood against partition and also the British, been brought on board on a larger enough front, would it have helped? However, there was a very real difficulty here—a worsening communal situation, it made such a united opposition an impossibility.

It is on account of these many questions that I still fail to understand why was India partitioned in 1947? Or the manner in which it was done. Of course, I have knowledge of the broad mechanics of it but not any deep understanding or acceptance of the attendant rationalizations, those fundamentals which made us choose this awful vivisection as our preferred option. It is over sixty years since this divide took place but it is still, unquestionably, the outstandingly defining event of the twentieth century, for India and for Pakistan.

Pakistan and Bangladesh both now established, independent states, of course, have total acceptance, and good wishes for achieving a stable polity with a thriving economy, and a social order that gives them comforting internal peace. We have all been born of Partition; we were one, India, Pakistan and Bangladesh, up till the third quarter of 1947, now we are three separated entities, but are we truly all that different? I cannot help querying so.

However, 'sowing questions', cautions Michel de Montaigne wisely in his *Essays of Experience,* 'make[s] the world teem with uncertainty'.[2] It is difficult to disagree with the wisdom of this nugget, primarily because too 'many interpretations clearly disperse truth'. Yet where does our 'truth' then lie?

Even Gandhi, ceaselessly searching for 'Truth' had found in our partition a very great tragedy. He had, in that fateful year of 1946, in Noakhali, jotted on a scrap of paper, using a pencil stub: 'I don't want to die a failure. But I may be a failure'.[3] Jinnah, too, failed, his life ending tragically just over a year of partition, (11 September 1948). He had had to settle for a 'moth-eaten' Pakistan, and that, too, he failed to mould into a working state, leave alone a shining example of that implausible theory of 'Muslims as a separate nation'. Consequently, the divided lands and people of India, Pakistan, later also Bangladesh have become a subcontinent in which 'peace has abandoned' us all; has it done so for ever? I wonder, for if it has, then that would be a disaster of untold dimensions; but then, have we needed the resource to prevent that? I think by constant questioning, by attempting to discover our own verities, not the handed-down versions we could prevent a repetition of the great errors of our past.

'Muslims—A Separate Nation'?

That is why these become the principal questions: why Partition and how are 'Muslims a separate nation'? Unarguably, all this had started just over a hundred years ago, (Simla delegation, 1906), with separate electorates but it is on this narrow foundation had finally got built the assertion of separate 'nation-hood' on which Mohammad Ali Jinnah had achieved that near impossible, of willing into being what he enunciated: 'Muslims are a separate nation'. That 'nation' came into existence on 14 August 1947. That controversial call through a persistent repetition of which Jinnah succeeded in carving out a separate land, how do we now, ex-post facto assess it? Did the birth of Pakistan conclusively prove Jinnah's thesis? Or was there actually a rejection of this thesis in the emergence of Bangladesh? This, and other similar ones are rather worrying questions. Did Jinnah's death empty the core of this idea? Also, this concept, propounded by Jinnah and the path on which he had set his creation—Pakistan—does the reality of it tally with those early fundamentals? With the coming into being of Pakistan did Jinnah's journey end? Or is the past of his idea actually a forerunner of our future?

Towards the end (1940-47) Jinnah, was both a self-avowed and the actual political leader of almost the entire Muslim community of undivided India. He had started his political life as an early champion of Hindu-Muslim unity, along with total commitment to the cause of freedom from the British. During that period he stood unambiguously for a united India; yet when he sought a Muslim 'nation', that was through partition, a division, and only in terms of a separation from India, whether internal or external, but as a separate entity. M.R.A. Baig, for some years Jinnah's secretary, has written in *Jinnah:* 'Islam, as such, came very little into his thinking, and if asked how mere belief in a common faith', by people of essentially the same ethnic stock could make a nation; he always gave the example of 'Americans [having proven] that nationalism was purely subjective. If the Muslims thought themselves a nation, [well then] they were a nation, and that was all there was to it'. This was not just a lawyer's argument, it was Jinnah's assertion of his belief in the 'power of faith, which he held to be the foundation of nationhood'. Even though this kind of reasoning remains riddled with infirmities, for Jinnah this was the needed and the only philosophical (at least so it sounded) platform, a kind of a much needed ideological 'cap', wearing which an idea [such as this] could be pushed. His opposition was not against the Hindus or Hinduism, it was the Congress that he considered as the true political rival of the Muslim League, and the League he considered as being just an 'extension of himself'. He, of course, made much of the Hindu-Muslim riots (1946; Bengal, Bihar, etc.) to 'prove the incapacity of Congress Governments to protect Muslims; and also expressed fear of "Hindu Raj" to frighten Muslims into joining the League, but during innumerable conversations with him I can rarely recall him attacking Hindus or Hinduism as such. His opposition, which later developed into almost hatred, remained focused upon the Congress leadership.'[4]

The Muslim community for Jinnah became an electoral body; his call for a Muslim nation his political platform; the battles he fought were entirely political—between the Muslim League and the Congress; Pakistan was his political demand over which he and the Muslim League could rule. Religion in all this was entirely incidental; Pakistan alone gave him all that his personality and character demanded. If Mr Jinnah was necessary for achieving Pakistan, Pakistan, too was necessary for the fulfilment of Mr Jinnah.

Phillips Talbot, as an eyewitness, (and he is perhaps the only one still alive) has assessed: 'Jinnah organised and hastened the development of Muslim solidarity with master strategy. By shrewd, brainy bargaining, cold-blooded astuteness, an absolute refusal to be panicked, and perceptive recognition of the strengths and weaknesses of both himself and his opponent, he has turned every opportunity to the advantage of the League. In negotiations he has consistently proved a match for the Congress high command with all its talent. "I am constitutionally and by long habit a very cold-blooded logician," he told an adulatory Muslim gathering last November'. No one could have analyzed him better.

Talbot continues: 'Jinnah is all in all in the League. As I write, nearly a month has passed since the British declaration that India will be free next year. In these weeks no important Muslim Leaguer has publicly expressed his reaction to the statement. The reason? Jinnah has kept mum, probably as a matter of tactics. In the United Provinces the deputy leader of the League Assembly Party told two of us in January that he favoured a coalition in the provincial ministry with the Congress Party and that, left to himself, he could swing his party to the same view. "But if Mr Jinnah said a word opposing this scheme," he added, "I would not have a vote with me".'[5]

And yet a great flaw remained; the tragic difficulty of the Muslims that were not part of this newly created Pakistan, either they did not or could not migrate; or they had chosen to stay back in India, or perforce had to. What about these Muslims? Would a separate nation be needed for them also? As A.G. Noorani, a prominent jurist, a perceptive and sympathetic observer of such causes and the history of that period has commented in *The Muslims of India:* 'Incredibly, some prominent members of the Muslim League demanded separate electorates in the Constituent Assembly of India even in the fundamentally altered situation, and thus fuelled distrust of Muslims which [then] pervaded significant sections in the Assembly. That is a measure of their incapacity for serious reflection and their utter incompetence in leadership'.

The fault, according to Noorani, lay also with Mohammad Ali Jinnah who in his total preoccupation with Pakistan and its creation did nothing to prepare the 'Muslim community as a whole about the new and emerging situation'. Mohammad Raza Khan, a prominent Muslim Leaguer, has recorded ruefully in his memoirs:[6] 'About the end of July 1947, the Muslim members of the Central Legislative Assembly met Mr Jinnah who was also the leader of the Muslim League Party in the Assembly. It was for the last time...for he was then arranging to leave for Karachi. [This] was their farewell meeting. Many members expressed concern about the future of the Muslims in India. When they sought his advice about their future, and that of the Muslim League, he refrained from saying anything specific. He, however, told them they had enough experience under his leadership, and they would have to evolve their own policy and programme. They had to decide things for themselves in the new set-up, and in the changed circumstances. But he made it clear, in no uncertain terms, that they should be "loyal" to India, and that they should not seek to ride two horses.'[7]

On 15 December 1947 the residual Muslim League in India adopted a resolution about reviving itself. Gandhi advised them not to, instead to lend their support to the Congress party.[8] This was wise counsel, welcomed even by Suhrawardy.[9] Sadly, though, Azad failed to rise to the occasion, a demoralized and confused Muslim community in India was his to lead, he did address them, in that much acclaimed oration of 23 October 1947 at the Jama Masjid, but that speech was far too layered over with the language of taunt and reproach, 'I hailed you; you cut off my tongue'. (See Appendix II).

Leaders of the Muslim League in the Constituent Assembly[10] had then, rather mindlessly, demanded not only a reservation of seats but separate electorates as well. This provoked Sardar Vallabhbhai Patel into delivering remarks that would have, on any other occasion been better left unsaid, but then with the country's partition wounds still raw, any such claim of reservations being raised again rubbed those wounds afresh and made them bleed all over again. The Sardar, in pain and in anger, admonished: 'I do not know whether there has been any change in their (the Muslims) attitude to bring forward such an amendment, even now, after all this long reflection and experience of what has happened in this country. But I know this that they have got a mandate from the Muslim League to move this amendment. I feel sorry for them. This is not a place today for acting on mandates. This is a place today to act on your conscience and to act for the good of the country. For a community to think that its interests are different from that of the country in which it lives, is a great mistake. Assuming that we agreed today to the reservation of seats, I would consider myself to be the greatest enemy of the Muslim community because of the consequences of the step in a secular and democratic State....[Those] who do not trust the majority, cannot obviously come into the Government....Accordingly, you will have no share in the Government. You will exclude yourselves and remain perpetually in a minority. Then, what advantage will you gain?'

Is that why there is in this a sense of disappointment and tragedy? Perhaps yes, but also perhaps because we continue to repeat the great errors of those epochal decades. Take 'minoritism', again. M.J. Akbar, in an erudite and magisterial essay analyses the challenge of it convincingly, in a yet to be published work *The Major Minority:* 'At what point in the story of the last thousand years did Indian Muslims become a minority? The question is, clearly, rhetorical. Muslims have never been in a numerical majority on the Indian subcontinent'.

Also then 'Did Indian Muslims consider themselves a minority during Mughal rule, which was finally buried, more than a hundred years after it had become impotent, in the rubble of the war of 1857?... Muslims formed only 11 per cent of the population of the most powerful Muslim princely state in the British era, Hyderabad; 84 per cent were Hindus. Did the Muslims of Hyderabad consider themselves a minority as long as the descendants of Nizam-ul Mulk, a Mughal governor who carved out an independent state from the shards of empire in 1723, ruled them? No.

'A minority, therefore, is not a consequence of numbers, but a definition of empowerment. As long as Muslims identified with the stare, were confident that they could expect economic benefits as well as jobs in the bureaucracy, judiciary and military, and their *aman-i-awwal* (liberty of religion) was protected, demographic figures were irrelevant'. That is why they were then psychologically not a minority, and yet, continues Akbar: 'In 1948, [as soon as] the Nizam was deposed and Hyderabad was absorbed into the new...Union of India...the same Muslims suddenly began to think of themselves a minority?' Why? An answer to this would settle a number of questions, I think.

It is in this, a false 'minority syndrome' that the dry rot of partition first set in, and then unstoppably it afflicted the entire structure, the magnificent edifice of an united India. The answer (cure?), Jinnah asserted, lay only in parting, and Nehru and Patel and others of the Congress also finally agreed. Thus was born Pakistan. However, minoritism in India stayed back and has now actually become even more emphasized, more acute, for we now have a precedent to follow, which with us is more binding than even constitutional provisions; suicidal, no doubt but we persist in flagrant masochism. In Pakistan it found new sectarian designs to assert minoritism, as in Bangladesh, too, though, in reality the Hindu of an undivided Bengal, had actually assented to a division of Bengal. So in all this what have we resolved? I can't find any answer; for this entire episode of the breaking up of India in 1947 is one of those rare conundrums of history which appears to be an answer but in reality is very far from it. Such paradoxes have no answers, but as in life so in politics and in history, too, paradoxes quite often resolve contradictions.

Islam and the Nation Concept

The late Girilal Jain, in a very learned and elegantly written dissertation entitled 'The Hindu Phenomenon' has given expression to his thoughts: 'Some Muslim scholars, he writes, have questioned the validity of the concept of Islamic state as distinct from Muslim state, the first being an ideological proposition which has never materialized in Muslim history because no Muslim state has ever been theocratic and the second being a fact of history in the past 1400 years. It would be recalled that the possibility and desirability of an Islamic state, that is, a state based on the Quran and the Hadith, had become a major issue of world-wide debate in view of the triumph of the Khomeini led revolution in Iran, in 1979'.[11]

In terms of facts, all this is irrefutable. The power struggle in the Muslim world has been as violent and unprincipled as anywhere else in the world; Muslim rulers have as a rule been as pleasure-loving and self-seeking as their counterparts elsewhere. 'But these facts need to be placed in....proper perspective. This cannot be done unless we grasp the central point that Islamic society, as Gai Eaton has put it in his *Islam and the Destiny of Man* is theocentric and not theocratic'.[12] The distinction is important and it is truly extraordinary that it has been missed in most of the writings on Islam.

The centrality of the state in human affairs is a modern development. Traditional societies regarded the state as no more than a necessary evil since large societies could no longer be managed on the old tribal basis. In the case of 'Hindus, this proposition is widely accepted despite the theories modern apologists have propagated in the past one century. It is generally accepted that as a self-regulating community, the Hindus have not been unduly dependent on the State and indeed that they have managed to preserve their identity under prolonged foreign rule on that strength' [alone].

To return to the question of this distinction between theocentrism and theocracy, it should scarcely be necessary to define theocentrism. However, it has become necessary to do so in view of the confusion that prevails. So it needs to be emphasized that for the Muslims, all sovereignty vests in God and that, indeed, nothing whatever exists or can exist outside of Him. It follows that God is the sole legislator; to quote Gai Eaton again, the Quranic insistence that 'there is no god but God' can be interpreted to mean that 'there is no legislator but the

Legislator'. That is precisely why for the Muslims their laws have to be derived from the Quran and the Sunnah of the Prophet. And they have been so derived in the past fourteen centuries. That is what has given the Ummah the unity it has possessed despite all the political turmoils it has passed through. That would also explain why jurisprudence and not theology has been the main preoccupation of Islamic scholarship.

The central issue, [therefore] in Islam has not been whether the state can be separated from religion but whether society can be separated from religion. It is because the answer to the second has to be firmly in the negative that the answer to the first has also to be in the negative. In posing the first question—whether the state can be separated from religion—without simultaneously posing the second—whether society can [also] be [so] separated from religion—scholars have, to use the old cliché, sought to put the cart before the horse. The modern mind just cannot comprehend Islam, precisely because it is a totality. Islamic society is rooted in the religion of Islam; it is not the other way about. The point needs to be heavily underscored that Islamic society is wholly unlike Christian society in terms of which it is judged. Unlike [Prophet] Muhammad, Christ did not give his people the law; Christians inherited the Roman law; in plain terms, Christianity did not represent a break from the Graeco-Roman past except in the field of religion narrowly defined. Islamic law is not rooted in pre-Islamic Arab traditions; it is rooted in the Quran and the Sunnah of the Prophet. As such Islamic society was a new 'creation' even if old materials had gone into its making in the sense Christian society was not a new 'creation'. [Sanatan Dharma, which is now, also and mostly though rather loosely termed as Hinduism, is a similar totality. But that is another issue, and I cannot even touch upon that here.]

As Islam stepped out of the spartan Arab setting in its formative period, its rulers were bound to succumb to the ways of the Byzantinian and the Sassanid empires they inherited, and they so easily succumbed. The glorious Muslim civilization that we admire and the Muslims take great pride in was, however, in no small measure the product of this development.

One aspect of this great civilization has not attracted the attention which, in my view, it deserves and about which we have commented in an earlier chapter. It created a divide between the Persianised, sophisticated and pleasure-loving upper crust and the pious and the ordinary Muslims, a rift which has not healed despite Islam's insistence on equality. This rift could have proved fatal for Islam, especially in the context of the introduction of the Aristotlean rationalist 'poison' into Islamic philosophy, if the state had acquired the kind of power it now enjoys in society. Islamic society has survived because over much of its history the state has been so marginal to it.

The gulf between Islamic exotericism as represented by the *ulama* and Islamic esotericism as represented by the Sufis of different orders is too wide to be glossed over. The great Ghazzali* sought to play a major role in integrating Sufism with Sharia, but this chasm was too wide even for him. Reluctantly we have to leave this highly engrossing dissertation here and proceed with the analysis that we have been engaged in an examination of Jinnah's journey from one end of the spectrum to the other; from unity to division.

Partition and Afterthoughts in India

This Partition of India first into two states, then subsequently three when Pakistan, too, split, (India, Pakistan, Bangladesh) could, of course, not leave India free of its many after effects. It is instructive that after thoughts about partition had begun to assail successor states early. Nehru, one of the principal architects, in reality the draftsman of India's partition began questioning himself, his actions, his thoughts soon enough. Mohammad Ali Jinnah died too soon after he had carved out a Pakistan in the face of near impossible circumstances to re-examine what he had done. But he, too, had begun to recognize the enormity of this partition, of what had happened, though, unfortunately we have not any written testament from him to inform us of his inner thoughts. His pre-1947 statements and the often quoted 11 August 1947 speech are in reality but indicators of his thoughts, not any definitions. [see Appendix I of this chapter]

This repeated partitioning of the land, inflicted deep wounds on India's psyche. In a seminar titled 'Our Republic Post—6 December 1992', held on 6 March 1993, late Bashiruddin Ahmed, then the vice

---

* Al-Ghazzali was born in Tus, Khurasan in Northeast Iran, which was destroyed by the conquering Mongols in 1389. He studied theology, philosophy, logic, and natural science. In Baghdad he joined the court of the Saljuks where he met many scholars and poets, patronized by the Persian wazir (minister of the court), Nizam Al-Mulk.

chancellor of Jamia Millia Islamia[13] had shared with other participants his views: 'I am once again sort of going back to what I call the "first principles". Emphasizing [these] "first principles" does not help always, but nevertheless it, I suppose, makes clear what is the direction in which we want to move. Notwithstanding all that, why is it that we had 6 December?[14]....I think one of the reasons why we had 6 December was primarily because there was an "unfinished agenda" of the national movement.

'Basically, the way I look at it is that the direction in which Indian nationalism was evolving was a direction that was culturally very Hindu and, I think, for a variety of reasons that evolution of nationalism in that direction got interrupted. There was necessarily a kind of ad hocism that crept in, and that ad hocism is our handling of the situation of what is Indian nationalism. It crept in essentially because of Partition....That was the time to dampen fires, and we had at the helm of affairs Jawaharlal Nehru, and he [was] ideologically committed to the notion of a modern secular state....Panditji's presence—his enormous influence—did not resolve the issue. It kept it in abeyance....Once this remarkable social transformation took place, once this enormous middle-class emerged and villages became accessible, then it was possible to raise this question of what is Indian nationalism?[15] Partition was after all a direct consequence of "separate electorates" and took in its train "various charters of demands like Jinnah's famous fourteen points. [Which is why] any expression of Muslim grievances or of the Muslim" identity now reminds India of that, and causes discomfort. Muslims' positive contribution to a secular ideal, "as distinct from protests against injustices" remain unconvincing. And yet, all are ready to exaggerate the dangers, raise apprehensions and garner the vote, not one to counsel sagely....It is obvious that whatever may be the future of India, and even if there is a regular partition, the different parts of India will have to cooperate with each other in a hundred different ways.'

It is a sad afterthought that despite all these reflections about 'union plus independence or disunion' etc., Nehru finally became a proponent of partition. And, it is not as if Independence of the country on 15 August 1947 eliminated all such 'after-thoughts' from his mind. After all, shortly after Independence, Gandhi was assassinated. Besides, as a by-product of partition the human suffering, loss of lives and uprooting was truly unprecedented; an empty recital of figures of the dead—or the uprooted does not, indeed cannot adequately convey the dimension of human suffering. Stanley Wolpert in *Shameful Flight* reports that 'Nehru too, after the catastrophic killings and uprootings that the land went through during those terrible days of 'freedom', told Mountbatten, on the eve of the latter's departure: 'It is difficult for me or anyone to judge of what we have done during the last year or so. We are too near to it and too intimately connected with events. Maybe we have made many mistakes, you and we. *Historians a generation or two hence, will perhaps be able to judge what we have done right and what we have done wrong...* [I] believe that we did try to do right, and therefore many of our sins will be forgiven us and many of our errors also.'[16]

Did he do right or did Mountbatten do right? Great doubts assail us in response, and the answer is not always as forgiving as Nehru, or others had then assumed, or might still do. However, it has to be said, and with great sadness, that despite some early indications to the contrary, the leaders of the Indian National Congress, in the period between the outbreak of war in 1939 and the country's partition in 1947, showed in general, a sad lack of realism, of foresight, of purpose and of will.

Corresponding with the late Nawab Sahib of Bhopal, Nehru replied on 9 July 1948, just a few weeks after Bhopal had questioned him about this partitioning of the country: 'It has been our misfortune', he wrote, 'the misfortune of India and Pakistan, that evil impulses triumphed.... I have spent the greater part of my adult life in pursuing and trying to realize certain ideals....Can you imagine the sorrow that confronts me when I see after more than thirty years of incessant effort the failure of much that I longed for passionately?.... I know that we [are] to blame in many matters Partition came and we accepted it because we thought that perhaps that way, however painful it was, we might have some peace....Perhaps we acted wrongly. It is difficult to judge now. And yet, the consequences of that partition have been so terrible that one is inclined to think that anything else would have been preferable....All my sense of history rebels against this unnatural state of affairs that has been created in India and Pakistan....There is no settling down to it and conflicts continue. Perhaps these conflicts are due to the folly or littleness of those in authority in India and Pakistan....Ultimately, I have no doubt that India and Pakistan will come close together...some kind of federal link. There is no other way to peace. The alternative is...war.[17]

This is a remarkably candid and very moving letter, almost 'confessional'. Such afterthoughts, starkly honest appraisals of his own acts, judgments upon himself were both Nehru's great strength as a human being, and his great failing as the first prime minister of a newly independent India.

The Partition that Robbed Us All of Peace

'We thought...we might have some peace,' Nehru had poignantly shared with the late Nawab Sahib of Bhopal. His surmise was tenuous, hardly justifiable: that this partition of India on the basis of faith—Hindu and Muslim, ought finally to resolve our communal discord and usher in an era of lasting peace was hopelessly off centre. Of course, it did not; instead 'peace' abandoned us. But then, how and why did partition rob us of it? Why, instead of our being left with unending peace, we got endowed with constant tension and conflicts?

This thought is in some manner central to our enquiry about Jinnah's journey; it has a direct bearing, for it is born directly from that unsustainable assertion of Muslims being a 'separate nation'. The basic and structural fault in Jinnah's notion remains a rejection of his origins; of being an Indian, having been shaped by the soil of India, tempered in the heat of the Indian experience. Muslims in India were no doubt subscribers to a different faith but that is all; they were not any different stock or of alien origin. The Muslims were willingly Indian, in every conceivable manner, for so long as they ruled over parts of India. It is the subsequent, slow decay of their rule, year after year, until that final, forceful and violent usurpation of both power and sovereignty from the last Mughal emperor that sowed seeds of uncertainty and insecurity in their minds. After which, came many events and then finally Jinnah with his persistent advocacy of separation resulting finally in the vivisection of 1947.

With Montford Reforms, which had introduced elections, though with ownership of property as the qualifying requirement for voting rights in local bodies like municipalities, (1909-19) an opportunity had presented itself to the Muslims, there was at last an opening offered. It was instantly seized. 'Reservation' became the starting point and with a granting of that status the Muslims were recognized and set apart as a distinctively different political category again. Thereafter, from reservation to special percentages, one-fourth to one-third to minority rights; to where in majority its preservation (Punjab/Bengal); to parity, and finally to partition—this was one continuous, ever increasing demand charter, almost an evolutionary flow sheet. Partition had to be claimed, yes, but for what? Was it for security, communal order, peace—which of these was the impulse that most energized this call of partition? As none of these were sufficiently sustainable points for a division of India, there then arrived the thesis: 'Muslims are a separate nation'. On first hearing, this sounded so absolutely, totally, illogically wrong, so unacceptable; and yet, it acquired a beguiling resonance, through constant repetition as if some high principle was being enunciated, any refutation of which would be both unjust and a complex task when and if attempted; besides this slogan, though ersatz, was sufficiently high sounding. Ultimately, both the Congress, the League and the departing British tried so much, so assiduously, so continuously, so hard and for so long to break India, that India had finally to divide. And in the end the physical act of partitioning became just a shabby, graceless and an indefensibly crude 'give and take' of numbers: 'You have this, I'll take this'. And thus was fractured the great unity of this ancient land; a divide that could simply not bring any peace in its wake; it first compartmentalized and then tightly sealed Hindu-Muslim animosities, cementing festering grudges into near permanent hostilities; what was domestic—Hindu-Muslim, became international—India-Pakistan; we made global our domestic disagreements. For Pakistan, it became the policy plank—'perpetual and induced hostility towards India that became its premiere state policy', it could scarcely be otherwise.

Mohammad Ali Jinnah was, to my mind, fundamentally in error proposing 'Muslims as a separate nation', which is why he was so profoundly wrong when he simultaneously spoke of 'lasting peace, amity and accord with India after me emergence of Pakistan'; that simply could not be. Perhaps, late General Ziaul Haq was nearer reality, when asked, as to why 'Pakistan cultivated and maintained this policy of so much induced hostility towards India?', he replied (some say apocryphalically, but tellingly) that, 'Turkey or Egypt, if they stop being aggressively Muslim, they will remain exactly what they are—Turkey and Egypt. But if Pakistan does not become and remain aggressively Islamic it will become India again. Amity with India will mean getting swamped by this all-enveloping embrace of India.' This worry has haunted the psyche of all the leaders of Pakistan since 1947.

I share here some thoughts about how Pakistan has fared post-1947. Since birth it has been accompanied by high drama, often troubled by dark and imaginary shadows of history, also myths; some grandiose dreams and plans, therefore often intense emotionalism, and a sad absence of cold, phlegmatic logic. Inevitably therefore, the 'idea of Pakistan' has often got usurped, which is why Pakistan's friends have so often become its masters, and which is also why the 'state' of Pakistan continues to remain fragile, so unsure, so tense. However, there were other factors, too. Pakistan, founded on the notion of separateness, a 'nation' distinctly apart from India, could do no more than to continuously affirm its Islamic identity. It therefore adopted the identity of being an Islamic Republic. This seemingly direct and logical evolution from 'Muslims as a separate nation', to Pakistan as an 'Islamic State' was neither direct, nor evolutionary as might at first sight appear. In reality this has impeded Pakistan's coming into its own, evolving into a modern, functioning state. Sadly, a reasoning and credible national identity eludes it still. From becoming an Islamic state, Pakistan ultimately, again perhaps inevitably, had to become a 'jihadi state', and when set on this path—it also then became, again perhaps inevitably, the epicentre of global terrorism; the chosen house of all the names associated with this global scourge: Al Qaeda and Osama bin Laden and Taliban and so on.

However, this partition had made Pakistan start 'life' with great administrative disadvantages too. Upon attaining Independence, India, freed of British rule, had a continuing identity, a functioning administrative structure, and in that immense spread of its land sufficient mass, enough resilience and cushion to absorb multiple shocks, repeatedly, as it had done so often through history. Not so in Pakistan; the challenges that it faced upon independence were formidable. After all, Pakistan had been no more than a 'negotiating idea, a tactical ploy to obtain greater political role for the Muslims of India so that they could become arbiters of their own political and social destiny, instead of leaving it in the 'unreliable political hands of a Hindu Congress'.

Besides, no one, not even Jinnah knew, or had ever defined, Pakistan; the cry was always in the name of Islam. That is why when this dream of Pakistan finally became a reality, no one was prepared for it. There existed no prior assessment of problems or priorities, for no one had known what the final shape of Pakistan was going to be. Yet, 14 August could not wait, and Jinnah dared not ask for a deferment.

In less than two months provinces had to be divided, civil and armed services bifurcated and assets apportioned. 'This telescoped time table created gigantic problems for Pakistan, which unlike India had not inherited a capital, a government, the financial resources to establish and equip its administrative, economic and military institutions. The migration of millions of refugees imposed its own burdens on this fledgling state with an awesome burden of rehabilitation.' This comment, from a former Pakistani diplomat would be one amongst many, of the multiple challenges that then faced Pakistan. For a fledgling Pakistan a quick release from these problems lay in a psychological diversion, a 'confront India' approach; that was so obvious an escape, but sadly it led nowhere then, and cannot, pragmatically assessed, lead anywhere even now.

That is when, with the benefit of hindsight, I believe, India needed to give more, it needed to accept with greater generosity (of spirit, too) what had separated from its own body. This was, and is, an extremely difficult call; the trauma of a searingly cruel partition having cauterized the sensibilities of an entire subcontinent, generosity could not, does not come easily. The manner of carving out the land, the shattering of the psyche of an entire generation (more than one, perhaps) and that unprecedented uprooting of so many millions made any accommodation of the other's needs almost a superhuman demand, so at least it was in the beginning. Pakistan was starting on its journey of statehood neither with any abundance of options nor with the goodwill of an amicable settlement, a willing partition of assets amongst disputant brothers. Great bitterness got added to what was already a very bitter partition. Under these circumstances could India have been more understanding? This now becomes largely an academic query. However, for Pakistan, a major challenge lay in just standing on its own feet. There was practically no industry, the market for its agricultural produce lay in India. Pakistan produced three-fourths of the world's jute but all the processing mills were now in India. The non-Muslim entrepreneurial class had moved away, carrying their capital with them, uncertain of the future in this new state. The monetary assets apportioned to Pakistan were held by the Reserve Bank of India, and given the hostile environment the transfer of these was not taking effect smoothly.[18]

Despite there being just one idea of Pakistan, a separate nation for Muslims, the movement for it actually bequeathed to this struggling state a number of identities. One was clearly Indian, in that the principal supporters of Pakistan, its pillars, were Indian and identified themselves so culturally, though they were and remained totally opposed to any suggestion of a Hindu India. This is a sensitive and a difficult aspect of the entirety of India-Pakistan relations, particularly about 'national identity'. What we routinely call India's identity, axiomatically will continue to incorporate so many aspects of what is also today a 'Pakistan identity', just as Pakistan will retain an 'Indianness' in their identity, as today's construct of that part of North India which is analogous to and is an adjunct of it, or East Bengal (Bangladesh now) being exactly that in the East Pakistan naturally both rejects this aspect of its identity and yet revels in it, too. This is Pakistan's continuing identity struggle, though it is largely overlooked; sadly, however, it cannot be rejected. How possibly can the reality of one's geography be shed, sloughed off; or a common historical past be totally erased, yanked out—and then do what with the gap left behind?

There are other ideas of Pakistan; some have worked, others not. Pakistan aspired at one time to be 'a modern extension of the Mughal dynasty', but such aspirations grossly misread both their present and an historical reality. The Mughals were able to rule a part of North India for almost 350 years, only because they early established a political coalition with the other dominant political force of that period—the principal Rajput kingdoms of Rajputana. Pakistan, wanting then to be a legatee: of British India in the tradition of the Raj, got inverted and, most unfortunately, Pakistan is now much more of a 'rented state' than even when it was part of the British Empire. Dreams of cultural links with Central Asia (which links India has had through centuries) do not make Pakistan a boundary land between the 'teeming masses of India and the vastness of Central Asia'; it just cannot be that link (except now as an outpost for Central Asian terrorists) because the geographical, historical and cultural logic is too, different. In Pakistan's case, its aspirations sadly are much greater than the accompanying reality.

'A Fractured Freedom'

No matter how viewed, India's independence from the British Raj was beyond doubt a 'fractured freedom. Independence came to India and Pakistan in 1947 but accompanied by a cataclysmically violent, pain-filled breakup of the land and its people. Then also occurred such an inhuman uprooting of countless millions as had not ever been experienced, even in this land of great and tragic events. What had for centuries been their homes these millions trudged their way across un-drawn lines mostly on foot, to a strange new land as refugees. What was left behind was bitterness, a deeply wounding trauma which continues to torment the psyches of successor countries, till today.

Amongst those very seriously troubled was Gandhi, who in his sunset years and had begun to give in to uncharacteristically pessimistic ruminations: 'I don't want to die a failure. But I may be a failure.'[19] For Gandhi this fractured freedom from the British was a telling failure, for he had been robbed of his public life's central purpose: Hindu-Muslim unity. Time and again he now gave voice to despairing thoughts: 'Partition has come in spite of me. It has hurt me. But it is the way in which the partition has come that has hurt me more.'[20]

However, with so many working against India's unity, partition had to come. The utter weariness and fatigue that had then seized all; the British, Nehru, Jinnah, even Patel had to tell. Though, Gandhi alone continued to oppose what from the beginning he had termed as a 'vivisection'; but he was by then a rather lonely crusader, withdrawn, and separated from his own creation—the Congress party of those days that political instrument which he had honed to efficiency as his chosen instrument in 'his fight for India's freedom.' It was galling for him to recognize that this instrument—the Congress—had now accepted India's partition, also that his principal lieutenants did so almost without consulting him, leave alone his consent.

We cannot still help reflect, again, how tense and consequential had become the personal angularities between Jinnah and Gandhi; but so much more sharply between Quaid and Nehru. Between these latter two the differences got so bitter as to actually become a factor in the country's vivisection; this fracturing of freedom. The Congress, led by Nehru, was the political party that agreed to partition; then later as the occupant of the seat of authority, and as the head of government of the day, he was clearly guilty of failing totally in his duty of preventing the bloodshed of million of innocents. The fratricidal killing was of such unprecedented dimensions that the blood that then soaked our land continues till today to entrap Hindu-Muslim relations into congealed animosities. What were essentially domestic differences between these two communities got internationalized on 14 and 15 August 1947, they became issues of global concern. This inter-communal matter got converted into an India-Pakistan issue, a question for the UNO to be engaged with. How criminally shortsighted! That is why Gandhi till the last had continued to plead for 'independence' first, 'Pakistan' after that. Jinnah would not agree, but then sadly, neither did Nehru, nor Patel go along with the Mahatma.

Jinnah, as the pre-eminent voice of the Muslims of India, certainly from about 1937 onwards, wanted a share of India's sovereignty when it arrived to a recognizable seat in the decision making apparatus of independent India; given that, he had repeatedly said the 'Muslims of India would abandon all claims to a separate nationhood': obtaining for the Muslims of India a large enough presence in the central legislature was for him 'the core'. Plus, of course, enough provinces that were governed by the Muslim League (Punjab, Sindh, NWFP, Bengal, Jammu and Kashmir) so that a permanent safeguard could be built against the remaining Hindu majority provinces from overwhelming them. Nehru, thought differently, unlike the commonly held perception he was not then any multi-cultural pluralist, he did indeed stand for equal rights, but accompanied by majority rule, resulting in secular governance with uniform and equal citizenship. However, post-partition this last, a uniform and equal citizenship, would be extremely difficult to implement in practice, particularly after the emergence of a 'Muslim Pakistan', for then it would be near impossible to have a really equal citizenship, and Nehru knew that. That is precisely why this query, again: Could we not have avoided this partition? Which in turn, gives rise to questions like: What was that one single critical event, if there was indeed such a single event that caused an irrecoverable loss of will to keep India united but still win freedom from the British? Or was it really the utterly sapping fatigue of those years of freedom struggle which just wore the leadership all down, broke them into submission? If that then where the centre of gravity of our partition lies: in fatigue? Then who is responsible for giving in to fatigue? These are cruel and painful questions to raise but they have to be asked.

Opinions on this point have differed and will no doubt continue to as no totally objective view is possible. How can there be? Besides, of course, we are all judging ex post-facto now. Perhaps that is why it is so much easier for us to comment that there were many missed opportunities when the balance could easily have been tipped in the other direction, in Seervai's words from the book *Partition of India: Legend and Reality*—'without penalties, perils and burdens flowing from a Pakistan separated from India?'

Viewed from that angle, examined as dispassionately as possible, it appears that the great tragedy of partition was not inevitable. It became so, in addition to the many factors mentioned earlier, because of Jinnah's continued rigidity, his fixed stand on an ever increasing charter of demands for the Muslims, an ever larger share of power for them in independent India. Personal relations and particular temperaments obviously bulked large, and if one sees partition as a consequence of a clash of political judgments then clearly Jinnah and Nehru are central to how this clash ultimately got defined and how it finally brought about this great tragedy.

A counter to such observations asserts that this notion of 'Partition' being the consequence of any one single set of human interactions is totally wrong, for it is unacceptably simplistic. Temperaments, personality, and character obviously played a very important role, like for instance this abrasive friction between Jinnah and Nehru, also their continuing hostility. However, that simply could not have been the only factor that resulted in our partition. Yet Nehru continues to be blamed for India's drift to partition, and cited as illustrative of this are: at different moments, his totally incomprehensible tactlessness, so often childish impetuosity bordering on the naïve, but can only these be held as factors responsible?[21] What certainly pushed the situation towards partition was Nehru's inability to restrain himself, to always give his views to the press, and in a manner that almost on every occasion generated huge contention and multiple controversies, wiping out all earlier achievements. Time and again this happened prior to Independence; sadly it happened on several critical occasions post-partition, too, but that is another account. Late in 1943, in his Ahmednagar jail diary, Nehru had privately given words to his views about the Quaid: 'Jinnah offers an obvious example of an utter lack of the civilized mind. With all his cleverness and ability, he produces an impression on me of utter ignorance and lack of understanding and even the capacity to understand this world and its problems...instinctively I think it is better to (give) Pakistan or almost anything if only to keep Jinnah far away and not allow his muddled and arrogant head from interfering continually in India's progress'.[22] With such extreme views what else could have followed but an extremely painful separation?

Yes, that certainly contributed, but what else? Where does the 'centre of gravity' of India's partition lie? Was it the Quit India Movement of 1942-45, and its visible lack of success that so demoralized Congress leaders that they had neither any more wish nor much stamina left to carry on with this fight for India's unity? Annie Besant, in the early 1920s, in those Home Rule League days, when parting politically from Gandhi, had commented: 'The success of the non-cooperation movement would lead the Congress into a blind alley from which it would not be possible...to extricate....'[23] This presciently sharp observation got proven right. Whenever Gandhi stopped his 'non-cooperation movement', the Congress high command did not know what to do next, all of them floundered in answering an entirely legitimate query: 'What do we do now?'; Gandhi had his programmes and issues even outside of the civil disobedience movement and however faddist they might have then appeared, or do so till today, they imparted to his actions a central purpose, a certain direction, a moral unity. However, what of the others? They only followed, and if and when they did initiate action or a programme it was always too limited in its spread and too short in duration. Perhaps all this frequent jail-going had instilled in the Congress ranks, being mostly Hindu, a complacent sense of permanent martyrdom; they assumed that this jail-going 'sacrifice' would suffice by itself, and would surely be recognized, as a meritorious act, therefore rewarded by a 'will' higher than that of the British Raj. However, through being in jail so frequently the Congress leaders, without realizing, were actually avoiding responsibility. Compare their secluded activity of jail life between 1942-45 to Jinnah's consolidation of his leadership during the same period; and this was when Jinnah's constituency was in comparison minuscule, but in this sphere of Muslim support he soon enough made the League the sole representative, and he became the only authority, the 'sole spokesman'. Jinnah dented Congress strongholds like the NWFP; but the reverse never happened, not once. Here we have to ask, why not? Why could not the Congress win over any of the Muslim majority provinces? These provinces chose instead to part from India but not ever did they transfer allegiance to the Congress. Why? Was it because the Congress was so recognizably, so beyond dispute Hindu in character? Then why their continuing charade of pretending to represent the Muslims, too.

The Government of India Act of 1935 was a British Act; we welcomed it then, perhaps missing its deeper import, which is surprising considering the galaxy of jurists that the freedom movement had. Being British the Act clearly safeguarded their interests, and had provisions for British interference and actual decisions on matters that Indian patriots believed were entirely India's preserve, like decisions of war and peace. Of course, no legislative measure could (or can) ever provide bridges to cover Hindu and Muslim divides, but by then it was clear that retaining Indian unity simultaneously gaining freedom from the British was impossible unless we accepted wide enough federal foundations; and here lay the rub for this was anathema to Nehru's centralizing approach and policies. It is astonishing what great distance separates this 'centralizing' Nehru from the author of the *Discovery of India*, who he had approvingly quoted: 'Union plus independence or disunion plus dependence'.

That is why this was the great error; that one great dividing decision: not consenting to dominion status and a decentralized, yet united, and a federal India, when that was so clearly ours to attain. This failure goes a long way back. To the decades of early twentieth century, to that Gandhi-Nehru discord on this very issue in the twenties, even to Balfour, 1926.[24] That being so a nagging thought surfaces: Then why lament now? Because, unless we recognize those great errors, those many missteps that finally brought us to where we are today we will continue to repeat our mistakes, to flounder always in this morass of inherited wrongs.

There was yet another opportunity, the Cabinet Mission of 1946, the Mission offered a constitution that could have maintained the unity of India, but at a price, of having up to three 'groupings' in a federal India. This was the sort of constitution for which the Joint Memorandum of 1934[25] could have naturally and steadily prepared the ground. Congress' attitude to even this last effort remained questioningly evasive, therefore, discouraging and this too, finally fell by the wayside. In the end the only course that remained was to break, to partition, and from what was one

India there now got carved out a Muslim part, and by implication, an India that was now denominationally separated but not termed as such or as Hindu India and neither was it so defined. India was finally divided by a swift, massive, unheeding surgical cut. After all, that is what Jinnah had warned, and Mountbatten too, and following him were Nehru and Patel, who if not actually wanting it had certainly consented to let partition happen. When Leonard Mosley, many years later had asked Nehru, 'Why?' he had responded candidly but also with great inherent pathos: 'We were tired men and had been in prison for too long'.*

Jinnah, on the other hand, was and remained fixed and unwavering in both his aim, also the means to achieve them. He worked for freedom from British rule but simultaneously, he sought a special status and special rights for the Muslims, working ceaselessly for both these aims. He recognized that the attainment of freedom from the British was 'unlikely unless Hindus and Muslims united', for such unity he believed the senior partner, Hindus, had to give more; it is they, Hindus, who he felt 'must provide the needed assurance to the Muslim' minority that their rights would be safe in a self-governing India. He perfected the art of negotiating from a position of weakness, for either he had learnt it or experience had taught him the implacable and exasperating power of a 'No', endlessly repeated, and a 'demand sheet' that kept growing endlessly longer until finally when he ran slap into the sign board of 'No Road Ahead', then 'Pakistan', with no accompanying territorial definition was presented as a solution. Besides, he was by then, and he knew it too, terminally ill. He had to hurry, for time now, was not on his side.

The British, too, were in a hurry, they wanted to go, they wanted out, for they, too, were by then utterly weary of the ravages of the Second World War, of the many discomforts that afflicted a post-Second World War life in Britain, above all of this endless squabbling amongst Indians. They wanted now to simply escape from India. There were other factors, too, for such a precipitate withdrawal by the British. The

---

* 'We were tired men and we were getting on in years too. Few of us could stand the prospect of going to prison again—and if we had stood out for a united India as we wished it, prison obviously awaited us. We saw the fires burning in the Punjab and heard of the killings. The plan of Partition offered a way out and we took it.... We expected that Partition would be temporary, that Pakistan was bound to come back to us.'— Nehru in an interview with Leonard Mosley. [*The Last Days of British Raj*, London, Wiedefeld and Nicholson, 1960, p. 285.]

Palestine mandate had by then ended. With VE day and the cessation of hostilities on the mainland of Europe, pressure had begun to mount upon the British to admit displaced Jewish refugees from Europe. The Jewish underground forces in Palestine too, had by then united and were launching concerted attacks on British forces. On 22 July 1946 the Irgun[26] had blown up the King David Hotel in Jerusalem, headquarters then of the British Forces, killing ninety-two. The UN had also by then created the UN Special Committee on Palestine on 15 May 1947, and it became clear that a UN mandated partition plan dividing Palestine, would soon follow. The British were being crowded out from the Middle East, too; an unusual and a very uncomfortable position for that one time great power to be in.

However, why was the Congress party in such great hurry? Is it because their entire leadership was also utterly fatigued by then? In the interim government the Congress had tasted power and it begun to be sensed that they were now not so transparently willing to shed 'power', but most sadly that was so even if in consequence of this meant a partition of India. Nehru admitted as much to Mosley but that rather sad confession was very many years later, besides that could scarcely be a condonation of a breaking up of India. The Congress also, always overestimated its strength, its influence and its leaders were extremely reluctant to accept Jinnah as the leader of not just the Muslim League and eventually of most of the Muslims of India. The Congress leadership, sadly, also lacked a befitting sense of reality. About two weeks prior to 15 August 1947, Mountbatten had shared an observation with Nehru and Patel that 'within a fortnight they would have full power and responsibility in India; did they realize', he enquired, 'the problems they would then have to face'?[27] Both leaders the men replied that they 'knew all that they had to do….' But did they in reality? Or were the Congress leaders then suffering from the courage of misplaced confidence, born of ignorance?

One of Jinnah's fail-safe negotiating tactics was to consistently charge the Congress leadership with not wanting any settlement with him, implicitly the League, though however many times the reverse would actually have been a more accurate charge. However, the Congress, too, was at fault for whenever its leaders felt that the British were about to come to some terms with them, they ignored Jinnah, and when the British paid no heed to the Congress, Jinnah, too, felt no urge to talk to the leaders of that rival party. This totally untenable and quite unreal equality between these two political parties, the Congress and the Muslim League, was a transparent British ploy, because it was beneficial to their own interests and of course, to Jinnah as well, for which reason he felt no urge to resist such machinations. Strangely, the Congress too, kept silent, it acquiesced, even though clearly it was a much larger political body and had so much more to lose.

The Congress remained stuck for very long to a fatally faulty view 'that the settlement of Hindu-Muslim problems could not be brought about just by the Congress—or a Muslim League, led by Jinnah, an external referee was definitely needed, hence the British. Gandhi's views were far apart but they no longer influenced the Congress. This divided the perceptions of the League and the Congress, it divided their approach, yet again benefiting the British for it gave them a special tool with which to dismember India; that of being a referee with the authority to finally divide the country. In the process Jinnah did not win Pakistan, as the Congress leaders—Nehru and Patel finally conceded Pakistan to Jinnah, with the British acting as an ever helpful midwife.

This assessment of the Congress role will no doubt be disputed, that is entirely understandable. However, I persist for we now view through the magnifying glass of retrospective sight, in consequence, our vision is clearer, far more focused, also a great deal sharper, too.

These two dates—14 and 15 August 1947—have by now become signposts marking an official end to a once great British Empire in India; these are now the symbolic markers of time, denoting an 'official' end of an united India, too. They also inform us about when this ancient, historical, geographical and cultural entity—India—having withstood so many onslaughts, through so many centuries, finally got vivisected by ourselves, when we acted in concert with an alien power.

It is this thought that stops me in my tracks, and I am struck by the petty preoccupations of most 'leaders' of those times, of whatever political hue, or faith, Hindu or Muslim; their being so totally consumed by the detail of commas, colons and such other trivia, their small legalisms; their commitments, it seems predominantly to the subjunctive or the subordinate clauses, never reaching for, never ever grasping the sweep of the larger text of those times; a blind and self-absorbed preoccupation with merely the detail of the draft, not the destructive dimensions or direction of it. As with Wavell, quoting two lines from

Browning: 'Now enough of your chicane of prudent pauses, sage provisos, sub-intents and saving clauses'.

I reflect, bewildered at those strangely arrogant presumptions of unshakable certainty about one's own opinions, an assumed infallibility of viewpoint, whether about faith or systems or whatever, which then so pervaded the political environs then that nothing else was focused upon: 'The [very] thought of dominion status suffocates and chokes me', Nehru had said.[28] Yet in August 1947 was it not just that? And now additionally, with an India that stood divided. Then, why all those intervening years of suffering, death and loss? How pitiably trivial our rivalries and petty point scoring now seem in contrast to the great and awesome tragedy of partition; the enormity of the human suffering that this splintering of the psyche of India has caused to our society, our people and to the ancient unities that had been built over several centuries of togetherness, whether that togetherness was in cooperation, contention or even occasional conflict. All these got shattered on grounds of several alien notions. We turned things, concepts, principles on their heads. Even India, its freedom had, I fear, in some perverted manner become secondary. 'My viewpoint, above all', was then the overriding concern. The goal of a united, independent India became subservient to that unsustainable notion—'Muslims are a separate nation', which finally the Quaid-i-Azam got even if it was 'moth eaten'. Yet, is that what he had really sought? Or was it a journey to just a notionally separate land? Then, how did we make two out of what even now remain, in so many ways as one; if not entirely in spirit, certainly so in name: Punjab remains Punjab in India as in Pakistan. Why? So does Bengal, why again? Now try calling these two ancient states by any other name.

At a certain level another extremely troubling question then arises: was Jinnah's journey of separation an attempt to somehow convert these casually drawn lines on inaccurate geographical maps into 'boundaries of faith'; and that, too in a land and amongst people whose entire lives are structured and lived on the strength of faith alone, of whatever hue or persuasion that be, and who remain culturally intermixed; diverse—yes, but united by a multitude of similarities; inseparable, because a common inheritance of such profound and enduring durability bonds them together that even time has not been able to grind dust. Besides, how can the quest have been so cynical? That cannot be, there must be more, why otherwise were so many multiple millions of humans so consumed by hatred, and of such fierce intensity that the fires of 1947 smoulder still. And the many millions that were then uprooted, the Hindus and the Muslims and the Sikhs—ultimately, why? And then an even more troubling question: Is the late Quaid's journey, at last, now finally over? Or has it only just begun? Has the separation ended or is it somehow endless, this growing apart? Also that quest for 'parity' which then divided us, has that now finally been realized for there is a separate land now, a sovereign, independent equal land: or has that, too, been redefined now and will continue to be reiterated in today's idiom, as a brand new, oven-fresh animosity?

Mohammad Ali Jinnah's own views, or response on some of these aspects (for they continue to assail us still) plus the ease and the offhanded insouciance with which he so often responded to some of them is greatly worrying, besides his thinking does come across as fractured, not threaded through with a fundamental unity, the bonding glue of irrefutable logic or principle, and this from a man who lived on logic.

In a press meet on 14 November 1946, in New Delhi, Jinnah when asked about the future of the communal situation in a yet to be Pakistan had said that 'this tension which exists—that one nation is going to rule the other—will cease. These minorities will then settle down as minorities, They will realize minorities can live only as minorities and not as a dominant body'. [There is deep irony here, 'minorities only as minorities'? what then of the example of the many demands, special status, parity etc.]

'Once they realize that they have to live as minorities, then I think you will have really a stable and secure government in Pakistan and Hindustan, Why should there then be a national quarrel? The position is reduced to a much smaller plane, that is how best can the minorities be protected and safeguarded in the two states?

'Unless you say we are reduced to bestiality I do not see any reason why the Muslim minority [sic! majority] in Pakistan should not deal with the minorities in a most generous way.' Jinnah dismissed 'Pan-Islamism' as an exploded bogey and declared, 'whatever others might say, I think that these two states of Pakistan and Hindustan by virtue of contiguity and mutual interests will be friends in this subcontinent.... They will go to each other's rescue in case of danger and will be able to say "hands off" to other nations. We shall then have a Monroe Doctrine more solid than in America...I am not fighting for Muslims, believe me, when I demand Pakistan', he said, adding 'Pakistan and Hindustan alone will mean freedom to both Hindus and Muslims'.[29]

Sadly I reflect, what then has happened to those noble thoughts? To all these many expectations? Was it a kind of premonition that had persuaded Gandhi, reflectively to jot that 'Jinnah had declared that in Pakistan the minorities would, if possible, have better treatment even than the Muslims, there would be no under-dog or upper-dog; if the Muslim majority provinces, where it was as good as Pakistan, became wholly independent of the British power and realized that ideal set forth by Jinnah in practice, the whole of India would welcome such an order, no matter by what name it was called, and the whole of India would be Pakistan'.[30]

The need then as now remains for a little more understanding, some greater accommodation of the other's viewpoint, accepting the limitations of imported concepts, notions and transient 'isms', for all those were eventually ground into dust by time; indeed by the very 'Indianness' of India. It is not as if India had then succumbed, rather time subdued us.

As for democracy, India effectively transformed this globally proclaimed instrument of equality into an effective device for dividing: How absolutely exceptional! Remarkable also this whole question of reservations, for Muslim or any other, as a means of affirmative action, as a supportive uplifting of those that are disadvantaged; we converted this also into an instrument of creating new, permanently compartmentalized identities; combative preserves of new privileges. Was this the destination that we had, in truth, sought—the great Quaid, Gandhi, or Nehru and the Congress? To travel permanently in combative compartments of separateness? After all, it was the same Jinnah who on 14 November 1946, in a press meet had spoken of an Indo-Pak 'Monroe Doctrine more solid than America's'. Or were they just words?

In this press conference, which amongst other things illustrated how ad hoc and ill thought this idea of Pakistan was. To advocate on the one hand, (as Jinnah did) a 'Monroe Doctrine more solid than America's,' but on the other casually proposing an 'exchange of populations'. This statement appeared as a single line item in the *Dawn* of 15 November 1946. Questioned about communal disturbances Jinnah said: 'This exchange of population will have to be considered seriously, as far as possible, specially after this Bihar tragedy'.

Of course, the painful history of South Asia cannot be altered, but that the Indian National Congress also acquiesced in this great tragedy of populations trudging into the unknown, still horrifies, it is doubly unfortunate that leaders of the freedom movement in 1947 failed posterity.

That is why there is a need to ask whether Jinnah actually reached that long sought after destination of 'Muslims as a separate nation?' Or was that at all his destination or the goal of his struggle? I hesitate to somewhat venture further on this dangerous territory, placed as I am, on the perch of this sharpened vision of hindsight, and also on the edge of the unlimited potentialities of this new century, a new millennium. It is Pakistan and the Muslims in India that have to respond to this. Jinnah's untenable notion of 'Muslims as a separate nation' was not any geographical destination, it simply could not be; it was much more the search for a defining concept; but that, too, in itself was an error of profound and telling dimensions. Which is why Jinnah got the land (even if moth eaten) but failed to create a 'state'; and failed so decisively in creating a 'nation'. He and the others (Mountbatten, also Nehru) had helped cut the land of India, surgically, and divide the people, but even they could not, surgically or otherwise, craft a 'nation' to come into being.

If, in Jinnah's mind, partition was a simple, pragmatic solution with the 'Two-Nation theory' as a temporary ideological justification, and with a marked sense of a continuing unity with India despite the partition, then partition, then the Congress, as an unconvincing advocate of unity, made little allowance for the diversities of and in India and, in effect, followed policies which impaired that unity. Little thought was given to autonomy, or how it should be spread in the Indian federation. The famous Jagat Narain Rai resolution of the All-Indian Congress committee, passed in 1942, opposed the grant of the right of secession to any member of the federation. However, in September 1945, the Congress Working Committee, while recalling this very resolution, said in the same breath that it could not think in terms of compelling the people in any territorial unit to remain in an Indian Union against their declared and established will. The person in the Congress party who had given some thought to this problem was

Maulana Azad. As he subsequently wrote in his memoirs, he had come to the conclusion that the Indian federation should deal with just three subjects: defence, foreign affairs and communications; thus granting the maximum possible autonomy to the provinces. According to the Maulana, Gandhi accepted his suggestion, while Sardar Patel did not. Maulana Azad had issued a statement on 15 April 1946, containing a masterly critique of the Pakistan demand and advocating instead a centre with very limited powers. However, there can be little question in the light of later events that this represented an expression of his personal opinion rather than the stand of the Congress.[31]

Lloyd and Susanne Rudolph whilst sharing thoughts on the subject with me have commented: 'Was Jinnah's articulation and pursuit of the "two nation" doctrine a political goal of establishing a separate and sovereign nation state or as a political strategy designed to share sovereignty in a multinational Indian state'. I think it is better read as a political strategy. Here is why.

Jinnah's finest hour was negotiating the Lucknow Pact in 1916 with Bal Gangadhar Tilak. He was hailed as a nationalist leader and the 'architect of Hindu-Muslim unity'. And he negotiated the pact with Congress as if the Muslim League and Congress were on par. This last was without any doubt a very significant concession by the Congress to the League. However, there was an unexpected and an unintended consequence of this: the rise of a variety of faith based ethnic nationalism which defined national identity only in terms of shared faith. This was a very damaging development, for once this ethnic nationalism captured the imagination of the Muslims in a society like India's, an eventual disaggregation or partition had to be the most likely consequence; another by-product then being the birth of 'politics of identity'.

There existed several examples of this. As Walker Connor has observed: 'Long before the nineteenth century, countries such as England, France, Portugal, Spain, and Sweden emerged as nation-states in polities where ethnic divisions had been softened by a long history of cultural and social homogenization'. Most speakers of Italian and German language were brought together as a nation state through a unification in the 1860s. But as late as the beginning of the Great War, most of the Central, Eastern and South-Eastern Europe was part of an empire and not any nation state—the Hapsburg, the Romanov and the Ottoman. Though these empires included a large number of ethnic groups, they were not multi-ethnic; not everyone amongst the populace had an equal status. This is where, conceptually, Gandhi was so right, Jinnah, Nehru and the British so wrong, for above all India is not, was not any eighteenth century Europe.

'Now, of course, we take the nation-state for granted as the "natural form of political association and regard empires as anomalies. But over the broad sweep of recorded history, the opposite is closer to the truth". There is of this yet another, explosive consequence. As Lord Acton recognized in 1862: "By making the state and the nation commensurate with each other in theory, [nationalism] reduces practically to a subject condition, all other nationalities that may be within the boundary...."' Not so much any reality but even the notion of it caused a psychological separation in a united India.

In reality ethnic disaggregation on a massive scale began on Europe's frontiers. 'In the ethnically mixed Balkans, wars to expand the nation-states of Bulgaria, Greece, and Serbia, at the expenses of the ailing Ottoman Empire were accompanied by ferocious interethnic violence.... World War I then led to the demise of the great turn-of-the-century empires, unleashing an explosion of ethno-nationalism in the process.... Out of the breakup of the Hapsburg and Romanov empires emerged a multitude of new countries. Many conceived of themselves as ethno-national polities, in which the state coexisted to protect and promote the dominant ethnic group.'

Our study of history must informs us that 'Winston Churchill, Franklin Roosevelt, and Joseph Stalin all concluded that the expulsion of ethnic Germans from non-German countries was a prerequisite to a stable postwar order'. As Churchill put it in a speech to the British parliament in December 1944: 'Expulsion is the method which, so far as we have been able to see, will be the most satisfactory and lasting. There will be no mixture of populations to cause endless trouble....A clean sweep will be made. I am not alarmed at the prospect of the disentanglement of population, nor am I alarmed by large transferences.' He cited the Treaty of Lausanne as a precedent, showing how even the leaders of liberal democracies had concluded that only radically illiberal measures would dominate the causes of ethno-national aspirations and aggression.'

The Imperial British had announced their intentions, about breaking ancient identities, our leadership was, however, not listening; it was not paying heed to these forewarnings. The end of the British Raj in 1947 brought about the partition of the subcontinent into India and Pakistan, along with an orgy of unprecedented violence that took hundreds of thousands of lives. Fifteen million people became refugees. Then, in 1971, 'Pakistan itself, originally conceived as the foundation of Muslims are a separate nation, "dissolved into" language divisions, Urdu and Bengali Pakistan and a Bangladesh'.

Yet it would be a mistake to think that because nationalism is partly constructed it is, therefore, fragile or infinitely malleable. Ethno-nationalism corresponds to some enduring propensities of the human spirit that are heightened by the process of modern state creation, it is a crucial source of both solidarity and enmity, and in one form or another, it will remain for many generations to come. One can only profit from facing it directly. However, this was a diversion and we must revert to the Lucknow Pact.

Surjit Mansingh summarizes the political circumstances and provisions of the Lucknow Pact: '...a scheme of constitutional reforms toward self-government presented jointly by the Indian National Congress [negotiated]...by the venerated Bal Gangadhar Tilak and the All-India Muslim League led by the dynamic Mohammad Ali Jinnah. Both parties had put forward demands for self-government during their concurrent sessions in Bombay in 1915 and set up committees to draft concrete proposals. Congress leaders sought unity, without which they could hardly advance their goals; Tilak [like Gandhi in 1946 and earlier, Lajpat Rai] wanted the British to leave as soon as possible and was sufficiently pragmatic by then to accommodate demands by the Muslim League for the sake of the larger cause. Jinnah too was anxious to bring the fledgling Muslim League and the experienced Congress together. Accordingly, the League pledged full support for Congress aims of self-government and a parliamentary system for India—which meant executive responsibility to an elected legislature; Congress accepted the League's demand for weighted representation and separate electorates for Muslims.'

Lloyd and Susanne continuing, add: 'The Lucknow Pact, a kind of constitution for India, recognized two nations and one state, what might be called a multi-national state that encompasses multiple sovereignties and, implicitly, a dynamic, bargaining relationship among them'.

Was Jinnah's subsequent bargaining strategy an attempt to maintain the goal of independence from British rule but with this independence vested in a multi-national Indian state capable of sharing sovereignty. It is these terms and conditions for sharing that were negotiated and renegotiated between 1916 and 1947 in a triangular bargaining, among the British Raj, the Congress with the Muslim League. Jinnah[32] at the time of the Nehru Report [1928] tried for a third of the seats in the Central legislature, and may have been willing to settle for a quarter of them if only he could get two more Muslim majority provinces [Sindh and Baluchistan]. During the end game of 1946, and the Cabinet Mission plan he accepted 'the multi-layered federal scheme [which included the Congress ruled NWFP grouped with Punjab in Part A and Assam grouped with Bengal in Part B], both of which Nehru couldn't swallow, and an Interim government with 6 Congress, 6 ML, one Sikh and 1 Depressed Classes ministers'.

Jinnah's position becomes clearer as the end of 1940 draws near. In negotiating the Lucknow Pact and his subsequent positions in recognizing and legitimizing the 'Two-Nation Theory' but 'not', Lloyd Rudolph asserts, *necessarily recognizing Muslims as a separate nation state.* 'It is more', he writes, 'in the context of recognizing and legitimizing a multi-national or pluralist state, a type of state that stands in marked contrast with the nation state, a state form taken to be the end point of the teleology of the modern state.' He continues reasoning that 'A multi-national state....shares sovereignty among a variety of actors. India's federal system, particularly its linguistic states, is a manifestation of a multi-national state that shares and bargains about sovereignty. Similarly, reservations for SCs, STs and for OBCs, as well as the 73rd amendment's creation of a third tier of local government [panchayat raj] manifestations of sharing and bargaining about sovereignty in a multi-national state. These developments are consistent with the kind of bargaining strategy that Jinnah adopted at the time of the Lucknow Pact and subsequently'.

[Note: For a more detailed study of the dialogue that the author exchanged with Lloyd and Susanne Rudolph, please read Appendix III to this chapter.]

That notwithstanding, now sixty-odd years after emerging as a new country, separated from India and as a sovereign entity, Pakistan has evolved; it now has a much greater and sharpened sense of its 'Pakistanness', a more enhanced consciousness of it being a distinctly separate country from India, and not just in contra-distinction to India.

Its induced and perpetual sense of hostility to India is now somewhat mellowed, it is more confident of itself, therefore, accommodative and is now ready to accept a greater understanding of the many onenesses and unities that bond India and Pakistan together. Or is it really ready? Dare I ask?

However, sadly, even this land for Muslims has not been the end of the journey. Pakistan went further along the path of Islamic exclusiveness, it opted to become an Islamic state, and this after having already separated on grounds of Islam. The country then adopted Sharia, as the foundational philosophy of its jurisprudence. From this to an acceptance of a law of apostasy, as part of the law of the land was inevitable, equally so then would become the transference of responsibility for interpreting law from courts of law to *maulvis* in the mosques. Tragically, Pakistan chose terrorism as an instrument of state policy, to be employed as a tool of external aggression. However, nemesis had to visit upon such policy planks; that malevolent energy of terror, by whatever name you choose to call it, once unleashed had to turn back upon its own creator and to begin devouring it. This has now converted Pakistan into the epicentre of global terrorism, sadly, therefore, Talibanization now eats into the very vitals of Pakistan. None of this was a part of Jinnah's dream of either 'Muslims as a separate nation', or that long sought after land of Pakistan.

Prof. Rosalind O'Hanlon has perceptively observed that upon partition in 1947, Pakistan suffered also from disabilities inherited from the days of the Raj: 'Punjab having been from the 1860s to 1947 the garrison province of the colonial state, its farmers and landlords nourished by generous agrarian policies, its landlords unchallenged by the kind of rural movements for social change that emerged elsewhere in India encouraged by the Congress or socialist parties. At independence, therefore, the most powerful institution in Pakistan was the army, and in the wider society, the powerful landed classes'. And that is what has remained, largely, not just in Punjab, but in reality in the whole of Pakistan.

It is also ironic in the extreme that Pakistan, mid-wifed by the West, as a strategic outpost to safeguard their (own) interests, ought today, more than sixty years after partition be for them the West, a 'fearsomely chaotic and dangerous country' posing the 'greatest challenge to their (West's) security'; and this metamorphosis is not a consequence of any one factor alone, like Islamic terrorism, though, currently that is most frequently cited. On the contrary, it is a compendium of many accumulated grievances, a deep sense in the minds and hearts of the citizens of Pakistan that they have been repeatedly betrayed, wronged continuously, decade after decade since 1947 by the West, also often by India, and it is this that has made Pakistan not a strategic outpost of western interests but in reality a great threat to the West.

The Indian subcontinent, from Burma to Afghanistan had almost always been a natural 'common market' for the movement of goods and people. Partition was not just a geographical and emotional vivisection of this subcontinent, in fact it amounted to, sadly and totally unnaturally, fracturing this common market of trade, commerce, and a free movement of people, too. It turned Indians, in their own subcontinent, into refugees, and the movement of goods in this region acquired a new term—that of 'smuggling'. India in consequence clearly lost the most; its land and its people; plus its political, cultural and social unity was torn asunder, but then that was not of concern to the Quaid-i-Azam.

As for Britain, as a post-Second World War country it gave up the 'jewel' in the crown of its Empire. I think, wisely and just in time, for it thus saved its own war-torn land and the people. The choice confronting them was stark: which was it to be—Empire or Britain? Or was there really ever any choice? That is why neither the choice made nor the method of implementing it was heroic, it was decidedly a 'scuttle', just short of being a rout. For this the British so clearly bartered India's interests, and in the process, (knowingly?) banished 'peace' entirely from this subcontinent. That peace is yet to return, as indeed is order, which also is yet to be fully re-established, for these two vital categories of governance (peace, law and order) do not feel welcome these days, in any of the successor countries. Was that the final British trade-off? The traders' spirit of the seventeenth century East India Company had come to the fore, again, as it had always done when pressed, it made India pay the price, yet again, for Britain's mistakes. It pains greatly to recognize that we agreed to this bargain and falsely called it a 'peaceful transfer of power'. For this 'transfer' India continues to pay, still, and that certainly was not amongst the chosen goals of Mohammad Ali Jinnah's journey as he travelled to become the Quaid-i-Azam of Pakistan. That was our own doing. As for the British, in the end as A.A. Gill mockingly comments in *The Angry Island Hunting the English*: 'The loss of Empire "broke England's heart but it couldn't tell anyone". So the English then experienced "what everyone who has been dumped experiences—a cataclysmic, middle-aged stumble of self-confidence, [but] nostalgia [has now] come to [their] rescue".'

Pakistan and its citizens have doubtlessly suffered grievously in the six decades of an independent existence. A break-up into two, in the emergence of Bangladesh; four military dictatorships during these decades; on top of which came the civilian governments that did not exactly serve the land, all this has inflicted upon the citizens of Pakistan untold hardships. There were then these several conflicts with India, each draining the land of resources. Whereafter arrived extremism. The country is now ravaged by all varieties of sectarian and provincial divisions, extremism and violence. And yet, it demonstrates a great vitality, enormous natural creativity and exuberance and, of course, always an outgoing heart warming hospitality. In comparison so much of the past pales, for Pakistan has overcome many near impossible obstacles. However, the dream of the late Quaid and the current reality do not entirely harmonize, which is a saddening comment for the land, for its people, in truth, merit so much more.

THE END?

There are now no more points left to score; all have already been scored, no great issues of partition left to resolve, except one: an inability to understand what, after all, did this partition achieve? Other than constant pain and the suffering of crores of humans, all around, which has now finally moulded itself into a kind of a sealed and an abrasive continuity. This has become ours, India's proverbial cross, also perhaps its greatness. And as we end writing about the epic journey of Mohammad Ali Jinnah from being the 'ambassador of Hindu-Muslim unity' to the Quaid-i-Azam of Pakistan, we need to share a reflection on a reality, that all historical narration is after all an account of the politics of those times. In which sense this attempt at Jinnah's political biography is exactly that, no more, no less. That notwithstanding, in the end, any assessment of who gained what in this traumatic partition becomes an empty exercise. For though Jinnah died in the after-glow of having found a 'new country', Pakistan, has remained a conceptual orphan, the result of a somewhat barren attainment; 'barren' because Pakistan itself, as both the progenitor and as the first born of the idea, has demonstrated that this notion of 'Muslims being a separate nation does not work'. It did so by breaking up on the issue of language; whereafter provincial identities and the many normal chores of routine, everyday existence like water or territory or boundary lines have asserted themselves.

The turbid sediment of our recent past, the agony of our blood encrusted partition continues to sour the present of Indo-Pak relations, still. Our sensibilities are now so splenetic that even the routine is a source of spiteful disbelief. Obviously, there is now no 'South Asian Monroe doctrine' of which Jinnah had spoken idealistically, instead we now have a near constant haze of simmering discord and mistrust. That is why I reflect: what if instead of this path of breaking apart and near continuous conflict, we had, instead, post-1947 partition chosen to work together, to wipe out contentions and now that finally there has been born a sovereign Pakistan, to fraternally stop looking at the past? Would that have brought back that lost 'peace' to our region? I cannot vouchsafe the outcome; indeed, who can? For, along with several other there is one central difficulty that India, Pakistan, Bangladesh face: our 'past' has, in reality never gone into the 'past', it continues to reinvent itself, constantly becoming our 'present', thus preventing us from escaping the imprisonment of memories. To this we have to find an answer, who else can or will?

The partitioning of India is the defining event of the twentieth century for this entire subcontinent. The searing agony of it torments still, the whys and what-fors of it, too. We relive the partition because we persist without attempts to find answers to the great errors of those years so that we may never, ever repeat them. Also, perhaps by recounting them we attempt to assuage some of our pain.

This is the account of Jinnah, the man and his heroic endeavours, and the others, too.

'And of these is a story written: but [then] Allah alone knoweth all.'

APPENDICES

Appendix to Chapter 1

Appendix I

THE SIMLA DELEGATION AND THE FORMATION OF THE MUSLIM LEAGUE

'The story starts with the arrival in India of King George V, as Prince of Wales, in 1905-6. Six Indian press representatives were selected to travel with the Prince. I happened to be one of them. I was then Editor of the *Alhaq*—the only Muslim Anglo-Sindhi weekly of Sindh. In the (sic) due course (February 1906), we reached Hyderabad Deccan, and there, one fine morning, we called on Nawab Imad-ul-Mulk, Moulvi Syed Husain Bilgrami. In the course of conversation, he whispered an anxious query whether we had been doing anything useful for the nation. He asked what we had found. The picture was very gloomy. The old and the young were both dissatisfied with their doom. The old were growling and grumbling in their own places, while the young were about to revolt against the authority of the Aligarh group of leaders. They were asked not to join the Congress, and they kept away from it. They were asked to remain loyal to Government, and they had been passing resolutions after resolutions of loyalty in their meetings. When they had had less of the Western education, they were more respected. The more their advancement in 'modern learning', the greater their fall. Their percentage in government services was steadily on decline. There was a time when three Muslim Judges graced the Indian High Court—Mr Mahmood in Allahabad, Mr Amir Ali in Calcutta and Mr Badruddin Tayabji in Bombay. Today (in 1906), with a larger number of graduates, pleaders, barristers and educated civilians, not a single Muslim has been found capable of occupying a Judge's seat in any of the High Courts in India. We went on like that for a long time, and then took leave of the Nawab'.

The same evening [Nawab Imad-ul-Mulk] said something on the following lines:

'Just after you left this morning, I received an invitation to tea for the afternoon from Sir Walter Lawrence (Chief of the Staff of the Prince of Wales). We have been very old friends. While he was Lord Curzon's Private Secretary, I was a member of the Viceroy's Council and we were together at Simla. When I went to him this afternoon, he asked me about the present condition of the country. You fiery young men put a spark into me this morning, and it kept on raging within me throughout the day. I unburdened myself before Sir Walter, and told him every word of what you said—and something more which I know and you know not. I told him frankly that our young men are getting out of hand. Don't ask us to control them unless you at once change your policy. Sir Walter told me they were perfectly justified in their attitude, and the government was certainly wrong in ignoring them. 'But it is never too late to mend,' he said. 'Do not let them join the Congress. They will suffer if they do that. Let them start a political organization of their own and fight their battle independent of the Congress. You keep control over the organization.' I said the Nizam Government Rules precluded me from taking part in politics. He said, 'let a big man, e.g. the Aga Khan, be its President merely for show. It is the Secretary who does the main work, controls and guides. You be the Secretary; and if your State Rules do not allow you, then let a nominal Secretary take that office and you do the real work behind the scenes. If you do not do that, Muslims will get crushed between two mill-stones. I promised to think over the matter. The wanted instructions were communicated to the Viceroy'.

The narrative continues:

'From here the Prince goes to Benares. From Benares he goes to the Terai Forest for a fortnight on a shooting trip From his shooting trip, he goes straight on to Aligarh in the middle of March (1906). At Aligarh you expect a huge gathering of Muslims from all parts of India. They have been invited there for the occasion. My friend, Mr Abdul Aziz, will write to his friends in the Punjab—men like Shah Din and Mohammad Shafi not to miss the occasion, as important matters were to be discussed and decided. I shall do the same with my friends in other parts of India, and both of us will exercise our influence in getting as many important men together as possible. We shall be at Aligarh a few days ahead of the Prince. You do the same. And when the people we want get there, we shall meet together and discuss matters in camera.'

The Nawab approved of the idea very much. 'But then', I continued, 'you have got to do something very important before we discuss the matter with others. You alone can do it. You have got to win the Aga Khan and Nawab Mohsin-ul-Mulk to your side. We know our people full well. If these two gentlemen oppose an idea, the rest of them are bound to oppose it and nothing will come out of the meeting. The Aga Khan has leanings towards the Congress. (In 1927 the Aga Khan disclosed the fact that towards the end of 1905, he was in favour of Muslims joining the Congress, as reported in *The Times of India*, 30 December 1927). He is not in favour of Muslims starting a separate political organization of their own. He thinks it is better to have one enemy than to have two; 'If you isolate yourself that way, you will have to fight against both the government and the Hindus'. As for Nawab Mohsin-ul-Mulk, he is definitely of the opinion that the glare of politics and the charm of novelty will dazzle the masses away from the Aligarh educational institution, and the M.A.O. College will lose its present popularity; that the Muslims are not yet sufficiently educated and are firebrands by temperament, and on that account it would not be advisable to introduce politics into the Muslim masses; and that the tragedy of 1857 should not be lost sight of. He thinks even now the governments are not so much afraid of the Hindus as of the Muslims. He is of the opinion that only a selected few of the Muslims should form themselves into a sort of a defence association and work secretly for the political emancipation of Muslims'.

Continuing the record states:

'Nawab Imad-ul-Mulk pondered over the subject for a while, put me some more questions, and ultimately decided to be at Aligarh five days before the Prince and try to bring both of them round, as the Aga Khan would be there too.

Here I may mention an incident which puzzled me. After finishing with Benares, since I had a fortnight's holiday, I went to Bombay for a week and saw Sir Pherozshah

Mehta. We know each other, and in those days when I went to Bombay, I invariably saw him. In course of conversation, while we were all alone, he told me: 'You Mohammedans are about to have a Congress of your own. There is no reason why you should not have it. You shall have my sympathy and support. But I tell you one thing. Remember it well. Your moderates will be our extremists. You will give a lot of trouble to the government and the Hindus. I shall be glad of it.' I did not say anything in reply. But I felt a bit embarrassed, and could not conclude whether he really knew anything about it or merely tried to pump me out.'

'We reached Aligarh five days ahead of the occasion. Within half an hour of our arrival there, Nawab Imad-ul-Mulk entered my tent, told me he had arrived 10 days ahead of the occasion and gave me the tidings that he had converted both of them.'

'To make (sic) a long story short, the proposed meeting took place in camera, and we all decided to have a political organization of our own. Then came the question of how to proceed. One of the gentlemen present said that sometime back Nawab Viqar-ul-Mulk had started a political organization, and called it the Muslim League. Although it never went beyond paper, and had not been heard of for long, present relations between Nawab Mohsin-ul-Mulk and Nawab Viqar-ul-Mulk were a bit strained, and the latter might misconstrue the proposed step as an act of antagonism against him. The matter was serious, so it was decided, on the proposal of Nawab Mohsin-ul-Mulk himself that a deputation be first sent to Nawab Viqar-ul-Mulk with a request to enroll all of us as members of his Muslim League if it functioned. If it had ceased to exist, let him and other of his following join the association we propose to start. The deputation was nominated and asked to report within a specified time. After this we all dispersed.'

'It was at this time that talk about the desirability of starting a 'Muslim Congress' became widespread, and different schemes of varying merits began to be hatched in different quarters. The spade-work was still on, when a Godsend opportunity arrived with the news of the impending Minto-Morley Reforms. Nawab Mohsin-ul-Mulk utilized the opportunity, and as a stepping stone in the direction of the permanent establishment of the proposed political association, he at once started organizing a Muslim Deputation to wait upon Lord Minto. He worked with lightning speed, Nawab Imad-ul-Mulk drafted the Memorial. Both the Nawabs received private assurances that the Viceroy's reply would be sympathetic. So the whole thing was done very secretly for fear of the Hindu Press, whose howls might spoil the atmosphere and the Viceroy might be compelled to become cautious in his reply. The public knew of the Deputation only at the eleventh hour and the contents of the Memorial became known only after the Aga Khan had read it.

Here again an incident took place which is worth mention. Before the eleventh hour arrived and the people knew anything about the Deputation, I went to Bombay on a private business of mine. There I happened to come across Mr Gokhale. He told me everything about the proposed Deputation, and gave me the contents of the Memorial drafted by Nawab Imad-ul-Mulk. I asked him bluntly if he had a spy in the Muslim camp. He told me he had received a copy of the address officially from the Viceroy!

Appendices to Chapter 2

Appendix I

MINTO-MORLEY REFORMS (1909)

In 1909 Indian nationalism was very different from what it had been in 1885 and 1892. Many of its exponents were now 'extremists', denouncing the British Raj. Lord Minto, Viceroy from 1905 to 1910, decided that, while 'extremism' should be firmly repressed, a further and a substantial concession should be made to the more moderate nationalists. Minto was met half-way by the Secretary of State. The outcome was the 'Morley-Minto Reforms' of 1909. By the Indian Councils Act of that year the principle of election at the Centre as well as in the Provinces was now recognized and legalized, but the constituencies were still to be communities and groups of various kinds and not general constituencies of the normal democratic type. A small official majority was retained at the Centre; but in all the Provinces the officials were outnumbered by the nominated plus elected members, and in Bengal the elected members had a clear majority. The possibility of Indians holding the highest offices in the administration was realized by the appointment of an Indian not only to each Provincial Executive Council but to the Governor-General's too.

Though the Act of 1909 brought the constitutional advance begun by the Act of 1861 to the threshold of representative government, the idea that this advance was comparable with what had happened in England or the Colonies was firmly rejected by the British statesmen and officials. The Legislative Councils were still regarded as Durbars rather than as parliaments. Lord Curzon's chief criticism of the new Councils was that they would inevitably become 'parliamentary bodies in miniature'.

Morley did not contest these arguments, and his conclusion was the same. 'If it could be said', he told the House of Lords, 'that this chapter of reforms led directly or necessarily to the establishment of a parliamentary system in India, I for one would have nothing at all to do with it.' There could be no analogy, he said, between Ireland and India or between Canada and India. He derided the idea that 'whatever is good in the way of self-government for Canada must be good for India' as a 'gross and dangerous sophism'. It was like arguing, he said, that, because a fur coat is needed in the Canadian winter, it is needed in the Deccan.

The process of developing a parliamentary system was as yet only in its earliest stages. Representative government was still a novelty and still incomplete and full representative government had existed in Canada for more than fifty years before it was converted into responsible government. It was not till 1916 that, in the new atmosphere created by the war, the Indian politicians proposed that they should take a hand in the government themselves and that proposal meant something much less than real responsible government.

'Throughout this period of advancing claims the Congress had not ignored the problem of the Muslim minority. The article of the constitution which allocated the seats for the All-India Congress Committee prescribed that 'as far as possible 1/5 of the total number of representative shall be Muslims. At the session of 1913 separate electorates were again condemned.

On the issue of separate electorate the Muslim leaders were equally unyielding. Separate electorates were, the indispensable safeguard without which they would not have acquiesced in the Reforms of 1909. But their disagreement with the Congress went deeper than that. Like Morley, they would have had nothing to do with those Reforms if they had been designed to lead on the colonial precedent towards a parliamentary system; yet that was precisely how the Congress, ignoring Morley's disclaimer, had interpreted them. This fundamental cleavage of opinion was soon made manifest. At a meeting of the Council of the Muslim League in 1913 the adoption of the Congress formula of colonial self-government as the constitutional objective was moved but found no seconder, and the League Council adopted in its place the formula, 'the attainment under the aegis of the British Crown of a system of self-government suitable to India'— a decision which the League confirmed. The President of the Council, Muhammad Shafi, denounced the Congress formula as inadmissible and unsound.

The old breach seemed to be widening when the outbreak of the war gave new strength and meaning to the idea of Indian nationhood. There was a move that the League and the Congress join forces to ensure that one to the results of the war should be a much larger measure of self-government in India. In the autumn of 1916, when it was known that the British authorities were also considering the question, nineteen members of the Indian Legislative Council, Hindu and Moslem, drew up an agreed plan of constitutional advance. And at the end of the year the pact was formally ratified at Lucknow.

Appendix II

THE OFFICIAL BRITISH OPINION ON THE MONTAGU-CHELMSFORD REFORMS

British opinion, like the Indian, had been affected by the war. For the first few years after the introduction of the Morley-Minto Reforms it was taken for granted that some considerable time would elapse before another advance could be justified. The British were yet not prepared to accept the colonial model as the guiding line of development in India. In a dispatch of 1911 mainly concerned with the establishment of a new capital at Delhi and with the reversal of Lord Curzon's partition of Bengal, the Central Government had declared itself in favour of gradually giving the Provinces a larger measure of self-government. This statement of policy had been welcomed not only the Congress but also by Mr Montagu, Under-Secretary of State for India prompting Lord Curzon to ask if the British Government were considering a further constitutional advance. But Provincial self-government did not necessarily mean self-government by Indians; nor had the dispatch raised any doubts as to the necessity of safeguarding 'the ultimate supremacy' of the government of India on which 'the maintenance of British rule in India depends'. Thus interpreted, Lord Crewe, the Secretary of State, in his reply could argue that there was nothing new in the policy of devolution from the Centre. The Congress, in other words, had wrongly interpreted the dispatch. But Lord Crewe went further. He alluded to the hopes expressed by Indian politicians, without the least 'taint of disloyalty' or any desire to break the British connection', of attaining in India 'something approaching the self-government enjoyed by those Colonies which have of late years received the name of Dominion'. 'I say quite frankly', he declared, 'that I see no future for India on those lines,' and he denied that the policy of devolution implied that 'anything of the kind is the hope or goal of His Majesty's ministers or of the present Government of India.'

Appendix III

LUCKNOW PACT

This agreement between the major political organizations, a striking expression of Indian nationalism, was only achieved through major concessions granted to both the sides. The Congress at last conceded separate Moslem electorates. It even acquiesced in their introduction in the Punjab and the Central Provinces, where they had not yet existed. Seats on the Councils were allotted to those electorates on a generous scale. In Bengal the Muslims were to obtain only three-quarters of the seats to which they would have been entitled on a purely numerical basis, and in the Punjab only nine-tenth but in both these Provinces this was great increase on the extent of Muslim representation under the Morley-Minto Reforms: in Bengal it was raised from 10.4 to 40 per cent, in the Punjab from 25 to 50 per cent. And in the other Provinces the Muslims were to obtain many more seats than they had then or would have on a population basis: in the United Provinces and Madras, for example, a 14 and 6.15 per cent Muslim population would have a 30 and 15 per cent representation. Muslim strength at the Centre was similarly increased by the allotment of one-third of the elections to the Council to separate Muslim constituencies. The Muslims were to surrender the additional advantage they had obtained in 1909 of also voting in general electorates; but by the more conservative or communal minded among them this may well have been regarded as no loss, since it emphasized and secured the distinction between the two communities. A final safeguard was provided by the application of the device adopted in the Congress constitution. No bill or resolution affecting a community should be proceeded with if three-fourths of the representatives of that community were opposed to it.

These were far more substantial concessions than the Muslims had been given by Morley and Minto to secure their acquiescence in the Reforms of 1909, and the League on its side acquiesced in the joint proposals for a further liberalization of the Councils. The cardinal points of me Congress-League Scheme, as it was called, may be summarized. as follows: i) the Provinces should be freed as much as possible from Central control in administration and finance; ii) Four-fifths of the Central and Provincial Legislative Councils should be elected, and one-fifth nominated; iii) Not less than half the members of the Central and Provincial Governments should be elected by the elected member of their respective Legislative Councils; iv) The Governments, Central and Provincial, should be bound to act in accordance with resolutions passed by their Legislative Councils unless they were vetoed by the Governor-General or Governors in Council and, in that event, if the resolution were passed again after an interval of not less than one year, if should in any case be put into effects; v) The Central legislative Council should have no power to interfere with the Government of India's direction of the Military affairs and the foreign and political relations of India, including the declaration of war, the making of peace and the entering into treaties; vi) The relations of the Secretary of State with the Government of India should be similar to those of the Colonial Secretary with the Governments of the Dominions, and India should have an equal status with that of the Dominions in any body concerned with imperial affairs.

This scheme was proof that the Indian politician's mind was not purely critical and unconstructive, but it had one major defect on account of which, it never materialized. It did nothing to remedy the inherent weakness of purely representative government. On the contrary, it aggravated it by giving the elected majorities much greater power to embarrass and obstruct their governments, without being able to remove those governments and shoulder their responsibilities themselves. Whatever the strength of their opposition those governments, most of whose members would not be chosen by or accountable to them, would remain in charge of the whole field of administration. While, therefore, the scheme was an encouraging manifestation of Hindu-Muslim accord in the work of advancing Indian self-government, it could not be assumed that its Muslim supporters had conquered their distrust of the representative principle. On balance, the real power would still be exercised not by the leaders of Hindu or Muslim majorities, but by neutral officials who, at any rate as long as India had not attained the same status as the Dominions, would still under the legitimate control of a distant and neutral parliament. The agreement on the scheme was unquestionably a triumph for Indian nationalism, and the Congress accompanied its adoption of it with a plea that the British Government should declare in intention 'to confer self-government on India at an early date', and that in any reconstruction of the imperial system 'India shall be lifted from the position of a dependency to that of an equal partner in the Empire with the self-governing Dominions'.

Appendix to Chapter 5

Appendix I

THE ELECTIONS OF 1937

With able leaders, an effective organization and a simple yet attractive programme, the Congress won a notable victory at the polls early in 1937. Of the 1585 seats in the provincial legislatures the Congress contested 1161 and won 716. The Congress victory is all the more impressive when it is borne in mind that of the 1585 seats less than half, 657, were 'general' or open, that is not allotted to a separate, closed elect group such as Muslims, Sikhs, Christians, Europeans, Anglo-Indians and landholders. Of the eleven provinces in British India the Congress secured a clear majority in six, and was the largest single party in three others.

By contrast, the Muslim League won only 109 of the 482 seats allotted to the Muslims, securing only 4-8 per cent of the total Muslim votes. It did not win a majority of seats in any of the four Muslim-majority provinces. In fact, its performance in certain Muslim-majority provinces was far worse than that in the Muslim-minority provinces.

(1937), Cmd. 5589. 2	Total number of seats in the Legislative Assembly	Seats won by the Congress in the elections of 1937
Assam	108	35
Bengal	250	54
Bihar	152	95
Bombay	175	88
Central Provinces	112	71
Madras	215	159
N.W. Frontier Province	50	19
Orissa	60	36
Punjab	175	18
Sind	60	8
United Ptovinces	228	133

3 Provinces	Total number of seats allotted to the Muslims in the Legislative Assembly	Seats won by the Muslim League in the elections of 1937
Assam	34	9
Bengal	117	39
Bihar	39	—
Bombay	29	20
Central Provinces	14	—
Madtas	28	10
N.W. Frontier Province	36	—
Orissa	4	—
Punjab	84	1
Sind	33	3
United Provinces	64	27

Appendices to Chapter 6

Appendix I

THE CRIPPS MISSION PLAN, 1942

Immediately upon the cessation of hostilities, steps shall be taken to set up in India, in the manner described hereafter, an elected body charged with the task of framing a new Constitution for India.

His Majesty's Government undertake to accept and implement forthwith the constitution so framed subject to the right of any province of British India that is not prepared to accept the new constitution to retain its present constitutional position, provision being made for its subsequent accession if it so desires.

With such non-acceding provinces, should they so desire, His Majesty's government will be prepared to agree upon a new constitution, giving them the same political status as the Indian Union, and arrived at by a procedure analogous to that here laid down.

These provisions were further amplified by Sir Stafford Cripps in a letter to the Secretary of the Muslim League, quoted in a later resolution of the League:

> 'The method of ascertainment proposed in the Cripps Plan is election on a broad franchise and the representatives so elected coming together with the fullest freedom of decision. The question of accession will be put to the vote of each Provincial legislature. If the majority voting for accession is less than 60%, the minority will have the right to demand a plebiscite of the adult male population of the province.'

Appendix II

THE C.R. FORMULA, 1943

Basis for terms of settlement between the Indian National Congress and the All-India Muslim League to which Gandhi and Jinnah agree and which they will endeavour respectively to *get* the Congress and the League to approve:

1. Subject to the terms set out below as regards the Constitution for Free India, the Muslim League endorses the Indian demand for Independence and will cooperate with the Congress in the formation of a provisional Interim Government for the transitional period.
2. After the termination of the war, a Commission shall be appointed for demarcating contiguous districts in the north-west and east of India, wherein the Muslim population is in absolute majority. In the areas thus demarcated, a plebiscite of all the inhabitants held *on* the basis *of* adult franchise or other practicable franchise shall ultimately decide the issue of separation from Hindustan. If the majority decide in

favour of forming a sovereign state separate from Hindustan, such decision shall be given effect to without prejudice to the right of districts on the border to choose to join either state.
3. It will be open to all parties to advocate their points of view before the plebiscite is held.
4. In the event of separation, mutual agreement shall be entered into for safeguarding Defence and Commerce and Communications for other essential purposes.
5. Any transfer of population shall only be on an absolutely voluntary basis.
6. These terms shall be binding only in case *of* transfer by Britain of full power and responsibility for the governance of India.

Gandhi was amongst the first Congress leaders converted to Rajagopalachari's point of view. In February 1943, while Gandhi was on his 21-day fast at the Aga Khan palace, detained since 9 August 1942, Rajagopalachari met him and obtained his approval for the formula. On 8 April 1943, he put this proposal before Jinnah in a slightly altered form. The altered formula is known as the C.R. Formula, having taken after the name of its author, Chakravarti Rajagopalachari.

Appendix III

GANDHI'S OFFER AS REVEALED IN HIS LETTER TO JINNAH, 24 SEPTEMBER 1944

The areas should be demarcated by a Commission approved by the Congress and the League. The wishes of the inhabitants of the areas demarcated should be ascertained through the votes of the adult population of the areas or some equivalent method.

If the vote is in favour of separation, it shall be agreed that these areas shall form a separate state as soon as possible after India is free from foreign domination and can therefore be constituted into two sovereign independent States.

There shall be Treaty of Separation which should also provide for the efficient and satisfactory administration of foreign affairs, defence, internal communications, customs, commerce and the like, which must necessarily continue to be matters of common interest between the contracting parties.

The treaty shall also contain terms for safeguarding the rights of minorities in the two states.

Immediately on the acceptance of this agreement by the Congress and the League the two shall decide upon a common course of action for the attainment of independence of India.

The League will, however, be free to remain out of any direct action to which the Congress may resort and in which the League may not be willing to participate.

Appendix IV

THE DESAI FORMULA

The Congress and the League agree that they will join in forming an interim government in the Centre. The composition of such a government will be on the following lines:

(a) an equal number of persons nominated by the Congress and the League in the Central Executive (the persons nominated need not be members of the Central Legislature);
(b) Representatives of minorities (in particular the Scheduled Castes and the Sikhs);
(c) The Commander-in-Chief.

The Government will be formed and function within the framework of the existing Government of India Act. It is, however, understood that if the Cabinet cannot get a particular measure passed by the Legislative Assembly, they will not enforce the same by resort to any of the reserve powers of the Governor-General or the Viceroy. This will make them sufficiently independent of the Governor-General.

It is agreed between the Congress and the League that if such interim government is formed, their first step would be to release the Working Committee members of the Congress.

The steps by which efforts would be made to achieve this *end* are at present indicated to take the following course:

On the basis of the above understanding, some way should be found to get the Governor-General to make a proposal or a suggestion that he desires an interim government to be formed in the Centre on the agreement between the Congress and the League, and when the Governor-General invites Mr Jinnah and Mr Desai either jointly or separately, the above proposals would be made declaring that they are prepared to join in forming the Government.

The next step would be to get the withdrawal of Section 93 in the provinces and to form, as soon as possible, provincial governments on the lines of a coalition.

Appendix V

WAVELL ON GANDHI-JINNAH TALKS 30 SEPTEMBER 1944

The Gandhi-Jinnah talks ended on a note of complete futility. I must say I expected something better. I did not expect statesmanship or a practical solution, but I did think the two would have got down to something, if only the best way to embarrass the G. of I. Anything so barren as their exchange of letters is a deplorable exposure of Indian leadership. The two great mountains have met and not even a ridiculous mouse has emerged. This surely must blast Gandhi's reputation as a leader. Jinnah had an easy task, he merely had to keep on telling Gandhi he was talking nonsense, which was true, and he did so rather rudely, without having to disclose any of the weaknesses of his own position, or define his Pakistan in any way. I suppose it may increase his prestige with his followers, but it cannot add to his reputations with reasonable men. I wonder what the effect on H.M.G. will be. I am afraid it will increase their dislike of any attempt at a move.

Gandhi offered Jinnah the maimed, mutilated Pakistan of the Rajagopalachari formula, but without real sincerity or conviction. Jinnah rejected the offer and bluntly told Gandhi that the division of India was only on his lips and did not come from his heart.

Moreover Gandhi insisted that any division of India could only take place after the British had left, which was in line with the general Congress aim of wresting control from the British first and settling with the Muslims, Princes, etc. afterwards. Jinnah believed that once the British had gone, the Hindus would never agree to the division of India and that the Muslims would have to fight a civil war to get even a mutilated Pakistan.

Appendices to Chapter 8

Appendix I

THE WAVELL PLAN, 1945

Broadcast of June, 1945, after Wavell's return from England:

'I have been authorized by His Majesty's Government to place before Indian political leaders proposals designed to ease the present political situation and to advance India towards her goal of self-government.

'This is not an attempt to obtain or impose a constitutional settlement.

'His Majesty's Government had hoped that the leaders of the Indian parties would agree amongst themselves on a settlement of the communal issue which is the main stumbling-block, but this hope has not been fulfilled.

'I propose, with the full support of His Majesty's Government, to invite Indian leaders both of central and provincial politics to take counsel with me with a view to the formation of a new Executive Council, more representative of organized political opinion.

'The proposed new Council would represent the main communities and would include equal proportion of caste Hindus and Muslims. It would work if formed under the existing Constitution. But it would be an entirely Indian Council, except for the Viceroy and the Commander-in-Chief, who would retain his position as a war member.

It is also proposed that the portfolio of External Affairs which has hitherto been held by the Viceroy should be placed in charge of an Indian member of the Council so far as the interests of British India are concerned.

'A further step proposed by His Majesty's Government is the appointment of a British High Commissioner in India as in the Dominions, to represent Great Britain's commercial and other such interests in India.

'The Council will work within the framework of the present Constitution.

'The main tasks for this new Executive Council would be:

(1) to prosecute the war with Japan with the utmost energy till Japan is utterly defeated;
(2) to carry on the Government of British India with all the manifold tasks of post-war development in front of it until a new permanent constitution can be agreed upon and comes into force; and
(3) to consider, when the members of the Government think it possible, the means by which such agreement can be achieved.

'I also hope that it will be possible for ministries to reassume office and again undertake the tasks of government in the provinces now administered under Section 93 of the Constitution Act, and that these ministries will be coalitions.

'If the meeting should unfortunately fail, we must carry on as at present until the parties are ready to come together.

'With the approval of His Majesty's Government, and after consultation with my Council orders have been given for the immediate release of the members of the Working Committee of the Congress who are still in detention. I propose to leave the final decision about the others still under detention as the result of the 1942 disturbances to the new Central Government, if formed, and to the Provincial Governments.

Appendix II

THE MUSLIM LEGISLATORS' CONVENTION, 1946

Early in April, 1946, while the Cabinet Mission was in Delhi, Jinnah convened an All-India Muslim Legislators' Convention attended by about 400 members of provincial and central legislatures. Addressing the Convention, the League President said: 'We are prepared to sacrifice anything and everything but we shall not submit to any government formed without our consent. This Convention is going to lay down once for all, in unequivocal terms, what we stand for. We stand unanimously for Pakistan. We shall fight and die for it, if necessary, achieve it we must, or we perish.'

The resolution, unanimously adopted by the Convention said:

'This Convention of the Muslim League legislators of India, central and provincial, after careful consideration hereby declares that the Muslim nation will never submit to any constitution for a united India and will never participate in any single constitution-making machinery set up for the purpose.'

The Resolution demanded: first, that the zones comprising Bengal and Assam in the north-east and the Punjab, the North-West Frontier Province, Sind and Baluchistan in the north-west of India, namely, Pakistan zones where the Muslims are a dominant majority, be constituted into a sovereign, independent state and that an unequivocal undertaking be given to implement the establishment of Pakistan without delay;

> Second, that two separate constitution-making bodies be set up by peoples of Pakistan and Hindustan for the purpose of framing their respective constitutions;
> Third, that the minorities in Pakistan and Hindustan be provided with safeguards on the lines of the All-India Muslim League resolution passed on 23 March 1940 at Lahore;
> Fourth, that the acceptance of the Muslim League demand of Pakistan and its implementation without delay are the *sine qua non* for the Muslim League cooperation and participation in the formation of an interim government at the Centre.

Appendix III

MUSLIM LEAGUE'S MEMORANDUM TO THE CABINET MISSION

Muslim League's Memorandum:

(1) The six Muslim provinces (the Punjab, the N.W.F.P., Sind, Baluchistan, Bengal and Assam) to be grouped together as one group. It would deal with all matters except Foreign Affairs, Defence and Communications necessary for Defence, which may be dealt with by the constitution-making bodies of the Pakistan group and the Hindu provinces;

(2) A separate constitution-making body to be set up for the six Muslim provinces;

(3) There should be parity of representation between the two groups of provinces in the Union Executive and the Legislature, if any;

(4) It will be open to any province of the Group to decide to opt out *of* its group, provided the wishes of the people of that province are ascertained by a referendum;

(5) The two constitution-making bodies would decide whether to have a Legislature or not; they would also decide the method of providing the Union with finance, but in no event should it be by means of taxation;

(6) No major point affecting the communal issue to be decided except by the majority of the members of the two communities;

(7) No decision, legislative, or executive, or administrative shall be taken by the Union *in* regard to any matter of controversial nature except by majority of three-fourths;

(8) The Group and provincial constitutions would provide for safeguards concerning religion, culture and other manners affecting different communities;

(9) A province would have liberty to secede from the Union at any time after an initial period of ten years.

Appendix IV

CONGRESS PROPOSALS TO THE CABINET MISSION

(1) The Constituent Assembly to be formed of representatives elected by each Provincial by proportional representation;

(2) The Constituent Assembly to draw up a constitution for the Federal Union. This would consist of an All-India Federal Government and Legislature dealing with Foreign Affairs, Defence, Communications, Fundamental rights, Currency, Customs and Planning as well as such other subjects as on closer scrutiny, may be found to be intimately allied to them. The Union would have necessary power to obtain for itself the finances it required for these subjects;

(3) All remaining powers to vest in provinces;

(4) Groups of provinces may be formed if any provinces want them;

(5) No major point affecting the communal issue to be decided except by the majority consent of the representatives of the community affected;
(6) Provision to be made for the revision of the constitution;
(7) Unsettled disputes to be referred to arbitration.

Appendix V

THE CABINET MISSION PLAN, 1946

The Mission studied the Congress and the League proposals and came out with its own recommendations on 16 May 1946.

The Mission after advancing various arguments concluded: 'We are unable to advise the British Government that the power which at present resides in British hands should be handed over to two entirely separate sovereign states.'

The Cabinet Mission, therefore, recommended that the constitution should take the following basic form:

(1) There should be Union of India, embracing both British India and the States, which should deal with the following subjects: (a) Foreign Affairs; (b) Defence; and (c) Communications. The Union should have the powers necessary to raise the finances required for the above subjects.
(2) The Union should have an Executive and a Legislature constituted from British Indian and State representatives. Any question raising a major communal issue *in* the Legislature should require for its decision a majority of the representatives present and voting of each of the two major communities as well as a majority of all the members present and voting;
(3) All subjects other than the Union subjects and all residuary powers should vest *in* the provinces;
(4) That States shall retain all subjects and powers other than those ceded to the Union;
(5) Provinces should be free to form groups with executives and legislatures and each group could determine the provincial subjects to be taken in common;
(6) The constitution of the *Union* and of the groups should contain a provision whereby any province could, by a majority vote of its Legislative Assembly, call for a reconsideration of the terms of the constitution after an initial period of ten years and at ten-yearly intervals thereafter.

The Mission divided the Indian provinces into three sections into which the Constituent Assembly would be split up and the sections would proceed to settle the provincial constitution for the provinces and would also decide whether any group constitution would be set up for those provinces and, if so, with what provincial subjects the group should deal. Provinces would have the power to opt out of the groups on the vote of the first legislature elected under the new constitution.

The provinces were classified into three sections as follows. Against each province was given the representation allowed to it in the Constituent Assembly.

Section A
Madras, Bombay, United Provinces, Bihar, Central Provina: and Orissa — Total 187, Muslim 20, General 167, Sikh x

Section B
N.W.F.P., Punjab and Sind — Total 35, Muslim 22, General 9, Sikh 4

Section C
Bengal and Assam — Total 70, Muslim 36, General 34, Sikh x

To Section A was to be added one representative each from Delhi, Ajmer, Marwara and Coorg. The Princely States were to be given seats not exceeding 93.

After the provincial and group constitutions had been formed, the Sections and the Princely States would reassemble for the purpose of settling the Union Constitution.

The Mission also announced that an interim government having the support of the major political parties

Appendix VI

THE 3 JUNE 1947 STATEMENT

On 3 June 1947 Lord Mountbatten announced the final settlement of the British Government which contained the Plan of the Partition of India and the Transfer of Power to the Dominions of India and Pakistan. The Statement said:

> It is clear that any constitution framed by the Constituent Assembly cannot apply to those parts of the country which are unwilling to accept it.

The Statement laid down the following procedure as 'the best practical method of ascertaining the wishes of the people of such areas on the issue whether their constitution is to be framed: (a) in the existing Constituent Assembly; or (b) in a new and separate Constituent Assembly consisting of the representatives of those areas which decide not to participate in the existing Constituent Assembly.'

The Statement laid down this procedure:

The Provincial Legislative Assemblies of Bengal and the Punjab (excluding the European members) will, therefore, each be asked to meet in two parts, one representing the Muslim-majority districts and the other the rest of the province. For the purpose of determining the population of districts, the 1941 Census figures will be taken as authoritative.

The members of the two parts of each Legislative Assembly sitting separately will be empowered to vote whether or not the province should be partitioned. If a simple majority of either part decides in favour of Partition, division will take place and arrangements will be made accordingly.

Before the question as to the partition is decided, it is desirable that the representatives of each part should know in advance which Constituent Assembly the province as a whole would join in the event of the two parts subsequently deciding to remain united. Therefore, *if* any member of either Legislative Assembly so demands, there shall be held a meeting of all members of the Legislative Assembly (other than Europeans) at which a decision will be taken on the issue as to which Constituent Assembly the province as a whole would join if it were decided by the two parts to remain united.

In the event of Partition being decided upon, each part of the Legislative Assembly will, on behalf of the areas they represent, decide which Constituent Assembly to join.

The Legislative Assembly of Sind (excluding European) would take its own decision, but since Sind had no Hindu-majority district, it would not meet *in* parts.

In regard to the North-West Frontier Province, the Statement provided for a referendum to be made to the electors of the Legislative Assembly to choose between the existing Constituent Assembly and a new separate Constituent Assembly. A similar referendum was provided for the Sylhet district, which was the only Muslim-majority district in the Hindu-majority province of Assam, having a common border with East Pakistan.

Within a few days of the announcement of the Plan, the Working Committees of the Congress and the League formally accepted it.

Appendix VII

WAVELL – GANDHI – NEHRU – 27 SEPTEMBER 1946 POST-CALCUTTA KILLINGS

[Leonard Mosley in *The Last Days of the British Raj*]

'This,' he said to Gandhi and Nehru, 'is an appeal to you to help me to bring it about.'

Wavell put the question frankly to Gandhi and Nehru: *Will you give me the guarantee the Muslim League is asking for?*

He was almost immediately plunged into the most difficult argument he had ever had with Gandhi, who chose this day to be at his most polemical. Gandhi, the Mahatma, on that evening chose to speak to Wavell purely and simply as a Congress politician.

'Give me a simple guarantee that you accept the Cabinet Mission Plan,' asked Wavell.

'We have already said that we accept it,' replied Gandhi, 'but we are not prepared to guarantee that we accept it in the way that the Cabinet Mission set it out. We have our own interpretations of what they propose.'

Said Wavell: 'Even if those interpretations differ from what the Cabinet Mission intended?'

Replied Gandhi: 'But of course. In any case, what the Cabinet Mission Plan really means is not what the Cabinet Mission thinks but what the Interim Government thinks it means.'

Wavell pointed out that the Interim Government's opinion, as things were at the moment, would almost inevitably be pro-Congress and anti-Muslim League, since the League was boycotting the Government. How could it be unbiased?

Gandhi replied that he was not concerned with such bias. He was simply concerned with the legal bias of the discussion. Legally, this was a matter for the interim government to decide. Once the interim government was in power, such matters as the Muslim league's ambitions and artificial anxieties could be voted upon; but not before.

'But don't you see,' said Wavell, 'it will be a Congress Government! They are bound to be lacking in impartiality.'

Nehru interrupted at this point. 'You misunderstand the composition of the Congress Party, your Excellency, not, I may say, for the first time. The Congress is not pro-Hindu or anti-Muslim. It is for all the peoples of India. It will never legislate against the interests of the Muslims.'

Replied Wavell: 'But whose Muslims Pandit Nehru? Yours, the Congress Muslims, the so-called stooges? Or those of the Muslim League? Can't you see that the necessity of this moment is to satisfy the Muslim League that you are not trying to do them down? It is a moment—possibly the last we have—to bring the League and the Congress together. And all I ask is a guarantee. Will the Congress commit itself to a declaration, a declaration which will satisfy the Muslim League and assure the continuation of a stable and unitary government?' He reached into his drawer and pulled out a paper. 'This is what I have in mind.' This declaration ran thus: 'The Congress are prepared in the interest of communal harmony to accept the intention of the statement of 16 May [the Cabinet Mission statement] that provinces cannot exercise any option affecting their membership of the sections or of the groups if formed, until the decision contemplated in paragraph 19 (vii) of the Statement of 16 May is taken by the new legislature after the new constitutional arrangements have come into operation and the first general elections have been held.'

Gandhi handed it over to Nehru, who read it through and said: 'To accept this is tantamount to asking Congress to put itself in fetters.'

Wavell replies: 'So far the Cabinet Mission Plan is concerned, that is what I feel you should do. When Congress accepted the Cabinet Mission Plan in the first place, I cannot believe that you did so not knowing its implications. If so, why did you accept it at all? The plan for dividing the country into groups was implicit. You cannot now turn around and say that you did not realize that is what was intended.'

Gandhi: 'What the Cabinet Mission intended and the way we interpret what they interpreted may necessarily may not be the same.'

'This is lawyer's talk,' said Wavell. 'Talk to me in plain English. I am a simple soldier and you confuse me with these legalistic arguments.'

Nehru: 'We cannot help it if we are lawyers.'

Wavell: 'No, but you can talk to me like honest men who are interested in India's future and welfare. Dammit, the Cabinet Mission made its intentions as clear as daylight. Surely we don't need to go to law about that or split legal hairs, either. As a plain man, the situation seems to me simple. If Congress will give me the guarantee for which I ask, I think I can persuade Mr Jinnah and the Muslim League to reconsider their refusal to join the interim government. We need them in the government; India needs them, and, if you are seriously concerned over the dangers of civil war—and you must know as well as I that the danger is great—then you need them too. In the circumstances, I feel that it would be unwise, even perilous, if I allowed Congress to form an interim government on its own.'

Gandhi: 'But you have already announced that the government will come into being. You cannot go back on your word now.'

Wavell: 'The situation has changed. As a result of the killings in Calcutta, India is on the verge of civil war. It is my duty to prevent it. I will not prevent it if I allow Congress to form a Government which excludes the Muslims: they will then decide that

Direct Action is the only way, and we shall have the massacre of Bengal all over again.'

Nehru: 'In other words, you are willing to surrender to the Muslim League's blackmail.'

Wavell (with great heat): 'For God's sake, man, who are you to talk of blackmail?'

Appendix VIII

WAVELL – THE VICEROY'S JOURNAL ED. BY PENDEREL MOON

PRIVATE AND PERSONAL   (31 January 1947)

My dear Viceroy,

I have your letter of the 19th in reply to mine of the 8th. It is clear from what you say with regard to government policy that there is a wide divergence of view as to the course which should be followed during the interim period. I had hoped that it would have been possible for you to have returned here during January to discuss the situation which has arisen.

I am very conscious of the heavy burden which you have carried and of the great services which you have rendered during this difficult period. I know that you undertook this task from a high sense of duty.

You were, I understand, informed that your appointment was a war appointment and that while the usual term for a Viceroy is five years, this might not apply. I think that three years was mentioned. This has now expired. I know, of course, that prior to your appointment as Viceroy you had had the heavy strain of high commands in war and, as you say in your letter, you have had no rest. I appreciate that you desire a month or two's leave at home.

But the Indian problem is emerging on a new phase, which will be very exacting and may be prolonged. The next few months are of great importance.

In view of all these circumstances and of the fact that it is specially necessary that the Viceroy should be in full agreement with the policy of His Majesty's Government. I think that you may agree that the time has come to make a change in the Viceroyalty.

I recall that you expressed your readiness to retire in the event of disagreement on policy and this would seem to me to be the appropriate course to follow.

An announcement should be made with as little delay as possible in order to allow time for the appointment of your successor and for him to take over at the end of February or early in March. The normal announcement about your successor would be prefaced with the statement 'Field-Marshal the Viscount Wavell who accepted the Viceroyalty as a war appointment is now retiring.' I have not looked into details, but if as a result you are denied any leave of absence which you would normally have had, you may be sure that you will not suffer financially.

I should like to submit your name to His Majesty for the dignity of an Earldom in recognition of the self sacrificing and loyal service which you have displayed in your long and distinguished career in India both to the Indian people and to this country and the Commonwealth.

Your sincerely,
C.R. Attlee.

5 February 1947

My dear Prime Minister,

I have received your letter of 31 January, in which you inform me of your intention to advise his Majesty to terminate my appointment as Viceroy in a few weeks time.

As you say, my appointment was a war one and no fixed term of office was given me. I think you are in error about a term of three years having been mentioned; but the point is immaterial, since the three-year term passed several months ago without your giving any indication of wishing to make a change.

You are causing me to be removed because of what you term a wide divergence of policy. The divergence, as I see it, is between my wanting a definite policy for the Interim period and H.M.G. refusing to give me one. I will not at this time enter into further argument on this.

I do not of course question your decision to make a change. I have no desire except to serve the State to the best of my ability; obviously I cannot continue to do so if I have not the confidence of the government in power.

I think, however, that I am entitled to observe that so summary a dismissal of His Majesty's representative in India is hardly in keeping with the dignity of the appointment. It has been usual to give a retiring Viceroy six months notice of his replacement. I may recall to you that I wrote to you six months ago, at the beginning of August last, suggesting that you might now wish to replace the soldier by a politician, but that you gave no indication of any desire to make a change. Whether my conduct of my office since then has deserved dismissal at a few weeks notice is for others to judge.

You can hardly have failed to appreciate the inconvenience and expense which you are causing to me and to the whole of my large personal staff by directing me to leave at such short notice; and I hope that I shall be given at least till the second week in March, to avoid the indignity, as well as the inconvenience of a scuttle. I note what you say about my entitlement to leave. I too have not looked into details on this matter, but will do so and will communicate with the Secretary of State. I hope that the expense and dislocation unexpectedly caused to my personal staff will be recognized and considered.

It is desirable for official and personal reasons to know the name of my successor, who has presumably been selected, as early as possible. You will of course give me advance notice of date and terms of announcement.

I thank you for what you say about my services. and will gladly accept your proposal to submit my name for the dignity of and Earldom.

Yours sincerely,
Wavell

Churchill told Wavell that he wished to be free to make another appointment after three years, if that should be necessary, but that he hoped it would not be. Apart from this, no exceptional limit was placed on his tenure as Viceroy. Normally the post was held for five years.

Appendix IX

NOTE BY FIELD MARSHAL SIR C. AUCHINLECK

L/WS/1/1092: ff 51-6
TOP SECRET

GENERAL HEADQUARTERS,
DELHI,
11 May 1946

A NOTE ON THE STRATEGIC IMPLICATIONS OF THE INCLUSION OF 'PAKISTAN' IN THE BRITISH COMMONWEALTH

ASSUMPTIONS

1. It is assumed:

(a) That India divides into two independent autonomous States—Hindustan and Pakistan.

(b) That Pakistan may consist of two parts—a Western zone and an Eastern zone, or of a Western zone only, comprising Sind, Baluchistan, the NWF Province and the Western Punjab.

(c) That HMG in the United Kingdom decide to leave Hindustan to its own devices and to have no more intimate dealings with it than the diplomatic and commercial relations usual between two friendly sovereign powers. HMG undertake no responsibility for the defence of Hindustan.

(d) On the other hand, HMG in the United Kingdom agree to the inclusion of Pakistan in the British Commonwealth as an autonomous Dominion having the same status as Canada, Australia etc, and, at Pakistan's request, to lend her British sea, land and air forces and British personnel to aid in her administration and defence.

COMMONWEALTH STRATEGIC INTERESTS IN THE INDIAN OCEAN AREA

2. Vital Commonwealth strategic in the Indian Ocean area are:

(a) The oil supplies from Persia and Iraq.
(b) Control of the Western entrance to the Indian Ocean—the Red Sea.
(c) Control of the Eastern entrance to the Indian Ocean—Singapore and the Malacca Straits.
(d) Ability to use the air routes across Arabia, Iraq, the Arabian Sea. India, Burma and Malaya.

(e) The control of Ceylon, for use as a port of call and a naval and air base.

Should India be unfriendly or liable to be influenced by a power, such as Russia, China or Japan, hostile to the British Commonwealth, our strategic position in the Indian Ocean would become untenable and our communications with New Zealand and Australia most insecure.

3. A Hindustan outside the British Commonwealth might very well be tempted, in order to give effect to an inevitable urge to conquer and absorb Pakistan, and thus restore the unity of India, to throw in her lot with Russia. Russia with her taste for power-politics and gangster methods would be likely to take full advantage of any such tendency on the part of Hindustan.

A Russian influenced Hindustan might well constitute such a menace to the security of the British Commonwealth as to cause its early dissolution.

INFLUENCE OF A BRITISH CONTROLLED PAKISTAN ON HINDUSTAN

4. In theory it might appear that a Pakistan under British influence could act as a check to the hostile potentialities of an independent Hindustan. Even if Pakistan comprised North-East as well as North-West India, a proposition which seems extremely unlikely to materialize owing to the great difficulties inherent in it, it is very doubtful if Pakistan would have the necessary resources in raw material. Industrial production, manpower, and, above all the requisite space, to enable it to become a base for warlike operations against a Hindustan, supported and equipped by a hostile power such as Russia.

If as seems more than likely, Pakistan were to be restricted to North-West India, it would most certainly not be adequate as a base for operations on a grand scale.

5. As atomic energy develops and weapons of all sorts, whether on the sea, on the land or in the air, improve depth in the defence and adequate space for the dispersion of base installations, including industrial plants, must become increasingly essential in war.

A united India has these qualifications, as would an independent Hindustan. Pakistan even if it includes North-East India, could never possess them.

6. It follows, therefore, that Pakistan, whether it has two zones or the North-West India zone only, will not provide the means by which the British Commonwealth can hope to influence or coerce an independent Hindustan and keep it free of hostile foreign influences, so as to ensure the security of our communications through the Indian Ocean area.

If we cannot secure these vital communications, it would seem that the break-up of the British Commonwealth is likely to follow before very long.

THE PROBLEM OF THE DEFENCE OF PAKISTAN

7. (a) Apart from the question of safeguarding our communications in the Indian Ocean area, must be considered the probable reaction of an independent Hindustan to a Pakistan under British influence and included in the British Commonwealth.

(b) The separation of Hindustan from Pakistan instead of eliminating the fundamental enmity of the Hindu for the Muslim is likely to inflame it. Any attempt to establish a Pakistan zone in North-East India, which if it is to be effective at all, must include Calcutta and a very large Hindu population, is certain to be strenuously resisted by the Hindus.

(c) Should by some means or other, the Hindus be brought to agree to the setting up of such a zone, they will almost certainly at once stand planning and working for its eventual elimination and reunion with Hindustan. A Hindustan without Calcutta and the control of the Bay of Bengal is not a practical proposition and the realization of this by the Hindus will inevitably lead to war between Hindustan and Pakistan. In this event, HMG in the United Kingdom would be committed to fight for the retention of this zone by Pakistan and might well become involved in a world war on this account.

8. (a) The actual defence of North-East Pakistan from the purely military point of view would be an extremely difficult problem, as the area could in no sense provide the needs of an army or an air force adequate for its defence, and these would be almost entirely dependent on sea communications for their needs. These sea communications would be most vulnerable to attack by sea and air forces based on Hindustan and could in no sense be considered reliable.

Moreover the attitude of Burma, which would presumably be independent, cannot be predicted.

Burma influenced by China, as it always must be, might well be hostile to the British Commonwealth and see, in a quarrel between Hindustan and Britain, a chance of improving her position. The possibility of North-East Pakistan having to defend itself from attack from the West as well as from the East and South cannot be excluded, and would make the problem well nigh insoluble. There can be little doubt that the drain on the resources of HMG in the United Kingdom would be immense and incalculable.

(b) Even supposing that Pakistan consisted of a North-Western zone only, the strategic problems involved in its defence would be many and difficult to solve.

The North-West Pakistan area is not self-supporting in any way, except possibly as regards cereals, it has practically no raw material or industrial capacity and all war material would have to be provided from overseas for many years to come. It has one port only—Karachi—seaward and landward approaches to which are constricted and most vulnerable to air attack.

For many years to come, Pakistan cannot hope to produce officers and technicians for the land and air forces necessary for her own protection, though it should be possible to produce sufficient men of the right quality for such forces.

(c) Physically, North-West Pakistan, like most other countries, has advantages and disadvantages from the defence point of view.

Assuming that it will absorb or at any rate, dominate Kashmir, North-West Pakistan cannot be seriously threatened from the North, protected as it is by the Himalayas, though it might be vulnerable to a limited extent to air attack from bases in Sinkiang.

The deserts of Rajputana and Sind similarly preclude any large scale attack by land from the South, and this is true also of the approach from the West through the wastes of Mekran, though the possibility of offensive operations on these fronts by mobile armoured and mechanized forces supplied by air cannot be excluded.

Pakistan would, however, be open to attack by land on a large-scale from the North-West and South-East.

Good communications within a country to be defended are essential to successful resistance and North-West Pakistan would be reasonably well provided with railways and roads running towards her Eastern and Western frontiers, and she would have good lateral railway communications. Her weakness in respect of communications would lie in the fact that the Indus and the great rivers of the Punjab run from North-East to South-West at right angles to her main arteries of communication and because the bridges over them are few and far-between and vulnerable to air attack. This disadvantage would probably outweigh in modern war any advantage which these rivers might confer as lines of defence.

No power is nowadays likely to venture to attack another unless it is reasonably sure of having initial superiority in the air.

(d) Let us first take the threat from the North-West. The aggressor would be Russia, supported possibly by Persia and Afghanistan, possibly unwilling but sovietised and coerced.

The problem of the defence of India against Russian aggression is of course an old one, and the considerations involved in the problem of resistance to it have been, and still are, continuously under review.

In the circumstances we are now considering the problem takes a new aspect because here we have Pakistan as a sovereign Muslim state controlling its own destinies, whereas before, the ruling power was Britain, a non-Muslim state and, therefore, disliked, suspected and feared by Afghanistan, and, also Persia.

This change of affinities may it is true ease the problem of defence of the Western frontier of Pakistan to a considerable extent, but in view of the well-known powers of infiltration and seduction possessed by Soviet Russia, it would be unwise to rely on it as a permanent solvent of the defence problem.

It is true that, in the conditions likely to prevail in any future war, a land invasion on a large scale of North-West Pakistan, through Northern Afghanistan over the passes of the Hindu Kush and the defiles of the Khyber and the Kurram, is most improbable.

Any land offensive against Pakistan from the West is likely to be made *via* Kandahar against Quetta and the Bolan Pass with the object of severing the railways leading from Karachi into the interior of the country and, thus, depriving its armies and air forces of their only source of supply of munitions of war.

It is true that the communications leading from Russia to Kandahar and beyond it are as yet undeveloped and that their development would take time and could not pass unnoticed. Nevertheless, given proper preparation a rapid advance by mechanized and armoured forces supplied partly by air is not an impossibility, as was proved in the campaigns in the Libya in the recent war. Quetta is connected with the rest of Pakistan by a single line of railway running through a narrow defile and extremely vulnerable to air attack, besides being liable to periodic interruption by flood and earthquake. The approaches to Quetta from the West are much more suitable to the deployment and movement of mechanized forces on a wide front than are the approaches from the East through Sibi, although the Khwaja Amran range just West of Quetta does provide a defensive position of some value, but of little depth. The total length of frontier to be watched and defended by Pakistan is about 500 miles from Peshawar to Kalat. It must be assumed, therefore, that the British will be required to provide at least fifty squadrons of aircraft and ten divisions of troops to assist in the defence of the Western frontier of Pakistan against a determined Russian attack, as the forces which Pakistan would be able to maintain from her own very limited resources, must of necessity be small, however efficient they may be.

All these forces whether provided by Britain or Pakistan would be completely dependent for their maintenance, except perhaps as regards food, on the one port of Karachi and on one line of railway leading thence to the main zone of operations. As already pointed out, Karachi and the approaches to it are very open to air attack from the South and North-West, and the sea approaches would also be liable to submarine and surface attack by craft based in the Persian Gulf, which in the circumstances we are considering, would almost certainly be controlled by Russia.

The supply of the forces in the Middle East from 1940 to 1943 was difficult enough when shipping had to use the Cape route, but it would be easy compared with the problem of maintaining an army and air force operating on the Western frontier of Pakistan in a major war.

(e) The frontier between Hindustan and North-West Pakistan must run through the flat plains of the Central or Eastern Punjab, and thence through the equally featureless, from the defence point of view, deserts of Northern and the Southern Punjab, until it reaches the sea just south of Karachi.

Even if it were to follow one of the rivers of the Punjab such as the Ravi or the Sutlej, or even the Jumna, this would not give a fully defensible frontier.

The communications running from the interior of Hindustan towards the frontiers of Pakistan are reasonably good and capable of maintaining considerable land forces in the northern sector of the common frontier. Though less good in the western or Rajputana sector, where they consist of metre gauge railway lines, they could support light mobile forces capable of striking at the rich corn producing areas of the South-Western Punjab.

Pakistan then, would be open to heavy attack by land forces on a front of some 100 miles from Jullundur to Bhatinda, and to lesser attack by light forces on a front of about 500 miles from Bhatinda to Kotri on the Indus above Karachi.

As the initiative and choice of the point of attack would lie with the aggressor, the whole of this long front would have to be watched even though it might be possible to hold the bulk of the main land forces more or less centrally in reserve.

The weight of the attack by land which Hindustan would be able to deliver would depend on the extent to which she had developed her industries and resources and raw materials, which would certainly be much greater than those of Pakistan, and on the amount of assistance in personnel, arms and equipment, she had received from any overseas ally, such as Russia. Hindustan as a base for warlike operations on a big scale, whether on the sea, on land or in the air, is, and always must be, vastly superior to Pakistan, while her communications are far less concentrated and thus far less vulnerable to attack by sea or from the air. Hindustan in fact, would be an efficient base for modern war, which Pakistan can never be. Assuming then, that Hindustan is unlikely to attack until she had organized and equipped adequate air and land forces, which she can do as quickly if not more quickly than Pakistan, it seems certain, even if Hindustan attacked Pakistan without the overt aid of Russia, that Britain would have to provide large air and land forces to ensure the integrity of Pakistan.

All these forces would be dependent for their maintenance on the single port of Karachi and on the 800 miles of railway thence to Lahore and Bhatinda. These railways would be exposed to attack throughout their length by mobile enemy forces operating from bases in Rajputana and by air forces based on existing airfields in Kathiawar and Rajputana.

(f) If Pakistan were to be attacked simultaneously, as is possible, by Russia from the North-West and by Hindustan from the South-East, then the air and land forces which would have to be provided by Britain to ensure its defence, would be very large indeed, as big if not bigger than those absorbed in the defence of the Middle East before the forces of the Axis were expelled from North Africa. It is most unlikely that forces of this size could be maintained through the solitary port of Karachi, even if they could be provided by the British Commonwealth when it no longer has the manpower of India to draw upon as it had in the recent struggle.

CONCLUSION

9. (a) The inclusion of Pakistan in the British Commonwealth of Nations and the assumption by Britain or the British Commonwealth of the consequent responsibility for its defence could be justified on the following grounds:

(i) That it would enable us so to dominate and control an independent Hindustan as to prevent her or her potential allies from disrupting our sea and air communications in the Indian Ocean area.
ii) That it would aid us in maintaining our influence over the Muslim countries of the Near and Middle East and so assist us to prevent the advance of Russia towards the Indian Ocean and the Mediterranean.

(b) If the arguments contained in this note are being based on correct surmises, it seems perfectly clear that the first of these objects is unattainable, because of the large forces which its achievement would require, relative to the resources likely to be available to the British Commonwealth, at the outbreak of a major war.

If the first object cannot be achieved, it would be useless to attempt to achieve the second, because it would be quite obvious to all the Muslim countries, that Britain had ceased to be a power in Asia.

(c) If we desire to maintain our power to move freely by sea and air in the Indian Ocean area, which I consider essential to the continued existence of the British Commonwealth, we can do so only by keeping in being a United India which will be a willing member of that Commonwealth, ready to share in its defence to the limit of her resources.

C. J. Auchinleck

Both in this paper relating to external defence, and in a second paper written about the same time on 'India's Mongol Frontier', General Francis Tuker stressed the importance of the northern and north-eastern frontiers in the defence of India—he was convinced [and this in 1946] that China, not Russia, would become the main threat to the subcontinent. This frontier, especially the Himalayan section, had for centuries been regarded as impregnable, but with the coming of air power its strength had decreased and its importance increased; and with the development of nuclear weapons its importance had become even greater. [This was recorded in an essay 'Keeping the Peace in India, 1946-7: The Role of Lieut.-General Sir Francis Tuker in Eastern Command']

The vital area was the Tibetan plateau, which would be the base for any attempt to conquer eastern India, and it was therefore India's prime interest to prevent the military occupation by China of the Tibetan plateau. China had always claimed Tibet, her influence at Lhasa was greatly increasing, and moreover pro-Chinese Tibetans were infiltrating into Assam, Sikkim and Bhutan. 'There is no doubt that as British influence and power withdraws from India, so will Tibet...lean more and more towards China.' Rather than see a Chinese occupation of Tibet, India should be prepared to occupy the plateau herself, for an invasion of India by various routes through Tibet would be quite practicable with modern equipment. The old caravan route from Lhasa through Sikkim, and the 'Diwangiri' route could both be easily made passable for modern transport. For the same reasons it would be essential for India to keep the friendship and even active cooperation of the peoples of this frontier from Nepal to the Naga Hills, and particularly the peoples of Nepal. The presence of a large Gurkha contingent in the external defence force would help in this, attaching Nepal to the Indian, rather than to the Chinese interest. 'There is every reason why Nepal should insist that as she holds a great part of the Indian frontier, she should therefore be consulted in India's defence and be allowed to contribute her share.' [It needs to be reiterated and emphasized that this note expresses the view of Mary Doreen Wainwright, in 'Keeping the Peace in India, 1946-7: The Role of Lieut.-General Sir Francis Tuker in Eastern Command' General Tuker's service in India.

Appendix X

THE LONG-TERM PLAN

9. Unless during the present discussions we can get back to acceptance by Congress and League of the original plan of the Mission as intended by the Mission and not as intended by the Congress, H.M.G. must accept the fact that the Mission Plan is dead. They must also accept the fact that we have only a very limited period and a very limited power to substitute fresh arrangements.

10. The following courses are open to H.M.G., on the failure of the Mission Plan:

A. To re-establish their own authority and rule India for a further period. This course they have already ruled out as politically impossible.

B. To attempt to negotiate a fresh settlement. This could only be some sort of partition, and would at once bring us into conflict with Congress. It would imply our remaining in India to set up the Partition, it might be for some years. I do not think that this is a practicable policy.

C. To surrender to Congress as the Majority party, to acquiesce in all it does, while using the little influence which will remain to us for a little time to try and secure what fairness we can for the Minorities, the States and the Services.

I do not think this an honourable or a wise policy; it will end British rule in India in discredit and eventually an ignominious scuttle or dismissal by Congress. There is no statesmanship or generosity in Congress.

D. To announce that, having failed to bring about a settlement, we propose to withdraw from India in our own method and in our own time, and with due regard to our own interests; and that we will regard any attempt to interfere with our programme as an act of war which we will meet with all the resources at our command. But we should of course do our best to secure agreement while we remained, and in any event to hand over to established authorities, e.g. Provincial Governments.

This is in effect the Breakdown Plan; but it is intended for use not merely when widespread disorder has broken out, but for use in the event of a political breakdown and *before* disorder has broken out. The existence of this plan will also enable us to take a firm line with Congress, since we have a reasonable alternative on which to fall back; and may thus enable us to avert a political breakdown.

11. I recognize H.M.G.'s political difficulties; but Parliament must soon be informed of the realities of the Indian situation. I do not consider it is fair to leave Parliament, on whom the ultimate responsibility rests, to believe that the present situation can continue indefinitely; nor to His Majesty's servants in India to allow matters to drift on without a definite policy.

12. I therefore recommend H.M.G. to make the fullest use of the present discussions to try and restore the Mission plan to its original basis *as intended by the Mission*. If it fails in this, it must choose one of the courses outlined in para. 10 above. But it must be quite definite in its choice. Neither I nor the Governors, nor any responsible officials can act with any confidence or decision unless we know, quite clearly, what policy H.M.G. proposes to follow.

It will also, I feel, be impossible to carry out the present negotiations with any hope of success, unless H.M.G. have made up their mind whether or not they are prepared to stand up to the Congress.

Appendix XI

THE CONGRESS SUBMITTED PANEL OF 15 NAMES FOR THE PROPOSED EXECUTIVE COUNCIL

1. Maulana Abul Kalam Azad (Congress Muslim)
2. Asaf Ali (Congress Muslim)
3. Pandit Jawaharlal Nehru (Congress Hindu)
4. Sardar Vallabhbhai Patel (Congress Hindu)
5. Dr Rajendra Prasad (Congress Hindu)
6. M.A. Jinnah (Muslim League)
7. Nawab Mohammad Ismail Khan (Muslim League)
8. Nawabzada Liaquat Ali Khan (Muslim League)
9. Dr Shyamaprasad Mookerji (Hindu Mahasabha)
10. Gaganvihari Mehta (Hindu)
11. Rajkumari Amrit Kaur (Woman, Indian Christian)
12. Muniswami Pillay (Scheduled Class)
13. Radhanath Das (Scheduled Class)
14. Sir Ardeshir Dalai (Parsi)
15. A Sikh member (Tara Singh).

Appendix XII

Results of the 1946 Elections

Province	Muslim seats	Won by the League
Punjab	86	75
Bengal	119	113
Assam	34	33
Sindh	34	28
United Provinces	66	54
Bombay	30	30
Madras	29	29
Central Province	14	13
Orissa	4	4
Northwest Frontier	38	17
Bihar	40	34

[Craig Baxter – Page 178]

Appendix to Chapter 10

Appendix I

QUAID-I-AZAM'S MESSAGE TO HINDUSTAN 7 AUGUST 1947

Statement on the eve of his departure for Karachi from New Delhi

'I am grateful to all our friends and those who have sent me their kind messages of greetings and good wishes on the establishment of Pakistan. I wish I could reply to every one of them individually, but having regard to the fact that I have received thousands of messages, I am unable to do so and hope that they will excuse me, as it was impossible to acknowledge every message separately owing to the enormous pressure of work that we have to meet and give effect to the big issues involved in the division of India.

I bid farewell to the citizens of Delhi, amongst whom I have many friends of all communities and I earnestly appeal to everyone to live in this great and historic city with peace. The past must be buried and let us start afresh as two independent sovereign States of Hindustan and Pakistan. I wish Hindustan prosperity and peace.

Appendices to Chapter 11

Appendix I

MR JINNAH'S PRESIDENTIAL ADDRESS TO THE CONSTITUENT ASSEMBLY OF PAKISTAN

11 August 1947

Mr President, Ladies and Gentlemen!

I cordially thank you, with the utmost sincerity, for the honour you have conferred upon me—the greatest honour that is possible to confer—by electing me as your first President. I also thank those leaders who have spoken in appreciation of my services and their personal references to me. I sincerely hope that with your support and your cooperation we shall make this Constituent Assembly an example to the world. The Constituent Assembly has got two main functions to perform. The first is the very onerous and responsible task of framing the future constitution of Pakistan and the second of functioning as a full and complete sovereign body as the Federal Legislature of Pakistan. We have to do the best we can in adopting a provisional constitution for the Federal Legislature of Pakistan. You know really that not only we ourselves are wondering but, I think, the whole world is wondering at this unprecedented cyclonic revolution which has brought about the clan of creating and establishing two independent sovereign Dominions in this subcontinent. As it is, it has been unprecedented; there is no parallel in the history of the world. This mighty subcontinent with all kinds of inhabitants has been brought under a plan which is titanic, unknown, unparalleled. And what is very important with regards to it is that we have achieved it peacefully and by means of an evolution of the greatest possible character.

Dealing with our first function in this Assembly, I cannot make any well-considered pronouncement at this moment, but I shall say a few things as they occur to me. The first and the foremost thing that I would like to emphasize is this: remember that you are now a sovereign legislative body and you have got all the powers. It, therefore, places on you the gravest responsibility as to how you should take your decisions. The first observation that I would like to make is this: You will no doubt agree with me that the first duty of a government is to maintain law and order, so that the life, property and religious beliefs of its subjects are fully protected by the State.

The second thing that occurs to me is this: One of the biggest curses from which India is suffering—I do not say that other countries are free from it, but, I think our condition is much worse—is bribery and corruption. That really is a poison. We must put that down with an iron hand and I hope that you will take adequate measures as soon as it is possible for this Assembly to do so.

Black-marketing is another curse. Well, I know that black-marketeers are frequently caught and punished. Judicial sentences are passed or sometimes fines only are imposed. Now you have to tackle this monster, which today is a colossal crime against society, in our distressed conditions, when we constantly face shortage of food and other essential commodities of life. A citizen who does black-marketing commits, I think, a greater crime than the biggest and most grievous of crimes. These black-marketeers are really knowing, intelligent, and ordinarily responsible people, and when they indulge in black-marketing, I think they ought to be very severely punished, because the entire system of control and regulation of foodstuffs and essential commodities, and cause wholesale starvation and want and even death.

The next thing that strikes me is this: Here again it is a legacy which has been passed on to us. Along with many other things, good and bad, has arrived this great evil, the evil of nepotism and jobbery. I want to make it quite clear that I shall never tolerate any kind of jobbery, nepotism or any influence directly of indirectly brought to bear upon me. Whenever I will find that such a practice is in vogue or is continuing anywhere, low or high, I shall certainly not countenance it.

I know there are people who do not quite agree with the division of India and the partition of the Punjab and Bengal. Much has been said against it, but now that it has been accepted, it is the duty of everyone of us to loyally abide by it and honourably act according to the agreement which is now final and binding on all. But you must remember, as I have said, that this mighty revolution that has taken place is unprecedented. One can quite understand the feeling that exists between the two communities wherever one community is in majority and the other is in minority. But the question is, whether it was possible or practicable to act otherwise than what has been done. A division had to take place. On both sides, in Hindustan and Pakistan, there are sections of people who may not agree with it, who may not like it, but in my judgment there was no other solution and I am sure future history will record its verdict in favour of it. And what is more, it will be proved by actual experience as we go on that was the only solution of India's constitutional problem. Any idea of a united India could never have worked and in my judgment it would have led us to terrific disaster. Maybe that view is correct; maybe it is not, that remains to be seen. All the same, in this division it was impossible to avoid the question of minorities being in one Dominion or the other. Now that was unavoidable. There is no other solution. Now what shall we do? Now, if we want to make this great State of Pakistan happy and prosperous, we should wholly and solely concentrate on the well-being of the people, and especially of the masses and the poor. If you will work in cooperation, forgetting the past, burying the hatchet, you are bound to succeed. If you change your past and work together in a spirit that everyone of you, no matter to what community he belongs, no matter what relations he had with you in the past, no matter what is his colour, caste or creed, is first, second and last a citizen of this State with equal rights, privileges, and obligations, there will be no end to the progress you will make.

I cannot emphasize it too much. We should begin to work in that spirit and in course of time all these angularities of the majority and minority communities, the Hindu community and the Muslim community, because even as regards Muslims you have Pathans, Punjabis, Shias, Sunnis and so on, and among the Hindus you have Brahmins, Vashnavas, Khatris, also Bengalis, Madrasis and so on, will vanish. Indeed if you ask me, this has been the biggest hindrance in the way of India to attain the freedom and independence and but for this we would have been free people long long ago. No power can hold another nation and specially a nation of 400 million souls in subjection; nobody could have conquered you, and even if it had happened, nobody could have continued its hold on you for any length of time, but for this. Therefore, we must learn a lesson from this. You are free; you are free to go to your temples, you are free to go to your mosques or to any other place of worship in this State of Pakistan. You may belong to any religion or caste or creed that has nothing to do with the business of the State. As you know, history shows that in England, conditions, some time ago, were much worse than those prevailing in India today. The Roman Catholics and the Protestants persecuted each other. Even now there are some States in existence where there are discriminations made and bars imposed against a particular class. Thank God, we are not starting in those days. We are starting in the days where there is no discrimination, no distinction between one community and another, no discrimination between one caste or creed and another. We are starting with this fundamental principle that we are all citizens and equal citizens of one State. The people of England in course of time had to face the realities of the situation and had to discharge the responsibilities and burdens placed upon them by the government of their country and they went through that fire step by step. Today, you might say with justice that Roman Catholics and Protestants do not exist; what exists now is that every man is a citizen, an equal citizen of Great Britain and they are all members of the Nation.

Now I think we should keep that in front of us as our ideal and you will find that in course of time Hindus would cease to be Hindus and Muslims would cease to be Muslims, not in the religious sense, because that is the personal faith of each individual, but in the political sense as citizens of the State.

Well, gentlemen, I do not wish to take up any more of your time and thank you again for the honour you have done to me. I shall always be guided by the principles of justice and fairplay without any, as is put in the political language, prejudice or ill-will, in other words, partiality or favouritism. My guiding principle will be justice and complete impartiality, and I am sure that with your support and cooperation. I can look forward to Pakistan becoming one of the greatest nations of the world.

I have received a message from the United States of America addressed to me. It reads:

I have the honour to communicate to you, in Your Excellency's capacity as President of the Constituent Assembly of Pakistan, the following message which I have just received from the Secretary of State of the United States:

On the occasion of the first meeting of the Constituent Assembly for Pakistan, I extend to you and to the members of the Assembly, the best wishes of the Government and the people of the United States for the successful conclusion of the great work you are about to undertake.

Appendix II

SPEECH DELIVERED BY MAULANA AZAD AT JAMA MASJID OF DELHI ON 23-10-1947

My brethren,

You know what has brought me here today. This congregation at Shahjehan's historic mosque is not an unfamiliar sight for me. Here, I have addressed you on several previous occasions. Since then we have seen many ups and downs. At that time, instead of weariness, your faces reflected serenity, and your hearts, instead of misgivings, exuded confidence. The uneasiness on your faces and the desolation in your hearts that I see today, reminds me of the events of the past few years.

Do you remember? I hailed you, you cut off my tongue; I picked my pen, you severed my hand; I wanted to move forward, you broke off my legs; I tried to turn over, and you injured my back. When the bitter political games of the last seven years were at their peak, I tried to wake you up at every danger signal. You not only ignored my call but revived all the past traditions of neglect and denial. As a result the same perils surround you today, whose onset had previously diverted you from the righteous path.

Today, mine is no more than an inert existence or a forlorn cry; I am an orphan in my own motherland. This does not mean that I feel trapped in the original choice that I had made for myself, nor do I feel that there is no room left for my *aashiana* (nest). What it means is that my cloak is weary of your impudent grabbing hands. My sensitivities are injured, my heart is heavy. Think for one moment. What course did you adopt? Where have you reached, and where do you stand now? Haven't your senses become torpid? Aren't you living in a constant state of fear? This fear is your own creation, a fruit of your own deeds.

It was not long ago when I warned you that the two-nation theory was death-knell to a meaningful, dignified life; forsake it. I told you that the pillars upon which you were leaning would inevitably crumble. To all this you turned a deaf ear. You did not realize that my brothers! I have always attempted to keep politics apart from personalities, thus avoiding those thorny valleys. That is why some of my messages are often couched in allusions. But what I have to say today needs to be direct and to the point. The partition of India was a fundamental mistake. The manner in which religious differences were incited, inevitably, led to the devastation that we have seen with our own eyes. Unfortunately, we are still seeing it at some places.

There is no use recounting the events of the past seven years, nor will it serve any good. Yet, it must be stated that the debacle of Indian Muslims is the result of the colossal blunders committed by the Muslim League's misguided leadership. These consequences however, were no surprise to me; I had anticipated them from the very start.

Now that Indian politics has taken a new direction, there is no place in it for the Muslim League. Now the question is whether or not we are capable of any constructive thinking. For this, I have invited the Muslim leaders of India to Delhi, during the second week of November.

The gloom cast upon your lives is momentary; I assure you we can be beaten by none save our own selves! I have always said, and I repeat it again today; eschew your indecisiveness, your mistrust, and stop your misdeeds. This unique triple-edged weapon is more lethal than the two-edged iron sword which inflicts fatal wounds, which I have heard of!

Just think about this life of escapism that you have opted for, in the sacred name of Hejrat. Get into the habit of exercising your own brains, and strengthening your own hearts. If you do so, only then will you realize how immature your decisions were.

Where are you going and why? Raise your eyes. The minarets of Jama Masjid want to ask you a question. Where have you lost the glorious pages from your chronicles? Was it only yesterday that on the banks of the Jamuna, your caravans performed *wuzu*? Today, you are afraid of living here! Remember, Delhi has been nurtured with your blood. Brothers! Create a basic change in yourselves. Today your fear is as misplaced as your jubilation was yesterday.

The words coward and frenzy cannot be spoken in the same breath as the word Muslim. A true Muslim can be swayed neither by avarice nor apprehension. Don't get scared because a few faces have disappeared. The only reason they had herded you in a single fold was to facilitate their own flight. Today, if they have jerked their hand free from yours, what does it matter? Make sure that they have not run away with your hearts. If your hearts are still in the right place, make them the abode of God. Some thirteen hundred years ago, through an Arab *ummi*, God proclaimed. "Those who place their faith in God and are firm in their belief, no fear for them nor any sorrow." Winds blow in and blow out: tempests may gather but all is short-lived. The period of trial is about to end. Change yourselves as if you had never been in such an abject condition.

I am not used to altercation. Faced with your general indifference, however, I will repeat that the third force has departed, and along with it, its trappings of vanity. Whatever had to happen has happened. Politics has broken out of its old mould and a new cast is being prepared. If your hearts have still not changed and your minds still have reservations, it is a different matter. But, if you want a change, then take your cue from history and cast yourself in the new mould. Having completed a revolutionary phase, there still remains a few blank pages in the history of India. You can make yourselves worthy of filling those pages, provided you are willing.

Brothers! Keep up with the changes. Don't say, "We are not ready for the change." Get ready. Stars may have plummeted down but the sun is still shining. Borrow a few of its rays and sprinkle them in the dark caverns of your lives.

I do not ask you to seek certificates from the new echelons of power. I do not want you to lead a life of sycophancy as you did during the foreign rule. I want to remind you that these bright etchings which you see all around you are relics of the *qafilas* (caravans) of your forefathers. Do not forget them. Do not forsake them. Live like their worthy inheritors, and, rest assured, that if you do not wish to flee from this scene, nobody can make you flee. Come, today let us pledge that this country is ours, we belong to it and any fundamental decision about its destiny will remain incomplete without our consent.

Today, you fear the earth's tremors; once you were virtually the earthquake itself. Today, you fear the darkness; once your existence was the epicentre of radiance. Clouds have poured dirty waters and you have hitched up your trousers. Those were none but your forefathers who not only plunged headlong into the seas, but trampled the mountains, laughed at the bolts of lightning, turned away the tornados, challenged the tempests and made them alter their course. It is a sure sign of a dying faith that those who had once grabbed the collars of emperors, are today, clutching at their own throats. They have become oblivious of the existence of God as if they had never believed in Him.

Brothers! I do not have a new prescription for you. I have the same old prescription that was revealed to the greatest benefactor of mankind, the prescription of the Holy Quran: "Do not fear and do not grieve. If you possess true faith, you will gain the upper hand." The congregation is now at an end. What I had to say, I have said, briefly. Let me say once again, keep a grip on your senses. Learn to create your own surroundings, your own world. This is not a commodity that I can buy for you from the market-place. This can be bought only from the market-place of the heart provided you can pay for it with the currency of good deeds.

May God's grace be on you.

Appendix III

DIALOGUE BETWEEN THE AUTHOR, LLOYD AND SUSANNE RUDOLPH, PROFESSORS OF POLITICAL SCIENCE EMERITUS, UNIVERSITY OF CHICAGO

Author: There is here, a definitional difficulty, how exactly do you interpret 'Nation, State, Country'?

Lloyd and Susanne Rudolph: Confusion arises "from using nation and state interchangeably. This, if often done in social scientific and historical writing, as well as in writing for the public sphere. In Woodrow Wilson's time it was assumed that all nations aspired to be states if they were not states already. Nationalism and nation and statehood and sovereignty went together. The Ottoman and Austro-Hungarian [Hapsburg] empires suffered and collapsed in large part because newly created nations insisted on being sovereign states. Earlier, in the 18th century, in Sir William Jones' [and James Tod's] time for example, the word nation was used interchangeably with race [before there was 19th century racism], people and country. [For more on the transformation of nation as a people often defined by language to nation as race defined by biology/blood see Thomas Trautman's excellent, *Aryans and British India*.] In any case I think it significant that Jinnah spoke of a Muslim nation and of two nations but bargained for a share of sovereignty in the colonial and post-colonial state. In this he was like—indeed he may have shown the way—to linguistically "nations" in India such as Telegus, Maharashtrians, and others.

Author: You point towards a "multinational—a pluralist state". I am of the view and have expressed the thought, in writing, and in speech that India is a 'non-territorial nation' where, through history, it is not the State but society that has been at the cellular core of its nationhood. On so many occasions in India's history, there have been no State, or dysfunctional States, or even States in conflict with one another, but India has always been there an inextinguishable, constant.

Lloyd: Having spoken above of "India" encompassing many nations in the framework of nation and state discourse I would like to shift ground here to agree with you that one can talk about India as an 'imagined community," a term invented by Benedict Andersen in a book of the same name, and as "a state of mind," a phrase used by Amitav Ghosh in an essay some years ago to explain why India can't be defined, as was allegedly the case for "original" modern nation, revolutionary France, in terms of language, religion, culture or birth. But Sudipto Kaviraj warns us, in "The imaginary institution of India" (Subaltern Studies VII and elsewhere] against anachronism, imagining that the Indian nation as created by the words and actions of the nationalist movement from 1885 onward existed in that form in earlier centuries. The Regional Kingdom and the Subcontinental Empire in Indian State Formation, [extracts attached] which addresses the variable forms "states" have taken in Indian history. Although we must be beware of using the idea of India anachronistically [and avoid getting into the morass of where the Aryans came from, etc] I think a recent book lends credence to your notion "India has always been there....' That book is by the Sanskritist and literary scholar, Sheldon Pollock, for years our colleague and friend and now at Columbia, *The Language of the Gods in the World of Men: Sanskrit Culture and Power in Pre-modern India* [University of California Press, 2006?]. Sheldon Pollock examines how new literatures and identities took shape in response to and, in a sense, against Sanskrit literature [texts, ideas, civilizational ideas]. Still there was a continuity along with difference and contestation. I simplify; it may prove worth your time to consult this book.

Extracts of "The Subcontinental Empire and the Regional Kingdom In Indian State Formation".*

LLOYD I. RUDOLPH AND SUSANNE HOEBER RUDOLPH

CRITIQUE OF EXTANT STATE THEORY

State Formation in Asia and Europe: A re-conceptualization explanations of state formation, the state-society relationship, and stateness have been based on interpretations of the history of the West. The failure to take account of non-Western historical experiences presents critical obstacles to an understanding of the state in Asia. Social and political changes in Asia have been both like and unlike changes in the West. In fact, different social conditions and doctrines in Europe and India produced contrasting state types, the nation-state in Europe and the subcontinental empire in India. As Nettl put it:

> The European experience of stateness was essentially the product of a particularization or narrowing of sovereignty into ethnically homogeneous or at least ethnically defined areas.... Developing countries, on the other hand, have in common the extension of central authority across ethnic boundaries and particular, hitherto 'sovereign communities'.

The conceptions of state, society, and the relationship between them have been formulated differently in India from the way they have been in Europe. In Europe, the Greek idea of common citizenship and the Christian ideal of a community of believers contributed to the seventeenth-century concept of a civil society that ultimately shaped the process of state formation, which eventually led to the nation-state.

In contrast, classical Hindua thought of the *dharmasastras* (legal texts) recognized ordered heterogeneity. It rationalized and legitimized a society of distinct cultural and functional communities that shared a sense of brotherhood within themselves, but lived as races apart in their relationship to each other. State power was constrained by society's autonomous claims to self-regulation. Communities were not united to each other by fellow feeling—quite the reverse—and yet they constituted non-antagonistic strata whose cultural differences, social interaction, and functional interdependence were ordered and integrated within a larger social architectonic that the state was meant to uphold and protect.

For Brahmin social theorists, the *dharmasastra* was a means to assimilate the diverse customs of *mlecchas* (foreigners) within the customs of the Vedic/Aryan peoples as they moved down the Gangetic plain from their 'homeland' in the Punjab. Brahmin theorists used the same conceptions and techniques to assimilate waves of subsequent conquerors, Greeks, Sakas, Kushanas, Huns. The characteristic strategy of the law books was a compartmentalization of diversity, rather than homogenization.

An Asokan pillar of the Mauryan Empire enjoins: 'King Priyadarsi, Beloved of the Gods, honours men of all religious communities with gifts and honours...other sects should be daily honoured in everyway....' Islam, too, in its Indian environment, was obliged to recognize this mode of social integration. The twelfth-century conceptions of militant Islam of the early Turkic invaders entailed the conversion of conquered peoples, that is, homogenization rather than compartmentalization. In the event, Indian social reality proved more intractable than that of other peoples. The exemptions generally extended to people of the book, Jews and Christians, were extended first to Brahmins, and eventually to other Hindu subjects. Badaoni, writing in the sixteenth century as a contemporary about Akbar, the greatest of the Mughal emperors, tells us: 'As a result of all the influences which were brought to bear on his Majesty, there grew...gradually as the outline on a stone, the conviction in his heart that there were sensible men in all religions....' Rulers who violated the norm of upholding the laws and customs of social groups by intervening to change them, as Aurangzeb did in the later part of his reign and the British did just prior to 1857, endangered the (Page 11) foundations of the subcontinental empire. The British policy eventually echoed the practice of previous imperial states, subventions to and protection of all sects. These doctrines about religious diversity are relevant for other diversities, such as language, caste, and religion, as well.

This view requires both empirical and theoretical revision. Empirically, the most important revision has to do with what Indian rulers did recognize and protect: the customs, activities, and prerogatives of communities, castes, sects, status orders, and guilds (craft and commercial). While practice often departed from norm, state theory recognized that such social formations, far from being creations or instruments of the state, existed *prior* to the state, and were governed by their own laws and customs. It was the first duty of rulers to preserve and protect them. ...As to the question of property, this is a very controversial one among the English writers on India. In the broken hill country south of Krishna [sic], property in land does seem to have existed. ...In any case it seems to have been Mohamedens who first established the principle of 'no property in land' throughout the whole of Asia.

Religious ties of regional sects, popular pilgrimages, and periodic devotional festivals constituted vital channels of cultural communication. Trade networks, in which credit and cash transactions played a role, were, from the most ancient times, critical to linking villages to sub-regions and to the world. Nor was the Indian political landscape exhausted by the duality that both Marx and Henry Mayne posit, of an all-powerful and despotic state confronting a universe of passive isolates—the villages of India. In fact, as we have pointed out, the social and political space between the village and the state was richly populated.

History is made by Europe, regardless of whether it is made by creation or oppression. There were no world systems before European capitalism created one. Buddhism and Islam fail to qualify as international systemic forces because of their superstructural nature. Nor do the diffusion of administrative and political forms by Byzantium and Persia qualify. South Asia's extensive international trade before the sixteenth century drops out of view because Asia is by definition peripheral.

British rule, too, blended extra-continental ideas and institutions into indigenous state forms, even as it adapted and extended Mughal symbolism, ceremonials, and administrative arrangements. Utilitarian/autocratic ideas and practices that were unacceptable at home were applied in India to create a centralized and autocratic imperial state.

THE NATION STATE AND THE SUBCONTINENTAL EMPIRE IN EUROPE AND INDIA

J.P. Nettl pointed out that 'if the entry of the third world onto the stage of modern socio-scientific consciousness has had one immediate result (or should have had), it is the snapping of the link between state and nation. What were awkward exceptions (Switzerland, the Soviet Union, empires generally, and so on) have now become also a rule of non-nation-states.' India is a striking exemplar of the rule. It continued along the road Western Europe turned away from when it abandoned the Holy Roman Empire. India's historic concepts of stateness and collective representations of the political universe featured an imperial state. On the one hand, it aggregated diverse territorial, cultural, and functional communities. On the other, it featured a symbolic and institutional state domain. For Europe, the collapse of the Hapsburg, Tsarist, and Ottoman states after the First World War seemed to confirm for the Atlantic world the atavistic nature of the multinational imperial state form. It is in the period after the Second World War that Europe sought once more, through economic and political means, to approximate a subcontinental political order.

'By 1300 it was evident that the dominant political form in Western Europe was going to be the sovereign state.' By contrast, the doctrine and practice of the Indian state preserved subordinate jurisdictions. It included, rather than eliminated, layered and segmented social and political power, and created a socially constrained negotiated political order. This order was not merely a concession to the contingent and layered distribution of power among the regional kingdoms and local chiefs that prevailed through much of Indian history, or a consequence of limited technical means of control. It was also a principle of state formation and maintenance.

The doctrine of sovereignty, with its implied exclusive jurisdiction, was inimical to the sharing and layering of power among culturally diverse areas that made possible a multinational empire.

By the nineteenth century, the nation-state had become so powerful an ideology that the existence of diverse ethnic communities was obscured, and their claims de-legitimized or repressed.

The result of Woodrow Wilson's insistence on self-determination after the First World War 'was the closest approximation that modern Europe has ever had to an ethnographic map coinciding with a political map'.

The difference between state formation in Europe and India was affected by the relatively early stability state forms achieved in Europe, and the relative fluidity they retained in India through the eighteenth century. This fluidity was a product of the tension between the imperial state and the regional kingdom, and the mutual determination that affected system-level differences.

State formation on the Indian subcontinent took a different course. The prevalent state form on the Indian subcontinent under Mughal and British rule from the sixteenth through the mid-twentieth centuries was the subcontinental empire rather than the regional kingdom. This outcome was by no means clear during prior, non-imperial eras, when the regional kingdom was the dominant state form. Literary and artistic creativity, as well as dynastic and territorial loyalties, are associated with both regional kingdoms and imperial states. Nor were the Deccan states of Bijapur, Golconda, or the Chola and Vijayanagar southern empires necessarily destined to fail. If the subcontinental empire prevailed, it did so marginally rather than totally; the successor states of the British Raj and the states in India's federal system are contemporary expressions of the regional state form Mughal miniature paintings featured the emperor with a penumbra. Because the loyalty and obeisance he commanded was at once intensely personal and abstract, it created a separate state domain that dissolved and displaced loyalties to place, king, and community. Performances and exchanges amplified his presence: for the public, the daily royal audience in the *diwan-i-am* (hall of public audience); for the court attended by princes and nobles appearances in the *diwan-i-khas* (hall of private audience); and at frequent *darbars*; for the crown servants in the field, intimate personal exchanges—the gift of a *khilat* (robe said to have been worn by the emperor) to mark an appointment as his agent, letters from the emperor's hand, and the reciprocation of gifts by subordinates.

The British used Mughal ceremonies and language to revitalize the universalism and mystique of the imperial state, reviving in Victoria's time the imperial grandeur and patrimonial ties in jubilees and coronation ceremonies, and in rituals of loyalty between the Queen and her subjects. Their cultural policy featured English. Like Persian under the Mughals, it became the language of state administration, a mark of elite status, and the medium through which the political leaders of the subcontinent's disparate regions and communities deliberated and bargained.

Both the Mughal and British states formed alliances that recognized and legitimated the ordered heterogeneity of Indian society. Mughal marital, political, and military alliances with Rajput (Hindu) princes helped them to create and rule an empire. The Mughal court's patronage embraced Hindu aesthetic and literary products and, in the case of Akbar, Zoroastrian and Christian as well as Hindu religious practices. In turn, Rajput lifestyles, state administration, and art were infiltrated by Mughal forms and standards, even while Rajput rulers preserved their religious and political patrimony.

The inability of Mughal officials to recognize southern rulers as part of the system of ordered heterogeneity and incorporate them as collaborators in the task of ruling the imperial state was a significant cause of the deterioration and collapse of Mughal rule. The northern, Persian, and Persianized Mughal court nobility and officials had recognized without pain the geographically, ethnically, and linguistically adjacent Rajputs. Incorporating the Marathas proved troublesome yet possible, but Mughal nobles and officials lacked the cultural flexibility to treat as peers the 'hideous, black' and guttural sounding Poligars and other southern notables. Together with overextended lines of communication, logistical (Page 21) difficulties, and the exhaustion of resources, especially *jagirs*, to sustain an expanded and increasingly unproductive and ineffective army and bureaucracy, the inability to accommodate southern political elites helped to account for the Mughal failure in the south, and ultimately in the subcontinent. Ironically, British racial arrogance contributed to their superficial but comprehensive acceptance of Indian heterogeneity. All Indians became natives, an inferior species distinguished by a wide variety of esoteric and—for most—abhorrent beliefs and practices.

The instrumental and institutional variables that accounted for a viable state in India included centralized fiscal and administrative mechanisms in the hands of the Crown; patrimonial bureaucracies barred from control over the means of administration, and from appropriation and inheritance of office and estates; and military formations controlled by the Crown rather than by feudal lords or independent military entrepreneurs.

The Indian nationalist movement lent a sense of commonality to the separate communities of the subcontinent.

The Mughals had utilized a variable mixture of direct and indirect rule, relatively direct in areas such as Gujarat and Awadh, and indirect in Rajputana, where local rulers retained considerable autonomy.

The similarities and differences in Mughal and British ideas about the state-society relation can be seen in their contrasting policies *vis-à-vis* rulers in Rajputana, whose north Indian regional kingdoms both sought to dominate. Mughal rulers attempted to impose upon Rajput kingdoms a centralized *jagir* system, and establish asymmetrical bonds of loyalty between themselves and Rajput *rajas* comparable to those that integrated master-servant relationships at the Centre. Centralized, hierarchical relations characteristic of the Mughal state stood in marked contrast to relations within Rajput kingdoms. Decentralization and horizontal bonds of clan and lineage brotherhoods sustained relatively symmetrical relations between rulers, and greater and lesser noble subjects. Maharajas stood above their brothers within dynastic clans, but did so as representatives of the clan's senior lineages. Over time, Rajput rulers emulated Mughal ideas and practice by trying to remodel their relations with their clan brothers into a more hierarchical master-servant connection. Their nobles' response recapitulated their own resistance to Mughal claims, that is, variable compliance punctuated by sporadic revolts.

Despite the common use of prevailing Persian terms, Mughal and Rajput language usage evokes the contrasting perspectives of empire and regional kingdom. Mughal patrimonial bureaucrats and chroniclers used the terms *mansabdar* or *jagirdar* to designate regional or local officials, and *mansab, jagir,* or *watanjagir* for estates, terms that made clear that offices and lands were granted in support of state service and held at the emperor's pleasure. Rajput rulers used other terms, *raja* (ruler) or *zamindar* (local lord), and *desh, raj, watan,* or *mulk* (a ruler's hereditary homeland) to express their sense of independence with respect to authority and land.

If the Mughal emperors thought of Rajputs rulers as *mansabdars* (milirary and civil officials), dispensable servants dependent for their posts and perquisites on imperial will, the British thought of Rajput lords as a feudal landed aristocracy. Vassals of the Queen-empress, they were meant to be at the same time a governing class with rights and obligations.

ENDNOTES

Introduction

1. The Umayyad Dynasty was the first dynasty of caliphs of the Prophet Muhammad, who were not closely related to Muhammad himself, though they were of the same Makkah clan. The first dynasty reigned from AD 661 to AD 750. The Abbasids were the dynasty of caliphs who ruled the Islamic Empire from AD 750 until the Mongol conquest of the Middle East in 1258. The dynasty takes its name from its ancestor al-Abbas, the uncle of the Prophet Muhammad. In AD 750 the Abbasids defeated the Umayyads and transferred the capital of the Caliphate from Damascus to Baghdad, thereby shifting the empire's centre from Syria to Iraq.
2. Sitaram Goel, *Heroic Hindu Resistance to Muslim Invaders,* (636 AD to 206 AD), Voice of India, New Delhi.
3. Ibid.
4. Abul Qasim Ubaidullah ibn Abdullah ibn Khurdad-bih (a.k.a. Istakhri, Persian: was a medieval Persian geographer. Among his works were *Al-masalik al-mamalik* and *Sovar al-Aqalim.*
5. Gedrosia is a dry, mountainous country along the north-western shores of the Indian Ocean. It was occupied in the Bronze Age by people who settled in the few oases in the region. Gedrosia became famous in Europe when the Macedonian king Alexander the Great tried to cross the Gedrosian desert and lost many men.
6. *Rajatarangini* is a study of the treatment of gender, a twelfth century chronicle of Kashmir by the poet Kalhana.
7. Lloyd I. Rudolph, Susanne Hoeber Rudolph, *Postmodern Gandhi and Other Essays: Gandhi in the World and at Home,* the University of Chicago Press, co-published with Oxford University Press, India, 2006, p. 272.
8. Mushirul Hasan, *India's Partition: Process, Strategy and Mobilization,* in Mushirul Hasan (ed.), 'Introduction', Oxford University Press, India, 1993, p. 10, n. 36.
9. Lloyd I. Rudolph, Susanne Hoeber Rudolph, *Postmodern Gandhi and Other Essays: Gandhi in the World and at Home,* the University of Chicago Press, co-published with Oxford University Press, India, 2006, p. 64.
10. An Arabic word, translating in this case to mean a 'preface' or 'introduction' of Ibn Khaldun's planned world history, the *Kitab al-ibar* (Book of Advice) 1377 that recorded an early Muslim view of 'universal history'.
11. Excerpted from the Introduction to *The Muqaddimah, An Introduction to History* by Ibn Khaldun translated from the Arabic by Franz Rosenthal, abridged and edited by N.J. Dawood, Bollingen Series, Princeton University Press.

Chapter 1

1. Iqbal and Jinnah had advocated one Indian nationality, however, their stance of 'we' changed to 'they', this happening earlier for Iqbal than Jinnah. The Muslims of India as a separate nation became an object worth striving for. Iqbal's concept of nationality (Muslim nationhood) derived from his concept of what it meant to be a Muslim. His 'ideal' was a human unity anchored in Islamic values, which was therefore universal and territory free. The western concept, on the other hand, was territory bound, (and excluded religious considerations altogether). Iqbal rejected this notion as also the religiously 'mixed' Indian nationality. He became, in his twilight years, more emphatic and concrete in his proposals about a Muslim state.
2. Richard M. Eaton, *Indo-Muslim Tradition, 1200-1750: Towards the Framework of Study*, text of the Annual South Asia lecture delivered at School of Oriental and African Studies, London, on 22 November 2001, South Asia Research, 22, 1, p. 2, Sage Publications, 2002.
3. Armies of Turkish slaves and Afghans, led by Eastern Iranian chieftains of Ghur, east of Herat, dominated parts of the Indo-Gangetic plains between AD 1192 and 1206. By AD 1221, Ghurid power had all but disappeared in Afghanistan with their (Ghurid) troops in India being isolated by the Mongols under Chengez Khan. Iltutmish (1211-36), a Turkish slave established the Delhi sultanate, which was repeatedly threatened by the Mongols at the end of the thirteenth century. The Turk, Amir Timur (1370-1405) sacked Delhi towards the end of the fourteenth century ensuring the process of disintegration of the Delhi sultanate in to regional sultanates of Gujarat, Malwa and Jaunpur.
4. Writing in AD 1260 from Delhi, just beyond the Mongol's reach, India's most prominent historian of the age, Minhaj Siraj Juzjani, noted bitterly that 'the accursed' Chengez Khan had just overrun the Islamic heartlands in Central Asia, Iran, and Iraq and that 'the authority of the Muhammadan religion departed from these regions, which became the seat of paganism. He added, 'the Kingdom of Hindustan by the grace of Almighty God, and...the protection of the Iltutmishi Dynasty, became the focus of the people of Islam, and [the] orbit of the possessors of religion.' Also cited in Richard M. Eaton, *Indo-Muslim Traditions, 1200-1750: Towards the Framework of Study*, text of the Annual South Asia Lecture delivered at School of Oriental and African Studies, London, on 22 November 2001, South Asia Research, 22, 1, p. 3, Sage Publications, 2002.
5. As until the arrival of the Europeans on this soil the word 'India' did not exist. I have chosen to remain with Hind and Hindustan, moving to the word India only with the arrival of the British.
6. Benedict Anderson's book *Imagined Communities: Reflections on the Origin and Spread of Nationalism* a standard text on the theme of nations and nationalism, elaborates the concept of 'Imagined Communities'.... It is Anderson's point that communities are 'imagined' because the 'members of even the smallest nation will never know most of their fellow-members, meet them, or even hear of them, yet in the minds of each lives the image of their communion'. Gellner makes a comparable point when he rules that 'Nationalism is not the awakening of nations

to self-consciousness: it invents nations where they do not exist'. Gellner is... 'anxious to show that nationalism masquerades under false pretences, 'fabrication' and 'falsity', rather than to 'imagining' and 'creation'... The nation is imagined as limited because even the largest of them encompassing perhaps a billion living human beings, has finite, if elastic boundaries, beyond which lie other nations... No nation imagines itself coterminous with mankind... The most messianic nationalists do not dream of a day when all the members of the human race will join their nation in the way that it was possible, in certain epochs, for, say, Christians to dream of a wholly Christian planet.

'It [Nation] is imagined as *sovereign* because the concept was born in an age in which Enlightenment and Revolution were destroying the legitimacy of the divinely-ordained, hierarchical dynastic realm. Coming to maturity at a stage of human history when even the most devout adherents of any universal religion were inescapably confronted with the living pluralism of such religions, and the allomorphism between each faith's ontological claims and territorial stretch, nations dream of being free, and, if under God, directly so. The gauge and emblem of this freedom is the sovereign state. Finally, it is imagined as a *community*, because, regardless of the actual inequality and exploitation that may prevail in each, the nation is always conceived as a deep, horizontal comradeship. Ultimately, it is this fraternity that makes it possible, over the past two centuries, for so many millions of people, not so much to kill, as willingly to die for such limited imaginings.

'These deaths bring us abruptly face to face with the central problem posed by nationalism: what makes the shrunken imaginings of recent history (scarcely more than two centuries) generate such colossal sacrifices? I believe that the beginnings of an answer lie in the cultural roots of nationalism.' (http://www.nationalismproject.org/what/anderson.htm)

7. Ibid.
8. Max Weber (21 April 1864–14 June 1920), was a German political economist and sociologist, and was considered one of the founders of the modern study of sociology and public administration. The most well-known of his works is his essay '*The Protestant Ethic and the Spirit of Capitalism*'.
9. Max Weber did not research Islam exclusively; his notes on Islam were a sociological companion to his famous analysis of 'Protestant Ethic'. For him one of the factors responsible for preventing Islam from evolving naturally was its main carrier—'a warrior group'. Consequently, the content of the religious message of Islam was transformed into a set of values compatible with the needs of this 'warrior group'.
10. We must, hereafter, for ease of communication and understanding, begin to use *only* India for the country otherwise also known as Hind, Hindustan, Bharat, etc.
11. Richard M. Eaton, *Indo-Muslim Traditions, 1200-1750: Towards the Framework of Study*, text of the Annual South Asia Lecture delivered at School of Oriental and African Studies, London, on 22 November 2001, South Asia Research, 22, 1, p. 10, Sage Publications, 2002.
12. Ashraf (Arabic, plural of Sharif, 'noblemen') is a term used for Muslim Perso-Arab-Turkish immigrants into India, with sub-groups including Sayyids, Shaikhs and so on. The non-Ashraf Muslim castes comprise converts from high Hindu castes, mainly Rajputs, in so far as they have not been absorbed into Shaikh castes,

followed by the artisans such as *julahas* and the lowest converted, the untouchables.
13. Muslim peasants and artisans from rural areas.
14. Francis Robinson, *The Ulama of Farangi Mahall and Islamic Culture in South Asia*, Permanent Black, Delhi, 2001, p. 35.
15. Thomas R. Metcalf, *The Aftermath of Revolt: India 1857-1870*, Princeton, 1965, p. 298.
16. Sir George Campbell, *Memoirs of My Indian Career*, Vol. 1, London, 1893, pp. 243-4.
17. Report dated 20 December 1858 to the Sudder Board of Revenue, Proc. No. 31, N-WP, Rev. Procs., 14-30 April 1859, India Office Library Range 221, Vol. 24.
18. European intrusion in the late fifteenth century resulted in competition between the Moppillas of Malabar and the dominant Hindu castes for social and economic influence. The Moppillas, as a reaction to the British conquest and the consequent shift of balance in agrarian relations, had engaged in a long series of attacks on the Hindu-landed castes. The climax of these attacks, the rebellion of 1921-22, saw the Moppillas striving to bring Islamic ideology to an advanced state of practice by trying to establish an Islamic state.
19. Ref. No. 362 of Papers on Miscellaneous Subjects, Canning Papers.
20. Major William Hodson, a British solider, joined the Indian Army in 1845 and fought through the First Sikh War, subsequently holding a civil post in the Punjab. During the First War of Independence in 1857, he headed the Intelligence Department, and commanded an irregular cavalry regiment daringly, named later eponymously as Hodson's Horse. He took part in the sieges of Delhi, and at Lucknow. He captured the Mughal emperor, killed with his own hands the young princes, and a few months later fell while storming a palace in the city (1821-158).
21. S.N. Sen, *Eighteen Fifty-Seven*, Delhi, 1957, p. 116.
22. Peter Hardy, *The Muslims of British India*, Cambridge University Press, 1972, pp. 71-2.
23. Ibid., p. 73.
24. Ibid., p. 78.
25. Sadar Amin: Under the British administration of the period, the designation of the highest office any Indian could aspire for was that of a deputy collector in the executive and a sadar amin in the judiciary.
26. Sir Sayyid Ahmad Khan was born in October 1817 into a circle of Muslim gentleman, attached to the Mughal court at Delhi. His maternal grandfather had served the East India Company during the time of Lord Wellesley on the embassy of Iran. After the death of his father in 1838 Sir Sayyid entered the judicial service of the EIC. He rose to the position of 'sadar amin' or sub-judge by the year 1857, which was a watershed in his life and thought. He had tried to hold the district of Bijnor for the British. A majority of his works aimed at convincing the Muslims that western thought was not anti-Islamic.
27. Peter Hardy, *The Muslims of British India*, Cambridge University Press, 1972, p. 79.
28. Hadith (translit: al-hadith) is traditions relating to the words and deeds of Prophet Muhammad. The Hadith collections are conventionally regarded as the authoritative

tools for determining the Sunnah, or the Muslim way of life, by all traditional schools of jurisprudence.
29. Naqshbandi (Naqshbandiyya) is one of four major Sufi orders (*tariqa*) of Islam. The order, formed in 1380, is considered to be a 'sober' order, which believes in silent *dhikr* (remembrance of God) and *suhbat* (an intimate relationship between student and master). The word Naqshbandi is Persian, taken from the name of the founder of the order, Baha-ud-Din Naqshband Bukhari.
30. Sheikh Ahmad Sarhindi (b.971 in Punjab–d.1079 Hijri) was a scholar and follower of the Farouqi Chistia Order. He claimed his genealogical origins from Caliph Umar, a revered name in the early history of Islam. Sirhindi was an academic having studied logic, philosophy and theology from Mulla Kamal Kashmiri of Sialkot and Ḥadith from Shaikh Yaqub Saifi. He was also called 'Mujaddid alf-i-thani', or the Renovator of the Second Millennium [according to the Islamic calendar] after he protested against Akbar's sulhi-kul.

Shah Waliullah (1703-63), a cleric, had written to Najib-ud-Dowlah and Ahmad Shah Abdali to form an allied force against the Marathas in the Third Battle of Panipat. His formula for the revival of Muslim fortunes echoed Ibn Khaldun's 'that revival was possible only through a return to the pristine spirit of that original Islam'; in his case, he amended this to the rule of Sharia. He stressed the concept of *ijtihad*; individual reasoning was necessary to retain the vigour of every age, often being critical of unthinking orthodox jurists. His successors were Shah Abdul Aziz (author of the famous fatwa against the British in 1803), Shah Abdul Qadir, Shah Rafiuddin and Sayyid Ahmad Barelvi. Dadu Miyan and Titu Meer were influenced by this school.

Sayyid Ahmed Barelvi, a critical figure in the history of Indian Islam, was a disciple of Abdul Aziz, the son of Shah Waliullah. While Abdul Aziz declared India *dar-ul-harb* (land of war), seeking to purify Islam by purging it of Hindu practices, he did not institute *jihad* (holy war), which was Barelvi's contribution, one reason why his followers are known as Wahabis. According to some Muslim writers, *jihad* was limited to the Sikh durbar on the ground in effect that while the British allowed the Muslims the freedom to practise their religion, the Sikhs did not. There are some who disagree holding the view that Sayyid Ahmed limited the *jihad* to the Sikh durbar in the first instance as he was of the opinion that it being weaker of two was easier to dispose of. The second proposition is valid; Sayyid Ahmed was unsuccessful in overthrowing the durbar from his fastness in the Pathan territory as he had to spend his energy and resources in coping with the unruly Pathans and their shifting loyalties. However, the *jihad* continued even after the Wahabis had taken over Punjab and NWFP in 1849. They played a significant role in the First War of Independence in 1857 and in the establishment of the Dar-ul-Uloom seminary in Deoband, a major centre for training ulema in the subcontinent.
31. Sayyid Ahmed of Bareilly (d.1831) made efforts to spread Islam through an aggressive movement of 'revival and reform', aiming to rid it of Hindu practices, and to establish an ideal Muslim community where they could live according to the Holy law. Unfortunately, his movement became a *jihad* and he was killed in 1831, but his followers continued to create a stir in many parts of India till the end of the nineteenth century.

32. Nikki R. Keddie, *An Islamic Response to Imperialism—Political & Religious Writings of Syed Jamal ad-Din 'al-Afghani*, University of California Press, 1968, pp. 55-6.
33. Ibid., p. 56.
34. *Maqalat-i-jamaliyeh*, pp. 75-87; cited in ibid., p. 56.
35. Ibid., p. 57.
36. Ibid.
37. The Faraizi Movement, founded by Haji Shariatullah, came about in East Bengal in the first half of the nineteenth century (1830-57). It came about as a reaction to the agrarian policy and the consequent dealing of the zamindars by the British, concentrating on the depressed class of Muslims. The latter were coerced into giving up un-Islamic customs and practices and to act upon the commandments of the religion called Faraiz or duties, his followers hence being known as Faraizi. .
38. Dadu Mian, (d.1869) the son of Haji Shariatullah the founder of the Faraizi Movement, further popularised and strengthened the movement. Over time, his influence extended to the Muslim peasants and craftsmen of Bakerganj, Dhaka, Faridpur and Pabna districts. Khalifahs were appointed who would keep him informed about the goings-on in their jurisdiction. He vehemently opposed the taxes imposed on Muslim peasants by Hindu zamindars for the decoration of the image of goddess Durga particularly during the Puja celebrations. Dadu Mian was arrested during the First War of Independence of 1857 for organising the peasants of Faridpur districts against the British government. Mir Nasir Ali also known as Titu Meer was greatly moved by the plight of the Muslims of Bengal. He undertook a pilgrimage and thereafter devoted himself to the country, making Narkelbaria, a village near Calcutta (now Kolkata), the centre of his activities. Many oppressed Muslim peasants joined their hands in solidarity with Titu Meer to offer resistance to their Hindu landlord, Krishna Deva Raj. Titu Meer was successful in defeating Krishna Deva and set up a government. Seeing this, the British sent in a small army of 100 English soldiers and 300 sepoys to Narkelbaria. Titu Meer died in 1831 fighting this British force. His followers remained united and he served as a source of inspiration in the years ahead.
39. Peter Hardy, *The Muslims of British India*, Cambridge Press, 1972, p. 58.
40. Ibid., p. 59.
41. Shah Waliullah Dehlavi (1703–62) worked for the revival of Muslim rule and intellectual learning in South Asia. He despised the divisions and deviations within Islam and its practice in the subcontinent and hoped to 'purify' the religion and unify all Indian Muslims under the banner of the 'truth' (Haq).
42. He founded the Barelwi school in the late nineteenth century. This reformist group called for the revival of many old practices and was opposed to the Deoband school and its philosophy.
43. Peter Hardy, *The Muslims of British India*, Cambridge Press, 1972, p. 1.
44. *Struggle for Empire*, Bhartiya Vidya Bhawan, pp. 54, 82, Indian Antiquary, XIX, p. 219, Epigraphica Indica IV, 119.
45. The First Battle of Tarain was fought between Mohammad of Gaur and Prithviraj Chauhan, the ruler of Ajmer and Delhi in 1190-1. Mohammad Gaur, who was defeated, severely wounded, thereafter returned to Ghazni.

    The Second Battle of Tarain: Muhammad Gaur soon raised a stronger army to avenge his defeat, invading India in 1192. This time too, the battle was fought on the same field (Tarain near Thanesar). Mohammad of Gaur routed the Rajputs and Prithviraj Chauhan was captured and put to death.

46. Jazia was a tax paid by non-Muslim citizens to ensure their protection. They were not required to pay other dues like Muslims. Jazia was imposed for the last time during the reign of the Mughal emperor, Aurangzeb, who wanted to establish the fact that there could be an Islamic state even if the Muslim population was in a minority.

47. Jajmani was a reciprocal social and economic arrangement between families of different castes within a village community in India. Under this system, one family would exclusively perform certain services for the other, such as barbering or providing agricultural labour. These continued from one generation to another.

48. Sir William Wilson Hunter (1840-1900) was a member of the Indian Civil Service, besides being a statistician, compiler, and imperial historian. Entering the ICS in 1862 he opted for service in Bengal Presidency. He was appointed assistant magistrate and collector of Birbhum. Thereafter he was transferred to the Government of India in July 1869; was appointed compiler of the Bengal Gazetteer, and in January 1871, complier of the Gazetteer of India. From February of the same year, he officiated as under-secretary to the Government of India in the Home department. In September 1871 he joined the Government of India as director-general of statistics, a post that had been especially created for him. He spent half of the year from 1875 to 1881 in England for compiling the *Statistical Account of Bengal and the Imperial Gazetteer of India*.

49. Wahabism is the branch of Sunni Islam which is the official religion of Saudi Arabia, It was founded by Wahab, an eighteenth century literalist, who some equate to a Puritan or revivalist figure. It became the official religion of Saudi Arabia. It is particularly intolerant of Shia and Sufi faiths which it considers heretical.

50. The Nagari or Devanagari alphabet originated sometime in the eleventh century AD. Originally developed to write Sanskrit it later adapted to write many other languages. The name Devanagari is made up of two Sanskrit words: *deva*, which means god, brahman or celestial and *nagari*, which means city. The name is variously translated as 'script of the city', 'heavenly/sacred script of the city' or '[script of the] city of the Gods or priests'.

51. A renowned poet, Pratap Narain Mishra was born in 1856 at Baijegaon in Unnao district, Uttar Pradesh. He was well versed in Sanskrit, Urdu, Bengali and English. He was the editor of a monthly magazine titled *Brahmin* and wrote more than fifty books. *Prem Pushpawali, Man ki Lehar, Kali Kautuk, Bharat Durdasha* are some of his well-known works. He died in 1894.

52. Bhartendu Harishchandra is known as the founder of modern Hindi. With his immense capability and literary writings he left such an indelible imprint that his era is known as the Bhartendu Era. His contribution in the field of Hindi journalism was also considerable.

53. *Kavi Vachan Sudha* [Benaras], 8 August 1873, UPNNR, 1873.

54. Raja Shiv Prasad was a multi-linguist. A patron of the Hindi language, he championed the cause of introduction of Hindi in the courts, proper education of Hindi in schools and publication of Hindi books for students.

55. In 1828, Raja Ram Mohan Roy (1772-1833) founded an organisation called 'Brahmo Samaj', which sought reformation in India. Roy is known as the 'father of modern India'.
56. The Prarthana Samaj 'Prayer Society' in Sanskrit, was inspired by Keshab Chandra Sen in 1964. The aim of the society was the promulgation of theistic worship and social reform. Their goals included improvement in the conditions of women, depressed classes and remarriage of widows.
57. Arya Samaj was founded on 7 April 1875 at Bombay, India, by Maharishi Dayanand Saraswati. Its purpose was to move the Hindu Dharma away from fictitious beliefs, and go back to the teachings of Vedas. The goal of the Arya Samaj has always been, 'Krinvanto Vishvam Aryam' (Make This World Noble).
58. Dharma Sabha was an association of orthodox Hindus which was established in Calcutta in January 1830. The purpose of this Sabha was to defend the traditional Hindu religious and social system.
59. Bharat Dharma Maha Mandal was established in 1902 to follow the orthodox tradition of Sanatan Dharma.
60. Sanatanis are those who follow Vedic Dharmas.
61. The Hindu Sabha, a non-political organisation, was established in 1910 in south-east of Punjab. It is organised by a community for social reconstruction.
62. Sir Bampfylde Fuller was the first lieutenant-governor of Eastern Bengal and Assam. He held office from 16 October 1905 until he resigned on 20 August 1906.
63. The Agitation of Serajganj: A difference of opinion between the lieutenant-governor and the Central Government resulted in the resignation of Sir Bampfylde Fuller (August 1906).
64. Sir Verney Lovett, *History of Indian National Movement*, a naval officer.
65. Maulana Mohammad Ali (1878-1931), also known by his pen name Jauhar, was a leader of the Khilafat movement. He was an outstanding writer and orator, and contributed to all major English and Indian newspapers, in both English and Urdu. He launched the Urdu weekly *Hamdard* and the English, *Comrade* in 1911. He strived hard to expand the Aligarh Muslim University, which was then known as the Mohammedan Anglo-Oriental College, and was one of the co-founders of the Jamia Millia Islamia in 1920, which later moved to Delhi. Besides serving as the president of the Al-India Muslim League in 1918, he had also attended its founding meeting in Dhaka in 1906. He was an active member of the party till 1928.
66. Dr Hakim Ajmal Khan (1863-1927), was a renowned physician and educationalist and the founder of the Jamia Millia Islamia in Delhi. He holds the sole distinction of having been elected president of the Indian National Congress, the Muslim League and the All India Khilafat Committee.
67. The Persianised form of Hindi or Hindustani; a name derived from the 'Urdu-e-Mu'alla', a 'bazaar' outside Delhi Palace, where it evolved during the Khilji period. It was necessary that foreign Muslim troops, settled around Delhi, were able to use the local dialect. Allaudin Khilji had a book titled *Khalikbari* comprising Persian and Arabic equivalents of common Hindi words. What they spoke came to be known as Urdu, a mixture of Persian, Arabic and Hindi. For as many as five hundred years, Urdu remained just a spoken language, only later going on to become a written language. Urdu, written in Arabic script distinguished it from Hindi where the script is Devanagari. Up until the collapse of the Mughal Empire,

Urdu was not used in public offices and courts; it was only in the nineteenth century that Urdu began to replace Persian, finally acquiring prominence during Bahadur Shah Zafar's time, especially when he read out his own Urdu verses before his court. When the British usurped power, Urdu was the court language throughout northern India.

68. Nawab Waqar-ul-Mulk was born in 1841 in Moradabad, Uttar Pradesh, India. Sir Sayyid and Mohsin-ul-Mulk led the education movement of the Muslims, while Wiqar-ul-Mulk added a political dimension. He felt the need for a separate political platform as well as a political party for the Muslims working assiduously towards this goal.

    He became the joint secretary of the Muslim League when it was founded in 1906. He became disillusioned with the British after the annulment of the partition of Bengal; he wrote his famous article '*Musalmano'n kaa Ayendah Laiha-e-Amal*' (The future course of action for the Muslims) which was published in the Aligarh Institute Gazette as a public expression of his anti-British stance. He died on 27 January 1917. (http://www.brain.net.pk/~wisetech/50/bio/waqar.htm)

69. After serving as governor-general of Canada, Sir Gilbert John Murray Kynynmond Elliot, 4th Earl of Minto became the viceroy of India in 1905.

    Viscount Blackburn John Morley (1838-1923) was secretary of state for India. He was responsible for the extensive remodelling (1908-9) of governance in India by the introduction of the representative element.

70. A hereditary title of governor.
71. Enclosed with letter of 8 August 1906 from Minto to Morley, Morley Papers, India Office Library, EUR D 573, No. 9.
72. Peter Hardy, *The Muslims of British India*, Cambridge University Press, 1982, p. 154.
73. Ibid., p. 155.
74. The text of the Simla Deputation's Address and of Minto's Reply is given in full in Ram Gopal, *Indian Muslims: A Political History*, London, 1959, pp. 329-38.
75. Peter Hardy, *The Muslims of British India*, Cambridge University Press, 1982, p. 155.
76. Ibid.
77. 'MUSLIMS ON THE WHOLE AGAINST THE CONGRESS', Badruddin Tyabji to Allan Octavio Hume.
    Badruddin Tyabji presided over the Madras session of the Indian National Congress in December 1887. This was not liked by several leading Muslims led by Syed Ahmad Khan. A controversy arose. Several letters were exchanged between Tyabji and Syed Ahmad as well as other Muslims. Initially Tyabji tried to defend his action and even tried to plead that he had not accepted India as one nation in his presidential address. He also pointed out in his letters to Syed Ahmad that the Congress had agreed not to discuss any matter if the Muslim community was opposed to it. Even this did not satisfy Syed Ahmad and the others. They were powerful enemies and Tyabji backed out. In this letter addressed to A.O. Hume, who was secretary of the Congress, Tyabji suggests that the Congress, after the Allahabad session, may be prorogued for five years as its activities had generated great animosity between Hindus and Muslims. If after five years the animosity still continued, the Congress may be wound up, he writes. Hume, of course, did not act on his advice but Tyabji did not attend any Congress session after that.

My dear Hume,

I received your letter of the 20th with the enclosure from your Jabulpore correspondence. I delayed writing to you because what I am about to say is a matter of utmost importance and though I have long been thinking about it I thought it best to take still more time about it before communicating my views to you. I write to you, of course, as an ardent friend of the Congress desiring nothing so much as its success. You have no doubt been watching the movements of the Mahomedans; but still you are probably not so well acquainted with their feelings as I am. Again I have been discussing the matter with thoughtful members of the different communities who are all in favour of the Congress. What I write now, herefore, may be taken to represent the views not only of myself and other leading Mahomedans of Bombay, but such men as Mehta, Telang, etc. We are all of opinion that having regard to the distinctly hostile attitude of the Mahomedans, which is becoming daily more pronounced and more apparent, it is time for the friends, promoters and supporters of the Congress to reconsider their position and to see whether under the present circumstances it is or not wise for us to continue to hold Congress meetings every year. My own view is that the friction and bitterness which are caused by this agitation every year outweigh the advantages to be gained. If all the communities of India were unanimous, I think the Congress would be a very good thing and capable of doing a very great deal of good to the people of India. The prime object of the Congress was to unite the different communities and provinces into one and thus promote harmony. As it is, however, not only have the Mahomedans been divided from the Hindus in a manner they never were before but the Mahomedans themselves have been split into two factions, the gulf between whom is becoming wider and wider every day. The Nizam and all the principal men of the state such as Salar Jung, Munir-ul-Mulk, Fateh Nawaz Jung and above all Syed Hussain Bilgrami have joined the opposition led by such well-known men as Syed Ahmad, Ameer Ali and Abdul Latif. For the purpose of my present argument, I assume that all these men are wrong and that we are in the right. Nevertheless, the fact exists and whether we like it or not, we must base our proceedings upon the fact that an overwhelming majority of Mahomedans is against the movement. Against this array it is useless saying that the intelligent and educated Mahomedans are in favour of the Congress. If, then, the Mussalman community as a whole is against the Congress—rightly or wrongly does not matter—it follows that the movement *ipso facto* ceases to be a general or National Congress. If this is so, it is deprived of a great deal of its power to do good. It may no doubt be continued by the force and determination of some men; but it is not the same thing as if the Mahomedans had joined it as a body. I observe increasing bitterness between Hindus and Mussalmans and I observe also that a difference of views among the Mahomedan leaders produces friction and bitterness which leads to extremely evil consequences. The peculiar state of Mahomedan society renders it necessary that we should act together in all political matters but this friction comes in the way and I already find that even in Bombay we are not able to act in the same way as we did before. Under these circumstances, weighing the good against the evil, I have come to the conclusion after most careful consideration of which I am capable that it is time to cease holding Congress every year. I should like to make the Allahabad Congress as great a success as possible. I should like to have as large a representation of Mahomedans as possible and I should then like the Congress to be prorogued, say for at least five years. This would give us an opportunity—of reconsidering the whole position and if necessary of retiring with dignity and would at the same time give us ample time to carry into execution our programme, which has already become very extensive. If at the end of the five years our prospects improve, we can renew our Congress. If not, we can drop it with dignity, conscious of having done our utmost for the advancement of India and the fusion of the different races into one. A.G. Noorani, *Badruddin Tyabji*, New Delhi, Publications Division (Govt. of India), 1969, pp. 186-88.

78. V.V. Nagarkar, *Genesis of Pakistan*, Allied Publishers, 1975, p. 153.
79. Savel Zimand, *Living India*, Books for Libraries Press, Freeport, New York, pp. 142-43.
80. Peter Hardy, *The Muslims of British India*, Cambridge Press, 1972, p. 153.
81. Ibid., pp. 156-7.
82. Martin Gilbert, *Servant of India*, London, 1966, p. 51.
83. Harcourt Butler Papers, EUR F 116/65.
84. Ibid.
85. Peter Hardy, *The Muslims of British India*, Cambridge Press, 1972, p. 159.
86. Martin Gilbert, *Servant of India*, London, 1966, p. 189.
87. Ibid.
88. Harcourt Butler to Minto, 22 July 1909, enclosure to letter of 25 July 1909 from Minto to Morley, Morley Papers, India Office Library, EUR D573/21.
89. Ibid.
90. Peter Hardy, *The Muslims of British India*, Cambridge Press, 1972, p. 163.
91. Ibid.
92. *Pathway to Pakistan*, Lahore, 1961, pp. 137-8.
93. Peter Hardy, *The Muslims of British India*, Cambridge Press, 1972, p. 166.

Chapter 2

1. Diwan—high governmental posts, official, especially of Cabinet rank or of nobility.
2. Khoja is the name of an Indian caste comprising mainly Nizari Ismailis and some Sunnis and Shias split off the Ismaili community. In a larger sense, the name refers to the Indian Nizaris including some minor communities like the Shamsis in the area of Multan and some Momnas in northern Gujarat. Most Nizari activity seems to be centered around Sindh.

   The Khojas, active in commerce between India and East Africa from the seventeenth century onwards, could only settle in large numbers in East Africa post eighteenth century. The coming of the Aga Khan Hasan Ali Shah to India in 1840 led to an aggravation of earlier conflicts within the Khoja community concerning the rights of the Imam. A judgment in a law suit brought against the Agha Khan by ex-communicated members of the community in 1866 resulted in fully upholding the rights and authority of the Imam. This led to the dissidents separating from the community—the Sunni Khojas. The later dissidents, seceding

in 1877 and 1901, formed the Ithna Ashari Khoja communities in Bombay and East Africa.
3. Bohras are a Mustali subsect of Ismaili Shia Islam, and are based in India. Their spiritual leader is Dr Syedna Mohammed Burhanuddin. Bohras believe that the twenty-first Imam, Tayyab Abi l-Qasim, a direct descendant of Prophet Muhammad through his daughter 'Fatema', went into seclusion and established the offices of the Da'i l-Mutlaq, *Ma'oun* and *Mukasir*. The Da'i l-Mutlaq is the Imam's vicegerent, with full authority to govern the Dawoodi Bohra community in matters spiritual and temporal. During the Imam's seclusion, the Da'i l-Mutlaq was appointed by his predecessor in office. The *Madhun* and *Mukasir* were in turn appointed by the Da'i l-Mutlaq. A fundamental belief of the Dawoodi Bohras is that the presence of the secluded Imam is guaranteed by the presentation of the Da'i l-Mutlaq. Syedna Mohammed Burhanuddin has appointed Syedi Khuzaima Qutbuddin as his *Ma'oun* and Syedi Husain Husamuddin as his Mukasir.
4. Aqiqah: In its origin is a name for a custom among the Arabs in the time of the Prophet. In this custom, an animal is sacrificed and its blood poured upon the child's head, after which, the child's head is shaved. It was believed that till such an act was performed upon the child, the child remained prone to calamities and sufferings.
5. A high school founded by Khan Bahadur Hasanali Effendi, a pioneer educationist among the Muslims of Sindh.
6. Translates literally into 'locality' in Hindustani.
7. R.P. Masani, *Dadabhai Naoroji*.
8. Extracts from *My Brother*, Fatima Jinnah, ed. Sharif al Mujahid.
9. Jinnah's evidence before the Islington Commission; Minutes of Evidences, IOR, Volume 22, Column 7294.
10. Civil Suit No. 11 of 1896, District Courts, Karachi.
11. *Mohammad Ali Jinnah—An Ambassador of Unity. His Speeches and Writings, 1912-1917*, with a Biographical Appreciation by Sarojini Naidu and a Foreword by the Hon'ble the Raja of Mahmudabad, Ganesh and Company, Madras, 1918, p. 4.
12. Chimanlal Setalvad, *Recollections and Reflections*, Padma Publications, Bombay, 1946, p. 61.
13. M.C. Chagla, *Roses in December*, Bhartiya Vidya Bhavan, Mumbai, p. 41.
14. Gopalkrishna Gandhi (comp. and ed.), *The Oxford India Gandhi, Essential Writings*, Oxford, p. 690.
15. Lohanas, an ethnic group and urban, Hindu mercantile community of India mainly reside in Gujarat, and areas around Mumbai. The Lohanas originally, were part of the Kshatriya caste of Punjab that later migrated to Sindh and Gujarat, around 800 years ago. As administrators and rulers, Kshatriya Lohanas were assigned the task of protection, but over a course of time, as a result of economic and political exigencies, they engaged in mercantile occupations. Lohanas are still to be found in Afghanistan and Pakistan. In Afghanistan, they still maintain their religious identity and are known as Lokhathra, while those who retained their Hindu identity in Sindh are known as Sindhi Lohana. Lohanas who converted to Islam are known as Memons, and those who converted to Shia or Shiite Islam are known as Khojas. Many of them retain their Hindu names. The most celebrated and well-known

among them was Mohammed Ali Jinnah, whose father's name, in full, was Jenabhai Thakkar.
16. The Khwajahs or officially Khojas are (mostly) a Muslim community concentrated mainly in South Asia, but due to migrations over the centuries have spread over many parts of the globe. The word Khoja is a phonetic corruption of the word Khawaja, an Arabic/Persian title. In Pakistan, Khojas are concentrated in the province of Sindh and especially in the city of Karachi. In India, most Khojas live in the states of Gujarat, Maharashtra, Rajasthan and the city of Hyderabad.
17. G.E. von Grunebaum (ed.), *Unity and Variety in Muslim Civilization*, Chicago, 1955, p. 8.
18. *Mohammad Ali Jinnah—An Ambassador of Unity. His Speeches and Writings, 1912-1917*, with a Biographical Appreciation by Sarojini Naidu and a Foreword by the Hon'ble the Raja of Mahmudabad, Ganesh and Company, Madras, 1918, p. 3.
19. Sir John Poynder Dickson-Poynder Islington, (1866–1936) was the seventeenth governor of New Zealand who also served as aide de camp to Lord Methuen in the Boer War. Islington become chairman of the Royal Commission on Public Services in India (1912–14). In the House of Lords, he was undersecretary of state for colonies (1914–15), and India (1916–18), and for a brief period in 1917–18 had sole charge of the India Office.
20. Evidence before the Islington Commission, Minutes of the Evidence, India Office Records, Vol. 22.
21. The Anjuman-i-Islam, established in 1874 by a group of Muslims led by Justice Badruddin Tyabji, is a premier educational and social organization of India. Over its past history of 130 years it has been dedicated to the cause of education and social service. This organization works mainly for social service.
22. Bombay Gazette, 30 June 1903.
23. Bombay Gazette, 30 July 1904.
24. H.P. Mody, *Sir Pherozeshah Mehta: A Political Biography*, Volume I, Bombay, 1921, pp. 252-3.
25. Sharifuddin Pirzada (ed.), *Collected Works of Jinnah*, Volume I, pp. 33-5.
26. *The Englishman,* 3 July 1908. Cited in Syed Sharifuddin Pirzada, 'Quaid-i-Azam Mohammad Ali Jinnah as a Lawyer', in Prof. A.H. Rani (ed.), *Quaid-i-Azam and Pakistan*, Islamabad, 1979, p. 83.
27. It was a usual practice in the years preceding/following the year 1916 to convene meetings of the Muslim League and Congress in the same city and around the same time to allow delegates to attend the annual sessions of both the Congress and the Muslim League.
28. David Page, 'Mohammad Ali Jinnah and the System of Imperial Control in India 1909-1930: A Case Study in Political Leadership and Constitutional Innovation', in *M.A. Jinnah: Views and Reviews*, ed. M.R. Kazimi, Oxford University Press, Karachi, 2005.
29. Ibid.
30. Wakf-alal-aulad: A wakf-alal-aulad is the extent with which the property is dedicated for any purpose recognised by Muslim law as pious, religious or charitable.
31. Report of the 22nd Indian National Congress.
32. Viceroy: A representative of the monarch governed British India. The term derives from the Latin prefix vice, meaning 'in the place of' and French 'roi', meaning

king. His province was called a viceroyalty. A vicereine is a woman in a viceregal position or a viceroy's wife.
33. Syed Sharifuddin Pirzada (ed.), *The Collected Works of Quaid-i-Azam Muhammad Ali Jinnah*, Volume I, East and West Publishing Company, Karachi, 1984, p. 1; *Gujarati*, Bombay, 7 October 1906.
34. Ibid.
35. His Highness the Aga Khan, *The Memoirs of Aga Khan*, Simon & Schuster, New York, 1954, pp. 124-5.
36. S.M. Burke and Salim Al-Din Quraishi, *Quaid-i-Azam Mohammad Ali Jinnah: His Personality and His Politics*, OUP, Karachi, 1997, p. 96.
37. Ibid.
38. Ibid.
39. Ibid.
40. Ibid., p. 91.
41. Ibid.
42. Gokhale's Elementary Education Bill (1912): As a non-official member representing the Bombay Presidency in the Imperial Legislative Council, Gokhale moved a resolution for free and compulsory elementary education in India, which stated that compulsion should be applied only in those areas where thirty-three percent of the male population of school-going age were already in school. But his resolution was rejected on the basis that as there was no popular demand for it no additional taxes could be levied for the same.

The Primary Education Bill (1917): Gokhale raised the issue of primary education in the Viceroy's Supreme Legislative Council. He moved a resolution and while calling for a bill to implement this resolution, stated: 'It is at present universally recognized that a certain minimum of general instructions an obligation which society owes to its future members, and in the nearly the whole civilized world, every states trying to meet this obligation'. The Bill introduced by Gokhale failed to become law. Post independence, the salient features of the Bill not only became the law, but the 'Supreme Law' of the land viz. constitutional law.

Special Marriage Act: This Act was enacted in 1872.
43. Report of the 26th Indian National Congress; cited in Riaz Ahmed, *Quaid-i-Azam Mohammad Ali Jinnah: The Formative Years, 1892-1920*, pp. 92-3.
44. Stanley Reed (ed.), *The Indian Year Book 1914*, Bombay, 1915, p. 476.
45. Meston Papers, IOL, MSS.Eur.F.136/6.
46. *The Comrade*, 13 September 1913.
47. *Bombay Chronicle*, 8 September 1913.
48. *Bombay Chronicle*, 22 December 1913.
49. *Mohammed Ali Jinnah—An Ambassador of Unity, His Speeches and Writings 1912-1917*, with a Biographical Appreciation by Sarojini Naidu, p. 11.
50. Mohammad Ali and Shaukat Ali were two prominent pan-Islamists of India.
51. S.M. Burke and Salim Al-Din Quraishi, *Quaid-i-Azam Mohammad Ali Jinnah: His Personality and His Politics*, Karachi, OUP, 1997, p. 95.
52. Riaz Ahmed, *Quaid-i-Azam Mohammad Ali Jinnah: The Formative Years, 1892-1920*, National Institute of Cultural and Historical Research, Islamabad, 1988, pp. 120-1.

53. S.M. Burke and Salim Al-Din Quraishi, *Quaid-i-Azam Mohammad Ali Jinnah: His Personality and His Politics*, Karachi, Oxford University Press, 1997, pp. 123-26.
54. The League and the Congress had called special sessions at Calcutta during the first week of September 1920.
55. Ibid., pp. 127-30.
56. Ibid.
57. A.S. Iyengar, *All Through the Gandhian Era*, Hind Kitab Limited, 1950, pp. 29-30.
58. Cassim Mitha was a Muslim leader of Bombay and in Bombay politics, an adversary of Jinnah.
59. The Lucknow Pact [1916]. When All India Muslim League came into existence, it was a moderate and a modest organisation with a basic aim to establish friendly relations with the Crown. However, due to the decision of the British government to annul the partition of Bengal, the Muslim leadership decided to change its stance. In 1913, a new group of Muslim leaders entered the folds of the Muslim League with the aim of bridging the gulf between the Muslims and the Hindus. The most prominent amongst them was Mohammad Ali Jinnah, who was already a member of Indian National Congress. The Muslim League changed its major objective and decided to join hands with the Congress in order to put pressure on the British government. Lord Chelmsford's invitation for suggestions from the Indian politicians for the post First World War reforms further helped in the development of the situation.

As a result of the hard work of Mr. Jinnah, both the Muslim League and the Congress met for their annual sessions at Bombay in December 1915. The principal leaders of the two political parties assembled at one place for the first time in the history of these organisations. The speeches made from the platform of the two groups were similar in tone and theme. Within a few months of the Bombay moot, nineteen Muslim and Hindu elected members of the Imperial Legislative Council addressed a memorandum to the Viceroy on the subject of reforms in October 1916. Their suggestions did not become news in the British circle, but were discussed, amended and accepted at a subsequent meeting of the Congress and Muslim League leaders at Calcutta in November 1916. This meeting settled the details of an agreement about the composition of the legislatures and the quantum of representation to be allowed to the two communities. The agreement was confirmed by the annual sessions of the Congress and the League in their annual session held at Lucknow on 29 December and 31 December 1916 respectively. Sarojini Naidu gave Jinnah, the chief architect of the Lucknow Pact, the title of 'the Ambassador of Hindu-Muslim Unity'.

The main clauses of the Lucknow Pact were:

1. There shall be self-government in India.
2. Muslims should be given one-third representation in the Central Government.
3. There should be separate electorates for all the communities until a community demanded for joint electorates.
4. System of weightage should be adopted.

5. The number of the members of Central Legislative Council should be increased to 150.
6. At the provincial level, four-fifths of the members of the Legislative Councils should be elected and one-fifth should be nominated.
7. The strength of provincial legislative should not be less than 125 in the major provinces and from 50 to 75 in the minor provinces.
8. All members, except those nominated, were to be elected directly on the basis of adult franchise.
9. No bill concerning a community should be passed if the bill is opposed by three-fourths of the members of that community in the Legislative Council.
10. Term of the Legislative Council should be five years.
11. Members of Legislative Council should themselves elect their president.
12. Half of the members of Imperial Legislative Council should be Indians.
13. Indian Council must be abolished.
14. The salaries of the secretary of state for Indian Affairs should be paid by the British government and not from Indian funds.
15. Out of two under secretaries, one should be Indian.
16. The Executive should be separated from the Judiciary.

Although this Hindu-Muslim unity was not able to survive for more than eight years, and collapsed after the development of differences between the two communities after the Khilafat Movement, yet it was an important event in the history of the Muslims of South Asia. It was the first time when Congress recognised the Muslim League as the political party representing the Muslims of the region. As Congress agreed to separate electorates, it in fact agreed to consider the Muslims as a separate nation. They thus accepted the concept of the Two-Nation Theory. (http://www.storyofpakistan.com/articletext.asp?artid=A032&Pg=2)

60. E.S. Montagu was the secretary of state for India from 1917-23 while Lord Chelmsford was the viceroy from 1916-21. It was during their time that the Reforms of 1919, commonly known as Montagu-Chelmsford Reforms, were introduced in India. Montagu met the Indian leaders to discuss the then prevailing political conditions in India. The meetings with Jinnah have been described in his diary.
61. Indian Legislative Council Debates, 1918, 1919, p. 133, 7 September 1918.
62. Gandhi at the Gurjar Sabha reception, Bombay, 14 January 1915, *Collected Works of Mahatma Gandhi*, XIII, No. 8, p. 9, Publications Division, Ministry of Information, Delhi, 1964.
63. Riaz Ahmed, *Quaid-i-Azam Mohammad Ali Jinnah: The Formative Years, 1892-1920*, National Institute of Cultural and Historical Research, Islamabad, 1988, p. 122.
64. Ibid., pp. 120-2.
65. Dadabhoi Naoroji, the 'grand old man' of India had intended to spend the better part of his life in England trying to influence the public opinion on Indian self-rule. Pherozeshah Mehta, a nationalist, became the president of the Indian National Congress in 1890. To Gokhale, the youngest of the three, Naoroji and Mehta were heroes worth emulating. Naoroji, Mehta and Gokhale had been connected to Jinnah at one time or the other. Jinnah started his political career as Naoroji's

private secretary; his legal and political career was helped in no small measure by Mehta. In the early part of his political career, Jinnah was also known as a Muslim Gokhale.

66. In August 1917, Gandhi visited London, where he praised the British government's foreign policy, urged Indians to 'think imperially' and did a brief stint as recruiting sergeant for one of the Indian regiments.

67. *Bombay Chronicle*, 1 January 1916, pp. 147-8; Riaz Ahmed, *Quaid-i-Azam Mohammad Ali Jinnah: The Formative Years, 1892-1920*, National Institute of Cultural and Historical Research, Islamabad, 1988.

68. Gokhale's Scheme: Gopal Krishna Gokhale (1866-1915), the Congress veteran, two days before his death, is said to have prepared a pencil draft, of which three copies were made, one each being sent to Lord Willingdon, Pherozeshah Mehta and the Aga Khan. It saw the light of day posthumously in 1917, when it was published by Aga Khan in London and Srinivas Sastri in India, at the time of the Montagu declaration. Also called *Gokhale's Political Will and Testament* it impelled upon the British Government to announce recommendations on administrative reforms voluntarily and at once. In case the British government granted provincial autonomy to India, it would have implied that governors would have Executive Councils on which Indians would be appointed.

- Number of members of the Legislative Council to be between seventy-five and hundred, out of which four-fifths should be elected;
- The members to be elected by various interests, with some communities to have reserve seats;
- Muslims should have separate electorates;
- Members to have the right to express their opinion about the administration. The budget not to be passed without the approval of the Legislative Assembly with, however, the governor having veto power.

The importance of Gokhale's Testament lay in his solution of the communal impasse. He had accepted separate electorates to the Muslims, as they had come to stay under the Morley-Minto Reforms.

69. Riaz Ahmed, *Quaid-i-Azam Mohammad Ali Jinnah: The Formative Years, 1892-1920*, National Institute of Cultural and Historical Research, Islamabad, 1988, p. 148.

70. Sir George Lloyd to Montagu, 13 August 1920, Montagu papers.

71. 'Vilayat' is an Urdu word that means 'foreign land' in English. In nineteenth-century India its usage was restricted to mean, simply, 'Great Britain', but now, of course, it has a wider connotation.

72. Senior Indian Civil Servant of the period, Sir James Meston.

73. Montagu to Chelmsford, 11 January 1917, Vol. 18, No. 14, pp. 16-19, Chelmsford Papers.

74. The Ahmedabad Mill strike was barely over when Gandhi got involved in the Kheda Satyagraha. In Kheda district near-famine like conditions was developing. As the crops had failed and the farmers of Kheda were demanding that the land rent for the year should be suspended. Gandhi, along with the locals like Mohanlal Pandya and Shankerlal Parikh launched his satyagraha seeking redressal. It was during the campaign of Kheda satyagraha that Gandhi discovered Vallabhbhai Patel and it was through this campaign that satyagraha took firm root in the soil of Gujarat.

510   JINNAH: INDIA – PARTITION – INDEPENDENCE

75. Lord Willingdon to Edwin Montagu, Bombay, 30 April 1918, pp. 50-1, Montagu Papers, MSS Eur D 523/18.
76. Lloyd to Montagu, 12 June 1919, Montagu papers, MSS Eur. D 523/25.
77. Jinnah to Chelmsford; 28 March 1919.
78. Ibid.
79. Was Jinnah, perhaps subconsciously, seeking a platform and a role removed from the competitive prejudices of the Congress, appreciating that in the UK he would be recognised much more on his merit, and so much less as a Muslim? Was this also his sense of continuing somehow to preserve his Hindu-Muslim unity platform. Who can tell with any certainty.
80. Sir William Wedderburn (ICS) was chief secretary to the government of Bombay at the time of his retirement. In 1889, he presided over the fourth Congress held in Bombay. In 1893, he entered British Parliament as a liberal member. He believed in self-governance, and one of his chief contributions was his lifelong commitment on behalf of the Indian Reform Movement. The Montford Reforms can therefore be also regarded as a milestone in his lifelong journey.

Chapter 3

1. After the formation of the Indian National Congress, there was a definite feeling that the Muslims should not join it. The social changes brought in as a consequence of British policies had strengthened the communitarian consciousness of the Muslims. In late 1880s and early 1890s, a person no less than Badruddin Tyabji had, as president of the Indian National Congress suggested that the National Congress be wound up because of the communal feelings it was generating. Then the Bengal anti-partition movement and its Hindu symbols had tended to reinforce the communitarian consciousness of the Muslims. The movement was largely viewed as Hindu. The period after the Lucknow Pact had witnessed the rise of pan-Islamist feelings amongst the Muslims, giving a boost to their communal consciousness.
2. The Portuguese had repeatedly tried to gain control over the Kerala spice trade which for long had been controlled by the Muslims. This regular intervention largely accounts for the Mopilla tradition of violence and the gradual breakdown in the relationship between the Mopillas and the dominant caste Hindus. The European intrusion had brought into existence a competitive relationship amongst the Mopillas, the Malayah Rajas and the Nayar aristocracy for territorial and economic gains by eighteenth century. This competition was flaring into bloody incidents.

    The British conquest had tipped the balance in favour of the Hindu landed castes over their Mopilla tenants who had retaliated regularly against the Hindu landed castes to breakout of the economic stranglehold. These attacks had been carried out as ritual acts to gain martyrdom; on occasions they were expressions of religious drive alone. The climax to these attacks was the rebellion of 1921-22.

    The British conquest had tipped the balance in favour of the Hindu landed castes over their Mopilla tenants who had retaliated regularly against the Hindu landed

castes to breakout of the economic stranglehold. These attacks had been carried out as ritual acts to gain martyrdom; on occasions they were expressions of religious drive alone. The climax to these attacks was the rebellion of 1921-22.
3. Edwards Thomson, *The Reconstruction of India*, London, 1930, p. 141.
4. Khilafat was not an Indian issue; the Muslims gave it more support than they had given to any Indian cause, which Gandhi accepted as quite natural. In a statement published on 2 October 1921, he said: 'the brave [Ali] brothers are staunch lovers of their country, but they are Mussulmans first and everything else after, and it must be so with every religiously-minded man'. Their passionate involvement in the Khilafat agitation, therefore, did not inspire feelings of Indian nationalism in Indian Muslims, which would have strengthened Indian unity; it nourished instead the feelings of Muslim nationalism which in time developed into the demand for Pakistan.
5. Bande Mataram 9 September, 13 October 1921. Cited in G.R. Thursby, *Hindu-Muslim Relations in British India*, Leiden E.J. Brill, 1975, p. 133.
6. Guru-ka-Bagh, a Sikh shrine, is twenty kilometres from Amritsar. Sundar Das, a mahant, had by mutual negotiations made available the shrine to the apex Sikh committee. However, he later went back on it saying that although he had surrendered the gurdwara to the Shiromani Committee, the piece of land known as Guru-ka-Bagh attached to the gurdwara belonged to him. He objected to Sikhs pulling down trees on Guru-ka-Bagh for the community kitchen. The police, which was willing to oblige him, arrested five Sikhs on charges of trespassing on 9 August 1922, the arrests having been made on a confidential report received by the police. Those arrested were put through a hurried trial and sentenced to six months rigorous imprisonment. In spite of this, Sikhs continued hewing wood from Guruka-Bagh for the community kitchen. Those who came for firewood from Guru-ka-Bagh were mercilessly beaten up and dragged by their hair. The Sikhs silently suffered all this and went in larger numbers with each passing day to face the brutalities. Every day a batch of one hundred volunteers would start from the Akal Takht pledging to silently suffer their fate. They would be stopped on the way by the police and then beaten up; the Sikhs suffering stoically the beatings and with complete resignation.
7. Quoted in H.N. Mitra (ed.), *Indian Annual Register 1923*, Calcutta, 1923, pp. 943-4.
8. They were the Muslim counterparts to Hanuman akharas of Hindus which stressed on the physical aspects of training the Muslim youth. As an organisational unit point, they provided a focus for communal cohesion.
9. Strength, to deter the opposite religious community. 'Sangathan' meant the acquisition of strength through consolidation of communal resources. This word became a rallying cry of those Hindus who believed themselves to be lagging behind Muslims in mobilisation and militancy.
10. Contrary to commonly applied meaning, Muharram is not a particular day but names the first month of the Islamic calendar. It is one of the four months that have been designated as holy. Though not obligatory, fasting is advocated during this month of Muharram—especially on the tenth day of Muharram, called 'Ashura'.

It was in the month of 'Muharram' (approximate date 20 October AD 680) on the banks of Euphrates in Iraq at Karbala, that Imam Hussain, the grandson of the Prophet was killed. His death is mourned annually on the day of 'Ashura. Colourful *taziyas*, (replica of the martyr's tomb) are carried by mourners walking barefoot to the beat of drums. In a frenzy of grief, they beat their chests, sometimes even flagellating or whipping themselves.

11. Id-ul-Adha, (feast of sacrifice) in India popularly known as Bakr Id, is celebrated on the tenth day of the month Dhu'l Hijja. It is the sacrifice made by pilgrims and performed as part of the ceremonies of the great pilgrimage. While the pilgrims are making their sacrifices at Mina, the ceremony is observed simultaneously by Muslims everywhere.
12. R.C. Majumdar, *The History and Culture of the Indian People Struggle for Freedom*, Bhartiya Vidya Bhawan, Bombay, p. 43.
13. Caliph (also spelled calif [Arabic khalifa] 'deputy of God' or 'successor to his Prophet'), a Muslim ruler, is the title given to the temporal and spiritual head of the Muslim community after the death of Prophet Muhammad (AD 632). Following Muhammad's death, his friend and disciple Abu-Bakr became the first caliph. The first four caliphs, Abu-Bakr, Omar, Uthman, and Ali, along with Muhammad, are regarded by Sunni Muslims as the 'rightly guided' caliphs. The title thereafter became hereditary and was taken over by the Ottoman sultans in the sixteenth century, following their conquest of the last caliph in Cairo in 1517. It was also used in India. There is a deep-rooted disagreement over the status and legitimate line of caliphs and this is the main bone of contention between Shiite and Sunni Muslims.
14. The Entente and Associated Powers signed the Treaty of Sevres on 10 August 1920 and the Ottoman Empire after the First World War. The treaty was signed in Sèvres, near Paris. The Turkish War of Independence forced the former wartime Allies to return to the negotiating table prior to ratification and a new treaty was signed and ratified: the Treaty of Lausanne in 1923.
15. *Indian Constitutional Documents*, Volume 1, p. 7, *Pilgrimage to Freedom*, K.M. Munshi, Bhartiya Vidya Bhawan.
16. The origins of the Home Rule Movement and League lay in a rather reactive caution as the word *swaraj* (self rule) had acquired a totally unmerited identity, that of being 'seditious and dangerous'. Any activity even suggesting swaraj was suppressed. This led Bal Gangadhar Tilak and Annie Besant to immigrate the national movement with a different name, i.e., 'Home Rule'. In December 1915, Tilak held talks with his colleagues and on 28 April 1916, the 'Indian Home Rule League' was established with its headquarters in Poona, (now Pune). The principal objective remained unaltered: to 'attain Home Rule or self-government, within the British Empire, by all constitutional means and to educate and organize public opinion in the countrytowards the attainment of [it]'. Similarly, a Home Rule League was also founded by Annie Besant, on 15 September 1916, with its headquarters at Adyar, near Madras (now Chennai).

Thereafter, Tilak undertook an extensive tour of the country, appealing for unity. The goals of the League remained unaltered, of the British Empire and the elimination the stranglehold of bureaucracy of the Raj in India. In his public speeches, Tilak continued to assert emphatically that Home Rule was the only answer to India's political grievances, that 'liberty was the birthright of every man'. Annie Besant, too, toured the country generating immense enthusiasm. Her writings in the *Commonwealth* and *New India* attracted a large readership which prompted C.Y. Chintamani to remark: 'Annie Besant stirred the country by the spoken as well as the written word, as scarcely as any one else could....'

In June 1917, Annie Besant was interned for her political activities, news that moved Jinnah to join the Bombay Home Rule League as its president. It is ironical that even in those days of communal ease (Lucknow Pact), the political kaleidoscope of India saw most of its leaders employing such social idioms as invariably aroused suspicion and questions amongst Muslims: What are the true intentions of the attitude of Hindu leadership? From such suspicions, even Gandhi and Tilak were not exempt, besides they too could not think of inspiring people through any method other than religious appeal. Sample a comment of Gandhi on the long established dispute of cow slaughter between Hindus and Muslims in *The Statesman* of Calcutta: 'Rightly or wrongly, worship of cow is ingrained in the Hindu nature.... Let the truth be faced. It must not be supposed that Hindus feel nothing about the cow slaughter going on for the Europeans. I know that their wrath is today being buried under the awe inspired by the English rule. But there is not a Hindu throughout the length and breadth of India who does not expect one day to free his land from cow slaughter... But contrary to the genius of Hinduism as I know it, he would not mind forcing it even at the point of sword either to the Christian or the Mohammedan to abandon cow slaughter.' This did stand in complete contrast to the language and methods of Jinnah's politics in those years. Jinnah shunned 'religion' in politics; Gandhi on the other hand, was unabashedly Hindu in the political beliefs, idiom, utterances, and commitments.

Jinnah, though never in agreement with Tilak's style of politics, had always stood unwaveringly in defence of Tilak, earlier in 1908 in a court of law and subsequently in 1916, in the Central Legislative Assembly, after Tilak's return from his six year incarceration in the Mandlay Jail. Jinnah had also engaged intensively to bring a rapprochement between Gokhale and Tilak. Jinnah's growing relationship with Tilak resulted in Gandhi drifting apart from Jinnah. Events, in brief, in succeeding paragraphs have as their main characters these three great Indians.

The year 1917 was an eventful year in the annals of the League as the two Home Rule Leagues, of Tilak and Annie Besant, worked in close cooperation. There was also kind of a tacit understanding about territorial responsibilities, Tilak confining his activities to the Bombay presidency, and the Central Provinces, whereas the rest of India became Annie Besant's field of activity. Accordingly, branches of the Home Rule League were established all over the country, resulting in a considerably enhanced popular demand for Home Rule.

In March 1918, the Home Rule League had decided to send a delegation under the leadership of Tilak to England to acquaint the British public of the 'true' situation in India. However, even before this delegation could reach England, their passports were cancelled and they were all forcibly landed in Cape Town South Africa. A protest meeting was thereafter held in Bombay on 8 April 1918 with Jinnah presiding.

On 24 April 1918, a joint manifesto, on the growing menace of the war was jointly signed by Jinnah, Annie Besant, and Tilak. Then came the War Conference of Delhi, on which occasion ignoring most of the leading Indian politicians, Lord Chelmsford invited Gandhi along with a host of rajas, landlords, and merchants. Gandhi received the invitation while he was leading a no-tax campaign in Khera, Gujarat; still he accepted the invitation and attended the conference though Tilak, Annie Besant, and Ali Brothers were not invited to it. Gandhi addressed the War Conference on 30 April 1918, offering his support to the British war efforts. Jinnah, too, had attended this War Conference but when he tried bringing a resolution on constitutional reforms in this meeting, he was summarily overruled by the chairman with Gandhi then making scarcely any effort to assist Jinnah in his efforts.

Following the London meet, a Provincial War Conference was convened on 10 June 1918 in Bombay which had both Tilak and Gandhi participating and Lord Willingdon presiding. This conference instead of narrowing the differences between Gandhi and Tilak over the war efforts in reality emphasised them. Tilak would not participate and support the conference unless some promise was given by the British government for India's political emancipation, therefore, when he proceeded to speak in the Conference he was time and again ruled over by Lord Willingdon and when his efforts finally failed, he walked out. However, Gandhi did not following suit; he chose to remain a silent spectator. Jinnah had also risen to move amendments to the Resolution but was as usual ruled over and to which he finally said: 'I cannot support the whole of the Resolution.... I want to move an amendment. But no amendment will be allowed. This is a procedure which is unheard of... and I will not have it.' Indulal Yajnik, a predecessor to Mahadev Desai in his book *Gandhi as I Know Him* gives more than a hint of Gandhi's differences with Tilak: 'Mr Tilak's methods drove him to an entirely different path. As he set his heart on the fundamental issues of transfer of political power from Government to the people, he never found any necessity, or opportunity, of any personal or diplomatic negotiations with the [British] authorities. And while [these] authorities were [always] anxious to meet Mr Gandhi if possible and satisfy him on any issue, [however narrow] they [so] detested Mr Tilak [that] would not deign to meet him because he was the embodiment of [India's] protest against foreign rule in India.'

The influence of Gandhi had grown steadily even though Tilak and Annie Besant dominated their respective Home Rule Leagues. However, their workers would now invariably look to Gandhi for direction. Mrs Besant's League finally succumbed to the influence of Gandhi when its name was changed to Swaraj League, leading to its absorption in the Non-Cooperation Movement. When this happened, Jinnah resigned from the Home Rule League in October 1920. Dr Annie Besant, the founder, had already departed because, as she said, the League had 'become so intertwined with religion', with Gandhi being elected in place of her. Under Dr Besant, with Jinnah as a member, the slogan had been 'self government within British Empire'. Gandhi appealed for 'purna swaraj', complete freedom from all ties with Britain. Jinnah's reaction to this change was characteristic, the lawyer in him urging adoption of constitutional methods, of responsible government. When he protested that the meeting was not competent to change the Constitution of the League, the Chairman answered that it was 'open to any member... to resign his membership', if he could not abide by the 'altered constitution'. It was then that Jinnah, with nineteen other members, decided to leave.

Gandhi now focused on other issues. Tilak's activities had not particularly ingratiated him to the Muslims of India. However, Gandhi with his 'reformed Hinduism' hoped to secure that cooperation. In early 1918, he began his contact programme with the Muslims, opening correspondence with the government on the matter. It is this that approaches espouse that led him in subsequent years to Khilafat question which in his opinion was not necessarily a 'movement against the British'. His differences with Jinnah, too, were now numerous and being fundamental could not be glossed over. Gandhi was embarking on a path of agitation, totally alien to Jinnah. The religious elements of Khilafat, though paradoxically, acceptable even to a devout Hindu like Gandhi were entirely unacceptable to Jinnah who then did not perceive his politics as being bound in any fashion by the doctrinaire dictates of the narrow confines of Islam. (http://library.thinkquest.org/26523/mainfi les/homerule.htm)

17. *Indian Constitutional Documents*, Volume 1, *Pilgrimage to Freedom*, K.M. Munshi, Bhartiya Vidya Bhawan.
18. See Endnote 4.
19. *Indian Constitutional Documents*, Volume I, *Pilgrimage to Freedom*, K.M. Munshi, p. 22, Bhartiya Vidya Bhawan.
20. *Transfer of Power*, Vol. VI, p. 617.
21. Jinnah was opposed as non-cooperation entailed the Congress not cooperating with the government on the issue of legislature too. The Congress, therefore, boycotted the Council elections of 1920. Jinnah, though not supportive of non-cooperation, could not openly go against the policy of Congress and the Khilafatists. He, too, therefore could not participate in 1920 elections.
22. The Jallianwala Bagh incident and the repressive policy of the Punjab government which was unleashed post-massacre.
23. During the freedom struggle, the Swarajists represented extremists pitted against moderates of the Home Rule League. The study of British constitutional history had generated, among moderates, a love for and faith in Dominion status. Self-government under British promontory had been the goal of the moderate school, but the ideal of extremist or militant school was complete autonomy and elimination of all foreign control.

    Bal Gangadhar Tilak (1856-1920) and other extremists who wanted to adopt a policy of direct action and resistance, denounced 'the political mendicancy' of the moderates. During the anti partition agitation, in the first decade of the twentieth century Tilak wrote: 'The time has come to demand Swaraj or self-government. No piecemeal reform will do. The system of the present administration is ruinous to the country. It must mend or end'.

    'The term Swaraj,' said Bipin Pal (1858-1932; another extremist leader), 'was not merely a political but primarily a moral concept. The corresponding term in our language,' he said, 'is not non-subjection which would be a literal rendering of the English word independence, but self-subjection which is a positive concept. Self-subjection means complete identification of the individual with the universal.'

    Another Swarajist leader who, like Tilak, spoke of the ideal of swaraj was Aurobindo Ghose (1872-1950). 'We of the new school,' he said, 'would not pitch our ideal one inch lower than absolute Swaraj-Self-Government as it exists in the

United Kingdom.' In addition, he added, 'We reject the claim of aliens to force upon us a civilisation inferior to our own or keep us out of our inheritance on the untenable ground of a superior fitness.'

Lajpat Rai (1865-1928), along with Bal Gangadhar Tilak and Bipin Pal, constituted the swarajist triumvirate called 'Lal-Bal-Pal'. Lajpat, like the other extremists, believed that India must rely on her own strength and should not look to Britain for help.

The swarajists said that, however much Britain's rule might be improved or liberalised, it could never be as beneficial to Indians as self-rule. Their attitude was the same as that of the Irish Sinn Fein leader Arthur Griffith, who had said: 'I...in those who talk of ending British misgovernment we see the helots. It is not British misgovernment, but British government in Ireland, good or bad, we stand opposed to.' (http://www.congress.org.in/congress-the-freedom-movement.php)

24. The Bengal Pact of 1923 granted Muslims reservations in government and local body jobs. It was generous to Muslims recognising that communalism grew on grievances and these would not disappear till Indians took hardheaded decisions to allay them. The Bengal Pact gave C.R. Das a Muslim audience in Bengal. The offer was constructive, whatever one might think of its terms.

25. The most gruesome of episodes in 1926 was the Hindu-Muslim riots in Calcutta which broke out in May and again in July 1926. The trouble arose due to an Arya Samaj procession playing music while passing a mosque. In the riots that followed many were killed on both sides. Ultimately, when both parties were exhausted they made peace, though, the matter did not reach a crisis elsewhere as it had in Calcutta, there was considerable tension all over the country. The elections to the Legislatures were due in November 1926 and they were going to be held under this shadow of Hindu-Muslim riots.

26. Malwa is a region of Punjab and parts of Haryana between the Satluj and Yamuna rivers. The people of the region are known as Malwais and the dialect of Punjabi spoken in Malway is called Malwi.

Majha starts northward from the tight bank of river Beas and stretches up to the Wagha village which marks the boundary between India and Pakistan. Majha in Punjabi means the heartland. The region is divided into two districts, Amritsar and Gurdaspur.

27. The provincial government of Punjab was controlled by Muslims. The State Act favoured the Muslim agriculturists, far greater in number than the Hindus, who were essentially residents of towns and urban localities. The Act also favoured the large zamindars of western Punjab as against the small cultivators and the agricultural labour. This economic schism was reflected in communal discontent of the Hindus who tended to see in the Act a discrimination against them.

28. Arya Samaj a reform movement and religious/social organisation was formed in Bombay in 1875. The word 'Arya' means a noble human being, one who is thoughtful and charitable, who thinks good and does good actions.

29. The major anti-Hindu Kohat riots occurred in Kohat in NWFP, India in 1924. In three days (9-11 September) of rioting over 155 Hindus and Sikhs were killed, the others had to flee for their lives. Gandhi undertook a twenty-one days' fast for Hindu-Muslim unity in October 1924.

ENDNOTES 517

30. The elections of 1926 had taken place in an atmosphere of communal antagonism with Jinnah's Independent party suffering the most. In the previous Central Assembly, Jinnah had held the balance between the Congress and the government; in the new Central Assembly (1926), he was a leader without a following. To continue playing an important role in the Central Assembly, it was essential for him to find a new following. He did try for the leadership of the Muslim group.

31. After the elections of December 1923, the Bengal government had consistently alleged that there was a thorough identification of revolutionaries with the Swaraj Party. Lord Lytton would frequently alert Lord Reading of the dangers of revolutionary violence in Bengal. In 1923, the Bengal government had wanted extraordinary powers to deal with revolutionary menace, but this was refused by the Government of India. However, subsequently, the Viceroy's Council came to regard that the situation had altered and finally gave assent to the ordinance in October 1924.

32. Fazli Hussain, the leader of the Punjab Unionist Party and the first chief minister of the Punjab where the dominant ruling party was a secular alliance of landed gentry: Muslims, Hindu, and Sikhs, in the form of the Unionist Party. This Unionist Party was a political alliance of Muslim, Hindu and Sikh landowners. Hussain's right-hand man was Sir Chhotu Ram, a great Hindu (Jat) landowner. The third main figure in that ruling triumvirate was Sir Sundar Singh Majithia, the leader of Sikh landed interests.

33. The Muddiman Committee Report, officially known as the Report of the Reforms Enquiry Committee, 1924 was the product of the Government of India Act, 1919. Resolutions were pressed in the Imperial legislature, especially led by the Swarajists for the revision of the constitution to secure for India a full, self-governing, dominion status. Under the chairmanship of Sir Alexander Muddiman, the British government constituted a nine-member Committee who was enquire into the difficulties arising from, or defects inherent in, the working of the Government of India Act and the Rules thereunder in regard to Central Government and the governments of governors' provinces; to investigate the feasibility and desirability of securing remedies for such difficulties or defects, consistent with the structure, policy and purpose of the Act, or by such amendments of the Act as appear necessary to rectify any administrative imperfections. The Committee was able to, rather expeditiously, complete its work between August and December 1924 and submitted its report the following year in the month of September. (banglapedia.search.com.bd/HT/M_0347.htm)

34. Hailey, an Indian civil servant spent most of his life in India. He was the commissioner of Delhi, governor of Punjab and Uttar Pradesh as also the Home member in the Viceroy's Executive Council. He was considered very close to Lord Irwin.

35. See Endnote 29.

36. V.C. Joshi (ed.), *Lala Rajput Rai, His Writings and Speeches*, Volume ii, pp. 175-78 and 210-14, Delhi, 1966.

37. CWC, Volume xxvi, pp. 232-34.

38. *India Quarterly Register*, 1925, vol. I, p. 73.

39. Indian Legislative Assembly Debates, Volume 6, Part ii, pp. 940-41, 8 September 1925.

40. Halifax papers, 3: Irwin to Birkenhead, 24 March 1927.
41. *Indian Quarterly Digest*, 1927, vol. I, pp. 36-7.
42. Government of India, Home Political, 6/1927: Note by Maddiman, 24 May 1927.
43. Dr Ansari was a highly respected Muslim of the Congress as well as the Muslim League. The Nationalist Muslims, a party of which he was one of the most important members, played an important part in the national politics. Subsequently, by 1934, their influences gradually waned as politics became more polarized, with Jinnah urging liberal Muslim Leader based in Delhi to garner support for his faction of the Muslim League.
44. At the annual session of the Congress in Madras (1927), a resolution on Independence had been adopted.
45. AICC Papers, G60: Ansari to Jawaharlal Nehru, 29 March 1928.
46. All Parties Conference 1928, Report, p. 23.
47. Shuaib Qureshi and Sir Ali Imam to represent the Muslims: M.R. Jayakar and M.S. Aney for the Hindu Mahasabha; Sardar Mangal Singh for the Sikhs; G.R. Pradhan for the non-Brahmins; Sir Tej Bahadur Sapru, the liberal leader; N.M. Joshi the trade unionist; and Subhas Chandra Bose from Bengal. Of these, Jayakar took no part at all, and Sir Ali Imam, N.M. Joshi, G.R. Pradhan and Subhas Bose only made limited contributions.
48. *A Bunch of Old Letters*, pp. 60-61: Motilal to Gandhi, 11 July 1928, 'the members have all gone to their respective homes leaving Jawahar and myself to prepare the report and now we are hard at work at it'.
49. Maulana Shaukat Ali and Muhammad Ali were deeply interested in Islam and totally committed to the cause of freedom movement.
50. A Muslim landlord, politician from the United Provinces. Subsequently, his family had sided with the Congress in fighting the 1937 provincial elections.
51. (1) that one-third of the elected representatives of both the Houses of the Central Legislature should be 'Mussulmans';
    (2) that in the Punjab and Bengal, in the event of adult suffrage not being established, there should be reservation of seats for the Mussalmans on the basis of population for ten years, subject to a re-examination after that period, but they (Muslims) shall have no right to contest additional seats;
    (3) residuary powers ought to be left to the provinces and should not rest with the Central Legislature, in addition, some detailed recommendations about clauses and schedules in the proposed Constitution; (ii) Clause 13A embodied in the Supplementary report be deleted; (iii) that the division of subjects in Schedule I and II be revised;
    (4) that the Constitution shall not be amended or altered unless such a amendment or alteration is passed first by both the House of Parliament, separately, by a majority of four-fifths of those present and then by both the Houses, in a joint sitting, and again by a majority of four-fifths;
    (5) Communal representation to be implemented immediately; and
    (6) Embody, in the Nehru Report the Pact regarding Communal representation in Punjab in full.

52. Proceedings of the All Parties National Convention, pp. 76-7, Ansari Papers: A note in pencil headed 'modifications in the Nehru Report', setting out the reactions of the various groups within the sub-committee.
53. Proceedings of the All Parties National Convention, pp. 78-82.
54. Ibid., pp. 86-92.
55. Ibid.
56. Ibid., p. 93.
57. In March 1929 Jinnah drew up his famous Fourteen points which were:
    1. The form of the future constitution should be federal with the residuary powers vested in the provinces.
    2. A uniform measure of autonomy shall be granted to all provinces.
    3. All legislatures in the country and other elected bodies shall be constituted on the definite principle of adequate and effective representation of minorities in every province without reducing the majority in any province to a minority or even equality.
    4. In the Central Legislative, Muslim representation shall not be less than one-third.
    5. Representation of communal groups shall continue to be by means of separate electorate as at present, provided it shall be open to any community at any time to abandon its separate electorate in favour of a joint electorate.
    6. Any territorial distribution that might at any time be necessary shall not in any way affect the Muslim majority in the Punjab, Bengal, and the NWFP.
    7. Full religious liberty, i.e. liberty of belief, worship and observance, propaganda, association and education, shall be guaranteed to all communities.
    8. No bill or any resolution or any part thereof shall be passed in any legislature or any other elected body if three-fourth of the members of any community in that particular body oppose such a bill resolution or part thereof on the ground that it would be injurious to the interests of that community or in the alternative, such other method is devised as may be found feasible and practicable to deal with such cases.
    9. Sindh should be separated from the Bombay presidency.
    10. Reforms should be introduced in the North West Frontier Province and Baluchistan on the same footing as in the other provinces.
    11. Provision should be made in the constitution giving Muslims an adequate share, along with the other Indians, in all the services of the state and in local self-governing bodies having due regard to the requirements of efficiency.
    12. The constitution should embody adequate safeguards for the protection of Muslim culture and for the protection and promotion of Muslim education, language, religion, personal laws and Muslim charitable institution and for their due share in the grants-in-aid given by the state and by local self-governing bodies.
    13. No cabinet, either central or provincial, should be formed without there being a proportion of at least one-third Muslim ministers.
    14. No change shall be made in the constitution by the Central Legislature except with the concurrence of the State's contribution of the Indian Federation.

The council of the All-India Muslim League accepted fourteen points of the Quaid. A resolution was passed according to which no scheme for the future constitution of the Government of India would be acceptable to the Muslims unless and until it included the demands of the Quaid presented in the fourteen points.
   David Page, *Prelude to Partition—The Indian Muslims and the Imperial System of Control, 1920-32*, Oxford University Press, Delhi, 1982, pp. 131-2. (http://www.storyofpakistan.com/articletext.asp?artid=A037)

Chapter 4

1. 'A peace to end all peace', a phrase used by David Fromkin for his book *The Fall of the Ottoman Empire and the Creation of the Modern Middle East*, published by Owl Books, Henry Holt and Company, LLC, New York is a *New York Times* bestseller.
2. Ian Bryant Wells, *Jinnah: Ambassador of Hindu-Muslim Unity*, Seagull Books, 2006, pp. 165-6.
3. William Manchester, *Winston Spencer Churchill: The Last Lion*, Vol. I: *Visions of Glory, 1874-1932*, A Delta Book/Dell Publishing, 1983, pp. 845-6.
4. Refer Endnote 23 in Chapter 3.
5. 'Those who say religion has nothing to do with politics do not know what religion is'—Gandhi.
6. A chapter from the book—Lloyd I. Rudolph and Susanne Hoeber Rudolph, *Postmodern Gandhi and Other Essays: Gandhi in the World and at Home*, the University of Chicago Press, 2006.
7. Delhi Proposals: Considering separate electorates to be the main hindrance in improving Hindu-Muslim relations, Jinnah proposed that if the Hindus agreed to provide certain safeguards, the Muslims would give up this demand. Consequently, the proposals were formally approved at a conference held by the Muslims in 1927 at Delhi, and are now called 'The Delhi-Muslim Proposals'.
    1. The formation of a separate province of Sindh.
    2. Introduction of reforms in the North West Frontier Province and in Baluchistan on the same footing as in other provinces.
    3. Unless and until the above proposals were implemented, the Muslims would never surrender the right of their representation through separate electorates. Muslims would be willing to abandon separate electorates in favour of joint electorates with the reservation of seats fixed in proportion to the population of different communities, if the above two proposals were implemented to the full satisfaction of Muslims and also if the following proposals were accepted.
    4. Hindu minorities in Sindh, Baluchistan and the North West Frontier Province be accorded the same concessions in the form of reservation of seats over and above the proportion of their population as Muslims would get in Hindu majority provinces.
    5. Muslim representation in the Central Legislature would not be less than one-third.

6. In addition to provisions like religious freedom, there was to be a further guarantee in the constitution that on communal matters no bill or resolution would be considered or passed if three-fourth of the members of the community concerned were opposed to it.

These proposals were to be accepted or rejected in toto. So, in effect, the Muslims agreed to give up the separate electorates in form of the reservation of seats. Unfortunately, the Congress first accepted but later rejected the proposals.

8. Lloyd I. Rudolph and Susanne Hoeber Rudolph, *Postmodern Gandhi and Other Essays: Gandhi in the World and at Home*, the University of Chicago Press, 2006, p. 67.
9. Kalends were part of the Roman calendar, not of the Greek, so the "Greek calends" are "a date that will never happen".
10. Nehru in a letter to Gandhi on 11 January 1928.
11. The idea of the Conference of Muslim legislators was first mooted by Aga Khan in December 1927, but it was only after the publication of the Nehru Report that it was taken up enthusiastically at which stage Jinnah's colleagues in the Central Assembly like Sir Mohammad Yakub and Mr Fazl Rahimtoolah brought the scheme to fruition. [David Page, *Prelude to Partition*, p. 193, OUP, Delhi, 1982.]
12. Jinnah's Fourteen points. Please refer to Endnote 57 in Chapter 3.
13. See Motilal Nehru papers: Nehru to Gandhi, 14 August 1929.
14. Muddiman Committee: Please refer to Endnote 33 in Chapter 3.
15. A Select Committee is one made up of a small number of parliamentary members appointed to deal with particular areas or issue originating in the Westminster system of parliamentary democracy.
16. Irwin's note of interview with Jinnah of 31 October 1927, Halifax Collection, India Office Library (H.C., IOL), MSS.Eur.C.152/29.
17. Jinnah to Irwin, 31 October 1927, H.C., IOL, MSS.Eur.C.152/21.
18. *The Times*, London, 10 November 1927.
19. *The Manchester Guardian*, 15 November 1927.
20. *The Times of India*, 15 November 1927. Also cited in Jinnah-Irwin Correspondence, edited by Wahid Ahmad, Research Society of Pakistan, University of Punjab, Lahore, 1969, pp. 5-6.
21. *The Times of India*, 28 November 1927. Also cited in Jinnah-Irwin Correspondence edited by Wahid Ahmad, Research Society of Pakistan, University of Punjab, Lahore, 1969, p. 6.
22. *The Civil and Military Gazette*, Lahore, 4 January 1928.
23. Irwin to Birkenhead, 15 March 1928, H.C., IOL, MSS.Eur.C.152/29.
24. Irwin to the Archbishop of Canterbury, 29 November 1928.
25. The pronouncement of August 1917 spoke of 'the gradual development of self-governing institutions with a view to the progressive realization of responsible government in India'. That is also the term used in the Preamble to the Act; that is the term used in the Royal Warrant of Instructions which adds that 'thus will India be fitted to take her place among the other Dominions'. The term has its significance; we know that it was deliberately chosen. The Congress and the League had asked the Imperial Government to proclaim its intention to confer self-government on India at an early date and the Cabinet chose the present term. The expression used in the Act is a term of precision, conveying that the Executive in

India would be responsible to the Indian Legislature instead of to the British Parliament. If you analyse the term 'full Dominion Self-Government', you will see that it is of somewhat wider extent, conveying that not only will the Executive be responsible to the Legislature, but the Legislature will in itself have the full powers which are typical of the modern Dominion. 'I say there is some difference of substance, because responsible government is not necessarily incompatible with a Legislature with limited or restricted powers. It may be that full Dominion self-government is the logical outcome of responsible government, nay, it may be the inevitable and historical development of responsible government, but it is a further and a final step.' (Sir Malcolm Hailey, Home Member to the Government of India on the grant of full self-governing Dominion Status to India, 8 February 1924—Gwyer and Appadorai, p. 220) (http://www.houseofdavid.ca/simon.htm#impact)

26. Legislative Assembly Debates, 5 February 1924, p. 768.
27. Wahid Ahmad (ed.), Jinnah-Irwin correspondence, Letter to Lord Irwin, p. 41.
28. Nawab of Chhatari, Ahmad Sa'id Khan (b.1888): minister of Industries, UP, 1923-25; Home Member UP, 1926-33; acting governor of UP, 1928 and 1933; prime minister of Hyderabad 1947; leader of the Zamindar party and the Muslim League.
29. His Highness the Aga Khan, *The Memoirs of Aga Khan*, Simon & Schuster, New York, 1954.
30. The Nawab of Bhopal, Sir Hamidullah Khan (1894-1960): Chancellor of the Chamber of Princes, 1931-2 and 1944-7.
31. His Highness the Aga Khan, *The Memoirs of Aga Khan*, Simon & Schuster, New York, 1954, p. 231.
32. Ibid., pp. 233-4.
33. Stanley Wolpert, *Jinnah of Pakistan*, p. 120.
34. Ibid.
35. Ibid., p. 121.
36. Quoted in Joachim Alva, *Men and Supermen of Hindustan*, Bombay, 1943, p. 226.
37. *The Civil and Military Gazette*, 3 March 1936.
38. David Page, *Prelude to Partition—The Indian Muslims and the Imperial System of Control, 1920-1932*, Oxford University Press, Delhi, 1982, p. 229.
39. Ram Raj, also Ram Rajya: Gandhi had said, 'By Ram Raj, I do not mean Hindu Raj... I mean by Ram Raj, Divine Raj, the Kingdom of God'. Ram Rajya can be described as a state in which local entities control local resources and decision-making, the state respects people's opinion, ensures transparency, imposes reasonable taxes for providing security and infrastructure, coordinates, but does not interfere or exploit.
40. GI Home Political.33/x/1931: AICC Circular No. 12, 10 March 1931.
41. One-fourth of a Rupee since the Rupee was equivalent to be of 16 annas. This terminology has since long gone out of use. A 'four anna' would mean a 'primary' member.
42. Fazli Hussain Papers: Fazli Hussain to Sir Muhammad Iqbal, 1 May 1931.
43. His Highness the Aga Khan, *The Memoirs of Aga Khan*, Simon & Schuster, New York, 1954, p. 235.

ENDNOTES 523

44. The role played by Sir Ramsay MacDonald (1886-1927) in India's struggle for freedom remains to be analysed. He was prime minister of Great Britain in 1924 and again from 1929-35 and Leader of the Labour Party from 1911-14. He was popular in India and was invited to preside over the 1911 session of the INC but was unable to do so as his wife had died. He was one of the most vocal in condemning the Partition of Bengal. He later declared that the British Government was ready to recognize the all important principle of executive responsibility to the legislature, except for certain safeguards, notably Defence, External Affairs, the maintenance of tranquility in the realm and the guarantee of financial stability. MacDonald was responsible for introducing separate electorates, and Gandhi undertook a fast unto death in disapproval of the above given by MacDonald's 'Communal Award' to the depressed classes. MacDonald lamented that the 'hope of united India, an India conscious of a unity of purpose and destiny seems to be the vainest of the vain dreams'. He also played a notable part in the appointment of the Simon Commission. Winston Churchill tauntingly promised him 'his cordial cooperation in the Government's self-imposed task of carrying out the conservative policy of making the world wiser if not safer for capitalism'. Lloyd George called the MacDonald 'the last of the conservatives'. Even Jawaharlal Nehru was convinced that the British Labour Government under MacDonald would not be of any special benefit to the Indian National Movement. (http://www.congress.org.in/british-friends-of-india.php)
45. S.R. Bakshi, *Mahatma Gandhi: Congress and its Leadership*, Anmol Publications Private Ltd, 1990, p. 143.
46. Victor Trench, *Lord Willingdon in India*, 1934, p. 212.
47. It was a rule in Gandhi's ashram that all domestic chores (Gandhi's conception of a kind of collective farm where his religious order of monks could stay; also any other Hindu farm order where religious monks could stay and propagate culture) should be performed by the Ashramites themselves, including a reformed method of scavenging.
48. *The Collected Works of Mahatma Gandhi*, Delhi; Publications Division, Minisny of Educadon and Broadcasting, Government of India.
49. Durga Das, *India from Curzon to Nehru and After*, 1970, p. 159.
50. Jawaharlal to Gandhi, 11 September 1931, in J. Nehru, Selected Works, vol. 5, 1972-4, pp. 31-2.
51. Ibid.
52. Jawaharlal to Gandhi, 4 October 1931, in J. Nehru, Selected Works, vol. 5, 1972-4, p. 137.
53. Jawaharlal to Gandhi, 27 September 1931, in J. Nehru, Selected Works, vol. 5, 1972-4, p. 46.
54. Ian Wells, op. cit., p. 229.
55. Fazli Hussain to Jinnah, Papers, Vols. 16-17.

Chapter 5

1. Chaudhri Khaliquzzaman, *Pathway to Pakistan*, p. 141.
2. Quote from Sir Muhammad Yousuf, *Star of India*, 20 June 1936. Also cited in Muhammad Reza Kazimi, *Liaquat Ali Khan and The Freedom Movement*, p. 111, Pakistan Study Centre, University of Karachi, 1997.
3. Quaid-i-Azam Papers, Volume 1122, 167-168; *Star of India*, Calcutta, 11 August 1936.
4. *Star of India*, Calcutta, 29 May 1936, p. 3.
5. A.K. Fazlul Haq (1873-1962) was popularly known as Sher-i-Bengal. For more than half a century, he was at the forefront of all political activities pertaining to the Pakistan Movement making valuable contributions towards the political, social and educational uplift of the Muslims of the subcontinent. While practicing law in his hometown, Barisal, he realized that the Muslims in Bengal remained backward due to a lack of education. He slowly began to emerge as a young political leader. He was one of the four members of the committee that drafted the constitution of the All India Muslim League in 1906. By the year 1914 he became the leader of the Muslims of Bengal and attended the Lucknow Pact as the representative of the province. During the Non-cooperation Movement of 1919-21, his advise to the Muslim students was to concentrate on their studies and not get involved in politics at that stage. Besides defending thousands of Muslims who were accused of the riot cases before the Partition, he was also a delegate of the Round Table Conferences pleading the cause of the Muslims to get their share in the administrative affairs of the country. He was elected chief minister of Bengal in 1937. During the AIML session of 23 March 1940 that was presided over by Jinnah, Haq rose to move the historic Pakistan Resolution protecting the rights of the Muslims of India. (http://www.storyofpakistan.com/person.asp?perid=P077)
6. Khawaja Nazimuddin (1894-1964) was born in Dhaka and educated at M.A.O. College, Aligarh, and Trinity Hall, Cambridge. He became the provincial education minister in 1929 and spearheaded the Bengal Rural Primary Education Bill in 1930. In 1937, he was appointed as the Home Minister. He remained an active member of Coalition Cabinet of the chief minister, Fazlul Haq during 1937-41. After Haq resigned, Nazimuddin took over as chief minister on 24 April 1943. In August 1947, he was elected as the leader of the Muslim League Party of East Bengal. After Jinnah's death, on 11 September 1948, Nazimuddin was designated governor general of Pakistan. After the assassination of Liaquat Ali, Khawaja Nazimuddin was asked to step in as the prime minister.
7. The Krishak Praja Party led by Fazlul Haq dominated Bengali politics in the 1930s.
8. Chaudhri Khaliquzzaman, *Pathway to Pakistan*, p. 153.
9. Ibid., p. 157.
10. Ibid., p. 161.
11. B.R. Nanda, *Nehru, The Indian National Congress and the Partition of India, 1935-47*, George Allen and Unwin Ltd, London 1970, p. 157.
12. Z.H. Zaidi, *Aspects of the Development of Muslim League policy, 1937-47*, George Allen and Unwin Ltd, London, 1970, p. 245.

13. Munshi, op. cit., p. 46, Bharatiya Vidya Bhawan, Bombay, 1967.
14. S. Gopal, *Jawaharlal Nehru: A Biography*, Volume I, 1989-1947, Bombay, 1976.
15. Ibid., pp. 228-29.
16. The Muslim clergy.
17. The All-India Muslim Personal Law Board (AIMPLB) is an organisation constituted for the protection and continued applicability of the Muslim Personal Law (Shariat) Application Act 1937.
18. The Momin Conference, inaugurated in Bengal in 1911, aimed to revive the traditional crafts of the weavers as well as to promote self-respect, devout religious conduct and economic independence of the poor weavers.
19. For a further exposition of these ideas see also William Gould, *Hindu Nationalism and the Language of Politics in Late Colonial India*, Cambridge, 2005.
20. Presidential Address, 27 December 1936.
21. Jawaharlal Nehru, *Eighteen months in India*. Allahabad, 1938, p. 153.
22. Selected Works of Jawaharlal Nehru, Volume 8, 'The Share of the Constitution', (Speech), 6 March 1937, pp. 54-5.
23. Ibid., Presidential Address to the All-India Convention of Congress Legislators, 19 March 1937, p. 63.
24. Ibid., 'The Share of the Constitution', (Speech), 6 March 1937, p. 55.
25. V.P. Menon, *Transfer of Power in India*, Orient Longman, 1997, p. 56.
26. Maulana Abul Kalam Azad, *India Wins Freedom*, Orient Longman, 1998, p. 171.
27. M.J. Akbar, *The Shade of Swords: Jihad and the Conflict Between Islam & Christianity*, Routledge, 2003, p. 183.
28. O.P. Rathan, *Encyclopaedia of Political Parties*, Anmol Publication Pvt. Ltd, p. 674.
29. Though the provinces were to have the responsible government of the parliamentary type, but their governors would be armed with special powers for the protection of minorities and also to take over administration in the case of a breakdown. These were sometimes called 'Section 93' powers from the number of the relevant section of the 1935 Act.
30. John Glendevon, *The Viceroy at Bay: Lord Linlithgow in India, 1936-1943*, Collins, 1971, p. 75.
31. Ibid.
32. Ibid., p. 77.
33. Ibid.
34. Ibid.
35. Ibid., p. 78.
36. Ibid.
37. Ibid.
38. Ibid., p. 87.
39. Ibid., p. 119.
40. Ibid.
41. Chaudhri Khaliquzzaman, *Pathway to Pakistan*, p. 182.
42. Ibid.
43. Ibid., p. 191.

44. S. Qaim Hussain Jafri (ed.), Congress Leaders correspondence with Qaid-e-Azam, Bose/Subhash Correspondence, 14 May 1938, p. 5, Aziz Publishers, Lahore, Pakistan.
45. Ibid.
46. Ibid., p. 6.
47. Bal Gangadhar Kher was the first chief minister of Bombay Province. Known for his genial and unfailing good nature and keen sense of humour he had won the respect and esteem of Congressmen from Gandhi downwards. He passed away on 8 March 1957.
48. Chaudhri Khaliquzzaman, *Pathway to Pakistan*, 1938, p. 201.
49. Word used to literally signify 'rulers', 'state authority' or 'government' in Hindi.
50. Literally, small locality in Urdu.
51. To investigate Muslim grievances, the Muslim League formulated the 'Pirpur Report' under the chairmanship of Raja Syed Muhammad Mehdi of Pirpur. Other reports concerning Muslim grievances in Congress run provinces were A.K. Fazlul Haq's 'Muslim Sufferings under Congress Rule', and 'Sharif Report'.
52. Press Statement: *Star of India*, 7 July 1937: 'Jinnah condemns Congress Mass contact—Muslims no roadies: A large body of Congress, instead of placing before public their programme is attacking the policy and programme of Muslim League and.... That all those who are with Muslim League stand for political slavery and are allies of British...their toadies and flunkeys. Is this how Congress proposes to establish mass contact with Muslims? In my opinion, this policy of mass contact with Mussalmans by Congress is fraught with very serious consequences'.
53. *Nehru and the Partition of India 1935-47*, George Allen and Unwin Ltd., London, 1970, p. 163.
54. 4 September 1939; John Glendevon, *The Viceroy at Bay: Lord Linlithgow in India, 1936-1943*, Collins, 1971, p. 137.
55. Ibid., p. 138.
56. Under the India Act of 1935, a Federal government comprising representatives—both of British India and that of the Princely states, latter to be nominated by their rulers was to be set up. The Central legislature was to consist of two Houses—a legislative assembly and a Council of State. Diarchy was to be abolished in provinces and introduced at the Centre.

    The Federation could not be brought into force until half the princely states entitled to sit in the Council of States acceded. In the British Parliament, the Federal part of the bill had been bitterly opposed by Conservatives. In India, the Provincial part of the Act was generally approved and implemented. Despite several attempts, the Federation part of the India Act could never be implemented.
57. *The Viceroy at Bay*, p. 151.
58. Cited in V.P. Menon, *Transfer of Power*, pp. 59-60. Menon does not indicate the date of this statement but it appears to have been made shortly after Jinnah met Linlithgow on 5 October 1939.
59. Linlithgow Papers, Eur.F.125/6/15, Brabourne to Zetland, 19 August 1938, IOL. Sir Sikandar Hayat had also assured Brabourne that 'given a fair deal' by the British, the Muslims 'would stand by the British through thick and thin'.
60. John L. Dundas (ed.), *Essayez, The Memoirs of Lawrence, Second Marquess of Zetland*, London, 1956.

61. Ibid.
62. Jamil-ud-din Ahmad, *Speeches and Writings of Mr Jinnah*, ii, p. 245, Lahore, 1947, 6th Edition, 1964.
63. V.P. Menon, *Transfer of Power*, p. 437.
64. India Office Records, Political Department Collections—L/P&J/8/505. Note of an interview between Linlithgow and Jinnah on 5 October 1939.
65. Gowher Rizvi, *Linlithgow and India: Study of British Policy and the Political Impasse in India, 1936-43* (Royal Historical Society Studies in History), London, 1978; India Office Records Political Department Collections L/P&J/8/506, pp. 113-14, 4 November 1939.
66. IAR, 1939, ii, 411.
67. Linlithgow Papers—Eur.F.125/18/303, Telegram from Zetland to Linlithgow, 18 November 1939, also Gowher Rizvi.
68. Linlithgow Papers—Eur.F.125/18/511, Telegram from Linlithgow to Zetland, 28 November 1939, IOL.
69. *Hindustan Times*, Delhi, 3 December 1939.
70. Gowher Rizvi, *Linlithgow and India, A Study of British Policy and the Political Impasse in India, 1936-1943*, p. 115, Royal Historical Society Studies in History Series, No. 13, Royal Historical Society, London, 1978.
71. Linlithgow Papers—Eur.F.125/19/6, Telegram from Linlithgow to Zetland, 16 January 1940, IOL.
72. Lahore Resolution [1940] From March 22 to March 24, 1940, the All-India Muslim League held its annual session at Minto Park, Lahore.

On the first day of the session, Quaid-i-Azam Mohammad Ali Jinnah narrated the events of the last few months. In an extempore speech he presented his own solution of the Muslim problem. He said that the problem of India was not of an inter-communal nature, but manifestly an international one and must be treated as such. To him the differences between Hindus and the Muslims were so great and so sharp that their union under one central government was full of serious risks. They belonged to two separate and distinct nations and therefore the only chance open was to allow them to have separate states.

In the words of Quaid-i-Azam: 'Hindus and the Muslims belong to two different religions, philosophies, social customs and literature. They neither inter-marry nor inter-dine and, indeed, they belong to two different civilizations that are based mainly on conflicting ideas and conceptions. Their concepts on life and of life are different. It is quite clear that Hindus and Muslims derive their inspiration from different sources of history. They have different epics, different heroes and different episodes. Very often the hero of one is a foe of the other, and likewise, their victories and defeats overlap. To yoke together two such nations under a single state, one as a numerical minority and the other as a majority, must lead to growing discontent and final destruction of any fabric that may be so built up for the government of such a state'.

He further said, 'Mussalmans are a nation according to any definition of nation. We wish our people to develop to the fullest spiritual, cultural, economic, social and political life in a way that we think best and in consonance with our own ideals and according to the genius of our people.' On the basis of the above mentioned ideas of the Quaid, A.K. Fazlul Haq, the then chief minister of Bengal, moved the historical resolution which has since come to be known as Lahore Resolution or Pakistan Resolution.

The Resolution declared: 'No constitutional plan would be workable or acceptable to the Muslims unless geographical contiguous units are demarcated into regions which should be so constituted with such territorial readjustments as may be necessary. That the areas in which the Muslims are numerically in majority as in the North-Western and Eastern zones of India should be grouped to constitute independent states in which the constituent units shall be autonomous and sovereign'.

It further reads, 'That adequate, effective and mandatory safeguards shall be specifically provided in the constitution for minorities in the units and in the regions for the protection of their religious, cultural, economic, political, administrative and other rights of the minorities, with their consultation. Arrangements thus should be made for the security of Muslims where they were in a minority'.

The Resolution repudiated the concept of United India and recommended the creation of an independent Muslim state consisting of Punjab, N.W.F.P., Sindh and Baluchistan in the northwest, and Bengal and Assam in the northeast. The Resolution was seconded by Maulana Zafar Ali Khan from Punjab, Sardar Aurangzeb from the N.W.F.P., Sir Abdullah Haroon from Sindh, and Qazi Esa from Baluchistan, along with many others.

The Resolution was passed on 24 March. It laid down only the principles, with the details left to be worked out at a future date. It was made a part of the All-India Muslim League's constitution in 1941. It was on the basis of this resolution that in 1946 the Muslim League decided to go for one state for the Muslims, instead of two.

Having passed the Pakistan Resolution, the Muslims of India changed their ultimate goal. Instead of seeking alliance with the Hindu community, they set out on a path whose destination was a separate homeland for the Muslims of India. (http://www.telepk.com/pakistan/lahore-resolution/pakistan-asvisualized-by-chaudhry-rahmat-ali.asp)

73. The celebration of 23 March as 'Pakistan Day' did not start before 1956. At first it was celebrated as 'Republic Day' to mark the passage of the first constitution and emergence of Pakistan as an independent republic similar in importance as '26 January' for India. However, when Gen. Ayub abrogated the constitution and established martial law in 1958, he was faced with a dilemma. He could not let the country celebrate a day commemorating the constitution that he had himself torn apart, nor could he cancel the celebration altogether. A way-out was found by keeping the celebration, but giving it another name: 'the Pakistan Resolution Day'.
74. *Manchester Guardian*, 2 April 1940.
75. Presidential address, All-India Muslim League, Delhi session, 24 April 1943.
76. Speech at the Punjab Muslim League conference, Sialkot, 30 April 1944.
77. Presidential address, All-India Muslim League, Delhi session, 24 April 1993.
78. See Humayun Kabir, *Muslim Politics 1942-1947*, but this view has been challenged in discussion.
79. Chaudhri Khaliquzzaman, *Pathway to Pakistan*, pp. 255-6.

80. Presidential address, All-India Muslim League, Delhi session, 24 April 1943.

Chapter 6

1. C.H. Philips and Mary Doreen Wainwright (eds.), *The Partition of India: Policies and Perspectives 1935-1947*, George Allen and Unwin Ltd. London, p. 388.
2. C.R. Atlee, *As it Happened*; R.G. Coupland—*Diary: 1941-1942*; Notes on Meetings of India Conciliation Group Sub-Committee Meeting with Nehru, 14 July 1938; Irene Harrison-Agatha Harrison: An Impression of Her Sister (1956), for a general account of the Indian Conciliation Group.
3. Notes on Meetings of India Conciliation Group Sub-Committee Meeting with Nehru, 14 July 1938, Friends' House, London. Nehru was speaking to the India Conciliation Group, which, at Gandhi's behest, had been set up in 1931 to promote 'mutual understanding between Great Britain and India'. It consisted largely of Quakers. Cripps stepmother was a Quaker. At Friends' House in September 1938 Nehru insisted that 'the first step to be conceded is the acceptance of the right of India to determine her own Constitution (India Conciliation Group Notes—3 September 1938).
4. Cripps to Sir Findlater Stewart, 24 November 1939, L/PO/252/16, and enclosure.
5. R.J. Moore, *Churchill, Cripps and India, 1939-45*, Clarendon Press, Oxford, 1979, pp. 9-10.
6. Ibid., p. 11.
7. Diary kept by Cripps and Geoffrey Wilson, 1939-1940, in possession of Maurice Shock, Leicester University, 11 December 1939. Liaquat Ali Khan's three solutions correspond broadly to the three major British answers to the Indian problem in the 1940s: Cripps's 'local option' (1942), the Cabinet Mission's three-tier scheme (1946), and Mountbatten's Partition Plan (1947).
8. Diary kept by Cripps and Geoffrey Wilson, 1939-40, in possession of Mr Maurice Shock, Leicester University, 15 December 1939; also cited in R.J. Moore, *Churchill, Cripps and India, 1939-45*, Clarendon Press, Oxford, 1979, pp. 12-13.
9. R.J. Moore, *Churchill, Cripps and India, 1939-45*, Clarendon Press, Oxford, 1979, p. 13.
10. Cabinet Conclusion, 59(39)8, 25 October 1939.
11. R.J. Moore, *Churchill, Cripps and India, 1939-45*, Clarendon Press, Oxford, 1979, p. 22.
12. Ibid., p. 28.
13. Ibid.
14. Linlithgow to Zetland, 13 February 1940, Zetland Collection, India Office Library, London.
15. Simon to Chamberlain, 13 February 1940, Prime Minister's Office Files, Public Record Office, London—1/414.
16. Ibid.
17. Ibid.

18. Churchill to Chamberlain, 20 February 1940, Prime Minister's Office Files, Public Record Office, London.
19. Cripps to Nehru, 18 March 1940, Jawaharlal Nehru Collection, Nehru Memorial Library, New Delhi.
20. India Conciliation Group, Notes, 24 May 1940; Cripps to Agatha Harrison, 20 May 1940, India Conciliation Group Box 47 (Cripps).
21. Cable of 16 July 1940—Private Officer Papers, India Office Library, London; also cited in R.J. Moore, *Churchill, Cripps and India, 1939- 45*, Clarendon Press, Oxford, 1979, p. 35.
22. War Cabinet, 30 July 1940, WP(40)295, including Churchill to Linlithgow, 28 July 1940 (Cable). Ibid. Also cited in R.J. Moore, *Churchill, Cripps and India, 1939-45*, Clarendon Press, Oxford, 1979, p. 36.
23. The British Government's Offer of 8 August 1940, Gwyer & Appadorai, Documents, ii, 504-505.
24. Leopold Amery's Speech in the House of Commons, 1 August 1942.
25. Guy Winant to Secretary of State, Cordell Hull, 4 November 1941, Foreign Relations of the United States: Diplomatic Papers, 1941, iii, 181-182.
26. The then US ambassador to Britain.
27. Ibid.
28. R.J. Moore, *Churchill, Cripps and India 1939-1945*, Clarendon Press, Oxford, 1979, p. 42.
29. Ibid.
30. Sir George Ernest Schuster, (1881-1982), Knight colonial administrator; Finance member of the Viceroy's Executive Council 1928-1934.
31. Kanji Dwarkadas, *Ten Years of Freedom*, Bombay, Popular Prakashan, 1968, p. 62.
32. Ibid., p. 63.
33. Ibid.
34. Ibid.
35. Ibid.
36. Ibid.
37. Ibid., p. 64.
38. Ibid., p. 64.
39. Ibid., p. 65.
40. Ibid., pp. 194-195.
41. Ibid., p. 67.
42. Ibid.
43. Mahmud Husain, 'Dacca University and the Pakistan Movement, in *The Partition of India: Policies and Perspectives 1935-1947*, C.H. Philips and Mary Doreen Wainwright (eds.), George Allen and Unwin Ltd, London, 1970, p. 371.
44. Kanji Dwarkadas, *Ten Years of Freedom*, Bombay, Popular Prakashan, 1968, p. 69.
45. Comment about Wavell by Pyarelal, p. 276.
46. Motilal C. Setalvad, *Law and Other Things*.

Chapter 7

1. Penderel Moon (ed.), *Wavell: The Viceroy's Journal*, Oxford University Press, 1973.
2. Ibid.
3. R.J. Moore, *Churchill, Cripps and India, 1939-1945*, Clarendon Press, Oxford, 1979, p. 140.
4. *Wavell: The Viceroy's Journal*, 7 and 8 October 1943, pp. 22-23.
5. Wavell to Churchill, October 1944, *Transfer of Power*, Volume V.
6. Wavell to Amery, 1 December 1944, TOP, Vol. V, 260.
7. *Wavell: The Viceroy's Journal*, pp. 110, 111, 112.
8. Ibid.
9. Ibid., pp. 115-116.
10. Ibid.
11. Amery to Field Marshal Viscount Wavell, 12 July 1945, *Transfer of Power*, Volume V, pp. 1236-1239.
12. David John Colville, 1st Baron Clydesmuir PC GCIE (13 February 1894–31 October 1954) became governor of Bombay, a post he held until 1947. He acted as viceroy and governor-general of India, in 1945, 1946 and 1947. On his return from India he was raised to the peerage as Baron Clydesmuir, of Braidwood in the County of Lanarkshire. From 1950 to 1954 Lord Clydesmuir served as a governor of the BBC.
13. Penderel Moon (ed.), *Wavell—The Viceroy's Journal*, Oxford University Press, 1973.
14. The election process started with nominations from 10 December 1945 and could be completed fully by 20 April 1946.
15. Punjab: Total strength of the House: 175 (Figure source taken from Post-War Upsurge of Freedom Movement and 1946 Provincial Elections in India); Sho Kuwajima, p. 268, April 1992.
16. Nawab Iftikhar Hussain Khan of Mamdot (1906-69), was the son of Sir Shah Nawaz Khan. He succeeded his father as provincial president of the Muslim League and assembly member from Ferozepur Central. He opposed Khizr Khan Tiwana both before and after the 1945-6 election leading the party in its successful campaign to oust Khizr in 1947. After independence he became chief minister of West Punjab, 1947-8, but soon fell out with his colleagues and left the League in 1950 to form Jinnah Muslim League.
17. H.M. Seervai, *Partition of India: Legend and Reality*, Oxford University Press; Karachi, 2005.
18. *Transfer of Power 1942-7*, Vol. VI, pp. 155-57, the post-war phase: 1 August 1945-22 March 1946 (68 Sir E. Jenkins to Mr Abell Telegram, Wavell Papers, Political Series July-Sep 1945, pp. 65-7). Printed in England for Her Majesty's Stationery Office, first published 1976.
19. *Transfer of Power*, Vol. VI, pp. 155-57, 172.
20. Ibid., Vol. VII, pp. 433-434.
21. Ibid., pp. 476-479.
22. Ibid., p. 466.

23. Kanji Dwarkadas, *Ten Years of Freedom*, Bombay, Popular Prakashan, 1968, p. 179.
24. Ibid.
25. Madhu Limaye, *Indian National Movement its Ideological and Socio-economic Dimensions*, Radiant Publishers, New Delhi, 1989, p. 308.
26. Sher Mohammad Garewal (ed.), Jinnah-Wavell Correspondence, 1943-47, Research Society of Pakistan, University of Punjab, Lahore, 1986.
27. *Transfer of Power*, Vol. VII, pp. 784-785.
28. Ibid., pp. 785-786.
29. 12 June 1946, QAP, File No. 14, p. 1; TOP, Vol. VII, p. 885.
30. QAP, File No. 14, p. 5; TOP, Vol. VII, p. 945.
31. Paragraph 8, considered by Wavell to have been introduced in the 16 June 1946 statement mentioned this stipulation. Subsequently, Jinnah accused the viceroy of a breach of faith when the Cabinet delegation asked for time before going ahead with the Interim Government formation.
32. TOP, Vol. VII. No. 562, p. 971.
33. QAP, File No. 14, pp. 14-17; TOP, Vol. VII, pp. 974-77.
34. QAP, File No. 14, pp. 33-34 A; TOP, Vol. VII, pp. 988-89.
35. *Transfer of Power*, Vol. VII, pp. 1032-36.
36. Ibid., pp. 1036-38.
37. QAP, File No. 14, p. 58; TOP, Vol. VII, p. 1077.
38. Kanji Dwarkadas, *Ten Years of Freedom*, Bombay, Popular Prakashan, 1968, p. 182.
39. Interview given by Jinnah to API, Hyderabad (Deccan), 13 July 1946.
40. QAP, File No. 20, pp. 9, 10, 11; TOP, Vol. VIII, pp. 98-9.
41. *The Indian Annual Register*, 1946, Vol. II, p. 228.
42. Stephens, op. cit., p. 107.
43. The Council had met from 27 to 29 July 1946.
44. The text of the 29 July 1946 Resolution of the All-India Muslim League Council.
45. Waheed Ahmad (ed.), *The Nation's Voice—Speeches, Statements, Interviews of Jinnah*, pp. 209-214.
46. Nehru quoted in *The Statesman*, 18 August 1946, p. 1.
47. Leonard Mosley, *The Last Days of the British Raj*, London, Weidenfeld and Nicolson, 1971.
48. Ibid.
49. Penderel Moon (ed.), *Wavell—The Viceroy's Journal*, Oxford University Press, London, 1973, p. 341.

Chapter 8

1. Wahid Ahmad (ed.), Annotated speeches, statements, interviews and messages of Jinnah, Volume V, Quaid-i-Azam Academy, 2001, pp. 321-22.
2. Ibid., p. 319.
3. Ibid., p. 323.

4. Ibid., p. 324.
5. Ibid., p. 326.
6. Ibid., p. 329.
7. H.D. Sharma (ed.), *100 Best Letters, 1847-1947*, Rupa & Co., pp. 396-99.
8. Patel admitted this to Kanji Dwarkadas in a meeting on 31 December 1946 at Ahmadabad. Quoted in Kanji Dwarkadas, *Ten Years of Freedom*, Bombay, Popular Prakashan, 1968, p. 201.
9. Ibid., 197.
10. Ibid., p. 199.
11. Ibid.
12. Ibid., p. 205.
13. Ibid., pp. 207-8.
14. Ibid., pp. 209-10.
15. Ibid., p. 216
16. Collected Works of Mahatma Gandhi, 20 and 25 March 1947, pp. 124-25.
17. Kanji Dwarkadas, *Ten Years of Freedom*, Bombay, Popular Prakashan, 1968, p. 210.
18. Ibid., p. 211.
19. Ibid., p. 211.
20. Leonard Mosley, *The Last Days of the British Raj*.
21. Ibid.
22. Ibid.
23. *Transfer of Power*, Vol. X, p. 771. Differences between the two were briefly the following: (i). A general exchange of presentation, to meet Nehru's views which presents the existing Constituent Assembly as fulfilling the Cabinet Mission's Plan and any new Constituent Assembly as a group of dissentient elements. (ii). Removal of the proposal that the decisions be taken by representatives of legislative assemblies on the basis proposed in the Cabinet Mission Plan. (iii). Adherence to the existing Constituent Assembly or to a new and separate one. The option to remain independent dropped.
24. Kanji Dwarkadas, *Ten Years of Freedom*, Popular Prakashan, Bombay, 1968, pp. 211-12.
25. Ibid., p. 213.
26. Ibid.
27. 'Vilayat'—Urdu word roughly translating for 'foreign land' in English.
28. The history of the Kohinoor diamond (Weight: 108.93 carats: Cut: round brilliant cut diamond) begins in the fourteenth century. At that time it was reported to be in the possession of the rajas of Malwa, later getting into the hands of Babur, the founder of the Mughal dynasty in 1526. Over the next two centuries the diamond was one of the most prized possessions of the Mughal emperors. In 1739, Nadir Shah of Persia invaded India and the treasures of the Mughals fell into his hands, reportedly exclaiming 'Koh-inoor' i.e. 'mountain of light' when he set his eyes on it.

The 'Koh-i-noor' remained with the Persian dynasty, although many attempts were made to gain ownership of it. Later, a Persian king fled with it to the Sikh court, and Ranjit Singh, Lion of the Punjab, took the stone and wore it as an embellishment. It was thereafter placed in the Lahore treasury. After the Sikh Wars, it was taken by the East India Company as part of the indemnity levied in 1849, and was subsequently presented to Queen Victoria at a sparkling levee marking the Company's 250th anniversary.

29. *Transfer of Power*, Vol. VII, pp. 734-5.
30. Ibid., pp. 805-6. Vol. IX, The fixing of a time limit, ed. Penderel Moon, Printed in England at her Majesty's Stationery Office, first published 1980.

General Sir Francis Ivan Simms Tuker, KCIE CB DSO OBE was a British Indian Army officer. Born in 1894 and educated at Brighton College, of which he was in later life a governor, Tuker served in the Indian Army and was most well-known for commanding the Indian 4th Infantry Division during the Western Desert and Italian Campaigns of the Second World War. On 14 July 1945 he was put in command of the Indian IV Corps in Burma and held this post to the end of the war. He died in 1967. There is a memorial tablet to him in the chapel of Brighton College, above which hangs his sword. Tuker's nickname in the army was 'Gertie'. He is known for a number of books on military history that he wrote: *The Pattern of War, While Memory Serves* and *The Yellow Scarf*.

Chapter 9

1. Field Marshal Lord Alanbrooke, *War Diaries*, first published in Great Britain, 2001, p. xiv.
2. Woodrow Wyatt, *Confession of An Optimist*, Collins, London, 1985, p. 162.
3. H.M. Seervai, *Partition of India: Legend and Reality*, Oxford, 2005.
4. Ibid.
5. Saleem Qureshi (comp. and ed.), *Jinnah: The Founder of Pakistan*, Oxford, fourth impression, 2003, pp. 15-16.
6. Volume X, p. 945.
7. *Transfer of Power*, Vol. X, 22 March–30 May 1947, printed in England, first published in 1981.
8. Seervai, p. 97 *ante*.
9. H.V. Hodson, 'The Role of Lord Mountbatten', in *The Partition of India: Policies and Perspectives 1935-1947*, C.H. Philips and Mary Doreen Wainwright (eds.), George Allen and Unwin Ltd, London, 1970, p. 121.
10. Record of Meeting between Jinnah and Mountbatten, 23 June 1947, TOP, Vol. XI, No. 311, p. 580.
11. Meeting of the Special Committee of the Indian Cabinet, 26 June 1947, TOP, Vol. XI, No. 354, p. 650.
12. Mountbatten to Listowel, 9 June 1947, TOP, Vol. XI, No. 120, p. 226.
13. On the personal staff of Sir Stafford Cripps along with Woodrow Wyatt, the British Labour MP Major Short was considered an expert on Sikh affairs.
14. *Transfer of Power*, Vol. XII, No. 326, p. 492.
15. Ibid., Vol. XI, p. 292.
16. Ibid., Vol. X, No. 456, dt. 16 May 1947, p. 843.
17. TOP, Vol. XII, No. 318, Message from Sir C. Radcliffe to Sir George Abell, p. 483.

18. Statement by Christopher Beaumont in 1989, Appendix IV, Ansar Hussain Khan, *The Rediscovery of India, A New Sub-continent,* London, Sangam, 1995.
19. TOP, Vol. XII, Enclosure to No. 81, p. 117.
20. Maulana Abul Kalam Azad, *India Wins Freedom,* New Delhi, Orient Longman 1959, 1988, p. 226.
21. Note by Auchinleck, 15 August 1947, TOP, Vol. XII, No. 486, p. 734.
22. From Ayesha Jalal's adaptation of Sardar Jafri's poem, *Khoon ki Lakeer.*
23. Penderel Moon, *The British Conquest and Dominion of India*, Part II (1858-1947), India Research Press, New Delhi, First Indian Edition 1999, p. 1167.
24. Ibid., pp. 1194-1195.
25. Unsung RSS heroes of Partition days—II, extracted from piece by V. Sundaram, retired IAS officer on the site http://www.newstodaynet.com/2006sud/06jul/1807ss1.html.
26. Mountbatten Papers, Viceroy's Interview No. 168; 24 July 1947, 5.15 pm.
27. Penderel Moon (ed.), *Transfer of Power,* pp. 322-25, Vol. XII, 8 July-15 August 1947, printed in England, 1983.
28. H.M. Seervai, *Partition of India: Legend and Reality,* Oxford, 2005, p. 135.
29. Ibid., p. 137.
30. Ibid., p. 139.
31. Ibid., p. 139.
32. Ibid.
33. Ibid., pp. 138-139.

Chapter 10

1. Maj.-Gen. S. Shahid Hamid, *Disastrous Twilights: A Personal Record of the Partition of India,* Barnsley: Leo Cooper, 1986, pp. 228-29.
2. 10 September 1948.

Chapter 11

1. Rudyard Kipling, *The City of Brass,* 1909.
2. Michel de Montaigne, Essays, 'Of Experience', pp. 994-995.
3. Gopalkrishna Gandhi (compiler and editor), *The Oxford India Gandhi, Essential Writings,* Oxford University Press, 2008, p. 615.
4. M.R.A. Baig, *Jinnah,* Khuda Baksh Oriental Library, Patna, p. 19.
5. Phillips Talbot, *An American Witness to India's Partition,* Sage Publications, 2007, pp. 240-41.
6. A.G. Noorani, *The Muslims of India: A Documentary Record,* OUP, India, 2003, p. 3.
7. Mohammad Reza Khan, *What Price Freedom,* Chennai, 1969, pp. 321-22, quoted in A.G. Noorani, *The Muslims of India.*
8. A.G. Noorani, *The Muslims of India,* Introduction, p. 7, also in Chapter 1 of the same book—Document 7.

9. Ibid., Chapter 1—Document 8.
10. Constituent Assembly of India Debates, 26 May 1949, Report on Minorities etc., p. 350, Book No. 3.
11. The Islamic Revolution of Iran, a widespread uprising in 1978-9 in which Islamic fundamentalists and their supporters overthrew Muhammad Reza Shah Pehlavi of Iran. The revolutionaries were led by an exiled religious leader, Ayatollah Ruhollah Khomeini, who dismantled the Shah's secular (nonreligious) monarchy and established the Islamic Republic of Iran. The new republic rejected Western influences and was guided by Shia Islamic teachings.
12. **Theocentric:** (adj.) having God as a central focus. **Theocracy:** (n.) a system of government in which priests rule in the name of God or a god. **The theocracy:** The commonwealth of Israel from the time of Moses until Saul became King.
13. Bashiruddin Ahmed, was the vice chancellor of Jamia Millia Islamia University between 1992-96 and also a nominated member of Consortium for Educational Communication.
14. The Babri Mosque was constructed by Babur, the first Mughal emperor of India in Ayodhya in the sixteenth century. Before the 1940s, the mosque was called Masjid-i Janmasthan ('mosque of the birthplace'). It stood on Ramkot ('Rama's fort') Hill (also called Janmasthan (birthplace). It is believed that Babur's commander-in-chief Mir Baki destroyed an existing temple at the site, which Hindus believe was the temple built to commemorate the birthplace of Rama, an incarnation of Vishnu and ruler of Ayodhya. This was demolished in a riot, on 6 December 1992.
15. Jaswant Singh, *Our Republic Post 6 December 1992: A Dialogue*, New Delhi, Rupa & Co., 2008, pp. 24-25.
16. H.M. Seervai, *Partition of India: Legend and Reality*, Oxford, p. 159.
17. Nehru to Nawab of Bhopal, 9 July 1948, SWJN, VII (1998), pp. 5-6.
18. As mentioned on page 11 of the book *Pakistan: Between Mosque and Military*, Husain Haqqani, 2005, Carnegie Endowment for International Peace.
19. Gopalkrishna Gandhi (compiler and editor), *The Oxford India Gandhi, Essential Writings*, Oxford, p. 615.
20. Ibid., p. 644.
21. Cited by Sunil Khilnani in his essay on 'Nehru's Judgement', in Richard Bourke and Raymond Geuss (eds.), *Political Judgement: Essays in Honour of John Dunn*, Cambridge, Cambridge University Press, 2008.
22. Ibid.
23. Kanji Dwarkadas, *Ten Years of Freedom*, Bombay, Popular Prakashan, 1968, p. 219.
24. The Balfour Declaration of 1926, named after the British Lord president of the Council, Arthur Balfour, Earl of Balfour, was the name given to a report resulting from the 1926 Imperial Conference of British Empire leaders in London. It states that the United Kingdom and the Dominions: '...are autonomous Communities within the British Empire, equal in status, in no way subordinate one to another in any aspect of their domestic or external affairs, though united by a common allegiance to the Crown, and freely associated as members of the British Commonwealth'.

25. That the Provinces of British India were divided into three numbered alphabetically, as under, comprising of the Provinces mentioned against each:
Group A—Madras, Bombay, United Provinces, Bihar, Central Provinces and Orissa;
Group B—Punjab, North-West Frontier Province, Sind and Baluchistan
Group C—Bengal and Assam.
26. Irgun Zvai Leumi (National Military Organization), also known as Etzel group, was found in Jerusalem. Led by Avraham Tehomi, it advocated armed Jewish insurrection against British rule and war against Palestinian Arabs. Menachem Begin became leader of the Israeli terrorist Irgun, which was engaged in a campaign against the British in Palestine. Irgun commanded the bombing at King David Hotel and the British embassy in Rome.
27. Kanji Dwarkadas, *Ten Years of Freedom*, Bombay, Popular Prakashan, 1968, p. 220.
28. Lloyd I. Rudolph and Susanne Hoeber Rudolph, *The Road Not Taken: The Modernist Roots of Partition, of Postmodern Gandhi and Other Essays: Gandhi in the World and at Home,* Chapter 2, New Delhi, Oxford University Press, 2006.
29. Ref. Extract from *Dawn* of 15 November 1946; pp. 74-75 of *Transfer of Power*, Volume IX—The fixing of a time limit; 4 November to 22 March 1947. Printed in England for Her Majesty's Stationery Office in 1980.
30. Gopalkrishna Gandhi (compiler and editor), *The Oxford India Gandhi, Essential Writings*, Oxford, p. 621.
31. A.G. Noorani, 'The Cabinet Mission and its Aftermath', in *The Partition of India: Policies and Perspectives 1935-1947*, C.H. Philips and Mary Doreen Wainwright (eds.), George Allen and Unwin Ltd, London, 1970, p. 105.
32. Cited in Chapter 3, p. 124.

INDEX

A

Abell, George, 322, 337, 359, 360, 368
Adult suffrage, 126, 159, 238, 243
Advocacy of separation, 424
Aga Khan Palace Detention Camp, 260
Agriculturist Party, 181, 183
Ahmed, Shafaat, 150
Ahmedabad Session (1921) of the Congress, 78
Ahmedia, 154
Ahmednagar jail diary, 431
Aiyar, Sri P.S. Siwaswamy, 107
Akbar, M.J., 417
Al Qaeda, 426
Al-Ghazzali, 421
Al-haq, 39
Ali, Chaudhuri Rahmat, 189, 217
Ali, Maulana Mohammad, 38, 75, 92, 107. *See also* Jauhar, Mohammad Ali
Ali, Maulana Shaukat, 38, 92, 102, 103, 107, 124, 159. *See also* Jauhar, Shaukat Ali
Ali, Syed Raza, 115
Aligarh Anglo-Muslim College, 173
Aligarh Institute Gazette, 25
Aligarh Movement, 24, 28
All-India Congress Committee, 88, 264, 290
All-India Muslim Conference, 141
All-India Muslim League Parliamentary Board (AIMLPB), 180
All-India Radio, 363, 364
Aman-i-awwal (liberty of religion), 418
Ambedkar, B.R., 96, 152, 257
American hegemony, 130
Amery, Leopold, 244, 245, 250, 260, 285, 286, 297
Amrita Bazar Patrika, 227

Anand Bhawan, 184, 185
Anderson, Benedict, 15
Aney, M.S., 123, 223
Anjuman-i-Islam, 63, 64, 74
Ansari, M.A., 78, 120, 134, 158, 159, 162, 215
Anti-British freedom movement, 228
Anti-Hindu: feeling, 44; poem, 102
Anti-Muslim policy, 230
Anti-partition: agitation, 36; movement, 37
Aqiqah, ceremony of, 53
Arab revolt in Palestine, 93
Arabian Sea, 51
Archbishop of Canterbury, 146
Arya Samaj, 36, 111
Arya Samajists, 36, 90, 96
Ashraf, K.M., 185
Atlantic Monthly, 92
Azad, Maulana Abul Kalam, 111, 185, 186, 187, 188, 194, 199, 208, 215, 216, 247, 252, 276, 281, 305, 306, 307, 309, 311, 317, 319, 324, 325, 336, 338, 339, 357, 370, 372, 382, 383, 386, 387, 392, 417, 441

B

Baig, M.R.A., 235, 236, 414
Bakr Id, 102
Balfour Declaration, 93
Balfour, Lord, 237
Baluchistan, 2, 119, 147, 164, 233, 310, 357, 379, 444
Banerjee, Surendra Nath, 82, 88
Bangladesh, 10, 410, 412, 413, 414, 419, 421, 428, 443, 447, 448
Barelwis, 29
Basu, Bhupendra Nath, 72

INDEX

Battle of Tarain, 31
Bay of Biscay, 1
Bengal Boundary Commission, 379
Bengal Pact, 110
Besant, Annie, 78, 83, 91, 432
Bharat Dharma Maha Mandal, 36
bin Laden, Osama, 426
bin Qasim, Mohammad, 1, 2, 11
Birkenhead, Lord, 117, 118, 144, 145
Birla, G.D., 239
Black flags, 256, 326
Boer War, 88, 133, 285
Bolitho, Hector, 63, 67, 126, 175, 179, 396
Bombay Chronicle, 88
Bombay Muslim Students' Union, 174
Bombay Presidency Association, 64, 70
Bombay Presidency, 36, 61, 71, 83
Bombay Provincial Conference, 82
Bose, Subhas, 208, 209, 210, 211, 214, 215, 216, 317, 339
Boundary Commission, 375, 376, 377, 378, 379, 380, 381
Brahmo Samaj, 36
British Civil Service, 172
British Commonwealth of Nations, 155, 237
British educational system, 48
British imperialism, 94, 199
British Labour party, 143, 145, 257, 313
British paramountcy, 203
Burrows, Sir Fredrick, 313
Butler, Sir Harcourt, 43, 44, 45, 73
Bux, Allah, 259
Bux, Dr Ilahi, 402, 405

C

Cabinet Mission, 236, 265, 297, 300, 302, 307, 308, 309, 310, 311, 312, 314, 316, 319, 321, 322, 324, 325, 326, 330, 331, 335, 336, 338, 339, 342, 344, 345, 346, 347, 348, 351, 358, 359, 361, 383, 384, 385, 392, 433, 444
Calcutta killings (riots), 327, 331, 339, 349

Calcutta League, 121
Calcutta session of the Congress, 69
Caliphate of Umar, 30
Campbell, Sir George, 20, 354
Casey, Richard, 107
Caste-Hindu-Muslim parity, 290, 296
Causes of the Indian Revolt, The, 25
Chagla, M.C., 174
Chamberlain, Neville, 241, 242, 243
Chancery Bar, 375
Charkha, 79, 134, 137. *See also* Spinning *khadi*
Charter of demands for the Muslims, 431
Chatterjee, Partha, 196
Chauri Chaura, 135
Chelmsford, Lord, 43, 77, 91
Christian: depredation, 12; invaders, 14
Christianity, 11, 420
Church Mission School of Karachi, 54
Churchill, Winston, 131, 174, 241, 242, 243, 244, 245, 248, 249, 250, 251, 252, 253, 260, 284, 285, 286, 288, 297, 298, 350, 355, 356, 366, 369, 370, 373, 442
Civil Disobedience Movement, 110, 156, 159, 166, 217, 432
Columbus, 12
Colville, Sir John, 287, 302, 307
Commercial exploitation of India, 33
Communal Award, 166, 167, 168, 175, 212, 213
Communal: conflicts, 98, 99, 102; controversy, 201; fight, 393; representation, 70, 74, 75, 140, 168, 238, 255; riots, 102, 103, 219, 220, 221, 304, 331; tension, 103, 114, 206, 221, 224, 327
Communalism, 43, 76, 111, 172, 196, 197
Complete freedom/independence, see *Purna swaraj*
Congress Provincial: Committees, 88; governments, 239, 240
Congress Reception Committee, 64
Congress Swarajists, 110
Congress vs. the Muslim League, 69, 239

INDEX

Congress-Khilafat campaign, 100
Congress-League Joint Scheme of Reforms, 88
Congress-League settlement, 216, 264, 267, 339
Connor, Walker, 441
Constitution for dominion status, 149
Constitutional correctness, 291
Constitutional law, sharp points of, 372
Constitutional reformist, 81
Constitutional reforms, scheme of, 443
Constitutional rights, 91
Constitution-making body, 302, 308, 320
Council Reforms, 74, 76, 81, 98, 105, 108, 110
Cows, killing of during Id, 99
Cows, slaying of, 93
Cripps declaration, 286
Cripps Mission, 171, 236, 237, 249, 251, 253, 298, 299, 300, 355, 363
Cripps, Sir Stafford, 237, 238, 239, 240, 241, 243, 244, 249, 250, 251, 252, 253, 287, 288, 298, 300, 307, 308, 309, 311, 314, 315, 322, 326, 337, 339, 343, 344, 349, 355, 377, 384, 385, 394
Crown's treaties, 237
Curzon, Viceroy, 34

D

Dandi, 128. *See also* Civil disobedience movement
Das, C.R., 78, 110, 111, 112
Daulatram, Jairamdas, 116
Dawn, 395, 439
Defence Advisory Council, 255
Defence and external affairs, 204, 206
Delhi Madrasa, 29
Delhi Pact, 156, 157, 160. *See also* Gandhi–Irwin Pact
Deliverance Day, 230, 231
Demagogic denunciations, 221
Deoband, 28, 29, 97. *See also* Barelwis
Depressed classes, 99, 168, 267, 271, 444

Desai, Bhulabhai, 252, 280, 281, 282, 286, 287, 288, 322
Desai, Mahadev, 238, 252
Desai–Liaquat Pact, 280, 281, 288
Destructive and death-filled partition, 356
Devanagari, 35, 36, 389
Devolution of power, 76, 79, 80, 109, 129, 156, 157, 167
Dharma Sabha, 36
Direct Action Day, 314, 327, 328, 330, 331, 333, 349
Direct action programme, 169, 331
Direct Action Resolution, 327, 328, 330
Discovery of India, 43
Divide and Rule, policy of, 140, 371
Dominion Cabinet, 398
Dominion Constitution of India, 148
Dominion status, 92, 131, 132, 133, 134, 135, 136, 138, 139, 140, 141, 148, 149, 152, 153, 156, 171, 193, 224, 237, 238, 239, 242, 244, 245, 246, 251, 359, 369, 370, 374, 433, 437
Do-nothing policy, 249
Dufferin, Lord, 29, 30, 33
Dussherra, 102

E

East Bengal, 37, 256, 331, 379, 428
East India Company, 20, 33, 285, 408, 446
Economic or social objectives, 192
Elementary Education Bill, 72
Emotionalism, 327, 374, 426
Ethno-nationalism, 442, 443
Euphemism, 196
Extra-constitutional campaigns, 240

F

Factionalism, 76
Faraizi movement, 27
Fatehpur Sikri, 24
Federal Court, 335, 344, 345, 346, 347
Federal Finance Committee, 167
Federal Objective, 232

Feudalism and capitalism, 137
Field Ambulance Training Corps, 88
First Simla Conference, 289
First World War, 82, 87, 89, 90, 92, 94, 105, 107, 130, 133, 225, 363
Forcible: conversions, 349; marriages, 349
Fractured freedom, 410, 429
Frederick Leigh-Croft, 53, 54
Frontier Gandhi, 389
Frontier Province, 319

G

Gandhi, Mohandas Karamchand, 6, 44, 45, 51, 55, 59, 63, 66-69, 77, 78, 85-96, 99, 102-108, 110, 111, 112, 114, 115, 116, 117, 118, 125, 126, 127, 129, 131-142, 149, 150, 157, 158, 160-166, 168, 171, 172, 180, 195, 196, 199, 200, 202, 204, 205, 206, 208, 210, 211, 214, 215, 216, 223, 226, 227, 228, 229, 236, 238, 239, 241, 242, 243, 250, 251, 252, 256, 260, 262, 264, 265, 267-282, 287, 290, 291, 292, 293, 295, 296, 297, 304, 305, 306, 307, 311, 322, 326, 329, 330, 332, 333, 334, 335, 336, 337, 338, 339, 340, 341, 357, 360, 371, 372, 374, 383, 385-392, 405, 406, 407, 409, 410, 413, 416, 422, 429, 430, 432, 433, 436, 439, 441, 442, 443
Gandhi–Irwin Pact, 156, 159, 166, 193
Gandhi–Jinnah Talks, 263, 266
Gandhi-Nehru discord, 433
Ganesh Chaturthi, 104
Gedrosia, 2
Ghauri, Mohammad, 31
Ghosh, Sudhir, 338
Gidwani, Chothram, 386
Gill, A.A., 446
Gokhale scheme, 77
Gokhale, Gopal Krishna, 5, 41, 45, 64, 65, 68, 72, 73, 77, 82, 85, 86, 87, 88, 89, 92
Government of India Act 1919, 108

Government of India Act of 1935, 202, 203, 218, 233, 259, 433
Government of India Bill (1919), 84
Government of India Bill 1935, 85, 171
Great depression, 161
Great October Revolution, 130
Great Rann of Kutch, 51
Green, Martin, 69
Gurjar Sabha, 86

H

Habibullah, A.B. (Sonny), 179
Hadith, 23, 419
Haig, Sir Harry, 184
Haj pilgrimages, 51
Hali, Altaf Hussain, 24
Haq, Fazlul, 154, 184, 188, 206, 232, 233, 234, 254, 255, 256, 259, 282, 384
Hare, Sir Lancelot, 46
Harijan, 252, 256, 391
Harijans, *see* Depressed classes
Haripur Session of the Congress, 208, 212
Harishchandra, Bhartendu, 35, 36
Hassan Pir, 53
Hassan, Sir Wazir, 73, 76, 80, 183, 191, 202
Hastings, Warren, 285
Hayat-i-Javed, 24
Heathenism, 330
Hedgewar, Dr K.B., 103, 104
Hidayatullah, Sir Ghulam Husain, 188
Hindi and Devanagari script, campaign for, 36
Hindu intelligentsia, 38-39
Hindu Mahasabha, 99, 101, 103, 116, 117, 119, 124, 125, 139, 144, 153, 164, 165, 267
Hindu Sabha, 36, 45, 97, 101. See also Hindu Mahasabha
Hindu Sadhus, 96
Hindu Shahi, 3
Hindu: policy, 205; raj, 200, 415
Hindu-Muslim: accord, 75; animosities, 425; antagonism, 119; combine, 81;

conflicts, 98; cooperation, 80; divide, 76; feud, 242; Martyrs, 95; parity, 290; political equalism, 37; problems, 117, 160, 436; question, 104, 140, 185, 215, 209, 239, 250, 328; relations, 103, 110, 173, 430; riots, 322, 415; rivalry, 228; settlement, 126, 209, 210, 213, 266; strife, 102; tensions, 206; unity, 5, 10, 14, 61, 80, 82, 86, 87, 88, 94, 99, 100, 106, 107, 109, 118, 129, 131, 132, 134, 140, 173, 176, 214, 272, 362, 415, 429, 441, 447

Hindustan Times, 406

History of the Indian National Movement, 37

Hoare, Sir Samuel, 166, 168, 170, 241

Hodson, H.V., 21, 367

Home Rule League, 78, 83, 90, 91, 105, 106, 432

House of Commons, 55, 81, 131, 166, 169, 231, 248, 252, 307, 351, 355, 356

House of Lords, 46, 78, 117, 151, 227, 354, 355

Hunter Committee Report, 77

Hunter, Sir William, 33

Husain, Fazli, 113, 141, 147, 148, 150, 154, 158, 159, 162, 175

Hussain, Dr Zakir, 317, 318

Hussain, Maulvi Mushtaq, 73

I

Ibbetson, Sir Denzil, 44

Imperial and Provincial Councils, 25

Imperial Bank, 328

Imperial corridors, 38

Imperial Legislative Council, 80

Imperialism, 133, 134, 197, 248, 261

In Quest of Jinnah, 67, 179, 396

INA, 327, 328

Independence Day, 398

Independence of India Act 1946, 7

Independence of India Act of 1947, 356

India Independence Bill, 380

India Wins Freedom, 199

Indian Councils Act of 1909, 34, 44

Indian Diary, An, 83

Indian National Congress (INC), 33, 41, 56, 63, 65, 87, 132, 135, 384, 413, 415, 416, 418, 423, 425, 426, 429, 432, 433, 435, 436, 439, 440, 441, 443, 444, 445

Indo-Gangetic plains, 51

Indo-Persian chroniclers, 12, 14

Interim Government, 69, 236, 263, 272, 273, 280, 281, 282, 289, 312, 314, 316, 317, 318, 319, 320, 321, 322, 323, 325, 326, 328, 329, 334, 336, 338, 340, 343, 347, 371, 374, 385, 392, 397, 435, 444

Internecine conflicts, 225

Irwin, Lord, 119, 122, 131, 133, 141, 143, 145, 146, 148, 149, 155, 156, 158, 160, 166, 193

Islam in Hindustan, advent of, 11, 275, 408

Islamic law, 420. *See also* Sharia

Islamic Literature, 256

Islamic reform, 28

Islamic terrorism, 446

Islamic traditions (Indo-Islamic), 10, 16, 17

Islington, Lord, 62

Ispahani, M.A.H., 257, 316

J

Jain, Girilal, 11, 419

Jajmani, 32

Jallianwala Bagh massacre, 105, 144

Jama Masjid, 21, 92, 417

Jamiat-ul-Ulema, 191, 194, 195

Jauhar, 2

Jauhar, Mohammad Ali, 41, 73, 90, 99

Jauhar, Shaukat Ali, 90

Jayakar, M.R., 112, 118, 126, 150, 152, 170, 279, 296

Jazia, 32

Jenkins, Evan, 305, 306, 380, 382

Jewish refugees, 435

K

Kadir, Ghulam, 18
Kafir, 14, 29
Kali, the goddess, 38
Kanpur mosque incident (riots), 73
Karachi session of the Congress, 74
Kashmiri descent, Muslim of, 158
Kathiawari principality, 53
Khalifa of Islam, 13, 105
Khalifa, abolition of the, 77, 99, 105, 107, 132
Khaliquzzaman, Chaudhri, 47, 158, 159, 178, 180, 181, 182, 183, 185, 186, 191, 192, 200, 208, 216, 217, 219, 232, 233, 257
Khan, Aga, 42, 61, 70, 73, 75, 77, 120, 141, 151, 152, 153, 155, 162, 163, 164, 165, 171, 172, 175
Khan, Badshah, 309
Khan, Khan Abdul Ghaffar, 387
Khan, Maulvi Khalilullah, 24
Khan, Maulvi Samiullah, 24
Khan, Nawab Abdullah, 73
Khan, Nawabzada Liaquat Ali, 181, 182, 183, 239, 280, 281, 282, 287, 288, 316, 343, 344, 347, 348, 393, 395, 397
Khan, Shaffat Ali, 163
Khan, Sir Sayyid Ahmad, 15, 22, 23, 24, 25, 26, 27, 41, 64, 179
Khan, Sir Sikandar Hayat, 188, 205, 206, 223, 232, 234, 240, 253, 255, 257
Khan, Sir Zafrullah, 150, 154, 163
Khan, Syed Mehdi Ali, 24
Kher, B.G., 214
Khilafat Committee, 102, 178, 217
Khilafat Conference, 77, 92, 178
Khilafat: movement, 92, 94, 100, 105, 107, 178, 225; agitation, 90, 99, 107, 131, 132, 178
Khilafatists, 98, 121, 142, 158, 195
Khoja Community, 60, 61
Khomeini, 419
Kidwai, Rafi Ahmed, 182, 185, 191
King Edward VII, coronation ceremonies of, 64
King George V, 151
Kitchlew, Dr Saifuddin, 101, 120
Knighthood, 65
Kohat, 102; tragedy, 103; riots, 111
Kripalani, Acharya, 180, 372, 387, 392
Krishak Praja Party, 184, 254

L

Lahore formula, 182
Lahore resolution, 121, 233, 235, 268, 272, 273, 274, 276, 277, 279
Lahore Session of the Congress, 159
Lajpat Rai, Lala, 25, 42, 78, 100, 103, 116, 443
Land reform, 185
Language divide, 34
Lateef, Nawab Abdul, 24, 35
League Assembly Party, 416
Liaquat–Desai formula, 282
Liberal Federation, 125
Linlithgow, Lord, 5, 202, 203, 204, 205, 206, 207, 223, 224, 225, 226, 227, 228, 229, 230, 231, 241, 242, 244, 245, 246, 247, 248, 250, 258, 259, 260, 262, 284, 294
Lloyd, Sir George, 90, 91
Lok Sevak Sangh, 69
London Times, The, 406
Lothian, Lord, 167, 203, 204
Lucknow Muslim League Council, 124
Lucknow Pact, 80, 82, 88, 106, 107, 114, 116, 119, 132, 134, 139, 141, 147, 191, 441, 443, 444

M

MacDonald, Ramsay, 43, 131, 141, 148, 156, 161, 168
Macpherson, John Molesworth, 59
Madan, T.N., 196
Madras Sappers and Miners, 364
Mahabir Dal, 101
Mahmud of Ghazna, 31
Mahratta Army, 18
Majeed, Maulvie Abdul, 95
Majoritarian communalism, 196

INDEX

Majoritarianism, 49, 115, 132, 141, 195, 239, 282, 305, 342
Majumdar, R.C., 383, 391
Malaviya, Pandit Madan Mohan, 15, 72, 78, 88, 91, 101, 116, 122, 144, 175
Mazhar-ul-Haq, 72, 73, 79
Meer, Titu, 27
Memorial Meeting, 95
Menon plan, 360
Menon, Krishna, 230, 237
Menon, V.P., 199, 226, 333, 359, 394, 397
Meston, Sir James, 73, 90
Metcalf, Thomas, 19
Mian, Dadu, 27
Military mutinies, 20
Minister without Portfolio, 343, 346, 348
Minoritism, 410, 417, 418
Minority syndrome, 418
Minto, Lady, 41, 42
Minto, Lord, 37, 38, 39, 40, 41, 43, 44, 45, 47, 70, 71, 72
Minto-Morley Reforms, 45
Mishra, Pratap Narain, 35
Mishra, Ram Gopal, 2
Mitchell, Christopher, 402
Mohammad bin Qasim, 1, 2
Mohammadan Anglo-Oriental College, 25
Mohammadan Anglo-Oriental Defence Association, 25
Mohammadan Educational Conference, 46
Momin Conference, 195
Mongol invasions, 13
Monroe Doctrine, 439, 440, 448
Montagu, Edwin S., 43, 80, 83, 89, 91, 92, 110
Montagu-Chelmsford Reforms, 81, 84, 108, 127, 131. *See also* Montford Reforms
Montford Reforms, 43, 81, 99, 108, 109, 424
Montford Report, 83, 85
Montgomery, Field Marshal, 370

Moon, Penderel, 235, 285, 333, 337, 362, 383
Moonje, B.S., 116, 122, 152, 174
Moplah rebellion, 101
Morley-Minto reforms, 47, 71
Mosley, Leonard, 333, 383, 391, 434, 435
Mosque Managing Committee, 95
Moth-eaten Pakistan, 4, 10, 264, 383, 409, 413, 437, 440
Mountbatten Plan of Partition, 359, 386
Mountbatten, Lord Louis, 354
Muddiman Committee, 113, 117, 142
Mughal aristocracy, 23
Mughal dynasty, 19, 23, 428
Muharram riots in Multan, 101
Municipal Amendment Act, 111
Munshi, K.M., 106, 190
Muslim deputation, 40
Muslim Khilafatists, 98
Muslim League, 4, 28, 39, 46, 47, 48, 50, 63, 66, 69, 71, 72, 73, 74, 75, 77, 78, 79, 80, 81, 82, 83, 87, 88, 89, 92, 103, 105, 113, 114, 115, 118, 119, 120, 121, 122, 124, 125, 126, 127, 133, 139, 140, 141, 144, 150, 156, 159, 175, 177, 178, 179, 180, 181, 182, 183, 184, 185, 186, 187, 188, 189, 190, 191, 192, 193, 194, 195, 198, 199, 200, 201, 202, 203, 204, 205, 206, 209, 210, 211, 213, 215, 216, 217, 219, 220, 221, 222, 223, 224, 225, 226, 227, 229, 230, 231, 232, 233, 236, 239, 240, 241, 243, 246, 247, 253, 254, 255, 256, 257, 258, 259, 260, 263, 264, 265, 266, 272, 274, 277, 278, 279, 280, 282, 286, 288, 289, 293, 294, 295, 296, 297, 298, 299, 302, 303, 304, 305, 308, 312, 313, 314, 316, 317, 318, 319, 322, 323, 324, 325, 326, 328, 329, 330, 331, 332, 335, 336, 338, 340, 342, 343, 345, 346, 348, 349, 350, 351, 358, 361, 371, 373, 374, 385, 386, 389, 391, 392, 394, 395, 398, 412, 413, 415, 416, 417, 430, 435, 436, 441, 443, 444

Muslim majority province, 37, 91, 110, 121, 139, 142, 188, 299, 300, 308, 311, 433, 439, 444
Muslim nation, 10, 15, 299, 300, 415
Muslim nationalism, 7
Muslim provincialism, 169
Muslim reform movements, 27
Muslim reformists, 27
Muslim separatism, 236
Muslim Unity Board, 178, 180, 195
Muslim Wakf Validating Act, 75
Muslim Wakfs, 72
Mussalahs, 32

N

Nadir Shah, 11
Nagpur Congress Resolution, 78
Nagpur riots, 104
Naidu, Sarojini, 5, 59, 61, 69, 74, 111, 162, 235
Nana Saheb, 20
Nanakchand, Lala, 96
Nanda, B.R., 385
Naoroji, Dadabhai, 41, 42, 55, 64, 69, 85, 87
Naqshbandi, 23
Narayan, Jayaprakash, 386, 387
Nath, Raja Narendra, 116
National Agriculturalist Party, 180, 181, 192
National Defence Council, 248
National Herald, 305
Nationalism, 214
Nationalist Muslims, 158, 159, 338, 397
Nawab Salimullah of Dacca, 46
Nazimuddin, Khwaja, 184, 232, 259, 288, 316, 333, 406
Nazism, 227, 249
Nehru, Jawaharlal, 10, 123, 127, 130, 132, 135, 139, 156, 172, 180, 183, 186, 196, 197, 204, 211, 214, 222, 238, 252, 258, 323, 357, 358, 378, 394, 409, 418, 421, 422, 423, 424, 429, 430, 431, 433, 434, 435, 436, 437, 439, 440, 442, 444

Nehru, Motilal, 78, 103, 112, 113, 115, 117, 118, 122, 123, 124, 126, 133, 134, 136, 140, 141, 142, 149
Nehruvian socialistic thinking, 193
New Statesman, The, 260
New York Herald Forum, 343
News Chronicle, 278
Noakhali killings, 305
Non-Cooperation Movement, 98, 99, 108, 113, 114, 158, 432
Non-cooperation, resolution on, 78
Non-violence, method of, 227
Noorani, A.G., 140, 416
North-West Frontier Province (NWFP), 35, 40, 102, 147, 153, 166, 188, 224, 233, 260, 299, 303, 310, 320, 323, 324, 342, 430, 432, 444

O

O'Hanlon, Rosalind, 104, 445
Olivier, Lord, 43
One-nation theory, 163
Operation Scuttle, 356
Orient Club, Bombay, 242
Ottoman Empire, 77, 90, 94, 105

P

Pakistan resolution, 217, 232, 233, 234, 235, 236, 243, 246, 282, 385
Pal, Bipin Chandra, 42, 78
Pan-Islamic activities, 90
Pan-Islamism, 439
Pant, Govind Ballabh, 185, 186, 187, 188
Parliamentary system, establishment of a, 46
Partition of Bengal, 47, 358
Partition of India, 5, 138, 191, 224, 359, 383, 384, 385, 386, 391, 392, 412, 421, 424, 435
Partition of India: Legend and Reality, 431
Partition Resolution, 390
Patel, Sardar Vallabhbhai, 4, 180, 193, 247, 251, 252, 325, 329, 336, 338,

349, 351, 356, 357, 358, 359, 374, 383, 385, 388, 389, 392, 394, 396, 397, 417, 418, 429, 430, 434, 435, 436, 441
Patel, Vithalbhai, 112, 149
Pathway to Pakistan, 178, 185
Peace Conference, 334, 381
Peaceful transfer of power, 333, 446
Pearl Harbour, 249 250
Perso-Islamic: culture, 17, 19; standards, 17; values, 28
Perso-Arabic script, 16
Personal enfranchisement, 41
Pethick-Lawrence, Lord, 307, 311, 322, 326, 337, 343, 344, 350, 384
Pherozeshah Mehta group, 41, 64
Philips, C.H., 4
Pilgrimage to Freedom, 106, 190
Pirpur Report, 221
Pirzada, Syed Sharifuddin, 59, 175
Political activism, 33, 37
Political bargaining and haggling, 125
Political pugnacity, 22
Political separateness, 46
Politics of Provinces, 255
Post-colonial era, 14
Post-Independence challenge, 409, 411
Post-partition relations, 397
Post-Second World War, 235, 434, 446
Praja Parishad agitations, 203
Prarthana Samaj, 36
Prasad, Dr Rajendra, 180, 184, 228, 241, 261, 359, 390, 392
Prasad, Raja Shiv, 35
Pratap, 322
Pre-Islamic Arab traditions, 420
Press Act, 98
Primary Education Bill, 72
Prince of Wales, 39
Princely states, 130, 139, 151, 152, 167, 172, 203, 204, 237, 251, 254
Principle of partition, 385, 388
Principles of democracy, 234, 311
Privy Council, 60
Pro-Hindi agitation, 35
Pro-Pakistan slogans, 331

Provincial autonomy, 83, 110, 112, 113, 114, 142, 147, 157, 188, 320, 335
Provincial Constitution, 193, 313, 344
Provincial Legislative Council, 75, 87
Provincial legislatures, 81, 85, 105, 159, 175, 178, 248, 288, 301, 302, 310
Provincial rivalries, 77
Public Services Commission, 62
Purna swaraj, 132, 134, 159, 193

Q

Qayum, Abdul, 96
Queen Victoria, 51, 366
Quit India Movement, 257, 258, 432
Quit India Resolution, 257, 264
Quran, 8, 16, 23, 95, 97, 419, 420
Quranic insistence, 419

R

Racial prejudice and discrimination, 60
Radcliffe Award, 374, 375
Rafi-ud-Din, Maulvi, 74
Raja Sahib of Mahmudabad, 72, 73, 76, 177, 179, 181, 182, 236, 257
Raja Sir Rampal Singh, 116
Rajagopalachari, C., 180, 236, 247, 254, 263, 338, 406
Rajatarangini, 3
Ram Lila, 102
Ram Raj, 156
Ram, Jagjivan, 318
Ramgarh Session, 243
Ramnavmi, 104
Rangila Rasool, 96
Rashid, Abdul, 96, 97
Rashtriya Swayamsevak Sangh (RSS), 103, 104
Rathore dynasties, 31
Reading, Lord, 112, 117, 118
Recollections and Reflections, 152
Reconnaissance mission, 203
Red Fort, Delhi, 23
Reformist movements, 23
Rejection of the 'grouping scheme', 337
Religious conservatives, 27

Religious nationalism, 26
Religious transformation, 32
Reserve Bank of India, 428
Revolution in Iran, 419
Riots in Delhi, 102
Roman law, 420
Roosevelt-Churchill Atlantic Charter, 248
Round Table Conference: First, 148, 152, 153, 155, 156, 203, 217
Round Table Conference: Second, 156, 157, 160, 161, 162, 163, 164, 166, 167, 168
Round Table Conference: Third, 167, 169, 170, 171
Rowlatt Acts, 91, 100, 108
Roy, Kiron Shankar, 269
Royal Commission, 118, 142
Royal Warrant, 144
Rudolph, Lloyd, 15, 132, 160, 441, 444
Rudolph, Susanne, 5, 67, 132, 441, 444
Russo-Japanese War, 90

S

Sanatan Dharm Sabha, 102
Sanatan Dharma, 420
Sangathan movement, 99
Sapru, Tej Bahadur, 72, 114, 123, 125, 126, 128, 133, 136, 140, 149, 150, 151, 152, 153, 170, 250, 257, 266, 276, 308
Sarhindi, Sheikh Ahmad, 23
Sastri, Srinivas, 72, 107, 151, 152, 153
Satyagraha, 149; agitational methodology of, 85; politics of, 68
Saunders, C.B., 18
Sayani, M.R., 82
Sayyid Ahmad of Bareilly, 23, 27, 28
Sayyid Mahmud-Beck scheme, 26
Second World War, 4, 88, 161, 223, 235, 236, 239, 249, 250, 284, 366, 375, 434, 446
Secularism and majoritarian democracy, 195
Secularism debate, 195
Seervai, H.M., 305, 370, 431

Self-governing principle, 43
Separate communal electorates, 71
Separate electorates for Muslims, 443
Separate Muslim homeland, 222
Separation mentality, 41
Sepoy Mutiny, 19
Setalvad, Motilal, 280, 281, 282
Setalvad, Sir Chimanlal, 60, 145, 152, 153, 361, 384
Shafi, Sir Mohammad, 114, 120, 121, 150, 151, 154, 158, 159, 163, 164, 165
Shah Nawaz, Begum, 164, 282
Shah Zafar, Bahadur, 18, 21
Shameful Flight, 423
Sharia, 27, 421, 445
Sharma, Nathuramal, 96
Sherwani, N.A., 158, 159, 194
Shraddhanand, Swami, 90, 92, 95, 96, 97, 99
Shuddhi (purification) movement, 99
Sikh Community, worsen the position of the, 347
Sikhistan, demand for, 267
Simla Conference, 236, 282, 289, 301, 302, 309, 311, 316
Simla delegation, 7, 34, 414
Simla Deputation, 38, 39, 41, 42, 43, 44, 46, 48
Simon Commission, 131, 133, 138, 142, 143, 144, 145, 146, 147, 148, 155
Simon, Sir John, 131, 241, 242
Sind Gazetteer, 60
Sindh Madrassah-tul-Islam, 54
Singh, Sardar Baldev, 343, 344, 347
Skeen Committee, 119
Smith, Dunlop, 43, 44, 45
Socio-economic solidarities, 194
Somnath temple, 51
South East Asia Command, 366
Sovereignty, 7, 13, 18, 130, 133, 139, 141, 203, 279, 408, 419, 424, 430, 441, 444
Spanish Civil War, 130
Special Marriage Bill, 72
Spinning *khadi*, 134
Stalin, Joseph, 244, 442

Statutory commission, 117, 122, 130, 131, 142
Struggle for Freedom, 383
Subdued optimism, period of, 271
Sufism, 23, 421
Suhrawardy, H.S., 328, 331, 417
Swarajists, 110, 112, 113, 114, 115, 131, 133

T

Taliban, 426
Talibanization, 445
Tandon, P.D., 185, 386
Tanzim, 102
Tatya Tope, 20
Tazia processions, 99
Thakurdas, Purushotamdas, 112, 124
Theocentrism, 419
Theory of 'Muslims as a separate nation', 5, 10, 11, 15, 25, 30, 37, 179, 273, 409, 410, 413, 414, 416, 424, 425, 426, 428, 430, 437, 440, 443, 444, 445, 448
Tilak, Bal Gangadhar, 42, 60, 64, 65, 68, 77, 82, 83, 87, 88, 89, 91, 107, 441, 443
Times of India, The, 42, 70, 97, 145, 406, 407
Tolstoy, 85
Tory government, 130, 144, 155
Treaty of Lausanne, 442
Treaty of Sevres, 77, 93, 105, 130
Triangular bargaining, 444
Tribune, The, 116
Turkic-Mongol destructions, 13
Two-Nation theory, 260, 273, 274, 299, 358, 385, 390, 440, 444
Two-party system, 220

U

Umayyads, 1
UN Special Committee on Palestine, 435
United Nations Relief and Rehabilitation Administration, 297
United Nations, 376
United Provinces, 36, 38, 46, 47, 73, 101, 109, 110, 116, 141, 150, 155, 157, 166, 184, 186, 187, 190, 201, 220, 222, 309, 416
UP Municipal Bill, 79

V

Vakeel, Abdul Rahman, 95
Vande Mataram, 229, 242
Viceroy of India, withdrawal of a, 363
Viceroy's Council, 72, 75, 76, 91, 246
Viceroy's Legislative Council, 71
Viquar-ul-Mulk, Nawab, 73

W

Wacha, Dinshaw, 64, 72
Wahabi influence, 35
Wahabi influence, 70
Wainwright, Mary Doreen, 4
Waliullah, Shah, 28, 29
War Cabinet, 244, 245, 251
War Consultative Committee, 246
Wardha 'Quit India' Resolution, 257
Wavell, Lord, 5, 236, 250, 252, 253, 262, 265, 283, 284, 285, 286, 287, 288, 289, 291, 292, 294, 296, 297, 298, 299, 300, 301, 302, 305, 306, 313, 314, 315, 316, 317, 318, 319, 321, 322, 325, 332, 333, 335, 336, 338, 339, 342, 343, 344, 351, 354, 355, 362, 363, 364, 367, 368, 370, 371, 383, 436
Wavell's scheme, 298, 300
Weber, Max, 15
Wedderburn, William, 92
White Hall, 90, 91, 408
White Paper on Indian Constitutional Reform, 173
Willingdon, Lord, 82, 91, 160, 166, 167, 168, 172
Wolpert, Stanley, 423
Woodrow Wyatt, 313, 338, 367

Y

Yakub, Mohammad, 120, 121
Young India, 107, 136, 138
Yousuf, Sir Muhammad, 181, 182, 183

Z

Zamindari, abolition of, 185
Ziaul Haq, General, 425
Zionist settlements, 94
Zoroastrianism, 11
Zulu War, 133